OMNIVOROUS PRIMATES
Gathering and Hunting in Human Evolution

OMNIVOROUS PRIMATES

Gathering and Hunting in Human Evolution

Edited by
Robert S. O. Harding and Geza Teleki

Columbia University Press
New York   1981

Library of Congress Cataloging in Publication Data

Main entry under title:

Omnivorous primates.

Bibliography: p.   Includes index.
1. Human evolution.   2. Hunting, Primitive.
3. Man—Animal nature.   4. Food habits.   I. Harding,
Robert S. O., 1931–   II. Teleki Geza, 1943–
GN360.046   573.2   80-23736
ISBN 0-231-04024-5

Columbia University Press
New York   Guildford, Surrey

Copyright © 1981 Columbia University Press
All rights reserved
Printed in the United States of America

Contents

Contributors

Diana C. Crader. Department of Anthropology, Wesleyan University, Middletown, Connecticut

Leslie G. Freeman. Department of Anthropology, University of Chicago, Chicago, Illinois

Richard A. Gould. Department of Anthropology, University of Hawaii, Honolulu, Hawaii

Reizo Harako. Meiji University, 1-9-1 Eifuku, Suginami-ku, Tokyo, Japan

Robert S. O. Harding. Department of Anthropology, University of Pennsylvania, Philadelphia, Pennsylvania

Brian Hayden. Department of Archaeology, Simon Fraser University, Burnaby, British Columbia, Canada

Claude-Marcel Hladik. Laboratoire d'Ecologie Tropicale du C.R.N.S., 91800 Brunoy, France

Glynn Ll. Isaac. Department of Anthropology, University of California, Berkeley, California

Richard G. Klein. Department of Anthropology, University of Chicago, Chicago, Illinois

Alan E. Mann. Department of Anthropology, University of Pennsylvania, Philadelphia, Pennsylvania

George Silberbauer. Department of Anthropology and Sociology, Monash University, Clayton, Victoria, Australia

Shirley C. Strum. Department of Anthropology, University of California, San Diego, La Jolla, California

Geza Teleki. Department of Anthropology, George Washington University, Washington, D.C.

David Webster. Department of Anthropology, The Pennsylvania State University, University Park, Pennsylvania

OMNIVOROUS PRIMATES
Gathering and Hunting in Human Evolution

Robert S. O. Harding and Geza Teleki

1.
Introduction

Philosophers in many societies have speculated about the origins of human behavior, but they have tended to concentrate on such fundamental issues as whether humans are born good and succumb gradually to evil or are born evil and struggle unsuccessfully to be good. The idea that human behavior, whether good or evil, might be influenced by millions of years of evolutionary history is a direct legacy of Charles Darwin's theory of natural selection, for if a species changes its physical structure over many generations in response to environmental conditions, the behavior with which each species adapts to these conditions must change as well. It thus became possible to think of behavior evolving, as well as physical structure, despite the fact that structural evolution could be verified in the fossil record whereas behavioral evolution could only be conjectured.

Once scientists acknowledged that contemporary human behavior had been molded by our evolutionary past, it then became a matter of great importance to reconstruct prehistory, to retrace human footsteps back into the distant past. Little systematic work of this sort was carried out at the end of the nineteenth and beginning of the twentieth centuries, however, and the nascent discipline of anthropology concerned itself mainly with cataloging fossil discoveries and comparing the cultures of living peoples. This era ended in 1924 with Raymond Dart's remarkable discovery of the manlike *Australopithecus africanus* at Taung in South Africa, for in the original report of his find Dart (1925) did not limit himself to a physical description of the fossil but suggested that the human line itself must have originated in country much like the open veld where the Taung fossil had been found. He reasoned that the abundance of food in the forests had offered no challenge to the apes, and thus they had remained apes; the open veld, by contrast, required "higher manifestations of intellect" (p. 199). Thereafter, Dart continued to include hypothetical reconstructions of australopithecine behavior in his vigorous attempts to convince the scientific world that these creatures were hominid rather than pongid (Dart, 1926, 1953, 1957, 1959). The ensuing controversy (W.E.L. Clark, 1967) generated a great deal of interest in the reconstruction of early hominid behavior, and although many of Dart's original hypotheses were never accepted, interest in this field remains high among paleoanthropologists (Isaac and McCown, 1976).

1

In distinguishing between humans and apes and assigning the australopithecines to one or the other category, one of the most obvious aspects of behavior to be reconstructed was subsistence, and from the beginning Dart assumed that the australopithecines differed from their pongid contemporaries in what they ate. As Dart wrote some years ago, "*Australopithecus* was terrestrial, troglodytic and predaceous in habit—a cave-dwelling, plains-frequenting, stream-searching, bird-nest-rifling and bone-cracking ape, who employed destructive implements in the chase and preparation of his carnivorous diet" (1940:177).

In short, *Australopithecus* was depicted as a meat-eater who depended on hunting for food, and the crucial behavioral difference between this early hominid and his nonhuman primate contemporaries was that he pursued, killed, and ate other animals. This australopithecine model was then generalized to include all early hominids, no matter what their taxonomic status, so the view that early humans depended on hunting for their survival, and that hunting in turn gave rise to many other unique forms of human behavior, has since become thoroughly entrenched in theories of human evolution.

Support for this "hunting hypothesis," as it has been called by one of its most outspoken advocates, Robert Ardrey (1976), has been sought in three main areas: in the archaeological record, in studies of the behavior of the living nonhuman primates, and in the subsistence patterns of those human groups which do not practice agriculture. Of these three, however, the archaeological record has provided most of the evidence used by advocates of the hunting hypothesis. Dart, for instance, relied on the masses of broken bone found in the breccias of Makapansgat and other South African sites for evidence that the australopithecines were carnivores, and hence (to his way of thinking) human. As Dart saw it, the australopithecines

were human in their cave life, in their love of flesh, in hunting wild game to secure meat. . . . These Procrustean proto-human folk tore the battered bodies of their quarries apart limb from limb and slaked their thirst with blood. . . . Man's predecessors differed from living apes in being confirmed killers: carnivorous creatures, that seized living quarries by violence, battered them to death, tore apart their broken bodies, dismembered them limb from limb, slaking their ravenous thirst with the hot blood of victims and greedily devouring livid writhing flesh. (1953:204, 209)

Having established the australopithecines' carnivorous habits to his own satisfaction, Dart proceeded, in a circular argument repeated by later writers, to establish that these creatures were hominids by comparing their purported behavior with his own rather dismal view of human history:

The blood-bespattered, slaughter-gutted archives of human history from the earliest Egyptian and Sumerian records to the most recent atrocities of the Second

World War accord with early universal cannibalism, with animal and human sacrificial practices or their substitutes in formalized religions and with the world-wide scalping, head-hunting, body-mutilating and necrophiliac practices of mankind in proclaiming this common bloodlust differentiator, this predaceous habit, this mark of Cain that separates man dietetically from his anthropoidal relatives and allies him rather with the deadliest of the Carnivora. (1953:208)

Despite Dart's sanguinary description of the events he believed had formed the South African bone accumulations, it was never fully established whether the australopithecines were predators or prey. In fact, an analysis by Brain (1970) seemed to show that they were the victims in at least one South African site. By contrast, there was little disagreement that hominids had been involved in creating some of the patches of bone debris uncovered at Olduvai Gorge, for these were associated with clearly utilized stone tools (M. D. Leakey, 1971). Although the part played by hominids in the death of these ancient animals has never been clear (see Isaac and Crader, in this volume), the discovery of tools associated with bone provided one of the most persuasive arguments in favor of the hunting hypothesis.

Circumstantial though it was, this evidence was especially appealing because an association had long existed in the minds of scientists between the emergence of the hominids, their use of stone tools as weapons, and an evolutionary reduction in the size of canine teeth in the hominid line. This association bore all the authority of Charles Darwin, who had stated:

The free use of the arms and hands, partly the cause and partly the result of man's erect position, appears to have led in an indirect manner to other modifications of structure. The early male forefathers of man were, as previously stated, probably furnished with great canine teeth; but as they gradually acquired the habit of using stones, clubs, or other weapons, for fighting with their enemies or rivals, they would use their jaws and teeth less and less. In this case, the jaws, together with the teeth, would become reduced in size. (1871:435)

Thus from Darwin's time onward, tools came to be thought of as *weapons*, even though no analysis of these mute stones had provided any clue to their original use. A typical example of this bias can be found in Ardrey's *African Genesis* (1961), where the reader will search the index in vain for references to tools; instead, there is only the brief notation, "*see* Weapons." From the use of tools as weapons, it was but a short step to a hypothesis in which tools made possible a hunting way of life.

The paleoanthropological preoccupation with hunting may have stemmed in part from the fact that the first prehistoric excavations were carried out in Europe, in deposits laid down in glacial times when the severe climate probably did make human populations especially dependent on animals for food. As Mann has suggested (personal communication), the abundant evidence for hominid exploitation of animals in the periglacial environments of the Upper Palaeolithic in Europe may have colored the way in which many subsequently discovered sites were interpreted, even if these newer sites were located in Africa and at much earlier time levels. Archaeology, at any rate, has provided the major evidential bulwarks for the hunting hypothesis, supplying concrete data in the form of stone tools and broken animal bones that can be tabulated, analyzed, and evaluated, whether or not the reasons for their original association have been established.

By contrast, hard data of this sort have been lacking until rather recently in the study of nonhuman primate behavior, the second source of evidence for the hunting hypothesis; as a result the primates have been useful only in a negative sense. If the hypothesis states that human primates can be distinguished from nonhuman ones by the fact that humans hunt animals and eat meat, then the corollary is that nonhuman primates subsist entirely on vegetable matter. This assumption, treated as if it were a fact, was used to support the hunting hypothesis. Morris (1967:31), for instance, declared that "we are vegetarians turned carnivores," while other primates are "typical forest-dwelling fruit-pickers." Similarly, Schaller and Lowther (1969:308) asserted that "all monkeys and apes are basically vegetarians, feeding on leaves, fruits, roots, and bark." It is never prudent to base an argument on the assumption that a behavior does not exist simply because it has never been observed (Teleki, in press), and it was certainly premature to make such claims at a time when field studies of the nonhuman primates were few and information on their diets was minimal.

African colobine monkeys have long been classified as "folivorous" because they have unusual digestive specializations for a leaf-eating diet (Napier and Napier, 1967). More than any others, these species have been responsible for the belief that *all* nonhuman primates are basically arboreal vegetarians. Yet it is becoming apparent that some, and perhaps all, colobine populations exploit a variety of plants and plant parts, including shoots, flowers, and fruits (Clutton-Brock, 1975a,b), as well as vertebrates (Struhsaker, 1975). In fact, any primate living in an equatorial habitat would find it virtually impossible to avoid consuming substantial amounts of animal matter along with plants; nearly every plant, and certainly every ripe fruit, is probably infested with invertebrates.

Other primates less specialized in their dietary patterns and feeding habits have also been misrepresented in the literature. To label gelada monkeys as "seed-eaters," for instance, may be useful shorthand for referring to a novel evolutionary hypothesis (C. J. Jolly, 1970) but is hardly a valid description of the complete gelada diet, which includes many plants and some invertebrates (Dunbar, 1977). Similarly, to call chimpanzees "frugivorous" simply because they eat large amounts of fruit in some seasons (Reynolds and Reynolds, 1965) obscures the fact that these apes eat at least 200 types of flora and 40 species of fauna at some study sites

(Wrangham, 1975, 1977). And to consider early hominids or modern humans as "carnivorous" in order to establish the value of analogies between social carnivore and human behavior (King, 1975; Peters and Mech, 1975; Schaller and Lowther, 1969; P. R. Thompson, 1975) disregards several facts: that most nonhuman primates are omnivorous (Harding, in this volume); that most band societies, especially the equatorial ones, only eat meat as a supplement to plant foods and rarely rely on hunting as the main source of food (Hayden, in this volume); and that the biological, behavioral, and psychological affinities of hominids lie with primates rather than social carnivores (Teleki, 1975).

In studies of omnivorous primates there has also been a frequent failure to distinguish between labels based on food intake, such as *insectivore* and *frugivore,* and labels based on the behavior performed while exploiting certain resources, such as *hunter* and *gatherer.* This issue is discussed elsewhere (Teleki, 1975), but we must stress that faunal resources can be gathered as well as hunted by omnivorous primates with complex and flexible behavioral repertoires. The distinction is an important one for those interested in tracing the evolution of primate predatory behavior (e.g., Rose, 1978), since the collection of insects, for example, may involve motor patterns exactly like those performed while collecting grass seeds. Nonetheless, some authors write about "hunting for prey" no matter what behavior is performed, as long as the food item is an animal (vertebrate or invertebrate), and serious comparisons are drawn between such activities as pursuit of large prey by chimpanzees and gathering of snails by translocated macaques (e.g., Estrada and Estrada, 1977; Estrada, Sandoval, and Manzolillo, 1978).

Were it not for the immense power of labels in regulating thoughts and forming concepts, often fixing inaccurate images in our minds well before solid evidence has been obtained, these would be no more than semantic problems. But once a dietary label and the concept it represents become firmly established in our theories and textbooks, a degree of validity exists which even hard evidence to the contrary cannot eradicate. Thus, having classified chimpanzees as "frugivores," we can no longer easily accept their omnivory, let alone their ability to prey on vertebrates with skill and persistence (see Reynolds, 1975; Gaulin and Kurland, 1976).

Unless we soon develop a precise set of terms for primate dietary patterns and feeding habits and arrive at a consensus on how and when to apply each term with maximum accuracy, misunderstanding is bound to prevail, inhibiting our ability to reconstruct human evolution and fostering notions of a "killer ape" ancestry (Ardrey, 1976) that are neither factually nor theoretically supportable (R. Leakey and Lewin, 1977). Although modern field studies of prosimian, monkey, ape, and human subsistence habits are beginning to use nutritional and behavioral data to generate more precise, more comparable results (see Lee and DeVore, 1968a, 1976; Clutton-Brock, 1977), for the time being we must concur with Hayden (in this volume) that most contemporary statements about dietary patterns remain suspect. Every book and article on this subject, including this one, must be carefully scrutinized for possible errors.

The third major source of evidence advanced in support of the hunting hypothesis is a homology drawn with contemporary band societies that subsist entirely by gathering and hunting for their food. In this line of reasoning, the hunting aspect of resource exploitation has been heavily emphasized while gathering has received little attention, to the point where many earlier writers omitted gathering completely when referring to these people as "hunters." One case in point is Elman Service's book, called simply *The Hunters* (1966). Another is the landmark volume edited by Lee and DeVore, *Man the Hunter* (1968a), in which several authors emphasized, however, the extent to which band societies depended on gathered vegetable matter (e.g., Lee, 1968). Others in that volume continued to emphasize the primacy of hunting in human evolution. Thus Washburn and Lancaster maintained that "our intellect, interests, emotions, and basic social life—all are evolutionary products of the success of the hunting adaptation" (1968:293) while Laughlin made what may be the most unequivocal formulation of the hunting hypothesis to be found in the scientific literature:

Hunting is the master behavior pattern of the human species. It is the organizing activity which integrated the morphological, physiological, genetic, and intellectual aspects of the individual human organisms and of the population who [*sic*] compose our single species. (1968:304)

One final aspect of the hunting hypothesis remains to be considered: a theory, most eloquently expressed in a 1969 paper by Schaller and Lowther, which rests on the *a priori* assumption that hunting and meat-eating have been central to the human adaptation since Plio-Pleistocene times, that is, for about two and a half million years. Observing that individual groups of the same primate species tend to behave differently in different habitats, Schaller and Lowther conclude that phylogenetically close animals such as primates make poor behavioral models for early humans. They suggest as more likely candidates the group-hunting social carnivores, which are described as being subject to the same environmental pressures that confronted the early hominids. King (1975) and P. R. Thompson (1975) have sounded variations on this theme, although King (personal communication) would include both carnivore and nonhuman primate models in the reconstruction of early human behavior. In a related development, the long-dormant theory that scavenging may have provided a transitional adaptation between a hypothesized vegetarian ancestor and hominids dependent on meat has recently been revived (King, 1975; Peters and Mech, 1975; Read-Martin and Read, 1975; Szalay, 1975). It is important to stress here that all these approaches are founded on the tacit assumption that the obtaining and eating of meat was the decisive adaptation in early hominid evolution: thus they lack any explanatory power if this assumption cannot be demonstrated.

It is quite clear that the hunting hypothesis has become firmly established in the popular and professional literature despite a number of flaws in its logical underpinning and criticisms of its validity (e.g., Perper and Schrire, 1977).

The extent to which hunting may have influenced our evolution is of interest not only to scholars committed to a particular theoretical position, however. We have stated that to understand current human behavior we must first understand the adaptations that underlie it; it has even been suggested that humans are facing the twentieth century with physiological and psychological equipment shaped under Pleistocene conditions.

We are convinced that most of the evidence and argument advanced in support of hunting as a "master behavior pattern" has never been rigorously tested on the basis of *all* the available information. In fact, the issue may never be resolved so long as those writing on either side of the question continue to rely on subsets of facts that support one particular position or prejudice. To this end, we asked highly qualified scientists to review the fields from which evidence for the hunting hypothesis has traditionally been drawn: paleoanthropology, primatology, and ethnography. Each of these areas is presented in as balanced a fashion as possible, with each section containing an introductory chapter that provides a general overview, as well as three other chapters that present concrete data from field studies.

The introduction to the paleoanthropology section reviews methods and techniques available for reconstructing the dietary patterns of the early hominids, and then discusses their limitations. The other chapters in this section are devoted to specific time periods, each author presenting information from the field to illustrate the kinds of evidence available. For the Pliocene and Lower Pleistocene, East Africa is the focus; the Iberian peninsula represents the Middle Pleistocene, and a South African site the Upper Pleistocene.

The primatology section is introduced by a survey of the natural diets of nonhuman primates in the wild, and reconsiders the traditional view that nonhuman primates are vegetarians. Since most of the surviving primates are arboreal animals, the next chapter discusses the evolution of dietary patterns in forest primates. The remaining chapters provide the most recent, detailed information available on predatory behavior in a troop of baboons at Gilgil, Kenya, and in a community of chimpanzees at Gombe National Park, Tanzania.

In the third major section, a wide-ranging review of band society diets is followed by a comparison of Aborigine groups in Australia with Indians of the Northwest Coast of America, and by ethnographic reports on the G/wi of Botswana and the Mbuti Pygmies of Zaïre.

Finally, paleontologists have provided provocative evidence from the fossil record which suggests that many large mammalian species may have become extinct during the Pleistocene. From this evidence, the notion has developed that Pleistocene extinctions, particularly those in the New World, were caused largely by overexploitations by human hunters (e.g., P. S. Martin, and Wright, 1967). Because this information is directly relevant to the hunting hypothesis, a review of the evidence and the premises on which it is based forms the last chapter of this book.

As editors, we have approached our task of assembling diverse information with a specific viewpoint, and our bias must be made explicit. In 1974, when we began to consider writing this book, we were not convinced that hunting was the "master behavior pattern" in human evolution, and when we solicited contributions we said as much. At the same time, we did not attempt to compel our contributors to conform to this view because, quite obviously, we also do not believe that hunting has had no effect whatsoever on human evolution.

Although diverse interpretations and conclusions appear in this book, the evidence here assembled has convinced us more firmly than ever that hunting was not *the* decisive factor differentiating the earliest hominids from their immediate predecessors. On the contrary, both groups probably subsisted, as their descendants do today, on an eclectic assortment of flora and fauna. As the hominids evolved greater manual dexterity, made more sophisticated tools, and developed more complicated social structures, they hunted larger animals in greater quantities, until by mid-Pleistocene times some human gatherer/hunters were capable of taking prey much larger than themselves.

This should not be taken to mean, however, that hunting was the fundamental adaptation for all human populations, even at this relatively late stage in hominid evolution. The primate evidence in particular suggests that subsistence activities wax and wane over time in different populations, so that a pattern may become preeminent under certain environmental conditions while remaining relatively unimportant under other circumstances.

We also feel strongly that it is a dangerous oversimplification to think of hunting as the most influential behavior in the evolution of humanity, if for no other reason than that hunting becomes equated with aggression, leading to the development of sociopolitical theories of human nature that appear to the unwary to be scientifically based (e.g., Ardrey, 1961, 1976; K. Lorenz, 1966). In fact, we see no reason why any single behavior should assume such importance, and hold instead that the human adaptation has been and remains a multifaceted one, incorporating the ancient primate subsistence patterns of collecting both plant and animal foods while preying upon vertebrates. Primates are indeed omnivores; from prosimians and monkeys to apes and humans, we share an adaptation which, in some members of the order, has developed further into dietary specialization.

We hope that this book, in which evidence from all relevant fields has been assembled in one place for the first time, will encourage readers to adopt a balanced view of the role of hunting in human evolution, and to reconsider many of the premises about human uniqueness that originally stemmed from the hunting hypothesis.

Alan E. Mann

2.
Diet and Human Evolution

Thought: why does man kill? He kills for food. And not only food: frequently there must be a beverage.—*Woody Allen,*
Without Feathers

In proportion as man grows sensitive through civilization or through disease, he should diminish the quantity of cereals and fruits, which are far below him on the scale of evolution, and increase the quantity of animal food, which is nearly related to him in the scale of evolution, and therefore more easily assimilated.—*George Beard, M.D.,* Sexual Neurasthenia, *1898*

One of the most important activities engaged in by an animal is the search for and consumption of food. Many organisms have the biochemical machinery to synthesize virtually all the compounds needed for maintenance and growth from simple chemicals taken directly from the environment, and for them this is a rather straightforward process. Mammals and other vertebrates, however, have lost the ability to synthesize many nutrients and must actively seek these substances in their environment. As a result, most mammals have evolved elaborate morphological complexes used in hunger-satisfying behaviors, and mammalian diets include foods that contain these necessary nutrients.

Perhaps because hominids have few obvious morphological specializations for obtaining food which are not shared with other mammals, it has been difficult to reconstruct the dietary patterns of our ancestors during the course of human evolution. Unlike carnivore dentitions, for example, which are clearly adapted for killing and for shearing meat, modern human teeth show no obvious adaptation to specific foods; rather, they seem in some ways to resemble the teeth of mammalian omnivores such as bears or pigs. Further complicating the issue is the bewildering diversity of modern human diets, which range from those based almost totally on animal tissue to those which are entirely vegetarian.

Yet understanding the kinds of foods that formed the diets of earlier hominids is central to the formation of a reasonable picture of human evolution. It is evident that many of the most important morphological

10

changes in human evolution, such as reduction in the size of the teeth and development of bipedalism, must be directly related to the ways in which these complexes were used in obtaining and preparing food. Thus our attempts to understand fully the evolutionary development of these changes will be limited if we do not know how they made hominids more successful in getting food.

The development of certain food habits may also have exerted a profound influence on the evolution of other behavior. For example, reconstructions describing early hominids as predatory carnivores have associated this adaptation with aggression (Ardrey, 1961; Dart, 1959; DeVore and Washburn, 1963; Pfeiffer, 1969), cooperation, altruism, and continual sexual receptivity in females (Morris, 1967; Washburn, 1968; Washburn and Lancaster, 1968; Wilson, 1975).

Clearly, greater knowledge of the evolution of hominid food habits is essential if we are to settle many of these issues. This article explores some basic problems that arise in studying the evolution of hominid diets. The objective is to understand the evolution of the dietary adaptations that characterize today's gatherer/hunters and that appear to have been firmly established by the Middle Pleistocene, judging by archaeological sites such as Terra Amata (de Lumley, 1969b) and Torralba/Ambrona (Freeman, 1975b, and in this volume). Accordingly, I concentrate on the evidence of early hominid morphology and adaptations in an attempt to determine if a general gathering/hunting adaptation was ubiquitous among early hominids, or if another pattern preceded it.

SOURCES OF INFORMATION

The materials that can be used to reconstruct earlier hominid diets are varied. Archaeological remains have provided the most important evidence, but the subsistence patterns of modern human gatherer/hunters, non-human primates, and even social carnivores have also been used as sources of information. Inferences may be drawn from analyses of the hominid dentition and related structures, and there have been recent suggestions that chemical analysis of the strontium content of a fossil hominid bone may show the extent to which animal or vegetable foods were part of the diet. To a marked degree, however, the nature of these data limits their usefulness, as I shall show.

The archaeological record is a highly selected information source; some materials preserve very well and are routinely found during excavation, while others either are not preserved or leave such subtle traces that they are missed. Many dietary reconstructions have been based exclusively on the recovered evidence, ignoring items that might originally have been present but that have disintegrated long since. Because vertebrate bones preserve better than plant materials or invertebrate exoskeletons, the basic diet during much of human evolution has been viewed in terms of an emphasis on a single food resource: mammals that are hunted (as defined by Laughlin, 1968).

Further, archaeological data do not always accurately reflect the reality of site occupation and food utilization (Chaplin, 1971:120–22). For example, mammal bones were collected from the historic Fort Ligonier site in western Pennsylvania (occupied between 1758 and 1766 by the British Army); comparison with the written records shows that the bone remains correspond to rations that "would have sustained only two men for the length of time of the known occupancy, or the entire garrison at full strength (4,000 men) for just one day!" (Guilday, 1970:186). The major reasons for this discrepancy are that the recovered sample is not complete, that some of the bones disintegrated and, most important, that salt pork (probably the single largest portion of the meat ration) left no archaeological trace at all.

In some instances, dietary patterns derived from one kind of archaeological material differ in significant ways from dietary reconstructions based on other evidence from the same site. Thus the diet of the peoples of the Tehuacan Valley of Mexico, reconstructed from the preserved flora and fauna, differs from the diet suggested by the preserved coprolites, in both kinds and percentages of animal and plant foods present (MacNeish, 1967:300–302).

The analysis of hominid dietary patterns as revealed in the archaeological record is further complicated by what may be termed the "snack factor." Even if an archaeological site preserves an unusually complete record of the foods eaten at that spot, an appreciable percentage of the diet may have been consumed elsewhere. For example, Robson and Yen (1976) report that the Tasaday fill about 78% of their protein needs but only about 27% of their energy needs from meals eaten at the camp; much of the rest is presumably eaten during the day, as individuals immediately consume food discovered during their daily rounds.

Because archaeological remains do not preserve a complete record of extinct activity patterns and are subject to various interpretations, analogies are often drawn with living gatherer/hunters to fill the archaeological blanks or to decipher clues that might otherwise be incomprehensible (Chang, 1967; Yellen, 1976).

The major problem with an analogical approach to reconstructing dietary patterns is the cultural and temporal distance between earlier hominids and modern gatherer/hunters. Today almost all people depend on agriculture for food, although nonsettled gathering and hunting has been the hominid way of life for most of our evolutionary history. Very few human populations now subsist entirely on gathered and hunted foods, and there is some dispute about how representative of earlier gatherer/hunter hominids these groups may be (Perper and Schrire, 1977) Contemporary gatherer/hunters exist for the most part in marginal environments (but see Silberbauer, in this volume), perhaps forced there by more powerful, agriculturally based neighbors. The earlier richness of the gatherer/hunters' subsistence may never be fully appreciated, given the context of their currently impoverished refuge areas.

It has also been observed that living gatherer/hunters use a number of very sophisticated weapons, such as poison darts, bows and arrows, snares, and traps, which may have been beyond the technological capabilities of all but our most recent ancestors. Can the subsistence patterns of these well-equipped humans legitimately be compared to those of earlier hominids who had Oldowan, Acheulean, or Mousterian tool kits?

how would these preserve however

lithic/preserve well

Modern humans are able to speak, an ability that may have been very important in conveying specialized information about foods to other members of a social group. There are few firm data documenting the origin of speech [Holloway (1969) suggests an early origin, while Lieberman and Crelin (1971) view it as a more recent development], but with its introduction a more complex relationship with the environment would have begun.

The large brains of modern humans provide the biological basis for what we think of as human behaviors, thoughts, and actions. Early hominids were doubtless capable of many of these behaviors, but their less complex nervous systems may have narrowed the range of actions open to them, and thus have limited their ability to exploit a wide range of environments and foods.

Shepard (1973) suggests that the development of agriculture, accompanied by a growing technological complexity, has so modified the value systems and world views of Western society that we may be incapable of fully understanding the gatherer/hunter way of life. He believes that these developments have led to the idea prevalent in the West that gatherer/hunters are unable to support themselves without periodic population reductions caused by severe food shortages. This, in turn, fosters the notion that gathering and hunting is a very unsatisfactory way to live.

There have been many attempts to use the subsistence patterns of nonhuman primates as a basis for the reconstruction of extinct hominid diets. Chimpanzees (Teleki, 1975; Mann, 1972), baboons (DeVore and Washburn, 1963), and gelada monkeys (C. J. Jolly, 1970, 1972) have served as models, but their value has been disputed. Some workers have argued that primate analogies have little meaning in the study of human evolution (e.g., Sahlins, 1960; White and Dillingham, 1973), since there is such a vast gulf between the large-brained, tool- and language-using hominids and the other primates; this criticism applies with even more force to social carnivore models. Although cercopithecoid examples may be inappropriate because of the long evolutionary separation between hominids and Old World monkeys, comparative data from chimpanzees, our closest living relatives, may well provide insights into the basic adaptation of the immediate pongid ancestors of the Hominidae. It has recently been suggested that the pygmy chimpanzee (*Pan paniscus*) may be an especially appropriate model for the early phases of hominid evolution (Zihlman et al., 1978). Such comparisons may identify those features that are uniquely hominid and those that hominids share with their pongid relatives. This information, in turn, may be useful in understanding the behaviors that have evolved in the hominid line. However, hominids and pongids have evolved separately for 5 to 15 million years, and nothing is known of the extent to which the chimpanzee has changed since it last shared a common ancestor with the hominids.

Several models of early hominid feeding patterns have been based on features of the dentition. C. J. Jolly (1970, 1972) suggested that there are many similarities between the dentitions of early hominids and the gelada monkey (*Theropithecus gelada*), and that the hominids may therefore have occupied an herbivorous niche like that now exploited by the gelada in East Africa.

Observing the differences in size of the posterior teeth in gracile and robust australopithecines, Robinson (1954, 1956, 1963) has hypothesized that the large back teeth of the robust forms are an adaptation for chewing large quantities of vegetable foods with relatively little nutritive value, a diet which may have resembled that of the gorilla. The smaller back teeth of the gracile australopithecine, by contrast, are more suggestive of an omnivorous, open-country adaptation. Wolpoff (1973a,b, 1976) has emphasized the large size of the back teeth in *all* early hominids; the summed area of the posterior teeth, when compared with rough estimates of body size, show that surface chewing areas were very large in proportion to body weight. He suggests that this large chewing area with its characteristic thick occlusal enamel is indicative of very heavy mastication, perhaps of seeds but also of roots and other items that are hard to chew.

Although morphological studies of this sort clearly can provide some interesting indirect information that is helpful in corroborating theories of dietary habits based on other data, the basically conservative nature of dental change remains an important problem. Chimpanzees and gorillas have rather different diets (Schaller, 1963; Teleki, 1975; Van Lawick-Goodall, 1968) but it is very difficult to distinguish their teeth, although some promising but elaborate techniques have been developed (e.g., Lavelle, 1975).

Recent investigations of occlusal wear in mammals, using scanning electron microscopy (Walker, Hoeck, and Perez, 1978), have been able to distinguish browsing from grazing mammals by their wear patterns, and this method may prove to be an extremely important tool for understanding hominid diets. However, it is unfortunate that the last items eaten before the sample is collected tend to leave the most obvious markings on the occlusal enamel (Walker, Hoeck, and Perez, 1978, and Walker, personal communication). Thus if early hominids had a diverse diet, a great many would have to be sampled to obtain an accurate picture. Even then, conclusions may be biased if the hominids from one site represent a particular seasonal feeding time or a particular specialization.

Another promising source of information about earlier dietary patterns is chemical analysis of the hominid bones themselves. Most current studies in this area have focused on the level of strontium in hominid bones, on the assumption that the bones of herbivorous animals will contain higher concentrations of strontium than those of carnivores. However, preliminary work (Boaz and Hampel, 1978; A. Brown, 1973; A. Fuchs, personal communication) suggests that much more basic analysis is needed before we know whether meaningful results are possible with this technique. We need to know more about the exchange of chemicals between buried bones and the surrounding soil, as well as the processes by which chemicals are incorporated into living bone. Research is also needed to establish the range of strontium concentrations in modern herbivorous and carnivorous mammals. Until this basic work is done, it will be unclear whether the strontium technique can provide general, unambiguous information about hominid dietary patterns.

Finally, we must consider how the culturally influenced food preferences of Western societies have shaped our view of earlier dietary adaptations. For instance, few discussions of the evolution of hominid dietary patterns mention insects as a possible source of high-quality protein (with adequate amounts of all the essential amino acids), yet insects have been and continue to be extremely important in the diets of many peoples (Bodenheimer, 1951; Meyer-Rochow, 1973; Oliviera et al., 1976). Similarly, it is possible to ask whether the widely held view that the early hominid diet was predominantly meat may also derive in part from modern Western food preferences. The second quotation introducing this article states a view that was widely held early in this century.

This brief survey of the available sources of data for reconstructing early hominid dietary patterns underscores the fundamental difficulties that plague any attempt to reach reasonable conclusions. Each source supplies some information, but none provides a full enough picture of evolving hominid food preferences. There is a pressing need to develop techniques that will yield unambiguous data, perhaps based on chemical or trace-element analysis of fossil hominid bones or on the application of scanning electron microscopy to tooth occlusal surfaces. For the present, we are necessarily limited to the information provided by archaeological remains, supplemented by indirect data from living nonhuman primates, gatherer/ hunters, and morphological analyses of dental complexes.

DIETARY NEEDS OF
MODERN HUMANS

Modern human beings require between 40 and 50 different nutrients for the maintenance of good health and growth. Some of these are needed in rather large amounts, while others are necessary only in trace quantities. These nutrients are generally divided into five classes: carbohydrates, fats, proteins, vitamins, and minerals. To be classed as a nutrient, each substance in each category must serve at least one of the following functions: to be oxidized to liberate energy; to maintain and build body tissues; and to regulate body processes. Although between 12 and 15 different minerals and about 14 vitamins are known to be used in the body (see tables 2.1 and 2.2), it has not been demonstrated that all of these substances are essential for humans; therefore the total number of nutrients said to be required by humans varies, depending on whether a particular authority considers a certain substance vital (see Bogert, Briggs, and Calloway, 1973:8–9; Scrimshaw and Young, 1976:52).

In the United States, the Food and Nutrition Board of the National Research Council (NRC) of the National Academy of Sciences has been responsible for determining recommended dietary allowances of essential nutrients (see tables 2.1 and 2.2). The designation of a substance as an essential nutrient and the level of its recommended daily intake are based on several factors, which include the observation that deficiency diseases will result from its absence or low intake, experimental studies on humans and other animals to determine its importance in metabolism and maintenance, and by reference to the amount which is consumed and maintained in the bloodstream and lost via excretion or through the skin.

It is possible that equally important nutrients have not yet been recognized. It is also possible that some human populations have specific nutritional requirements not found among the majority of living humans. The limited studies of nonhuman primate diets, both in the field and in captivity (e.g., Bilbey, 1968; du Boulay and Crawford, 1968; Portman, 1970b; Short, 1968; Thorington, 1970; and see Harding, in this volume) suggest that the nutritive needs of these animals are similar to those of modern humans in terms of the range of substances which are essential. It seems likely that the dietary requirements for good health have remained about the same throughout human evolution.

There is considerable disagreement, however, in the field of human nutrition concerning the precise amounts of many nutrients that should be

Table 2.1. Recommended daily allowances (RDA) of energy, protein, and vitamins

| | Body weight (kg) | Energy (Kcal) | Protein (g) | Water-soluble vitamins | | | | | | Fat-soluble vitamins | | |
				C (mg)	Thiamine (mg)	Riboflavin (mg)	Niacin (mg)	Folic acid (mg)	B_{12} (µg)	A (retinol) (µg)	D^a (µg)	E (mg)
Children												
1–3 years[b]												
NRC	13	1,300	23	40	.7	.8	9.0	100	1.0	400	10	7
FAO	13.4	1,360	16	20	.5	.8	9.0	100	.9	250	10	—
Adult												
males												
NRC	70	2,700	56	45	1.4	1.6	18.0	400	3.0	1,000	—	15
FAO	65	3,000	37	30	1.2	1.8	19.8	200	2.0	750	2.5	—
Adult												
females												
NRC	58	2,000	46	45	1.0	1.2	13.0	400	3.0	800	—	12
FAO	55	2,200	29	30	.9	1.3	14.5	200	2.0	750	2.5	—

Sources: Food and Nutrition Board of the National Research Council (1974), and Food and Agriculture Organization, World Health Organization (FAO/WHO, 1975).

[a]Vitamin D: 2.5 µg = 100 IU. The NRC lists no RDA for adults; 10 µg has no risk of toxicity.

[b]The NRC and FAO standards for other age groups of children cannot be compared because different age ranges are used.

Table 2.2. Recommended daily intake of essential elements for adults

	NRC	FAO	Schroeder
Elements			
Calcium	800 mg	400–500 mg	1.1 g
Phosphorus	800 mg		1.4 g
Potassium	2.5 g		3.3 g
Chlorine	*		5.1 g
Sodium	*		4.4 g
Magnesium	300–350 mg	200–300 mg	310 mg
Iron	10–18 mg[a]	5–28 mg[a]	13 mg
Trace Elements[b]			
Copper	2 mg	4.8 mg[c]	5 mg
Chromium	*	0.02–0.5 mg	3 mg
Fluorine	*	*	3 mg
Iodine	0.1–0.13 mg	0.1–.14 mg	0.1 mg
Manganese	*	2.3 mg	3 mg
Molybdenum	*	0.12 mg[d]	0.2 mg
Nickel	**	**	**
Selenium	*	*	0.01 mg
Silicon	**	*	0.3 mg
Tin	**	**	
Vanadium	**	*	*
Zinc	15 mg	5.5–22 mg	13 mg

Sources: For the NRC column, Food and Nutrition Board (1974); for the FAO column, WHO Expert Committee (1973) and Passmore (1974); and Schroeder (1973).

[a]NRC: adult males, 10 mg; adult females, 18 mg.

FAO: adult males, 5–9 mg; adult females, 14–28 mg.

[b]"Those elements that occur or function in living tissues in concentrations most conveniently expressed in mcg/g or mcg/litre [μg/g or μg/l] are generally considered as trace elements" (WHO Expert Committee, 1973:5).

[c]Based on recommended 80 μg/kg body weight for a 60-kg adult.

[d]Based on tentative recommendation of 2 μg/kg body weight for a 60-kg adult.

*Recommended intake not established.

**Possibly essential, but implications for human nutrition unknown.

included in the daily diet (Campbell, 1974; Durnin et al., 1973; Hegsted, 1972). As Scrimshaw and Young point out (1976), deficiency diseases will result from the absence or low intake of certain nutrients, but good health and well being, the other end of the scale, are very hard to define. Variability in nutrient requirements is well established in humans. The NRC, for example, recommends increased amounts of protein, calcium, and carbohydrates during pregnancy and lactation. High activity levels, as well as work in cold regions and other stressful environments, call for an increased intake of energy-producing foods. Recommended daily allowances of many nutrients are based on individual characteristics such as age, sex, height, weight, and occupation. However, while the daily allowance tables discriminate between different classes of individuals, the intakes recommended by the NRC "are intended to be above the estimated requirements of most individuals in the population" (Hegsted, 1972:256). Hegsted also notes that the recommended daily allowances represent an average requirement, and if some individuals or populations do not consume these amounts, we need not necessarily consider them under-nourished. Indeed, there have been differences in the recommended daily intakes of some nutrients as established by the NRC and by the Food and Agriculture Organization of the World Health Organization (FAO, WHO) (table 2.1).

The recommended daily allowances of calcium, protein, and vitamin C established by the NRC have been significantly higher than the allowances for these nutrients established by the FAO (tables 2.1 and 2.2). These differences "are related largely to the degree of ignorance in relating minimum requirements to recommended levels for optimal health" (Campbell, 1974:178). It may also be that the marked preference of Americans for foods high in calcium and protein has led to the establishment of excessively high recommended levels of these substances.

Scrimshaw and Young (1976) have observed that the nutritional needs of human populations with different geographic, cultural, and genetic backgrounds may vary considerably. Durnin et al. (1973) have suggested that the energy utilization of different individuals and populations varies so greatly that we do not really know the energy requirements of modern humans. They state that "studies in a number of countries suggest that some people, perhaps through some mechanism of adaptation, are able to be healthy and active on energy intakes which, by current standards, would be considered inadequate" (1973:418).

As observed earlier, Robson and Yen (1976) found in their analysis of Tasaday diets that about 78% of protein requirements and only about 27% of energy requirements (based on FAO tables) were provided by formal foraging and consumption at the camp. These figures do not take into account casual foraging away from camp, which the observers were unable to document fully and which no doubt contributed additional protein and energy to the diet. It is unlikely, however, that casual foraging would make up the discrepancy between the known food intake from formal foraging and the estimated dietary needs of the Tasaday individuals. McArthur (1960) also found deficits in energy intake (by FAO standards) among Australian Aborigines subsisting on naturally occurring foods, of 41% in one group and 48% in another. The excess protein in the diet of these Australians may help compensate for the lack of other energy foods, but this is not certain.

Studies in New Guinea (e.g., Bailey, 1963; Hipsley and Kirk, 1965;

Oomen, 1961) also show that actual energy and protein intakes were lower than the estimated requirements in many different groups, yet the people appeared to be in good health.

If there is little agreement on the optimal diet for all modern humans, the situation becomes even more complicated when we attempt to apply these data to the diet of earlier hominids. One important difficulty is that we know little about body size in earlier hominids; estimates for gracile australopithecines range between 18 and 37 kg (McHenry, 1976). If we use the NRC standard of 0.6 g of protein per kilogram of body weight per day, the protein needs of a gracile australopithecine would vary between 11 and 22 g per day—an appreciable range. Moreover, sexual dimorphism in early hominids may have been much greater than exists in modern humans, so individual dietary requirements may have been even more variable. Finally, little is known about the health implications of the short-term absence or low intake of certain nutrients, making reconstruction of hominid diets even more uncertain. Perhaps the most reasonable approach is to examine a number of essential nutrients whose limited availability or low concentration might have had a significant influence.

Although many essential nutrients are widely available in different foods and were therefore relatively easy for early hominids to obtain, others are found in only a few foods or in very small amounts in certain foods. Such nutrients include proteins, energy sources, essential fatty acids (especially linoleic acid), and vitamins B_{12} and C. These dietary constraints may have limited possible adaptations or use of specific environments by early hominids.

Proteins are essential to human health. Their constituent amino acids are used by the body to build and repair tissues and can be utilized for energy in the absence of other nutrients. Of the 20 common amino acids, 8 are considered essential, i.e., they cannot be synthesized in the body but must be supplied by foods. A ninth amino acid, histidine, is considered essential only for infants (National Research Council 1974). Most nutritionists consider only one sulfur-containing amino acid, methionine, to be essential, since it cannot be synthesized directly; however, Scrimshaw and Young (1976) also place the other sulfur-bearing amino acid, cystine, in the essential category, primarily because cystine can be synthesized only from methionine and because stress is placed on the diet when methionine must be utilized for both amino acids.

Protein is found in a variety of animal and plant foods, including vertebrate and invertebrate animal tissue, eggs, milk, seeds, beans, vegetables such as corn, asparagus, broccoli, cauliflower, potato, and kale, and grains such as rice, wheat, rye, and millet. Animal tissue, eggs, and dairy products contain enough of the eight essential amino acids to permit the body to synthesize protein. All other protein sources lack one or more of these essential amino acids. Adequate amounts of all eight must be consumed at fairly short intervals since spare or incomplete sets of amino acids are not stored long in the body but are metabolized for energy. Lack of one amino acid will result in decreasing utilization of all the others. "Poor quality" protein sources generally lack one or more of the following amino acids: tryptophan, methionine, lysine, or threonine. In modern agricultural societies where the main protein sources are vegetables, legumes, and grains, complementary foods such as rice (poor in lysine) and beans (with adequate amounts of lysine) are eaten together to achieve the necessary protein intake.

Presumably, nonagricultural hominid societies relying on the collection of a wide variety of foods, whether animal or vegetable, would be in a much better position to satisfy their protein needs than more specialized farming groups (Jerome, 1976). Unfortunately, there is little published information on the amino acid content of foods important in the adaptation of modern gathering/hunting groups such as the !Kung (Lee, 1973; Wehmeyer, Lee, and Whiting, 1969) or the Tasaday (Robson and Yen, 1976), but the few available reports do stress the high percentage of protein acquired from different sources in the diets of these peoples.

Modern international standards consider body weight and other factors in establishing daily protein requirements. In one study, Scrimshaw and Young (1976) discovered that a group of American undergraduate males achieved protein balance with the consumption of 0.57 g of protein per kilogram of body weight per day. While both the FAO tables and the most recent NRC standards now recommend between 0.5 and 0.6 g of protein per kilogram of body weight per day, it is still unclear whether this amount is needed by all populations. As noted earlier, some studies suggest that some modern human groups may remain fit with lower daily intakes of protein. Thus it is not possible at this time to conclude that the earliest hominids required daily protein allowances similar to those which international standards have established for modern humans.

Human energy requirements can be satisfied by the utilization of dietary protein as well as by fats and carbohydrates. Total energy need is strongly tied to an individual's body weight, height, age, sex, and activity levels, as well as to such environmental factors as temperature. The most efficient way for the body to gain calories to support basal metabolism and activity is through the direct oxidation of carbohydrates, protein, and fat from the diet. Body protein and stored fat, the latter primarily derived from dietary carbohydrates, are used when dietary sources are insufficient. Indeed, protein yields 5.65 Kcal/g and fat 9.45 Kcal/g, while carbohydrates yield only 4.1 Kcal/g (Bogert, Briggs, and Calloway, 1973).

In general, foods with a high energy value tend to have a high fat or low water content. Dairy products such as butter and cheese, fatty meats, many insects, nuts, and dried fruits are high in calories, while most fresh fruits and vegetables, high in water content, are relatively poor sources of energy.

It has been observed that the daily diets of modern gathering/hunting peoples are insufficient in calories, especially at certain times of the year, when compared with amounts recommended by the FAO and the NRC (Robson and Yen, 1976; Truswell and Hansen, 1976). Seasonal calorie deficits (according to FAO and NRC standards) in the diets of !Kung people of the Kalahari may result in thinner layers of subcutaneous fat at certain times of year and may be implicated in their somewhat smaller stature (Truswell and Hansen, 1976) and in controlling fertility (R. E. Frisch, 1973, 1975; Frisch and McArthur, 1974; N. Howell, 1976b).

It is very difficult to estimate energy needs in early hominids, not only because their body size has not been definitely established but also because the amount of work performed daily can radically alter energy needs. For example, the Food and Nutrition Board of the National Research Council (1974) estimates that a 70-kg modern adult uses up to 2.5 Kcal/min in "very light" activities (laboratory work, driving an automobile), and between 7.5 and 12 Kcal/min when engaged in "heavy work" (walking uphill with a load, climbing, felling a tree). Let us assume that a female gracile australopithecine weighing between 18 and 37 kg engages in some very light work, some light work, some moderate, and a little heavy work during the day. Although modern estimates of energy needs may not be appropriate, a very rough energy estimate for this australopithecine would be between 1,000 and 1,900 Kcal/day, depending on body size. Lee (1969, 1973) has estimated the daily energy requirements of the !Kung San as approximately 2,000 Kcal [average male weight is 47.9 kg, and average female weight, 40 kg (Truswell and Hansen, 1976:172)].

Although high intake of fats (particularly saturated fats) may contribute to the development of obesity and coronary disorders, dietary fat is essential for the maintenance of good health. Fatty acids are involved in many physiological activities, serve as a precursor for the prostaglandins, and are required for body cell maintenance and metabolism (Scrimshaw and Young, 1976; Bogert, Briggs, and Calloway, 1973; Food and Nutrition Board, 1974).

One of the most important fatty acids—the polyunsaturated linoleic acid—cannot be synthesized by the body and must be supplied by the diet. Linoleic acid is found primarily in vegetable fats, especially in nuts and seeds, and is also well represented in the fats of some insects (Oliviera et al., 1976). Its presence in animals is quite variable, since fatty acid composition in animals frequently reflects the fatty acids present in their diet (Lough and Garton, 1968). Ruminant digestive systems contain a bacterium that hydrogenates unsaturated dietary fats into saturated fats; hence the amount of unsaturated linoleic acid in ruminant meat is usually quite low. The fats of some amphibians (frogs, tortoises), some reptiles (lizards, pythons, crocodiles), and some birds contain relatively high proportions of linoleic acid. Most of the limited number of animals examined, however, contain only small amounts of linoleic acid. Rabbits, bushbucks (*Tragelaphus scriptus*), giant pandas (*Ailuropoda melanoleuca*), and one species of baboon (*Papio hamadryas*) contain higher amounts (Hilditch and Williams, 1964).

Deficiency of essential fatty acids has been found in humans and produces such effects as poor growth, dermatitis, poor reproductive performance, lowered caloric efficiency, and decreased resistance to a number of stress conditions (Food and Nutrition Board, 1974). Some early hominids may have consumed insufficient amounts of linoleic acid, particularly if they specialized in hunting ruminants or had diets that varied widely with the seasons.

It should be emphasized that the saturated fat in domestic ruminants— the marbling that gives the meat of Western grain-fed animals its distinctive, highly prized taste—is an artificial product of domestication. Non-domesticated ruminants do not possess this intramuscular fat, and the thick fat deposits of other animals such as seals and walruses (H. Draper, 1977) tend to consist largely of unsaturated fats (but not linoleic acid). Thus the taste preferences which have such importance in modern Western diets may not have been an important factor in determining dietary choices for early hominids, particularly in choosing between animal and vegetable foods.

Vitamin B_{12}, the largest and most complex vitamin yet discovered, is essential for vertebrates, and a severe anemia results from its deficiency. Unlike almost every other vitamin, B_{12} is not found in plant foods; the principal dietary sources are animal tissue and liver (Maugh, 1973). Although only a small amount of B_{12} is thought to be necessary daily (0.003 mg for an adult), its limited availability in foods may have had serious consequences for hominid groups who were strongly dependent on plant foods. Vitamin B_{12} deficiency has been observed in modern human vegetarians (Herbert, 1968).

Most mammals possess the biochemical machinery to synthesize vitamin C (ascorbic acid), but this ability has been lost in humans and in many other primates tested (Stone, 1965). Pauling (1970) hypothesized that the enzyme which is responsible for production of ascorbic acid and is found in the liver of other mammals was lost during primate evolution because ample supplies of this vitamin were present in the diet. Consequently, it would have been disadvantageous to maintain the biochemical machinery necessary for synthesizing it. Ritenbaugh (1978:115) has recently suggested, however, that some ability to synthesize vitamin C may still be present in modern humans, citing a single study which shows that the human placenta is capable of some synthesis.

Vitamin C is found widely in fruits and vegetables, but only small amounts are present in animal tissue. In a recent review of the Alaskan Eskimo diet, H. Draper (1977) noted that scurvy, a disease associated with vitamin C deficiency, is rare among these people, despite a lack of fruits and vegetables for most of the year. Draper believes that "the Eskimo practice of eating their food in the raw, frozen, or lightly cooked state was a critical factor in preserving the small amounts of vitamin C necessary to prevent scurvy (less than 10 mg per day)" (1977:310). This observation is interesting because it suggests that the discovery of fire, usually considered to have been a great advantage for hominids because it broadened the diet to include items needing to be cooked to soften or detoxify them, may also have had some serious disadvantages for any hominids subsisting largely on meat.

This brief discussion of nutritional factors suggests that the more varied the dietary base, the less likely are serious nutritional deficiencies. Similarly, it has been noted that a gathering/hunting adaptation, based on a seasonally diversified diet, is capable of providing much sounder nutrition than that available to many agricultural groups, who depend on one or two staple crops (Jerome, 1976; Lee, 1968; Truswell and Hansen, 1976). It is also apparent that gatherer/hunters living in environments rich enough to provide a wide variety of food sources take advantage of this bounty and make use of many different foods; for example, the !Kung (Lee, 1968, 1973) and the Hadza (Woodburn, 1968a). In food-poor environments such as the Arctic (Damas, 1972) and tropical forests like those inhabited by the Guayaki Indians (Clastres, 1972), the choice of food is more limited, the techniques for exploiting available sources more specialized, and the chances for nutritional deficiencies greater. But even in environments usually thought to be relatively deficient in certain foods, the inhabitants have often discovered effective techniques for maximizing scarce resources. Nickerson, Rowe, and Richter (1973) discuss the methods used by some North Alaskan Eskimos to exploit the sometimes abundant, but short-lived, appearance of plant foods. They report that six different varieties of berries and the shoots, buds, and leaves of willow, various roots, and wild spinach are gathered in season, with some being frozen or preserved in seal oil for consumption during the winter.

Thus one implication is that the broader the dietary base, the better the chance for adaptive success. However, it is also clear that nutritional factors alone do not preclude the possibility that early hominids were quite specialized in terms of diet. Individual populations could have been equally well nourished as carnivores (assuming that some of the meat was eaten raw or relatively uncooked, thus preserving vitamin C), or as herbivores (assuming that small amounts of insects were incidentally ingested with the vegetation to provide the needed vitamin B_{12}).

Nevertheless, given the available archaeological evidence and what is known of the dietary patterns of living gatherer/hunters and chimpanzees, it appears to me unlikely that all early hominids were almost exclusively carnivorous or herbivorous. It is more reasonable to suggest that the diet of most early hominids fell within the broad range of today's gatherer/hunter diets, but that within the wide spectrum of this adaptation, local environmental resources and seasonal scarcity may have forced some individual populations to become more dependent on vegetable or animal-tissue foods than others.

DIET AND ENVIRONMENT

A discussion of the evolution of hominid feeding patterns must include the environmental setting in which the hominids were adapting. Reconstruction of the prehistoric environment is an obvious first step in drawing up a list of the resources available for hominid exploitation and possible limitations on food preferences. Unfortunately, our knowledge of early environmental settings is incomplete and sometimes ambiguous. Even in those rare circumstances where the habitat seems to be clearly established, dietary interpretations differ greatly. One widely held interpretation is that early hominids evolved in open savannah, in the sense that this term is used by van Couvering and van Couvering (1976) to describe open-country, nonforest zones.

In announcing the discovery of the Taung child, Dart (1925:198) noted that geologists believed the current semiarid, treeless environment had probably not changed significantly "since Cretaceous times." In the same year, writing about his examination of the Taung fossil, Broom (1925:571) observed that "we can assert with considerable confidence that it could not have been a forest-living animal, and that almost certainly it lived among the rocks and on the plains, as does the baboon of today." Later discussions, which included the discoveries in the Sterkfontein Valley (for example, Barbour, 1949; Washburn, 1951), emphasized that there had been no great change in the climate since the australopithecines lived in the area, and that the associated animal fossils, baboons and antelope, were those of the plains and not the forest. The presence of a bipedal hominid on the open savannah appeared to be a logical association: hominids were thought to have evolved their specialized locomotion as a response to the treeless, open country (see Washburn, 1951, 1968).

One of the major problems in accepting a savannah habitat for early hominid evolution is the lack of any positive evidence to establish this association. Presumably, as Pilbeam and Simons (1965) have suggested, the hominids originated in the tropics of the Old World, but in what sort of habitat and under what circumstances is unclear. During the Miocene, Africa underwent a large-scale environmental transformation, with open woodland and savannah habitats increasingly replacing tropical forests (Andrews and van Couvering, 1975; van Couvering and van Couvering, 1976). It is possible that this environmental change served as the background for the origin of the hominids, and that the need to adapt to increasing amounts of open country created the selection pressures which led to their appearance. However, I must emphasize that there is no direct fossil evidence for this association [indeed, there are suggestions that the hominids did not appear until much later, perhaps 7 m.y. B.P. (Sarich, 1971)], and it remains to be fully demonstrated that the Hominidae actually originated in Africa, or that they are the product of the savannah.

Even though there is little substantive evidence for the hypothesis that the needs of life in the open country shaped the early evolution of the hominids, it continues to be supported by many scholars. There is little agreement, however, about what the hominids might have eaten in this habitat. Leopold and Ardrey (1974) have argued that there would have been only a limited number of vegetable foods available on the savannah to a mammal with few dental and digestive specializations, and thus early hominids are best viewed as predators. In contrast C. J. Jolly (1970, 1972), who also sees the early hominids as open-country forms, feels their diet was composed of "the seeds and rhizomes of grasses and the tough, dry fruits of savannah trees and shrubs, with the addition of many insects and leaves, occasional fleshy fruits from riverine forests, and some vertebrate meat. In other words . . . foods requiring fine comminution and hard grinding" (1972:10). Szalay, however, feels that the early hominid dental system is better seen as an adaptation to hunting and scavenging, with the cheek teeth with their thickened enamel being used for "cracking ribs, metapodials, joints, or for increased longevity, or for both" (1975:428).

Baboons and chimpanzees can and do move through a variety of habitats in their yearly round (Altmann and Altmann, 1970; Harding, 1976; Rowell, 1966; Suzuki, 1976; van Lawick-Goodall, 1968), as do many modern gatherer/hunters (Lee and DeVore, 1968b). It is highly probable that early hominids were at least as flexible as modern gatherer/hunters and nonhuman primates; yet the fossil record may never show this. Taphonomy, "the study of the transition (in all its details) of animal remains from the biosphere into the lithosphere" (Efremov, 1940:85, quoted by Behrensmeyer, 1975:476) has made important contributions to the understanding of the agencies responsible for the accumulation and composition of fossil bone assemblages. However, conditions in various habitats do not equally favor fossilization, but vary according to such factors as rainfall, temperature, humidity, type of major vegetative cover, amount of biological activity in the topsoil, depositional conditions favoring rapid covering of remains, and other features (Brouwer, 1966). In general, forest floors are very poor places for fossilization. Unless a forest animal falls into a context where rapid deposition of sediments is occurring—such as a stream—and the bones can be quickly removed from destructive agencies, its remains rapidly disappear. Only a small number of habitats offer optimal conditions for deposition of bony remains. Therefore, most fossil samples may derive from those environments most conducive to long-term preservation, even though these environments may have been exploited only marginally by hominids, or occupied for only brief intervals during the year.

Like baboons and chimpanzees, early hominids may have exploited many different environmental zones. As a result, it is extremely difficult to make broad generalizations about the dietary patterns of early hominids, based solely on environmental reconstructions. Examination of the evidence for the environmental context of the early fossil locales may provide us with *some* information useful in reconstructing early dietary patterns. Studies now in progress may be able to provide relevant environmental information from middle and late Miocene *Ramapithecus* sites in Pakistan and Hungary (Pilbeam, Meyer, et al., 1977; M. Kretzoi, personal communication), and these studies can be compared with preliminary descriptions of the environment of *R. wickeri* at Fort Ternan in Africa [K/Ar age of 14 m.y. B.P. from a tuff 30–40 feet above the fossil horizon (Bishop, 1967:40)] (Andrews and Evans, 1979; Andrews and Walker, 1976). The fauna at Fort Ternan was apparently mixed, with elements from open country, forest, and woodland represented in the sample. On the basis of represented faunas, Andrews and Evans (1979) suggest that the Fort Ternan environment during ramapithecine times was woodland in nature, comparable in some ways to Bed I at Olduvai, and different from the reconstructed forest environment of the early Miocene dryopithecine East African site of Songhor, perhaps indicating the beginning of an adaptive shift from forest to nonforest habitats.

Much more evidence is available for the environmental setting of the hominids of the latest Miocene, the Pliocene, and the early Pleistocene (about 5.5–1.5 m.y. B.P.). These hominids, grouped together here for convenience as australopithecines, are known from sizable collections in both East and South Africa.

As noted earlier, the discovery of the Taung fossil in South Africa was a major impetus for development of the "savannah hypothesis." Recent investigations of the South African sites have suggested, however, that earlier reconstructions of these areas as savannah may not be totally correct. At Taung, for example, Butzer (1974) has reanalyzed the geology of the australopithecine deposit and has shown that the breccia in which the immature australopithecine cranial material was discovered was formed much later than had been thought previously. Therefore, the environment may not have been as arid as Dart and others suggested, but received about as much rainfall as does the Sterkfontein Valley today.

Vrba's work on the bovids at Sterkfontein and Swartkrans (1974, 1975) suggests that the fossils from these sites accumulated under varying environmental conditions. She distinguishes an earlier phase, associated with the gracile Sterkfontein australopithecines, containing bovid fossils whose modern forms are "to a greater or lesser extent bush-loving and water-dependent" (1974:23) and a later phase, associated with the Swartkrans robust australopithecines, containing more open-country forms, suggesting less bush cover. She notes, however, that the presence of several fossil bovids in all phases indicates that grassland existed nearby during the accumulation of all the deposits.

On the basis of chert/quartz ratios and sand-grain angularity, Brain (1958) concluded that rainfall in the Sterkfontein Valley increased from gracile australopithecine times to the present, his results being somewhat at variance with Vrba's. It is interesting to note that the bovid fossil assemblages from the Sterkfontein Valley sites indicate that a variety of habitats existed in the area of the cave deposits. The nature of these South African fossil-bearing locales is also noteworthy—they are solution cavities deep in the dolomite hills. Australopithecine bones, along with the bones of other animals, pieces of stone, surface soil, and other debris, tumbled down a shaft and became incorporated in the breccia (Brain, 1958; Sampson, 1974; Tobias and Hughes, 1969). These accumulations probably took a reasonably long time to collect (in terms of mammal generations), with 20,000 years suggested as the interval for accumulation of the main Swartkrans robust australopithecine breccia (Brain, 1970).

Thus it is reasonable to question environmental reconstructions in the area of the australopithecine-bearing caves. All the late Pliocene–early Pleistocene Transvaal deposits, including those without australopithecine remains such as Bolt's Farm, are found in similar geological contexts (Brain, 1958; Cooke, 1963) and may represent the only possible local situation within this time span that favored fossilization. Australopithecines may have spent very little time in the areas near the caves, yet over the course of thousands of generations, individuals died or were killed in the neighborhood [possibly by predators, as Brain (1970) suggested for the Swartkrans site], and their bones eventually ended up in the cave breccia deposits. This may explain why there is such a high percentage of juvenile specimens in the Swartkrans sample (Mann, 1975). Any attempt to compare the demography of australopithecine samples from these sites with living populations is a dubious enterprise (Mann, 1975).

East Africa presents somewhat similar problems. Geological paly-nological, and taphonomic reports on the australopithecine sites at Olduvai Gorge (Hay, 1973, 1976), Lake Turkana (Behrensmeyer, 1975; Bonnefille, 1976a; Coppens et al., 1976; Johnson and Raynolds, 1976; Maglio, 1972), and the Omo Basin (Bonnefille, 1976b; Coppens et al., 1976;

Howell, 1976) suggest a generally mosaic character for the surrounding areas, with a variety of habitats close by. At Olduvai Gorge, the hominid sites are usually located along stream channels or along the shores of a perennial alkaline lake that fluctuated in length from 7 to 25 km. Apparently both savannah and well-watered, well-forested volcanic highlands were nearby (Hay, 1973, 1976). Pollen evidence from australopithecine levels at sites east of Lake Turkana reveals rainfall considerably greater than that today, with indications of more forest and bush vegetation and a more closed habitat (Bonnefille, 1976a). Behrensmeyer's taphonomic and geological studies (1975, 1976a) suggest that most hominid bones near Lake Turkana are found in contexts indicating that they were deposited along the lake margin or along stream channels. These locales also appear to have been rather heavily forested, with open country existing between water courses. The evidence is similar at Omo, with pollen samples from 2–3 million years ago suggesting forest at the higher elevations and wooded savannah and riverine forest within the Omo Basin itself. Savannah grasses occur throughout the sequence, however, and the pollen profile reflects apparent decreases in rainfall associated with changes in savannah grass types toward the end of this period (Bonnefille, 1976b).

In sum, the paleo-environmental evidence from a variety of early hominid locales strongly suggests that different habitats existed near the australopithecine finds, and it is difficult to conclude that early hominids were limited to any one zone.

In view of the ability of modern gatherer/hunters to exploit a number of habitats during a yearly round and the similar patterns observed in baboons and chimpanzees, early hominids may have seasonally exploited various habitats, with groups specializing in different food resources in separate geographic areas. This strategy would have the obvious advantage of increasing the range of food items available, thereby reducing the possibility of serious nutritional deficiencies. This suggestion leads, however, to the consideration of a difficult problem—whether this pattern applies equally to the various kinds of early hominids.

HOMINID MORPHOLOGY AND DIET

The earliest fossil evidence attributed to the Hominidae comes from Middle and Upper Miocene deposits in East Africa, South Asia, Europe, and the Middle East (Andrews, 1971; Andrews and Tekkaya, 1976; Andrews and Tobien, 1977; Kretzoi, 1975; L. S. B. Leakey, 1962, 1967, 1968; Pilbeam, Barry, et al., 1977; Pilbeam, Meyer, et al., 1977; Pilbeam and Simons, 1965; Simons, 1961, 1964, 1972, 1976; von Koenigswald, 1972; Walker and Andrews, 1973). Although many fossils have been collected from these areas, the hominid status of these specimens, generally assigned to the taxa *Ramapithecus punjabicus* (South Asia), *R. wickeri* (East Africa and the Middle East), and *Rudapithecus hungaricus* (Hungary) is still strongly debated (see the chapters on *Ramapithecus* in Tuttle, 1975a). Pilbeam, Meyer, et al. (1977) have suggested that it may be more appropriate to place *Ramapithecus, Sivapithecus,* and *Gigantopithecus* into a separate hominoid family, the Ramapithecidae, and that one or another member of this family was the ancestor of the australopithecines and later members of the Hominidae. They believe that these forms are part of a group which differed sufficiently from the Pongidae and the Dryopithecidae to warrant their inclusion in a separate family, and that their common features (including thick occlusal enamel, reduced canines, and shortened faces) reflect the evolution of a distinctive adaptation.

Morphological analyses of australopithecine fossils from East and South Africa have resulted in various interpretations of the number of early hominid taxa, their phylogenetic relationships, and their possible adaptive differences (Johanson and White, 1979; L. S. B. Leakey, Tobias, and Napier, 1964; R. Leakey and Walker, 1976; Robinson, 1954, 1963, 1967, 1968, 1972; Walker and Leakey, 1978; Wolpoff, 1973a,b). The discovery at East Turkana of crania with features similar to those of *Homo erectus* (e.g., KNM-ER 3733) in a level roughly contemporaneous with a hyperrobust skull (KNM-ER 406) demonstrates that at least two independent hominid lineages existed at one point (1.5–1.6 m.y. B.P.). In fact, as many as four independent hominid lineages may have coexisted in East Africa (and possibly South Africa as well) between about 3.0 and 1.3 m.y. B.P.

These problems of lineage raise several crucial questions. What, if any, where the differences in dietary adaptation among the various hominid groups? Did the robust South African australopithecine, *Australopithecus robustus,* share adaptive patterns with *A. boisei*, the hyperrobust form from East Africa? Did *A. africanus* and *A. robustus* belong to different lineages, or were they temporal segments of a variable species (Wolpoff, 1970, 1971, 1976), perhaps separated in time (Tobias, 1973a)? Was the group that includes *Homo habilis* and other fossils attributed to *Homo* from East Africa (R. Leakey and Walker, 1976) and from Sterkfontein (Hughes and Tobias, 1977) separate from the gracile australopithecine lineage, or did the gracile form evolve into the genus *Homo* (Tobias, 1976; Weiss and Mann, 1978)? An understanding of possible adaptive and dietary differences among the various australopithecine groups is essential for the resolution of these taxonomic questions.

It would also be extremely helpful to know the identity of the hominid form or forms responsible for the Oldowan industrial complex (Isaac, 1976a). The archaeological sites at Olduvai (Isaac and Crader, in this volume; M. D. Leakey, 1971), east of Lake Turkana (Isaac, 1978; Isaac and

Crader, in this volume), and the Omo Basin (Merrick, 1976), are the remains of hominid living floors. They contain scattered animal bones (sometimes thoroughly smashed), stone tools, and occasionally hominid bones and teeth. It is not clear which early hominid form or forms was responsible for these accumulations. Finally, it is interesting to consider the relationships between such well-studied hominid traits as small canines and bipedalism and the adaptation of the early hominids and whether these traits are as central to human evolution as is usually thought.

Answers to several of these questions seem relatively clear cut. First, the hyperrobust australopithecine *A. boisei* (known only from East Africa) and possibly the South African *A. robustus* possess a specialized masticatory system different from that of contemporary and later hominids. This masticatory complex is composed of premolars and molars with very large occlusal surfaces, anterior teeth that are small in comparison to the posterior teeth, and strongly developed masticatory muscles, including the anterior portion of temporalis and an anterior shifting of masseter fibers. These muscular changes permitted a more effective bite force over the posterior teeth and were accompanied by the development of a sagittal crest to provide increased attachment areas for temporalis, and by enlarged areas on the zygomatic arch for the attachment of masseter. These modifications of the masticatory complex all suggest that *A. boisei* and perhaps *A. robustus* were adapted to a niche different from that of other hominids. Present evidence suggests that *A. boisei* was limited to a period from about 2.0 to 1.5 m.y. B.P. It may thus be an evolutionary development from earlier *A. robustus* forms, gradually evolving into a specialized niche that evidently required very heavy masticatory force. This force could have been used for crushing bones, eating small objects, or masticating large amounts of food with relatively low nutritional value, such as the wild celery and bamboo that make up much of the mountain gorilla's diet (Schaller, 1963). At present, however, the exact nature of the robust australopithecine niche is not known, nor do we know the extent to which these creatures shared with other contemporary hominids such behaviors as tool-making and the use of a home base.

I favor a two-lineage view of hominid evolution, although obviously future research may show the hominid fossil record to be more complicated. One of these lineages consists of an earlier form of australopithecine, *A. afarensis* from Laetoli, Tanzania and Hadar, Ethiopia (Johanson, White, and Coppens, 1978; Johanson and White, 1979), which evolved into the gracile *A. africanus,* known from South Africa (Taung, Sterkfontein, and Makapansgat), possibly from the Omo Basin (Howell and Coppens, 1976), and possibly east of Lake Turkana as well (KNM-ER 1482 mandible), and eventually into the genus *Homo.* Robinson (1967) presents a convincing case for separating the *Homo habilis* sample from Olduvai Gorge into two parts. An earlier segment is composed of the Bed I habilines (for example, OH-7 and OH-24), which presumably are closely related to the gracile australopithecines, while a later segment from Bed II (for example, OH-13 and OH-16) is composed of specimens more closely resembling later members of the genus *Homo*. Thus, *H. habilis* would represent the transitional taxon between *Australopithecus africanus* and *Homo erectus.* Similarly, numerous fossils recovered from sites east of Lake Turkana and dating from 1.8 to 1.5 m.y. B.P. (between the KBS tuff and the Okote tuff) have morphological features which link them to *Homo habilis* (R. Leakey and Walker, 1976). Some of these fossils (KNM-ER 1470, 1590) have *Homo*-size brains with *Australopithecus*-size teeth and some the reverse, (KNM-ER 1805, 1813) suggesting various morphological stages between *Australopithecus* and *Homo*. The partial skull from Member 5 at Sterkfontein (formerly known as the Extension Site) probably also belongs in this group (Hughes and Tobias, 1977).

The second lineage represented in early hominid evolution includes the robust and hyperrobust forms, and may have speciated from the gracile forms during the period when the Makapansgat cave deposit was formed, since there are some examples of robust morphology in the Makapansgat sample (Howell, personal communication; Mann, 1970; Tobias, 1973b).

It is a tempting speculation, although unverifiable for the moment, to attribute the evidence for meat-eating, tool-making, and home bases (Isaac and Crader, in this volume) to the *A. afarensis/A. africanus/H. habilis* lineage. Thus the pattern of resource exploitation seen in later hominids would have been well established in those creatures whose morphology suggests that they are the evolutionary ancestors of the genus *Homo*. There is some evidence, however, that behavior in each lineage was equally complex. The sequence and timing of dental eruption in both the South African gracile and the robust samples resembles that found in modern humans. This, in turn, can be correlated with skeletal maturation, thus providing a means of determining the length of the period of skeletal growth and development. Similarities of skeletal growth suggest that both gracile and robust australopithecines—like modern humans—had a prolonged period of childhood. This extended childhood would have been adaptive in facilitating the transmission of learned behavior, perhaps including environmental information, from one generation to the next (Mann, 1975).

MODELS OF EARLY HOMINID
DIETARY EXPLOITATION

Any model of early hominid dietary patterns must propose dietary specializations to account for the morphological diversity described above, and several contrasting approaches to this problem have been developed.

Robinson (1954, 1967) felt strongly that each australopithecine lineage was adapted to a different environmental niche, whereas Wolpoff (1971) found it difficult to conceive of two hominid lineages, each bipedal with small canines, coexisting in the same environment. The behavioral flexibility characteristic of hominids, Wolpoff argued, would result in both forms competing for the same broad array of resources, and as a result he supported a single lineage hypothesis. Recently, Wolpoff (personal communication) has emphasized the large posterior teeth of both gracile and robust South African australopithecines, and while he acknowledges that the fossil evidence demonstrates the existence of two hominid lineages in East Africa, he continues to believe that the entire South African sample consists of one lineage. Summers and Neville (1978) have suggested that both hominid lineages were initially adapted to the same environmental niche, but that as a result of competition between them one lineage underwent rapid morphological changes, evolving biological and behavioral traits that adapted it to another niche.

I continue to be persuaded by Wolpoff's argument (1971) that two contemporary hominid lineages were unlikely to occupy the same broad niche. Thus it seems relatively clear that the specialized masticatory systems of the robust/hyperrobust forms are an adaptation to foods different from those exploited by the gracile/*Homo* group, as Robinson (1954) first proposed. The lack of a clear difference between the gracile and robust dentitions in South Africa (Wolpoff, 1970, 1971, 1973b) leads to the conclusion that originally only one lineage existed there. The robust line then speciated from this group at a later date, with the increasing size of the posterior teeth as one measure of its increasing divergence. Summers and Neville (1978), by contrast, propose that the gracile/*Homo* forms diverged from the robust line by means of character displacement.

If one assumes, as I do here, that no more than two independent hominid lineages existed at any given time, then two models of early hominid feeding adaptation may be proposed to account for the geographical distribution and morphological variability seen in the australopithecines. (If future research demonstrates that the hominid fossil record is more complicated, of course, greater diversity in hominid adaptations would necessarily follow.) These models may also help to explain the divergence of the hominids from an ancient pongid line.

In the first model, the evolution of the hominids as a separate lineage also represents the beginning of a broad-based feeding strategy, with all hominids in the direct ancestry of modern *Homo sapiens* characterized by unspecialized dietary patterns. The robust/hyperrobust line speciated from the gracile lineage in both South and East Africa in the later stages of the Pliocene, finally becoming extinct between 1.5 and 1.3 million years ago. These larger forms represented the evolution of a different adaptation, one based on a specialized masticatory complex.

Applying this model to the origin of the Hominidae, it is possible to speculate that the features which differentiate some members of Ramapithecidae (*Ramapithecus, Rudapithecus,* and *Gigantopithecus*) from the contemporary Dryopithecidae—thicker occlusal enamel, smaller canines, less facial prognathism (Pilbeam, Meyer, et al., 1977)—evolved as part of a new feeding specialization that may have included items such as seeds and roots, which require "fine comminution and hard grinding" (C. J. Jolly, 1972:10). Alternatively, these changes may be attributable to a scavenging adaptation (Szalay, 1975). *Both* views may be correct, and the anatomical changes Pilbeam has detected in the Ramapithecidae may have permitted the hominid diet to expand to include many diverse foods. The hominids would then have been able to exploit a range of habitats and foods and, with the addition of tools, to develop an adaptation not limited to vegetable or animal foods, but including both. In short, the broad-based pattern of food exploitation characteristic of later humans may have been established very early in hominid evolution.

Hypotheses that propose more specialized dietary adaptations for the earliest hominids (small-object feeders, vegetarians, carnivorous predators) do not take into account the behavioral flexibility of either the living gatherer/hunters or the nonhuman primates, particularly the chimpanzee. The australopithecine evidence, including paleo-environmental reconstructions, stone tools [first found at Hadar, dated some 2.5 m.y. B.P. (Taieb et al., 1978)], and the archaeological evidence for meat-eating (Isaac and Crader, in this volume), suggests that the early hominids were not limited to any particular environment but exploited several diverse habitats through a seasonal or yearly round. To be sure, hominids in a given geographic area may have emphasized or remained in one zone longer than their conspecifics elsewhere, and for this reason it may be difficult to use paleo-environmental data to reconstruct what may have been a very complicated pattern of adaptation.

This first model has the advantage of including the known morphological, environmental, and archaeological data, while remaining within the limits established by the adaptive patterns of closely related living forms. In its dietary diversity, it also provides a basis for sound nutrition. In 1953, Bartholomew and Birdsell suggested a list of foods that an early hominid equipped only with a digging stick could obtain. These included berries, fruits, nuts, buds, shoots, shallow-growing roots and tubers, fruiting bodies of fungi, most terrestrial and the smaller aquatic reptiles, eggs, nesting birds, some fish, mollusks, insects, and all small mammals, including the burrowing ones. This diverse diet, obtainable in different habitats and at different seasons, is very close to that of the Gombe National Park chimpanzees (Teleki, 1975; van Lawick–Goodall, 1968) and living gatherer/hunters (Hayden, in this volume). Knowledge of environmental resources and their seasonal location is vital to this adaptation, and the evolution of a prolonged childhood dependency period would have had obvious advantages in transmitting such information from one generation to the next, even among small-brained hominids.

This model of early hominid dietary patterns views the gracile/*Homo* lineage as made up of environmentally complex forms, subsisting on a wide variety of plant and animal foods and exploiting them at different seasons in different habitats. It is questionable whether tools initially were directly involved with this adaptation, for hominid tool-making abilities need not have been greater than those of the chimpanzee. As I noted elsewhere, however (Mann, 1972), the diverse feeding pattern proposed as the hominid adaptive niche may be directly related to the use of tools. I suggested that the initial development of the hominid pattern from a pongidlike baseline was founded on the crucial importance of tools in the acquisition of important food items. For example, as Coursey (1973) pointed out, a simple digging stick would materially increase the number of hypogeous (underground) foods available to an early hominid.

An alternative model views the first hominids not as diverse feeders but as specialized animals, perhaps feeding on small objects, as C. J. Jolly (1970, 1972) suggests, with some additional plant and animal foods broadening the pattern. In this second model, the robust and hyperrobust forms are seen as maintaining the ancient hominid pattern, while the gracile/*Homo* lineage evolved the attributes that led to a broad-based feeding strategy (Summers and Neville, 1978). Since the smaller forms would have made use of a greater selection of foods, they would have had a competitive advantage and, over time, would have outcompeted the robust line for available resources. The evolutionary expansion of the posterior dentition in the robust forms could have been an initial response to this competition, although ultimately a futile one. It should also be noted that this model implies a greater antiquity for multiple australopithecine lineages than is supported by the available fossil record.

The obvious problem with such models is that they are concerned with extinct forms which do not have exact living analogues, and, like the combinations of morphological attributes of these forms, their adaptive patterns may prove to be unique. Chimpanzees, after all, have undergone a great deal of evolutionary change since they last shared a common ancestor with hominids and therefore may not be valid models for them. This question, already raised at the beginning of this article, cannot be answered directly. The important point, however, is that more than one equally plausible model for the adaptation of extinct forms can be formulated, and we must view these models within the context of the available data.

Although both the models I have proposed are consistent with the morphology of the early hominids and their geographic and temporal distribution, paleontological and archaeological evidence tends to favor the first model. Moreover, the fact that both pongids and living gatherer/ hunters pursue a diverse feeding strategy strongly suggests that the early hominids, intermediate in time between the hominid/pongid divergence and modern *Homo sapiens,* would have had similar adaptations. While it is possible that the lineage which culminates in *Homo sapiens* originated with a group of specialized feeders, present evidence suggests that this model is less likely than one which proposes a continuity in subsistence patterns from the time of *Ramapithecus* to the present.

Glynn Ll. Isaac and Diana C. Crader

3.
To What Extent Were Early Hominids Carnivorous? An Archaeological Perspective

The adaptive strategies of recent humans who live without agriculture are outside the range of those found among other primates, or indeed among other mammals. These hunter/gatherers (or gatherer/hunters) consume a combination of vegetable and animal matter which is so diverse that they surely qualify as omnivores. But that term may be misleading in some ways, since what is commonly involved is not casual eclecticism but an intensive dual approach to food acquisition. Many such groups engage in a vigorous and selective system of predation which is comparable only to that of the largest members of the order Carnivora, while at the same time harvesting a wide range of gatherable plant and animal foods such as roots, fruits, nuts, grains, leaves, eggs, and invertebrates. Other large mammals with a comparable dietary range are few, and those that do exist, such as the bears, are generally far less predatory than most nonagricultural modern humans (Herrero, 1972; Jonkel and Cowan, 1971; Pearson, 1975; E. Walker, 1968).

On careful scrutiny, the subsistence practices and the social organization of nonagricultural humans are found to be intertwined in an intricate way. Humans usually, perhaps invariably, live in social groups within which some food is actively shared. Generally, somewhat different contributions to the sharing system are made by different age and sex classes of these groups. The acquisition of flesh (meat or fish) is commonly the principal contribution of mature males, although females may also take part in this aspect of subsistence. The gathering of other foods is often the responsibility of adult females, but all members of the society participate at times in this activity.

One can go on to argue that many of the other distinctive dimensions of human behavior are interconnected with this socioeconomic system. Division of labor and food sharing are facilitated by an ability to transfer information through language. Furthermore, the existence of stable family groups within which the males help to feed and rear offspring has particular significance when male and female subsistence activities have differing emphases. Food sharing, when coupled with language and family ties, may also encourage the development of the complex chains of reciprocal obligation and exchange that characterize almost all recent human societies.

The foregoing is a cursory sketch of some characteristics of human socioeconomics in which our species differs from other primates. Even without consideration of phylogeny or the fossil record, this scheme inevitably suggests that the adoption of meat-eating by our protohuman ancestors may at some stage have had a crucial formative and facultative influence on the course of human evolution. This belief is highly plausible and is widely held by anthropologists on the basis of synchronic comparisons between modern humans and their living primate relatives. If the validity of the model is to be tested, we need to seek data on the subsistence of ancestral hominids. Such data can be obtained only through paleontological and archaeological research.

Speculation about the subsistence patterns of our early hominid ancestors is abundant, and in many models of human evolution an involvement in hunting and a significantly carnivorous diet are prominent. However, there is a spectrum of opinion on this matter. At one extreme, writers such as Dart (1953) and Ardrey (1961, 1976) hold that meat was the principal food of Plio-Pleistocene hominids and that early human adaptive patterns pivoted on hunting success. At the other extreme, authors such as Geist (1975) Perper and Schrire (1977), and Tanner and Zihlman (1976) have argued either that the early hominids did not hunt or that hunting was an unimportant activity. Another interpretation regards meat as important but hypothesizes that it was obtained by scavenging (e.g., Binford, personal communication; J. D. Clark, 1959:71; Read-Martin and Read, 1975). Clearly, distinguishing the relative probabilities of these alternative models depends on access to information on what hominids were doing and what they ate at formative stages in their phylogeny.

In the dynamics of human evolution, there are two intersecting dimensions of variation: (1) the degree of which meat[1] was a component of the diet, and (2) if meat was a component, the proportion acquired by hunting[2] relative to scavenging or "gathering." In fact, in considering any given stage of human evolution, the model must be elaborated immediately, as we need to allow for variation between contemporary populations in different circumstances, whether geographic, environmental, seasonal, or even "cultural."

Most scientists concerned with the study of the last few million years of human evolution assume that the lineage ancestral to mankind was to a degree "carnivorous" and that this dietary involvement had a significant influence on the trajectory of change. We regard this view, when not pushed to extremes, as very reasonable and very plausible. However, it is beginning to be incorporated into the literature as established knowledge in a way that it should not be. "Early man, the hunter" is in danger of becoming a fact by default. In this chapter we critically examine the evidence and as many alternative models as ingenuity and space allow.

At the outset of an inquiry such as this one, it is important to be realistic. There is little chance that we can prove, in a literal sense, either that early hominids were exclusively carnivorous or that they never ate a scrap of meat. We can only seek sufficient evidence for the working hypothesis that they were carnivorous to a large degree—or, alternatively, determine that the hypothesis is purely speculative.

One approach to the question is to view prehistoric research as an investigation probing back from the recent past into successively earlier and earlier stages of human and protohuman development. Given that recent humans are far more intensive flesh-eaters than any other living primates, the question can be rephrased: When did hominid meat-eating start to intensify, and how much interpopulation variation has there been at each successive stage? As we go back in time, for each major phase we ought to ask if there is clear evidence that at least some hominid subsistence patterns involved the eating of significant amounts of meat.

The first step back in time takes us to the nonagricultural societies of the Upper Pleistocene, that is, the last 100,000 years or so. For these societies, the answers to our questions are unambiguous. In many but not all regions, human artifacts of this age are very often incorporated in middens with impressive amounts of broken, burnt bone. The case for substantial meat-eating by some humans in this time range is well proven (see Klein, in this volume). If we move farther back in time to the early Pleistocene and late Pliocene, to the span covering 700,000 to 3,000,000 years B.P.,[3] evidence is relatively scant. But aspects of its conformation, especially the recurrent associations between artifacts and broken animal bone, do look familiar and suggestive. Does this necessarily mean that these early hominids, too, were meat-eaters? This is the major question which this chapter seeks to answer, and in the pages which follow, a review of specific evidence for meat-eating is undertaken. We assume throughout that plant foods formed a major part of hominid diets even though there is little direct evidence for this. Gathered foods are also discussed.

LINES OF EVIDENCE

In a search for *direct* evidence for early hominid dietary habits, the following sets of clues can be considered:

Anatomy and physiology
  1. The morphology of hominid fossils, especially dentition and mastication, as well as limbs and locomotion.

2. Wear and damage on teeth.
3. Chemical composition of fossilized bone or tooth.
4. Growth and nutrition patterns evident in hominid fossils.

Environment
5. Habitats occupied, as judged from the location of hominid fossils and artifacts.
6. The relative abundance of hominids compared with other classes of animals, as judged from fossil finds.

Archaeology
7. Artifacts with a recognizable function in the acquisition of food.
8. Materials identifiable as prehistoric food refuse or as feces.
   a. By far the commonest evidence of this kind is patches of broken bones associated with discarded artifacts.
   b. In some instances, associations between hominid and other animal bones have been claimed as evidence of hominid meat-eating.

All these potential lines of evidence are important, but most are inherently inconclusive as ways of determining whether early hominids ate significantly more meat than other primates do. Items 1 and 2, which depend on fossilized skeletal remains, illustrate this point well. In modern humans, the same kind of dentition and masticatory apparatus serves adequately among populations of tropical gatherer/hunters for whom meat is only a subsidiary component of the diet, and among Arctic hunters for whom meat is a staple. Clearly, we cannot appeal to the evidence of fossil teeth to settle the questions that confront us, although the teeth do suggest some limits to interpretations based on other lines of evidence. For example, the flat-crowned cheek teeth of all hominids have thickened enamel and are quite unlike those of any of the Carnivora, except for superficial resemblances to the teeth of omnivorous or non-meat-eating members of the order, such as bears and the aardwolf (*Proteles cristatus*) (Dorst and Dandelot, 1970). Given the morphology of hominid and human teeth, then, it is unlikely that our phylogeny includes any prolonged period of exclusively carnivorous diet, Ardrey (1976) notwithstanding. The analogies between aspects of tooth morphology in hominids and various omnivorous species, such as bears and pigs, are suggestive, but arguments from such morphological analogies hold no promise of settling the issue.

Studies of wear patterns on the fossil teeth of early hominids are a promising potential source of paleodietary evidence (Tobias, 1967; A. Walker, Hoeck and Perez, 1978; Wallace, 1973; Zihlman and Tanner, in press), but few results are yet available. However, we should recognize in advance that although scratch and chippage patterns may well indicate vegetable components in diet, the eating of meat itself is unlikely to leave particularly distinctive traces. Tooth wear patterns may show that meat was *not* the exclusive food of a given fossil hominid, but they are unlikely to help us determine whether meat comprised 0%, 5% or 20% of its food. (See also Mann, in this volume, for discussion of these questions.)

Regarding item 3, Toots and Voorhies (1965) pointed out that carnivore tissues, including bone and teeth, tend to have less strontium as a trace ingredient than do those of herbivores. Clearly if the ratio of strontium to other minerals in bone does not vary too much within an area and is not unduly distorted by postmortem processes, then strontium content might serve as an indicator of the diet of fossil animals. Recently, Boaz and Hampel (1978) have followed up this long-neglected lead, but their results do not conform to expectations. Although this first attempt at finding a chemical discriminant has failed, the approach remains an interesting one for future research.

Study of growth and development rates and patterns, item 4, is an aspect of paleoanthropology that is bound to become more important as the sample of specimens expands (Tobias, 1967; Mann, 1975). Eventually we may learn something from signs of trauma and malnutrition, and our understanding of human evolution may then include knowledge of interrelations between subsistence patterns, social arrangements, longevity, and child rearing. But currently the information is quite insufficient to guide us in reconstructing dietary habits.

Items 5 and 6, habitats occupied and the relative abundance of hominids, must ultimately have been related to trophic patterns. As such, they are important parts of any model of early hominid adaptation, but these spatial and numerical relationships are only indirect evidence for diet since similar configurations can result from very different subsistence systems. Available data of this sort can fit equally well in models of hominid life that involve complete dependence on meat, the opposite, or anything in between. Thus, neither habitat preference nor the relative frequency of fossil hominids in relation to other taxa can settle the question confronting us.

Item 7, the function of distinctive artifacts, remains to be considered. In recent prehistoric times, specialized tools such as projectile points or grindstones can be telling clues to subsistence habits, but the kinds of generalized stone tool kits that survive from early prehistoric times do not lend themselves to such inferences. As we shall see, stone artifacts play an important role in those models of early hominid behavior that postulate significant consumption of meat, but although the artifacts may reinforce the belief that the early hominids were hunters, they cannot be used as conclusive evidence.

This leaves us with the last item on the list, food refuse and feces, as our only real hope at present of obtaining tangible evidence for testing the hypothesis that early hominids were to a significant degree carnivorous. The clues subsumed under item 8 depend on our ability to identify certain fossil organic materials as residues of early hominid feeding activities, either discarded, inedible refuse or, more rarely, fossil feces. For the later periods of prehistory the archaeological study of refuse has proved a highly informative source of evidence for reconstructing diet and economy, so that seeking clues of this kind in the Plio-Pleistocene simply constitutes an extension of these research methods back in time.

The recognition of organic remains as food refuse normally depends on a significant association between these materials and other undoubted traces of human activity, such as shelters, structures, hearths, an abundance of discarded artifacts, or some combination of these. For late Pleistocene or Recent settlement sites, these indicators are so common that designating appropriate associated organics as food refuse is not controversial. However, it is predictable that as one probes back into earlier and earlier stages of human and protohuman development, one will reach phases in which some marker traces are missing and others are less clear. In other words, we may expect that the signals will be ambiguous. The question, then, is how far back we can follow the trail of clearly identifiable, bone food refuse.

MODELS OF HOMINID SUBSISTENCE

Every line of argument is dependent on assumptions or inferences made explicitly or implicitly at different levels. It is useful to visualize different kinds of models in terms of three sequential levels of interpretation. The lowest level concerns interpretation of hard evidence (finds). For example, what is the behavioral meaning, if any, of an association between the bones of potentially edible animals and discarded artifacts? This question leads the researcher to consider carefully the processes that preserve specimens singly or in clusters, and hence the meaning of dispersal patterns within fossiliferous beds. If it can be shown in any instance that natural mechanisms such as water currents or carnivore feeding are unlikely causes of accumulation, one might adopt the working hypothesis that the particular coincident concentration of bones and artifacts was caused by meat-eating activities of the tool-makers. Given this working hypothesis, models of various possible subsistence strategies involving meat can be developed and tested, and their technological, ecological, and sociological implications considered, thus leading to a third level in which models of evolutionary dynamics can be formulated which involve competition among individuals, leading to differential rates of reproductive success and hence to changes in gene frequency and evolutionary change.

CLASSIFICATION OF SITES

As we have seen, the most promising line of direct evidence for early hominid meat-eating comes through recognition of associations between artifacts and the bone remains of potentially edible animals. But before one can use this as evidence, it is necessary to examine the ways in which bones and artifacts have been found to occur, and to assess how the archaeologist recognizes "significant association."

In discussing functional relationships between artifacts and bones recovered from ancient sediments, we must envision a three-dimensional configuration. The material is dispersed horizontally over the landscape and may also be dispersed vertically through sediments. Both the artifacts and the bone specimens may be dispersed or concentrated in relation to either the horizontal or the vertical dimension, or both. Concentrations and dispersions of artifacts and bones may or may not coincide. Figure 3.1 illustrates some of these permutations, according to the following scheme for classifying sites (Isaac, 1978; Isaac and Harris, 1978). Categories A, B, and C refer only to vertically concentrated occurrences, or "floors," while categories G and O include both vertically diffuse and vertically concentrated configurations.

Type A.   Sites containing a concentration of artifacts but little or no bone materials.
Type B.   Sites in which artifacts are found with bones of the carcass of a single large animal.
Type C.   Sites in which a concentrated patch of artifacts and a

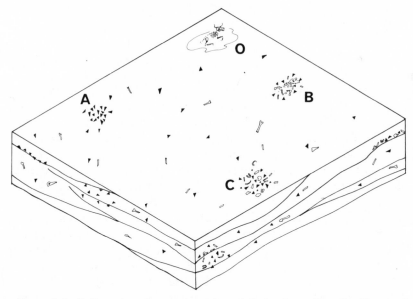

Figure 3.1. A diagrammatic representation of the configuration of artifacts and bones as they are preserved in the sedimentary formations of Eastern Africa. Each forms a scatter over the surfaces of the ancient landscape and each occurs in clusters of various kinds. The classification of cluster types is explained in the text.

concentration of bones from several species of animals coincide.

Type D. Sites in which artifacts, with or without bones, are locally abundant but are dispersed through an appreciable thickness of sediment that lacks detectable individual horizons.

Type G. Sites in which materials have been transported and re-deposited in another geological context.

Type O. Sites containing osteological material only. In these cases it is particularly difficult to demonstrate active hominid involvement in the process of accumulation.

Categories B and C are thoroughly familiar to archaeologists, though they usually are given labels that prejudge their interpretation; type B occurrences are referred to as butchery sites, and type C occurrences as camps or occupation sites.[4] Occurrences of type A, other than so-called factory sites, have received less attention from paleoanthropologists, perhaps because they are tacitly assumed to be sites of type C from which bone has disappeared by decay. This may be a valid inference in many cases, but it cannot be made for all such occurrences; some may be sites where bone was never present in any quantity.

All the archaeological evidence currently available involves the use of stone artifacts as markers of places where tool-making hominids were active. It is entirely reasonable to envisage a pre–stone tool phase of hominid evolution of which meat-eating was an important component, but because of the present lack of evidence this possibility is not discussed here.

SOME POSSIBLE EVIDENCE

Almost all direct evidence of protohuman life in the period before 700,000 years ago comes from a very small number of geographic areas, namely Java,[5] northwest Africa, the East African Rift Valley, and the Transvaal in South Africa. The series of fossil remains from Java is important for our understanding of anatomical developments, but as yet there are few data on ecological context and none are from excavations of archaeological sites in the fossiliferous beds. At present Java contributes little or nothing to the solution of the problem at hand. Similarly, there are a number of fairly early hominid fossils from North Africa, and some, such as the Ternifine specimens, may conceivably be as much as 700,000 years old. Ternifine and two other archaeological sites, Ain Hanech and STIC at Casablanca, contribute potential evidence of early diet, but detailed data are not available (see Balout, 1955:159–73; Biberson, 1961:156–84).

Thus we are left with the Transvaal and the Eastern Rift Valley as sources of direct field evidence against which to test the hypothesis that the early hominids were meat-eaters. The record in these two areas has been preserved by very different mechanisms. In the Transvaal, hominid fossils have been found during the excavation of deposits that accumulated in caves and fissures. They occur jumbled with numerous bones of other animals. In a few instances, some scattered artifacts do occur among the bones, but only in Sterkfontein, Member 5 (= "Extension Site"), is there an assemblage of at least several hundred flaked stones. The question is; Were the nonhominid bones at these sites accumulated in whole or in part by the hominids as food refuse? Raymond Dart (1957) inferred that they were, and his view has been widely publicized (Ardrey, 1961, 1976), but we now realize that the processes whereby bones accumulate in caverns and fissures must also be taken into account. Many of the bone assemblages in question are unlikely to be middens accumulated by hominids (Brain, 1958, 1976a).

Along the Eastern Rift, hominid fossils, numerous nonhominid fossil bones, and artifacts occur together in the deposits of large sedimentary basins. In layer after layer, the material is preserved as a series of scatters and clusters over the basin floors. In this region the claim for early hominid meat-eating has been based largely on the spatial conjunction of concentrated patches of hominid artifacts with concentrated patches of the bones of potentially edible animals—i.e., the eighth line of evidence listed above (Isaac, 1969, 1971; M.D. Leakey, 1971; Speth and Davis, 1976). However, a skeptical investigator might well ask how the mere conjunction of artifacts and bones demonstrates that the bones are the food refuse of the tool-makers. A complete answer to this problem would require studies of the various processes which cause concentrations of bone to accumulate.

Table 3.1 lists potential evidence for early hominid meat-eating, subdivided according to two axes of variation. The horizontal axis distinguishes among circumstances of preservation, and the vertical axis categorizes the main characteristics of the context.

In our view the best evidence for meat-eating comes from sites in categories III and IV, and selected test cases of these are discussed next in some detail. The appendix reviews the evidence from other sites in table 3.1.

TEST CASES

From our search for definitive evidence of early hominid involvement in meat-eating, Olduvai Gorge and Koobi Fora emerge as the best available test cases, and we here present a critical and detailed review of the evidence from these sites. The possible outcomes of such tests of the meat-eating hypothesis form a graded series: (1) Meat-eating might be demonstrated in some instances, *beyond all reasonable doubt,* as having been a part of the early hominid subsistence base. (2) Meat-eating might be postulated as the

Table 3.1. Selected sites that preserve evidence of hominid ecology and activity, from the time range 5–0.7 m.y. B.P. The table is a matrix showing kinds of evidence preserved (categories I–V) and the circumstances of preservation (A–C)

Kinds of evidence contained in the geological formation	EVIDENCE PRESERVED IN:			Significance for testing meat-eating hypotheses
	Caves and fissures A	Sedimentary strata of major basins of deposition B	Other C	
I. Hominid and other vertebrate fossils (no artifacts yet confirmed by excavation)	Makapan gray breccia Taung Sterkfontein Mbr 4	Lothagam Kanapoi Laetolil Hadar Chemeron Djetis Beds (Java) Trinil Beds (Java)		In general, do not provide evidence for or against hominid meat-eating
II. Hominid and other vertebrate fossils, plus sparse artifacts	Swartkrans Mbr 1 Swartkrans Mbr 2 Kromdraai B	?late Hadar ?Kanam		In general, do not provide evidence for or against hominid meat-eating
III. Hominid and other vertebrate fossils plus concentrated patches of artifacts and bones	Sterkfontein Mbr 5	Olduvai Beds I–III Koobi Fora Formation Melka Kunturé	Ternifine (a spring-vent site)	Bone concentration *may* be food refuse and may imply meat-eating
IV. Vertebrate fossils plus patches of artifacts with associated bone		Ain Hanech Casablanca STIC 'Ubeidiya Gadeb		Bone concentration *may* be food refuse and may imply meat-eating
V. Patches of artifacts without significant associated vertebrate bones		Shungura Mbr F Peninj Chesowanja?		Do not provide evidence for or against hominid meat-eating

Sources: References for sites not otherwise treated in the text are as follows: for Lothagam, Kanapoi, and Chemeron, see Howell (1972, 1979) for summaries and bibliographies; for Kanam, see L. S. B. Leakey (1935), S. Cole (1963), Howell (1972); for Gadeb, see Clark and Kurashina (1976); for Ternifine, see Balout (1955), Jaeger (1975); for 'Ubeidiya, see Bar-Yosef (1975); for Peninj, see Isaac (1967b), Howell (1967b), Howell (1972); for Chesowanja, see Bishop (1975).

best of several explanations for the observed configurations of some Lower Pleistocene archaeological sites. This would suffice as a legitimate *working hypothesis*, but one would be obliged to test other subsistence models. (3) Evidence for meat-eating might be found to be very weak or lacking.

Demonstration that the early hominids definitely did *not* eat any significant amount of meat would be at the furthest extreme in this series, beyond grade 3. However, given the nature of the evidence, such an outcome is extremely unlikely. Postulation of a diet without any meat is equivalent to a null hypothesis. Evidence can show that the null hypothesis is in some specifiable degree improbable (grades 1 and 2), but the converse is not true—the proposition in itself is not proven by lack of evidence. Thus, even if our test cases turned out to be type 3, it would still be legitimate to consider meat-eating as a possible component of Lower Pleistocene subsistence. In that case, however, the hypothesis would remain highly speculative, and supportive evidence would have to be derived from indirect sources such as primate behavior studies, ethnography, and general evolutionary considerations.

Recognizing a co-occurrence of artifacts and bones as significant evidence of hominid meat-eating depends on fulfillment of one or more of the following test conditions.

Condition 1. The density of both the bones and the artifacts is anomalously high compared to the background density of both (fig. 3.1), and no agency or circumstance other than hominid transport can account for their co-occurrence. It is particularly important to guard against the possibility that the stones and bones have been swept together by water currents.

Condition 2. At least some bones show damage or modification characteristic of hominid actions, especially distinctive breakage patterns, cut-marks, or traces of burning.[6]

Condition 3. The composition of the bone assemblage with regard to species, age, sex, or body parts differs from expectation in a way that can only be explained satisfactorily as the result of hominid action.

Solid results in these test conditions would confirm the hypothesis that the tool-making hominids accumulated the bones in connection with their subsistence activities. The logic is quite clear, but at present these tests must be applied *intuitively,* since systematic research on background densities, on the distinction between "natural" versus human-induced bone fractures, and on the composition of natural bone assemblages is just beginning.

Olduvai Gorge

The sedimentary sequence exposed in the eroded walls of the canyon at Olduvai provides the longest combined record that we have of fossil hominids and the archaeological indicators of their technology and culture.

Mary Leakey's (1971) monograph on Beds I and II gives archaeological details and the results of preliminary osteological analyses for more than 20 sites. Olduvai Gorge provides by far the largest body of evidence bearing on both the technological capabilities and the behavior of early protohumans, and is thus the crux of any review of evidence for meat-eating in the Plio-Pleistocene.

The eroding walls of Olduvai Gorge provide access to fossils and artifacts scattered throughout the sediments. The sites are varied in their characteristics, and their configurations approximate the types discussed earlier and shown in figure 3.1. Type B and C sites are patches of stones and bones preserved on an old land surface; each of these may be a trace of an individual episode of activity on the part of the tool-making hominids. All these concentrations presumably represent foci of intensive usage over a limited span of time and may provide the kind of evidence for meat-eating that involves the fewest complications in interpretation. By contrast, type D sites, where both the artifacts and bones are dispersed through an appreciable thickness of sediment, must represent recurrent episodes of artifact discard and bone emplacement, stretching across centuries or even millennia. The possibility that the bones, like the tools, were carried to the spot and discarded by the hominids remains strong, but it is perhaps one degree more difficult to evaluate than is the case with discrete floors.

Table 3.2 shows the main Olduvai sites as reported by Mary Leakey (1971), classified by type, and the potassium-argon chronology and paleomagnetic stratigraphy (Hay, 1976). Several occurrences that we have listed as type D might, if one had access to all the excavation records, prove to be floors plus a small admixture of vertically diffuse material from above and below. The table shows that slightly more than half the sites are vertically diffuse.

There follows a series of brief individual descriptions of selected sites that may help to test the hypothesis about meat-eating.[7] Accompanying the descriptions are tables showing the number of taxa represented at each site (table 3.3), the relative proportions of the main macrofaunal taxa (table 3.4), the relative proportions of mammalian skeletal parts (table 3.5), the proportions of identifiable bones to nonidentifiable fragments (table 3.6) (the percentage of nonidentifiable fragments usually provides an approximate indication of the degree to which the bones have been broken up), the proportions of artifacts, manuports (unmodified stones transported by hominids), and bone (table 3.7), and the densities of bones and artifacts per square meter for the sites (table 3.8). Table 3.10 provides comparative data from several localities, while table 3.11 provides taxonomic lists for the sites.

The Zinjanthropus Floor at FLK. This site is of vital importance to an investigation of early hominid meat-eating. Excavation has revealed a dense patch of discarded stone artifacts that coincides with a dense patch of broken bones, a clear example of a type C site (figure 3.2). The stone artifacts and bones occur within a thin layer that appears to represent a weak paleosol, which makes it seem highly unlikely that the concentration of either the stones or the broken bones could have been caused by water currents. Distinct patterning can be discerned within the scatter; there is a marked concentration of flaking debris and broken bones toward the center. According to Mary Leakey, this may represent the interior of a windbreak or sheltered area. The localization of material may imply either one spell of occupation lasting several weeks, or recurrent occupations that were so close in time that the ephemeral features which caused activity to center there did not shift in the intervals between visits.

The material lies scattered over the area, as shown in figure 3.2. The bone is unweathered, but most of it has been broken. Skulls are in fragments. Three articulated series of bones have been found close to each other, as if they were still joined by sinew at the time of deposition. A number of bones at the site bear tooth marks, as if they had been chewed by scavengers. The bone material is far more broken up than is common at other Bed I sites; about 60% of all the 3,510 specimens are unidentifiable fragments (table 3.6). The composition of the bone scatter is varied, with at least 16 taxa of relatively large mammals represented among an assortment of other fauna (see tables 3.3, 3.10, and 3.11). Until detailed faunal analysis has been completed, it will not be clear what proportion of this assemblage, if any, should be regarded as normal background.

The existence of the Zinj floor was revealed when excavations were carried out adjacent to the spot where the cranium of *Australopithecus (Zinjanthropus) boisei* (Olduvai Hominid 5) had been found. The skull is part of the bone assemblage at the site, as are fragmentary remains attributed to *Homo habilis* (Olduvai Hominid 6).

The assemblage of artifacts from the Zinj floor is distinctive compared to other Oldowan sites, because 92% of the 2,275 specimens are unretouched flakes and flake fragments, without visible use-damage; 73 flakes show sign of use. Only 60 objects are classifiable as shaped tools, of which about half are core tools (choppers and polyhedrons) and half are scrapers. About 62 (3%) are nodules, cobbles, and blocks showing battering and signs of heavy-duty use.

Several higher stratigraphic levels at the Zinj FLK site have yielded very-low-density scatters of bones and artifacts that are interesting primarily as indicators of background densities. Level 15 contained 9 artifacts and 259 bones, and level 13 contained 11 artifacts and 187 bone specimens; by contrast, 2,470 artifacts and 3,510 bone specimens were

Table 3.2. Major sites in Beds I and II of Olduvai Gorge, showing stratigraphic sequence and a classification according to type (see text)

| | Vertically concentrated (= "floor") | | | Vertically diffuse | |
	Type C	Type B	Type A	Type D	Geologically redeposited
Upper Bed II					BK
			TK upper floor	TK upper tuff	
			TK lower floor	TK intermed.	
					TK channel
	SHK Annex			SHK main	SHK main, channel
Middle Bed II				MNK main	
			FC W floor	FC W tuff	
			EF-HR		
				MNK skull	
				HWK E 3–5	

Lemuta Member		**FLK N** *Deinotherium*	**HWK E 2**
Lower Bed II	HWK E 1		FLK N 5,4,3
	FLK N 1–2		
Bed I	FLK Zinj	FLK N 6	DK 1–3
	FLK NN 1		
	FLK NN 3		
	DK 1		
Basalt flow			

Source: Based on M. D. Leakey (1971).

Notes: Sites in Beds III and IV are not included because comparable reports on faunal remains are not yet available. Bed I dates from 1.9–1.65 m. y. B.P.; Bed II dates from 1.65–1.2 m.y. B.P. The site labels are abbreviations of names given to the sites, often recording who first found them. Thus FLK stands for Frieda Leakey Karonya (*karonya* being the Swahili for a small gully or canyon). N, S, E, and W stand for compass directions and refer to parts of sites. Numbers refer to levels or layers within a site.

Table 3.3. Number of taxa represented in bone remains associated with artifacts at Olduvai Gorge

Sites	Mammalian families	Genera of large mammals	Genera of small mammals	All mammalian genera	Reptiles	Birds	Amphibia	Fish	Other	Hominids
Type C										
HWK E 1	7	14	—	14	2	≥1	—	—	—	
FLK N 1–2	17	16	13	29	7	P	4	—	—	
FLK Zinj	12	16	8	24	8	≥1	3	2	4	A,H
FLK NN 3	11	7	13	20	9	≥1	4	2	—	H
Type B										
FLK N *Deinotherium*[a]										
FLK N 6	12	13	10	23	5	—	3	—	—	
Type A										
FC W floor	5	5	—	5	3	—	—	—	—	
EF-HR	6	7	—	7	1	—	—	—	—	
Type D										
TK all levels	8	13	—	13	1	—	—	—	—	
SHK all levels	9	22	1	23	—	≥1	—	2	1	
MNK main	10	21	1	22	2	≥1	1	2	—	
FC W tuff	5	5	—	5	1	≥1	—	1	—	indet.
MNK skull	8	8	1	9	2	≥1	1	1	1	H
HWK E 3–5	7	9	—	9	2	P[b]	—	—	—	
HWK E 2	11	14	2	16	4	P[b]	1	—	1	
FLK N 3	17	15	18	33	4	P	4	P	—	
FLK N 4	15	11	18	29	4	P	1	P	1	
FLK N 5	13	13	15	28	6	P	3	P	—	indet.
DK all levels	15	27	2	29	7	≥2	2	2	1	H
Geologically redeposited										
BK (?)	11	28	1	29	4	≥1	1	2	—	A

Source: Based on M. D. Leakey (1971), appendix B. For comparison, see table 3.10.

Key: P, various unidentified remains of that taxon were present.

A, *Australopithecus boisei* was in direct association.

H, *Homo habilis* or *H. erectus* was in direct association.

[a] No data.

[b] Reported by M. D. Leakey (1971) but not listed in appendix B.

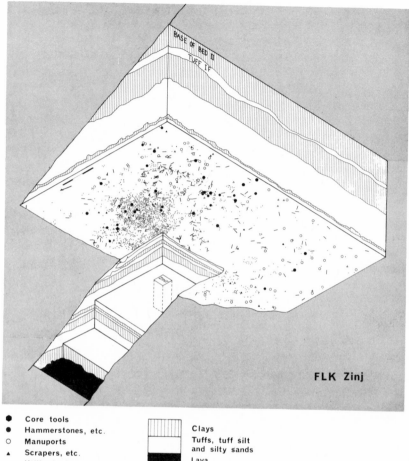

BASE OF BED II
TUFF IF

FLK Zinj

- ● Core tools
- ● Hammerstones, etc.
- ○ Manuports
- ▲ Scrapers, etc.
- △ Utilized pieces
- · Flakes, etc.
- ⟋ Bones, identifiable
- ⟋ Bones, non-identifiable

Clays
Tuffs, tuff silt
and silty sands
Lava

Figure 3.2. The FLK "Zinjanthropus" site seen in isometric perspective. As the diagrammatic representation shows, excavation has opened a "window" into the stratified layers of Bed I. An area of the old lake-margin floodplain has been uncovered, exposing a dense concentration of stone artifacts which closely coincides with a dense concentration of broken bones. The figure is based on plans and sections in M. D. Leakey (1971), to which readers should refer for details. The plinth marked *Zinj* indicates the spot, on the outcrop of the horizon, where the cranium of *Australopithecus boisei* was found eroding out, in 1959. Details of the step trench and trench walls are schematic. The scale at left on the horizon is in meters; the arrow points north.

Table 3.4. Percentages of major macrovertebrate taxa among identifiable bone remains at Olduvai Gorge. The figures on the left are relative to the total of macromammal remains. The three columns on the right give the percentages of mammals, chelonians, and crocodiles relative to the overall macrovertebrate total

	Percentages within Mammalia												
	Bovidae	Equidae	Suidae	Carnivora	Hippopotamidae	Proboscidea	Giraffidae	Rhinocerotidae	Primates	Mammalia	Chelonia	Crocodylidae	Number of specimens
Type C													
HWK E 1	81	8	5	1	1	2	3	—	—	99	1	—	319
FLK N 1 & 2	79	3	7	11	P	—	—	P	P	100	P[a]	—	1,721
FLK Zinj	78	7	8	2	—	—	P	—	5	90	8	2	675
FLK NN 3	70	3	10	17	—	—	—	—	—	17	82	1	1,893
Type B													
FLK N 6	40	P	15	1	P	43	P	—	—	100	—	—	478
Type A													
FC W floor	38	38	6	—	15	2	—	—	—	81	5	14	58
TK all levels[b]	46	28	11	1	7	P	3	4	—	100	—	—	215

Type D												
MNK Main	49	22	8	1	14	P	3	2	P	94	3	3	677
FC W tuff	53	19	7	—	19	2	2	—	—	98	2	—	91
MNK skull	69	5	14	—	7	2	—	2	—	36	57	7	216
HWK E 3–5	77	9	3	4	3	—	2	2	—	99	1	—	214
HWK E 2	65	3	7	2	2	14	1	6	—	84	3	13	541
FLK N 3–5	72	2	8	15	P	P	2	P	P	99.6	P[a]	P[a]	2,542
DK all levels	73	3	12	2	2	1	1	1	4	18	17	65	8,085
Geologically redeposited													
BK	56	19	9	1	2	1	8	2	2	95	2	3	988
Mean % for Olduvai	64.0	10.2	8.5	5.4	4.2	3.8	1.8	1.2	0.6				
Standard dev.	14.2	11.0	3.1	7.1	6.1	10.6	2.1	1.7	1.5				

Source: Based on M. D. Leakey (1971, table 4); percentages have been rounded to the nearest whole number.

Note: No data available for FLK N *Deinotherium*, EF-HR, SHK all levels.

[a] P = present but less than 0.5% of total.

[b] TK upper and lower floors are of type A, but the small amounts of fauna from them are not reported separately in the Olduvai monograph.

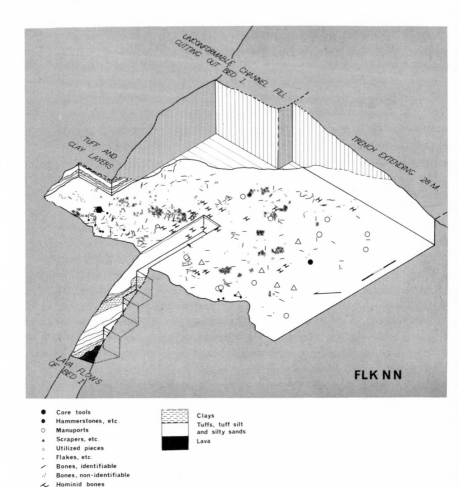

- ●   Core tools
- ●   Hammerstones, etc.
- ○   Manuports
- ▲   Scrapers, etc.
- △   Utilized pieces
- .   Flakes, etc.
- ╱   Bones, identifiable
- ⌐   Bones, non-identifiable
- ⚡   Hominid bones
- ⋊   Tortoise bones

Clays
Tuffs, tuff silt
and silty sands
Lava

Figure 3.3 The FLK NN site, seen in isometric perspective. As in the case of the "Zinjanthropus" site, an area of the ancient lake-margin floodplain has been uncovered by excavation, which has exposed a concentration of bone remains, especially chelonian bones, plus a number of stone artifacts. The places where pieces of hominid bones were discovered are marked *H* (Olduvai hominids 7 and 8, *Homo habilis*). The patch of material did not extend far beyond the limits of the area shown; a large trench extending southeastward proved sterile. Any easterly or westerly continuations of the floor have been destroyed by recent erosion or by a late Quaternary channel cut, now filled with unconformable sediments. This partly schematic figure is based on M. D. Leakey (1971), to which readers should refer for details. The scale at right on the floor is in meters; the arrow points north.

recovered from a comparable area of level 22, the Zinj floor. Clearly the density of stone and bone at that horizon is anomalously high.

Site FLK NN, Level 3. This site is probably of type C, but the density of bone is low enough that interpretation is more doubtful than in the previous case. Once again, studies of variations in background density are needed as a standard of reference. The site was discovered when hominid bones came to light during a paleontological excavation. Subsequently, large cuttings exposed more than 200 m^2 of a series of buried, old land surfaces stratified within middle Bed I. Level 3, the lowest, contained the most material, including Olduvai Hominids 7 and 8.

Excavation revealed a thin layer of clay above Tuff IB, with the bones and artifacts scattered on and in the upper surface of the clay. They had been buried in turn by another thin layer of tuff (volcanic ash), which is effectively sterile. Figure 3.3 shows the distribution of material on the exposed central area of the paleosol. Other trenches extending away from this area demonstrated that the same surface elsewhere had no material. There is no particular pattern to the overall distribution, although there are patches of chelonian bones within the scatter, each patch representing a single disintegrated tortoise shell. Mary Leakey (1971:250–51) reports a minimum of 17 patches, adding that "careful scrutiny of the carapace and plastron fragments has been carried out, but apart from a very few small indentations, such as could have been caused by a pointed stone, no signs of damage are visible. It seems likely that the shells were not broken open, but fell apart after they had lain in the open for a time." Clearly, experimental work is needed to evaluate any interpretation of the tortoise shells as food refuse. Speth and Davis (1976) have suggested that the remains imply a particular season of occupation.

The other faunal remains at the site are dominated by bones of bovids (70% of the mammal bones), carnivores (17%), and suids (10%) (see tables 3.3 and 3.4). There are numerous microfaunal remains in all these sediments, and Mary Leakey points out that their occurrence in level 3 does not prove that they were food refuse. All the bones appear to be less broken than at other sites, only 6% being nonidentifiable fragments, but this figure rises to 17% if reptile bones are excluded from the calculations as being identifiable even in small fragments. Mary Leakey reports that "a considerable number of coprolites, together with tooth marks on some of the bones (including the hominid right parietal and astragalus), indicate that scavengers were active after the site had been abandoned" (1971:43). It is conceivable that the bones at this site were largely or entirely accumulated by carnivores.

The artifacts consist of 36 flakes and flake fragments, mainly of quartz, 2 utilized flakes, 5 chipped quartz blocks, 1 lava hammer stone, and 4 lava core tools (2 choppers, 1 polyhedron, and 1 heavy-duty scraper).

Table 3.5. Percentages of body parts of larger mammals at Olduvai Gorge

	Number of specimens	Crania and cranial frags.	Horn cores	Maxillae	Man- dibles	Isolated teeth	Verte- brae	Ribs & rib frag
Average skeleton		1	1	1	21	22	19	
Non-archaeological sample of background								
FLK NN 2	401	1	1	1	4	19	4	18
Type C								
HWK E 1	375	2	3	2	3	23	10	9
FLK N 1–2	2,018	3	1	1	3	15	8	10
FLK Zinj	1,023	4	0	1	11	20	9	23
FLK NN 3	476	9	0	3	5	15	18	17
DK 1	190	5	1	1	2	35	10	11
Type B								
FLK N 6	529	2	1	1	3	27	17	17
Type A								
TK upper floor	132	5	2	—	2	52	1	12
TK lower floor	105	—	—	—	5	39	5	4
FC W floor	61	5	—	—	—	41	3	5
Type D								
MNK main	854	3	1	1	3	41	7	5
FCW tuff	101	4	3	—	1	62	1	—
MNK skull (H.13)	70	10	—	1	—	41	4	9
HWK E 3–5	223	1	0	0	2	42	9	2
HWK E 2	520	4	2	2	2	34	10	6
FLK N 3	933	5	2	1	5	17	8	7
FLK N 4	727	2	1	0	5	21	8	1
FLK N 5	1,161	3	2	1	3	24	4	3
DK 2	1,084	8	2	1	3	33	6	7
DK 3	628	7	1	1	4	32	8	9
Geologically redeposited								
BK	1,313	5	1	1	5	28	7	12
Other sites								
FLK N 13	144	2	5	3	7	18	12	4
FLK N 15	146	1	1	—	6	19	4	10
FLK NN 1	162	2	2	2	6	43	14	3

Source: Based on M. D. Leakey (1971, table 8); percentages have been rounded to the nearest number.

The overlying levels contain much less material than level 3. Level 2 contains only bone fragments and might serve as an example of the background density of nonhominid-accumulated bone assemblages in Bed I (see tables 3.7 and 3.8).

The bovid remains on all FLK NN levels are predominantly waterbuck (*Kobus* sp.). The site was close to the lake margin, and the waterbuck are

Pelves	Humeri	Radii	Ulnae	Meta-carpals	Femora	Tibiae	Meta-tarsals	Meta-podials, indet.	Podials, patellae, fibulae, sesamoids	Limb-bone shafts
1	1	1	1	1	1	1	1	1	12	—
1	3	3	2	3	0	2	3	0	24	6
3	3	4	3	3	1	4	5	1	14	7
3	3	3	2	3	2	4	5	2	22	7
2	2	2	2	2	1	2	3	0	13	3
1	2	2	2	2	1	1	0	0	14	6
1	1	1	1	1	2	—	3	1	23	—
2	2	2	2	2	1	1	2	0	16	2
5	2	1	—	2	2	—	1	—	9	5
3	3	1	2	1	2	—	4	4	16	12
2	2	2	—	—	—	2	3	12	15	8
2	1	2	2	2	1	2	2	2	16	4
2	2	1	—	2	—	—	1	3	15	3
1	3	—	3	6	—	—	1	7	13	—
1	1	3	0	3	1	3	2	1	21	2
2	1	2	0	2	0	1	2	2	25	5
5	4	2	2	4	2	3	2	1	24	6
2	2	2	1	2	2	1	3	2	40	5
2	2	2	2	3	2	3	3	3	33	4
2	2	2	1	2	1	2	1	3	20	1
1	3	1	1	2	2	2	2	4	16	2
2	3	2	2	2	1	3	3	1	13	7
2	6	4	1	4	1	7	1	1	5	13
1	3	4	2	5	1	8	6	1	13	12
3	3	2	1	3	2	1	5	1	4	3

thought to have been part of the immediate local fauna. Thus, even if the remains were food refuse, they do not constitute evidence of long-distance food transport.

Site FLK N, Level 6. At this level, some 130 artifacts and manuports were found at a type B site, in apparent association with much of an elephant skeleton (*Elephas recki*). According to Mary Leakey (1971:62), the material lay encased in a bed of "dark greyish-brown silty clay with white streaks," which was 45–60 cm thick.[8]

Only some 35 m² of the horizon was accessible to excavation, and the elephant skeleton filled a large part of that zone (fig. 3.4). The artifacts were closely associated with the elephant bones. Very few bones of other animals were recovered, and presumably they were simply part of the general background.

The cause of the elephant's death could not be determined. The bones are somewhat disarranged, as though the carcass had been partly pulled apart by scavengers or hominids. It appears that the body had lain on its left side. The bones are as large as those of many adult individuals among modern African elephants, but various epiphyses are unfused. Since male elephants continue to grow well into adult life, the individual was not necessarily immature (Laws, 1966).

The assemblage of 130 introduced stones consists of the following: core tools (4%); utilized heavy stones (14%); utilized flakes and flake fragments (4%); flakes and flake fragments without visible damage (73%); and manuports (5%). In view of the fine-grained encasing matrix, it is almost certain that neither the remains of the elephant carcass nor the introduced stone were transported by stream action. Both were deposited at the same spot within the relatively short span of time in which the layer was

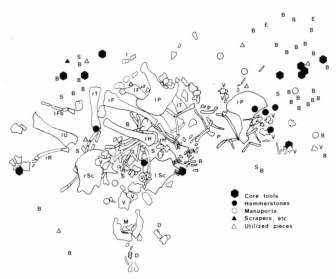

Figure 3.4. A plan of FLK N, level 6, a site of type B. A large part of the skeleton of an elephant was uncovered by excavation, with artifacts lying among the bones. Redrawn from M. D. Leakey (1971). Elephant bones: *D*, tooth; *F*, femur; *Fb*, fibula; *H*, humerus; *M*, mandible; *P*, pelvis; *R*, ribs; *Sc*, scapula; *T*, tibia; *U*, ulna; *V*, vertebra. Prefix *r*, right; prefix *l*, left. *B*, bovid bone; *S*, suid bone.

Table 3.6. Identifiable and nonidentifiable bones and bone fragments (excluding microfauna) in the archaeological sites at Olduvai Gorge

Sites	Number of specimens	Identifiable to taxon (%)	Identifiable to skeletal part but not taxon (%)	Noniden-tifiable fragments (%)	Corrected % Nonidentifiable fragments (ex-cluding turtles and crocodiles)[a]
Type C					
HWK E 1	425	75	14	11	11
FLK N 1–2	3,294	52	9	39	39
FLK Zinj	3,510	19	12	69	70
FLK NN 3	2,158	88	7	6	20
Type B					
FLK N 6	614	78	8	14	14
Type A					
FC W floor	127	46	11	43	47
Type D					
TK all levels	459	47	18	35	38
MNK main	1,723	40	10	50	52
FC W tuff	254	36	5	59	60
MNK skull (H.13)	378	57	7	36	44
HWK E 3–5	269	80	5	16	16
HWK E 2	631	86	11	3	5
FLK N 3	1,254	64	10	26	26
FLK N 4	929	71	5	22	22
FLK N 5	2,210	48	5	47	47
DK all levels	9,984	81	4	15	43
Geologically redeposited BK (?)	2,957	33	13	54	55

Source: Based on M. D. Leakey (1971, table 3); percentages have been rounded to the nearest whole number. For comparison see table 3.10.

Note: Data are not available for FLK N *Deinotherium,* EF-HR, and SHK all levels.

[a]In this column reptile bones have been excluded because even small fragments may be identifiable.

deposited. On the face of it, this site would seem to provide good evidence of "butchery" activities by tool-making hominids, but other possibilities cannot be entirely eliminated (see below).

Site FLK N, II Layer (Deinotherium Butchery Site). Thirty-nine introduced stones were found among the skeletal remains of a *Deinotherium* carcass, encased in a gray-green silty clay bed at the base of Bed II.

Table 3.7. Relative proportions of artifacts, bones, and manuports at Olduvai sites

Sites	Number of specimens	Artifacts (%)	Manuports (%)	Bone (%)	Ratio of Artifacts/ Bone	Reciprocal Ratio of Bones/ Artifact
Type C						
HWK E 1	742	21	22	57	.36	2.8
FLK N 1 & 2	4,709	26	4	70	.37	2.7
FLK Zinj	6,076	41	2	58	.70	1.4
FLK NN 3	2,230	2	1	97	.02	44.9
Type B						
FLK N 6	744	17	1	83	.20	4.9
Type A						
TK upper floor	5,549	93	3	4	22.5	.04
TK lower floor	2,321	93	1	6	14.7	.07
FC W floor	1,562	76	16	8	9.3	.11
EF-HR	556	94	—	6	15.4	.07
Type D						
MNK main	7,038	63	13	25	2.6	.39
FC W tuff	1,034	65	10	25	2.7	.38
MNK skull						
(H.13)	1,134	61	6	33	1.8	.55
HWK E 3–5	3,442	58	34	8	7.4	.14
HWK E 2	965	32	2	65	.49	2.0
FLK N 3	1,464	12	3	86	.14	7.3
FLK N 4	1,013	7	2	92	.07	13.9
FLK N 5	2,390	6	1	93	.07	14.6
DK all levels	11,182	11	—	89	.12	8.3
Geologically redeposited						
BK (?)	10,177	67	4	29	2.3	.44
TK channel	1,485	97	0.4	3	33.4	.03
Other						
FLK 13	198	6	—	94	.06	17.0
FLK 15	268	3	—	97	.04	28.8
FLK NN 1	309	5	6	89	.06	17.2
FLK NN 2	481	—	—	100		

Source: Based on M. D. Leakey (1971, table 6).

No plan of this type B site has yet been published.[9] It appears that the carcass lay with its limbs extending down into the clay, suggesting that the animal may have died while mired in a swamp. Many of its bones are in articulated position, but some are displaced as much as 2.5 m. The artifacts are scattered among the bones, with one chopper actually located within the pelvis, and the bone in general is poorly preserved. Cut-marks and artificially induced breaks have not been reported and probably could not be detected even if they had been present at the time of burial by sediment.

The assemblage of 39 introduced stones is as follows: core tools (15%); subspheroid stones (3%); utilized/chipped heavy forms (23%); undamaged flakes and fragments (18%); manuports (41%). Clearly this assemblage could represent a set of utensils discarded during the hacking up of parts of a deinothere carcass, but it contains fewer sharp flakes than one would have expected for such an activity (see J. D. Clark, 1972a). The density of artifacts in this instance is not so high as to constitute a definite anomaly.[10] Although this site probably represents an example of hominid meat-eating, it is not impossible that the co-occurrence of the skeleton and the stones could be fortuitous. We regard this site as less satisfactory evidence than that of the FLK N 6 elephant.

Site EF-HR. This type A site contains stratified sands, gravels, clays, and clayey tuffs between the Lemuta Member and Tuff IIC. The horizon containing artifacts occurs at the interface of a gravel bed and an underlying clay. According to Mary Leakey (1971:124), "the available evidence indicates that the site represents a small temporary camp on either side of a shallow water course." The site may not represent an original living floor, since the material was perhaps rearranged during the emplacement of the sands and gravels.

Only 34 fragmentary bone specimens were recovered, in addition to a complete cranium of *Giraffa jumae.* Other faunal specimens include bovids, two distinct equids, and single specimens of a carnivore, a rhinoceros, a suid, and a tortoise (see tables 3.3 and 3.8). The site is clearly of type A (artifacts plus very little bone), serving to show how low the bone-to-artifact ratio can be at some early sites.

Site FC West Floor. This site, also type A, contains a particularly rich concentration of artifacts associated with a paleosol overlying a clay bed. Although there are no heavily rolled specimens, some are either weathered or abraded, suggesting that there has been some displacement by water action. The horizontal distribution of the remains shows two distinct concentrations: one is a roughly circular area approximately 2 m in diameter, and the other is an oblong patch, nearly 3 × 4 m. Because one end of the latter patch has been damaged or destroyed by erosion, it may originally have been somewhat larger.

Table 3.8. Density of bone and artifact specimens at Olduvai sites

Site	Overall density, number per m², 9-cm levels	Artifacts per m²	All bones per m²	All bones minus reptile bones per m²
Type A				
TK upper floor	70.38	65.66	2.96	2.96
TK lower floor	55.91	51.89	3.52	3.52
FC W floor	88.70	67.2	7.10	5.85
EF–HR	12.53	11.76	0.78	0.78
Type B				
FLK N 6	3.54	0.59	2.93	2.93
Type C				
HWK E 1	7.71	1.60	4.42	4.42
FLK N 1–2	18.09	4.63	12.64	12.64
FLK Zinj	19.61	7.75	11.33	10.21
FLK NN 3	10.66	0.23	10.32	2.14
DK 3	5.46	—	—	—
Type D				
BK	5.16	3.45	1.50	1.43
FC tuff	7.43	4.83	1.83	1.83
MNK main	4.84	3.03	1.19	1.19
MNK skull	4.20	2.55	1.40	0.27
HWK E 3–5	18.73	10.83	1.46	1.46
HWK E 2	1.29	0.42	0.84	0.84
FLK N 3	9.02	1.06	7.71	7.71
FLK N 4	4.51	0.30	4.14	4.14
FLK N 5	4.29	0.27	3.97	3.97
DK all levels	1.68	0.18	1.50	0.50
Occurrences accounted as indicative of "background" densities				
FLK NN 1	1.28	0.067	1.14	0.78
FLK NN 2	0.97	0	0.97	0.97
FLK 15	0.35	0.012	0.34	0.34
FLK 13	0.15	0.008	0.14	0.14

Source: Based on M. D. Leakey (1971, table 5).

Note: For sites of types A, B, and C (butchery sites and "floors"), the artifacts and bones are contained in layers no more than 0.3 feet thick (9 cm). The densities express the number of items per square meter on the "floor." For sites of type D (vertically diffuse), to make the values comparable the densities have been expressed as densities per square meter per 9-cm thickness (i.e., number ÷ (total thickness/0.09 m) ÷ area).

Faunal remains are well preserved but relatively scarce in this level—only 127 specimens, or 7.5% of the total occupation debris. The composition of this small bone assemblage is shown in table 3.4. On the basis of the low bone-to-artifact ratio (see table 3.7), the occupation floor at FC West clearly represents a site of type A. Judging by the good condition of the bone materials, this may be a site where no great quantity was ever present.

Sites HWK E, Levels 2, 3–5.[11] Level 2 does not represent an occupation surface. Artifacts and bone debris are scattered vertically throughout 2 m of clay, but they are more concentrated near the base and about midway up the level. Although this level is best classified as vertically diffuse, type D, the two concentrated layers may represent separate occupations. The faunal remains in level 2 were more plentiful and better preserved than in any of the other horizons of this site (see tables 3.3–3.6). The lower part of the layer contained a high proportion of *Elephas* and *Deinotherium* remains, including teeth, the associated bones of a forefoot, and other postcranial bones. This layer was rich in avian remains and also included scattered bones of other taxa such as bovids, equids, and hippos. The upper part of the layer contained little besides parts of a rhinoceros skeleton associated with a few artifacts. In the entire level, crocodile remains amounted to 13% of the identifiable material. Large coprolites (hyena or lion size) were present, along with snake, amphibian, and rodent bones and a shell fragment belonging to a large gastropod. In contrast with the usual situation on living floors, the entire level contained only 3.6% of unidentifiable bone fragments.

Levels 3–5 do not seem to represent living floors but rather a complex series of partly redeposited materials. Since there were no appreciable typological or proportional differences in the artifacts from the three levels, Mary Leakey (1971:96, 110–11) treats them as a unit. Faunal remains are less plentiful relative to artifacts and are markedly more fragmentary than those from levels 1 and 2 (see tables 3.7 and 3.8). This difference may be in part a consequence of transport and redeposition processes. It is entirely possible that this and many other type D sites represent the continued operation of the processes that led to sites of type C—but anthropological interpretation is complicated by their greater stratigraphic thickness. Usually the material is not so dense that the sites can be treated as analogous to a deep, stratified midden.

Site BK. The BK site is situated approximately 8 m higher in the Bed II sequence than site SHK. The deposits consist of a series of tuffs, silts, sands, and gravels filling an old river channel, part of which has been destroyed by a modern gully. The maximum depth of the channel in the excavated areas was 2.6 m. Because of the complexity of the cut-and-fill bedding, all attempts to establish a sequence within the channel proved impossible. The whole deposit, including the artifacts and bones, has therefore been considered a single unit. It is uncertain whether BK is a complex type D site (vertically diffuse) or type G site (partially geologically redeposited). Since the material is associated in channel deposits, we suggest the latter. Mary Leakey (1971:199) notes that although a few of the artifacts and bones from the coarser horizons are rolled, these form a negligible proportion of the whole assemblage. Apparently the artifacts were not transported far enough to become abraded, and they probably derive from material discarded on the adjacent bank of the river or in the riverbed itself.

The faunal remains recovered from BK are extremely diverse (see tables 3.3–3.6). They include 29 mammalian taxa (plus Olduvai Hominid 3: one canine and one molar of *Australopithecus boisei*), 1 bird, 4 genera of reptiles, 1 amphibian, and 2 fish. If the bones are food refuse, which is uncertain, several features of the faunal material may provide interesting insights about hominid dietary behavior. Quantitative analysis of the faunal remains by M. D. Leakey (1971) included only those specimens recovered during the 1963 excavation, although a great deal of material had been obtained in previous excavations (table 3.11). In 1963, the 2,957 bone specimens represented 29.1% of all archaeological specimens.

During the 1956 excavation, many partially articulated remains of *Pelorovis oldowayensis,* representing 24 individuals of a genus of large, extinct bovids, were recovered in the clay filling of a depression that apparently represents a swamp or quiet backwater adjoining the main river. One virtually complete skeleton, mostly articulated as though joined by sinew at the time it became embedded, was found standing vertically in the clay, with the limb bones at a lower level than the head and trunk. It appears that the animal died in a standing position after becoming engulfed in mud. Because choppers and other tools, including one biface, were found nearby, Mary Leakey (1971:199) supports Louis Leakey's original suggestion that the animals had been driven into the swamp by hominids and then slaughtered (see also S. Cole, 1963:131). This interpretation is plausible enough, but other possibilities need to be considered. Instances elsewhere of mass deaths due to epidemics, drought, severe cold, and migration are not uncommon, and the resultant carcasses may at times be concentrated at water sources (Behrensmeyer, 1976b; Hill, 1975; A. Root, in the film *The Year of the Wildebeest;* Shipman, 1975). The occurrence of so many artifacts as a general scatter in the vicinity weakens the argument that the implements are in direct functional association with the *Pelorovis* remains. However, if the interpretation suggested by Louis and Mary Leakey is tentatively accepted, then the BK site may contain evidence of hunting by game drives, a method not otherwise in evidence in early sites. Alternatively, it is possible that the hominids simply came across these animals after they were bogged down and butchered them without having to drive them into the swamp. We regard anthropological interpretations of this site as very insecure.

Koobi Fora Formation

Sedimentary outcrops of the Koobi Fora Formation appear in an area of nearly 2500 km² on the east side of Lake Turkana (formerly Lake Rudolf). Numerous hominid fossils and a rich archaeological record have been recovered from many parts of the formation, which spans about 3 to 1.3 m.y. B.P. (see Coppens et al., 1976, for references on geology, paleontology, and archaeology). Hominid fossils have not been found under circumstances that provide direct evidence of meat-eating but, in a number of instances, concentrations of stone artifacts are accompanied by quantities of broken bones. Therefore, these sites potentially meet test conditions 1 and 2, described earlier, and they deserve to be considered in detail.

In the Lower Member, three sites have been excavated: KBS, which is of type C; HAS, type B; and NMS, type A. The artifact assemblages are similar to the "Oldowan" of Olduvai Gorge but have been designated as the *KBS Industry* (Isaac 1976c; Isaac and Harris, 1978). More than 50 sites have been discovered in the Upper Member, and those that have been excavated have yielded samples of a distinctive industry, the *Karari Industry* (Harris and Isaac, 1976). Analysis and interpretation of these sites is still in progress (J. W. K. Harris, 1978); until this work has been completed, the data, although potentially relevant to this review, cannot be included. Archaeological research at Koobi Fora is not so far advanced as at Olduvai, but it does show that the site types and the co-occurrences of artifacts and bones observed by Mary Leakey at Olduvai recur in other areas of East Africa where conditions of preservation are favorable. Only two of the Koobi Fora sites are considered here. These were excavated under the direction of one of us (GLI), with J. Barthelme, D. Crader, J. W. K. Harris, and J. Onyango-Abuje serving as site supervisors at different times.

Site KBS. At the Kay Behrensmeyer site (KBS),[12] artifacts and bones occur in beds of the KBS tuff which choked a distributary channel traversing the floodplain of a delta then being formed at the shores of the proto–Lake Turkana. The specimens are concentrated on and just above an interface where fine-grained, unbedded tuff silt rests on tufaceous sand. The mode of occurrence and the presence of leaf casts in the encasing silts indicate extremely quiet conditions and minimal disturbance (see fig. 3.5). We thus adopt the working hypothesis that the concentration of material in the site was not caused by water flow along the channel. However, we

Table 3.9. Characteristics of faunal remains from archaeological excavations in the lower member of the Koobi Fora Formation ("East Rudolf")

	KBS	*HAS*
A. Taxonomic list		
Fish		
Catfish	a few cranial plate fragments	a few cranial plate fragments
Polypterus	1 scale	—
Crocodilians		
Crocodile	7 teeth	—
Euthecodon	2 teeth	1 tooth
Rodents		
Porcupine	2 teeth	—
Suids		
(undetermined)	12 fragments	—
Hippopotamus	13 fragments	some tooth fragments (numerous teeth and bones of a single hippo occur on outcrop of layer)
Giraffids	2 fragments	
Bovids		
Antidorcas recki	3 teeth	1 tooth
Kobus cf.		
ellipsiprymnus	4 teeth	1 tooth
Aepyceros	1 tooth	1 tooth
Damaliscus spp.	3 teeth	
Alcelaphini		1 tooth
Cephalophini	1 tooth	
Bovidae indet.	>30 tooth fragments	>10 tooth and podial fragments

propose to test this hypothesis by means of experiments and further analyses.

The tool-making hominids apparently occupied the dry, sandy bed of a seasonally active distributary channel in which water flow had effectively ceased. Perhaps the spot was attractive because larger trees and bushes lined the watercourse, as is common today on the Omo, the Ileret, and the Turkwell deltas. The leaf impressions in the sediments encasing the archaeological material lend support to this interpretation.[13]

The scatter of broken bones at the sites is not spectacular, but the density is significantly higher than anything encountered in many geological test trenches cutting into the tuff outside the artifact concentration. As table 3.9 shows, the animals represented include at least one individual each of porcupine, pig, gazelle, waterbuck, and giraffe. In addition, several pig and

Table 3.9 (*continued*)

	KBS	HAS
B. Number of taxa represented (for comparison with Olduvai data in table 3.3)		
Mammal families	5	≥2
Genera of large mammals	≥9	5
Genera of small mammals	0	—
Reptiles	2	1
Birds	—	1
Amphibia	—	—
Fish	2	1

C. Degree of fragmentation as represented by percentage of nonidentifiable fragments (see table 3.10)

	% identifiable to taxon	% nonidentifiable fragments
KBS	~10	~90
HAS	~ 5	~95

D. Proportions (%) of bones, artifacts, and manuports

	N^a	% Bones (B)	% Artifacts (A)	% Manuports	Ratios A/B	B/A
KBS	1199	88	12	0.4	.132	7.59
HAS	481	75	25	0.6	.328	3.05

E. Densities of artifacts and bones per unit area of excavation

	Size of area	Overall densities per m^2	Average of artifacts per m^2	Average of bones per m^2
KBS	54 m^2	22.2	2.57	19.54^a
HAS	33.5 m^2	14.4	3.58	10.75^a

[a]The total numbers of bone pieces at KBS and HAS are 1,055 and 360, respectively. The first is estimated to be subject to a 10% correction and the second to a 20–30% correction for splinters formed by recent fracture. More detailed analysis is in progress.

hippo tusks are present, perhaps introduced for use as tools. Many of the taxa are represented by only a few fragments, and so we cannot be sure about their dietary significance. There are also many hundreds of small, nonidentifiable bone fragments; these constitute the best *prima facie* evidence that there is a co-occurring concentration of bone and artifacts at this horizon.

The artifacts recovered at KBS include a fairly small series of core tools, including some classic choppers, two discoids, a polyhedron, and a scraper on a split pebble, and a much larger series of flakes and flake fragments. The debitage is morphologically varied, including some flakes (and

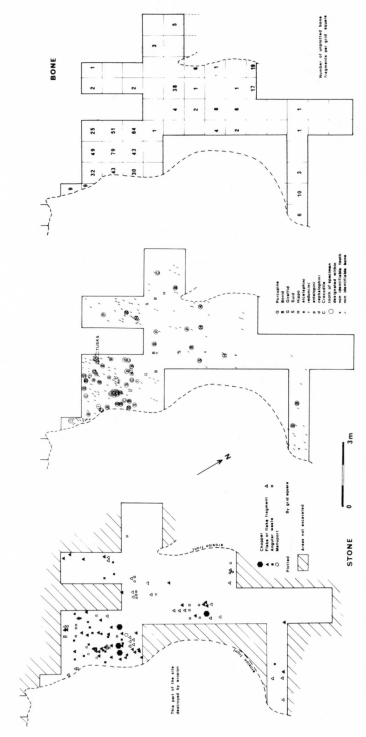

Figure 3.5. Plans of KBS in the Koobi Fora Formation, a site of type C. The site was discovered because erosion had cut into an area where artifacts and bone fragments were clustered on an old land surface buried by layers of sediment. Trenches were excavated to recover material from the uneroded beds; the three trench plans show the distribution of different classes of archaeological finds.

perhaps one blade) up to 6 or 7 cm in length, as well as numerous small flakes and chips down to less than 1 cm long. The presence of pieces small enough to be blown away by the wind, if not handled with care, probably indicates that at least some of the flaking was done at this spot and that disturbance during the covering of the site by sediment was minimal.

Site HAS. This "hippo and artifact site" (HAS)[14] was found by Richard Leakey 1 km south of KBS. The archaeological horizon is again stratified within an outcrop of the KBS tuff, which represents the fill of a choked delta distributary channel (fig. 3.6).

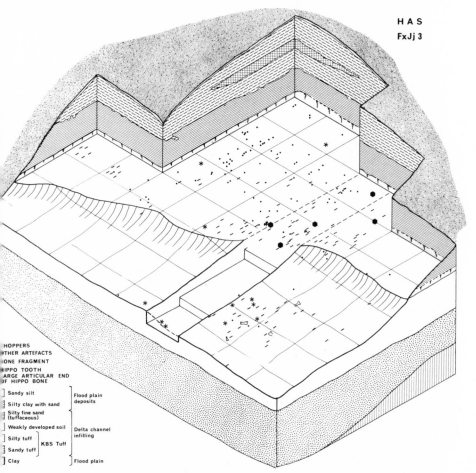

HAS
FxJj 3

:HOPPERS
:THER ARTEFACTS
:ONE FRAGMENT
:IIPPO TOOTH
:ARGE ARTICULAR END
:OF HIPPO BONE

] Sandy silt	Flood plain deposits
⫶ Silty clay with sand	
⫶ Silty fine sand (tuffaceous)	
] Weakly developed soil	Delta channel infilling
] Silty tuff ⎫ KBS Tuff	
⫶ Sandy tuff ⎭	
] Clay	Flood plain

Figure 3.6. An isometric block diagram of the HAS site, Koobi Fora. Fossil hippopotamus bones and artifacts were found on the surface where erosion had cut into the site (*right foreground*). Excavation into undisturbed, layered sediments at the outcrop revealed a buried old land surface with a concentration of artifacts and a few weathered hippopotamus bones.

Table 3.10. Comparative data from examples of later sites

| | | Indicators of the degree of fragmentation | | |
Sites	Total no. of bone pieces	% Identifiable to taxon [a] (+ skeletal parts where not differentiated)	% Identifiable to skeletal part only	% Nonidenti
Late Pleistocene–Holocene				
Caves and rockshelters				
Bushman rock shelter	4,028	2.5	29.9	67.6
(Brain, 1969b)				
Andrieskraal 1	11,056	19.6		80.4
(Hendey and Singer, 1965)				
Chencherere	66,847	3.9		96.1
(Crader, in prep)				
De Hangen				
(Parkington and Poggenpoel, 1971)[b]				
Open sites				
Gwisho B	195,415	1.1	4.7	94.2
(Fagan and Van Noten, 1971)				
Gwisho C	30,687	0.7	3.7	95.6
(Fagan and Van Noten, 1971)				
GrJi 1 (Gifford et al., in press)	162,426	2	6	92
Upper Pleistocene/Middle Stone Age				
Kalkbank	3,619	52.1	30.4	17.5
(Cooke, 1962; Dart and Kitching, 1958)				
Duinefontein 2, horizon 2	311			
(Klein, 1976c)				
Cave of Hearths	"thousands"			
(Cooke, 1962)				
Middle Pleistocene				
Olorgesailie: I3	14,600	5	—	95
DE/89[b]	13,800	12	15	85
(Isaac, 1966)				
Sidi Zin, all levels				
(Vaufrey, 1950)[c]				
Cave of Hearths	"particularly few"			
(Cooke, 1962)				
Plio-Pleistocene examples (see tables 3.3, 3.6, 3.9)				
FLK Zinj	3,510	19	12	69
FLK NN 3: all bones	2,158	88	7	6
mammals only	595	55	25	20
KBS	1,199	3	7	90
Range of all Olduvai and KBS sites	425–9,984	3–88	4–18	3–90
Nonarchaeological				
Andrieskraal 2	1,105	57.9		42.1
(Hendey and Singer, 1965)				
Swartklip 1				
(Klein, 1975b)[b]				

[a] The level of taxonomic precision attained in identifications varies. "Taxon" refers, in different entrie family, to genus, and to species. The numbers are thus minimum numbers, since greater taxonc resolution could only increase an entry.

[b] Overall counts not given.

[c] Only taxonomic lists available.

able 3.10 (*continued*)

			Numbers of taxa represented[a]				
ge mammals	Small mammals	Reptiles	Birds	Amphibians	Fish	Other	Total no. of species/genera
13	2	3	2	—	—	2	22
12	6	2	2	—	—	—	22
28	6	2	—	—	1	—	37
12	8	3	1	1	1	8	24
25	4	2	1	—	—	—	32
21	1	1	1	—	—	—	24
13	—	—	—	—	—	+	17
13	—	—	—	—	—	—	13
9	2	1	1	—	—	—	13
21	3	2	2	—	—	—	28
9	—	1	1	1	2	—	14
12	—	1	1	1	2	—	17
11	—	—	—	—	—	—	11
16	2	—	—	—	—	—	18
16	8	8	1	3	2	4	42
7	13	9	1	4	2	—	36
9	—	2	—	—	2	—	18
5–28	0–18	0–9	0–72	0–4	0–2	0–4	8–42
13	2	1	2	—	—	—	
20	7	2	2	—	—	—	31

By the time the site was discovered, erosion had cut into it, uncovering a large number of hippopotamus bones that were beginning to fragment as a result of exposure to weathering. The right fore and hind limbs are represented, as well as foot bones from both sides. Only sparse, fragmentary remains of the axial skeleton have been recovered, plus various teeth. The material was identified by the late Shirley Coryndon (1976) as *Hippo-*

potamus "Species C" nov., an extinct form known only from parts of the Lake Turkana basin. A scatter of stone artifacts was found among the hippo bones at the surface. Excavation subsequently confirmed the existence of a type B site. In 1970, a few artifacts and badly weathered bones were recovered from a small area of paleosol. During 1971, a much larger area revealed a patch of about 120 artifacts scattered over about 15–20 m^2. Bone was also present here, especially in the corner of the cutting adjacent to the surface scatter of hippo bones and teeth. However, the bone was very badly preserved.

Excavations undertaken in 1972 explored the lateral extent of the artifact-and-bone-bearing horizon. Extensions were made at the northeast corner and at the western margin. Both these cuttings rapidly ran out of the artifact-bearing zone, thus demonstrating that the material recovered in 1971 comes from a discrete patch of artifacts and weathered bone, the outcrop of which is exactly contiguous with the patch of hippo bones previously exposed by erosion.

Since the old ground surface on which the artifacts rested is now known to slope in the direction of the patch of hippo bones, it seems very probable that the bones formerly lay in a hollow within the choked and largely silted-up channel. Artifacts were found among these hippo bones and also on the elevated bank adjacent. It thus seems highly probable that this is a type B site. However, we must stress that the only large portions of hippo bones to be found were on the outcrop of the site, not in the excavation.

The artifacts consist largely of small flakes and flake fragments, plus 1 polyhedron and 2 unclassifiable pieces, but the surface finds include 3 or 4 small choppers. The assemblage is less varied than that of KBS, and it is possible that this greater uniformity reflects the more restricted range of activities appropriate to a butchering site (see Clark and Haynes, 1969). Bone remains of animals other than the hippo occur in such small quantities that they could well be part of a general background scatter.

COMPARISONS WITH LATER PREHISTORIC ACCUMULATIONS

Before we attempt to assess the behavioral significance of early prehistoric artifacts and bone remains, it would seem wise to compare the characteristics of the early bone assemblages with those from more recent prehistoric sites. Table 3.10 summarizes some comparative data from a variety of sites.

Most of the assemblages in table 3.10 are of late Pleistocene or Holocene age; only three Middle Pleistocene ("Acheulean") cases have been included (Orlorgesailie, Sidi Zin, and the Cave of Hearths). Four of the entries pertain to caves and rock shelters, for which we have no early Pleistocene counterparts. In all East African cases, the faunal remains are predominantly those of wild animals, presumably obtained by hunting and scavenging, although at one site (Nakuru GrJi 1) some remains of domestic animals are also present. We have also included data for Swartklip I, which is probably a carnivore accumulation, and Andrieskraal 2, which is believed to be a porcupine accumulation. Examples of data from Olduvai and Koobi Fora (the KBS sites) are presented according to the same format, to facilitate comparison.

The data in tables 3.3, 3.6, 3.9, and 3.10 show clearly that the percentage values recorded for these categories of specimens at the very early sites overlap the values for undoubted recent human bone-refuse deposits, although gross abundance of bone is far greater at those recent sites where stable localized amenities, such as the shelter of a cave or the proximity of a spring, led to repeated superimposed occupations.

The recent bone middens tend to show a higher proportion of nonidentifiable bone splinters than do the early sites.[15] The degree of bone pulverization indicated by these values is probably attributable to the breaking up of bones for marrow extraction, but note that fragmentation due to weathering and trampling has not been distinguished. Low fragmentation indices may argue against a hominid role in accumulation of materials, but other possible factors need to be considered as well: (1) fine mesh screens are more often employed on Later Stone Age sites, and this may have led to the recovery of more small, unidentifiable fragments; (2) preservation factors, including trampling on an intensively used site, may raise the proportion of small splinters; (3) there may have been an increase through time in the intensity of dismemberment and bone smashing techniques; (4) the use of pots or vessels in some late-period sites may have necessitated greater bone fragmentation; (5) the early sites are open, while many of the later sites are rock shelters. Shelters are more likely to preserve small bones.

During the course of our review we found more taxa represented at many of the Olduvai sites than we would have expected at a hominid occupation site. However, table 3.10 shows that high taxonomic diversity is usual among food-refuse assemblages at African sites.

Comparison of quantitative data from early and later sites, where the bone refuse undoubtedly accumulated as a result of meat-eating, shows that it is entirely possible for the early assemblages to represent food refuse. However, the numerical values also overlap with those for assemblages attributable to nonhuman agencies. The question thus remains open, and it is necessary to examine further the intrinsic features of the early archaeological data in order to try to reach a conclusion.

TOWARD A VERDICT

Now that we have summarized the circumstantial evidence from the Olduvai and Koobi Fora test cases, and have compared these cases with more recently deposited bone refuse, we can move toward a verdict on the question: Does archaeological evidence support hypotheses of early hominid hunting or meat-eating?[16] The chosen test cases should meet the three conditions set forth earlier, which can be reformulated as questions.

Criterion 1. Do artifacts and bones coexist in an anomalously high concentration at any of the test sites? Table 3.8 summarizes the density data for artifacts per square meter, bones per square meter, and combined densities at the Olduvai sites. These measures only have anthropological significance for vertically concentrated occurrences, for which transport of the stones and bones by nonhominid agents such as water currents or carnivores can be shown to be a highly improbable explanation. Figure 3.7 shows the data as frequency histograms and as a rank-ordered series, from least to most dense.

Clearly many of the test case sites yield high concentrations of artifacts and bones, but the density values at which occurrences become anomalously concentrated must be evaluated on the basis of more objective criteria. Ideally the observed values should be compared with background values for the paleo-landscape around each site. The values of bone concentrations at the archaeological sites should also be compared with the densities of bone collected at present-day campsites.

Unfortunately, very few systematic data are available on the densities of bone at the living sites of current hunter/gatherers. However, from plans published by Yellen (1977) and Gifford (1977), we have been able to make estimates. We have computed the densities per square meter from the numbers of bones in areas within the camps which are, in our judgment, equivalent to the areas normally excavated by archaeologists when they dig early stone age open-air sites. The results for a series of eight Dobe !Kung camps that contained 100 or more bones when mapped by Yellen (1977) ranged from $0.5/m^2$ to $4.6/m^2$, with a mean of 1.7 and a median of 1.3. The magnitude of occupation ranges from 7 to 30 days and from 7 to 26 persons. Values for four hunter/fisher camps mapped by Gifford (1977) are 0.1, 0.3, 0.6, and 40.7 bones per square meter. Occupation intensities were 14 people for 10 days; 8 people for 7 days; 2 people for 40 days; and 8 people for 4–5 days, respectively. The peak value derives from site 20, where fish bones, terrapins, and the dermal scutes from several crocodile carcasses led to a very high value. The equivalent figures for Olduvai sites of type A, B, or C (table 3.8) range from 0.8 to $12.6/m^2$, with a mean of 6.2 and a median of 4.4. Thus, the Olduvai and Koobi Fora sites contain densities of bone that

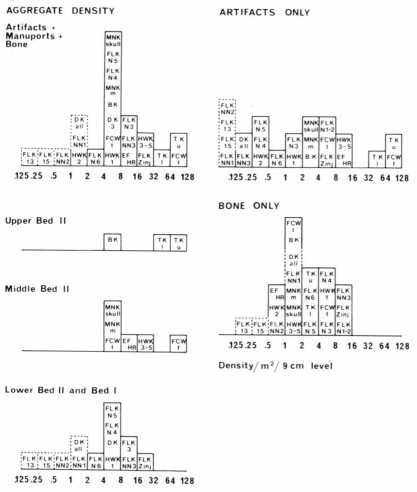

Figure 3.7. Histograms showing the densities of specimens recovered by excavation from the early sites at Olduvai. The histograms on the left show overall densities (artifacts, manuports, and bones) for each of three stratigraphic intervals and for the whole series. Those on the right show the frequency distribution of artifact density and of bone density. The dotted lines distinguish three occurrences for which evidence that hominids induced the concentration is particularly doubtful. DK is all shown in broken lines because this is an aggregate entity including DK 3, which is also shown. All values are based on data in M. D. Leakey (1971, table 5), but the values are converted to densities per unit area. Where the thickness of deposit yielding the material exceeds 9 cm (0.3 ft), the densities have been calculated as the density per square meter per 9-cm level.

Table 3.11. The representation of animal taxa in bone assemblages from Olduvai Gorge Beds I and II

	DK 2-3	DK 1	FLK NN 3	FLK NN 2	FLK NN 1	FLK Zinj	FLK N 6	FLK N 5
Mollusca	·	·	—	—	—	×	—	—
Fish	×	×	×	×	—	×	—	—
Amphibia	×	×	×	·	—	×	×	×
Reptilia								
Chelonia	×	×	×	—	×	×	—	×
Crocodilia	×	×	×	—	—	×	—	×
Squamata	×	×	×	×	×	×	×	×
Aves	×	×	×	—	—	×	—	—
Insectivora	—	—	×	×	×	×	×	×
Chiroptera	—	—	×	—	—	—	—	—
Primates								
Galago spp.	×	—	—	—	—	×	—	—
Simopithecus cf. *oswaldi*	·	·	×	—	—	—	—	—
cf. *Cercocebus* sp.	—	—	—	—	—	—	—	—
Papio sp.	×	—	—	—	—	—	—	—
Primate indet.	—	—	—	—	—	—	—	—
Rodentia	×	—	×	×	×	×	×	×
Lagomorpha	—	—	—	—	—	×	—	×
Carnivora								
*Thos mesomelas	×	×	—	—	—	×	—	—
Otocyon recki	—	—	×	—	—	—	—	—
Canidae indet.	—	—	·	·	—	—	—	—
Viverridae spp.	×	—	×	×	—	—	—	—
Crocuta sp.	×	·	—	—	—	×	—	—
Felis cf. *serval*	—	—	—	—	—	—	—	—
Panthera spp.	—	—	—	—	—	—	—	—
Felidae indet.	×	—	—	—	—	—	—	—
Machairodontinae indet.	×	—	—	—	—	—	—	—
Carnivora (not specified)	—	—	—	—	×	—	—	—
Proboscidea								
Deinotherium cf. *bosazi*	×	—	—	—	—	—	—	×
Elephas recki (early & evolved)	×	×	—	—	—	—	×	×
Perissodactyla								
Equus cf. *oldowayensis*	×	—	·	·	·	×	×	×
*Stylohipparion sp.	—	—	—	—	—	×	×	×
Ceratotherium simum	×	×	—	—	×	—	—	—
Diceros bicornis	—	—	—	—	—	—	—	—

Table 3.11. (*continued*)

FLK N 4	*FLK N 3*	*FLK N 2*	*FLK N 1*	*HWK E 1*	*HWK E 2–5*	*MNK skull*	*EF–HR*	*MNK main*	*FC W floor*	*FC W tuff*	*SHK*	*TK*	*BK*
×	—	—	—	—	×	×	—	—	—	—	×	—	—
—	—	—	—	—	—	×	—	×	—	×	×	—	×
×	×	×	×	—	×	×	—	×	—	—	—	—	×
—	—	×	×	×	×	×	×	×	×	×	—	—	×
—	—	×	×	×	×	×	—	×	×	—	—	—	×
×	×	×	×	—	×	—	—	—	—	—	—	×	×
—	—	—	—	×	—	×	—	×	—	×	×	—	×
×	×	×	×	—	×	—	—	—	—	—	—	—	×
—	×	×	·	—	—	—	—	—	—	—	—	—	—
—	—	—	—	—	—	—	—	—	—	—	—	—	—
—	—	—	—	—	—	—	—	·	—	—	—	—	—
—	—	—	—	—	—	—	—	—	—	—	—	—	×
—	—	—	—	—	—	—	—	—	—	—	—	—	—
—	—	—	·	·	—	—	×	—	—	—	—	—	—
×	×	×	×	—	×	×	—	×	—	—	—	—	—
×	·	·	·	—	—	—	—	—	—	—	—	—	—
—	×	—	—	—	—	—	—	—	—	—	—	—	—
×	×	—	—	—	—	—	—	—	—	—	—	—	—
—	—	—	—	—	—	×	—	×	—	—	—	×	—
×	×	—	×	—	—	—	—	—	—	—	?	—	—
×	—	—	×	—	—	—	—	—	—	—	—	×	—
—	—	—	—	—	—	—	—	—	—	—	×	—	—
—	—	—	—	—	—	—	—	—	—	—	—	—	2 spp
—	—	—	×	—	—	—	—	—	—	—	—	—	—
—	—	—	—	—	—	—	—	—	—	—	?	—	—
—	—	—	—	×	×	—	×	—	—	—	—	—	—
—	—	—	—	×	—	—	—	—	—	—	—	—	—
—	—	—	—	×	×	×	—	×	×	—	×	×	×
×	×	×	×	×	×	×	×	×	·	·	×	×	×
×	×	×	×	·	×	×	(×)	×	·	·	×	×	×
—	×	·	·	—	×	×	×	×	·	·	×	×	×
—	—	—	—	—	—	—	—	×	—	—	—	—	×

Table 3.11 (*continued*)

	DK 2-3	DK 1	FLK NN 3	FLK NN 2	FLK NN 1	FLK Zinj	FLK N 6	FLK N 5
Artiodactyla								
Mesochoerus spp.	2 spp	—	—	×	—	2 spp	×	—
Potamochoerus spp.	×	—	×	—	—	—	—	—
Metridiochoerus spp.	×	—	—	—	—	×	—	—
Notochoerus spp.	×	—	—	—	—	×	—	—
Stylochoerus spp.	—	—	—	—	—	—	—	—
Suidae indet.	—	—	—	—	×	—	—	—
Hippopotamus spp.	×	×	—	—	—	—	×	×
Giraffa spp.	×	—	—	—	—	—	×	—
Libytherium olduvaiensis	×	—	—	—	—	—	—	—
**Strepsiceros* spp.	·	·	·	·	×	×	×	×
*Strepsicerotini indet.	·	·	—	—	—	×	—	—
Pelorovis oldowayensis	—	—	—	—	—	—	—	—
Bovini (small) indet.	·	·	—	—	—	×	×	—
Kobus spp.	·	·	×	×	·	×	—	×
Redunca sp.	—	—	—	—	—	—	—	—
Hippotragus gigas	·	·	—	—	×	—	—	—
Oryx sp.	—	—	—	—	—	×	—	—
Hippotragini indet.	—	—	—	×	×	—	×	×
Parmularis altidens	·	·	—	—	—	×	×	×
**Xenocephalus* sp.	·	·	—	—	—	—	—	—
Beatragus antiquus	—	—	—	—	—	—	—	—
Gorgon olduvaiensis	—	—	—	—	—	—	—	×
Aepyceros sp.	—	—	—	—	—	—	—	—
Damaliscus spp.	—	—	—	—	—	—	—	—
Alcelaphini indet.	·	·	·	·	·	×	—	—
Neotragini indet.	—	—	—	—	—	—	—	×
Gazella spp.	·	·	—	—	—	×	×	×
**Phenacotragus recki*	—	—	—	—	—	—	—	—
Antilopini indet.	·	·	—	—	—	—	—	—
**Pultiphagonides africanus*	—	—	—	—	—	—	—	—
Bovidae indet., sp. nov.	—	—	—	—	—	—	×	×
Bovidae indet. or not specified	—	—	—	—	—	—	—	—

Source: Based on M. D. Leakey (1971, appendix B).
Key: * = taxon name to be changed
· = recorded for site, but level not certain
? = probable identification
(×) = probably present

Table 3.11. (*continued*)

FLK N 4	FLK N 3	FLK N 2	FLK N 1	HWK E 1	HWK E 2–5	MNK skull	EF–HR	MNK main	FC W floor	FC W tuff	SHK	TK	BK
—	—	—	×	×	—	×	—	×	—	—	×	2 spp	×
—	—	—	—	—	—	—	—	—	—	—	—	—	×
—	—	—	—	—	—	—	—	×	—	—	×	×	×
—	·	·	·	—	×	·	—	·	—	—	×	—	×
—	—	—	—	—	—	—	—	×	—	—	2 spp	—	2 spp
—	—	—	—	—	×	—	×	—	×	×	—	—	—
×	—	·	·	×	×	×	—	×	×	×	×	×	2 spp
×	×	·	·	×	×	—	×	×	—	—	—	×	2 spp
—	·	·	·	×	×	—	—	×	—	×	×	×	×
×	×	×	×	×	×	—	—	×	—	—	×	—	×
—	—	—	—	—	—	—	—	—	—	—	×	—	—
—	—	—	—	×	—	—	—	×	—	—	×	—	×
—	·	·	·	×	×	—	—	×	—	—	×	×	×
×	×	—	—	×	×	—	—	×	—	—	×	—	×
×	—	—	—	—	—	—	—	—	—	—	—	—	—
—	—	—	—	—	—	—	—	—	—	—	—	×	×
—	—	—	—	—	—	—	—	—	—	—	—	—	—
×	×	×	×	—	×	—	—	×	—	—	—	—	—
×	×	×	×	—	—	—	—	—	—	—	—	—	—
—	—	—	—	×	—	—	—	×	—	—	×	—	×
—	×	—	—	—	—	—	—	—	—	—	—	—	—
—	—	—	—	—	—	—	—	—	—	—	×	—	×
—	—	—	—	—	—	—	—	—	—	—	—	—	×
—	—	—	—	—	—	—	—	—	—	—	2 spp	—	×
—	—	—	—	×	×	—	—	—	—	—	—	—	×
—	—	—	—	—	—	—	—	—	—	—	—	—	—
×	×	×	×	×	—	—	—	—	—	—	—	—	×
—	—	—	—	—	—	—	—	—	—	—	×	—	×
—	—	—	—	—	—	—	—	—	×	—	×	×	×
—	—	—	—	—	—	—	—	—	×	—	×	—	×
—	—	—	—	—	—	—	—	—	—	—	—	—	—
—	—	—	—	—	—	×	×	—	×	×	—	—	—

Notes: Thos mesomelas = Canis mesomelas
Stylohipparion = Hipparion
Libytherium olduvaiensis = Sivatherium
Strepsiceros = Tragelaphus
Strepsicerotini = Tragelaphini
Xenocephalus = Megalotragus kattwinkeli
Phencotragus recki = Antidorcus recki
Pultiphagonides africanus = Connochaetes africanus

are as great or greater than some values for the short-term occupation of current foraging societies. Quantitative information on the densities of nonhumanly induced bone scatters are available only in forms that make comparison with the archaeological data virtually meaningless.[17]

For the Koobi Fora sites at which direct field evidence has been collected, we can report with confidence that the artifact density at each site is truly a conspicuous positive anomaly. Mary Leakey (1971) does not directly discuss the question of background information at the Olduvai sites, but she repeatedly implies that these sites are conspicuous anomalies. The same inference can be drawn from R. L. Hay's report (1976). Although these conclusions are not seriously doubted by scientists who have field knowledge of the areas in question, they should be brought under control by the collection of systematic data on background density variation, perhaps involving surveys of erosion cuts as well as random square excavations.

The only Olduvai site that currently provides a control measure is FLK NN, level 2, which is a horizon with bones but no artifacts. Assuming that this was not a hominid-induced aggregate, we can compare the density value there with those of other putative hominid bone-refuse accumulations. As can be seen from table 3.8, the density value of $0.97/m^2$ is among the lowest of the Olduvai series, being matched only by EF-HR ($0.78/m^2$) and FLK NN, level 1 ($1.14/m^2$). The first of these is a site of type A; the second is doubtful as an archaeological site because of the low incidence of artifacts. The FLK Zinj floor emerges as the best-documented site of type C, with densities for both artifacts and bone which are close to the upper limits of observed values. This is clearly a coincident positive anomaly for the densities of both artifacts and fragmented bone. Other sites such as FLK N 1–2, DK, FLK NN 3, HWK E 1, and KBS (see table 3.9) can also provisionally be so regarded.

Criterion 2. Do any of the sites show patterns of bone damage that are strongly indicative of the action of protohumans? Cut-marks would be the most satisfactory direct indicators, but no careful search for them has been reported, and we have to fall back on bone breakage as potentially symptomatic. Table 3.6 summarizes the degree to which the bones at the Olduvai sites have been fragmented. Some comparative data from other later-period archaeological sites appear in table 3.10. A greater range of variation among the sites is again apparent, and a problem again arises regarding the degree of fragmentation above which an occurrence can be regarded as more highly comminuted than is normal in natural bone aggregates.

Data on the normal natural situation are sparse, but we have culled some indicators from taphonomic research on recent bone by Behrensmeyer

(1975) and Hill (1975). Other relevant data include those collected by Isaac (1967a), Klein (1975b), and Sutcliffe (1972) from hyena lairs. Compared to these varied results, the Olduvai and Koobi Fora sites are unusual in the degree to which the bone has been fragmented. Concentrations of broken bone in which more than 15–20% is unidentifiable bone splinters seem to be distinctive features of (1) human food refuse; (2) carnivore lairs at which bone is recurrently chewed; (3) some cave deposits, which may well be fossil examples of category 1 or 2; (4) deposits where weathering and soil pressures have broken up the bone (Klein, 1977a).

The degree of bone fragmentation observed at the early East African archaeological sites is consistent with the hypothesis that the bone *was* food refuse, but other agencies may also have been responsible in whole or in part.[18]

Criterion 3. Do any of the test sites show patterns of bone composition which indicate accumulation due to protohuman activity? Table 3.3 shows the number of taxa identified at each of the Olduvai sites under discussion, and table 3.11 lists the species of larger mammals represented. Each site contains a fairly typical range of savanna macrofauna. No conspicuous anomaly is evident. Although the number of taxa represented at the Olduvai sites is very high, it does not exceed that observed at undoubted human occupation sites (see table 3.10). Species composition does not by itself establish the role of hominids in creating the accumulations.

Table 3.5 shows the relative percentages of large-mammal body parts at Olduvai. If these data are arranged in stratigraphic order, then certain trends emerge. In particular, there is a marked rise through time in the teeth/vertebrae ratio, which has been suggested by Behrensmeyer (1975) as a useful index of the degree of distortion of a bone sample by transport and weathering processes. It seems very likely that conditions of preservation were optimal in Bed I times and harsher in later times. If this change is taken into account when interpreting the record, the proportional composition of bone remains by taxon and by body part is compatible with, but does not confirm, the hypothesis that the bones were wholly or partly accumulated as food refuse.

In summary, we find that even after ultracritical review, there is good *prima facie* evidence for the involvement of early tool-making hominids in meat-eating. First, there are a number of instances in which anomalously high densities of bones coincide with high densities of discarded artifacts, under circumstances where water flow seems unlikely to have washed the stones and bones together. Second, in many instances the aggregations of bone show a degree of fragmentation that is unusual in the natural bone aggregates observed thus far on open terrain.

The co-occurrence of artifacts and fragmented bones is a reliable indicator of the habitations of later prehistoric and recent humans, and the notion that many of the Plio-Pleistocene sites represent early instances of analogous protohuman behavior seems highly plausible to us. However, before adopting this as a working hypothesis, we should consider as many alternative explanations as possible. Patches of discarded artifacts and fragmented bones may coincide for any of the following reasons.

1. Tool-making hominids may have frequented the sites, repeatedly bringing, using, and discarding stones and artifacts. They may also have brought bones encased in meat to these sites, and broken the bones in the process of eating meat and marrow.

2. At slightly different times both tool-making hominids and carnivores may have frequented the same restricted locality—for instance, a grove of shady trees. The hominids may have discarded stone tools, while the carnivores brought bones and broke them up by chewing.[19]

3. Tool-making hominids may have been attracted to places such as waterholes where quantities of bones were lying around, and the hominids' recurrent or prolonged activity in the vicinity may have created a coincident scatter of artifacts.[20]

4. Tool-making hominids may have habitually collected and broken dry bones for some reason other than meat-eating, perhaps for tool use.

5. Both artifacts and bones may have been swept together from initially dispersed and separate locations by stream action or flash floods. This alternative applies only to those sites associated with channels or depressions.

6. Given the formation of both stone artifact concentrations and bone concentrations in ancient landscapes, some could come to coincide purely by chance.

A similar list of alternative hypotheses can be given for instances where a cluster of artifacts coincides with the bones of a single large carcass (site of type B). Each hypothesis carries its own test implications, and the stage of research has now been reached where we and others are searching for evidence that will show, for a series of sites, that some of these potential explanations of the coincident accumulations of artifacts and bones can either be eliminated or shown to be highly improbable. While we await the results of more rigorous tests, we tentatively conclude that meat-eating by hominids is the best of several possible explanations for the Plio-Pleistocene sites. We still do *not* regard meat-eating by early hominids as an established fact, but we believe the evidence is strong enough to justify our retaining the working hypothesis. Acceptance of this proposition in turn raises other questions: Did the early tool-makers acquire meat by hunting or by scavenging? If both, can we determine the relative proportion of each? Assuming that gathered foods such as plants, insects, and eggs were as important in prehistoric hominid diets as in current human diets, can we assess the proportion of meat intake relative to these other foods? What may have been the ecological, sociological, and evolutionary implications of meat-eating in a protohuman subsistence economy?

SOME SPECULATIONS ON EARLY HOMINID BEHAVIOR AND SUBSISTENCE

Hunting versus Scavenging

Data from comparative zoological and ethnographic studies present archaeology with a challenge. The larger social carnivores of Africa, such as the lion and the hyena, acquire meat both by hunting and by scavenging (Kruuk, 1972; Schaller, 1972; Schaller and Lowther, 1969). Contemporary hunter/gatherers in Africa, such as the !Kung, the Hadza, the Gal Dies, and the Bisa, all do likewise (Lee, 1968; Woodburn, 1968a; Marks, 1976; Gifford, 1977). However, it appears that even the nonhuman primates that are sometimes active predators either do *not* scavenge (chimpanzees: Teleki, 1973a) or do so very rarely (baboons: Harding, personal communication; Strum, in this volume). The question confronting archaeologists, therefore, is: When did protohuman behavior come to include opportunistic scavenging? Were the early hominids more like modern humans and carnivores or more like modern predatory primates in this regard?

Elizabeth Vrba (1974, 1975) has recently proposed some criteria for ascertaining differences between bone assemblages acquired by hunting and by scavenging. She suggests that a hunted primary assemblage (one that is brought into caves by predators, either hominids or carnivores) is likely to contain a significant percentage of juveniles,[21] and furthermore that if one predatory pattern predominates, most carcasses should fall into a restricted body-weight range. In contrast, a secondary assemblage (one that is brought into caves by scavengers, either hominids or carnivores) is likely to contain only a low percentage of juveniles, since the carcasses of young animals are quickly destroyed by primary predators. Equally, the body weights in the scavenged assemblage are likely to be highly variable, for scavenging may lead to a more random, opportunistic sampling of game animals than does hunting.

In an attempt to apply these generalizations, Vrba first arranged the bone materials of the Blaaubank Valley in chronological order and then noted the observed values for the frequency of juvenile bovids and the size variation among the game animals represented. She concluded that the bone assemblages from the three earliest sites—Sterkfontein Type Site (= Member 4), Swartkrans A (= Member 1), and Kromdraai A—represent primary assemblages accumulated by large, actively hunting carnivores. The three later sites—Kromdraai B, Swartkrans B, and Sterkfontein

Dump 16—seemed to Vrba to represent the results of hominid predation because the presence of both *Homo* and stone artifacts is known or inferred, and because the bones of smaller animals predominate. The Sterkfontein Extension Site (Member 5) assemblage stands chronologically between the earlier and later sites and contains a markedly low percentage of juveniles. This suggests a scavenged assemblage and, since numerous artifacts are present, hominids are strongly implicated as the agents. The sequence that emerges is a first phase in which carnivore activity is predominant in the caves, followed by a second phase of hominid occupation in which scavenging preceded active hunting. These interpretations are highly tentative, and they are complicated by the fact that the cave deposits lack definable occupation floors. The study is important, however, since it seeks *direct* evidence rather than speculative hypotheses regarding the hunting/scavenging question.

Detailed data, such as the frequency of juvenile bones, which would allow us to apply Vrba's criteria in East Africa are not yet available.

Regarding sites of type B, need one suppose that pachyderms such as the elephant at Olduvai FLK N 6, the hippo at Koobi Fora HAS, or the deinothere at Olduvai FLK N II were killed by the makers of the stone tools found among their bones? Even if we accept the idea that the tools were functionally associated with the fresh carcass, we cannot say that these sites constitute solid evidence of hunting. Pachyderms that die of natural causes may constitute a bonanza for any scavenger who can break through the tough hide with sharp sticks, stone flakes, and jagged stone choppers.

Tables 3.3, 3.4, and 3.11 show that the Olduvai sites characteristically contain a very wide range of mammalian taxa. However, even without full access to quantitative data, Mary Leakey (1971) proposed that the preponderant forms are medium to large ungulates. With the exception of tortoises, small animals are not conspicuous among the bones that seem to be food refuse—yet Later Stone Age and modern African gatherer/hunter diets are likely to include numerous hyrax, hares, spring hares (*Pedetes*), porcupines, dikdiks, and steenbok (Brain, 1969b; Lee, 1968; Woodburn, 1968a). Although one could argue that the paucity of this middling-small grade was more consistent with a scavenging rather than a hunting origin, the argument could not pretend to be conclusive. Thus, we favor the view that the early tool-making hominids were opportunistic scavenger/hunters and that, given the simplicity of technology at the time, the flesh of medium ($\geqslant$50 kg) and large ($\geqslant$200 kg) prey was probably obtained more by scavenging than by hunting.

The Importance of Other Foods in Early Hominid Diets

Outside of the Arctic and cold temperate regions, gatherer/hunters who do not depend heavily on fishing have a diet consisting of more than 50%

gathered foods, of which the bulk are plants (B. Hiatt, 1970; Lee, 1968; Teleki, 1975). Models of the early hominid diet that contain smaller proportions of plant food seem inherently much less probable than those that recognize the importance of foods other than meat. At present archaeology can provide very little direct evidence. Nonetheless, some aspects of the archaeological record may eventually prove informative: Some type A sites (artifacts present, but little or no bone) may have been locales where tool-makers set up a base of operations but where they did not eat meat in any quantity. However, many type A sites may really be type B or C sites where conditions were unfavorable to the preservation of bone. We need to develop taphonomic, geological, and geochemical criteria for distinguishing sites where bone was never present from those where it is secondarily absent.[22] The location of archaeological sites within a mosaic of paleohabitats may be an indicator of land-use patterns, and these patterns may in turn be used to interpret the accessibility of various potential food types (J. D. Clark, 1972b; Isaac, 1972, 1976a; Vita-Finzi and Higgs, 1970). Foley (1977) has suggested that archaeologists compile "isocal" maps of potential caloric energy available from different classes of food that would have been available in the vicinity of archaeological sites. This compilation has yet to be made for the early sites, but clearly it could be highly informative.

In summary, it can be said that while the archaeological evidence is insufficient, it is at least consistent with modern hunter/gatherer dietary patterns, in which varied fruit, vegetable, and insect foods make up more than 50% of the total food intake.

Technological Skills

So far, we have treated artifacts simply as physical markers of places where tool-making hominids were active and as the means whereby certain fossilized bone concentrations can be recognized as being associated with hominid activity. Archaeologists clearly seek to gain more information from artifacts than this.

Data on current hunter/gatherer band societies strongly suggest that tools and other equipment used in subsistence activities greatly extend the range of foods available. Humans extract deeply buried tubers by use of digging sticks. With the aid of cutting and bashing tools, they gain access to the meat, skin, and marrow of animals as large as, or larger than, themselves. By contrast, baboons and chimpanzees feed only on prey animals smaller than themselves, which they can dismember, divide, and eat with their hands and teeth (Teleki 1973a, 1975).

Humans obtain a far wider range of flesh, including fish and fowl, than does any nonhuman primate (cf. Harding, in this volume; Teleki, 1974, 1975), and use throwing stones, throwing sticks, stabbing and throwing spears, clubs, snares, and nets to do so. Humans also use many techniques of preparation to gain access to foods not as readily available otherwise: cooking, grinding, and baking grass seeds, cracking hard nuts, leaching toxins, etc. While less than exhaustive, this list stresses the importance of material culture in gaining access to many nutritious resources in addition to the fruits, leaves, and insects that are also eaten by primates such as the chimpanzee.

Equipment is involved in yet another aspect of the modern human adaptive mode, namely *gathering*,[23] by which we mean *acquisition with postponed consumption*. Collection of tubers, fruits, nuts, insects, fungi, and foliage for later meals is really feasible only with the aid of containers such as trays, bags, baskets, or pouches. Lee has called this set of subsistence aids "the basic human invention."

The problem that now confronts us centers on the role of equipment in the adaptation of very early hominids. Deplorably little information is available, but a few useful observations can be offered from an archaeological perspective. Only stone artifacts and very few *ad hoc* bone tools have been recovered from early hominid sites, but it is highly probable that among the most important functions of stone artifacts was the manufacture of simple wooden equipment. The core tools (choppers, etc.) can be used to hack off fresh hardwood branches, which can then be trimmed and sharpened into digging sticks, spears, and so on, by using sharp flakes with or without secondary retouch.[24] The early stone tool kits are fully adequate to assist in the acquisition of meat from large carcasses, simple flake forms being particularly effective for this work (see reviews by J. D. Clark, 1972a; Clark and Haynes, 1969; Gould, 1968a). Isaac (1976b,c) also reports on a demonstration of the usefulness of simple flakes by the present-day inhabitants of the Koobi Fora area. Traces of fire and of grinding equipment, which would indicate extensive feeding on parched grains or baked crushed grains, are absent from the sites under consideration.[25]

Most of the early sites have yielded substantial numbers of manuports (see table 3.7). These stones were transported to the sites and eventually abandoned without being demonstrably modified, though some do show signs of battering and of use as hammers and anvils. It is possible that the smaller manuports were carried about for use in throwing. The larger stones may well have served as hammers and pounders for cracking nuts and marrow bones, and for pulverizing fibrous foods. The rough-surfaced stone artifacts classified as polyhedrons, subspheroids, and spheroids were probably pounding and hammering tools (J. D. Clark, 1970; M. D. Leakey, 1971).

If one turns from discussion of the ways such artifacts *can* be used to consideration of direct evidence for *how* they actually were used, much less can be said. To be sure, associated sets of core tools and flakes were made and discarded in the vicinity of pachyderm carcasses. This constitutes circumstantial evidence for the use of these artifacts in getting at meat and offal, or perhaps for obtaining skin and gristle left by other predators. Beyond this, little exists in the way of direct evidence. Some type A sites may conceivably have been places where plant foods were consumed, or where meat was brought after having been stripped off the bone (the *schlepp* effect of Perkins and Daly, 1968). Binford (1972) has observed that an abundance of handaxes tends not to be associated with abundant bone, implying that these ubiquitous tools were used mainly in activities not associated with meat consumption (see Freeman, in this volume; Isaac, 1971, 1975).

Studies of damage from use, such as those carried out by Keeley (1977), Semenov (1964), and Tringham et al. (1974) are currently in progress but the results have not yet been reported.

Habitats and Site Locations

Most of the evidence for hominid subsistence activities between 3–4 and 0.7 m.y. B.P. comes from regions that today are neither forest nor extreme desert. In general, the early sites are found in the varied habitats that we may conveniently, but vaguely, classify as savannah—regions with a heterogeneous cover of grassland and woodland, interspersed with ribbons and patches of riverine or mountain forests. The available paleo-environmental data strongly suggest that the early sites were formed in similar but slightly moister savannah, or grassland-woodland, habitats (see Bonnefille, 1972; Butzer, 1971a, 1978; Isaac, 1975).

The overall impression gained from the many situations in which traces of Plio-Pleistocene hominids occur is that these protohumans ranged widely over varied environments, favoring terrain with a mosaic of swamps, grassland, and woods rather than homogeneous expanses of forest or steppe. Models of early protohuman subsistence patterns should therefore incorporate feeding modes that would take advantage of habitat diversity.

Archaeologists have long been interested in the possibility that early hominids exhibited seasonal patterns of range utilization (e.g., J. D. Clark, 1970:84–86; Howell and Clark, 1963; Kleindienst, 1961). Speth and Davis (1976) have recently suggested that most of the lakeside sites at Olduvai were occupied during the dry season, based on the presence of significant amounts of tortoise remains at only 4 out of 22 hominid sites. They argue, in part by analogy with data for the !Kung of Botswana, for whom tortoises are a wet-season dietary item, that the ratio of dry- to wet-season sites at Olduvai is about 18 to 4. The approach is interesting but by no means conclusive. Before it can be incorporated as a working hypothesis, we need to know more about the seasonality of tortoise behavior along the swampy margins of a permanent, fluctuating lake, and about the incidence of chelonians in prehistoric sites, as expressed in the minimum numbers of individuals rather than the incidence of bone pieces. Statistical considerations also enter into the question. One can ask whether 4 wet-season sites relative to 18 dry-season ones are a significant departure from expectation, given 4 wet months and 8 dry months per year. The χ^2 value is 2.27 with 1 degree of freedom ($p > .10$). The data as they stand do not seem to preclude year-round hominid usage of the basin floor, with each site being occupied only briefly.

In summary, then, the available data indicate that one or all species of early hominids ranged all over the low-lying floors of sedimentary basins, probably exploiting a wide range of food resources. Presumably these same hominids also ranged over the surrounding hills, valleys, and plateaus, and it is entirely possible that the different hominid species had different land-use patterns which overlapped mainly around water holes, lakeshores, and river channels. Behrensmeyer (1976a,b, 1978) has made a provocative effort to discern such land-use patterns.

Socioeconomic Models

If we accept the working hypothesis that early tool-making hominids sometimes transported food to campsites, or temporary home bases, where they also made and discarded stone tools, then we face the challenge of developing models of probable socioeconomic systems that incorporate such behavior. The following alternatives might be considered.

Model 1. Early tool-making hominids lived in social groups within which food was shared. Each day, individuals or subgroups traveled separately over different parts of the home range which were accessible from a temporary base camp. At the end of each excursion, food that was surplus to the immediate needs of the foragers was brought back to be shared with some or all other group members at the campsite, and thus food refuse and tools accumulated at the home base.

Model 2. The same as Model 1, except that the food brought back was fed exclusively to infants, not to any adults.

Model 3. Early tool-making hominids moved over their home range in nomadic fashion, with each adult feeding himself or herself. Small bands formed under shade trees adjacent to feeding grounds, and some high-quality foods such as scavenged or hunted meat were carried from open terrain into the shade for consumption without active sharing. The members of these social groups also carried stones about and engaged in the manufacture and use of tools in these same areas.

The first alternative is the one that anthropologists tend to accept most readily, because the behavior patterns occur almost universally in ethnography, the Ik of Uganda being one of the few alleged exceptions

(Turnbull, 1973). Model 1 also stands in contrast to the socioeconomic behavior of other living primates.

All of these are hypothetical scenarios, and although one may use them to arrive at the most sensible working hypothesis, they certainly do not aid in eliminating all alternatives. In fact, it is difficult to envision suitable archaeological tests for the relative credibility of subtly distinct alternatives such as the first two just listed. Perhaps when we have better surveys of the distributions of archaeological material in the landscape and have mapped the distributions of various subsistence opportunities, including scavenging and hunting opportunities, we will be able to adopt or reject other models, such as number 3. Then again, the distinctions may be too subtle for archaeology to resolve.

Having duly noted these precautions, we can attempt some elaboration of Model 1. As we see it, the pivotal ingredient is *active food-sharing,*[26] with some food being transported to a shifting but well-identified spatial focus that can be termed a *home base.* In the versions of this model practiced by living peoples, *division of labor* between *hunter-scavenger-fishers,* who are preferentially male, and *gatherers,* who are preferentially female, is virtually universal. The system cannot operate without some simple *equipment and tools,* namely containers for carrying food and knives to cut up carcasses. The whole complex is interconnected with an evolutionary change in anatomical-locomotor arrangements, namely *bipedalism,* which facilitates *carrying* things about. A social system involving exchange of energy in the form of transported food puts a premium on the ability to exchange information and to make arrangements regarding future movements of group members (Isaac, 1976a–d, 1978). It also increases the importance of regulating social relations among individuals. All these influences might be expected to favor the evolutionary development of an effective communication system, such as protolanguage, and of sharpened sociointellectual capabilities (Humphrey, 1976).

In current band societies, food-sharing is part of a broad range of reciprocal expectations and responsibilities (see Mauss, 1954). Characteristically, food-sharing involves a social network of relationships. The fundamental module is commonly a family group comprising one or more females mated with one or more males and their dependent offspring. Sharing among adults within the family and the feeding of juveniles characteristically involve different inputs from males and females—which may help to account for the evolutionary advantages of pair bonding. Different degrees of sharing may also extend into the wider reaches of society, often following lines of recognized kinship. There is no way at present to judge how social bonds and exchange networks operated between early hominids as they became involved in the cooperative acquisition of food, but it is probable that mating bonds and kin ties were important from very early stages.

Model 1 implies that certain of the fundamental innovations differentiating human from nonhuman primate behavior had begun to be established by Plio-Pleistocene times (i.e., 2 m.y. B.P.), but it does *not* mean that the tool-making hominids of that time would be recognizable as "human." We surmise that language and systems of cultural rules and codes were at a level that would make us react to these hominids as nonhuman, were we to confront living representatives. In fact, they probably represented a mode of life that has no living counterpart.

One might ask why it is so important to know whether meat was a significant component of early hominid diet. Is it any more important to know this than to know whether the hominids ate tubers or consumed honey? The answer is in part that there has grown up a strong tradition both inside science and among the general public that hunting has had a crucial formative influence on the evolutionary development of human nature (e.g., Ardrey, 1961, 1976; Dart, 1953; Morris, 1967; Tiger and Fox, 1971). This tradition clearly has its roots outside science (cf. Rousseau, 1755) and is also perhaps psychologically related to the biblical injunction that gave mankind "dominion over the fish of the sea, and over the fowl of the air, and over the cattle" (Genesis 1:26; cf. Perper and Schrire, 1977:448).

The view has often been expressed that the gradual development of many important human abilities, including technological skill, insight, ability to cooperate, mobility, and the ability to plan, has been advanced by a pattern of natural selection which over many generations favored the most successful hunters. This view in its simplest form would be valid only if it were true that hunting success was an important prop for protohuman subsistence during the long span of evolutionary development.

As we have attempted to show, there is enough evidence to indicate that the acquisition and consumption of meat may have been a more intensive activity among early hominids than it is among any living nonhuman primates. This is far from certain, however, and the archaeological evidence emphatically does *not* indicate, contrary to what Ardrey (1976) so strenuously maintains, that early hominids were critically dependent on meat as their main item of diet. Thus, although we suspect that the importance of meat *per se* has probably been exaggerated, we would argue that increased involvement in the acquisition of meat may have been more important in human evolution than we can assess simply from the caloric value of the meat consumed. Increased involvement in meat-eating may well have established an asymmetry in early hominid social life that in turn made division of labor and the development of reciprocal social obligations an advantageous adaptive trend. In many current hunter/gatherer societies, meat acquisition and consumption seem to have quasi-symbolic overtones and to affect status as well as nutrition (Hayden, in this volume).

The hunting model for the dynamics of protohuman differentiation has been widely promoted, and even where not explicitly espoused it is often implicitly accepted.[27] Only recently have some authors explored the possibility that the appeal of the hunting model stems very largely from naive male bias in the interpretation of the record (Morgan, 1972; Tanner and Zihlman, 1976; Zihlman and Tanner, in press). These authors propose that a crucial step in the development of cumulative behavioral differences between evolving protohumans and the hominoid common ancestor of apes and humans was the inception of the practice of gathering plant foods for delayed consumption. This, they suggest, was primarily a female activity involving clusters of older females and their female descendents. Later, more mobile roving males tended to attach themselves to these groups and to contribute such meat as they could acquire.

This model has the virtue of redressing the imbalance of the fashionable male-oriented hunting models and of incorporating explanations for many important fundamental aspects of human behavior. However, in our view it poses a difficult problem: Why would a predominantly vegetarian primate find it advantageous to postpone consumption of fruits or roots instead of consuming them as they were obtained? We are skeptical about Zihlman and Tanner's suggestion that it may have been advantageous to acquire such foods in haste and then to take cover so as to minimize exposure to predators. However, it is possible that if hominids fed extensively on items that had to be prepared with equipment, such as nuts needing to be opened with nut-cracking stones, then it might be easier to collect the food and go at intervals to the apparatus. Alternatively, feeding in the shade may have been important. On balance, though, we feel that it remains difficult to understand what vital advantages would accrue in breaking away from the presumed primitive pattern of nomadic self-feeding observed among most nonhuman primates.

In devising models of early stages in the evolution of a system in which food-sharing became a pivotal ingredient, meat does have critical importance: it is a highly concentrated, highly portable form of nourishment. Portions of a carcass are readily carried and are an important food prize when consumed at the destination. We thus favor a model in which the active delivery of some meat to fellow members of a social group developed in a reciprocal relationship with the practice of transporting and sharing some surplus plant foods. We see the model as representing a functionally integrated behavioral complex, in which any attempt to isolate one or another component as an initial or prime mover is probably misleading.

SUMMARY

We have reviewed such tangible archaeological evidence as is available for the significance of meat in the diet of some hominids during the Pliocene and Lower Pleistocene. Our findings can be summarized as follows:

1. The most convincing positive evidence consists of the patches of discarded artifacts and broken bones that have been excavated at Olduvai and in the Koobi Fora Formation.
2. The evidence at these sites is good but not conclusive. Meat-eating, as a part of early hominid diet, should be regarded as one useful working hypothesis, not as an established "fact."
3. Many other sites from the same time range provide evidence which tends to corroborate the hypothesis of hominid meat consumption, but the evidence has not yet been reported in such a way that the sites can be used as test cases, e.g., Sterkfontein Member 5, Melka Kunturé (various subsites), Ain Hanech, Ternifine, Casablanca STIC, and 'Ubeidiya.
4. It is not possible as yet to determine the proportion of bone refuse accumulated as a result of hunting rather than scavenging. We surmise that both were involved and that scavenging may have been a particularly important means of obtaining the meat of medium- or large-sized animals. Smaller prey may also have been scavenged, but studies have shown that carnivores often consume such animals in a matter of minutes and therefore they would not be as readily available to hominid scavengers.
5. Ethnographic, primatological, and ecological considerations lead us to surmise that foods such as tubers, roots, fruits, nuts, eggs, insects, and other small animals were quantitatively the main items of early hominid diet.
6. Some sites that lack bone, in spite of apparently favorable conditions of preservation, may attest to situations in protohuman life where meat was not a significant part of the diet, owing to seasonal, locational, or accidental factors. We cannot yet test this proposition rigorously.
7. The configuration of archaeological evidence strongly suggests that some meat was occasionally carried to central locales or "home bases." We have no direct evidence for the transport of plant foods, but we speculate that these too were carried.

If a model of early hominid subsistence involving a combination of intensive gathering of plant foods and opportunistic hunting/scavenging is adopted as a working hypothesis, it may help account for certain other important innovations in human evolution. Partial division of subsistence labor between females and males, mediated by food-sharing, would become advantageous. Language would fill a need for exchange of information about the past and future, a need that does not exist to the same degree in nonhuman primates. Finally, the development of long-term mating bonds between females and males, combined with the establishment of joint responsibility for sustaining offspring, would have more socio-economic advantages than is the case among most other primates.

Although, in our view, hypotheses of "hunting" by early hominids cannot by themselves account for the innovations, it seems very likely that the portability and high food value of meat helped establish an adaptive complex that involves the transport and sharing of food obtained by the complementary endeavors of different members of the same society. This in turn may well have led to spiraling developments in communications, networks of reciprocity, and mechanisms of intragroup cooperation. Nonetheless, meat-eating by early hominids remains a working hypothesis, not an item of sure knowledge. Given the importance of the superstructure that one is tempted to build on the hypothesis, continued, rigorous testing is clearly essential. We need more excavated examples of well-preserved sites, and more detailed studies of site formation processes.

POSTSCRIPT

Since this review was written, a new round of research has been undertaken to deal with the problems discussed here. In particular, Richard Potts is thoroughly reexamining the faunal remains from Olduvai, while Henry Bunn is completing a full osteo-archaeological analysis of bone assemblages from the Koobi Fora sites as well as making detailed studies of bone assemblages from selected Olduvai sites and from various carnivore lairs. Ellen Kroll is studying spatial arrangements within these sites, and Nic Toth has studied potential usage and, with Lawrence Keeley, use wear.

It is already plain that all these studies will contribute greatly to the resolution of the problems and uncertainties discussed in this article. The workers who have conducted the studies must report their specific findings, but perhaps we may give preliminary indications of results. Several lines of new evidence point clearly to extensive involvement by tool-using hominids in dismemberment of carcasses, the accumulation of bones and their breakage. These findings do tend to sustain the working hypothesis advocated in our conclusion.

The need for revision also emerges. For instance, the new research results make us less sure that the concentration of stones and bones at KBS was not swept together by water flow.

The possibility that all the Koobi Fora sites might simply be mechanical jumbles of stones and bones swept together by water currents has been raised since we first submitted our article (e.g., Binford, 1978). We mention this possibility but in most cases dismiss it as unlikely because of the fine-grained sedimentary context of most of the sites discussed. Perhaps the question should have received more extensive discussion. Suffice it to say here that research begun in 1977 by Kathy Schick is testing this explanation of how the sites formed and that the results of her work along with the findings of Bunn, Kroll, and Toth should deal with Binford's legitimate doubts more decisively than we could have without access to new data.

APPENDIX

In the main text we have focused on Olduvai Gorge and Koobi Fora as test cases. In this appendix other selected important instances cited in table 3.1 are briefly reviewed. The categories are explained in the table.

Makapan Limeworks Cave (Category 1)

This south African site occupies a pivotal position in discussions of early hominid subsistence. Raymond Dart (1957) and his co-workers recovered fragmentary hominid remains and a densely packed jumble of other bones from "grey breccia," an occurrence of type O in our classification, and inferred that *Australopithecus africanus* had been responsible for the bone accumulation, i.e., that these hominids had been active hunters, or "killer-apes." He also observed that the proportional representation of the various body parts of antelopes, the predominant species in the cave, departed markedly from the proportions of one bone to another in an intact antelope skeleton. From this evidence, Dart argued that the assemblage showed deliberate selection of bones which could be used in various ways—as clubs, rasps, piercing tools, and so on. His term for the practice of using selected bones was the "osteo-donto-keratic" (bone-tooth-horn) culture. The argument has clear logical validity, and it has been taken up by various authors (Ardrey, 1961, 1976; Read-Martin and Read, 1975; Tobias, 1968; Wolberg, 1970). However, it was also plain from the start that information was needed on the processes whereby bone accumulates, in order to test the overall validity of the argument (Washburn, 1957).

The more detailed work recently undertaken at Makapansgat will undoubtedly provide important new information. Meanwhile, the studies of C. K. Brain demonstrate the need for extreme caution. Brain (1967, 1969a, 1976a) has shown that bone assemblages where hominid tool use is not a factor have the same kinds of distorted relative proportions of body parts as do the Makapan assemblages. Others have found similar patterns elsewhere among natural bone assemblages (Behrensmeyer, 1975; Hill, 1975; Isaac, 1967a; Shipman and Phillips-Conroy, 1977; Sutcliffe, 1972). These data do not prove that the australopithecines did *not* use bone tools; they merely leave us without any clear positive evidence that they did so.

Other alleged evidence of hominid activity in the cave includes particular bone damage patterns, bones rammed into one another, and perhaps most importantly, a series of depressed fractures in skulls, especially baboon skulls (see summary by Tobias, 1968). In our view it remains highly uncertain whether these occurrences really do indicate hominid hunting, or even an extensive hominid role in forming the bone accumulation (cf. Klein, 1975b, 1977a). Possible artifacts have been reported from deposits in the main bone-bearing breccias at Makapan (Brain, van Reit Lowe, and Dart, 1955), but their status remains uncertain. Others have been recovered in quantity from solution cavities in the upper levels (Maguire, 1968), but it is not all clear that these can be used to demonstrate that tool-making hominids lived in the cave (Mason, 1965; Sampson, 1974).

All claims that Makapan provides direct evidence of extensive austra- lopithecine meat-eating, involving both hunting and scavenging, depend ultimately on a premise that the hominids were responsible for the bone accumulations. Brain's data (1969a, 1976a,b, 1978), both on recent accumulation processes and on other prehistoric sites such as Swartkrans, show that other alternatives need to be considered. It seems possible, perhaps even likely, that the bones accumulated mainly through the action of large carnivores, gravity, and colluvial slope wash. Hominid bones possibly are represented simply as part of the broad faunal spectrum being sampled. Until a range of alternative hypotheses has been tested, the Makapan evidence cannot be used either for or against the proposition that early hominids were significantly carnivorous.

Hadar (Category I)

A wealth of paleontological evidence, including hominid fossils, has been recovered in recent years from a major sedimentary basin near the entry of the Ethiopian Rift Valley into the Afar Depression. The part of the succession that has been studied and dated seems to be between 2 and 4 million years old (Johanson and Taieb, 1976; Taieb et al., 1976). Research is still in progress, and the preliminary reports which are available do not describe any assemblages of animal bones whose association with the hominid remains might indicate that the bones were food refuse. Artifacts have recently been discovered in the upper part of the sequence (Roche and Tiercelin, 1977), and these are associated with bone accumulations.

Conditions of preservation in the Afar are such that we can expect the area to contribute varied data on early hominid diet and ecology, but the available information cannot be used to test the hominid meat-eating hypothesis.

Swartkrans (Category II)

It is now known that the deposits filling the Swartkrans cavern system in South Africa were formed during three distinct episodes widely separated in time (Brain, 1976b; Butzer, 1976). The classic *Australopithecus robustus* material comes from the oldest fossiliferous breccia (member 1), which also contains a very few scattered flaked stones, but these seem to be incidental inclusions. Brian (1970) has shown that in this instance the bone accumulation probably formed in a sink-hole shaft. Under these circumstances it is impossible to identify any of the bones as refuse from hominid feeding. Furthermore, Brian (1970, 1976b, 1978) has shown that the assemblage resembles a carnivore accumulation more than a human one in such features as the preferential preservation of hyrax cranial bones and the virtual absence of postcranial bones. Animal carcasses (including hominids) that had been preyed upon by leopards were also present.

The member 2 breccia, formed as a long-term infilling of solution channels, contains artifacts of Acheulean form and bone remains, plus the *Homo (Telanthropus)* mandible. Vrba (1975) interprets the bones as an accumulation by hominids who hunted small game, but the scant available data do not permit this to be used as a test case to scrutinize the early hominid meat-eating hypothesis.

Sterkfontein (Category III)

A partly filled-in cavern system is now exposed by erosion near the top of a low dolomite hill above the Blaaubank River, very near Swartkrans and Kromdraai. Recent work has shown that the stratigraphy of the site is more complex than was previously believed (Partridge et al., unpublished data). In only two members is the paleoanthropology sufficiently well known to allow their consideration in relation to the problem of early hominid diet. Member 4, formerly the "type site," has yielded most of the hominid (*Australopithecus africanus*) specimens recovered from Sterkfontein, but no stone tools have yet been found in this layer. The bone assemblage includes a fair number of large carnivore remains, especially those of saber-tooth felines, and a careful study of the assemblage has led Elizabeth Vrba (1975) to conclude that it accumulated at or near a carnivore lair. There are no *prima facie* grounds for regarding any of the bones as indicators of hominid involvement in meat-eating. Member 5, formerly the "extension site," has yielded both stone artifacts and hominid remains, including a recently discovered partial cranium attributed to *Homo* (Hughes and Tobias, 1977). An assemblage of 286 artifacts was excavated by Robinson from this member (Mason, 1962; Robinson 1962), along with a series of fragmentary bones.

More fauna and artifacts, thought to have come from member 5, have been recovered from adjacent solution cavities and from quarry dumps. Vrba (1975) has studied the fauna and has concluded that the bone assemblage was probably accumulated by hominids through a process involving extensive scavenging. This layer may well provide potential evidence of early hominid diet, but the problems and uncertainties are too great for it to be used, as yet, as a test case.

Melka Kunturé (Category III)

At Melka Kunturé, Ethiopia, there is a small sedimentary basin containing numerous sites that have been under excavation since 1965. Oldowan, Developed Oldowan, and Acheulean sites, as well as Middle and Late Stone Age horizons, have been excavated (Chavaillon, 1976a). We will consider here only the Oldowan, Developed Oldowan, and Lower Acheulean sites—that is, Gombore I, Garga IV, and Simburro III.

Gombore I contains several stratified levels of which only the most recent, level B, is a living surface. Level B actually consists of three sublevels that are not always distinguishable, but the main sublevel, B2, appears to be a true occupation floor. It is claimed that there has been little or no movement of the material by water action, since flaked pieces that fit together are rarely separated horizontally by more than 1 m. The distribution of remains on the floor shows a marked clustering of material in some areas, whereas other portions are almost entirely barren, and there is a possible shelter in the eastern portion of the site. The fauna appears to be typical food debris: vertebrae, ribs, and limb bones predominate, while cranial and dental elements are rare. Hippos are most abundant, but equids, bovids, and suids are also present. Carnivores, crocodiles, and fish are very rare. Based on the character of the artifacts, Gombore IB is considered a "workshop" (*atelier de taille*) by Chavaillon (1976a), but until quantitative data are available it will not be possible to determine whether the site belongs to type A or type C in our classification system.

Garba IV, one of the richest sites at Melka Kunturé, has been described by Piperno and Bulgarelli Piperno (1974–1975). One of the Developed Oldowan levels, level D, seems to be a type C occurrence. Four-fifths of the 45-m^2 excavated area was thickly strewn with river pebbles, stone artifacts, and bones, occasionally forming concentrations up to 30 cm thick. The lithic material includes numerous unutilized river pebbles of lava, which are probably manuports. Tool types include an abundance of various flake tools, as well as cores, choppers, *rabots,* polyhedrals, two handaxes, and two cleavers.

Although quantitative data are not yet available, the faunal remains in level D form a varied assemblage. Bovids of all sizes, from gazelle to buffalo, are the most numerous and are represented by horn cores, mandibles, isolated teeth, and fragmentary limb bones. Hippopotamus is also well represented by numerous remains of scapulae, pelves, vertebrae, limb bones, and many teeth, including tusks which apparently have been flaked. Two kinds of equid are present, one large and one small, and are represented by numerous teeth, some limb bones, and a mandibular symphysis. Suids are rare but, on the basis of those which have been found, H. B. S. Cooke (cited in Piperno and Bulgarelli Piperno, 1974–1975) has suggested that level D may be between 1.2 million and 700,000 years old. Also present but rare are elephant, carnivores, a large porcupine, and crocodile. The presence of numerous bovid horn cores and hippo tusks led Chavaillon (1976b) to suggest that these elements were used as implements or weapons.

Simburro III, located about 5 km from the other sites, consists of a series of sands, gravels, and tufaceous clays that contain Lower Acheulean artifacts. Of the three or four archaeological layers, one of the middle levels is a vertically diffuse occurrence, whereas the others may be occupation floors. One level contains the remains of *Pelorovis oldowayensis* and may document a butchery episode.

It is certain that some of the sites at Melka Kunturé provide good additional instances of association between artifacts and bones, but until more detailed information on the material recovered has been published, we have not felt able to incorporate these sites in rigorous tests of the meat-eating hypothesis.

Ain Hanech (Category IV)

The deposits at Ain Hanech, in Tunisia, are at the summits of a series of river and lake sediments approximately 200 m thick. Some layers are sterile whereas others contain bones as well as artifacts that were attributed to the "Pebble Culture" by Balout (1955). The fauna from these horizons is very similar, and its character indicates a late Villafranchian age, probably between 1 and 2 m.y. B.P. (Arambourg, cited in Balout, 1955; Jaeger 1975). The artifact assemblages are dominated by faceted spheroids, but choppers and flake forms also are present. The whole assemblage is somewhat similar to the Developed Oldowan of Olduvai Gorge. Bifaces occur in the beds immediately overlying the Pebble Culture horizons. Unfortunately we have no information on the pattern of association of the artifacts and bones or on the degree to which bones have been fragmented. A faunal list is available in Balout (1955:163). It includes various proboscideans, rhinoceros, hippopotamus, equids, suids, giraffes, carnivores, and 6 species of bovids.

The Ain Hanech occurrences may well represent archaeological manifestations of early hominid meat-eating, but with the information available they cannot be used as test cases.

Shungura (Category V)

Archaeological sites of Lower Pleistocene age have been found in the Shungura Formation in the Omo Valley of Ethiopia. A number of quartz and lava artifacts are present, either singly or in low-density scatters, on the surface of eroded outcrops in members C, D, E, and F. Five *in situ* occurrences have been excavated in member F (Chavaillon, 1976a; Merrick and Merrick, 1976; Merrick et al., 1973) and one in the upper portion of member E at Omo 84 (Chavaillon, 1975). One site was provisionally reported as belonging to member C but is now believed to be in member E, with an age of about 2.2 m.y. B.P. (J. Chavaillon, personal communication). The five excavated sites in member F probably date between 2.04 ± 0.1 and 1.93 ± 0.1. m.y. B.P. (Brown and Lajoie, 1971). Three of these sites are associated with stream channels and undoubtedly have been geologically redeposited (Merrick and Merrick, 1976). Although a few fragmentary bones are found in association with the artifacts, the bones are not particularly abundant, and both stones and bones appear to be secondarily derived. The remaining two sites are possible occupation surfaces but are located in fine silt and clay deposits representing floodplain or marginal backswamp environments. Bone has not been recovered from these sites and very probably would not have been preserved even if it had once been present. None of the five sites can be used in testing hypotheses about early hominid meat-eating.

NOTES

1. Throughout this paper, "meat" is used to refer to the flesh of tetrapod vertebrates, excluding fish, birds, and invertebrate animal protein.

2. A gradation exists in the applicability of the term "hunting," which is *not* synonomous with predation. The pursuit of fairly large, highly mobile prey is clearly hunting. As the quarry becomes smaller and less mobile, the pursuit becomes less and less like hunting. In our definition, acquiring a nestling bird is not hunting, nor is the digging up of small burrowing animals.

3. The Matuyama-Brunhes geomagnetic polarity reversal which occurred 700,000 years ago provides a convenient boundary between the Lower and Middle Pleistocene (Butzer and Isaac, 1975), and hence also delineates the coverage of this article.

4. The interpretations implied by the labels are in most instances very plausible, but we propose to facilitate critical inquiry by using only the alphabetic terms.

5. It is possible that some of the Chinese fossils are more than 700,000 years old, but they are not yet well dated. Choukoutien, of major importance in the history of human subsistence, is almost certainly of Middle Pleistocene age.

6. Neither of the last two indicators has yet been reported for artifact-associated bone from sites of the age range under consideration, but careful searches are now in progress for the first time.

7. It should be stressed that Mary Leakey regards the faunal analysis on which the subsequent discussion is based "merely as a preliminary report, to be amplified when taxonomic identifications and more detailed analyses of the distribution patterns on the living floors have been carried out. For the present only the relative abundance or scarcity of the principal groups of larger animals have been recorded, together with the common or rare occurrence of certain parts of the skeleton. Since it is clearly impossible to estimate the number of animals represented in any context unless taxonomic identifications have been carried out, no attempt has been made to count the minimum number of individuals" (M. D.

Leakey, 1971:248). The review presented here will clearly need revision when the additional analyses have been completed and reported, but in the meantime, notwithstanding the reservations she expressed, consideration of her data from Olduvai is vital for any discussion of the factual evidence for early hominid meat-eating.

8. This thickness is greater than that usually allowed for a single horizon, but the occurrence of bones from a single carcass strongly suggests that the site can be treated as representing a single occupation event.

9. There is a good photograph in the *National Geographic* (L. S. B. Leakey 1961:580), which has also been reproduced in M. D. Leaky (1976:430). The site profiles imply that the trench was about 13×6 m at this level.

10. The density at the deinothere horizon is close to the average density for the entire body of sediments containing the FLK N archaeological levels 1-6.

11. Levels 2 and 3-5 at HWK E have been grouped together, since they all represent vertically diffuse occurrences.

12. Sases Catalogue no. FxJj 1 (C. M. Nelson, 1971).

13. The leaf casts have not yet been specifically identified, but inspection of the overall morphology of the best specimens led Dr. J. Gillett (personal communication) to suggest that there were *Ficus*-like.

14. Sases Catalogue no. FxJj 3 (C. M. Nelson, 1971).

15. This we take to be an approximate indicator of degree of fragmentation.

16. We have avoided discussing the problem of how many hominid species existed during the time range in question, since the purpose of our inquiry is to determine whether or not early tool-making hominids ate meat. If more than one hominid species made tools, then it is also possible that more than one created bone food refuse.

17. A. K. Behrensmeyer (1976b) has provided some survey data on the incidence of bones at Amboseli in Kenya, a game park with habitats somewhat analogous to those prevailing at Olduvai at the time under review. She reports aggregate densities of bones per square kilometer which, when converted to average values per square meter, are as follows: (a) swamp habitat, $0.0062/m^2$; (b) dense woodland, 0.0026; (c) open woodland, 0.0019; (d) grassland, 0.0029; (e) playa lake bed, 0.0012; (f) bush, 0.0010. Clearly, these are average values only and we need to be concerned with maximum natural concentrations, their frequency of occurrence, and their circumstances.

18. Of relevance here is a personal observation by Isaac that small patches of bone splinters, each apparently the leavings or regurgitation of a single hyena as a result of chewing a single bone, are dispersed across the East African landscape. These patches are usually very small and widely spaced, and could be mistaken for human bone refuse only if a great many occurred very close to each other *and* if this composite patch coincided with a patch of artifacts.

19. Note that this explanation is made less likely by the differences in habits of humans and large carnivores. Lions and hyenas are primarily nocturnal; during the day, wild dogs and hyenas take shelter in burrows rather than under shade trees.

20. The problem here is to find a reason for the attraction. Presence of edible insect larvae or pupae? Plant growth induced by carrion decay? Scraps of edible skin and gristle, or marrow in dry bones? To be sure, some of these scenarios would be variants of meat-eating.

21. This conforms with the primatological data reviewed by Teleki (1975), who stresses that predatory monkeys and apes prey mainly on infants and juveniles of all hunted species.

22. For discussion of these suggestions, see Isaac (1971, 1975) and Butzer (1975).

23. We are dissatisfied with the terminology proposed by Teleki (1975), in which omnivorous nonhuman primates are labeled collector/predators. The *Oxford English Dictionary* defines the verb *collect* as "to gather together into one place . . . to gather in . . . , to assemble, accumulate." Clearly it is only in the stomachs of chimpanzees that

most of their food is collected. The problem is our lack of a word that specifically distinguishes peripatetic selective feeding, which is what chimpanzees do, from gathering with postponed consumption, which is so characteristic of humans, beavers, squirrels, ants, and so on. Humans may, of course, also feed while moving (Gould, 1969b, and in this volume; Hayden, in this volume; Lee, 1968).

24. In response to a challenge from R. E. Leakey in 1976, Isaac replicated KBS-style core tools and flakes and used them to make two digging sticks. There are also ample data from Australia to show that very simple tools can be used to make a wide range of wooden equipment (Gould, Koster, and Sontz, 1971; Mulvaney, 1969).

25. Tests for the presence of fire at the early sites in East Africa have so far proved negative or inconclusive. The oldest definite signs of controlled fire come from sites where conditions of preservation have conserved charcoal. These are in Eurasia and are about half to three-quarters of a million years old (see Butzer and Isaac, 1975).

26. We distinguish *active food sharing* from the kind of behavior reported for chimpanzees (Teleki 1973a, 1975; van Lawick-Goodall, 1968, 1971). "Sharing" is in part a misleading label for what has been filmed and reported among chimpanzees; that would be better designated as "tolerated scrounging."

27. One of us pleads guilty to having overstressed this model in previous papers (Isaac, 1969, 1971).

Leslie G. Freeman

4.
The Fat of the Land:
Notes on Paleolithic Diet in Iberia

In discussing the difficulty of interpreting prehistoric behavior from the evidence in the archaeological record, Christopher Hawkes characterized the study of technology as easy, inferences about subsistence economics as operationally laborious but relatively simple and straightforward, reasoning about social-political institutions as much harder, and the study of religious institutions and spiritual life as hardest of all (1954:161–62). It is scarcely possible to dispute his general diagnosis, which expresses a basic tenet of prehistoric research. Nevertheless, Hawkes' statement hides a paradox; in specific cases a great deal is known about other aspects of subsistence-related technological systems, but there is very little unambiguous evidence for diet during the Paleolithic period, simple though that study theoretically ought to be. The subject is far knottier than is generally granted, and authors who undertake to produce an original synthesis of dietary data find themselves forced by the nature of the subject to speculate more than they might wish.

The deficiencies of our dietary analyses are not solely due, as is so often the case in Paleolithic research, to any absolute paucity of potentially relevant data, for data of certain kinds are abundant in many sites, although we often fail to collect them. Good prehistorians are generally aware, at a theoretical level, of the potential of the data, and appropriate data-gathering techniques are available. Several simple, readily practicable, and often inexpensive methods for recovering information relevant to the study of Paleolithic diet exist, such as flotation (Struever, 1968). Even though no methods can yield more than partial pictures of dietary practices, their consistent application to Paleolithic site sediments would increase our recovery of such information by several orders of magnitude.

Major obstacles to the study of dietary evidence stem, in my opinion, from two factors. First of all, it is unfortunately true that the study of Paleolithic prehistory bears at least its share of scientific inertia. Its practitioners usually profess an interest in reconstructing prehistoric lifeways, recognizing the great potential importance of information derived

104

from the study of contextual evidence (including the topographic situation of the site, the nature of contained sediments, chemical, radiological, and biological residues, and the positional and numerical relations of recovered data). In practice, however, most of us still place overwhelming emphasis on the analysis of artifacts in stone and bone and the chronological ordering of artifact assemblages, relegating to a secondary position the study of all contextual materials except those useful in climatic reconstruction or dating. Unfortunately, stone and bone tools studied as such provide little evidence of diet.

The collection procedures required for maximal recovery of Paleolithic dietary information are undeniably time-consuming. For example, at the Mousterian site of Abric Agut, in eastern Spain, for every bulk sample that yielded seeds when subjected to flotation, there were 25 that yielded none; furthermore, we were overjoyed that our recovery ratio was so high. Obviously, an intensive attempt to gather dietary data requires a substantial shift in the mental set and excavation priorities of the average Paleolithic prehistorian, who has been trained to dig to recover artifacts and identifiable bones, and to invest only a minimum effort in collecting suites of samples for sediment, pollen, and chronometric analyses. Intensive sampling for dietary study also demands additional personnel on the field and laboratory teams and thus increases excavation costs. Perhaps it is understandable (though not excusable) that such sampling has not been a customary part of the average Paleolithic excavation.

Even in those rare cases where materials with significance for dietary studies are routinely collected by prehistorians, they are ordinarily gathered for other reasons, and their potential contribution to the study of subsistence is frequently ignored or undervalued. So, for example, faunal material lacking the diagnostic characteristics which permit species identification is simply discarded by many investigators, often without counting or weighing the fragments or examining them for marks of intentional human activity. Only because all such specimens from the Mousterian levels at Cueva Morín, in Cantabrian Spain, were carefully examined were we able to discover that the bones from Upper Level 17 are not primarily food remains.

A second set of considerations is at least as great an obstacle to the study of Paleolithic diet. Excavators who have conscientiously collected samples of contextual materials for analysis sometimes discover to their great frustration that specialists competent to identify the remains and explain their significance are impossible to find or are not interested enough to help. This problem still plagues our work at Cueva Morín.

These two factors have interacted to produce an unsatisfactory state of affairs in which the total amount of solid evidence available is insufficient to support broad generalizations about subsistence patterns.

THE LIMITS AND POTENTIALS
OF DIETARY DATA

Although we often assume that certain categories of organic material recovered from Paleolithic sites are residues of meals eaten by prehistoric people, that assumption may be unwarranted in any specific case. Some such items may be the raw material or by-products of manufacturing processes unrelated to diet. Evidence about food, fuel, and raw material *acquisition* (hunting/gathering operations, butchering techniques) is commonly reported as though it were direct evidence for *consumption,* which, of course, it is not.

Data potentially relevant to dietary studies often have ambiguities that can only be resolved after thorough and thoughtful study. Some of the reasons for these ambiguities are outlined below.

The prehistorian reads the records of the past in its relics and the situations in which they are discovered. For the most part, only the relatively imperishable relics remain, but the recovered items may provide no evidence at all about diet, or the picture they present may be biased, owing to its incompleteness.

True residues of human activities in an archaeological site are never a fair sample of all the imperishables resulting from those activities, because a single site is not an entire prehistoric settlement system. Furthermore, prehistorians never recover a fair sample of all imperishables in a single level; some always go unrecognized, and imperishability in the archaeological sense is a relative condition anyway. In addition, the materials recognized as important at any stage of our discipline's development are almost never distributed uniformly over the surface of an undisturbed archaeological level, and because we very seldom excavate a level completely, we always miss some of them. This injects another element of bias into our interpretation. Even if we could recover an unbaised sample of all diet-related imperishables produced by an extinct human society, it would not give a complete idea of the diet of the times, since a large proportion of any past meal may have consisted of foodstuffs that do not leave anything we now recognize as a durable material trace (beverages, boned meat, greens, ground meal, and so on).

For present purposes, we may distinguish two kinds of prehistoric evidence. When a substance in which we are interested is itself recovered, the evidence for its presence is unequivocal and may be called primary. Sometimes the substance itself no longer exists in recognizable form, but other indications of its presence, such as traces of chemical decay products, may be detectable with appropriate procedures. This evidence is of course, secondary, but in rare cases it may be virtually as unequivocal as primary evidence. Crosscutting this distinction is another, which can only be made when the purpose of the investigation is known. That is the dichotomy, familiar from legal usage, between direct and circumstantial evidence. In dietary studies, we try to determine what was actually consumed by past human groups; any direct evidence depends on proving that the material in question really found its way to the human gut. As a result, there are just two kinds of direct evidence for food consumption. When a body is as well preserved as those of the Tollund, Grauballe, or Borre Fen corpses, an actual analysis of stomach contents may be possible (Glob, 1969:56–57; Helbaek, 1969:207–8); no such miracle of preservation is known for the Paleolithic period. The only other direct evidence for food consumption is the presence of food remains in hominid fecal material (coprolites). A few possible hominid coprolites have in fact survived from very remote periods (R. Leakey, 1971:67; de Lumley, 1966), but they are very rare and none is identified with certainty from the study area discussed here. Even where it does occur, such direct evidence can never provide a complete picture of past diet; it only gives us partial information about the represented meals, which are in turn an infinitesimally small proportion of all the meals eaten by the individuals in question.

In the overwhelming majority of cases where primary evidence of potential food materials is recovered, we still have no more than circumstantial evidence of their consumption. The strongest kind of circumstantial evidence would be the discovery of hominid tooth-marks on the material, but I know of no unequivocal case of such data from a Paleolithic site. I am sure that among the masses of unidentifiable bone fragments from Paleolithic sites some will eventually be found with convincing tooth impressions, but finding them will require much closer attention than is ordinarily extended to bone debris.

The primary materials with dietary potential that one may ordinarily hope to recover, with care and luck, from at least some sites are the range of durable animal, plant, and edible mineral remains. For animals these include bones, teeth, antlers, mollusk shells, otoliths, scutes, carapace and plastron fragments, and (rarely) hair, horn, scales, and bits of beetle elytra. For plants, carbonized plant material and opal phytoliths (microscopic remains of the siliceous skeletons of plants) are our primary evidence. Unfortunately, species identification from some of these materials (phytoliths, for example) is still so difficult and our knowledge about them so rudimentary that their analysis has not yet made the contribution we hoped for a few years ago. Pollen is ordinarily no more than secondary evidence for the presence of plants in a site and is very unreliable, circumstantial evidence at that, since it is ordinarily transported to the site by currents of air or water, or on the bodies of animals or people, or on clothing, or enters in other ways beyond conscious human control. However, when pollen from a plant species occurs in sediments in large clumps, the deliberate transportation of flowers to the site may be indicated, as has been claimed for a Mousterian level at Shanidar (Leroi-Gourhan, 1975). Edible mineral salts, easily leached from archaeological levels, may perhaps be recovered from dry sites someday.

Prehistorians do a much better job of collecting most kinds of primary evidence of plant and animal remains in the levels they excavate than they do with the trickier collection of secondary evidence. However, secondary evidence is extremely important to sound interpretation, since a number of materials would be undetectable otherwise. Among the most important kinds of secondary evidence for dietary studies are chemical traces and microbial spores and particles (Burrows 1968; Graczyk, 1971; Graham, 1962; J. Jay, 1970). For years, it has been recognized that the decay of organic materials (bone, kitchen wastes, fecal material, etc.) in an occupation horizon results at least temporarily in detectably higher phosphate levels than those characterizing adjacent layers that had lesser organic content. Under appropriate conditions the higher phosphate values may persist for millennia, and a stratigraphic profile will show the relative intensity of organic detritus accumulation in each level. Such information is quite crude compared to the results of chemical studies made possible by modern technology. Spectroscopy (Britton and Richards, 1969), X-ray diffraction studies (Brothwell et al., 1969), and neutron activation analysis (Jervis et al., 1963) can detect and measure tiny quantities of trace elements, permitting the recognition of such characteristic and complex molecules as amino acids in archaeological horizons.

Spores of certain microbes (some bacilli, yeasts, molds, and fungi) persist in recognizable form in Paleolithic horizons, and it is theoretically possible that some prehistoric spores can be identified and perhaps even cultured. Since some microbes (obligate parasites and obligate saprophytes) are only associated with one or a very few specific host media, concentrated patches of these forms would suggest the former presence of long-vanished animal or plant tissues. Even virus particles may someday be identified in Paleolithic horizons. The major obstacle to the search for Paleolithic microbes is the great difficulty of securing uncontaminated samples, but the prospect of recovering evolutionarily antecedent forms of "antibiotic" microbes has enough potential to interest large pharmaceutical companies, and with their help we may hope to see important advances in "prehistoric microbiology."

Food consumption is the last stage in a variable sequence of subsistence-related events, some of which may provide other kinds of circumstantial evidence relevant to dietary reconstructions. Food acquisition is the first step in the sequence. Food may of course be eaten immediately where it is acquired. Unless such foraged meals are detected as coprolites or stomach contents, they leave no durable trace in the archaeological record. Among some societies today, much of the total dietary intake is consumed on the spot (Hayden, Mann, in this volume); this is especially true for small, perishable items such as berries or shellfish. In some groups where there is a pronounced division of food-acquisition activities by age and sex, during certain seasons children and women may regularly satisfy their major dietary requirements for days at a time in this way. Prehistorians must always be aware of the possibility that they are recovering remains of the meals of just one segment of the population, and so their observations may have only partial validity for the society as a whole. At present there is no apparent way out of this dilemma.

When food items are not consumed as they are being collected, they may be brought to what will later become a recognizable archaeological site. This may be anything from an ephemeral resting place used while certain activities are undertaken at some distance from the group's headquarters, to its temporary or permanent "living area" or base camp. In this case, durable remains of diet-related activities may perhaps accumulate at the site. Where a temporary surplus of foodstuffs is available, a society may develop special techniques for storage over shorter or longer periods. Storage pits, "silos," cairns, or tanks may be constructed to contain these materials and protect them from competitors, large and small. Careful study of such features may provide evidence that they were indeed used for foodstuffs instead of serving some other purpose, but the proof is not easy. Nor are all the possible food-storage devices represented in the archaeological record, since food may be kept in perishable containers such as boxes or skin bags, or may be protected by suspending it high in the air, or placing it on a platform atop a post or in a tree. Nevertheless, the features that do survive may provide significant evidence of subsistence practices.

Perishable foodstuffs also need to be preserved if they are to be stored beyond the normal period of their "palatability." Opinions about palatability vary widely from group to group, of course, and prehistorians must keep their own ethnocentric biases from influencing their interpretations in this context. There eventually comes a time, however, when most biotic materials in most environments become so rotten that they are toxic to humans. Many societies have discovered techniques that effectively delay this decay process for appreciable periods.

Where there are cold seasons, foods may be preserved by chilling, because near-freezing temperatures slow down the metabolism of food-spoilage microorganisms. Roots and tubers may be kept in dark, humid containers at 6° C for several months. At temperatures of 0° C, fresh meats will keep for a week or more, and at −18° C most meats other than organs may be kept up to two years and on thawing will have virtually the same palatability as when they were first frozen (J. Jay, 1970; Paul and Palmer, 1972).

Heat will also slow or halt the microbial spoilage of food, since high temperatures can destroy all or most of the decay organisms present. One advantage of the "perpetual stewpot," where fresh food is added to the pot each time a portion is eaten, is that the food is regularly reheated. Unfortunately, direct evidence of food preservation by these techniques would be unrecognizable in most Paleolithic sites.

Since the metabolic processes of microorganisms require water, food may be preserved by drying. If food is dried by the sun or the heat of a fire, direct archaeological evidence of the process is unlikely to result. However, drying may be done by plasmolysis, which occurs when the food is surrounded by high (hypertonic) concentrations of salt or sugar. In some cases, residues of those substances might survive but by themselves would be no more than circumstantial evidence of food preservation. Residues of other chemical substances used to kill microbes or retard their growth might eventually be recoverable. Wood smoke, for example, contains antimicrobial chemicals (aldehydes, alcohol, phenol, cresol, and others) that add their action to the preservative effects of drying and heat (J. Jay, 1970:117).

Undesirable microbial action can also be slowed in certain cases by subjecting foods to the intensive growth of specific microorganisms that the human gut tolerates. This encouraged growth results in a controllable fermentation, which produces an unfavorable environment for the un-desirable decay-producers. Sour cream, pickles, yogurt, cheese, and alcoholic beverages are familiar fermented foods on our tables, but the process is not restricted to modern industrial society. Some food-gathering peoples, especially in northern latitudes, use controlled fermentation to preserve meat, fish, and berries. Traces of the microorganisms responsible for fermentation, or the lactic and acetic acid resulting from their metabolism, may someday be recovered from Paleolithic sites.

Most human foods may be consumed raw, without special preparation. Infrequently, hunter/gatherers use foodstuffs that must be treated in special ways before they become edible. In California, several genera of highly nutritious acorns are so rich in tannic acid that this substance had to be removed before the acorns could be eaten. Sometimes the nuts were hulled and buried for long periods. Alternatively they could be dried and ground into meal with mortar and pestle; the meal was placed in baskets or shallow basin-shaped depressions and then repeatedly soaked with water. As the water passed through the meal, it leached out the bitter tannins. The cyanic acid in wild plum pits and buckeyes was removed in the same way (Kroeber, 1953).

Cooking is the most widely used technique of food preparation. Primary evidence that potential foodstuffs have been subjected to the action of fire is widespread, in the form of charred animal remains. Carbonized plant remains are more rare but have been found in Paleolithic contexts. These materials may have been burned for other reasons, either accidentally, or as part of the food-preservation process, or because they were used as fuel. But, where such material is abundant, we should be able to rule out one or more of the possible explanations on the basis of the nature of the materials, the pattern of charring, and the contexts in which the items were recovered.

Fireplaces are ordinarily no more than circumstantial evidence of cooking, since fires may also have been used to provide warmth and illumination. In addition, from at least Solutrean times, fires were used to make flint more workable in the tool-making process, especially when pressure-flaking was involved. Thus, caution should be exercised in interpreting the remains of fireplaces as indicating that food was cooked. Paleolithic hearths are often not informative—although they exist in considerable variety, most seem to be variants of the open fireplace, with or without draft trench or reflector. Possible exceptions are the hearths at two Upper Paleolithic sites in the Corrèze (Coumba del Boitoü and le Pré-Neuf), which contained slab-walled chambers that may be ovens, and the pits that may be ovens on the peripheries of a large hearth at Dolní Věstonice (see Breuil and Lantier, 1959:104; Klíma, 1963:125; Perlès, 1976:680–81). Occasionally, large patches of partially carbonized vegetation have been found, and these might be the remains of smoldering fires built to smoke meats, although other interpretations are possible.

These lengthy introductory remarks illustrate both the wide range of data about diet which can be recovered (at least theoretically) from Paleolithic sites, and the many interpretive problems the prehistorian faces. We must always be wary of conclusions based on isolated finds. Reliable information can be obtained only where a number of lines of evidence converge.

Paleo-environmental reconstructions provide us with the data needed to assess the past potential of a region for hominid subsistence. They afford much background information about resource availability that may clarify the hard evidence of actual behavior. Naturally, even the most reasonable attempts at assessing the potential offerings of the area accessible from a site will not tell us what actually happened in history; at best they show us what might have been. There has recently been a resurgence of interest in studying the environment as a key to understanding past behavior (see, for example, Higgs, 1975; Higgs and Vita-Finzi, 1972). The approach taken by the "site catchment analysts" (who seem to assume that whenever a resource is available, it will be exploited) glosses over both the known complexities of hominid behavior and the great difficulties involved in reconstructing prehistoric environments in useful detail. Nevertheless, it is self-evident that we cannot properly evaluate the finds from an occupation level unless we see them in the context of their relationship to the prehistoric environmental setting.

OBSERVATIONS ON TERMINOLOGY

There is a real danger that any synthesis of Paleolithic prehistory which attempts to paste together our fragmentary glimpses of the past into a single bigger picture will be misleading, because these isolated glimpses may actually show us parts of different, unrelated pictures which should not be combined. However, as data accumulate over time, it becomes increasingly difficult to evaluate or remember details that are not integrated into a simpler conceptual structure, no matter how imperfect the structure may eventually prove to be. I have therefore devised a loose classification of Iberian Paleolithic assemblages, which follows.

The *industrial complex* is the most abstract and encompassing division in this classification. Defined on the basis of very general similarities in artifact form, the complex is the largest set of assemblages that Paleolithic prehistorians have generally agreed are similar. Complexes are widespread in space and time, but the early ones have a greater spatial and temporal extent that the later ones; for example, the Acheulean complex (a set of assemblages usually including characteristic tools called bifaces) is found in Africa, Europe, and part of Asia for more than a million years, whereas the later Solutrean complex is known in the strict sense only from France and Spain, and lasts only a few thousand years.

A complex may be divided into *facies,* or subcomplexes of assemblages that resemble each other closely in the proportional representation of specific artifact types which are believed to have different functions. When functions are known or can be presumed with some certainty, the facies may be given a functional designation (quarry/workshop facies, hunting/ butchering facies, etc.). In other cases, various distinctive designations may be used (facies A or B, denticulate, etc.). A facies may have as broad a geographic distribution and as long a duration as the parent complex it represents. In its application to Mousterian facies, my use of the word deliberately differs from that of Bordes, who intends a stylistic distinction when he says "facies" (e.g., Bordes, 1968).

Pattern is the term used here to designate differences that identify groups of regionally distinctive materials. The pattern is a regionally restricted set of lifeways that may include peculiar tool-making techniques, distinctive forms for functionally equivalent tools, the utilization of different resource bases, settlement patterns, and exploitative strategies, and the presence of one or a few special artifact types unrepresented in adjacent regions. Like their analogues, the ethnographic culture areas, patterns seem to coincide with major "natural regions," large geographic areas that share certain basic environmental characteristics in contrast to those of other regions. In the Iberian Peninsula, if one disregards agricultural practices and linguistic/cultural distributions, there seem to be 10 or 11 such regions today: (1) southern Portugal; (2) Galicia and northern Portugal; (3) Cantabria; (4) the Pyrenees; (5) the Ebro basin (to Zaragoza, Huesca, and Teruel); (6) Cataluña; (7) Valencia (approximately coincident with the provinces of Castellon, Valencia, and most of Alicante); (8) Levante (Murcia, some of Alicante, and Almeria); (9) Andalusia; (10) the Meseta (Extremadura, Leon, the two Castiles). Some authorities would split the Meseta into a northern and a southern part, others would separate the Basque provinces (Vizcaya, Guipuzcoa, Alava) from Cantabria, and still others consider the western Iberian littoral as a unit (Dantín Cereda, 1948; Lautensach, 1967; de Terán et al., 1968). Ordinarily, the modern 10-fold division also seems to adequately describe regions that existed in past warm climatic phases, and even grosser divisions are often indicated. Distinctive groups of assemblages sometimes occupy less space than a major natural region: such areas are called *subregional style zones*.

Some complexes change notably through time (the Acheulean is an example). Temporally distinctive aggregates of assemblages from a single complex are called *phases* (such as the Earlier Acheulean Phase). However, it is not yet possible to recognize such temporal divisions in all complexes.

A *site* is a local concentration of detritus from human occupation, ordinarily from a few square meters to several hundred square meters in extent, although some open-air sites may occupy several hectares. A site may contain any number of superimposed occupation horizons. The *occupation horizon* is an undisturbed or almost undisturbed, relatively short-term accumulation of the products and by-products of human activity, contained in a level of geological deposits, while an *assemblage* is the set of all artifacts recovered from a single occupation horizon. Sometimes a site may have numerous geological levels containing abundant vertically diffuse scatters of artifacts but no occupation horizons at all. These sets of tools are referred to as *collections*. The term *industry* may refer to the set of artifacts in an assemblage which are made in one material but may also mean the set of artifacts in a single material which we know from a pattern, phase, or facies.

DIET-RELATED INFORMATION
FROM PALEOLITHIC IBERIA

In the Iberian Peninsula, large-scale modern investigations have been undertaken since the 1960s with the specific aim of understanding the development of hominid lifeways and human-environmental interactions during the Pleistocene. Consequently, circumstantial evidence about diet is becoming increasingly abundant.

Evidence Prior to the Mid-Pleistocene

There are no hominid occupations in the Iberian Peninsula that can be shown convincingly to antedate the mid-Pleistocene. Claims for greater antiquity are rumored for some assemblages rich in choppers and chopping tools in the province of Gerona (Puig d'en Roca and Cau del Duc de Torroella, for example), and for the vicinity of Cádiz (El Aculadero). However, the latter lacks the diagnostic faunal (or other) elements that would permit a precise assessment of its relative age, while the former are guess-dated solely on the typology of the recovered lithics, and Lower Paleolithic typological usage in Gerona is inconsistent and nonstandard at best (Canal and Soler, 1976; Carbonell, 1976).

The Acheulean Complex (prior to ca. 100,000 B.P.)

Lower Paleolithic sites in Iberia, all of which seem to be assignable to the Acheulean complex of industries, become reasonably abundant sometime in the mid-Pleistocene, although no exact chronometric dates are yet available. I have discussed most of these occurrences elsewhere (Freeman 1975b). The majority of the stratified occurrences were excavated so badly that one cannot determine whether they were undisturbed occupation horizons or mixed batches of derived material brought together in alluvial deposits. However, it seems probable that the Earlier Acheulean Phase of mid-Pleistocene hominid occupation in Iberia was essentially restricted to zones of open vegetation (especially grassland) along the coasts and major stream valleys.

In the last two decades modern excavations were undertaken at two large Acheulean sites in the province of Soria (Torralba and Ambrona), and in the 1970s Santonja and others excavated two smaller sites (JR-AR-01 and JR-AR-02) in the Aridos quarry in a 15/20 m terrace of the left bank of the Jarama river, 18 km southeast of Madrid (Freeman, 1975a; Freeman and Butzer, 1966; Santonja et al., n.d.). The only reliable diet-related data for mid-Pleistocene Iberia come from these four sites.

When synthesized with the most reliable data from the best older work, the information from these sites (all in the Tajo drainage of Spain's Central Meseta) yields a picture of regional Earlier Acheulean lifeways that we may call the Meseta Pattern. When more information becomes available, a Gallego/Lusitanian Pattern and a Mediterranean Pattern may also be definable for the Earlier Acheulean Phase.

In the Meseta Pattern, two kinds of specialized sites can now be recognized: quarry/workshop stations, such as Pinedo, and kill/butchery sites (the four localities mentioned above). Although one would also expect to find "living sites," no occupation is yet identifiable as such, which suggests that populations may have camped in areas that have since been subject to intensive erosion—the surfaces of the *parameras* or dissected uplands near the Torralba/Ambrona sites, for example.

In the hunting/butchering facies of this pattern, bifaces are not numerous (usually not more than 10–15% of all the shaped tools in stone). Cleavers and cleaver-flakes are abundant within the biface series. Picks, "screwdriver"-ended forms, pieces skewed at butt and tip, and minimally retouched flat tabular forms are also represented in the biface series. There is conclusive evidence of deliberate bone-working by percussion flaking, and the bone industry includes pieces made from juvenile elephant tusk tips, sharpened adult tusks, and flaked scraper and denticulated forms. There is also a reasonably well developed industry in wood (especially pine); a spearpoint, several wedge-shaped objects, and skewerlike pieces were recovered at Torralba. The wooden pieces are frequently shaped by charring, at least in part, and small fragments of charcoal are abundantly disseminated over the surfaces of both the large sites. The occupants imported some stone raw material or finished tools (sometimes in large sizes) from several kilometers away, although the locally available limestone also was used extensively. Quartzite and chalcedonous flint, the other major raw materials, usually were quarried as rolled cobbles from alluvial deposits, and larger tools were at least roughed out at the quarry. The large numbers of split cobbles, flakes, and discarded defective roughouts at Pinedo and several of the Manzanares/Jarama sites testify to these practices (Freeman 1975a).

Each level at Torralba and Ambrona yielded the bones of several individual animals of different species. If these animals died and were processed by humans simultaneously, as seems to be the case, the most economical explanation of their presence would seem to be that the animals were taken in game drives, probably conducted by large groups of people (perhaps with the aid of fire). According to this interpretation, large animals were driven through the lush valleys into natural traps provided by the marshes and ponds along the valley bottom. For at least the largest species, the preliminary disjointing was performed where the animals were killed. The tusks and mandibles were detached from elephant skulls, as were the horncores from the large bovids. Skulls of these large species were battered open, exposing the brain.

The large joints and slabs of meat produced by this process were carried a short distance to higher ground, where apparently several small groups were independently engaged in reducing them to smaller cuts. Wooden and bone "wedges" and bifacial stone implements and sidescrapers were used and abandoned at this processing stage, although they were rarely left behind in the "primary butchering" area. Fire also was used. The body parts represented in the areas used for this activity suggest that each work party had access to approximately the same kinds and quantities of meat.

In the third processing stage, undertaken still farther from the marsh edge, hunks of meat were reduced to yet smaller sizes. Repeated differences in areal contents suggest some specialization of activities at this stage; elephant and bovid skull fragments seem to have been processed in one area, and ribs, scapulae, vertebrae, and marrow bones in another. Patches of charcoal are relatively abundant, as are larger wooden objects, and the lithic inventory is richer in retouched flakes, utilized flakes, denticulates, perforators, and notches than are those of the two other processing stages.

Although no deliberately prepared fireplaces are recognizable at either Torralba or Ambrona, there is one large accumulation of tiny, partly carbonized wood splinters and other vegetal material that may be the remnants of a smudge or smoldering fire. This unique feature is accompanied by small bone fragments and abundant vestiges of the stone-knapping process (small flakes and debris, probably produced during the retouching of working edges rather than the primary stages of tool manufacture). The patch of half-burnt vegetal material could conceivably be the remains of a meat-smoking fire, although analogous features at Kalambo Falls, in Africa, have been interpreted as burnt bedding (J. D. Clark, 1960:314), and other functions, such as repelling insects are also possible.

Several considerations suggest that the Torralba/Ambrona accumulations are the residues of food procurement and processing activities. First, a number of bones bear the marks of slicing by stone tools. Second, the meatier body parts are extremely underrepresented. Third, the marrowbones are broken, the braincases of even the most robust animals have been battered to bits, and larger mandibles have been cracked open, exposing the blood vessels and nerves lying in the mandibular and mental foramina and canals. These breakage patterns occur on bones, which are so large that no carnivore of the time could possibly be implicated in their production. Fourth, very few of the broken bones are deliberately shaped tools, while most of the fragments suitable as raw materials for tool-making (tusk, cervid antler, etc.) were abandoned intact with the rest of the bone debris. This suggests that the few bone tools manufactured at Torralba were expedients produced for use in the butchering process. Finally, some bone fragments are quite charred, but there are not enough such pieces to indicate the use of bone as fuel, nor does the pattern of charring suggest that. Natural deaths or predation by animals might have produced a part of the Torralba/Ambrona bone accumulations. However, the evidence seems to us to indicate that human activity was responsible for the bulk of these remains.

The bone residues at Torralba and Ambrona are not those one would expect if the meat had been eaten on the spot. Exactly those body parts which would have made up the bulk of edible meat are notably under-represented, and what we find seems to be the waste left behind when the most desirable body parts were removed to some other place to serve as food, clothing, and raw material.

The species represented at Torralba, where our analysis is farthest along, are given in table 4.1. There are several superimposed occupation levels at the site, and some of them are quite small. For this and other reasons, the total species list is broader than the list for any single occupation. In 1962 and 1963, we excavated 10 major short-term occupations and many smaller horizons. The total number of individual animals whose remains were recovered in those two years is at least 115, but the largest number from any single horizon is only 15. Table 4.2 summarizes the occurrences, by genus, in the eight most extensive levels excavated during the 1962 and 1963 field seasons.

For several reasons, I believe that the lion, the lagomorph, and the small carnivores found at Torralba are probably not hominid food residues. First, the bones are not charred or cut. Second, for other species, several bones were recovered for each identified individual, but for these species, typically a single bone or at most two (the same is true for the birds). These remains, then, do not have the same characteristics as those of the creatures which were clearly processed by humans. However, all the recovered animals are considered edible, so they are included in the discussion that follows.

The Torralba / Ambrona sites are sometimes characterized as "specialized big-game hunting" or "specialized elephant-hunting" camps. The table shows that, even allowing for differential preservation, the majority of recovered species represented at Torralba were large animals, and if we consider anything bigger than a rabbit or a fox to be big game, the phrase "big-game hunting" fits. But to call the Torralba hunters *specialized* is another matter. There is least reason to call them specialized elephant hunters. As the table shows, our minimum estimate of 69 animals from the eight levels tabulated includes only 22 elephants.

Table 4.1. Total fauna known at Torralba

Elephas (Parelephas) trogontherii	*Rangifer* sp.
Elephas (Paleoloxodon) antiquus	*Eucladoceras / Euctenoceros*
Dicerorhinus hemitoechus	*Felis* cf. *leo*
Equus caballus	*Canis* cf. *lupus*
Bos primigenius (primitive form)	Carnivorae indet.
Dama sp. (more primitive than	Lagomorphae indet.
D. clactoniana)	Aves (probably Anatidae and
Predama (?)	Ciconidae)
Cervus elaphus	Mollusca indet.

Table 4.2. Mammals in eight occupation horizons at Torralba (preliminary estimates of minimum numbers)

Occupation	Elephas	Dicero- rhinus	Bos	Euclado- ceras	Cervus	Equus	Dama	Felis	Small carnivores	Lago- morphs	Total, by level
1	5	1	1	—	3	3	1	—	1	—	15
2	3	1	1	—	1	1	1	—	—	—	8
3	4	1	2	1	1	2	1	—	—	—	12
4	3	—	1	—	1	2	1	1	—	—	9
5	1	—	1	—	1	1	—	—	—	—	4
6	1	—	1	—	1	1	1	1	—	1	6
7	3	—	1	—	2	1	1	—	—	—	8
8	2	—	1	—	2	2	—	—	—	—	7
Total, by species	22	3	9	1	12	13	5	2	1	1	69

Note: Identifications were by E. Aguirre and others.

Furthermore, the species taken by Torralbans are quite variable in size. If the animals are sorted into groups on the basis of body size,[1] as has been done in table 4.3, the proportion in each group may be calculated. Then, the formula cited in note 1 will provide a numerical index of the relative diversity of the faunal spectrum across the size categories. The value obtained, using 6 categories, can only vary from 0.167 (highly specialized) to 1.0 (completely diversified). The index of diversity in the capture of animals of different sizes for the eight combined Torralba levels in table 4.2 is 0.70 (see table 4.3), indicating substantial diversity rather than size specialization.

Table 4.3. Sizes of captured animals, potential meat yield, and diversity indices for Torralba (Lower Paleolithic) and Morín (Middle Paleolithic)

	No. of individuals	Percent	Weight of meat (kg)	Percent
Torralba				
Very large	25	36	83,625	91
Large	9	13	4,000	4
Large medium	16	23	2,715	3
Average medium	12	17	1,200	1
Small medium	5	7	312.5	0.3
Small	2	3	5	0.005
Total	69		91,857.5	
Species diversity	0.71		0.20	
Morín 17				
Very large	2	8	3,636	45
Large	6	24	2,400	30
Large medium	7	28	1,260	16
Average medium	7	28	670	8
Small medium	2	8	45	1
Small	1	4	12.5	0.2
Total	25		8,023.5	
Species diversity	0.73		0.51	
Morín 15				
Very large	—	—	—	—
Large	1	14	400	57
Large medium	1	14	180	26
Average medium	1	14	100	14
Small medium	—	—	—	—
Small	4	57	25.2	4
Total	7		705.2	
Species diversity	0.43		0.40	

Note: Owing to rounding, totals do not always equal 100%. Size categories and the index of species diversity are defined in note 1 to the text.

The Torralba fauna has never seemed to me to indicate an intentional concentration on big-game hunting. Although really small animals are almost unrepresented, that may simply be because the smaller species would have been hard to see and secure in the marshy vegetation along the valley bottoms. Thus, at Torralba, "big-game" hunting may have been an expedient strategy dictated by a combination of environmental conditions, technology, and the organization of personnel in the hunt. Within the limits thus imposed, the hunters seem to have been opportunistic, taking all animals of any species, age, or sex that came within range.

The animals butchered at Torralba represent an immense quantity of edible meat. And there is no doubt that the overwhelming bulk of that meat would have been provided by the very large animals. A quick calculation of the proportions of potential meat yield indicates little diversity (index 0.20), with the largest species producing over 90% of the total. If the faunal remains are a fair indication of the abundance of different kinds of meat in the Torralbans' diet, the data indicate that the Acheulean hunters were rather specialized elephant eaters, if they were not specialized elephant hunters.

There is no way to prove that most or any of the meat represented by the Torralba kills were eaten, but I think it a fair assumption that some, probably the major part, was, and that it was at least the intention of the hunters to eat as much as possible of the bounty produced by their efforts. Impressive quantities were certainly available. Carcasses that would have yielded a total of over 13,600 kg of meat were recovered in Occupation 7 alone. If we estimate a consumption of 2.25 kg of meat per day per person, that amounts to more than 6,000 man-days of meat rations (see Freeman, 1975b).

I have suggested that the total social group from which the hunters were drawn might have varied in size from 25 to as many as 100 persons. If meat consumption per person per day was as high as I have (unrealistically) suggested, and if we also assume that the group intended to consume all the available edible meat, 100 active adults could have been fed for 60 days. However, if the Torralbans intended to use the meat taken in this game drive over such a long period, some techniques of preservation and storage must have been known to them. Otherwise the meat would have begun to spoil and to attract carnivores and scavengers. The Torralbans could not reasonably have hoped to consume more than a small fraction of the food they worked so hard to procure unless they preserved it. Given what we know of the environment at that time, the most accessible technique would have been drying, with or without the aid of fire and smoke.

As noted earlier, evidence for the presence of fire is abundant in the Torralba sediments; it includes very many small bits of charcoal and several large fragments of charred wood. However, with one possible exception, nothing suggesting a deliberate fireplace was recovered. The exception, the large, partly burned "smudge" in Occupation 8, would have been a quite adequate source of smoke and gentle heat for meat preservation. (If it was general practice to butcher and bone the meat in several stages, proceeding at last to treat it over smoking/drying fires well back from and upslope of the mucky marsh edge, we are fortunate indeed to have recovered one such feature at Torralba since erosion has subsequently cut away most of the areas where they were probably located.) Other circumstantial evidence for the use of fire in food processing comes from the fact that several partially charred bone fragments were found. In proportion to the thousands of other bone fragments, burnt pieces are rare indeed, and that fact suggests that they may result from accidents in the fire-drying process rather than from a cooking stage of food preparation through which most meat might have been expected to pass if it was all to be consumed immediately.

The visual appearance of the burnt bones can be used as an index of the heat to which they were exposed. The nature of the discoloration on the Torralba bone fragments (which are blackened, but not further calcined) indicates that they were subjected to temperatures of 300–350° C. Open woodburning fireplaces generate heat up to 600–700° C (Coles, 1973:135), and bones subjected to such heat intensities soon change color further, becoming blackish-gray to whitish-gray (Bonucci and Graziani, 1976). This seems to me to be an additional indication that the Torralba bones were not deliberately burned or even long exposed to the hottest part of the fire.

At Ambrona, one elephant skull was recovered which had undergone more elaborate treatment than the smashing characteristic of such finds. After the braincase was opened and the mandible removed, a fire was lit on or under the palate. The bones of the roof of the mouth were charred in the process. We do not know if this operation was intended to cook the flesh of the palate for immediate consumption, or to tenderize it so that it would come free from the bone with less effort, or for some other reason. Nor can we tell whether the "cooking" involved the trunk or not.

Thousands of bits of charcoal and hundreds of fragments of plant materials (among which are a few bits of bark and grass) were recovered in excavations of the Torralba/Ambrona sites. It is noteworthy that this mass of organic material did not include a single seed, fruit, or nut. All the potentially diet-relevant material from the two sites is animal. Of course, that does not indicate that the Mesetan Acheulean hunters ate nothing but meat. However, it does suggest strongly that the activities undertaken at these two butchering stations were concerned mainly with the procurement and processing of meat. Whatever edible vegetal materials may have been obtainable in the vicinity of those stations were ignored while those activities went on, or, if collected, they were not processed at the site in ways that left durable residues there.

The location and elevation of the Torralba and Ambrona sites are such that, today, the climate can be bitterly cold in winter, and nights stay quite cool even in summer. During the full glacial period when the sites were utilized, the mean annual temperature of the region was about 10° C lower than it is now, which would make fire, good shelter, and heavy clothing essential to survival during the winter months. However, the presence of migratory birds (Anatidae in one Torralba level and a stork in another) suggests a warm-season utilization of the horizons where they occur, and perhaps one may generalize this to the site as a whole. If Torralba and Ambrona were warm-season camps, we know nothing concrete about Mesetan activities during the harsher part of the year, and can only speculate that the Acheulean hunters might have moved down the Tajo (Tagus) to the coast, and then possibly farther south in the peninsula. In any case, it seems clear that the kinds of food-acquisition activities we can detect at Torralba and Ambrona may have taken place only periodically, and perhaps on a seasonal basis.

All the potential food remains from the two sites are animal, and the kinds of activities involved in procuring these resources may have been the responsibility of a limited segment of the society (the able-bodied hunters and anyone else involved in processing the meat) rather than its membership as a whole. If that is the case, we have no evidence whatever of the part played by other social groups in food procurement, or of the kinds of places where those activities might have been performed. In my opinion, our picture of subsistence-related activities undertaken by societies of the Mesetan Pattern of the Earlier Acheulean Phase in Iberia is extremely fragmentary, and is likely to remain so for some time.

JR-AR-01 and JR-AR-02, two sites in terraces of the Jarama river near Madrid, seem to me to be assignable to the Mesetan Pattern, although I have not seen the recovered materials from either. Both are known only from small exposures, and the excavators have assigned the deposits to a period when the climate was not unlike that at present. Judging from the faunal list they present, the occupations should perhaps be attributed to a mid-Pleistocene interglacial just subsequent to the Torralba/Ambrona cold phase. At JR-AR-02, excavators found a partial vertebral column, scapula, and humerus of a single individual of *Paleoloxodon antiquus* in anatomical connection, and in association with 28 stone tools; nearby, in earth which fell from this horizon during modern gravel-quarrying operations, 2 bifaces and 2 cleaver-flakes were recovered. JR-AR-01 is, in certain respects, more interesting. The small stone tool assemblage lacks Acheulean diagnostics but includes the tips of two bifaces removed when the tools were resharpened, as well as hammerstones, natural-backed knives, primary flakes, and trimming flakes. The faunal list is extensive, including an adult *Paleoloxodon antiquus*, a beaver, a wolf, and a stag (*Cervus elaphus*), as well as abundant small fauna. The small fauna is

Table 4.4. Small fauna from JR-AR-01

Oryctolagus cf. *cuniculus*	Emydidae indet.
Lepus sp.	Colubridae indet.
Eliomys quercinus (large)	*Lacerta* sp.
Cricetulus (Allocricetus) bursae	
Microtus brecciensis	Anatidae indet.
Arvicola sp.	*Alectoris rufa* sive *barbara*
Apodemus cf. *sylvaticus*	*Perdix paleoperdix*
Crocidura sp.	*Porzana porzana*
Chiroptera indet.	*Columba palumbus*
	Columba livida sive *oenas*
Discoglossus pictus	*Corvus monedula*
Alytes sp.	*Strix aluco*
Pelobates cultripes	Passeriformes indet.
Hyla sp.	
Bufo bufo	Gastropoda indet.
Rana ridibunda	Pisces indet.

Source: Data are from Santonja Gómez, López, and Perez González (1978).

indicative of a marshy riverine environment, including ponded, slow-moving, or still waters and reedy banks, and patches of open vegetation interspersed with extensive stands of deciduous forest. The species recovered are listed in table 4.4.

The abundance of birds, reptiles, amphibians, and small and micro-mammals in the JR-AR-01 fauna is striking and might at first suggest that hominids of the Earlier Acheulean Phase were quite eclectic in their dietary preferences, and that they had already developed efficient means for taking fish and birds. However, I do not think that is the case. With the exception of the gastropods (which probably will prove to be pond-dwelling, riverine, and riverbank species, naturally to be expected in these sediments), the beaver (also a local denizen), the owl, *Strix aluco* (which may have nested nearby), and the large fauna listed above (which may well be human prey), the remaining species, of which there are at least 27, read almost exactly like an ornithologist's monograph on the diet of the black kite, *Milvus migrans*. These marsh-side dwellers nest in colonies, preferring to build in oaks or other deciduous trees, and their nests and the ground beneath them become littered with the remnants of their meals. Delibes' excellent study of the feeding habits of the black kite in the Doñana reserve (1975) gives species lists so similar to that from JR-AR-01—fish, mollusks, reptiles including turtles, amphibians, the same sorts of birds, and mammals of sizes up to and including rabbits—that the likeness can scarcely be coincidental, especially when we consider that the site environment was precisely the sort preferred by these raptors. This suggestion could be tested by a study of the condition of the bone remains.

For the present, I suggest that the fauna from JR-AR-01 is a complex assemblage resulting from the spatial coincidence of at least two major agencies of accumulation: the predatory and food-processing activities of humans (and perhaps large carnivores) and the predatory and feeding behavior of kites. At the two Jarama sites the remains that probably accumulated as the result of human activities seem essentially similar to those at the Torralba/Ambrona site complex; at JR-AR-02 a kill site/preliminary disjointing area is perhaps represented, whereas the remains at the other site seem more characteristic of later stages in the butchering process. Whether the excavated areas are parts of larger occupation horizons like those at Torralba or represent activities undertaken by smaller groups acting independently is not determinable.

Middle Paleolithic Patterns (from ca. 100,000 to 35,000 B.P.)

Human occupation in Iberia undoubtedly continued without interruption from Middle through Upper Pleistocene times. Disturbed and poorly collected sites, apparently quarry/workshop areas and probably bracketing this long period, are known on all Iberian coasts and in terraces along the major rivers. Sites like Tahivilla (Cádiz) seem to show a persistence of certain lithic types (cleaver-flakes, picks) into the Late Acheulean. There are two Acheulean cave occupations (both at one site, El Castillo in Santander), but faunal evidence from the early excavation of these horizons is so poorly reported as to be virtually useless for our purposes. I have briefly described the lithic collections from these levels (Freeman, 1975b). The evidence for Late Acheulean behavior patterns in Iberia is too fragmentary to synthesize here.

The Middle Paleolithic is another situation entirely. Although some feel otherwise, I see no reason why all the Iberian Middle Paleolithic cannot be embraced in the Mousterian complex. Within this complex, both facies and patterns can be recognized.

At present, the only Middle Paleolithic horizons from Iberia which have been dated are: the Carigüela (Granada) Mousterian horizons, where a thermoluminescence technique was applied to burnt flint, yielding age estimates from 48,000 to 28,000 B.P. (Göksu et al., 1974), layer G, the topmost Mousterian level at Gorham's Cave, where carbon-14 ages of 49,200 ± 3,200 and 47,700 ± 1,500 B.P. were obtained (Waechter, 1964), and level IVb at Els Ermitons, where a tentative date of "around 35,000 years" resulted (Muñoz and Pericot, 1975:27). In two of these cases, dating is problematical—the thermoluminescence technique used at Carigüela is still considered experimental (and the 28,000 B.P. date is unacceptably young), while the Gorham's Cave dates are so close to the upper limit of the carbon-14 technique that they probably are best regarded as minimum estimates rather than approximate ages—and the Ermitons date has not been confirmed. That being the case, there is no way at present to subdivide the Iberian Mousterian into phases; in fact, there is little evidence for such a division, although in some regions some facies do show changes through time.

The evidence suggests that there are at least five major patterns in the Iberian Mousterian: the Cantabrian, the Andalusian, the Suboriental (Valencian/Levantine), the Catalan, and the Mesetan (a Pyrenean pattern seems to exist in France, and may also be present in Spain). Good excavations are still rare; as they accumulate, new patterns may be recognized and some may prove to be further divisible.

The Mesetan Pattern. In the Mesetan Pattern, Levallois technique is common, both in cave occupations and open-air stations. The open-air occurrences include quarry/workshop facies, in which flakes and the few finished tools may be very large in size. Casares, an informative and reasonably well-excavated cave site, yielded a series of small assemblages that may be attributable to the Ferrassie Mousterian facies (Beltrán Martínez and Barandiarán Maestú, 1968). Exposures at Casares were small, the faunal lists only provide counts of bone fragments from each species and level, and the authors devote a minimum of space to their discussion, so the lists are not very useful for our purposes. The list for level 4 consists of at least one individual each of rhinoceros, large bovid, *Sus, Equus, Cervus,* cave lion, *Capra, Rupicapra, Capreolus, Canis lupus, Lynx, Crocuta, Vulpes, Felis sylvestris, Castor fiber, Oryctolagus cuniculus,* an indeterminate toad, and birds. If all these animals were taken by humans, the Casares Mousterians would have been wide-spectrum opportunists in their food-collecting patterns. Representative species from open country, forested areas, rocky uplands, and valley bottoms are all present. The index of size diversity for this assemblage is 0.60, indicating almost as great a spread as for the Acheulean occupations examined earlier. If this datum is meaningful, it might indicate either that larger animals were becoming less abundant or were harder to hunt in the kinds of terrain and vegetation cover near the site, and that the Mousterian hunters were becoming more aware of the range of resources available in their environment and making more use of that range. Nevertheless, the vast bulk of available food would have been provided by the rhinoceros.

The cave of La Ermita, in Burgos, contained two occupation horizons with fauna and artifacts attributed to the Quina variant of the Charentian facies (Moure and Delibes, 1972). Level 5b, which yielded the richest fauna, contained bones of a bat (*Miniopterus* sp.), and some indeterminate dove-sized birds, as well as rabbit, wolf, fox, wild horse, red deer, chamois, ibex, and a large bovine. Although individual counts are not presented in the report, this fauna is less varied than the collection from Casares level 4. At both sites the bulk of meat yielded by the animals represented would have come from one or two species. If these animal remains do provide an indication of the kinds and proportions of meat in the hominid diet, the "main course" in most Mesetan Mousterian meals must have been about as monotonous as it probably was for their Acheulian ancestors. There is no evidence at all for the sorts of vegetal food that may have been consumed by Mousterians of the Meseta.

The Ebro Pattern. The only reasonably well known Mousterian site from the Ebro pattern is the Eudoviges rock-shelter, where several levels of Charentian facies Mousterian (Quina variety) were found (Barandiaran, 1975). Unfortunately, faunal preservation was very poor at Eudoviges, and only a very few bones were identifiable. These included a rhino, a cervid, and a wild horse. The complete faunal list from this site might have been about as varied as those for the Mesetan Pattern.

The Suboriental Pattern. We are not well informed about potential subsistence-related materials available to the peoples of the Suboriental Pattern. Most known sites of this pattern are in caves and shelters, and some are reasonably well excavated (Cochino, El Salt, El Pastor). There are also open-air quarry/workshop sites. Lithic assemblages are composed primarily of small tools, among which sidescrapers predominate. The only facies so far recognized is a sidescraper-rich Typical Mousterian, with varying representation of Levallois technique and types. The sidescraper series usually includes a number of pieces with abrupt "backing" formed by cortical surfaces or breaks. Such pieces are present but much rarer in other Iberian patterns of this complex. The Cochino fauna has never been described (Soler Garcia, 1956). Unfortunately, one of the most important sites of this pattern, Còva Negra, was so poorly excavated that its abundant faunal data are almost useless (Viñes Masip, Jordá Cerdá, and Royo Gómez, 1947). Although birds, rodents and reptiles (*Testudo*) are present, they are rare in a fauna which includes elephants, rhinoceros, bovids, equids, cervids, goats, sheep, suids, and remains of Neanderthal man. The Còva de la Pechina also yielded horses, wild cattle, cervids, and ovids (Jordá Cerdá, 1947).

The Andalusian Pattern. This pattern is known from excavations in the cave of Carigüela (Granada) and the sites of Devil's Tower and Gorham's Cave on Gibraltar. Results of the recent reexcavation of Carigüela are still not completely published; a short note has appeared (Almagro et al., 1970), but apparently the excavation coincided in large part with a previously disturbed part of the site, and little new has been offered. Stone tools from this site are attributed by de Lumley (1969a) to the sidescraper-rich Typical Mousterian. The fauna from Spahni's earlier excavations (García Sánchez, 1960) was never completely published, but it includes at least Merck's rhinoceros, wild horse, red deer, bears, spotted hyena, *Panthera pardus, Capra ibex,* and remains of Neanderthal man.

The sites on Gibraltar are more informative for our purposes. Devil's

Tower, excavated by Dorothy Garrod a half-century ago, contained human remains, and for that reason her work has been widely cited (Garrod et al., 1928). Unhappily, the excavation fell far short of modern standards. The site, a fissure, is interesting because the recovered fauna was exceptionally varied. The earliest horizon in the site is a raised beach, formed when sea level reached 9 m above its present stand. The beach, which also forms the base of the Gorham's Cave sequence, is part of a horizon of beaches and platforms found at essentially the same altitude throughout southern Spain and the coasts of the Maghreb. This high sea stand has been dated by Stearns and Thurber (1967) at 125,000 ± 10,000 B.P., which would indicate that both sites were habitable at any time after the earlier part of the Last Interglacial; the nature of the sediments and fauna would be consistent with an Interglacial age for Mousterian horizons at Devil's Tower, at least.

I have not seen the stone tools from Devil's Tower, but illustrations (Garrod et al., 1928) suggest that the assemblages may be assignable to Ferrassie Mousterian or sidescraper-rich Typical, depending on the degree to which Levallois technique, which is abundantly illustrated, was employed. The Gorham's Cave collections contain few finished stone tools but many cores, utilized flakes, and unretouched flakes and blades, suggesting that the activities undertaken at this site may have been quite specialized (stone tool manufacture and butchering are among the likelier possibilities). The shaped stone tools could be assignable to the Typical Mousterian. Flaking debris, split cobbles, and choppers are abundant in nearby disturbed open-air quarry/workshop sites between Gibraltar and La Linea.

At Devil's Tower, there are five Mousterian levels in sands and eolianites. We have lists by level of the recovered mollusks (table 4.5) but only composite lists for birds and mammals (table 4.6).

At first glance, the faunal spectrum is surprisingly broad. However, there is internal evidence that many of the forms are unrelated to human occupation. For example, terrestrial mollusks from level 6 include almost all the forms found in any later horizon, but level 6 seems to have accumulated before the first humans set foot on the site. The snails are precisely those one would expect to find today in a cave or fissure on the Rock, if natural vegetation conditions prevailed nearby. The represented species are virtually all denizens of dry places, rocks, cliffs, and grottoes. Consequently, the land snails cannot be used as evidence for diet. Some of the marine mollusks, such as *Tritonium, Pecten* and *Lucina*, ordinarily live at considerable depths and are unlikely to have been noticed by people except as empty shells thrown up by storms onto nearby beaches, *Patella* (limpets) and *Mytilus* (mussels) might have been deliberately collected by Mousterian cave-dwellers, but raised beaches from Algeciras to Tarifa

Table 4.5.　Molluscan species from Devil's Tower

Marine	Terrestrial
Level 2	
Patella vulgata (abundant)	*Rumina decollata* (very abundant)
P. ferruginea	*Helix alonensis* (very abundant)
Mytilus edulis (abundant)	*H. marmorata* (abundant)
	H. semipicta
	H. calpeana
	H. cemenelea
	Hyalinia (?) *navarrica*
Level 3	
Patella vulgata	*Helix alonensis*
P. ferruginea	*H. marmorata*
Mytilus edulis	*H. calpeana*
Lucina borealis	*H. aspersa*
Tritonium nodiferum (fragment)	*Buliminus montanus*
Level 4	
Patella vulgata	*Rumina decollata*
Mytilus edulis	*Helix alonensis*
Tritonium nodiferum (fragment)	
Level 5	
Patella vulgata	*Rumina decollata*
P. ferruginea	*Helix alonensis*
P. depressa	
Mytilus edulis	
Pecten jacobaeus	
Level 6	
Spondylus gaederopus	*Helix calpeana* (very abundant)
	H. alonensis (abundant)
	H. marmorata
	Hyalinia (?) *navarrica*
	Buliminus (?) *montanus*
	Rumina decollata

Source: Data are from Garrod et al. (1928).

include these species in great numbers (as well as *Lucina, Pecten jacobaeus, P. maximus,* and *Chlamys varia*). The possibility that many of the marine mollusks at Devil's Tower were incorporated in the sediments by natural agencies other than human activity cannot be ruled out.

The fact that some mussels in level 2 are burnt could indicate their occasional consumption by humans but could also result from the accidental incorporation of empty shells in fires lit for other purposes. If there were a large number of charred mussel shells, and charring occurred on the outside of the shell only, a case could be made that the valves were held together by the living animal while burning took place. If, on the other hand, the inner surfaces of the valves are as charred as the outer surfaces, one might reject with more confidence the suggestion that charring resulted from cooking mussels for human meals. Unfortunately, Garrod does not provide enough information to resolve this question.

Table 4.6. Fauna from Devil's Tower Mousterian Levels

Mammalia	Aves
Bos primigenius	*Falco peregrinus*
Equus sp.	*F. eleonorae*
Ursus arctos	*F. subbuteo*
Cervus elaphus	*F. tinnunculus*
Sus scrofa	*F.* (?) *cenchroides*
Felis pardus	*Haliaëtus albicilla*
Capra pyrenaica	*Hieraëtus fasciatus*
Canis lupus	*Hieraëtus pennatus*
Lynx lynx	*Gyps fulvus*
Crocuta crocuta	*Oidemia* (?) *fusca*
Meles meles	*Mergus* cf. *serrator*
Felis sylvestris	*Puffinus diomedea*
Hystrix cristata	*P. puffinus*
Oryctolagus cuniculus	*Sterna sandvicensis*
Eliomys quercinus	*Phalacrocorax carbo*
Apodemus sylvaticus	*P. graculus*
Arvicola sp.	*Larus fuscus*
Pitymys sp.	*Alca impennis*
Talpa europaea	*Cepphus grylle*
Crocidura russula	*Columba livia*
Myotis myotis	*C. oenas*
Nyctinomus teniotis	*C. palumbus*
	Alectoris (?) *petrosa*
Reptilia	*Pyrrhocorax graculus*
Testudo ibera	*P. pyrrhocorax*
	Fringilla cf. *coelebs*
Pisces	*Passer* sp.
cf. *Lates*	*Turdus viscivorus*
	Turdus cf. *merula*
	Turdus sp.
	Hirundo rustica
	Apus melba
	Picus viridis

Source: Data are from Garrod et al. (1928).

Note: Avian species names have been brought into conformity with usage in Peterson, Mountfort, and Hollom (1962) where possible.

Nor is the list of birds (table 4.6) a sure indication of human dietary practices, although it does include several marine species that probably nested locally and are not difficult to capture while nesting (puffins, auks, gulls, etc.). They might well have fallen prey to early hunters, but they might equally well have died in the site itself while it was not occupied by people. More than 60% of the remaining avian species are raptors or carrion-eaters, among which are forms, so ferocious or so large, or both (eagles, hawks, buzzards), that is does not seem likely that Mousterian hunters were able to capture them. Such birds are only infrequently represented in Upper Paleolithic sites and are not sought as staple dietary items by any living hunting group I know of. These raptors regularly hunt migrating birds from resting stations or nests on cliffs like those at Gibraltar. The remaining 40% of the species found at Devil's Tower are just the sorts of birds they normally hunt. As a result, the bulk of the Devil's Tower avifauna should probably be excluded from the list of Mousterian dietary items, while we admit the possibility that the site's occupants may occasionally have been fortunate enough to take a seabird or two and may have eaten the carcasses of any dead birds they found.

Most of the smaller mammals in the Devil's Tower fauna may also be the remains of raptor meals. The bats (*Myotis, Nyctinomus*) typical cave-dwellers. Since the minimum number of mammals present is not given, one can say only that large open-country forms, forest inhabitants, and alpine animals are included. The occurrence of *Hystrix cristata* is unusual, although this porcupine is quite easy to hunt. The ibex could possibly have been taken from a population on the Rock itself. The species list is considerably richer in carnivores than the average Mousterian occupation, suggesting that part of the accumulation may be a carnivore lair.

At Gorham's Cave, which was better excavated, there were some 6 m of Mousterian or probably Mousterian occupations (levels G through U). The lower horizons (T to K) are assigned to the cold "Würm I" stadial because they overlie a Last Interglacial beach and include much wind-blown sand,which could only have accumulated when the adjacent foreshore was much wider than it is today, implying a substantial drop in mean sea level. Layer G would have been deposited during "Würm II" (Waechter, 1964; Zeuner, 1953). This interpretation, while not unreasonable, rests entirely on Zeuner's study of sediments, since the faunal lists from Mousterian horizons are climatically uninformative.

Waechter (1964) provides lists of animal remains, broken down into bone totals for each species and level (table 4.7). Minimum numbers of individuals are not estimated, but occurrence of individuals in the different size categories would probably give a diversity index of 0.60 to 0.75 (very diverse), judging by the magnitude of the bone counts. Deer and ibex are abundant, and rabbit is especially so, a useful criterion for differentiating

Table 4.7. Fauna from selected Mousterian levels at Gorham's Cave (no. of bones and shells)

	Level G	Level K	Level M
Mammalia			
Dicerorhinus sp.	—	2	1
Bos. cf. *primigenius*	5	5	11
Equus caballus	—	—	8
Cervus elaphus	52	29	53
Panthera pardus	1	6	2
Ursus arctos	—	3	1
Capra cf. *ibex*	11	162	132
Canis lupus	—	2	1
Crocuta crocuta	5	5	4
Lynx lynx	5	2	2
Felis sylvestris	1	—	1
Oryctolagus cuniculus	94	187	178
Erinaceus sp.	1	—	—
Mollusca			
Mytilus edulis	32	3	—
Patella coerulea	109	49	45
P. ferruginea	—	6	5
Monodonta articulata	11	—	—
Semicassis undulata	—	—	2
Helix marmorata	1	—	—

Source: Data are from Waechter (1964).

Note: *Sus scrofa* is present in several other Mousterian horizons. Hyena coprolites are present in many Mousterian levels and are abundant in level K, probably indicating that some of the bones in that level, at least, may be the remains of carnivore meals.

the Mediterranean Mousterian patterns from those in the rest of the peninsula. However, many rabbits provide little meat in comparison with a single deer, ibex, cow, or rhinoceros, and in some levels most of the available meat would have come from the rhinoceros. All the major Mousterian levels contained marine mollusks, and the species that are best represented (*Mytilus* and *Patella*) are reasonably easy to find and collect. It seems quite likely that they were gathered for human consumption. That in turn increases the probability that some marine mollusks from Devil's Tower are also food remains. (Since mollusks yield so little meat per individual, it is unlikely that they were a mainstay of the diet). Fragments of *Testudo* were found in several levels; this species should also be included in the potential food resources at Gorham's Cave.

Evidence for fire is abundant at both sites. In layer G at Gorham's Cave, pine charcoal, probably from *Pinus pinea,* and several fragments of pine cones tentatively attributed to that species were found. Unfortunately, this evidence does not tell us whether pine nuts were collected for food or whether the cones simply served as fuel.

The data from the Gibraltar sites seem to me to represent the persistence of opportunistic exploitative strategies. The potential meat sources at both sites are animals that would have been accessible and noticeable in the immediate vicinity. The animal species lists are quite varied, possibly indicating a considerable broadening of the resource base as well as a dawning awareness that there were a great number of potentially exploitable biotopes in the local environments. Unfortunately, there is no information about plant resources exploited by Mousterian peoples in Andalusia.

The Catalan Pattern. For Catalonia, a somewhat similar pattern emerges. The Catalan Mousterian pattern is found in caves and shelters of varying sizes, and open-air sites are known from the terraces of major rivers and the seashore. Many of the open-air sites seem to be quarry/workshop areas, and some sites in Gerona that are now called Lower Paleolithic may well be Mousterian workshops.

There are very few well-excavated Mousterian sites, and only two (Abric Romaní, Barcelona, and Els Ermitons, Gerona) have been reasonably well published (de Lumley and Ripoll, 1962; Muñoz and Pericot, 1975). Catalan Mousterian facies include a Typical Mousterian, with at least two subvarieties (one rich in choppers and chopping tools), a Denticulate Mousterian, a possible Charentian (at Ermitons), and an as yet undescribed facies with high percentages of backed blades (probably a regional Mousterian of Acheulian Tradition). The latter facies is known, so far, only from a small exposure in Arbreda I, which has not yet been completely studied (Soler, 1976c). Quality of manufacture is extremely variable, and in some Denticulate Mousterian levels the tools are extremely crude. Some of this variation may be due to local differences in the quality of raw materials, since the Catalan Mousterians, like their Suboriental counterparts, seem to have relied almost exclusively on stone sources close to the sites they occupied.

Finished stone tools are relatively poorly represented in most sites, and in levels of the Denticulate facies they are usually scarce and widely dispersed. Abric Agut, a tiny shelter in the province of Barcelona, is unique in the extent to which its occupants utilized apparently unsuitable raw materials for making stone tools. The Agut Mousterians made much use of poor-quality, crumbly limestone (travertines and stalactite fragments) and a very flaky shale as expedient raw materials. If similar tools were present in other Catalan Mousterian horizons, they have gone unrecognized.

Extensive faunal lists are available for one Typical Mousterian horizon (level 5 at Mollet I in Gerona) and the Denticulate Mousterian horizons at Abric Romaní (a much larger shelter only half a kilometer from Abric

Agut). The varied Mollet fauna (table 4.8) does not seem to have been gathered from a single animal community, including as it does both reindeer and fallow deer, two forms that normally are not found in a single occupation level (Vila, 1976). This suggests that the excavators may have confused several levels. The fauna contains animals of a wide range of sizes and includes creatures from both open habitats and deciduous forest. If the identification of *Rangifer* is correct, the level probably accumulated during a cold stadial of the Würm/Weichsel glaciation; the rest of the fauna would be appropriate to a temperate period that was perhaps somewhat moister than the present.

For Abric Romaní, faunal lists are still not completely published. Snails (both freshwater and dry-terrestrial species) are noted in the sediments and, given their environmental requirements, it seems likely that the climate was relatively benign during the Mousterian occupations, most of which are attributed to the "Würm II/III" interstadial (de Lumley and Ripoll, 1962:7). The published mammalian fauna from the richest level (9) includes abundant *Equus caballus, Cervus elaphus,* possible *Dama, Crocuta crocuta,* and *Lynx pardina,* but with rabbits also well represented (Ripoll, personal communication; de Lumley and Ripoll, 1962; Ripoll and de Lumley, 1964). This fauna is far less varied than that from Mollet I. Neither total bone counts nor estimated minimum numbers of individuals are yet available for the Abric Romaní Mousterian. At least one hearth was found, a fireplace in a pit in level 10.

Abric Agut and Abric Romaní are both found in the east face of the Capelló, a platform of lacustrine travertines and tufas nearly 0.75 km² in area, which rises to 60 m above the Noia river. The two sites are about 500 m apart, following the wall of the Capelló. They apparently were occupied simultaneously, which implies that the inhabitants of Romaní could scarcely have been ignorant of Agut and the people who occupied it; in fact,

Table 4.8. Mammals from Mollet I, level 5

Elephas antiquus	*Dama dama*
Dicerorhinus kirchbergensis	*Panthera pardus*
D. hemitoechus	*P. leo*
Bos primigenius	*Capreolus capreolus*
Bison priscus	*Canis lupus*
Equus caballus	*Crocuta crocuta*
E. hydruntinus	*Lynx pardina*
Cervus elaphus	*Vulpes vulpes*
Ursus arctos or *prearctos*	*Erinaceus europaeus*
Sus scrofa	*Oryctolagus cuniculus*
Rangifer tarandus	

Source: Data are from Vila (1976).

it seems reasonable to suggest that Agut may have been utilized by people who lived at Romaní.

New excavations were begun at Abric Agut in 1976. Although the site has been seriously disturbed by modern clandestine excavators, areas of intact Mousterian deposits still remain. There were four superimposed Denticulate Mousterian occupations, each consisting of one or more discrete lenses of occupation debris measuring about 2 m or less in average diameter. Stone artifacts are extremely scarce in these distributions, and finished tools are even rarer. Most artifacts are unretouched flaking debris, flakes, and cores. Pieces in flint and quartzite are generally small and reasonably well finished, while those in the other raw materials (sandstone, travertine, stalactite, shale, and quartz) are surprisingly crudely made. Although the latter are recognizable as finished tools and can be sorted into classes well enough, their crude appearance suggests that the manufacturers were either unskilled or hurried, or both.

Judging from the small size of the "activity areas" at Abric Agut and the meagerness of their archaeological contents, the site must have been occupied only sporadically, for brief periods of time, by a very small number of people. Abric Romaní was most likely the major encampment occupied by people who visited Agut. We do not know if Agut was an informal way-station where people rested on their way to or from Romaní, a "playground" for Neanderthal youngsters, an area where certain people were periodically isolated from the rest of society, or a place where it was convenient to undertake some special but infrequent economic operation. A human premolar and three molars, all heavily corroded were found in 1909, and another small fragment of a tooth that seems to be human was recovered in 1976.

Although the faunal remains from Abric Agut are still being analyzed, over 4,900 bone fragments were recovered, including approximately 120 bird bones, 70 "average medium" mammal bones (including remains of *Cervus*), 35 "small medium" mammal bones (probably including a smaller deer), 80 indeterminate rodent bones (probably including dormice and microtines), 94 lagomorph bones (probably *Oryctolagus*), and 3,500 micromammal bones (probably including shrews, other insectivores, and bats). Many of the bird bones, some of the rodents, and most of the "micromammals" may be the remains of pellets regurgitated by diurnal raptorial birds that nested above the site in the tufas of the Capelló, as they do today. Very few of these tiny bones are burnt, as opposed to the lagomorph bones, many of which are charred. The lagomorphs, "average medium," and "large medium" animals are evidently human food refuse. Each category contains at least some bones showing butchering marks or traces of burning. Snails of several species were also recovered. All seem to be natural residents of the site, and probably none was a human food resource.

Excluding the birds, snails, and micromammals, I would estimate that the Abric Agut fauna from all levels totals 15–30 individual animals, that the index of diversity will prove to be quite restricted (in the range of 0.30–0.35), and that the low index is due to the concentration on rabbit as a main food item at Abric Agut. Some levels yielded no other probable "food animal" than rabbit.

A number of samples from the Agut Mousterian were subjected to flotation, in the hopes of recovering macrobotanical remains. Twelve whole or fragmentary seeds were recovered from two very localized patches in adjacent 1-m squares in one level. Kathleen Volman, of the Department of Botany, Texas A & M, who is studying the Agut macrobotanicals, found 7 of these seeds intact enough to attempt an identification; the groups certainly represented are Leguminosae (6 specimens, of which 4 may be *Vicia/Lathyrus* spp.), and Chenopodiaceae (1 specimen, possibly *Beta* sp.). We hope that a more precise identification of more of the specimens will prove possible.

All the recovered seeds are carbonized, and some of the remains are quite fragmentary. Their occurrence in restricted patches suggests to me that they were deposited in human feces which subsequently disintegrated and disappeared. As far as I know, this is the first successful attempt to recover seeds from Mousterian horizons by flotation, although there may prove to be edible macrobotanicals in the still unstudied flotation samples from the 1968–1969 field seasons at Cueva Morín.

The seeds from Abric Agut come from plant forms with wide distributions, but one characteristic they share is a tolerance for disturbed ground (paths, slopes, sandy areas, riverbanks). This suggests that plants may have been collected nearby, along the banks of the Noia and on the slope between the river and the site.

It might be argued that these seeds came from plants which grew on the site and were accidentally burned, or that they are parts of plants used as fuel. Three observations oppose these arguments. First, the plants identified do not make particularly good fuel (the vetch seeds are protected by pods), and much better combustibles would have been readily available. Second, the plants involved drop their seeds right beneath them; it seems improbable that plants from two families with different environmental requirements grew so closely together that, when burned, they dropped their seeds into the same small area. Third, a fire intense enough to char a half-dozen legume seeds would certainly have burned at least one plant entirely, if it did so, we should have recovered many more seeds.

Seeds from representatives of each plant taxon identified could have been collected simultaneously in July and August. That edible seeds of several kinds were collected at the same time may be yet another reflection of the opportunistic food-gathering strategies and eclectic tastes of Mousterian peoples.

Although I suspect that the seeds were eaten soon after collection, I cannot prove that assertion. Nevertheless, no features that might have served as storage facilities were identified at either Abric Romaní or Abric Agut.

No true hearths were found at Agut, but there is much charcoal at the site. The patterns of charring on the bones are consonant with cooking meat over an open fire. The seeds certainly were not intentionally carbonized; they may have been overroasted or accidentally charred during parching.

At Abric Agut, we have apparently recovered the remains of an ephemeral campsite or way station, visited sporadically by very small groups of people (probably five or less) who perhaps were part of the larger population that occupied nearby Abric Romaní. The purpose for which Abric Agut was utilized is still unknown, but during the course of that occupation, snacks or major meals could have been consumed, the meat often consisting of rabbit. At some time during the 24-hour period before visiting the site, an individual apparently ate a meal including legumes and grains of several species, some of which were accidentally charred before they were eaten. The charred seeds were deposited, probably in feces, on the site. This reconstruction admittedly is based entirely on circumstantial evidence, and is therefore speculative, but it is nevertheless consonant with all evidence and considered to be quite probable.

The Cantabrian Pattern. This Mousterian pattern is best known from the province of Santander, and includes many more sites and occupations than any other Mousterian pattern from the Peninsula. Cantabria offers a vast diversity of environmental zones in a relatively small space, and even during the harshest climatic episodes of the Pleistocene, it afforded a richness of exploitable resources that is unparalleled elsewhere in Iberia. Cantabria, from the Pyrenees to approximately the city of Oviedo, is a region of classic montane karst, offering innumerable caves and shelters suitable for human habitation. In fact, we know very little of open-air Mousterian occupations in Cantabria. There are certainly some disturbed quarry/workshop areas along the shore, and Unquera (Alcalde del Rio, Breuil, and Sierra, 1911) may have been an open-air hunting/butchering site, but the collections are lost and the site, along a railroad cut, seems to have been completely destroyed. A few surface scatters of Mousterian artifacts have been recognized but do not seem to be associated with any intact stratigraphy, and their significance is still unclear.

The Mousterian occupation of Cantabria evidently began quite early. At Cueva Morín, this complex first appears in levels apparently assignable to Lower Pleniglacial Würm. The earliest horizon (a Denticulate Mousterian occupation?) is associated with sediments that suggest humid, temperate conditions analogous to those at present. One Denticulate Mousterian level (lower 17) and two cleaver-flake-rich Typical Mousterian horizons (upper 17, 16) accumulated during a subsequent Lower Pleniglacial cold phase. The remaining levels, two with cleaver-flake-rich Typical (15, 14/13) and two with Denticulate Mousterian (12, 11) formed during a new warm phase, probably Hengelo (Butzer, 1971b). At El Pendo, human occupation may have begun even earlier, but there is not enough artifactual material in the earliest levels to permit their assignment to any specific complex of industries. It is clear that Cantabrian assemblages representing a single facies are relatively indifferent to major climatic change, since both Denticulate Mousterian and cleaver-flake-rich Typical may be found in deposits indicating either cold or temperate climatic conditions. There does not seem to be any direct relationship between the abundance of any specific tool type and the abundance of individual animals of any species. This implies that artifacts were not specifically tailored for use on a particular raw material. They were probably designed instead for efficiency in specific operations (such as chopping or fine slicing) that could be applied to a variety of raw materials.

The lithic industrial facies now recognized in Cantabria include the Denticulate Mousterian (at El Conde, La Flecha, El Pendo, and Morín), the Quina Charentian (Castillo Mousterian Beta), and both sidescraper-rich and "normal" variants of Typical Mousterian, either of which may be found accompanied by a regional index type (the cleaver-flake) that seems to set Cantabrian assemblages off stylistically from their counterparts elsewhere in Iberia.

There is little good flint in Cantabria, and when it occurs it is used to the utmost. Even the smallest pieces often have multiple working edges, and often three or four working edges will be found on a triangular or prismatic-sectioned piece. So-called Quinson points (triangular-sectioned pieces with two converging scraper edges meeting on one "dorsal" surface, the other two faces forming two "bases" at right angles to one another), and convergent denticulates on the same plan are quite common. The better raw materials for little tools occur as small rolled stream-cobbles, and pieces made on segments of cobbles abound. Quartzite of fine to medium granularity is a major raw material, and tools made of it show considerable virtuosity. However, in the absence of other suitable stone, coarse-grained quartzite may dominate the assemblage, as it does at El Conde in Oviedo. In Mousterian assemblages, Denticulate tools made of good raw material are smaller on the average than those of other facies. There is often a marked size dichotomy in tools from the other facies, may small implements accompanying a few really large ones. Limestone, coarse-grained quartzites, and especially ophites are used for the larger bifacial tools and most Levallois flakes. In all Cantabrian Pattern assemblages, finished tools are less abundant than unretouched pieces and cores, but artifacts usually are densely packed onto the occupation surface, so that even small exposures yield many retouched tools. Most Cantabrian Mousterian assemblages contain substantial proportions of notches and denticulates, and regional Denticulate Mousterian assemblages have a higher proportion of serrate-edged tools than is usual in other parts of the world.

Several large, flattened circular grindstones (18–20-cm diameter) were recovered from one Mousterian horizon at Castillo. Smaller grindstones are known from other occupation levels. Apparently, such objects may occur in assemblages of any facies. We do not know what material may have been processed with these implements. Dried meat, vegetable foods, and coloring matter have all been suggested.

Cantabrian Mousterians often collected highly unusual rocks and minerals, sometimes using them as blanks for tool manufacture (such as the worked quartz crystals at Castillo and an iron oxide scraper at Morín), sometimes keeping them unaltered, perhaps as curiosities (as seems to be true for the galena found in the Castillo Mousterian).

There is some evidence of fire in all facies, and in the upper Denticulate Mousterian horizon at Cueva Morín we found a single large hearth that had contained an intense fire, reddening 15–20 cm of the earth underlying it. This level (11) contained many heat-fractured ("potlidded") and burnt flint artifacts and several small fragments of bone burnt to a grayish-black (or even whitish) color, cracked, and distorted, indicating that they had been heated to at least 550–650° C (Bonucci and Graziani, 1976). While open fires regularly reach such temperatures, they are considerably higher than those indicated by charred bone earlier, and may indicate a different kind of application of fire to animal remains than has been encountered in any of the earlier cases we have examined.

Faunal assemblages from Cantabrian Pattern horizons are quite variable (table 4.9). In general, the species lists from Denticulate Mousterian levels are poorest (Morín 12, El Conde 6, La Flecha). The Castillo Beta faunal list is only partial, as I have explained elsewhere (Freeman, 1973). The nature of the (presumably) Mousterian facies represented in Lezetxiki is still not certain. The fauna from that level is extremely rich (Altuna, 1972), but I do not believe it is a reliable indication of hominid diet. The exceptional number of cave bears and other carnivores suggests that the site served as a den for these animals and that hominid occupation residues probably contributed only a small part of the faunal remains.

We still have little evidence concerning the nature of the activities undertaken in most Mousterian occupation levels. Morín upper level 17 is an exception. I have suggested elsewhere that it is a specialized (perhaps seasonal) hide-working area, and that many of the bone fragments found in the occupation level are hide-working tools or blanks for manufacturing

Table 4.9. Mammals from selected Mousterian levels in Cantabria

	Morín Upper 17	Morín 16	Morín 15	Morín 12	Lezetxiki VI	Castillo Beta	El Conde 6	La Flecha (no. of bones)
Dicerorhinus hemitoechus	2	—	—	—	—	—	—	—
D. kirchbergensis	—	—	—	—	1	1	—	—
Equus caballus	7	1	1	—	3	6	1	25
Bovinae indet.	6	1	1	—	6	5	—	18
Capra ibex	1	—	—	1	1	1	—	1
Cervus elaphus	5	1	1	—	2	16	—	11
Cervus sp.	—	—	—	—	—	7	—	—
Megaloceras sp.	—	—	—	—	1	—	—	—
Capreolus capreolus	1	—	2	—	2	—	—	—
Rupicapra rupicapra	—	—	—	—	2	—	1	—
Sus scrofa	1	—	—	—	1	—	—	—
Ursus spelaeus	—	—	—	—	13	—	—	—
Ursus arctos	—	—	—	—	2	—	—	—
Ursidae indet.	—	—	—	—	—	—	—	2
Panthera spelaea	—	—	—	—	2	—	—	—
P. pardus	—	—	—	—	1	—	—	—
Lynx lynx	—	—	—	—	1	—	—	—
Vulpes vulpes	—	—	—	—	2	—	—	—
Canis lupus	1	—	—	—	2	—	—	2
Crocuta crocuta	1	—	—	—	—	—	—	—
Meles meles	—	—	—	—	2	—	—	—
Lepus sp.	—	—	—	—	2	—	—	—
Rodentia indet.	—	—	2	—	4	—	—	—

Source: Data are from Altuna (1971, 1972, 1973), Freeman (1973, 1977), Freeman and González Echegaray (1968).

such tools (González Echegaray and Freeman, 1978; see also Semenov, 1968:156–71). In a recent article, Straus (1976) maintains that the upper level 17 fauna is only the remains of butchering operations, and that the retouching on most of the so-called bone tools is simply the result of bone-breaking for marrow extraction. However, that opinion is not substantiated by the evidence and does not accord as well with the data as does our own interpretation. The bone fragments from upper level 17 were especially selected and treated for a specific nondietary purpose. Although they undoubtedly came from carcasses that were eaten somewhere (perhaps on the unexcavated terrace in front of the site, or in one of the many other caves nearby), these bones are probably not reliable indicators of proportions of animal food in the human diet at that time. Most other Mousterian occupations at Morín have little in the way of faunal remains.

The larger faunal lists from Cantabrian Mousterians sites suggest a persisting "opportunistic" exploitation of the environment. Large "open-country" ungulates (bovids, horses) are regularly represented, and rhinos were taken with some frequency. Meat provided by these animals would have been at least as abundant as that from all other species combined, in most levels. In colder periods, the most numerous animals in the faunal lists are grassland and open-parkland species, while during warmer phases (at Castillo, for example), forest dwellers tend to increase in proportion, as one would expect. An occasional boar was taken (a piglet at Morín) but in general the more dangerous animals (bears, large felids, boars) seem to have been avoided.

Sites near broken uplands have occasional ibex and chamois, but not enough to indicate their systematic exploitation. For what it is worth, the index of size diversity for the levels where it can be calculated or estimated varies from 0.34 (the partial collection for Castillo Beta) to 0.73 (Morín upper 17), with most values at about 0.45.

There is one bird in a Denticulate Mousterian horizon in Cantabria: an alpine chough (which may not have been intentionally hunted) in El Conde 6. There are also occasional mollusks. In addition to the terrestrial forms known to frequent caves, there are two individual limpets (*Patella vulgata* and *P. aspera*) and one oyster (*Ostrea edulis*) from Morín 16. They may represent a beginning interest in the littoral and estuarine environments a short distance from the site, without any attempt to exploit them seriously. These species are easily collected, shallow-water or splash-zone residents.

There are not many individual animals in most occupation levels [the outstanding exception is Castillo, an immense site where exceptionally large exposures (100–150 m²) are available for both major Mousterian horizons]. Whether such large, intensively occupied sites as Castillo were used by larger human groups than small sites like Cueva Morín cannot now be determined. However, there is no inherent reason why the Castillo region would not support large population aggregates, at least on a seasonal basis. Most sites occupied by Iberian Mousterians are much smaller, which suggests that the social groups that occupied them were ordinarily not much larger than a single nuclear family.

Synthetic Overview:
Lower and Middle Paleolithic

If the scanty documentation available from four sites in the Central Meseta is at all typical, Middle Pleistocene Acheulean inhabitants of the Iberian Peninsula seem to have based their hunting operations in well-watered lowland areas where grasses, sedges, and reeds were the dominant ground cover. Perhaps this kind of situation was most favorable for spotting and pursuing game. Although relatively large social groups may have been able to aggregate periodically and conduct large-scale "opportunistic" game drives, and remains suggesting such activities are widespread at least in the Tajo drainage, human populations do not seem to have been large enough to require a broad resource base. Most of the meat in the Acheulean diet during this period probably consisted of elephant and rhinoceros, with wild cattle and horses providing some variety. The small numbers and small body size of other prey would have restricted the amounts of meat available from those sources. Staple food animals were the largest, slowest-breeding, slowest-maturing species, and it is probably no accident that their numbers apparently decreased significantly even in purely paleontological localities by the earlier Upper Pleistocene. There is suggestive evidence that open fires were already used for roasting and perhaps drying or smoking meat. We know nothing of the vegetable foods that probably were utilized, perhaps in great quantity, by Iberian Acheulean hunters. Our data, as far as they go, suggest that this exploitative/subsistence pattern was relatively uniform, and in my opinion nothing about this picture (other than the presence of fire) is particularly surprising or innovative when compared with the best-documented, broadly contemporary Acheulean sites in Africa (e.g., Olorgesailie, Isimila, and parts of the Olduvai sequence).

The Mousterian patterns described show both similarities to and differences from this Acheulean behavior. There is no doubt that opportunistic exploitative strategies persisted. There is no evidence to indicate any concentration on one or a few species to the neglect of others. Large numbers of animals are typically found in two situations: either there are relatively large numbers of many species, indicating intensive or long-lasting use of a particular site, or there are large numbers of the very small species (the mollusks), in which case the rest of the faunal spectrum is diverse, not impoverished. Where there are few species in the fauna, the collection is either small (El Conde 6) or biased (Castillo Beta). Nor are the species lists as diverse as they become in the Upper Paleolithic. Mousterians seem to have neglected many potential food resources in their environments, even whey they were apparently aware that those resources existed.

Some regions occupied by Mousterian peoples (e.g., Cantabria) were relatively lush and offered an abundance of large game animals all year. In such settings, Mousterian peoples could live comfortably by a combination of plant gathering and hunting the larger lowland-dwelling herbivores, and the picture of subsistence practices that emerges is not much different from our reconstruction of Acheulean behavior. However, Cantabrian Mousterians apparently did not often kill the largest, fiercest carnivores and suids, nor did they regularly invest much energy in chasing alpine animals over the difficult terrain of their upland habitat. Even so, they were interested enough in the diversity of nearby resources to take such animals when they came in contact with them, and occasionally to exploit the most readily available marine creatures in the immediate littoral zone.

Spanish Mousterian hunters explored aspects of the hominid niche that were apparently ignored by their mid-Pleistocene ancestors and, in so doing, established a solid human presence in areas that evidently had not been permanently colonized before. The southern Mediterranean shore of Iberia probably was always rather poorly endowed for big-game hunting. However, to foodgatherers who had learned to expand their resource base by increasing their reliance on rabbits, rodents, shellfish, birds, and seeds when there were not enough large mammals to provide the protein they needed, even the poorest parts of Andalusia provided a rich larder. The lesson was learned well by Mousterian peoples along the Mediterranean coast.

Some areas, such as the lower Ebro basin, seem to have remained inhospitable, but Iberian Mousterians managed an effective colonization of much of the peninsula by tailoring their tastes (though apparently not their tool kits) to each region's major offerings. It is no surprise that regional differences in lifeways became much more marked during the Mousterian than they ever had been before. If we restrict our vision to stone tool assemblages, it is easy to overlook those differences, though they are present. However, they stand out quite clearly once we focus on the total constellation of reconstructed behavioral systems.

I do not deny that Acheulean assemblages from far-removed places may have quite distinctive characteristics. However, one can also find extremely similar Acheulean assemblages from widely separated areas (some assemblages from India look a good deal like some African or Spanish ones, for example). Regional distinctions are large-scale and very coarse-grained; the differentiated areas are nearly continental in size. In the Mousterian, by contrast, regional diversity has become much more finely focused.

The diet of Mousterian peoples differed from region to region. In lush areas like Cantabria, where humans could concentrate on the resources that gave the highest yield for a tolerable investment (given the available technological and organizational means at hand), meals probably did not vary much: rhinoceros, "beef," and horsemeat may have been the usual sources of meat. In poorer environments, such as Catalonia or Andalusia, the subsistence base was wider, and there probably was more meal-to-meal variety in meat consumption than in Cantabria. Sometimes rabbits and rodents may have served as the staple meat for considerable periods, and there may have been long stretches of time when inland populations in these regions had little or no meat in their diets, a situation that surely was rare (or unknown) in Cantabria. It is puzzling that no subterranean storage features have yet been recognized in any Iberian Mousterian site. Mousterian "storage pits" are known from French sites (Peyrony, 1930, 1934) and I expect that they will eventually be found in Spain.

It is difficult to identify critical subsistence resources for this period. In Cantabria, Barcelona, and Gerona, at least, water was relatively abundant throughout the Pleistocene. Availability of water may periodically have been a limiting factor for human occupation in other regions, and perhaps kept people out of some regions entirely.

Although this overview of food habits is based on a series of insights into short-term behavior patterns from the study of a few individual occupation levels, these reconstructions take on an appearance of long-term normalcy that is almost certain to be deceptive. We really do not know whether rabbit was a dietary staple at Abric Agut all year round, or if it was a lean-season resource used only when all else failed. Nor can we pinpoint those critical food resources whose absence would have precluded continued human occupation in a region. Perhaps the question is trivial, for who is to say whether the foods one eats for 11 months of the year are more critical to survival than the lean-season rations that permit human life to endure during the remaining month when the normal staples are exhausted. It may well be that, given the technological means and population sizes of that time, Mousterian subsistence practices used so little of the potential of any region that any single resource could have been sacrificed without causing famine. Certainly that seems true for Cantabria.

Diet in the Earlier Upper Paleolithic (from ca. 35,000 to 18,000 B.C.)

Although there are many Upper Paleolithic occupations in much of the Iberian Peninsula, they are mostly known from inadequately controlled excavations. The Cantabrian region is the single outstanding exception to this rule. Interest in sites in the province of Gerona is now reviving, and we may hope to learn much about Upper Paleolithic behavioral adaptations in that region within the next few years. It is still too early to predict the sorts of knowledge to be gained, but one can say with confidence that regional differences between patterns of Upper Paleolithic complexes do exist and seem to become more marked over time. However, from the Chatelperronian to the Solutrean, Cantabria remains the major source region for Upper Paleolithic studies.

There is only one unmistakable Chatelperronian level in the Iberian Peninsula: Morín 10 (González Echegaray et al., 1971). Faunal remains from that level are too scarce for our purposes and obviously will not support claims that the appearance of the first Upper Paleolithic industrial complexes in Spain was marked by a major break in subsistence strategies.

Aurignacian occupations are relatively numerous in Cantabria: there are nine horizons in Santander, three in Oviedo, and three in Basque country for which estimated minimum numbers of individuals of each mammalian species in the fauna are now available (Altuna, 1972; Freeman, 1973; Straus, 1977). Faunal lists for the six levels at Cueva Morín also include counts of mollusks by species (Madariaga de la Campa, 1971); since this site is generally representative of the Iberian Aurignacian, I shall concentrate on it.

There are two broad kinds of Aurignacian assemblages at Morín. The earlier levels include assemblages designated "Archaic Aurignacian," which are rich in Dufour bladelets and nosed and keeled endscrapers. An important complex of structures, including a semi-subterranean hut foundation, a posthole alignment, and a series of graves, was found in one of these horizons (Freeman and González Echegaray, 1970; González Echegaray et al., 1971, 1973). This level (8a) is the most suitable representative of the Cantabrian Archaic Aurignacian for our purposes. A later, Classical Aurignacian is also found at Morín, in levels 7, 6, and lower 5. [These assemblages are described in detail by González Echegaray et al. (1971, 1973).] The fauna of lower level 5, typical of the Classical Aurignacian, is described in tables 4.10 and 4.11. These two varieties of Aurignacian industries may be either facies or phases: we still cannot say which is most likely, although at Morín there is some temporal difference between them. The Archaic Aurignacian is found in temperate deposits (probably representing the Denekamp/Arcy interstadial), and the various stages of Classical Aurignacian embrace two subsequent cold episodes and an intervening warm period in Upper Pleniglacial Würm.

As representative of the available information concerning Upper Perigordian (Gravettian) horizons, I have selected two other levels at Morín: upper level 5, deposited under cold climatic conditions dating to 18,760 ($\pm$ 340) B.C., and level 4, in temperate deposits. These levels contained a very late kind of Perigordian, probably best compared to the phase called Perigordian IV in France (González Echegaray and Freeman, 1978; González Echegaray et al., 1971, 1973). For three other Gravettian levels in Iberia (one at Bolinkoba and two at Lezetxiki, all in Basque

Table 4.10. Mammals from selected Aurignacian and Perigordian horizons in Cantabria (estimated minimum number of individuals)

	Morín "structures"	Morín lower 5	Morín upper 5	Morín 4
Elephas sp.	—	—	—	1
Equus caballus	2	3	4	4
Bovinae indet.	3	3	3	2
Capra ibex	1	2	3	3
Cervus elaphus	7	10	9	10
Capreolus capreolus	1	6	5	4
Rupicapra rupicapra	1	1	1	1
Sus scrofa	2	—	1	—
Panthera pardus	—	1	—	1
Lynx lynx	—	1	—	1
Felis sylvestris	—	1	1	1
Vulpes vulpes	—	1	—	1
Canis lupus	1	1	1	1
Crocuta crocuta	—	—	1	—
Lepus europaeus	—	1	1	1
Talpa sp.	—	—	—	1
Arvicola sp.	—	1	1	1
Rodentia indet.	—	—	—	2
Species Diversity	0.46	0.59	0.57	0.57

Source: Data are from Altuna (1971).

Table 4.11. Mollusks from selected Aurignacian and Perigordian levels in Cantabria

	Morín "structures"	Morín lower 5	Morín upper 5	Morín 4
Terrestrial forms				
Helix lapicida	1	—	—	—
Hyalinia sp.	1	—	—	—
Indet. terrestrial gastropods	8	—	—	—
Marine forms				
Patella vulgata	2	—	—	2
P. aspera	3	—	—	—
Patella sp.	7	1 (+)	1 (+)	3
Littorina littorea	5	—	—	—
L. obtussata	—	—	—	1
Monodonta lineata	1	—	—	—
Nassa reticulata	—	—	—	1
Crassostrea angulata	10	—	—	1
Ostrea edulis	—	—	—	2
Indet. oyster	9	—	—	—
Scrobicularia plana	3	—	—	—
Solen sp.	1	—	—	—
Mytilus edulis	2	—	—	—
Tapes decussatus	7	—	—	—
Cardium sp.	—	—	—	1

Source: Data are from Madariaga de la Campa (1971).

Note: (+) indicates at least the preceding number, perhaps one or two more.

country) there are published lists of estimated minimum numbers of mammals (Straus, 1977), but our information concerning them is still not as complete as it is for the Morín horizons.

In the earlier Upper Paleolithic horizons just described, almost all our evidence comes from faunal lists, even though hearths have been described for some levels. These vary from small basin-shaped depressions, sometimes containing fire-cracked rock, to the more complex hearth with sloping draft trench found on the floor of the Aurignacian hut in level 8a at Cueva Morín. The latter implies a rather sophisticated if impressionistic appreciation of the physics of combustion in enclosed areas, and the relationship to seasonal changes in draft patterns along the cave floor (González Echegaray and Freeman, 1978; González Echegaray et al., 1971). Hearths associated with the hut and burial complex in this Aurignacian level contained charred, checked, and sometimes calcined bone fragments, suggesting that temperatures were as high as any that can be attained in simple open fireplaces, but there is no evidence of more intense heating, even in the hearth with attached draft trench. Two irregular "storage pits" (whose functions are not as clear as their name implies) were found in another Aurignacian level at Morín. The major dimension of one was 40 cm, that of the other 1 m, and both were about 0.5 m deep and absolutely jammed with fragmentary bones and stone tools. The fill they contained was clearly not stored food remains but "garbage." However, true food-storage pits are sometimes jammed with debris just before a campsite is abandoned.

In fill deliberately packed between two of the graves in the Morín structural level, we found several fragmentary hazelnut shells next to a pair of large double-pitted hammer/grindstones. Suggestive as this find was, it is not entirely reliable as dietary evidence. Some of the nutshells had been gnawed open by a rodent, perhaps a microtine (see Bang and Dahlström, 1975:125–29), and it is therefore possible that the Aurignacian cave occupants, piling earth near a grave, accidentally incorporated the remains of rodent meals in their work.

The species lists (table 4.10) are more diverse than is usual for reliably excavated Mousterian horizons in Cantabria, and the body size of animals appears to become more diversified over time. In the Morín series, the "size diversity" index increases from 0.46 to 0.57–0.59, and for two Gravettian horizons (Bolinkoba E and Lezetxiki III) the index varies from 0.44 to 0.66. Most individuals in any level at Morín are generally those with "average medium" body sizes (goat, deer, boar). Bovids would usually have provided more meat than any other species, but there would have been more variety in meat meals than in the past; beef would have made up only 40–50% of the total, deer would have provided from 25 to 35%, horsemeat about 15%, and other mammals together around 10% of the meat available for consumption. Morín 4 is unusual: remains of an elephant were recovered from that level, and would have yielded more meat than all other animals combined; but elephants and rhinos have also been found in Aurignacian and Perigordian horizons elsewhere, so this case is not unique. Compared with Mousterian levels, these faunal lists include more small animals. Even though small animals were apparently not major food sources, this evidence is interesting because it parallels the information provided by the mollusks (table 4.11).

Most levels of this age contained few or no mollusks, but there are important exceptions such as the Morín "structure" level. That horizon contained at least 10 species of marine mollusks, and although no species is abundant enough to have been more than a very minor constituent of Aurignacian diet, enough specimens are present that they probably cannot be explained away as curios collected on the beach. Oysters are the most numerous shellfish, followed by limpets, carpet shells (*Tapes*), and periwinkles (*Littorina*). The species list implies that the resources of the splash zone, the intertidal zone, both rocky and sandy coastal bottoms, and muddy estuaries were regularly but not intensively exploited. While all of these forms can be collected in shallow water, some are burrowers; they are never visible and would certainly have had to be dug or raked from bottom sediments. There is no evidence of burning on the shells, which is intriguing. Although many of the species can be eaten raw, limpets are virtually impossible to chew if uncooked. Given the state of the shells and the nature of the fireplaces we recovered, the only likely cooking techniques are quick grilling atop hot stones or boiling, and the latter is the only process that would tenderize limpets adequately.

In sum, these data suggest a continued opportunism in food-gathering strategies, but one in which a much wider variety of resources was taken than had earlier been the case. These prehistoric Cantabrians were "settling into" the region, to use a phrase coined by Braidwood and Willey (1962).

Until some 20,000 years ago, the impact of humans on their environment in Iberia was the merest foreshadowing of later disruptive effects. Even so, at no time in their history can hominids be ignored as potential agents of environmental change: it is suggestive that local populations of cave-dwelling carnivores, in direct competition with humans for food and living space, declined or vanished by the earliest Upper Paleolithic, and elephants and rhinos suffered a similar decline soon after. Nevertheless, humans still were not exerting strong pressures on their environment. They seem to have survived by long-term reliance on the same dietary staples that had served their Mousterian predecessors, supplementing them from time to time with a number of peripheral resources. Their numbers had not increased to the point where there was any real danger that a reasonable investment of energy in subsistence-related activities might not be repaid by the expectable yield. In a sense, Mousterian adaptations seem to have been designed to harmonize with the natural setting, disturbing it as little as possible in the process.

The unprecedented extent to which Archaic Aurignacian humans changed the sites they lived in shows that Upper Paleolithic people had a fundamentally different attitude toward their environment. They began to practice major alterations on their surroundings to tailor them more closely to their needs, rather than accepting natural conditions as given, as their predecessors had done. For example, when they first occupied Cueva Morín, they cleared away literally tons of accumulated debris from previous occupations, leveling the floor and changing the shape of the available space to suit them. They then dug pits, huts, postholes, and other structures into the cave floor, altering the site surface in ways Mousterian peoples had never done. Their behavior seems to indicate an attitude of dominance by mankind over nature. With this development, a chain of action and reaction was started which would have important implications for human survival. A new awareness of the variety of nature, first acquired during the earlier Upper Paleolithic, was soon put to serious use.

Diet during Later Phases of the Upper Paleolithic (from ca. 18,000 to 8.500 B.C.)

A number of carbon-14 dates on Lower Magdalenian horizons in Cantabria cluster near 14,000 B.C., which sets a *terminus ante quem* to Solutrean occupation in that region, at least. The earliest Solutrean assemblages in Spain are typologically comparable to the French Middle or Late Solutrean, depending on the particular region in question. [Les Mallaetes in Valencia may have an Early Solutrean horizon; the level dates to 19,760 B.C. Unfortunately, the fauna from this site has not been studied (Fortea Pérez and Jordá Cerdá, 1976).] The so-called Iberian Solutrean, characterized by small, bifacially retouched, stemmed points, certainly deserves recognition as a distinctive pattern or set of related patterns; such assemblages extend across Iberia to the Portuguese coast south of the Cantabrian mountains.

The classic Iberian Solutrean site is still Parpalló, in Valencia. The earliest Solutrean levels there date to approximately 18,200 B.C., but the stemmed-point levels are probably later, as at Les Mallaetes, where similar artifacts are dated to 14,350 B.C. (Fortea Pérez and Jordá Cerdá, 1976). Unfortunately, no detailed study of the mammals from Parpalló has yet appeared. At best, one can document the presence and apparent relative abundance of bones from each species, from Pericot Garcia's monograph (1942). Rabbit and ibex are said to be extremely numerous, with horses and red deer next in order of importance. The list of mammals is quite varied, and my estimate of the index of size diversity suggests considerable spread, due to the abundance of small elements. I am confident that the diversity index would not be less than about 0.45, and while it seems likely to range as high as 0.55, I am less confident of the upper limit, which could easily go as high as 0.65.

The report on the mollusks from this site (table 4.12) is somewhat more useful. Mollusks from the Parpalló "middle Solutrean" level are extremely varied, including forms from estuaries, the splash zone, and both rocky and sandy/muddy bottoms. Burrowing species are well represented, but most surprising is the presence of fair quantities of free-swimming forms that live at some depth below low tide (the scallops *Pecten* and *Chlamys*). Their numbers suggest that they probably were intentionally exploited, which

Table 4.12. Mollusks from Solutrean and Magdalenian faunas at Parpalló

	Solutrean	*Magdalenian "III"*
Helix sp.	11	10
Neritina sp.	6	—
Patella sp.	2	—
Cerithium vulgatum	—	3
Trivia sp.	—	1
Littorina obtussata	—	1
Dentalim sp.	147	6
Nassa mutabilis	12	—
N. incrassata	1	—
N. gibbosula	2	—
Purpura lapillus	52	1
Cassis sp.	1	—
Murex brandaris	—	1
Turritella sp.	1	6
Melanopsis sp.	7	2
Albea candidissima	—	1
Lucina sp.	—	1
Pectunculus sp.	4	15
Arca sp.	1	—
Cardium edule	9	38
C. erinaceum	6	2
C. exiguum	1	—
C. oblongum	—	2
C. tuberculatum	—	5
Lutraria lutraria	1	1
Chlamys sp.	3	2
Pecten jacobaeus	20	23
P. maximus	10	11
Donax trunculus	—	2

Source: Data are from Pericot García (1942).

would require free-diving or the use of nets. Dogwinkles (*Purpura*) and cockles (*Cardium*) are probably also of some dietary relevance. Several kinds of small burrowing snails are represented, but there is one form (*Neritina*) which is so small that it seems unlikely to have been gathered for its nutritive value. Instead, it may have come to Parpalló in a load of the seaweed on which it grazes. Seaweeds could have had any of several uses: larger mollusks could be packed for transport in damp seaweed, or steamed in seaweed over an open fire, and of course many varieties of marine algae are themselves highly nutritious and quite palatable when cooked. In any case, the range of molluscan species is broader than that for any other Spanish Solutrean horizon with which I am familiar, and the fauna as a whole suggests that the Parpalló Solutreans were exploiting a greater variety of littoral and terrestrial habitats than their Cantabrian contemporaries.

A second Iberian Solutrean site, the cave of Ambrosio in Almería, had two levels with tools like those from Parpalló (one of the Ambrosio horizons contained large hearths) and a fauna in which rabbit was the predominant animal (Ripoll Perelló, 1961). Apparently, concentration on rabbit is a recurrent feature of Paleolithic subsistence strategies in the Mediterranean region. There is a rather small faunal list for another site, Cau de les Goges in Gerona, but this is perhaps expectable, since it was excavated many years ago. The list is of interest primarily because it contains the cold-climate indicator *Mammuthus primigenius,* the woolly mammoth. Evidently, this site was occupied when the climate was cold enough for the mammoth to survive in Gerona. Rabbits were also recovered from this occupation.

There are considerable differences among Cantabrian Solutrean faunal assemblages (table 4.13). Some species lists are extensive: from Altamira, for example, we have at least 12 mammalian species and 2 or 3 kinds of birds. The faunal collection, recently restudied, also included about 300 *Patella vulgata* and about 75 *Littorina littorea* shells, although this is probably a smaller number than the excavators recovered (Altuna and Straus, 1975; Breuil and Obermaier, 1935:178–96). Other lists, like that for El Cierro in Asturias, are much more restricted. Morín level 3 falls between these two extremes. High proportions of forest-dwelling forms are found in most levels in Santander and Asturias, but in Basque sites alpine animals may be the predominant forms. The large number of ibex in Bolinkoba D suggests some concentration on that species, but most meat would have been provided by bovines and equids in almost all of the Cantabrian levels (El Cierro is the exception).

The size diversity index also seems to show two distinct exploitative patterns: one is a reasonably wide-spectrum hunting strategy, and diversity indices for such horizons as Morín 3, Altamira, and Bolinkoba D (table

Table 4.13. Fauna from selected Solutrean horizons

	Altamira	Morín 3	El Cierro	Bolinkoba D	Aitzbitarte	Cau de les Goges	Parpalló
Mammuthus primigenius	—	—	—	—	—	×	!
Equus caballus	8	2	3	1	3	×	×
Bovinae indet.	5	1	2	3	2	—	!!
Capra ibex	2	1	1	16	1	—	!
Cervus elaphus	20	5	21	2	9	×	—
Rangifer tarandus	1	—	—	—	1	—	×
Capreolus capreolus	1	3	1	—	1	—	—
Sus scrofa	2	—	—	—	—	—	?
Rupicapra rupicapra	2	—	—	2	6	—	×
Phoca cf. *vitulina*	1	—	—	—	—	—	—
Ursus sp.	5	—	—	2	—	—	×
Lynx lynx	—	—	—	—	—	×	×
Vulpes vulpes	2	—	—	6	1	—	×
Canis lupus	—	1	—	—	—	—	—
Meles meles?	—	—	—	7	—	—	—
Mustela nivalis	—	—	—	—	3	—	—
Mustela putorius	—	—	—	—	1	—	—
Mustela erminea	—	—	—	—	1	—	—
Lepus sp.	—	—	—	—	—	—	?
Oryctolagus cuniculus	×	—	—	—	—	×	!!
Misc. Rodentia	—	1	—	16	105	—	—
Misc. Insectivora	—	1	—	—	67	—	—
Misc. Aves	3	1	—	—	—	—	—
Pisces indet.	—	—	—	—	—	—	?
Index of Species Diversity	0.49	0.56	0.24	0.42	0.21		

Source: Data are from Altuna (1971, 1972), Altuna and Strauss (1975), Pericot García (1942), Soler García (1976a), and Strauss (1974).

Note: Estimated minimum numbers of individuals are given, where known. Presence is indicated by ×, and abundance by !

4.13) are moderately high (0.42–0.56). Despite the large number of caprids at Bolinkoba, the total of individual animals is reasonably uniformly spread over several size categories.

The other pattern is that illustrated at El Cierro, where the size diversity index is very low (0.24) because 75% of the animals in the level are red deer (which could have provided almost 60% of the available meat in this horizon). This may indicate the beginning of the concentrated exploitation of one or a few species that I have called wild-harvesting (Freeman, 1973:39, 1975a:255).

I distrust the index as an indicator of specialization in hunting strategies at Aitzbitarte, however; the number of rodents and insectivores is so high that it swamps the larger elements. The small index in the Aitzbitarte case may be an artifact of the excavators' confusing animals living in the site or brought in by raptorial birds with species that were human prey.

Earlier I had thought that the first evidence for wild-harvesting occurred in Lower Magdalenian occupations, but this picture is changing as a result of L. Straus's Solutrean studies and Altuna's revision of key faunal collections. In the Solutrean, this strategic exploitative shift seems to have been largely restricted to terrestrial resources; mollusks are usually rare or absent from the faunal assemblages, and even where they are quite abundant, as at Cueto de la Mina or Altamira, they do not seem to form concentrated shell-heaps.

Some levels, like that at Aitzbitarte, have a good representation of burrow-dwelling and nocturnal carnivores. These creatures were present in Aurignacian and Perigordian levels, but more sporadically. They may have been sought primarily as sources of pelts rather than food.

Hunting such creatures with any hope of success requires a thorough knowledge of their characteristics and habits, and special tools and techniques for each species. The Solutrean period marks the earliest time when one can make a case for such "resource-oriented" rather than "technique-oriented" adaptations, in my opinion. In Solutrean assemblages, special tool types, such as small tanged and stemmed weapon points, make their appearance in considerable numbers, and the special forms in the Iberian Solutrean may in fact be related to the hunting of small game. Traps, which must be specially designed for the species they are to catch, were probably required to take the furbearing carnivores. Before the Solutrean, the evolution of lithic assemblages seems to lead to the more efficient adaptation of different kinds of tools to different kinds of primary operations (slicers become better slicers, crushers better for crushing, and so on), regardless of the nature of the specific resource on which that operation was performed. From the Solutrean onward, we have increasing evidence for the special tailoring of specific tools to particular resources.

Once toolkits are specifically designed with a particular set of resources in mind, assemblages from regions with markedly different sets of important resources are bound to reflect that difference in their makeup. This must result in more marked and obvious distinctions between assemblages representing different regional patterns than had existed before, when tools were tailored to operations rather than resources. That, in fact, seems to be true for Solutrean (and later) interregional differences in France, but the evidence outside Cantabria is still not abundant enough to permit us to further define patterns or subregional style zones in the later Upper Paleolithic in Spain.

The evidence we have suggests that outside Cantabria, dietary practices during the Magdalenian followed the earlier Solutrean model, perhaps expanding the resource base even further at sites like Parpalló (tables 4.12, 4.13). The "Magdalenian III" horizon at Parpalló has been dated at about 12,850 B.C. (Fortea Pérez and Jordá Cerdá, 1976), which seems too recent to be equated with the French Magdalenian III, but some Cantabrian dates also suggest a long survival of this cultural manifestation, which may prove to be a facies rather than a phase of the Magdalenian. *Dama* (fallow deer) is probably present in this level (Pericot García, 1942:268–72). At Bora Gran (Gerona) a relatively diverse Late Magdalenian faunal list is reported, including reindeer and the predictable rabbit. (The level has been dated to about 9,520 B.C. ± 500 years.) Magdalenian levels in Basque country also seem to follow a regional trend, in which there are often good proportions of alpine animals in an otherwise varied faunal assemblage (table 4.14). However, these levels may prove to be similar to that from Rascaño discussed below.

There are occasional fish and bird bones in several Magdalenian horizons, and rare remains of crustaceans and sea urchins in others. The birds identified include long-legged wading species, suggesting that fowling may have taken place along coasts and estuaries. Salmon/trout vertebrae and bones of perchlike fish are among the documented fish remains. Although Cantabrian Upper Paleolithic peoples are likely to have known about the periodic spawning runs of species such as salmon, eels, and lamprey, fish bones are never reported in great numbers. If these species were harvested while spawning, their skeletons were disposed of outside the sites. There is no doubt that late Paleolithic peoples were extremely interested in birds and fish. There are numerous depictions of salmonids, pleuronectids (flatfishes), birds, and eels in mobile art and wall art.

The case for specialized wild-harvesting adaptations, in which one or a few very productive species are exploited at the expense of others [pushed back in time by Straus (1977) to the Solutrean], will stand or fall largely on the results of new excavations. The current work of G. Clark and L. Straus at La Riera, of A. Moure at Tito Bustillo, and the recent excavations of J. González Echegaray and I. Barandiarán Maestú at Rascaño will certainly contribute essential evidence on the topic.

Table 4.14. Mammalian fauna from selected Magdalenian horizons

	El Juyo 1978/79		Altamira	Bora Gran	Ermittia	Morín 2	Tito Bustillo		
	6	4					1a	1b	1c
Equus caballus	2	2	4	X	1	3	3	4	3
Bovinae indet.	1	2	4	—	1	1	2	1	2
Capra ibex	3	2	1	—	13	3	6	6	3
Cervus elaphus	38	17	19	X	3	9	9	15	17
Rangifer tarandus	—	—	—	X	2	1	—	1	—
Capreolus capreolus	2	3	2	—	1	2	1	—	—
Rupicapra rupicapra	—	—	2	—	2	3	2	4	1
Sus scrofa	1	1	—	X	2	2	—	—	—
Phoca hispida	—	—	—	—	—	—	1	—	1
Phoca vitulina	—	—	—	—	—	—	1	—	—
Panthera pardus	—	1(?)	—	—	—	—	—	—	—
Lynx	—	—	—	X[a]	—	—	—	—	1[b]
Canis lupus	1	1	—	—	—	—	—	1	—
Vulpes vulpes	—	1	—	—	1	—	1	1	1
Mustela erminea	—	—	—	—	—	—	—	1	—
Mustela putorius	1	—	—	—	—	—	—	—	—
Lepus sp.	—	—	—	—	1	1	—	1	—
Oryctolagus cuniculus	—	—	—	X	—	—	1	—	—
Erinaceus europaeus	1	1	—	—	—	—	1	—	1
Misc. Rodentia	X	X	—	—	3	1	5	5	12
Misc. Insectivora	X	X	—	—	1	5	1	—	1
Species Diversity	0.23	0.36	0.39	—	0.36	0.49	0.54	0.44	0.46

Source: Data are from Altuna (1971), Altuna and Straus (1975), Klein (n.d.), Moure et al. (1978), Soler Garcia (1976b), and Straus (1975, 1977).
Note: Estimated minimum numbers of individuals are given, where known. Presence is indicated by X.
[a] *Lynx lynx.*
[b] *Lynx pardina.*

Although some Cantabrian "Earlier Magdalenian" horizons (broadly equivalent typologically to the Magdalenian III in France) yielded varied faunas, there is a sizable group for which faunal lists are restricted and in which a single species provides 60% or more of the individual animals represented. That is the case for level 6 at El Juyo (1978/79 excavations), dated ca. 13,000 B.C., and one level at Altamira (table 4.14), dated to around 14,000 B.C. In all horizons at El Juyo, red deer would have provided the bulk of available meat; even at Altamira, *Cervus* would have yielded more meat than any other species. The size diversity indices reflect this specialization; they range from 0.23 to 0.39 at absolute maximum.[2]

There is a major difference between the subsistence practices documented for Magdalenian levels and those indicated by the El Cierro fauna. Magdalenian deposits often contain great numbers of mollusks of one or a few species, enough that the excavators refer to the levels as shell middens. At El Juyo, level 8 (the upper part of level IV in the older literature) is such a midden, consisting mostly of *Patella vulgata* and *Littorina littorea*. Janssens and González Echegaray described the level as follows:

The study of the food remains in the ash layers of the site indicates that the inhabitants of El Juyo primarily subsisted on shellfish, meat from the hunt being of secondary importance. The great proportional representation of molluscs with respect to slaughtered animals (cervids, bovids, horses, etc.) is manifestly evident, to the point that the richest levels (IV–VI in Trench I and III–IV in Trench II) were true shell middens composed of thousands and thousands of shellfish remains: *Patella* and *Littorina*. (1958:86)

At Altamira, too, the Magdalenian III levels yielded abundant shellfish remains (Breuil and Obermaier, 1935:180). G. Clark sampled and dated an apparently Magdalenian shell midden in Asturias, which contained abundant *Patella* and *Littorina*. The midden at La Lloseta was dated to 13,706 B.C. ± 412, consonant with an Earlier Magdalenian age of deposition (G. Clark, 1971:238, 246). This site is coastal, and El Juyo and Altamira are only about 5 km from the present coast. It seems safe to conclude that such sites document the practice of wild-harvesting, which had been extended to selected marine resources (as well as terrestrial ones) by around 14,000 B.C., and that this practice continued in some sites in Cantabria throughout the Magdalenian. However, we must be cautious about the suggestion that meat played a lesser part than shellfish in the diet at El Juyo. The mammals in El Juyo 8 represent more than 4,000 kg of potentially edible meat. It would take 80,000–150,000 limpets to match this.

Not all Magdalenian faunal lists lend themselves to the "wild-harvesting" interpretation. Some levels (such as Morín 2) have varied faunal collections, implying broad-based subsistence patterns. At Tito Bustillo, the spectrum of mammalian resources in the three divisions of level 1 widens with time, and comes to include 2 kinds of seals as well as 9 terrestrial animals. Moure (personal communication) has recovered an unidentified seed from these levels, which also contain 15 molluscan species (the greatest number from any single Upper Paleolithic level in the Cantabrian region). However, enough mollusks in two of the species have been recovered to suggest that wild-harvesting techniques were being applied to coastal resources (table 4.15). Some of the mollusks are so small that they probably entered the site attached to seaweed (Madariaga de la Campa, 1976).

For some time, a seasonal aspect to wild-harvesting has been suspected. It seems possible that Magdalenian hunters might seasonally have entered the broken uplands of Cantabria to concentrate on capturing the "alpine" species, ibex and chamois. Rascaño, a specialized ibex-hunting camp during the Lower Magdalenian, would represent this stage of the year's

Table 4.15. Nonmammalian fauna from selected Magdalenian horizons in Cantabria

	Altamira	Morín 2	Tito Bustillo 1a, 1b, 1c
Terrestrial gastropods	—	1 (+)	—
Patella vulgata	very many	4	3,365
Patella sp.	—	7	—
Calyptraea chinensis	—	—	1
Littorina littorea	very many	—	1,907
L. obtussata	—	—	172
Cyclostrema serpuloides	—	—	1
Gibbula sp.	—	—	1
Nassa reticulata	—	—	11
N. incrassata	—	—	2 (+)
Purpura lapillus	—	—	5
Aporrhais pes-pelicani	—	—	1
Buccinum sp.	rare	—	—
Trivia europaea	—	—	28
Mytilus edulis	—	4	17
Tapes decussatus	—	2	—
Scrobicularia plana	—	1	—
Cardium norvegicum	—	—	1
Cardium sp.	—	1	1
Pecten maximus	—	—	2
Crustacea indet.	—	—	several
Pisces indet.	several	—	several
Aves indet.	several	—	—

Source: Data are from Breuil and Obermaier (1935), Madariaga de la Campa (1971, 1975, 1976).

activities. At Rascaño, there are enormous concentrations of ibex bones, some still articulated (González Echegaray, 1977). The station is clearly a hunting/butchering camp, where the prey from intensive hunts were dismembered, the carcasses stripped of the choicest cuts, and the meat possibly processed for consumption elsewhere. (The light weight of a gutted ibex carcass would permit its transport from the kill-spot to the site, which may have been located close to some natural or artificial trap.) "Near-industrial" quantities of meat were processed at Rascaño, as I understand it.

At other times, the population or some segment of it may have moved to coastal sites like El Juyo to gather shellfish (which, because they are so perishable and are toxic when spoiled, were probably consumed immediately) and to hunt red deer (and possibly to prepare the meat for storage and future consumption). It is suggestive that red deer are most densely aggregated and easiest to hunt during the rutting season in September–October, and that this period coincides with the maximum spring tides during the autumnal equinox, when shellfish would have been easiest to gather. However, there is no evidence yet for seasonality in the faunal inventories from the most recent (1978/79) excavations at El Juyo. The site may have been used as a base camp or periodically revisited during the year (or we may still find evidence that it was a seasonal station as analysis progresses). Naturally, subsistence activities at almost any season might have included variably intensive plant-collecting, perhaps by groups of people who also actively engaged in hunting.

Large, decorated caves like Altamira and Castillo might have served as periodic centers of assembly where ceremonies were conducted on behalf of the congregated population of a large surrounding area. When not engaged in intensive seasonal activities, Magdalenian peoples might have lived in smaller social units in base camps where the accumulated surplus of the seasonal "harvests" was consumed. This is one possible explanation for the extremely varied faunal lists from some Magdalenian sites.

If this model is appropriate, over the course of a year the diet of most Magdalenians could have been quite varied, including several different kinds of plant foods, many varieties of meat and shellfish, and at least some sea urchins, crustaceans, and birds. Red deer seems to have been the major meat staple, over the long run. During the periods when particular wild resources were being harvested, meals might have been rather monotonous.

There is no evidence that Magdalenian peoples prepared their food any differently from their Solutrean predecessors. Large open hearths in firepits are found in some sites, and smaller ones, surrounded by rings of stones, are noted at others. The very large quantities of shellfish in some sites, and the small size of some species that probably were eaten, are strong circumstantial indications that boiling was a regularly used cooking technique, and this in turn suggests that soups and stews probably were prepared. No suitable containers have survived, but liquids can be boiled over an open fire in a skin or gut bag, a wooden trough, or a bark bucket, all of which are extremely perishable. It is also possible to boil liquids without subjecting the container to direct heat; heated stones are simply placed into the liquid. (This practice survives today among Spanish Basques.)

During the later Upper Paleolithic, Cantabrian populations began to use certain resources intensively, at least on a periodic basis. There is direct evidence of the effects of increased human pressure on these resources. Madariaga de la Campa (1976) summarizes studies which show a steady decrease in the average length of limpets (*Patella vulgata*) in Paleolithic levels at Castillo, from 48 mm in Aurignacian levels to 42 mm in the Magdalenian. While a few very large specimens still occur in the Tito Bustillo Late Magdalenian fauna, the average size of the species at that site is only 39.2 mm. Average annual size increments are known for the species in Scotland, where individuals reach a length of 22.5 mm their first year, 38 mm their second, 43 mm the third, and 46.5 mm the fourth (Madariaga de la Campa, 1975:94–96, 1976:211–12, 221). These calculations suggest that Aurignacian food-gatherers were collecting specimens about 4 years old on the average, but by the Late Magdalenian, local population turnover took place every 2 years. We know from other evidence that maximum population size for this species lags a year behind the maximum ratio of *Fucus* algae to individuals, which suggests that if populations were extensively cropped in a particular year, the second year following would probably be the best time to harvest them again (Chapman, 1964). During the post-Paleolithic Azilian and Asturian, the mean size of individual limpets in some sites is so low as to suggest annual cropping, perhaps combined with special techniques for encouraging the local accumulation of spawn on easily collectible substrates (G. Clark, 1971:454; de la Vega del Sella, 1923; Freeman 1975a:255).

All but the very largest nonhuman predators in Pleistocene Iberia which prey on the larger ungulate species (ibex, deer, bovines, etc.) specialize in very young, very old, or incapacitated individuals rather than healthy, prime-age adults (see Mech, 1970:246–63). The big cats (panthers and lions) are the only exceptions to this rule. What is more, nonhuman predators, even the social carnivores, seldom kill more than a single animal at a time. This makes hominid hunting practices in Iberia look much different from the behavior of any of the large carnivores. Even at the very earliest sites in the peninsula, such as Torralba and Ambrona, human hunters, whom we believe to be responsible for most of the accumulated bones, were not limited in their choice of prey to the young, the weak, and the aged, even when dealing with such formidable prey as the huge proboscideans. In their capacity to capture animals of all ages and conditions, including prime adults, hominids were more like the big cats than like wolves or hyenas. But, in their capacity to kill the very largest animals and their use of plant foods (which must have been extensive even if it is still largely undocumented), humans were exploiting a much greater breadth of resources than the big cats. If my suggestion that they were hunting by means of large-scale, opportunistic game drives is correct, humans had so far surpassed the big cats in hunting ability as to have become truly incomparable to any other carnivore.

By the latest Paleolithic, and particularly in some Cantabrian Solutrean and Magdalenian levels, there are indications that humans were effectively utilizing a much wider range of wild resources than was ever indicated in the earlier archaeological record. Human foragers had also learned to tailor their equipment to the extracted resources and to focus their organized effort on the periodic harvesting of a few selected, particularly productive species. Klein's detailed study of the faunas from El Juyo (n.d.) suggests that, at least by the Magdalenian, people were able to slaughter whole herds of red deer, probably by means of species-focused drives or surrounds.

The most reasonable explanation for the food acquisition practices documented for the later Upper Paleolithic in Cantabria is that resources were becoming scarce, owing to increases in the size and density of human populations in the region, with some of the apparent increase possibly due to immigration from other regions. The general similarity of Upper Paleolithic artifact assemblages from Cantabria and southwest France has been taken to indicate physical migration of populations. But such similarities in artifact assemblages may equally well result from "stimulus diffusion" or information flow between the two regions. Where wild resources are as abundant as they were in Cantabria, and emigration is denied or checked by the presence of other populations in neighboring regions, intrinsic human population growth over a few generations might easily suffice to put pressure on the local resources. A. Osborn (1977) presents an interesting discussion of a model of this sort applied to Peruvian prehistory.

Information about the size of home ranges exploited by late Upper Paleolithic human populations would be extremely useful. The available data are ambiguous, as usual, but they afford some basis for an educated guess about (seasonal) range size, if we assume that the people at El Juyo cropped the local red deer population as efficiently as they could. Blaxter (1975) estimates that wild ungulate populations will stand an annual cropping rate of some 15% at maximum. If the fauna from El Juyo level 6 represents a single season's red deer harvest (and this is admittedly a big "if"), the local population of *Cervus elaphus* would therefore have had to number at least 253 animals. In favorable environmental conditions, such as those which probably obtained along the Cantabrian coast, densities of red deer may run as high as 1 animal in every 10 hectares; so a deer population as large as our estimate would require 2,530 ha or 23.5 km² total range (a circular area about 5.5 km in diameter). Ranges this small, or even up to four or five times as large, would allow for seasonal occupation of the coast of Santander by 12 to 25 local groups of the size of that at El Juyo. Judging from the number of Magdalenian sites in the region, such figures are not unreasonable. If we go still further, guessing that the El Juyo social group might have numbered 15–25 individuals, the population size for the whole Cantabrian coast (and, by implication, the region) might have been no larger than 1,000–4,000 persons, which seems well within the possible limits of regional carrying capacity for hunter/gatherers; if anything, this estimate seems low. These figures are entirely speculative, and are advanced here only because nothing better is available. But, as shaky as they are, the figures are 5 to 10 times larger than my most optimistic estimates of earlier Upper Paleolithic or Mousterian populations.

SUMMARY AND CONCLUSIONS

The earliest undisturbed human occupations now known from the Iberian Peninsula seem to be restricted to alluvial plains and grasslands. These are precisely the situations where primary production is highest and large herbivores most abundant (Kormondy, 1969). The correlation of earlier Acheulean sites with such settings is not surprising, since hunting strategies at that time seemed to concentrate on larger herbivores. Nonetheless, subsistence strategies were opportunistic, and the range of species taken was greater than that for any other predator. Periodically, relatively larger aggregates of hominids apparently could assemble and undertake large-scale drives, accumulating sizable quantities of meat in the process. Meat may have been dried or smoke-dried to preserve it. Open fires could have been used for roasting meat, as well. No storage features have been recovered. Plants were employed as raw material, but no evidence of their use as food has survived, although it is probably safe to assume that several kinds were eaten, since the human gut and dentition are not those of a specialized carnivore. Until the earlier Upper Pleistocene, humans were probably very rare animals in the Iberian landscape.

Mousterian peoples established a human presence in many parts of the Iberian Peninsula which their predecessors seemingly did not penetrate. They were found virtually throughout the peninsula, along alluvial plains and wherever forest–grassland mosaics occur. In poorer regions, they extended their subsistence activities to the exploitation of mollusks from the supralittoral and intertidal zones.

A. Osborn (1977) claims that marine ecosystems are less productive than terrestrial ones, and that collection of resources from marine environments requires the investment of intensive labor, making such creatures as mollusks second-rate foods. At a very gross level of analysis, this reasoning may be correct. However, estuaries in temperate zones (and there are many estuaries on Spain's coasts) have among the highest documented levels of primary productivity to be found in nature, and other kinds of supralittoral and littoral biotopes compare favorably in primary productivity with montane forests, dry grasslands, and higher mountain slopes (Kormondy, 1969). Furthermore, littoral environments abound in comestible detritus-eaters, such as mussels, some snails, and clams. Along Cantabrian coasts, there are mussel beds yielding as much as 30–50 kg of animals per square meter, and densities of 500–900 periwinkles (*Littorina littorea*) per square meter are not uncommon (Madariaga de la Campa, 1976). At least some littoral environments are rich potential sources of food for humans.

The littoral-estuarine zone may be harder to exploit than alluvial flats or forest-grassland mosaics, but it is no accident that sporadic and finally intensive exploitation of marine resources seems to have kept exact pace with the use of alpine resources in Cantabria. The regular exploitation of both biotopes began at the same time (as early as the Mousterian in some regions), then intensified progressively to the peaks documented by some of the later Paleolithic occupations.

The catch, and consequently the diet, of some Mousterian food-collectors was more varied than it had been for their earlier ancestors, although beef and horsemeat remained dietary mainstays in Cantabria. The first solid evidence for the use of vegetable foods also comes from this period. Mousterian peoples continued to use opportunistic exploitative strategies, exploring environmental potential in at least a desultory fashion to a greater depth than had Acheulean food-collectors in the Peninsula. Food preservation and cooking techniques probably continued to be much the same.

Earlier Upper Paleolithic peoples expanded the number of subsistence resources markedly. Vegetable foods undoubtedly continued to be eaten, although evidence to prove this is virtually lacking. The number of lowland terrestrial resources used was increased, the taking of furbearing animals for meat or pelts began, animals that were extremely dangerous to hunt appear more regularly in faunal inventories, and a more systematic exploitation of alpine and coastal biotopes began. In the Archaic Aurignacian, possible food-storage facilities are recognized for the first time in Iberia. The molluscan fauna from some sites strongly suggests that some food may have been grilled over hot stones or steamed in seaweed. New kinds of hearths were invented, capable of generating intense heat, but there is no evidence that their potential for producing high temperatures was realized. Salt, from seawater, could scarcely have been unknown as a seasoning, and brine-curing may now be added to the list of possible preservative techniques.

Given the age and sex distribution of the most numerous terrestrial prey, it seems that hominids hunted in much different fashion from other predatory animals. Organized game drives such as those I believe were conducted at Torralba are beyond the capacity of social carnivores, or for that matter of any predator other than humans. Nor can any facultative predator, no matter how catholic its tastes, successfully hunt as wide a variety of game: humans are able to capture and consume virtually any nontoxic animal large enough to catch their eye. They can digest a wide range of plant foods and convert them directly to body tissue and energy. They have developed techniques of cooking and food preparation that convert less digestible substances into more digestible ones. They have learned to preserve food and store it over the lean season as necessary. In short, they are supreme omnivores, unique in the animal kingdom. Modeling early hominid behavior on that of any specific group of social carnivores can only end in showing us how different from them we have always been.

As human populations expanded, pressure on resources increased, and new and more efficient subsistence strategies were originated. The number of food items used during the course of the year was further augmented in Solutrean and Magdalenian levels. Seeds, nuts, and perhaps even algae were utilized. Alpine animals (especially ibex), red deer, limpets, periwinkles, and probably other species were exploited intensively.

It is hard to see how the quantities of small mollusks represented in some collections could have been cooked efficiently except by boiling. Once introduced, boiling would add gruels, soups, and stews to the diet, and simultaneously provide a useful technique for reheating foods as a short-range preservative measure. If food was boiled, evaporation could not have been unknown, and with this technique, quantities of salt could have been produced for use as a seasoning and for dry-salting foods.

Most important of all, the technique of periodic (probably seasonal) cropping of especially productive resources (wild-harvesting) was introduced. The new relationships with animals which this technique generated would almost certainly have produced effects similar to the game-conservation procedures implied by rational resource management, whether the hunters were conscious of the fact or not; otherwise, the unrestrained application of the wild-harvesting procedure would have exhausted the primary dietary resources in short order.

By the end of the Paleolithic, Iberian peoples had evolved intricate and sophisticated interrelationships with a variety of environments. In some settings, human populations were apparently maintained at relatively high levels by economic systems that relied on conscious or unconscious management and perhaps even deliberate manipulation of breeding reserves of those species which served, at least seasonally, as critical dietary resources. Such systems depend on attitudes and techniques which foreshadow those essential to food-production, and I should not be at all surprised to find that some Mesolithic populations in Iberia were encouraging, selecting, improving, and cultivating suitable local resources well before agricultural complexes derived from the Near East arrived on the scene.

Dietary evidence from the Iberian Peninsula is scanty and circum-stantial, and after examining it we are left with far more questions than answers. Nevertheless, the outlines of Pleistocene dietary practices have begun to appear. The most striking conclusion they suggest is that subsistence-related behavior during the Iberian Paleolithic was extremely variable from place to place and time to time, and became progressively more so. In retrospect, this conclusion seems almost tautological. However, it directly contradicts the now-popular assertion that man's long history as a hunter immutably fixed the direction of his social, psychological, and cultural evolution in a narrowly circumscribed rut, from which escape is impossible. Our species' long food-collecting apprenticeship did open particular vistas to the future, but those vistas are far wider than such simplistic models assume. We use shorthand labels such as "hunting" as though they signified unitary economic processes, but they really do not. "Hunting" is not a single set of behavioral patterns and attitudes, but thousands of different sets, many of which have little in common. Food-gathering demanded from our hominid forebears intelligence, inventive-ness, cooperation, information exchange, and adaptability. These are the hallmarks of the modern human condition. What we learn from close reading of the record of the prehistoric past is just how variable our trajectory to the present has been; that, in turn, suggests that we need not be pessimistic about our species' future potential.

Acknowledgments

I owe many of the ideas in this paper to discussions held over the years with J. González Echegaray, J. Altuna, B. Madariaga, G. Neuman, and R. Klein. R. S. O. Harding's comments on the first draft were most useful. Comparison of the Iberian data with Klein's South African material has also called my attention to the similarities and differences between carnivore accumulations and earlier Paleolithic archaeological bone series. Some of the ideas expressed here first appeared in two earlier articles (Freeman, 1973, 1975a). We owe the bulk of the corpus of Spanish mammalian identifications to J. Altuna, and B. Madariaga has been the major source of malacological observation and commentary for Iberia in recent years. In two recent articles, L. Straus (1976, 1977) has reviewed and critiqued my earlier work, adding important new observations. Our ideas about Pleistocene diet in Iberia have not changed as much in the last 5 years as they will in the next 5, when many of our young Spanish colleagues will take to the field to search for new information more seriously and insistently than has been done in the past.

NOTES

1. The size categories used throughout this paper are the following:

Very large species ($>$ 1000 kg): elephants, rhinos.

Large species (500–1000 kg): bovines.

Large medium–sized species (200–500 kg): *Felis* cf. *leo, Panthera, Eucladoceras, Equus, Ursus.*

Average medium-sized species (100–200 kg): *Rangifer, Cervus, Capra, Sus.*

Small medium-sized species (40–100 kg): *Rupicapra, Dama, Canis lupus, Phoca, Crocuta.*

Small species ($<$ 40 kg): *Capreolus, Vulpes, Felis sylvestris, Oryctolagus, Meles, Leupus,* most mustelids, rodents, insectivores.

These categories are rough estimates based on the literature (see Freeman 1973, 1975b).

The formula $1/(\Sigma_i p_i^2)n$, where p is the proportion of animals in each group and n the number of categories, apparently was originally suggested by Simpson. It was developed by MacArthur (1972:113, 170–73, 197–98), who shows that it is equally applicable to calculating the diversity of species in a research area, of resources in different areas, or of resource utilization by a species. It was used by Delibes Castro (1975:194) as an index of "niche breadth." I have applied it to size categories simply because in the very early periods the habitat tolerances are unknown, and species are present which are not represented in later levels. Size categories maximize comparability of Paleolithic occupations from Middle through Upper Pleistocene time ranges.

Richard G. Klein

5.
Later Stone Age Subsistence at Byeneskranskop Cave, South Africa

The main source of information about the subsistence of prehistoric peoples is the analysis of food debris preserved in their sites. In some situations, this debris includes remains of plants, but much more often the only preserved food wastes are animal bones. When analyzed in as much detail as possible (to learn the minimum number of individuals of each species, their ages and sexes, which of their skeletal elements are present, and so forth), bones can provide a wealth of interesting information, not only about subsistence at any given time but also about long-term subsistence changes that probably reflect alterations in the environment or in the ability of people to exploit animal resources. This article illustrates the potential of archaeological bone analysis, using as an example the bone assemblage excavated at Byeneskranskop 1 in the southern Cape Province of South Africa.

To place the results of this analysis in context, some background information on southern African prehistory is necessary. In southern Africa, the information available on prehistoric subsistence comes largely from the Upper Pleistocene and Holocene, roughly the last 130,000 years. People living in the earlier part of this period, from perhaps 130,000 to 50,000 or 40,000 B.P., made stone artifacts that are generally designated Middle Stone Age (MSA). Although it is still not clear whether all the stone artifact assemblages postdating the Middle Stone Age share enough technological and typological features to be grouped in a single culture-stratigraphic unit, for convenience I refer to all post-MSA stone industries as Later Stone Age (LSA). Defined in this way, the LSA in southern Africa began perhaps 50,000–40,000 B.P. and ended at various times, depending upon the place. In the north and east, especially in Rhodesia, the Transvaal, the eastern Orange Free State, Natal, and the northern Cape Province of South Africa, the LSA was terminated by the arrival and dispersal of Bantu-speaking, Iron Age agriculturalists, beginning about 2,000 B.P. In the south and west, especially in the western Orange Free State and in the southern and western Cape Province, including the area of Byeneskranskop 1, the LSA persisted longer and was eventually truncated by the spread of

166

Europeans, mainly from the vicinity of Cape Town, beginning in the latter half of the seventeenth century.

My own research, devoted primarily to faunal remains from sites in the southern Cape, has led to several conclusions (Klein, 1974a, 1975a, 1977a): (1) During the last glacial (approximately 70,000–10,000 B.P.), the southern Cape contained substantially more grassland than existed during the preceding interglacial (roughly 130,000–70,000 B.P.) or during the Holocene (the last 10,000 years); (2) Middle Stone Age peoples were less effective at exploiting local animal resources than their Later Stone Age successors; (3) Later Stone Age peoples were at least partly responsible for the extinction of several large mammalian species in the southern Cape roughly 10,000 years ago; and (4) the introduction of domestic sheep to the southern Cape between 2,000 and 1,600 B.P. led to differences in the way Later Stone Age peoples dealt with the indigenous fauna. This report on the Byeneskranskop 1 faunal analysis should be read against the background of these conclusions or working hypotheses.

EXCAVATION AND STRATIGRAPHY
OF BYENESKRANSKOP 1

Byeneskranskop Cave 1 (34° 35'S, 19° 28'E) is roughly 160 km east-southeast of Cape Town, near Gansbaai, in the southern Cape Province of South Africa (fig. 5.1). For several years, the South African Museum has had a small collection of animal bones from this site (called "Eyre's Cave" in the catalogue). F. R. Schweitzer undertook the first controlled excavation in 1973 and extended it in 1974 and 1976, showing that the site contains approximately 3 m of undisturbed LSA deposits, within which a minimum of 19 different layers could be isolated. Radiocarbon dates obtained at the Council for Scientific and Industrial Research Laboratory

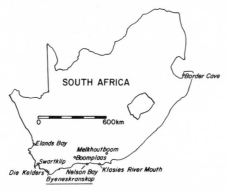

Figure 5.1. Locations of the main sites mentioned in the text.

in Pretoria, the University of Washington Laboratory in Seattle, and the Isotopes Laboratory in New Jersey indicate that layer 19 (the lowest) is probably about 12,500 years old, layer 14 about 9,700 years, layer 9 about 6,400 years, layer 5 about 4,000 years, layer 2 about 3,500 years, and layer 1 about 3,200 years and younger. Further dates are now being determined and may lead to some revisions of this chronology, but it is clear that the sequence at Byeneskranskop is more or less continuous from the terminal Pleistocene through the early and middle Holocene, a time span of 10,000– 11,000 years.

Schweitzer's preliminary analysis of the Byeneskranskop artifacts indicates that at least four and perhaps five discrete LSA culture-stratigraphic units are represented: unit A in layer 19, unit B in layers 18–14, unit C in layers 13–10, unit D in layers 9–6, and (a tentative) unit E in layers 5–1. The small convex scrapers and backed elements characteristic of the Wilton Industrial Complex appear first in unit D, and the contrast between this unit and the underlying one (C) is particularly clear. Broadly speaking, units A, B, and C may be grouped as "Pre-Wilton" LSA occupations and units D and E as Wilton ones. The carbon-14 dates discussed above suggest that the Wilton replaced the Pre-Wilton at Byeneskranskop roughly 6,400 B.P. Elsewhere in the southern Cape, the comparable replacement appears to have occurred between 8,000 and 7,500 B.P. (H. J. Deacon, 1972, 1976; J. Deacon, 1974; R. Klein, 1974a, 1975a), and the apparently anomalous Byeneskranskop date is currently being checked, using fresh samples.

Schweitzer's excavations have also provided substantial quantities of animal remains, including shells of intertidal mollusks and bones of fish, reptiles, birds, and mammals. Schweitzer is studying the shells and fish bones, G. MacLachlan the snake remains, G. Avery the bird bones, and D. M. Leakey-Avery the bones of micromammals (mainly insectivores and rodents, most of which were probably introduced into the site by owls). I am studying the tortoise and larger mammal remains, most of which were probably brought in by Later Stone Age people. I have not yet analyzed the 1976 sample, but the data from that sample will be included in a final report accompanying the full description of the stratigraphy, artifacts, and other aspects that Schweitzer is preparing. This article is thus a preliminary report, based on the 1973–1974 samples.

SORTING, COUNTING, AND IDENTIFICATION

I sorted the Byeneskranskop bones in the Department of Cenozoic Palaeontology of the South African Museum, with the immediate goal of assigning as many bones as possible to body part and species. With that information in hand, I then intended to calculate the minimum numbers of individuals of each species by noting the frequency of the most abundant body parts. Wherever feasible, I divided examples of a body part assigned to a species between lefts and rights and, further, between those with fused and those with unfused epiphyses. I then added the higher number (left or right) with fused epiphyses to the higher number with unfused epiphyses to obtain the minimum number of individuals represented by that body part. Excepting atlases and axes, which I counted individually, I assigned vertebrae of each taxon only to gross categories (cervicals 3-7, thoracic, lumbar, and sacral) and divided by a number appropriate to the taxon and vertebral category (e.g., 5 for cervical vertebrae 3-7 of all species; 1, 7, and 5, respectively, for the thoracic, lumbar, and sacral vertebrae of most bovids). Similarly, depending on the taxon, I sorted phalanges as finely as I could (generally into firsts, seconds, and thirds; where possible into rights and lefts, epiphyses fused or unfused), and again divided by an appropriate figure to obtain a minimum number estimate (for example, for bovid right first phalanges with epiphyses fused, the divisor was 4).

Like every other southern African faunal assemblage I have studied Byeneskranskop contains a substantial amount of fragmentary bovid postcranial material that I cannot assign to species. As Brain has done in these circumstances (1974, see also 1969c), I have divided the bovid postcranial fragments among four size categories: small, small medium, large medium, and large (see also R. Klein, 1975b, 1976a, 1977b). These categories are defined in the note to table 5.1. Minimum individual counts for bovid species were established solely on the basis of securely identified cranial material—mainly teeth. Most bovid teeth occurred as isolated specimens rather than in jaws with the other teeth, and therefore I recorded both position in the mouth and degree of wear. This allowed me to obtain not only overall minimum individual counts, but also estimates of the numbers in different age categories within each bovid species (table 5.10). Since degree of wear must be judged subjectively, these age distributions are only approximate, but I believe they may reasonably be compared to others that were similarly derived; any gross similarities or differences that emerge may be considered nontrivial.

Not even teeth enabled me to distinguish consistently between some closely related bovid species of similar size. In particular, I was forced to use a composite category to include material that could belong either to hartebeest (*Alcelaphus buselaphus*) or to an extinct subspecies of the black wildebeest (*Connochaetes gnou*) that once lived in the southern Cape. I was able to separate grysbok (*Raphicerus melonatis*) from the closely related steenbok (*R. campestris*) when I had fairly complete mandibles (the inferior margin of the mandible is much straighter in the steenbok; see R. Klein, 1976b), but I could not separate isolated teeth or maxillae of the two species. This led me to count grysbok and steenbok mandibles separately, but to use a single composite category (*Raphicerus* spp.) to incorporate all the dental material.

As with bovid postcranial bones, I found it impossible to separate suid

Table 5.1. Larger mammals and tortoises in Byeneskranskop Cave (minimum numbers of individuals)

									Levels										
	1	*2*	*3*	*4*	*5*	*6*	*7*	*8*	*9*	*10*	*11*	*12*	*13*	*14*	*15*	*16*	*17*	*18*	*19*
Papio ursinus, baboon	1	—	—	1	1	2	1	—	1	1	1	—	—	1	—	—	—	—	—
Homo sapiens, man	1	—	—	1	1	1	1	—	—	—	—	—	—	—	—	—	—	—	—
Canis cf. *mesomelas*, jackal	1	—	1	1	1?	—	—	—	—	1?	—	—	—	—	—	—	—	—	—
Mellivora capensis, honey badger	—	—	—	—	—	—	—	—	—	1	—	—	—	—	—	—	—	—	—
Aonyx capensis, clawless otter	1	—	—	—	1	—	—	—	—	—	—	—	—	—	—	—	—	—	—
Herpestes ichneumon, Egyptian mongoose	2	—	—	1cf	1	—	—	1cf	—	—	—	1cf	—	—	—	—	—	—	—
H. pulverulentus, gray mongoose	1cf	—	—	—	1cf	2	1	1cf	—	—	—	—	—	—	—	—	—	—	—
Atilax paludinosus, water mongoose	—	—	—	—	—	—	—	—	—	—	—	—	—	1	—	—	—	—	—
Hyaena brunnea, brown hyena	—	—	—	—	1cf	—	—	—	—	—	—	—	—	—	—	—	—	—	—
Felis libyca, wildcat	1	—	1cf	1cf	1	—	—	—	—	—	—	—	1	—	—	—	—	—	—
Felis cf. *caracal*, caracal	—	—	—	1	—	1	—	—	1	—	—	—	—	—	—	—	—	—	—
Panthera pardus, leopard	—	—	—	—	1	—	—	—	—	—	—	—	—	—	—	—	—	—	—
Arctocephalus pusillus, Cape fur seal	2	—	—	1	1	2	1	—	—	1	—	1	—	—	—	—	—	—	—
Loxodonta africana, elephant	—	—	—	—	1	1	1	—	—	—	—	—	—	—	1	1	—	—	—
Procavia capensis, rock hyrax	—	—	—	—	—	1	1	—	1	—	—	—	1	—	1	1	—	—	2
Diceros bicornis, black rhinoceros	1cf	—	—	—	1cf	1	—	—	1	—	1	1?	1cf	1	1	1	1?	—	2
Equus cf. *quagga*, quagga	—	—	—	—	—	—	—	—	—	—	1	—	1	1	1	1	2	—	2
Equus cf. *capensis*, "giant Cape horse"	—	—	—	—	—	—	—	—	—	—	—	—	—	—	1	—	—	—	1
Potamochoerus porcus, bushpig	—	2	2	1	2	—	—	—	1	1	—	—	1	1	—	—	—	—	—
Phacochoerus aethiopicus, warthog	—	2	2	1	2	—	—	—	1	1	—	—	1	—	1	—	—	—	—
Suidae—general, pigs	—	—	—	—	1	1	1	—	1	1	—	—	1	1	1	1	1	1	1
Hippopotamus amphibius, hippopotamus	—	—	—	—	—	1	1	—	—	—	—	—	—	—	—	—	—	—	—

Raphicerus melanotis, grysbok	2	2	—	3	8	2	1	—	—	—	—	—	—	1	—	—	1	—	—
R. campestris, steenbok	—	3	1	1	2	1	—	—	—	—	—	—	—	2	2	2	1	—	—
Raphicerus spp., grysbok/steenbok	6	—	6	—	18	7	4	3	4	1	—	2	1	2	2	1	2	1	1
Oreotragus oreotragus, klipspringer	3	—	1	1?	3	—	—	—	1?	—	1?	—	—	—	—	—	—	1	1
Pelea capreolus, vaalribbok	—	—	1?	—	—	1	1	—	—	—	—	—	—	2	—	—	2	—	—
Redunca arundinum, southern reedbuck	—	—	—	—	1	1	1	—	1	—	—	2	—	—	—	—	—	—	—
R. fulvorufula, mountain reedbuck	—	—	—	—	—	—	—	1	1	1	—	1?	—	—	—	—	—	—	3
Hippotragus leucophaeus, blue antelope	—	—	—	—	1	—	—	—	1?	2	—	1	3	1?	—	1	—	1	—
Damaliscus cf. *dorcas*, bontebok	—	—	—	—	—	—	—	—	—	1	—	—	—	—	1?	—	—	1	—
Connochaetes/*Alcelaphus*, wildebeest/hartebeest	—	1	—	—	2	—	—	—	1	1	2	3	5	2	3	1	1?	2	1
Taurotragus oryx, eland	—	1?	—	—	—	2	2	—	1	1	—	—	—	—	—	—	1	1	2
Syncerus caffer, Cape buffalo	2	2	1	1	2	2	2	2	3	1	1	2	2	1	1	1	1	1	2
Ovis aries, sheep	2	—	—	—	—	—	—	—	—	—	—	—	—	—	—	—	—	—	—
Bovidae—general, bovids																			
Small	9	4	7	7	21	7	4	3	5	1	1	2	1	2	2	2	1	2	1
Small medium	2	1	—	—	1	1	1	1	1	1	—	1	1	1	1	1	1	2	1
Large medium	2	2	2	3	3	2	2	1	2	3	3	6	8	3	5	1	2	2	4
Large	3	3	1	2	2	2	4	3	4	1	—	2	2	—	1	1	1	1	4
Lepus sp., hare	—	—	—	—	1	—	—	—	1	—	—	—	—	—	—	—	1	—	1
Hystrix africae-australis, porcupine	—	1	—	—	—	—	—	—	2	1	2	1	1	1	2	1	—	—	1
Bathyergus suillus, dune mole rat	12	5	3	14	23	8	4	3	2	2	1	1	1	1	2	1	1	—	11
Chelonia, tortoises	75	48	37	55	150	94	40	38	111	61	39	60	75	90	41	29	18	8	62

Note: In the context of this article *small* bovids include grysbok, steenbok, and klipspringer; *small medium* ones include vaalribbok, mountain reedbuck, and sheep; *large medium* ones include southern reedbuck, blue antelope, bontebok, and wildebeest/hartebeest; and *large* ones include eland and Cape buffalo; "cf" indicates a probable but not certain assignment of bones to the species listed.

postcranial remains consistently between the two species that are definitely represented by teeth (*Potamochoerus porcus* and *Phacochoerus aethiopicus*). I have therefore based the suid minimum-number estimates strictly on teeth and have assigned the postcranial material to a single composite suid category (table 5.1).

Finally, my inexperience in dealing with tortoise bones and the inadequacy of available comparative specimens has forced me to deal with a single gross category (Chelonia). The initial sorting of the tortoise material into body parts was undertaken by M. Schoch. On the basis of obvious morphological differences among homologous bones, there are at least two and probably more tortoise species represented. One species, clearly much more abundant than the others, is probably *Testudo angulata,* still quite common locally. The minimum individual counts for tortoises are based on counts of limb bones, divided among presumed species and between lefts and rights. In every level, the humerus proved to be the most common limb bone. The tortoise remains are discussed only briefly in what follows, but I plan a more detailed study incorporating the 1976 sample.

PALEO-ENVIRONMENTAL IMPLICATIONS OF THE BYENESKRANSKOP FAUNA

Table 5.1 presents the minimum numbers of individuals for the mammalian species and tortoises represented in the various layers of Byeneskranskop, and demonstrates a clear tendency for larger, gregarious grazers to be concentrated in the Pre-Wilton layers (10–19) and smaller, nongregarious browsers or mixed feeders in the Wilton ones (1–9). This is brought out more clearly in table 5.2, where the composite frequency of the most common small browsers (grysbok/steenbok) is compared directly with the composite frequency of the most prominent large grazers (alcelaphine antelopes and equids). I have found the same contrast between the Pre-Wilton and Wilton in every southern Cape fauna I have examined (see R. Klein, 1974a, 1975a); it almost certainly reflects widespread vegetational change from a mosaic with substantial grassland to one dominated by scrub, bush, and fynbos (Cape macchia), similar to the historically known vegetation of the southern Cape. At other sites, the pertinent carbon-14 dates indicate that this vegetational change coincides broadly with the Pleistocene–Holocene transition, 12,000–8,000 B.P., a further reason to suspect that the carbon-14 determination of 6,400 B.P. for the appearance of the Wilton at Byeneskranskop is too recent.

The decrease of hare relative to dune mole rat in the Wilton levels (table 5.2) may reflect either a reduction in grassland or the terminal Pleistocene-early Holocene rise in sea level, which probably increased the habitat

Table 5.2. Grysbok/steenbok versus alcelaphine antelopes and equids, hares versus mole rats, and seals versus bovids, equids, and suids in the Wilton and Pre-Wilton deposits of Byeneskranskop 1 (figures are minimum numbers of individuals taken from table 5.1)

	Wilton (layers 1–9)	*Pre-Wilton* (layers 10–19)
Grysbok/steenbok	52	12
Alcelaphine antelopes and equids	5	31
Hares	3	7
Mole rats	74	21
Seals	8	2
Bovids, equids, and suids	95	78

Note: In the Wilton layers, alcelaphines and equids are significantly less common than grysbok/steenbok ($\chi^2 = 31.36, p < .001$) and hares are significantly less common than mole rats ($\chi^2 = 8.28, p < .01$). Seals are relatively more common than bovids, equids, and suids in the Wilton levels, but the contrast with the Pre-Wilton ones is not significant ($\chi^2 = 1.45, p > .2$).

favorable for mole rats (dunes) near the site. At present the coastline is about 5 km away, but during the late Pleistocene, when sea level fell by as much as 120 m, it was up to 25 km distant. Sea-level change is surely reflected in the rarity or absence of shells and bones of fish, seabirds, and seals in the lowest levels of the site. So far, I cannot show that the lower frequency of seals in the Pre-Wilton as compared with the Wilton levels is statistically significant (table 5.2), but statistical demonstration will probably be possible after analysis of the 1976 sample. This will require especially large samples from Byeneskranskop because the site probably has never been closer to the coast than its present distance. People therefore never brought as many seals back to the site as they did to coastal caves such as Nelson Bay (R. Klein, 1972) and Elands Bay (Parkington, 1977).

Once the 1976 sample has been analyzed, the total sample size may be large enough to permit a multivariate statistical analysis of species frequency variation through time, in order to check and perhaps amplify the paleo-environmental conclusions I have already drawn. To test the possibilities, I have undertaken a pilot analysis, augmenting the available Byeneskranskop data with comparable ones from the MSA levels of the nearby site of Die Kelders, which are probably between 75,000 and 55,000–50,000 years old (Tankard and Schweitzer, 1974, 1976). The matrix actually submitted to analysis is reproduced here as table 5.3, and is limited to species that were reasonably well represented at Byeneskranskop, Die Kelders, or both. I used principal components analysis in order to isolate groups of species that covary from level to level.

The results of the analysis and some further particulars on the technique

Table 5.3. The matrix of species (minimum numbers) submitted to principal components analysis

	Byeneskranskop				Die Kelders (MSA)			
	1–5	6–9	10–13	14–19	NEV	MJA	MJB	RAY/TDZ
Cape fur seal	4	4	2	—	4	4	2	7
Rock hyrax	1	3	1	4	15	37	13	8
Quagga	—	1	2	7	—	1	—	—
Grysbok/steenbok	34	18	4	8	12	77	18	10
Klipspringer	7	—	—	1	2	5	4	2
Vaalribbok	—	1	—	—	5	10	2	—
Southern reedbuck	—	1	3	2	1	3	2	—
Blue antelope	1	1	7	4	—	4	2	—
Wildebeest/hartebeest	3	1	1	9	2	3	2	1
Eland	—	3	—	3	6	6	3	8
Cape buffalo	7	9	6	4	—	2	—	—
Dune mole rat	57	17	5	16	33	80	81	17

Note: For further information, see the text and the note to table 5.4. The Byeneskranskop minimum numbers (by cultural unit) were compiled from table 5.1. The Die Kelders minimum numbers are from Klein (unpublished data). Both sets of data are from youngest to oldest, reading from left to right.

Table 5.4. Varimax-rotated four-component solution of the species frequency variation in table 5.3

	Components			
	1	*2*	*3*	*4*
Cape fur seal	*−0.83*	0.15	0.23	−0.32
Rock hyrax	0.04	*0.85*	0.50	0.07
Quagga	*0.74*	−0.26	−0.01	−0.24
Grysbok/steenbok	−0.08	*0.98*	−0.07	0.03
Klipspringer	−0.40	0.60	−0.29	0.41
Vaalribbok	0.05	*0.88*	0.40	−0.02
Southern reedbuck	*0.87*	0.38	0.11	0.12
Blue antelope	*0.90*	0.14	−0.21	−0.06
Wildebeest/hartebeest	*0.87*	−0.23	−0.23	−0.16
Eland	−0.35	0.19	*0.88*	−0.20
Cape buffalo	0.11	−0.13	*−0.86*	−0.30
Dune mole rat	−0.00	0.02	0.12	*0.96*
Eigenvalue of initial component	4.60	3.16	1.59	1.33
Percentage of variance explained	38.3	26.3	13.3	11.1

Note: The analysis was performed on the University of Chicago's IBM 370/168 computer using the method "PA 1" and other appropriate options of the subprogram FACTOR (Nie et al., 1975). Only initial components with eigenvalues greater than 1.00 were selected for rotation and interpretation (the eigenvalue of the fifth initial component was 0.66). A species that has a "loading" of ⩾.71 on a component (shown in italics) has more than 50% (>.71 × .71) of its frequency variation explained by that component. This means that species that have loadings of ⩾.71 on the same component are probably varying together in a systematic way. A high negative loading implies a strong inverse frequency relationship with species that have high positive loadings on the same component. Table 5.3 exhibits too little frequency variation among too few provenience units to be totally appropriate for principal components analysis, but even so the results strongly support the paleo-environmental interpretations suggested on other grounds in the text.

are presented in table 5.4. Although the small number of observations (levels), the relatively limited extent to which some species vary, and other factors make a precise interpretation of the results impossible, it is fair to say that my interpretations are supported. In particular, the analysis suggests clearly that a group of the more prominent grassveld creatures (hartebeest/wildebeest, quagga, southern reedbuck, and blue antelope) are varying together and independently of a covarying group of smaller animals (grysbok/steenbok, klipspringer, vaalribbok, and rock hyrax) that share a preference for browse, for rocky, broken relief, or for both. Seals fail to associate clearly with any other species but show a strong inverse relationship with the grazers, as would be expected if rises in sea level generally coincided with a shrinkage in grassland. The mole rat also fails to associate with other species, perhaps because its frequency is determined more by strictly local factors than are the frequencies of the other species. The apparent occurrence of an inverse relationship between eland and buffalo is more difficult to explain but may well reflect cultural rather than paleo-environmental factors. (Table 5.3 shows that this relationship is largely due to the great numbers of eland in the MSA levels of Die Kelders, and I believe this has cultural significance.)

CULTURAL IMPLICATIONS OF THE BYENESKRANSKOP FAUNA

The rise in sea level that brought the cave within easy reach of the coast in Wilton times obviously affected the way its occupants used the site, but the roughly simultaneous reduction in the amount of grassland appears to have had an even greater impact. Unlike the Pre-Wilton peoples (levels 19–10), who hunted mainly large, gregarious, grazing mammals that probably roamed over large ranges in response to seasonal changes in precipitation and temperature, Wilton peoples devoted more attention to small, nongregarious, nonmigratory browsers. Thus Wilton hunter/gatherers probably occupied smaller, more closely nested home ranges, relying more on plant foods, particularly geophytes (perennials that overwinter below the soil surface), which probably had increased substantially as a result of environmental change. Plant remains were preserved only at the very top of the Byeneskranskop sequence, but the remarkable Wilton deposits at Melkhoutboom in the southeastern Cape demonstrate that geophyte exploitation was a very important aspect of subsistence from the earliest Wilton onward (H. J. Deacon, 1976).

In the context of subsistence changes probably caused by environmental change, the ratio of tortoise to mammal individuals deserves attention. Table 5.5 shows that cultural units B, C, and D resemble each other in the frequency of tortoise versus mammal remains and differ significantly from units A and E, which in turn resemble each other. If the larger numbers of all taxa anticipated from analysis of the 1976 sample show that A is more like E in other respects as well, at least some of the kinds of environmental change inferred above may have occured more than once during the LSA occupation of Byeneskranskop. Whatever the outcome, figure 5.2 shows that the frequency relationship between tortoises and mammals is probably a complicated one: there seems to be a strong frequency correlation in the upper levels of the site (roughly 1–8), but little or no correlation in the lower levels (roughly 9–18). There is little frequency covariation in levels where the principal mammals are large, gregarious, migratory grazers, but frequencies correspond closely in levels where the principal mammals are small, nonmigratory "ground game"—precisely the sorts of creatures one

Table 5.5. Tortoises and mammals represented in the major cultural units of Byeneskranskop Cave 1 (minimum numbers, and percentages in parentheses)

	A (1-5)	B (6-9)	C (10-13)	D (14-18)	E (19)
Tortoises	365 (70)	283 (78)	235 (80)	186 (79)	62 (67)
Mammals	157 (30)	80 (22)	59 (20)	50 (21)	30 (33)

	χ^2	p
A vs B	6.64	.01-.001
A vs C	9.14	.01-.001
A vs D	6.00	.02-.01
A vs E	0.13	.8-.7
B vs C	0.23	.7-.5
B vs D	0.00	.98-.95
B vs E	3.88	.05-.02
C vs D	0.00	.98-.95
C vs E	5.50	.02-.01
D vs E	4.05	.05-.02

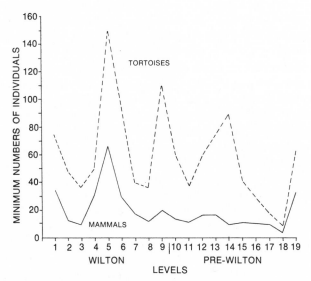

Figure 5.2. Minimum numbers of tortoises and mammals represented in the various levels of Byeneskranskop Cave 1.

would be likely to encounter on a systematic hunt for tortoises. Thus Wilton people may have been relatively more systematic (less opportunistic) in their exploitation of tortoises, generally more successful in obtaining mammals on a regular basis, or both. I should add that even though the tortoise to mammal ratio is generally higher in the Pre-Wilton levels, the average individual mammal found there is much larger. Therefore, the actual dietary contribution of tortoises was probably considerably smaller (relative to mammals) than in the Wilton.

Finally, it is important to point out the presence of domestic sheep (*Ovis aries*) at the very top of the Byeneskranskop sequence (see table 5.1). At the nearby site of Die Kelders, sheep bones are definitely present in deposits dating to 1,600 B.P. and may even occur in the earliest LSA occupation of the site, dating to 2,000 B.P. (Schweitzer, 1974, 1976; Schweitzer and Scott, 1973); thus the earliest Byeneskranskop sheep probably falls in the 1,600–2,000 B.P. range. The analyzed bone sample from the Byeneskranskop sheep layer is too small for comparison with the samples from the pre-sheep layers, but a meaningful comparison may be made between the Byeneskranskop pre-sheep layers and the ones with sheep at Die Kelders. The Die Kelders faunal sample containing sheep is far larger than the Byeneskranskop pre-sheep sample, yet many of the wild species found at Byeneskranskop have not been positively identified at all (R. Klein and Scott, unpublished data, as reported in Schweitzer, 1976). I have also observed a wider range of well-represented wild species in the pre-sheep levels at Nelson Bay Cave and Boomplaas, suggesting that herders either hunted less than their predecessors or were more casual about it, perhaps taking only those wild creatures found close to a site.

The 1976 sample, much of which was obtained from the top of the sequence, may make an age–sex analysis of the Byeneskranskop sheep possible. The age and sex compostion of the Die Kelders "flock" (composed almost entirely of subadult males, with a scattering of old females), led Schweitzer (1974) to conclude that the people at Die Kelders were probably herders rather than thieves.

In addition to an LSA fauna with sheep, the Die Kelders site contains an MSA fauna that is probably between 75,000 and 55,000–50,000 years old; it, too, may be fruitfully compared to the Byeneskranskop sample. In earlier papers (R. Klein, 1975a,c), I pointed out similarities between the MSA faunas from Die Kelders and Klasies River Mouth, the only other southern Cape site that so far has provided a large fauna of this age. In both, eland are the most common larger bovids, and suids are rare or absent, in contrast to LSA faunas from nearby sites. Table 5.6 makes this point clearly for Die Kelders and Byeneskranskop. If animals' responses to attack were arranged along a continuum from relatively docile to relatively fierce, eland and pigs would be located at opposite ends; I believe that the

Table 5.6. Minimum numbers of individual eland, other bovids, and suids present in the LSA layers of Byeneskranskop and the MSA layers of Die Kelders

	Byeneskranskop	*Die Kelders*
Eland	7	28
Other Bovids	153	207
Suids	15	0

Note: Comparing eland with other bovids, $\chi^2 = 5.79, p = .02-.01$; comparing suids with all bovids, $\chi^2 = 18.54, p < .001$.

greater frequency of pigs and lower frequency of eland in LSA sites reflects the enhanced ability of LSA peoples to capture dangerous prey, perhaps with snares or long-distance projectiles such as the bow and arrow. In contrast to the Die Kelders and Klasies MSA faunas, the Byeneskranskop LSA contains large numbers of fish and flying birds, seabirds for the most part, but also some terrestrial and freshwater fowl (G. Avery, personal communication). Since we know from the substantial amounts of seal and penguin bone found that that Die Kelders and Klasies were near the coast in MSA times, this evidence suggests that their inhabitants were technologically incapable of active fishing and fowling. The detailed data necessary to support this generalization are being developed by Poggenpoel and Schweitzer (fish) and Avery (birds).

The Byeneskranskop fauna is similar in other respects to the Die Kelders MSA as well as to all the other southern African archaeological faunas I have examined. For example, large carnivores (especially lion, leopard, and hyena) are poorly represented here, as at other archaeological sites, probably because people and carnivores tend to avoid one another. Carnivores are present at Byeneskranskop (29 of 213 animals, or 13%) in frequencies comparable to those I have found in other southern African archaeological faunas (Klein, 1980), although they appear in substantially greater proportions in the single nonarchaeological fauna I have studied in detail: Swartklip, roughly 100 km west-northwest of Byeneskranskop. Here the deposits are early Upper Pleistocene in age and were almost certainly accumulated by large carnivores, probably hyenas (Klein 1975b). This fauna contains a significantly higher frequency of carnivores (46 of 205 individuals, or 22%) than Byeneskranskop or other archaeological sites, and large carnivores are as well represented. This suggests that the carnivores who accumulated the Swartklip bones preyed on other carnivores more often than either MSA or LSA hunters did.

Finally, in an attempt to make inferences about hunting behavior and subsistence strategies, I have compared the age distribution of various bovids at Byeneskranskop (table 5.7) and at several other southern African

Table 5.7. Minimum numbers of bovid individuals of various dental ages in the Byeneskranskop fauna

	I	II	III	IV	V	VI	VII	Totals
	Younger ⟶ *Older*							
Raphicerus melanotis, grysbok	5	4	3	4	—	3	2	21
R. campestris, steenbok	1	—	—	2	—	1	—	4
Raphicerus spp., grysbok/steenbok	14	13	5	12	1	18	2	65
Oreotragus oreotragus, klipspringer	1	—	—	3	2	3	—	9
Pelea capreolus, vaalribbok	—	1	—	1	—	—	—	2
Redunca arundinum, southern reedbuck	3	—	—	2	—	1	—	6
R. fulvorufula, mountain reedbuck	—	—	—	—	2	—	—	2
Hippotragus leucophaeus, blue antelope	3	3	1	2	—	2	2	13
Damaliscus cf. *dorcas*, bontebok	1	1	—	—	—	—	1	3
Connochaetes/Alcelaphus, wildebeest/hartebeest	9	2	1	2	1	7	2	24
Taurotragus oryx, eland	—	1	—	2	—	1	—	4
Syncerus caffer, buffalo	6	—	1	4	1	13	—	25
Ovis aries, sheep	—	—	1	—	1	—	—	2

Note: The dental ages are defined as follows: (I) dP4 erupting to erupted, but essentially unworn; (II) M1 erupting to erupted, but essentially unworn; (III) M2 erupting to erupted, but essentially unworn; (IV) M3 erupting to erupted, but essentially unworn; (V) P4 erupting to erupted, but essentially unworn; (VI) P4 in early to mid wear; and (VII) P4 in late wear. In contrast to the wild bovids that dominate the Byeneskranskop fauna, sheep were probably characterized by eruption of P4 before M3. As a consequence, the sheep dental ages were defined by transposing M3 and P4 in the list above. The result is still seven ages, arranged I to VII from younger to older.

sites (both MSA and LSA). Sample sizes were large enough to allow the following comparisons:

1. Byeneskranskop grysbok/steenbok with grysbok/steenbok at Nelson Bay (LSA), Elands Bay (LSA), Die Kelders (MSA and LSA taken separately), and Klasies 1 (MSA).
2. Byeneskranskop blue antelope with blue antelope at Nelson Bay (LSA) and Klasies 1 (MSA).
3. Byeneskranskop wildebeest/hartebeest with wildebeest/hartebeest at Nelson Bay (LSA), Klasies 1 (MSA), and Border Cave (MSA and LSA taken together).
4. Byeneskranskop Cape buffalo with buffalo at Nelson Bay (LSA), Klasies 1 (MSA) and Border Cave (MSA and LSA taken together).

To make a chi-square test possible, I compressed the dental age distributions to three broad categories: (1) dental age category I, including only newborn animals; (2) dental age categories II and III, including older calves that probably had not reached sexual maturity; and (3) dental age categories IV–VII, the near-adults and adults, all of which are likely to have been sexually mature.

The comparisons for grysbok/steenbok revealed only one significant difference, between Byeneskranskop and Klasies 1 (MSA). Klasies 1 has only one individual in the newborn category (out of 53 total grysbok/steenbok), and in this respect is significantly different from all the other sites providing reasonably large grysbok/steenbok samples. I am not sure how to interpret this. Differences in season of occupation are not likely to be involved, since grysbok and steenbok are not and probably never have been seasonal breeders to any marked extent (Mentis 1972:73–76). Nor is a major cultural difference likely, since the Die Kelders MSA contains an even higher proportion of newborn grysbok/steenbok (26 of 100 individuals) than Byeneskranskop. The problem may be sampling bias at Klasies 1, where the relatively wide-meshed screens used in excavation may not have trapped the teeth of very young grysbok/steenbok, most of which probably occurred as small, isolated specimens.

I found no significant differences between the age distributions of blue antelope and buffalo at Byeneskranskop and at other sites. Byeneskranskop does contain a significantly higher proportion of newborn wildebeest/hartebeest than the other sites, however, indicating that both the Byeneskranskop people and the animals involved are frequently near the site when calves were born, which may not have been true for the people, the animals, or both at the other sites. It would obviously be interesting to know if people only visited Byeneskranskop seasonally, but to establish this from the bovid evidence would require much larger dental samples. These could be analyzed for multimodality in crown height distribution, which would suggest that individuals of one or more species were not being brought to the site all year long. Most of the larger bovid species at Byeneskranskop probably were seasonal breeders, so that more extensive dental samples may one day allow demonstration of seasonal occupation.

THE IMPLICATIONS OF BODY-PART FREQUENCIES

The numbers of different skeletal elements by which bovids and other creatures are represented at Byeneskranskop are given in figure 5.3 and table 5.8, respectively. The main determinants of body-part frequencies are: the introduction or removal of various body parts from the site by its LSA inhabitants; and pre- and postdepositional destructive pressures, as the bovid body-part data clearly demonstrate. Figure 5.3, supported by chi-square results in the caption, shows that there are statistically significant or near-significant differences in body-part frequencies among bovids of different sizes. In very general terms, the small bovids tend to be well represented by a wider variety of their body parts than are the larger bovids. This makes sense if the LSA people often brought small bovids

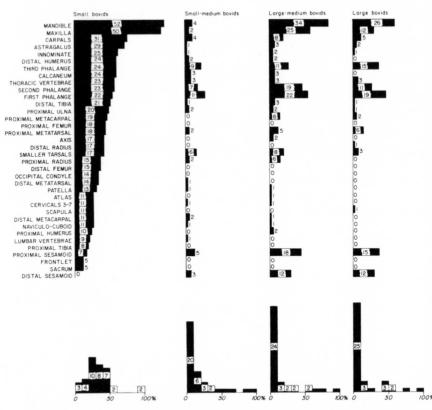

Figure 5.3. *Top*, minimum numbers of different-sized bovids represented by different skeletal elements. *Bottom*, the frequency of each body part within a bovid size class has been calculated as a percentage of the most common part and arranged in histograms by 10% intervals. For example, 3 small-bovid parts were represented 0–10% as well as the mandible. The histograms show that the small bovids tend to be well represented by a wider range of body parts than the larger bovids.

home intact but usually butchered larger ones at the place where they were killed, carrying away only selected parts. The figure suggests that the large bovid body parts most likely to reach the site were heads and feet. I have observed the same pattern at various other southern Cape sites (Klein, 1980); Byeneskranskop is unusual only in that the pattern of small medium bovid bodyparts more closely resembles that of the large medium and large bovids than it does the small bovid class. In the other faunas I have studied, the relative frequencies of various small medium bovid body parts tend to resemble those of small bovid ones. I have no explanation for this anomaly at Byeneskranskop, but it may be related to the fact that the fauna contains relatively few small medium bovids.

Table 5.9 presents the minimum numbers of individuals represented by different major regions of the skeleton for each Byeneskranskop bovid size category and provides some pertinent ratios between these regions. It is apparent from the table that divergence of ratios from 1.00 is more marked for the large bovids than for the small ones. Once again, this suggests that there was a greater tendency for the small bovids to be taken intact to the site, while only selected parts of larger ones were regularly brought home. The table makes the further point that larger bovid heads (perhaps mainly mandibles) and feet, rather than limb bones and vertebrae, were generally brought there.

Although small bovids were probably returned to the site intact more often than large ones were, the frequency of various small bovid body parts still differs significantly from the anatomically expected frequency (figure 5.3, table 5.9). This is almost certainly a consequence of their differential durability when subjected to predepositional forces (such as butchering, burning, and chewing) as well as postdepositional ones (such as leaching and trampling). Brain (1967, 1969a) has pointed out that the distal epiphysis of the bovid humerus is denser and fuses earlier than the proximal epiphysis. If both epiphyses were subjected to more or less the same destructive pressures, the distal humerus would be expected to outnumber the proximal one in a bone assemblage. For the same reason, the bovid distal tibia would be expected to outnumber the proximal, the proximal femur the distal, and the proximal radius the distal. The discrepancies in frequency between the opposite ends of both the humerus and the tibia would be expected to be greatest, since the differences in density and times of epiphyseal fusion are especially great between the opposite ends of these bones. The Byeneskranskop bovid limb bones show the pattern of discrepancies that would be expected if differential durability were playing an important role in determining frequencies (table 5.10).

The factors that account for frequencies of bovid body parts also account for those of other creatures, but only the mole rats are numerous enough to be considered. Most of the substantial frequency discrepancies among mole rat body parts noted in table 5.8 probably reflect differential durability factors. This will be discussed further in the final report on the fauna, which will be based on the larger numbers resulting from inclusion of the 1976 sample.

EXTINCT SPECIES IN THE BYENESKRANSKOP FAUNA

The lowest level of Byeneskranskop contained an upper molar of the very large equid, *Equus capensis*. The species is also known in a terminal Pleistocene context at Elands Bay Cave (Klein 1974b; Parkington 1977) but has never been recorded in Holocene or later sites. I believe it probably became extinct in the terminal Pleistocene or early Holocene, along with

Table 5.8. Minimum numbers of nonbovid individuals represented by different skeletal elements in Byeneskranskop 1

	baboon	man	jackal	honey badger	otter	Egyptian mongoose	Cape grey mongoose	water mongoose	brown hyena	wildcat	caracal
Occipital condyle	1	—	—	—	—	1	1	—	—	—	—
Maxilla	7	1	}3	—	1	1	—	—	—	}2	—
Mandible	—	1		1	1	1	3	1	—		—
Atlas	—	1	—	—	—	—	—	—	—	—	—
Axis	—	—	—	—	1	—	—	—	—	—	—
Cervicals 3–7	—	—	—	—	—	—	—	—	—	—	—
Thoracic vertebrae	—	—	—	—	—	—	—	—	—	—	—
Lumbar vertebrae	—	—	—	—	—	2	—	—	—	—	—
Sacrum	—	—	—	—	—	—	—	—	—	—	—
Clavicle	—	—	—	—	—	—	—	—	—	—	—
Scapula	—	—	—	—	—	—	—	—	—	—	—
Humerus: proximal	—	—	—	—	—	—	1	—	—	—	—
distal	—	—	—	—	—	3	1	—	—	—	1
Radius: proximal	—	—	—	—	—	—	—	—	—	—	—
distal	—	—	—	—	—	—	1	—	—	—	—
Ulna: proximal	—	—	—	—	—	1	—	—	—	—	—
distal	—	—	—	—	—	1	1	—	—	—	1
Carpals	2	—	—	—	—	—	—	—	—	—	—
Metapodials	2	1	1	—	1	2	—	—	—	1	2
Phalanges	3	2	1	—	1	—	—	—	1	3	3
Innominate	—	—	—	—	—	—	1	—	—	—	—
Femur: proximal	—	—	—	—	—	—	1	—	—	—	—
distal	—	—	—	—	—	—	1	—	—	—	—
Tibia: proximal	—	—	—	—	—	—	—	—	—	—	—
distal	—	—	—	—	—	—	—	—	—	—	1
Patella	—	—	—	—	—	—	—	—	—	—	—
Calcaneum	—	—	—	—	—	1	—	—	—	—	—
Astragalus	—	—	—	—	—	—	—	—	—	—	—
Other tarsals	1	—	—	—	—	—	—	—	—	—	—

Table 5.8 (continued)

	leopard	fur seal	elephant	rock hyrax	rhinoceros	quagga	"giant Cape horse"	hippopotamus	suids	hare	porcupine	dune mole rat
Occipital condyle	—	—	—	—	—	—	—	—	—	—	—	19
Maxilla	—	5	3	5	9	10	1	—	11	1	3	56
Mandible	—	1	—	3	—	—	—	3	—	5	—	86
Atlas	—	—	—	—	—	—	—	—	—	—	—	8
Axis	—	—	—	—	—	—	—	—	—	—	—	13
Cervicals 3–7	—	1	—	—	—	—	—	—	—	—	—	8
Thoracic vertebrae	—	1	—	—	—	—	—	—	—	1	—	11
Lumbar vertebrae	—	—	—	—	—	—	—	—	—	—	—	17
Sacrum	—	—	—	—	—	—	—	—	—	—	—	4
Clavicle	—	—	—	—	—	—	—	—	—	2	—	6
Scapula	—	—	—	—	—	—	—	—	—	—	—	26
Humerus: proximal	—	1	—	—	—	—	—	—	—	—	—	23
distal	—	—	—	—	—	—	—	—	—	—	—	34
Radius: proximal	—	2	—	1	—	—	—	—	—	—	—	6
distal	—	—	—	—	—	—	—	—	—	1	—	12
Ulna: proximal	—	—	—	—	—	—	—	—	—	—	—	31
distal	—	—	—	—	—	—	—	—	—	—	—	22
Carpals	1	2	—	1	—	—	—	—	3	—	—	—
Metapodials	—	2	—	1	—	—	—	—	5	4	1	9
Phalanges	—	7	3	—	1	1	—	—	8	1	—	—
Innominate	—	—	—	—	—	—	—	—	—	—	—	25
Femur: proximal	—	—	—	—	—	—	—	—	—	—	—	33
distal	—	—	—	—	—	—	—	—	—	1	—	33
Tibia: proximal	—	1	—	—	—	—	—	—	—	—	—	24
distal	—	—	—	—	—	—	—	—	—	—	—	22
Patella	—	—	—	—	—	—	—	—	—	—	—	6
Calcaneum	—	—	—	—	—	—	—	—	—	—	—	11
Astragalus	—	1	—	1	—	—	—	—	—	—	—	3
Other tarsals	—	—	—	—	1	1	—	—	—	—	—	—

Table 5.9. Minimum numbers of different-sized bovids represented by major skeletal regions in the fauna from Byeneskranskop Cave 1

	Small	Small medium	Large medium	Large
Mandible	50	2	25	12
Maxilla	52 (.96)	4 (.50)	34 (.74)	26 (.46)
Most abundant cranial element	52	4	34	26
Most abundant postcranial element	31 (1.68)	11 (.36)	22 (1.55)	19 (1.37)
Most abundant axial element[a]	25	3	3	3
Most abundant appendicular element[b]	31 (.81)	11 (.27)	22 (.14)	19 (.16)
Most abundant limb bone[c]	24	2	6	1
Most abundant foot bone[d]	24 (1.00)	11 (.18)	22 (.27)	19 (.05)
Most abundant forelimb bone[e]	31	4	8	5
Most abundant rear-limb bone[f]	24 (1.29)	6 (.67)	8 (1.00)	6 (.83)

Chi-square values

Maxilla/mandible	Small	Small medium	Large medium	Large
Small	—			
Small medium	.106	—		
Large medium	.423	.000	—	
Large	2.743	.149	.730	—

Cranial/postcranial	Small	Small medium	Large medium	Large
Small	—			
Small medium	5.328	—		
Large medium	.003	4.230	—	
Large	.122	3.200	.009	—

Axial/appendicular	Small	Small medium	Large medium	Large
Small	—			
Small medium	1.641	—		
Large medium	*6.763*	.102	—	
Large	*5.320*	.023	.073	—

Forelimb/rear-limb	Small	Small medium	Large medium	Large
Small	—			
Small medium	.372	—		
Large medium	.027	.009	—	
Large	.110	.036	.025	—

Limb bone/foot bone	Small	Small medium	Large medium	Large
Small	—			
Small medium	*3.696*	—		
Large medium	*4.906*	.001	—	
Large	*10.437*	.155	1.381	—

Notes: For the definition of the size categories, see table 5.1. Figures in parentheses are ratios between the first and second elements of a pair. Italicized χ^2 values are significant at the .05 level or below.

[a] Vertebrae and innominates.

[b] Scapula, limb bones, carpals/tarsals, metapodials, and phalanges.

[c] Humerus, radius, ulna, femur, and tibia.

[d] Carpals/tarsals, metapodials, phalanges, and sesamoids.

[e] Excluding scapula, but including carpals and metacarpals.

[f] Excluding innominate, but including tarsals and metatarsals.

Table 5.10. Minimum numbers of different-sized bovids, as represented by proximal and distal ends of major limb bones

	Small	Small medium	Large medium	Large	Totals
Humerus					
proximal	7	—	2	—	9
distal	18	2	2	—	22
Radius					
proximal	11	2	6	—	19
distal	12	—	—	1	13
Femur					
proximal	15	—	—	—	15
distal	10	—	—	—	10
Tibia					
proximal	7	—	—	—	7
distal	17	1	3	1	22

Note: For definition of the bovid size categories, see table 5.1.

the giant buffalo (*Pelorovis antiquus*), the "giant hartebeest" (*Megalotragus priscus*), and five or six additional species or subspecies of larger mammals. One such mammal, a wildebeest at least subspecifically distinct from the extant *Connochaetes gnou,* may also be represented in the available Byeneskranskop sample, but I would need more complete dentitions or horncores to be sure. A second extinct form, a large reedbuck at least subspecifically distinct from the extant *Redunca arundinum,* is more certainly present at Byeneskranskop and appears to continue there well into the Holocene. This suggests that the pattern of southern Cape mammalian extinctions may be more complex in its timing than I had thought. I suggested earlier (Klein, 1974b) that these large mammals became extinct because of changes in the environment between the last glacial of the Pleistocene and the Holocene, combined with the actions of Later Stone Age hunters. The environmental change (a reduction in grassland, leading to fewer animals with smaller ranges) cannot have been the only cause of these extinctions, because the same animals had survived a similar environmental change that occurred about 130,000 B.P., in the transition from the penultimate glacial to the last interglacial. The contrast between faunas of the Middle and Late Stone Age, discussed above, suggests that the crucial difference 10,000 years ago was the presence of more competent big-game hunters.

SUMMARY AND CONCLUSIONS

Analysis of the Byeneskranskop mammalian fauna and tortoises allows the following conclusions.

1. The Pre-Wilton vegetational setting of the site contained substantially

more grassveld than the Wilton or historic one. The Pre-Wilton occupants depended more on large, migratory plains game, the Wilton ones more on small, nonmigratory ground game and probably also on plants (especially geophytes). Both the Pre-Wilton and Wilton inhabitants ate tortoises in large numbers, but tortoises clearly were more important as a reliable dietary staple in Wilton times. The faunal data may be used to suggest differences in Pre-Wilton and Wilton settlement and demographic patterns. Relying to a great extent on large, migratory, gregarious grazers, Pre-Wilton peoples would probably have had to roam over large home ranges, while Wilton peoples, concentrating on small, solitary, nonmigratory browsers and on plants, were probably more sedentary, with smaller, more closely nested home ranges.

2. Following the terminal Pleistocene–early Holocene rise in sea level that brought the coast to within 5–6 km of Byeneskranskop, Later Stone Age peoples began to use it as a base for the exploitation of coastal resources. This is shown by the appearance or greatly increased frequency of molluscan shells and bones of fish, seabirds, and seals in the Wilton levels. Seal bones, however, are not as common at Byeneskranskop as in Wilton sites located directly on the coast, almost certainly because it was uneconomic to transport such large animals that far inland.

3. Supplemented by observations on other southern Cape faunas, the Byeneskranskop data suggest that Later Stone Age people exploited animal resources more effectively than their Middle Stone Age predecessors. In particular, they hunted more dangerous terrestrial prey (especially pigs) with greater frequency, and were actively engaged in fishing and fowling, which Middle Stone Age peoples were not.

4. Sheep bones are recorded only from the very top of the Byeneskranskop sequence. On the basis of information obtained at the nearby site of Die Kelders and at other southern Cape sites, it is probable that the oldest sheep bones at Byeneskranskop are between 2,000 and 1,600 years old. So far, the Byeneskranskop bone samples which include sheep are small, and detailed comparisons are not possible with the pre-sheep bone samples from the site. However, comparison of the Byeneskranskop pre-sheep samples with the large bone sample including sheep at nearby Die Kelders suggests that a much less varied range of indigenous species was hunted locally after the introduction of sheep. It is also possible that some indigenous species became less numerous as a result of range alteration caused by sheep.

5. As at other sites, the Byeneskranskop body-part frequency data suggest that smaller prey were often brought to the site intact, whereas larger ones were usually butchered elsewhere and only certain parts (mainly skull and foot elements) were regularly returned to the site. After reaching the site, certain body parts survived disproportionately, owing to differences in durability.

6. The discovery of an unquestionable *Equus capensis* tooth in the lowest level of Byeneskranskop confirms the survival of this large species of equid into the terminal Pleistocene, as already indicated at Elands Bay Cave. At least one and perhaps two other extinct mammalian taxa are found in the available Byeneskranskop sample. One of these may have survived later near Byeneskranskop than it did elsewhere in the southern Cape, suggesting that the local pattern of terminal Pleistocene extinctions may have been more complex than I had suggested earlier.

Acknowledgments

I thank F. R. Schweitzer for making the Byeneskranskop fauna available to me. Q. B. Hendey kindly provided study facilities in his department at the South African Museum. J. Deacon and F. R. Schweitzer made helpful comments on a draft of the manuscript. My presence in South Africa was made possible by a generous grant from the National Science Foundation.

Robert S. O. Harding

6.
An Order of Omnivores:
Nonhuman Primate Diets in the Wild

Evolutionary theories that tie the origin of the hominids directly to the development of hunting (Dart, 1953; Ardrey 1961, esp. 1976) have all relied, explicitly or implicitly, on the premise that the creatures ancestral to the hominids subsisted entirely on plant foods. Underlying these theories has been the widespread assumption that all nonhuman primates were and are vegetarians. Evolutionary hypotheses of this sort have become increasingly untenable in recent years, however, as reports of extensive predatory behavior by nonhuman primates have become available. Recent field studies of chimpanzees and baboons are salient examples (Teleki, Strum, in this volume), although predatory behavior in primates had been reported earlier (e.g., Dart, 1963; DeVore and Washburn, 1963; Goodall, 1963b). It is now clear that several primate populations make regular and substantial use of precisely that type of food which the early theories described as instrumental in the emergence of the hominids.

If the diets of these particular nonhuman primates are more broadly based than we had thought, then how accurate is it to characterize contemporary primate diets in general as "vegetarian"? Chimpanzees probably eat more fruit, and the colobine monkeys of Asia and Africa eat more leaves, than any other kind of food, but is it correct to call chimpanzees "frugivorous" or colobines "folivorous"? Because some human populations include large amounts of meat in their diet, should we label humans as "carnivorous"? As Teleki points out (1975:127 ff.), such terms are first used as shorthand references to a particular dietary specialization but then gradually become inclusive descriptions of an animal's entire diet. Essential elements of the diet are ignored, and the result is a generally misleading impression of what a group or population actually eats. As this article shows, diversity rather than specialization is typical of primate diets.

A knowledge of the extent of which primate diets are diversified is important because we cannot draw a valid evolutionary analogy when the underlying premise is at best poorly understood. Thus it makes little sense to propose that a dietary shift and the subsequent change in selection pressures gave rise to an entire new family of organisms, when the original

191

diet cannot be reconstructed and very little is known about the supposedly analogous natural diet of living primates.

Yet it would be a mistake to ignore dietary factors completely in considering primate evolution, for virtually everything primatologists have studied can be linked in some way to the things which primates eat: anatomy, behavior, and even social organization can all be seen as interlocking adaptations that enable primates to obtain and utilize food items as efficiently as possible. Although the original diet of our prehuman ancestors may never be known, we can compile what is known about natural primate diets in the wild and thus provide a sound basis of fact from which evolutionary theorization may proceed with more confidence. This article presents the results of a survey of nonhuman primate diets, in order to determine the extent to which primates in general are truly omnivorous, or conversely, the extent to which they specialize in particular types of food. As a corollary, the importance of specific kinds of food in primate diets is examined.

DIETS AND ADAPTATION

Many recent evolutionary theories have stressed the reproductive advantage accruing to individuals that possess specific anatomical or behavioral adaptations, which then spread in succeeding generations (Emlen and Demong, 1975; Moss, 1972). Although reproductive strategies are clearly of the utmost importance, the role played by feeding strategies in the evolutionary molding of primate anatomy and behavior is equally important (Schoener, 1971), for in order to reproduce at all, an animal must first be able to find enough food to survive.

Dentition is one of the most obvious anatomical reflections of dietary preference. For example, Kay discusses the functional significance of molar conformation in relation to diet and shows that primates which eat large amounts of insects have well-developed shearing crests on their molars (Kay, 1973, 1978), presumably to pulverize the hard chitin of insect exoskeletons. More herbivorous and omnivorous primates, by contrast, have a more bunodont crushing and shearing dentition, with rounded cusps—those which eat more leaves having longer shearing blades than those which prefer fruit, presumably to process the extra fiber contained in their diets.

Dietary preferences may also be correlated with the gut morphology of some primates (C. M. Hladik, 1966, 1967, 1968; C. M. Hladik and Chivers, 1978a). The leaf-eating colobines, for instance, have large, sacculated stomachs containing symbiont bacteria that enable them to digest mature leaves (Bauchop and Martucci, 1968). Such specializations, however, are rare.

Locomotor anatomy and behavior can also be seen as direct adaptations to food-getting. The retia mirabilia, specialized networks of blood vessels in the limbs of the lorisine primates, make a slow-climbing and grasping kind of locomotion possible, thus enabling these animals to approach insect and small animal prey without alarming them (Osman Hill, 1972), while the closely related galagos attain a similar end through rapid, saltatory motion (A. Walker, 1969). Ellefson (1974) regards gibbon morphology and brachiating locomotion as being basically a feeding adaptation.

The links between social organization and diet are elegantly explored by L. Klein and D. Klein in their study of four sympatric neotropical primate species (L. Klein, 1972; L. Klein and D. Klein, 1975). For instance, they point out that the tendency of spider monkey subgroups to fragment and recombine into different subgroups can be correlated with the seasonal availability of dispersed fruits, and that quick-moving squirrel monkey troops are well suited for flushing out the hidden insect prey they seek. Likewise, the semisolitary social organization of the orangutan can be viewed as a necessary consequence of the animal's great size and its major food source, widely dispersed fruits (Rodman, 1973b).

The distribution of food in space and time clearly affects the ranging behavior of the primates who must locate it in order to survive. To take extreme examples, hamadryas baboons travel an average of 13.2 km daily in their harsh environment (Kummer, 1968), while gorillas need to move only a few hundred meters each day to obtain the food they need (Schaller, 1963). The amount of time required to locate, process, and consume food items places limits on the amount of social activity possible for a given species, as Teleki has shown in the case of one chimpanzee population (1977a). Finally, the clumping or wide dispersal of food is known to have significant effects on social behavior: e.g., aggression rates rise when mangabeys converge on large jackfruits (Chalmers, 1968).

METHODS OF COLLECTING DIETARY DATA

Research into primate diets has increased greatly in recent years (Clutton-Brock, 1977; C. M. Hladik and Chivers, 1978), as a result of a growing interest in primate ecology and the tantalizing possibility, never fully realized, that primates might be classifiable into ecological as well as phylogenetic grades (Crook, 1970; Eisenberg, Muckenhirn, and Rudran, 1972). Nonetheless, data on primate diets are both scant and patchy when compared with the amount of information available on social behavior. A major reason for this situation has been the relative difficulty of collecting dietary data. For the primatologist whose major interest is the natural diet of wild primates, three avenues are open, each of which has its drawbacks.

The first avenue is the analysis of the stomach contents of wild-shot primates (Charles-Dominique, 1971; Fooden, 1964; C. Jones, 1970). The value of this method lies in the certainty with which an investigator can identify dietary items; however, it is not possible to tell how much of each item was ingested, nor is it at all certain that the stomach contents accurately reflect everything that has been eaten. Chitinous insect parts, for instance, survive better in the intestinal environment than do many other types of food. The main disadvantage of this kind of analysis, of course, is that the animal must be killed before the contents of its stomach can be analyzed, and this step is almost impossible to justify in view of the shrinking primate populations throughout the world.

Fecal analysis (e.g., Suzuki, 1969), the second method available, can be carried out without disturbing the primate populations involved, but as an analytic tool it has all the other drawbacks of stomach-content analysis. Nevertheless, fecal analysis may be of greater value in the near future because laboratory techniques now being developed may make it possible to expand the number of dietary items that can be identified. For instance, meat consumption may soon be detectable through laboratory testing (Dimuzio, n.d.).

Most of the available data on natural primate diets in the wild has been collected by observational methods (e.g., A. Hladik and C. Hladik, 1969; Wrangham, 1977). Depending on the thoroughness of the individual observer, this method can produce a reasonably accurate tally of the items eaten and quantities consumed while the observer is watching, but limits to and differences in human observational abilities may result in an incomplete picture of the primate diet. Then, too, the relative amounts of different foods ingested have often been estimated by recording the amount of time an animal spends feeding on each item. Such records include not only the time spent chewing but the period necessary to prepare each item, and this can be quite misleading. For instance, in certain seasons baboons spend a great deal of time digging for the underground corms of sedge plants, each corm measuring little more than 5 mm in diameter. The total amount of time spent in this activity may indicate something about the attraction which these corms have for baboons, but the proportion of feeding time spent in procuring and eating them cannot be translated directly into proportion of diet.

Given these disparate methods of obtaining data on natural primate diets, there are several levels of information available in published reports of field studies.

1. *Lists of food species.* This is by far the most widely available kind of information, often obtained by field researchers as a by-product of their major research on other topics. Such lists may be accompanied by rough estimates of amounts consumed or a ranking of foods by preference.

2. *Quantitative measures of amounts eaten.* These may be obtained by

calculating the amount of time spent feeding on each item or by measuring stomach contents, approaches which are likely to bias the data, as noted above. A more accurate method is to estimate the size of an average morsel and then to count the number of times such morsels are brought to the mouth.

3. *Biochemical analysis of food items.* This level of investigation makes it possible to determine not only what and how much an animal eats, but also the nutritive value of its food. But whereas some crude analyses (e.g., bomb calorimetry) can be undertaken in the field, more sophisticated testing can be extremely expensive, and in some instances tedious and time-consuming procedures may be required in order to obtain a sample large enough to be tested. For instance, acacia seeds are a favorite baboon food, but only the seed itself is eaten, not the seedcoat or the pod. Processing enough acacia pods to obtain the 1 kg of seeds necessary for analysis may take more time than a fieldworker has available. As a result of the expense and time involved, biochemical analysis has been infrequently used until relatively recently [e.g., research on baboon diets carried out by Stuart Altmann (personal communication) at Amboseli National Park, in Kenya, in 1976].

Rarer still have been attempts to analyze samples of the same food item collected at different times in the diurnal and annual (seasonal) cycles, although we now know that plant parts differ in both nutritive content and toxicity according to degree of maturity and time of day. Not only are immature plant parts richer in protein than older ones, but toxic levels are also lower in the immature fruits and leaves of those plants in which secondary compounds have evolved as antipredator devices (Janzen, 1975). Diurnal fluctuations exist as well: intense sunlight may concentrate toxic alkaloids in plant tissues (Cates and Orians, 1975), and thus early morning feeding may be very beneficial to primates who forage on certain plants.

4. *Estimates of nutritional requirements.* In order to understand fully the natural diets of wild primates, it is necessary to determine their nutritional requirements; this can only be done under controlled conditions in the laboratory. The steps that might be taken include the following.

a. Measuring metabolic rates as animals perform routine activities under experimentally varied conditions of temperature, humidity, direct solar radiation, and wind velocity.

b. Administering precisely controlled amounts of food and water, analyzed for vitamin and trace element content, followed by analysis of excreta to determine what proportion of the diet can be utilized and what proportion cannot be.

c. Studying the interactions of the intestinal microenvironment and the various internal parasites which primates harbor, as a means of assessing the effect of these parasites on the nutritional requirements of their hosts.

Further analyses may be devised by the ingenious researcher, but it is striking that, to date, most laboratory research on primate diets has been aimed either at human nutritional problems or at ways of keeping laboratory and zoo populations healthy, not at understanding the diets of wild primates. Some data on metabolic rates and diet are available from field studies (e.g., Coelho, 1975), but there is still much room for innovative research in this area.

5. *Estimates of distribution and seasonal availability of resources.* This kind of information has become more available as interest in the study of primate ecology has grown. Its main value is the insight provided into the mechanism of choice: why a primate chooses to eat what it does when it does, considering the competition of conspecifics and other animals, as well as the limits imposed by seasonal availability of food items.

Information from all these categories was, theoretically, available when this survey of natural primate diets in the wild was made. In practice, however, most field reports have confined themselves to the first category—lists of foods eaten and rough estimates of their relative amounts. Quantitative measures of what is eaten and ecological surveys (the second and fifth categories) are sometimes available but still uncommon, while studies providing quantitative nutritional requirements (the third and fourth categories) are no more than a handful in number. No study, to my knowledge, integrates all five levels of information. In addition, the quantity of data varies widely from species to species: contrast, for instance, the information available on such well-studied primates as chimpanzees and baboons with the few reports on some of the forest cercopithecines.

With such a wide variation in quality and quantity of available data, two approaches are possible in correlating what is known of wild primate diets. The first is to include only those species on which significant amounts of quantitative data are available. This approach has been used most successfully by Hladik (1975, and in this volume), working from his own carefully collected and rigorously tested data on primate species in Central America, Sri Lanka, Gabon, and Madagascar. The primates Hladik has studied are sufficiently diverse—phylogenetically, geographically, and ecologically—that he can draw reasonable inferences about primate evolution from a relatively small sample.

A second approach is to acknowledge the unevenness of the available data but to include as much information as can be gleaned from a survey of the literature, in an attempt to make up in completeness of coverage for what is lost in precision. This approach obviously makes an analysis in any depth difficult, and statistical testing all but impossible. Nevertheless, this method is used here, because quantitative comparisons are not necessary to establish the points at issue: that the various primate species are not exclusively vegetarian, particularly when an entire annual cycle is considered; that the order Primates as a whole is omnivorous; and that the family Hominidae is no exception to this overall primate pattern.

METHODS OF COLLATING DIETARY DATA

Every available report that contained information about natural primate diets in the wild was scanned, and individual food items were noted along with their relative importance in the diet of each primate species. The various kinds of food were then combined into the following categories: *A*, Animal foods, including vertebrate and crustacean flesh, plus eggs. *B*, Invertebrates. *C*, Fruits and berries. *D*, Seeds and nuts. *E*, Soft plant parts, including immature leaves, buds, shoots, and flowers. *F*, Mature leaves.[1] *G*, Roots and grasses. *H*, Tree parts, including bark, gums, decayed wood. *I*, Human crops.

Different symbols were used in table 6.1 to indicate the relative importance of food categories in a species' diet. The symbol $\boxed{X}$ was used whenever field records listed a category as a principal source of food. This symbol was used more than once for an individual species whenever several food types were described as equally significant major dietary components. The symbol $\textcircled{X}$ was used to designate foods of secondary importance. When the field report made no attempt to evaluate the role of a particular food in a primate diet, a plain X was used. None of these symbols is intended to imply anything about absolute quantities consumed.

Primate species were used as the basic units of study because not enough data could be found to make interpopulation comparisons possible throughout the order. Species were grouped by higher taxa following the classification of Napier and Napier (1967), and individual species were omitted only when reliable dietary information could not be located.

Space limitations made it necessary to eliminate from the final list of works consulted a number of references that actually were read. Some of the older sources, such as the work of Humboldt and other nineteenth-century naturalists, were not included in the list. A number of articles in regional publications that are available only in major libraries were omitted as well.[2] If articles by different authors mentioned the same dietary information, the source with the most comprehensive data was selected for inclusion in the list. Not every paper by a given author on the diet of a particular primate species could be included, and the criterion of comprehensiveness was applied here as well. Selection of this sort clearly is subjective, and many valuable studies could not be included. Finally, some pertinent information must inevitably (if inadvertently) have been excluded; I would be grateful to learn of any new data that can significantly extend this compilation.

Table 6.1 presents the results of the survey. The reader should bear in mind that the emphasis is on types of food which each primate species is known to eat, and that a blank spot on the table does not necessarily mean that the species concerned does not eat that particular item. In other words, the table represents the *minimum* amount of variability in primate diets, and more extensive field studies coupled with more thorough work should result in filling in many of the blank spaces.

CONCLUSIONS

The data are summarized in histogram form in figures 6.1 through 6.14, which show the proportion of species in various major taxa whose diets contain each of the 9 food categories. Thus, for instance, 118 of the 129 primate species surveyed, or 91%, have been reported to eat fruit (figure 6.1).

Eclecticism is the rule among primate diets. Only two species, the tree shrews *Dendrogale melanura* and *Tupaia tana,* have been reported to subsist exclusively on one category of food (insects, in this case). This is expectable, for in their anatomy tree shrews are not unlike the ancestral insectivore from which the primate order is presumed to have evolved, and insects are the major food source for every tree shrew species surveyed.

All the other primate species have much more varied diets, however; an average primate diet contains between 4 and 5 of the 9 possible categories. At the opposite end of the spectrum from the tree shrews are those species which use food from all 9 categories: *Cercopithecus aethiops, Pan,* and the *Papio* species. It should also be noted that, despite the occasional dietary specialization of individual species, the same 4 food categories—fruits, soft plant parts, mature leaves, and insects—are the items found most frequently in the diets of each of the major taxa: the prosimians, Old World monkeys, New World monkeys, and apes.

When primate diets are ranked by food category, the following conclusions emerge.

A. *Animal foods.* More than one-third (37%) of all primate diets contain vertebrate or crustacean flesh or eggs.

B. *Invertebrates.* Prosimians are the heaviest consumers of invertebrates (72% of all prosimian diets surveyed include invertebrates), but it should be stressed that invertebrates are eaten by every major primate group, even the "folivorous" colobines. The unavoidable implication is that insect-eating is not only an ancient but a consistent trait throughout primate evolution.

C. *Fruit.* The most widely used type of food, fruit is found in 90% of all primate diets. Even among prosimians, whose diets contain substantial proportions of insects, more eat fruit than any other food category (81% of all prosimian diets).

D. *Seeds and nuts.* These items are important components of the diets of Old World monkeys (59%), but are less significant to New World monkeys, prosimians, and apes. Seed-eating may thus be a relatively recent primate adaptation, associated with colonization of habitats that are either relatively rich in this resource or poor in some of the other primate staples such as fruits, soft plant parts, and insects.

E. *Soft plant parts.* This category is also heavily utilized by Old World monkeys, with cercopithecine and colobine monkeys participating almost equally (92% and 94% of diets). Immature leaves, buds, shoots, and flowers are second only to fruit, being found in 79% of all primate diets.

F. *Mature leaves.* This food category is of special interest to the Old World monkeys, a conclusion that would seem inevitable given the leaf-eating specializations of the colobine monkeys. However, other Old World monkeys also consume mature leaves (they are found in 79% of all cercopithecine diets), while the comparable figures for other major taxonomic groups vary between 58% and 70%.

G. *Grasses and roots.* Only Old World monkeys and apes appear to make any use of this kind of food, and less than one-third of the diets in each of these two groups include grass or roots.

H. *Tree parts.* Consumption of barks, gums, and rotted wood varies between 50% (prosimians) and 7% (New World monkeys) of all diets.

I. *Human Crops.* The exploitation of this resource (where it is available), is much more widespread than expected, but is still limited to the Old World monkeys (52% of all diets), the great apes (75%), and to one prosimian family, the Lorisidae (11%).

Table 6.2 compares the proportionate representation of food categories in the aggregate of all primate diets surveyed (taken from figure 6.1) with the frequency with which each category was listed in table 6.1 as a major food source ([X]). The discrepancy between the two columns in table 6.2 demonstrates how misleading it is to categorize a primate's diet by its major component. Thus, while only 45% of all species might be labeled "frugivores" based on their major source of food, the fact is that 9 out of every 10 species eat at least some fruit. Similarly, while it is true that neither meat nor human crops are the major resource for any primate species, 37% and 25% of all species eat these foods. Finally, if the primates who eat either vertebrate (category A) or invertebrate (category B) foods or both are lumped together, it is evident that at least 69% of all primate species deliberately eat nonvegetable foods. (Accidentally eaten invertebrates, such as the larvae that often infest the fruit of *Ficus*, are never included in estimates of insect consumption, and yet under some circumstances they may contribute substantially to the diet.) Primates, then, can only be described as omnivores; they are definitely not vegetarian animals.

I have not attempted to assess quantitatively the relative importance of various items in each primate's diet. Because of the uneven quality of the information available, I have listed only the types of food primates eat, indicating, where possible, which types can be considered primary food sources. Thus I have not confronted some of the most fundamental issues in primate dietary research today: What are the nutritive requirements of each species? What is the nutritive content of each item eaten? And, by extension, what are the exact quantities of each food consumed? With few exceptions, such data are not available; yet it is in precisely these areas that research must be undertaken if we are to come to a full understanding of diets and the role they play in the evolutionary development of primate anatomy and behavior. Such research is complex, costly, and difficult, and will require the participation of many different branches of science if it is to be successful. Anatomists, biochemists, ecologists, ethologists, and physiologists must all contribute to the joint effort.

Not until a basis of quantitative data has been collected from this kind of research can evolutionary hypotheses tracing the ultimate origin of mankind to changing diets be much more than speculative. In the meantime, although the data presented here only begin to probe the complexity of this subject, they nevertheless make it clear that the natural diet of almost every living wild primate is characterized by great diversity. There is no reason to suppose that the diet of the common ancestor of humans and apes differed in any major way. Substantial amounts of animal food must already have been present in the diet of our prehominid ancestors.

These data suggest that the capture and consumption of invertebrates is a behavioral trait which arose very early in the evolution of the order Primates. The hunting of small vertebrates could have developed out of this trait, as natural selection gradually improved the anatomical capability of such behavior. Under these circumstances we need not search for the roots of primate hunting among techniques used for plant exploitation, as M. D. Rose has suggested (1978). Instead, we can postulate an evolutionary continuum that begins with the eating of small, mobile insects, progresses to capture of the larger orthopterans and coleopterans, and thence to predation on small vertebrates (cf. Cartmill, 1974). There is every reason to suppose that this latter behavioral trait was widespread within the primate order well before the Pliocene, when the first of the hominds developed.

If meat-eating is not a radical innovation of our earliest ancestors, then hunting cannot be the major adaptation which first set them on the pathway to modern humanity. Thus, the extreme theories that attribute the many forms of present-day human aggression, including war and murder, to this hypothesized innovation (Ardrey, 1961; Lorenz, 1966) can no longer be sustained. The causes for the emergence of the hominids must be sought in a more complex adaptational shift, of which diet was only a part.

Acknowledgments

My principal debt is to Claudia Fishman, upon whose shoulders fell most of the burden of searching out and reviewing the hundreds of sources checked to provide the data for this chapter. Similar thanks are due to Sharon Kolasinski for her painstaking bibliographic work. Both provided valuable advice and criticism as well. I am grateful to Richard Kay for opening the door to many sources not previously considered and for sharing his work, both published and unpublished. Finally, I would like to acknowledge the help of Steven Gaulin, who provided me with some of his own findings, especially his review paper with M. Konner (1977).

NOTES

1. When authors did not distinguish between mature and immature leaves, both items were counted as part of the diet. This arbitrary step may have biased the data; since mature leaves are harder to digest (thus less likely to be eaten), this category of food may be overrepresented.

2. For readers interested in pursuing these two avenues of research, Kay (1973) includes a valuable compendium of many of the older and less easily obtained sources.

Table 6.1. Survey of Primate Diets

	A	B	C	D	E	F	G	H	I
PROSIMII									
TUPAIIDAE									
1. *Anathana ellioti*	—	⊠	⊗	—	—	—	—	×	—
2. *Dendrogale melanura*	—	⊠	—	—	—	—	—	—	—
3. *Ptilocercus lowii*	×	⊠	—	—	—	—	—	—	—
4. *Tupaia glis*	×	⊠	—	×	×	—	—	—	—
5. *Tupaia minor*	×	⊠	×	×	—	—	—	—	—
6. *Tupaia montana*	—	⊠	×	×	×	×	—	—	—
7. *Tupaia tana*	—	⊠	—	—	—	—	—	—	—
8. *Urogale everetti*	×	⊠	×	—	—	—	—	—	—
Totals	4	8	4	3	2	1	0	1	0
LEMURIDAE									
Cheirogaleinae									
9. *Cheirogaleus major*	—	⊗	⊠	—	—	×	—	—	—
10. *Cheirogaleus medius*	—	⊗	⊠	—	—	×	—	—	—
11. *Microcebus coquereli*	—	⊠	×	—	×	×	—	×	—
12. *Microcebus murinus*	—	⊠	⊗	—	×	⊗	—	×	—
13. *Phaner furcifer*	—	×[1]	×	—	—	⊗	—	×	—
Lemurinae									
14. *Hapalemur griseus*	—	—	—	—	⊗	⊠	—	×	—
15. *Lemur catta*	—	—	⊠	—	⊠	⊠	—	×	—
16. *Lemur macaco*	×	×	⊗	×	⊠	⊠	—	×	—
17. *Lemur mongoz*	—	—	⊗	×	×	⊠	—	—	—
18. *Lemur rubriventer*	—	—	×	—	⊗	⊠	—	—	—
19. *Lemur variegatus*	—	—	×	—	×	×	—	—	—
20. *Lepilemur mustelinus*	—	—	×	—	⊗	⊠	—	×	—

[1]Secretions.

Key: A. Animal foods, including vertebrate and crustacean flesh, plus eggs.
   B. Invertebrates.
   C. Fruits and berries.
   D. Seeds and nuts.
   E. Soft plant parts, including immature leaves, buds, shoots, flowers.
   F. Mature leaves (both mature and immature leaves counted when authors did not distinguish between them).
   G. Roots and grasses.
   H. Tree parts, including bark, gums, decayed wood.
   I. Human crops.

⊠ This category described in field records as a main source of food.
⊗ This category listed as a secondary source of food.
× Relative importance of this food category not described.

Table 6.1. (Continued)

	A	B	C	D	E	F	G	H	I
INDRIIDAE									
21. *Avahi laniger*	—	—	⊗	—	⊠	⊠	—	×	—
22. *Indri indri*	—	—	⊗	—	⊠	×	—	—	—
23. *Propithecus diadema*	—	—	×	—	⊠	×	—	×	—
24. *Propithecus verreauxi*	—	—	⊠	—	⊗	⊗	—	×	—
DAUBENTONIIDAE									
25. *Daubentonia madagascariensis*	—	⊠	⊗	—	—	—	—	×	—
Total, Madagascar lemurs	1	7	16	2	14	17	0	11	0
LORISIDAE									
Lorisinae									
26. *Arctocebus calabarensis*	—	⊠	×	—	—	—	—	×	—
27. *Loris tardigradus*	×	⊠	×	—	×	—	—	—	—
28. *Nycticebus coucang*	×	⊠	×	—	×	×	—	×	—
29. *Perodicticus potto*	×	×	⊠	—	×	×	—	⊗	—
Galaginae									
30. *Galago alleni*	×	⊗	⊠	—	—	×	—	×	—
31. *Galago crassicaudatus*	×	⊠	⊠	—	—	×	—	—	×
32. *Galago demidovii*	—	⊠	⊗	—	×	×	—	—	—
33. *Galago elegantulus*	—	⊗	×	—	—	—	—	×	—
34. *Galago senegalensis*	—	⊠	—	×	×	×	—	×	—
Totals	5	9	8	1	5	6	0	6	1
TARSIIDAE									
35. *Tarsius bancanus*	×	×	⊠	—	—	—	—	—	—
36. *Tarsius spectrum*	×	⊠	—	—	—	—	—	—	—
Totals	2	2	1	0	0	0	0	0	0
ANTHROPOIDEA									
CALLITRICHIDAE									
37. *Callimico goeldii*	—	×	×	—	—	—	—	—	—
38. *Callithrix* spp.	×	×	×	×	×	—	—	×	—
39. *Cebuella pygmaea*	×	⊠	⊗	—	×	—	—	×	—
40. *Leontideus rosalia*	×	⊠	⊗	—	—	—	—	—	—
41. *Saguinus fuscicollis*	—	⊠	⊠	—	—	×	—	—	—
42. *Saguinus geoffroyi*	—	⊗	⊠	—	×	×	—	—	—
43. *Saguinus oedipus*	×	⊠	⊗	—	—	—	—	—	—
44. *Saguinus tamarin*	×	⊠	—	—	—	—	—	—	—
Totals	5	8	7	1	3	2	0	2	0

Table 6.1. (Continued)

	A	B	C	D	E	F	G	H	I
CEBIDAE									
45. *Alouatta seniculus*	—	—	⊗	—	⊠	⊠	—	—	—
46. *Alouatta villosa*	—	—	⊠	×	⊠	⊠	—	×	—
47. *Aotus trivirgatus*	×	—	⊠	—	⊗	⊗	—	×	—
48. *Ateles belzebuth*	—	—	⊠	—	—	×	—	×	—
49. *Ateles geoffroyi*	—	×	⊠	×	—	⊗	—	—	—
50. *Ateles paniscus*	×	—	×	×	—	×	—	—	—
51. *Brachyteles arachnoides*	—	—	×	—	×	×	—	—	—
52. *Cacajao calvus*	—	—	×	×	×	×	—	—	—
53. *Cacajao melanocephalus*	—	—	×	—	—	—	—	—	—
54. *Callicebus moloch*	×	×	⊗	—	⊠	⊠	—	—	—
55. *Callicebus personatus*	—	—	×	—	—	—	—	—	—
56. *Callicebus torquatus*	—	×	⊠	×	×	×	—	—	—
57. *Cebus albifrons*	—	—	—	×	×	×	—	—	—
58. *Cebus apella*	—	⊠	⊠	×	×	×	—	—	—
59. *Cebus capucinus*	×	⊗	⊠	—	×	×	—	—	—
60. *Cebus nigrivittatus*	—	×	×	—	—	—	—	—	—
61. *Chiropotes albinasus*	×	—	×	×	×	×	—	—	—
62. *Chiropotes satanas*	×	—	×	×	×	×	—	—	—
63. *Lagothrix lagotricha*	—	×	⊠	×	×	×	—	—	—
64. *Pithecia pithecia*	×	×	⊠	×	—	×	—	—	—
65. *Saimiri oerstedii*	—	⊗	⊠	—	×	×	—	—	—
66. *Saimiri sciureus*	—	⊗	⊠	×	—	×	—	—	—
Totals	7	10	21	12	14	19	0	3	0
CERCOPITHECIDAE									
Cercopithecinae									
67. *Cercocebus albigena*	×	⊗	⊠	×	×	×	—	×	×
68. *Cercocebus galeritus*	×	×	⊠	×	⊗	⊗	—	—	—
69. *Cercocebus torquatus*	—	×	⊠	×	×	×	—	×	×
70. *Cercopithecus aethiops*	×	×	⊠	⊗	×	×	×	×	×
71. *Cercopithecus ascanius*	—	⊗	⊠	—	×	×	—	×	×
72. *Cercopithecus campbelli*	—	×	⊠	—	×	×	—	—	×
73. *Cercopithecus cephus*	×	×	⊠	×	⊗	⊗	—	—	—
74. *Cercopithecus denti*	—	—	—	—	×	×	—	—	—
75. *Cercopithecus diana*	—	—	⊠	—	—	—	—	—	—
76. *Cercopithecus erythrotis*	—	—	×	—	—	×	—	—	—
77. *Cercopithecus lhoesti*	—	—	×	—	—	×	—	—	—
78. *Cercopithecus mitis*	×	⊗	⊠	⊗	×	×	—	—	×
79. *Cercopithecus mona*	—	×	×	×	×	×	—	—	—
80. *Cercopithecus neglectus*	—	×	⊠	⊠	⊗	⊗	—	—	—
81. *Cercopithecus nictitans*	—	×	⊠	⊗	⊗	×	—	—	—
82. *Cercopithecus petaurista*	—	—	×	—	×	×	—	—	—
83. *Cercopithecus pogonias*	×	⊗	⊠	×	—	×	—	—	—

Table 6.1. (Continued)

	A	B	C	D	E	F	G	H	I
84. *Cercopithecus* (*Miopithecus*) *talapoin*	X	⊗	⊠	X	X	X	—	—	X
85. *Erythrocebus patas*	X	X	X	X	X	X	X	—	X
86. *Macaca arctoides*	X	X	⊠	X	X	X'	⊠	—	X
87. *Macaca assamensis*	X	X	X	X	—	—	—	—	X
88. *Macaca cyclopis*	—	X	X	—	—	X	—	—	X
89. *Macaca fascicularis*	X	X	⊠	—	X	X	X	—	X
90. *Macaca fuscata*	X	X	X	—	X	X	X	X	X
91. *Macaca maurus*	—	X	X	—	—	—	—	—	X
92. *Macaca mulatta*	—	X	X	X	X	X	X	X	X
93. *Macaca nemestrina*	—	X	⊠	X	—	X	—	—	—
94. *Macaca radiata*	X	X	⊠	X	⊗	⊗	—	X	X
95. *Macaca silenus*	X	X	⊠	X	X	X	X	—	X
96. *Macaca sinica*	X	X	⊠	—	⊗	⊗	—	—	X
97. *Macaca sylvanus*	—	—	X	X	X	X	X	X	X
98. *Mandrillus leucophaeus*	X	X	⊠	X	X	⊠	X	—	X
99. *Mandrillus sphinx*	—	X	X	X	X	X	—	—	X
100. *Papio anubis*	X	X	⊗	⊗	X	X	⊠	X	X
101. *Papio cynocephalus*	X	X	⊗	⊗	X	X	⊠	X	X
102. *Papio hamadryas*	X	X	X	X	X	X	X	X	X
103. *Papio ursinus*	X	X	⊗	⊗	X	X	⊠	X	X
104. *Theropithecus gelada*	—	X	X	⊗	X	X	⊠	—	X
Totals	20	32	37	26	30	35	14	12	26
Colobinae									
105. *Colobus badius*	—	—	X	—	⊗	⊠	—	X	—
106. *Colobus guereza*	—	—	⊗	X	⊗	⊠	—	X	—
107. *Colobus polykomos*	—	—	X	X	⊠	⊠	—	—	X
108. *Colobus* (*Procolobus*)									
109. *verus*	—	—	X	—	⊠	⊠	—	—	—
Colobus satanas	—	—	—	⊠	⊗	⊗	—	—	—
110. *Nasalis larvatus*	—	—	⊠	—	X	X	—	—	—
111. *Presbytis aygula*	—	—	X	—	⊠	⊠	—	—	—
112. *Presbytis cristatus*	—	—	⊗	X	⊗	⊠	—	X	—
113. *Presbytis entellus*	—	X	⊗	X	⊠	⊠	—	X	X
114. *Presbytis geei*	—	—	⊗	—	⊠	⊠	—	—	—
115. *Presbytis johnii*	—	X	X	X	X	X	—	X	X
116. *Presbytis melalophos*	—	—	⊗	X	⊠	⊠	—	X	—
117. *Presbytis obscurus*	—	—	⊗	—	⊠	⊠	—	—	—
118. *Presbytis phayrei*	—	—	—	—	X	X	—	—	—
119. *Presbytis pileatus*	—	—	X	—	X	—	—	—	—
120. *Presbytis senex*	—	—	⊗	—	⊗	⊠	—	—	—
121. *Pygathrix nemaeus*	—	—	—	—	—	—	—	—	—
122. *Rhinopithecus roxellanae*	—	—	X	—	X	X	—	—	—
Totals	0	2	15	7	17	16	0	6	3

Table 6.1. (Continued)

	A	B	C	D	E	F	G	H	I
HYLOBATIDAE									
123. *Hylobates hoolock*	×	×	×	—	×	×	—	—	—
124. *Hylobates klossii*	—	—	×	—	—	—	—	—	—
125. *Hylobates lar*	×	×	⊠	—	—	⊗	—	—	—
126. *Hylobates moloch*	—	—	⊠	—	×	×	—	—	—
127. *Symphalangus syndactylus*	—	×	⊠	—	×	⊠	—	—	—
PONGIDAE									
128. *Gorilla gorilla*	—	×	⊠	—	⊠	⊠	×	×	×
129. *Pan paniscus*	×	×	⊠	—	—	×	—	—	—
130. *Pan troglodytes*	×	×	⊠	×	×	⊗	×	×	×
131. *Pongo pygmaeus*	—	×	⊠	×	⊗	⊗	×	×	×
Totals, Hylobatidae and Pongidae	4	7	9	2	6	8	3	3	3
Grand totals, all species in table	48	85	118	54	91	104	17	44	33

Table 6.2. Comparison of dietary frequency with major dietary components

Food category	Dietary frequency[a]	Major dietary components[b]
Fruit	90	45
Soft plant foods	79	9
Mature leaves	69	15
Invertebrates	65	23
Seeds	41	2
Animal foods	37	0
Tree parts	34	0
Human crops	25	0
Grasses, roots	13	5

[a] Percentage of surveyed species for which a given food category was listed in the diet.

[b] Among species for which a major food source was designated in table 6.1, the percentage in which a given food category was listed. When two or more types of food were described as major sources, each was weighted proportionately.

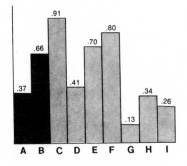

Figure 6.1.

Figure 6.1. Proportions of species, among all primates surveyed ($n = 131$), whose diets contained each of nine food categories. For all the figures in this article, the nine food categories are as follows: A, meat; B, insects; C, fruits; D, seeds and nuts; E, mature leaves; F, soft plant parts; G, roots and grasses; H, tree parts; I, human crops.

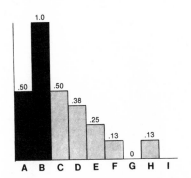

Figure 6.2. Diet of Tupaiidae surveyed ($n = 8$).

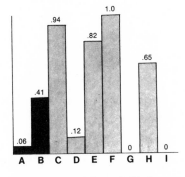

Figure 6.3. Diet of Madagascar lemurs surveyed ($n = 17$).

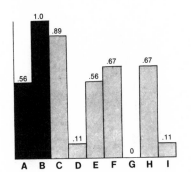

Figure 6.4. Diet of Lorisidae surveyed ($n = 9$).

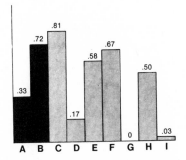

Figure 6.5. Diet of all prosimians surveyed, including Tarsiidae ($n = 36$).

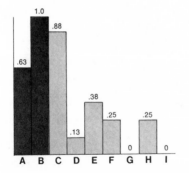

Figure 6.6. Diet of Callitrichidae surveyed (*n* = 8).

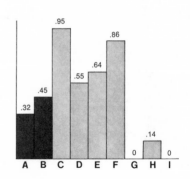

Figure 6.7. Diet of Cebidae surveyed (*n* = 22).

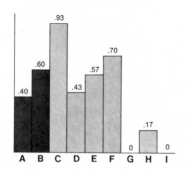

Figure 6.8. Diet of Platyrrhines surveyed (*n* = 30).

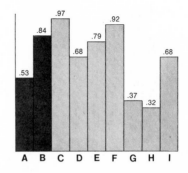

Figure 6.9. Diet of Cercopithecinae surveyed (*n* = 38).

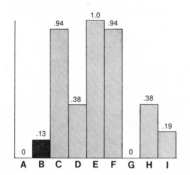

Figure 6.10. Diet of Colobinae surveyed (*n* = 18).

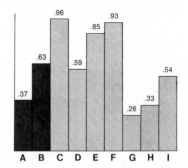

Figure 6.11. Diet of Cercopithecidae surveyed (*n* = 54).

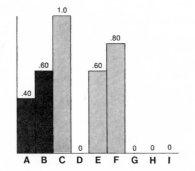

Figure 6.12. Diet of Hylobatidae surveyed (*n* = 5).

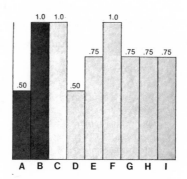

Figure 6.13. Diet of Pongidae surveyed (*n* = 4).

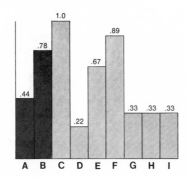

Figure 6.14. Diet of all apes surveyed (*n* = 9).

WORKS CONSULTED IN PREPARATION OF TABLE 6.1

PROSIMII

A. TUPAIIDAE
Anathana
  Chorazyna and Kurup, 1975
Dendrogale
  Napier and Napier, 1967
Ptilocercus
  Napier and Napier, 1967
Tupaia
  D'Souza, 1974
  Roonwal and Mohnot, 1977
Urogale
  Wharton, 1950

B. LEMURIDAE
Cheirogaleinae
Cheirogaleus
  Napier and Napier, 1967
  Petter, 1962a
Microcebus
  R. D. Martin, 1972, 1973
  Petter, 1962a,b, 1978
Phaner
  Petter, 1962a,b
  Petter, Schilling and Pariente, 1971,
    1975

Lemurinae
Hapalemur
  Petter and Peyrieras, 1970a, 1975
Lemur catta
  C. M. Hladik, 1978b
  A. Jolly, 1966
  Petter, 1962a,b
  Sussman, 1974, 1977
Lemur macaco
  C. M. Hladik, 1978b
  Petter, 1962a,b
  Sussman, 1974, 1975, 1977
Lemur mongoz
  Sussman and Tattersall, 1976
Lemur rubriventer
  Petter, 1962a
Lemur variegatus
  Petter, 1962a,b
Lepilemur mustelinus
  Charles-Dominique and Hladik, 1971
  C. M. Hladik, 1978b
  C. M. Hladik and Charles-
    Dominique, 1974

C. INDRIIDAE
Avahi
  Petter, 1962a,b
Indri
  Petter, 1962a,b
  Pollock, 1975
Propithecus
  A. Jolly, 1966
  Petter, 1962a,b
  Richard, 1974

D. DAUBENTONIIDAE
Daubentonia
  Petter, 1962a,b, 1965
  Petter and Peyrieras, 1970b

E. LORISIDAE
Lorisinae
Arctocebus
  Charles-Dominique, 1971, 1974, 1977
  Oates, 1969
  A. Walker, 1969
Loris
  Amerasinghe, Van Cuylenberg, and
    Hladik, 1971
  C. M. Hladik, 1975
  Roonwal and Mohnot, 1977
  A. Walker, 1969
Nycticebus
  Chivers, 1973
  Elliot and Elliot, 1967
  A. Walker, 1969
Perodicticus
  Bearder and Doyle, 1974
  Charles-Dominique, 1971, 1974, 1977
  Jewell and Oates, 1969
  A. Walker, 1969

Galaginae
Galago alleni
  Charles-Dominique, 1971, 1974, 1977
  Jewell and Oates, 1969
Galago crassicaudatus
  Bearder and Doyle, 1974
  Coe and Isaac, 1965
  Kano, 1971b
Galago demidovii
  Charles-Dominique, 1971, 1972, 1977
  Gartlan and Struhsaker, 1972
  Jewell and Oates, 1969
Galago elegantulus

Charles-Dominique, 1974
C. M. Hladik, 1978b
Galago senegalensis
Bearder and Doyle, 1974
Charles-Dominique, 1971
Sauer and Sauer, 1963

F. TARSIIDAE
Tarsius bancanus
Fogden, 1974

ANTHROPOIDEA
A. CALLITRICHIDAE
Callimico
Moynihan, 1976
Callithrix
Coimbra-Filho and Mittermeier,
1973b
Cebuella
Hernandez-Camacho, 1976
Izawa, 1975
Kinzey, Rosenberger, and Ramirez,
1975
Leontideus
Coimbra-Filho and Mittermeier,
1973a
Saguinus fuscicollis
Izawa, 1975
Saguinus geoffroyi
C. M. Hladik, 1975
C. M. Hladik, A. Hladik, et al., 1971
Saguinus oedipus
Hernandez-Camacho, 1976

B. CEBIDAE
Alouatta seniculus
Fooden, 1964
Izawa, 1975
L. Klein, 1972
L. Klein and D. Klein, 1975
Alouatta villosa
Carpenter, 1934
Coelho, 1975
Freese, 1976
Glander, 1975, 1977, 1978
A. Hladik and C. M. Hladik, 1969
C. M. Hladik, 1975, 1978a
C. M. Hladik, A. Hladik, et al., 1971
Richard, 1970
Aotus
A. Hladik and C. M. Hladik, 1969
C. M. Hladik, 1975
Ateles belzebuth

Izawa, 1975
L. Klein, 1972
L. Klein and D. Klein, 1975
Ateles geoffroyi
Carpenter, 1935
Coelho, 1975
Freese, 1976
C. M. Hladik, A. Hladik, et al., 1971
Richard, 1970
Ateles paniscus
Hernandez-Camacho, 1976
Brachyteles
Zingeser, 1973
Cacajao
Moynihan, 1976
Napier and Napier, 1967
Callicebus
Hernandez-Camacho, 1976
Izawa, 1975
Kinzey, 1977, 1978
Snodderly, 1978
Cebus apella
Fooden, 1964
Izawa, 1975
L. Klein, 1972
L. Klein and D. Klein, 1975
Thorington, 1967
Cebus capucinus
Freese, 1976
A. Hladik and C. M. Hladik, 1969
C. M. Hladik, 1975, 1978a
C. M. Hladik, A. Hladik, et al.,
1971
Chiropotes
Fooden, 1964
Thorington, 1967
Lagothrix
Hernandez-Camacho, 1976
Izawa, 1975
Zingeser, 1973
Pithecia
Fooden, 1964
Izawa, 1975
Saimiri
Baldwin and Baldwin, 1972
Fooden, 1964
Hernandez-Camacho, 1976
A. Hladik and C. M. Hladik, 1969
Izawa, 1975
L. Klein, 1972
L. Klein and D. Klein, 1975

Rosenblum and Cooper, 1968
Thorington, 1967, 1968

C. CERCOPITHECIDAE
Cercopithecinae
Cercocebus
Chalmers, 1968
Gartlan and Struhsaker, 1972
Gautier-Hion, 1978
C. Jones, 1970
Jones and Sabater Pi, 1968
Waser, 1974, 1975
Cercopithecus aethiops
Dunbar, 1974
Galat and Galat-Luong, 1976
Gartlan and Brain, 1968
Hall and Gartlan, 1965
C. M. Hladik, 1978a
Moreno-Black and Maples, 1977
Poirier, 1972
Sade and Hildrech, 1965
Struhsaker, 1967
Cercopithecus ascanius
Haddow, 1952
Kano, 1971b
Struhsaker, 1975, 1978
Cercopithecus cephus
Gautier and Gautier-Hion, 1969
Gautier-Hion, 1978
Gautier-Hion and Gautier, 1974
C. Jones, 1970
Cercopithecus diana
Booth, 1956
Napier and Napier, 1967
Cercopithecus erythrotis
Gartlan and Struhsaker, 1972
Cercopithecus lhoesti
Gartlan and Struhsaker, 1972
Cercopithecus mitis
DeVos and Omar, 1971
Gartlan and Brain, 1968
Kano, 1971b
Moreno-Black and Maples, 1977
Oatley, 1970
Struhsaker, 1975, 1978
Cercopithecus mona
Gartlan and Struhsaker, 1972
Gautier and Gautier-Hion, 1969
Cercopithecus neglectus
Gautier and Gautier-Hion, 1969
C. M. Hladik, 1978a
C. Jones, 1970

Cercopithecus nictitans
Gartlan and Struhsaker, 1972
Gautier and Gautier-Hion, 1969
Gautier-Hion, 1973
Gautier-Hion and Gautier, 1974
C. M. Hladik, 1978a
C. Jones, 1970
Cercopithecus pogonias
Gartlan and Struhsaker, 1972
Gautier-Hion, 1978
Gautier-Hion and Gautier, 1974
C. M. Hladik, 1978a
C. Jones, 1970
Cercopithecus (Miopithecus) talapoin
Gautier-Hion, 1966, 1971, 1973, 1978
Gautier and Gautier-Hion, 1969
C. Jones, 1970
Rowell, 1972
Erythrocebus
Hall, 1965
Macaca arctoides
Bertrand, 1969
Estrada and Estrada, 1976
Fooden, 1971
Macaca assamensis
Fooden, 1971
Roonwal and Mohnot, 1977
Macaca fascicularis
Chivers, 1973
Fooden, 1971
Furuya, 1965
Kurland, 1973
Poirier and Smith, 1974
Macaca fuscata
Iwamoto, 1974
Izawa, 1972
Koganezawa, 1975
Suzuki, 1965
Macaca mulatta
Lindburg, 1971
Neville, 1968
Puget, 1971
Macaca nemestrina
Chivers, 1973
Fooden, 1971
Macaca radiata
Roonwal and Mohnot, 1977
Simonds, 1965
Sugiyama, 1971
Macaca silenus
Roonwal and Mohnot, 1977

Sugiyama, 1968
Macaca sinica
C. M. Hladik, 1975
C. M. Hladik and A. Hladik, 1972
Macaca sylvanus
Deag and Crook, 1971
Taub, 1977
Mandrillus
Gartlan, 1970
Gartlan and Struhsaker, 1972
Grubb, 1973
C. M. Hladik, 1978a
Jouventin, 1975
Sabater Pi, 1972
Papio anubis
Aldrich-Blake et al., 1971
Crook and Aldrich-Blake, 1968
Harding, 1973a, 1975, 1976
Nagel, 1973
Ransom, 1971
Rowell, 1966
Papio cynocephalus
Altmann and Altmann, 1970
Papio hamadryas
Kummer, 1968
Nagel, 1973
Papio ursinus
Hall, 1962, 1963b
Theropithecus
Crook and Aldrich-Blake, 1968
Iwamoto, 1974
Dunbar, 1977

Colobinae
Colobus badius
Clutton-Brock, 1973, 1975a,b
Gunderson-Coolen, 1977
Nishida, 1972b
Struhsaker, 1975, 1978
Colobus guereza
Clutton-Brock, 1975a
Dunbar and Dunbar, 1974
Gautier-Hion, 1978
Groves, 1973
C. M. Hladik, 1978a
Moreno-Black and Maples, 1977
Oates, 1977
Struhsaker, 1975, 1978
Colobus polykomos
C. Jones, 1970
Sabater Pi, 1973
Colobus (Procolobus) verus

Booth, 1957
Colobus satanas
McKey, 1978
Nasalis
Kawabe and Mano, 1972
Kern, 1964
Presbytis aygula
Rodman, 1973a
Presbytis cristatus
Bernstein, 1968
Fooden, 1971
Medway, 1970
Presbytis entellus
C. M. Hladik, 1975, 1978a
C. M. Hladik and A. Hladik, 1972
Hrdy, 1974
Ripley, 1970
Rodman, 1973a
Yoshiba, 1968
Presbytis geei
Mukherjee and Saha, 1974
Roonwal and Mohnot, 1977
Presbytis johnii
Poirier, 1969, 1970
Roonwal and Mohnot, 1977
Presbytis melalophos
Chivers, 1973
Curtin, 1976, 1977
Harrison, 1962
Presbytis obscurus
Chivers, 1973
Curtin, 1976, 1977
Harrison, 1962
Presbytis phayrei
Fooden, 1971
Presbytis pileatus
Roonwal and Mohnot, 1977
Presbytis senex
Amerasinghe, Van Cuylenberg, and Hladik, 1971
C. M. Hladik, 1975, 1977a, 1978a
C. M. Hladik and A. Hladik, 1972

D. HYLOBATIDAE
Hylobates
Carpenter, 1940
Chivers, 1973
Ellefson, 1974
Newkirk, 1973
Rodman, 1973a
Roonwal and Mohnot, 1977
Tenaza and Hamilton, 1971

Symphalangus
Chivers, 1974, 1977
Chivers, Raemaekers, and Aldrich-Blake, 1975

E. PONGIDAE
Gorilla
Casimir, 1975
Fossey, 1974
Fossey and Harcourt, 1977
C. Jones and Sabater Pi, 1971
Kawai and Mizuhara, 1959
R. Osborn, 1963
Sabater Pi, 1977
Schaller, 1963
Pan paniscus
Badrian and Badrian, 1977
Nishida, 1972c, 1976
Pan troglodytes
Gartlan and Struhsaker, 1972
Goodall, 1963b
Hladik, 1973, 1977b
van Lawick-Goodall, 1968
McGrew, 1974, 1975

Reynolds, 1965
Reynolds and Reynolds, 1965
Struhsaker and Hunkeler, 1971
Sugiyama, 1973
Suzuki, 1966
Teleki, 1973a,b, 1974, 1975, 1977a
Wrangham, 1974, 1975, 1977
Pongo
Davenport, 1967
Galadikas-Brindamour and Brindamour, 1975
Horr, 1972
Mackinnon, 1971, 1973, 1974
Rodman, 1973a,b

F. *GENERAL TITLES OF VALUE*
Clutton-Brock, 1977
Hladik, 1975, 1978a
Hladik and Chivers, 1978a,b
C. Jones, 1972
Kay, 1973, 1978
Milton and May, 1976
Napier and Napier, 1967
Oates, 1969

Claude-Marcel Hladik

7.

Diet and the Evolution of Feeding Strategies among Forest Primates

Every living organism is just an abstraction when viewed apart from its physical and biological environment, for life is a continuous exchange of matter and energy. The trophic functions that regulate these exchanges can neither be measured nor understood outside their ecological context.

Unfortunately, a complete description of the trophic structure within an ecosystem is virtually impossible. The concept of *ecological niche* includes all the environmental parameters that Hutchinson (1957) described in terms of a theoretical hypervolume determined by the conditions compatible with life for a given species. Or, as Odum puts it (1971:234), an ecological niche includes the physical setting (habitat) of an organism as well as its functional role in the community (e.g., trophic position). Interaction between occupants of different niches in partly isolated habitats results in the evolutionary process (MacArthur and Wilson, 1967), and the present condition of a species reflects this evolutionary history.

Such theoretical notions have recently been applied to nonhuman and human primates (Hardesty, 1975; Hladik and Chivers, 1978), but the multitude of connections among the parts of an ecological system (and often the lack of data) make a linear approach unrealistic. Since the "dimensions" of the ecological niche are determined by specific adaptations in morphology, physiology, and behavior, separate analyses of these components is attempted here as a way to trace evolutionary trends.

DIETARY SPECIALIZATIONS

The simplest definition of diet is what a primate species actually eats in its natural habitat, although there is, of course, much more food available in terms of quantity as well as diversity than a primate will exploit under normal circumstances. The fact that primates choose to eat some foods and neglect others implies a selective response to stimulation (Hinde, 1966). This response can be fairly rigid in some species (e.g., colobines) and quite flexible in others (e.g., macaques and chimpanzees). Dietary flexibility may be illustrated by an ability to shift to artificial diets that differ from the natural ones and by the variable utilization of food resources during different seasonal cycles.

Comparative Measures of Primate Diet

In many recent field studies, primate diets have been investigated by quantitative methods based on the time spent feeding on various types of food. Precise comparison of diets in different species is generally impossible, however, if we refer only to temporal data, since feeding rates on different types of food are highly variable, even within a local population (C. M. Hladik, 1977a). Information on the quantity of food actually ingested is absolutely necessary for interspecific comparison and even for intraspecific comparison of populations dispersed over a large geographical range, as is the case with chimpanzees. In this type of quantitative investigation, the food ingested by different primates is measured by continuous observation (e.g., C. M. Hladik, 1973), and the total number of fruits, leaves, and so on ingested by one animal are counted. The weight of the ingested food can then be estimated from samples collected in the field. From such data, it is possible to construct a "dietogram" (fig. 7.1) to illustrate general patterns of food intake for the year. Such dietograms can show the annual mean of the different categories of food ingested as well as the variability (maximum and minimum ingested) during a 24-hour period. Dietograms for 15 primate species from Central America, Gabon, Madagascar, and Sri Lanka have been established with enough accuracy to allow significant interspecific comparison (A. Hladik and   C. M. Hladik, 1969; C. M. Hladik, 1973, 1977a,b; C. M. Hladik and A. Hladik, 1972). Other

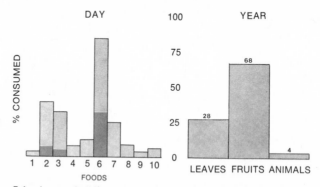

Figure 7.1. A sample "dietogram" illustrating the relative proportions of major food types ingested per day and per year by a small group of relocated chimpanzees in Gabon (after C. M. Hladik, 1973). 1, earth; 2, bark and twigs; 3, leaves and piths; 4, gums and flower buds; 5, immature fruits; 6, mature fruits; 7, seeds and arils; 8, ants, termites, and small arthropods; 9, large arthropods; 10, bird eggs, fledglings, and other large prey. The filled portion of the bars refers to minimum percentage consumed, the open bar to maximum percentage.

researchers such as Iwamoto (1978) are beginning to publish data based on the same system of direct observation, and these studies will eventually provide an accurate picture of diets on a regional scale.

Another type of record, based on measuring the stomach contents of many specimens shot in the wild, can also provide quantitative data on primate diets, although such studies may not provide a complete picture of a particular diet (see Harding, in this volume). If the sampling is thorough, however, as in the studies conducted in Gabon by Charles-Dominique (1966, 1977) and Gautier-Hion (1977, 1978), this method allows some comparisons of the mean quantities of food ingested.

To compare the dietary habits of many different primate species, however, it is necessary to include all data in a unique diagram. We therefore formulated a new method of dietary comparison (Chivers and Hladik, in prep.) based on three natural categories of foods. Each of the following categories is biochemically distinct, and these distinctions, in turn, require distinct specializations of the digestive tract.

Animals. Included here are all types of prey, vertebrate and invertebrate, as well as eggs, larvae, and insect secretions. Most of these foods have a high protein content, but in some cases lipids are predominant (e.g., caterpillars and some termites; C. M. Hladik, 1977b) and in others the sugar content is high (e.g., secretions of homopteran larvae; Petter, Schilling, and Pariente, 1971). In these cases, the caloric value is at least as high as that of protein, and the time of digestion is generally short.

Fruits. Mature and immature fruits as well as flowers are included in this category (for instance, wild figs, which are commonly eaten by primates, are actually inflorescences when immature). For brief periods, the nectar of some flowers is the main food of certain lemurs (Sussman, 1978). Arils, tubers, and seeds, also included, are generally rich in lipids, protein, starch, and other highly polymerized carbohydrates, and necessitate slightly more time for digestion than does the animal category.

Leaves. All foods high in fiber and cellulose content, as well as gums and other tree exudates, are included here. Among these, the young leaves of leguminous trees or herbaceous plants can be extremely rich in soluble sugars and/or protein (more than 50% of the dry weight is protein in some cases; Hladik and Viroben, 1974). By contrast, the composition of mature leaves is not very different from that of barks and twigs. All these materials contain long carbohydrate chains that can be broken down only by bacterial fermentation in some specialized part of the digestive tract.

Dietary Composition and Variability

The respective percentages of these three major food categories—animals, fruits, and leaves—can be plotted along three converging axes in a three-dimensional system, as shown in the right upper part of figure 7.2.

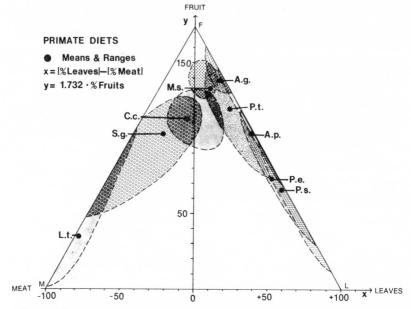

Figure 7.2. Annual means and ranges of the diets of nine primate species (*Loris tardigradus, Saguinus geoffroyi, Cebus capucinus, Macaca sinica, Ateles geoffroyi, Pan troglodytes, Alouatta palliata, Presbytis entellus, Presbytis senex*) within a triangle where point *M* represents 100% animals, point *F* 100% fruits, and point *L* 100% leaves, based on average 24-hour sample periods (Chivers and Hladik, in prep.).

Since the three variables are not independent (their sum is always 100%), the projection of any type of diet will fall within the triangle *MFL*, where point *M* represents a diet with 100% animals, point *F* a diet with 100 fruits, and point *L* a diet with 100% leaves. Therefore, it is more convenient to present only this *MFL* triangle, as shown in the main part of figure 7.2. Any point within this triangle corresponds to a given diet that would be rich in animals if close to *M*, rich in fruits if close to *F*, and rich in leaves if close to *L*.[1] Given the construction of the *MFL* triangle, the dietary values (in terms of percentages of the three categories) can be plotted along two new perpendicular axes, $0x$ and $0y$.[2] If the line $0L$ on the x axis $= +100$ and the line $0M = -100$, then $x = (\% \text{ leaves}) - (\% \text{ animals})$ and $y = \sqrt{3} \cdot (\% \text{ fruits})$ for any point within the triangle corresponding to a given diet.

After selecting nine primate species for which accurate dietary data are available (A. Hladik and C. M. Hladik, 1969; C. M. Hladik, 1973; C. M. Hladik and A. Hladik, 1972), I first plotted the mean values of their diets (solid arrows in fig. 7.2) and then outlined the short-term variations in dietary composition for rain-forest genera in Panama (*Saguinus, Cebus,*

Ateles, Alouatta) and Gabon (*Pan*), and for dry-forest genera in Sri Lanka (*Loris, Macaca, Presbytis*). The ranges of dietary variation shown in figure 7.2 give a simplified picture, since only three major food categories are represented. Given this level of generalization, it is not surprising that large overlaps occur between sympatric species. In such cases many other factors, especially choices of particular plant parts or species, allow each primate to feed on its own food resources.

Comparison of dietary variation among allopatric species is more illuminating. For instance, the capuchin (*Cebus capucinus*), the toque macaque (*Macaca sinica*), and the chimpanzee (*Pan troglodytes*) are three frugivorous primates that include large quantities of leaves in their diet and actively seek a maximum amount of insects, yet the ranges of dietary variation in these three species do not overlap significantly. Their positions within the triangle show a clear difference: the chimpanzee is the most folivorous, the macaque is more strictly limited to a frugivorous diet, and the capuchin eats the most animal matter. These three diets are generally characterized as omnivorous, but it is obviously better to use quantitative data to differentiate between them accurately.[3]

Digestive Morphology

Observational data on primate diets can also be compared and correlated with morphological data obtained from studies of digestive tracts (Chivers and Hladik, in prep.). Measurement of the surface areas and volumes of intestinal sections in primates and other wild mammals has eliminated problems inherent in an earlier, similar approach (Fooden, 1964; C. M. Hladik, 1967). For instance, the volume of potential fermenting chambers was calculated in 180 specimens, including 117 primates. Results were plotted on log/log scales, in relation to the body weight of the animals. Linear regressions were calculated separately for the species feeding mainly on animals and for those feeding on leaves (figure 7.3). Most primate species are located between these two regression lines, and the distance (d) from the middle (0) is an indicator of morphological tendency toward folivory or "animalivory." The transformed distance $TR_{(d)}$, which was obtained from the conditional antilogarithmic formula indicated on the figure, allows direct comparison with the actual dietary parameters (Chivers and Hladik, in prep.).

The species feeding mainly on fruits (especially primate species) are located between these two limits and can be compared to animalivores and folivores of equal body weight. This comparison yields a simple expression of the index of gut differentiation that will be about +100 for a pure folivore and around −100 for a pure animalivore. For most of the species tested thus far, the index of gut differentiation is virtually identical to the mean diet ($\bar{x}$) as defined in the preceding section, demonstrating the best possible

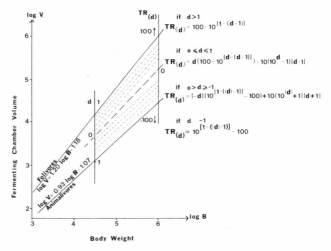

Figure 7.3. A comparison of different gut shapes in relation to different diets, with fermenting chamber volumes plotted against body weight, to eliminate allometric parameters. Regressions have been calculated for a set of species feeding mainly on animals, including primates and some other mammals, and for a set of folivores. Most primate species fall between these two regression lines, and the distance (*d*) from the middle is an indicator of morphological tendency toward folivory or animalivory.

correlation between diet and intestinal morphology, once body size has been taken into account.[4] Species with indexes near zero have the least specialized form of intestines, and their diets are correspondingly varied but predominantly frugivorous.

The digestive tracts of primates thus have morphological characteristics which are closely related to their diets. The extreme types can be recognized at a glance (C. M. Hladik, 1979). *Arctocebus calabarensis* is almost exclusively carnivorous (Charles-Dominique, 1977) and has a hind gut that is extremely short. By contrast, *Galago elegantulus,* which feeds mainly on gums, and *Lepilemur leucopus,* which eats mainly leaves, have a very large cecum and colon with marked embossing, and *L. leucopus* has the shortest small intestines (in proportion to body length) known in mammals. The situation is rarely so clear cut in the large, frugivorous primates. For instance, the barbary ape, *Macaca sylvana,* which feeds on plant shoots for several months of the year (Deag, 1974), has a hind gut larger than that of other macaques, but this becomes apparent only after measuring and calculating the indexes as shown above.

Primate teeth also reflect dietary adaptations. As in the preceding examples, the extreme types can be easily recognized (James, 1960) but many primate species that have no obvious dental specialization require refined quantitative analysis. Kay and Hylander (1978) present evidence that the anterior part of the mandible, and especially the incisors, are well developed in frugivorous primates. Folivores, by contrast, have less need to prepare food with the incisors but perform more mastication. Accordingly, in these animals the posterior part of the mandible is predominant and the molars include different features for shearing and crushing fibrous materials. This kind of study is crucial for the paleontologist, and it is unfortunate that many potential correlations between dental features and dietary habits cannot be investigated because precise data on natural primate diets remain unavailable.

Evolution of Dietary Habits

Primitive mammals probably fed largely on invertebrates, and it appeares that trophic chains were not very diversified at the beginning of the Paleocene.[5] Thus it is likely that early primates were predatory, feeding on invertebrates and small vertebrates, perhaps with some fruit supplementing the diet, as in extant *Microcebus* and *Galago* species (Charles-Dominique and Martin, 1970).

Frugivorous and folivorous primates evolved from this primitive stock, developing dietary specializations in relation to various ecological factors. In broad terms, the general trend of evolution led from the less specialized forms toward the more complex teeth and digestive tracts exhibited by folivores. The digestive tract is able to undergo rapid changes in the relative proportions of its different segments (C. M. Hladik, 1967), but there is no evidence that the major structural features of the digestive tract of the most specialized primates emerged more rapidly than those of the bones and teeth, which we can trace in the fossil record. Accordingly, dietary changes must have developed very slowly.

DIETARY ECOLOGY: FOOD AVAILABILITY AND FEEDING NICHES

Forest Production and Food Availability

The trophic levels characterizing an ecosystem are traditionally presented as an ecological pyramid in which producers form the bottom tiers and consumers the successive upper tiers (Odum, 1971:79–84). In the rain-forest habitats occupied by many primates, the primary production consists mainly of fruits, leaves, and wood. According to various measures (A. Hladik, 1978a; Leigh and Smythe, 1978), it is fairly constant in different rain forests throughout the world, exceeding 10 tons of dry litter per hectare per year. The successive tiers are much smaller, and represent the gross production of all the consumer organisms feeding on primary production. No precise measure of these upper tiers is available, but the order of magnitude of the secondary production is between 10 and 100 kg/ha per year. The top tier of predators must be 100 to 200 times smaller than the previous tier (Odum, 1971).

The amount of food produced in such a system will determine the carrying capacity of the environment for the consumer populations, which include all the primates. As primary consumers, the folivorous mammals (including a limited number of specialized primates) can be supported at the highest population and biomass levels. Leaf production, as measured from litter fall in different rain forests, is very high and constant—e.g., 7 tons of dry matter per hectare per year in Gabon (A. Hladik, 1978a), and 6 tons in Panama (Leigh and Smythe, 1978). Even in a dry deciduous forest in Sri Lanka, the order of magnitude is similar: 3 to 4 tons (C. M. Hladik and A. Hladik, 1972). Since a large part of this production can be cropped without detrimental effect on plants, the biomass of folivores is high and fairly constant across different habitats (Eisenberg, Muckenhirn, and Rudran, 1972; C. M. Hladik, 1975).

Fruit production is obviously smaller—e.g., 0.5 tons, dry weight, per hectare per year, in Gabon (A. Hladik, 1978a). Although most of the fruits can be eaten without diminishing overall production in the environment, because the seeds are not destroyed (A. Hladik and C. M. Hladik, 1969; C. M. Hladik and A. Hladik; 1967), the biomass of frugivorous animal populations will be much smaller than that of folivorous populations. The animalivores will, in turn, exhibit the lowest biomass because these organisms are all on the secondary-consumer trophic level. In each of these cases, the maximum carrying capacity of the environment is not necessarily attained. However, in field studies conducted in relatively stable environments, the observed primate populations tend to utilize a maximum of the available food resources (Charles-Dominique and Hladik, 1971; C. M. Hladik 1975; C. M. Hladik and A. Hladik, 1972), up to the limits set by seasonal variations. This is also true of most other vertebrate populations (Odum, 1971; Wilson, 1975).

Trophic Levels and Dietary Grades

The ecological model I have proposed for characterizing the most significant dietary differences between primate species can be refined by separating the organisms at each level into dietary grades by biomass (C. M. Hladik, 1975). In each grade, the biomass of a primate population is a measurable quantity that can be used to locate it on a graduated scale. Given that the diet of any primate species is a mixture of two or three of the major food types defined previously, the species' biomass is determined by the proportions of animals, fruits, and leaves consumed relative to the quantities available in the ecosystem. The source of dietary protein is another important aspect of this classification.

The following grades apply to primates but not necessarily to mammals in general.

Grade 1 includes the species at or near the top of the pyramid. These are usually the most "primitive" forms, which are predators on invertebrates and small vertebrates, although their diet is often supplemented by fruits and gums. Depending on the relative proportions of these elements in their diets, their biomass is generally between 10 and 100 g/ha (log biomass from 1.00 to 1.99).

Grade 2 includes the species feeding mainly on fruits, which thus require a supplement for dietary protein. This supplement is partly derived from animal food but also includes a certain amount of leaves. Many of the primates classified as "omnivores" fall within this intermediate grade, and their biomass, depending on the proportions of the different food categories eaten, is generally betweeen 100 and 1,000 g/ha (log biomass from 2.00 to 2.99).

Grade 3 includes the species utilizing exclusively primary production. They are located near the bottom of the pyramid, but at different intermediate levels according to the proportions of fruits and leaves in their diet. Leaves are their main protein resource, but all these species also utilize fruits to some extent. Fermentation is an important part of their digestive process, and different phylogenetic lines have developed different types of fermenting chambers—e.g., in the hind gut (such as *Lepilemur* and *Gorilla*) or in the stomach for the most specialized and ruminant-like Colobidae (Moir, 1967). According to the proportions of fruits and leaves in their diet, their biomass is generally between 1,000 and 10,000 g/ha (log biomass from 3.00 to 3.99).

Biomass and Diet

In keeping with the relative proportions of major food types in the diet, each primate species will tend to attain a fairly constant biomass in an undisturbed habitat because food production levels in different tropical forests have similar orders of magnitude. This conclusion is derived from comparison of a large set of field studies conducted at field stations where records of populations and observations on primate feeding behavior have been kept simultaneously (C. M. Hladik and Chivers, 1978).

Figure 7.4 shows how the primates at several field sites, ranging from wet to dry habitats, are ranked in terms of dietary grades. Such comparisons might be risky in some cases, especially when the population distribution is not homogeneous. Some behavioral factors not directly connected with food choices can result in differential utilization of certain parts of the habitat. In such cases, the biomass estimates apply to the range effectively utilized by each primate species, yielding a maximum biomass which can then be related to the food productivity of the habitat. It is clear that the

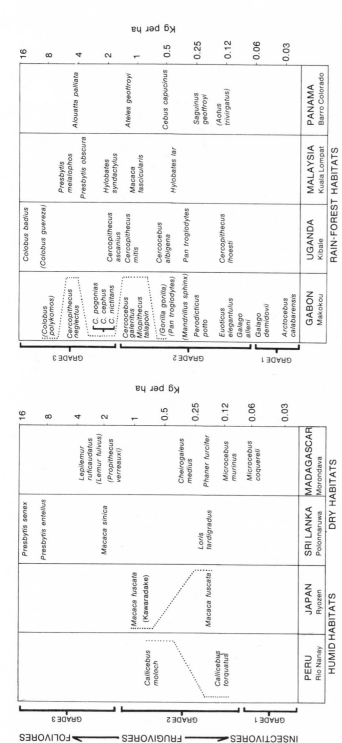

Figure 7.4. Comparison of biomasses (in kilograms of fresh weight per hectare) of sympatric primate species living at various field sites, with each species located on a vertical logarithmic scale according to maximum biomass observed, and with the corresponding dietary grades and major food types shown on the same vertical scale (after Hladik and Chivers, 1978b). Data from Gabon (Charles-Dominique, 1978; Gautier-Hion, 1978) and Peru (Kinzey, 1978) have been separated into two sets by a dotted line, with the species inhabiting the flooded areas listed on the left side. Data from Japan (Iwamoto, 1978) cover two different field stations with nonprovisioned troops of macaques. Sources for the other data are: Uganda (Struhsaker, 1978), Malaysia (Curtin and Chivers, 1978; MacKinnon and MacKinnon, 1978), Panama (A. Hladik and C. M. Hladik, 1969; Moynihan, 1976), Sri Lanka (C. M. Hladik and A. Hladik, 1972), Madagascar (Petter, 1978; Charles-Dominique, personal communication). The biomasses of species in parentheses are based on data obtained at other field sites.

biomasses of primates in grade 1 (animalivores) are extremely small, falling below 10 g/ha in a few instances, while those in grade 2 (frugivores) fall within a medium range. The maximum biomass is attained by species in grade 3 (frugivores/folivores), and is higher than 10 kg/ha for the most folivorous species. The differences affecting primate biomasses are clear and reliable enough so that the logarithm of primate biomass—in grams per hectare, within limits of 10 to 10,000 g—can be used as an expression of the dietary grade.

Food Niches for Forest Primates

At a few field stations the diet of different primate species has been quantitatively determined by equivalent field methods. These results are shown in figure 7.5, with each species represented by a separate dietogram.

In figure 7.5, comparison of the sympatric prosimians in the rain forest of Gabon with those living in the dry deciduous forest of Madagascar shows once again the fairly similar biomasses of species having equivalent diets even when there are major differences between the habitats. Another aspect to be noted is the larger number of primate species in Gabon (see fig. 7.4). The most evident consequence of this concentration of species is a narrower range of food choice for each, to reduce interspecific competition. For instance, *Arctocebus calabarensis* feeds mainly on caterpillars, while the two *Galago* species utilize other types of prey according to a more subtle mode of partition (Charles-Dominique, 1971, 1977). By contrast, in the dry forest of Madagascar a small number of primate species have a wider range of food resources available to each of them. In spite of a lower food production in this area, the biomasses of *Microcebus murinus* and *Cheirogaleus medius* can be high, because they have this wide range of food choices. Some monkeys can be compared in a similar way (fig. 7.5). In the dry deciduous forest of Sri Lanka, where a small number of species live together, the food niche is wide (C. M. Hladik and A. Hladik, 1972) and the biomasses are very high. This is true not only for the two species of *Presbytis* which feed mainly on leaves, but also for *Macaca sinica*, a frugivore with a dietary supplement of insects and young leaves. On the other hand, the species inhabiting the Panamanian rain forest are more specialized, utilizing narrow "food niches," owing to the presence of many other mammals. In this forest all the primate species feed mainly on fruits (A. Hladik and C. M. Hladik, 1969), with various dietary supplements determining the dietary grade: grade 2 for *Saguinus* and *Cebus,* and grade 3 for *Ateles* and *Alouatta.*

A "food niche" can be defined in terms of the range of foods chosen by a species, and is delimited by the ecological pressure exerted by the sympatric species that share the local resources. In the examples from Sri Lanka presented later in figure 7.6, the "food niche" is broad because there are

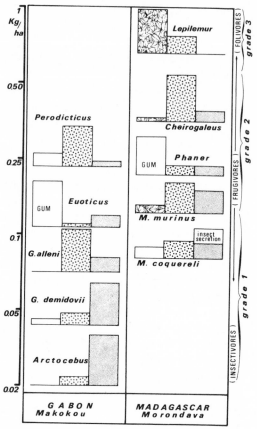

Figure 7.5. Comparisons of primate dietary habits, focusing on the nocturnal prosimians of the Gabon rain forest, the prosimians of the Madagascar dry forest, the monkeys of the Sri Lanka dry forest, and the monkeys of the Panama rain forest, with each primate represented by a dietogram showing intakes of leaves and gums (*left*), fruits (*center*), and animals (*right*), plotted against the relationships between biomasses and types of diet at different field sites (after C. M. Hladik, 1978).

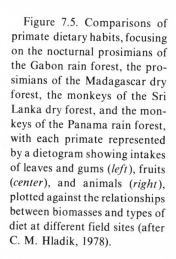

fewer species in habitats where food production is low. This explains why species of equivalent dietary grade can have similar biomasses in different environmental conditions.

Body Weights and Diet

The body weights and population densities of different primate species determine their biomass, but there is also a direct relationship between the dietary habits and body weights of prosimian (Charles-Dominique, 1971; C. M. Hladik, 1979) and simian primates (A. Hladik and C. M. Hladik, 1969; C. M. Hladik, 1978).

Small primate species (those weighing between 60 g, such as *Microcebus murinus,* and 250 g, such as *Loris tardigradus*) can feed exclusively on small prey, mainly invertebrates. Larger primates usually cannot fill their stomachs with small prey during the period when they are active, since

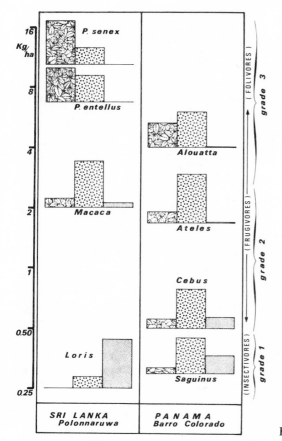

Figure 7.5 (*continued*)

chances of finding and collecting insects or invertebrates are approximately equivalent for any species. Interestingly, the average quantity of prey eaten is approximately equal, in terms of weight, for different primate species with similar foraging techniques. To satisfy their greater energy needs, however, the medium-sized species, such as *Saguinus geoffroyi* (500 g) and *Perodicticus potto* (1,000 g), add fruits or gums. The larger the body size, the larger will be the proportion of fruit in the diet. This pattern accounts for some of the dietary differences of species of increasing size.

For larger species, such as *Cebus capucinus* and *Macaca sinica* (2–3 kg), a diet of only insects and fruit would be protein deficient because the proportion of fruit (which has a very low protein content, about 5% of dry weight) would be high in order to meet calorie requirements. However, supplementary protein can be obtained by eating leaves, especially shoots and young leaves which are high in protein (C. M. Hladik, 1978).

If we now consider the largest primate species—which range from about 10 kg for *Indri indri, Alouatta palliata,* or *Hylobates syndactylus* up to 100 kg and more for *Gorilla gorilla*—it seems clear that intensive foraging for small prey would be of little benefit because such a small fraction of the total energy and dietary protein requirements could be obtained by this time-consuming activity. If morphological and physiological adaptations for digesting long-chain β-linked carbohydrates exist, the large primate species are likely to evolve in a direction that emphasizes feeding on leaves, a ubiquitous and plentiful food resource. The proportion of leaves in the diet will therefore be high for large species and, for those species unable to digest a large proportion of leaves, fruits will become the limiting factor because they are not as abundant as leaves.

Furthermore, digestion of leaves requires the kind of large fermentation chamber found only in the intestines of large mammals. The metabolism of these large mammals is low enough to match the limited energy available in such food resources as mature leaves (Parra, 1978). Conversely, small species need more energy per unit of body weight because their basal metabolism, as well as their expenditure of energy for locomotion, increases exponentially in inverse ratio to their weight (Tucker, 1970). Small primates need concentrated food resources yielding as much energy as possible, such as the fats and protein available in invertebrate prey (Portman, 1970a).

It is apparent that body size, "food niche," and digestive adaptations must evolve simultaneously. Behavioral adaptations, which can be as sophisticated as tool use, have been superimposed on these biological features. In some cases, these behavioral adaptations have considerably increased the efficiency of predation on invertebrates and small verte-brates, and thus some large primates can regularly supplement their basic diet of fruit and leaves with a variety of small prey.

Finally, it should be noted that population density—measured as the number of individuals in a given area—is not necessarily greatest among the leaf-eating forms; for instance, a group of 10 gorillas uses more than 30 km^2 of home range (Goodall, 1977), yet the highest primate population density has been observed in a folivorous form, *Lepilemur leucopus,* a relatively small prosimian that reaches 800 individuals/km^2 (Charles-Dominique and Hladik, 1971). To maintain this high a density, some accommodations must be made in social organization (Wilson, 1975), a subject discussed in a later section.

Adaptation to Ecological Niches

The "food niche" can be regarded as the core parameter of the ecological niche. One strategy for partitioning the limited resources available at any locality is time-sharing between diurnal and nocturnal species. This occurs, for example, in the rain forest of Gabon (see fig. 7.4), where nocturnal prosimians and diurnal simians both eat large amounts of the same fruit resources (Charles-Dominique, 1977; Gautier-Hion, 1978). In Madagascar, some nocturnal prosimians eat the same types of leaves and flowers as the sympatric diurnal prosimians, and the system of time-sharing, given equal access to these food sources, allows the nocturnal and diurnal forms to obtain reasonably equivalent amounts of food (Charles-Dominique and Hladik, 1971).

This temporal partitioning of food resources probably began early in primate evolution, for the ancestral animals evolving toward diurnality would have had to compete with diurnal birds of similar body weight that fed on insects and fruits. Charles-Dominique (1975) has argued that modern primates probably stem from nocturnal ancestors. When simian primates appeared in the Oligocene, they could compete with birds as diurnal feeders on fruits and insects in part because of new adaptations in hand structure and function (Bishop, 1964). These changes led to improved foraging techniques that enabled primates to open hard pods and strip bark from decaying trees, and, along with other adaptations, permitted utilization of food resources not available to birds of similar body size (C. M. Hladik, 1979).

The partitioning of available food between sympatric species can be approached by a more subtle strategy than the temporal separation of nocturnal and diurnal species. Space can also be partitioned horizontally and vertically, with many possibilities for settling into new ecological niches, as shown recently in a comparative review of space utilization by primates (C. M. Hladik and Chivers, 1978). Forest structure obviously affects feeding options and strategies, and the discontinuous nature of the rain forest permits many ecological specializations among the primates (A. Hladik, 1978a; Oldeman, 1974, 1977). The flooded zones, such as those along river banks, contain specific flora which can be the exclusive habitat of some species. In Peru, for instance, *Callicebus moloch* inhabits the low and moist parts of the forest (Kinzey, 1978); in Gabon the flooded zones intersecting rain forests are inhabited by *Miopithecus talapoin, Cercopithecus neglectus,* and *Cerococebus galeritus* (Gautier-Hion, 1978). In contrast, the other zones of the Peruvian rain forest are the exclusive habitat of a different *Callicebus* species, and in Gabon several *Cercopithecus* species utilize both flooded and nonflooded forest zones.

The spatial partitioning of food resources along a horizontal plane follows the cycles of regeneration that characterize the "primary" rain forest. Due to this regeneration process, the forest is actually a mosaic. Only 5–10% of a large area consists of small patches at the final stage of fully "mature" forest growth (Oldeman, 1974). The differential utilization of these regenerative stages was illustrated by Charles-Dominique's work

(1971, 1977) on rain forest prosimians of Gabon. *Arctocebus calabarensis,* for example, prefers zones characterized by the early stages of the regeneration cycle, where small interwoven lianas form favorite supports for locomotion and predatory feeding on caterpillars.

There is no vertical stratification in the primary rain forest (Rollet, 1974), at least in the sense that different horizontal layers have appeared in the schematic diagrams of many authors, although these strata do occur in other types of "specialized" forests (A. Hladik, 1978a). Nevertheless, some vertical stratification in the spacing of different primate species has been observed and measured (Gautier-Hion, 1978; Struhsaker, 1978). We again refer to Oldeman's analysis of the forest structure (1974) to clarify the meaning these differences have for various primate species. The forest consists of sets of trees with different architectural and physiological properties (the set of the present, growing and mature trees which intercept the most light; the set of the future, small trees which "wait" in the shade of an opportunity to grow; the set of the past, older trees, in senescence). If we look from bottom to top, there is a continuous change in the environmental conditions inside the forest (humidity and temperature), with an inversion surface occurring at a level between the set of the future and the set of the present. This vertical gradient of temperature and humidity, which is intersected by different types of tree crowns, must necessarily influence the vertical distribution of different entomological faunas. It is obvious, even without examining structural details, that the preferential utilization of a certain level by a given primate species corresponds approximately to opportunities to feed on particular resources (e.g., specific insects living in specific forest structures).

Studies of primate behavior in the context of these different forest structures are still very limited, but it is becoming evident that height alone is not a good indicator of structural changes. This explains why some of the differences found after considering only feeding heights of primates are neither clear nor useful. On the other hand, Charles-Dominique's study of prosimians in Gabon (1977) illustrates how precise information on forest structure can lead to insights about feeding strategy. At his site, all vertical levels of the forest canopy are exploited by *Galago demidovii* in an active search for insects. By contrast, *Galago alleni* concentrates its activity near the ground, jumping between small tree trunks and lianas while feeding on invertebrates. Competition between these two members of the same genus is thereby reduced or avoided. Even if the differences between other primate species are not as clear cut as this, one can expect that further ecological analysis will show similar patterns of spatial distribution in most habitats where several primate species are sympatric.

The feeding strategies of extant primates derive from successive and multiple adaptations in the past, and we probably will never be able to trace these in complete detail. Nevertheless, systematic analysis of contemporary feeding strategies, as presented in the next section, can explain some adaptations based on physiological and behavioral mechanisms, among which changes in social organization represent key adjustments to changing environmental conditions.

DIETARY SOCIOLOGY: BEHAVIORAL VERSUS PHYSIOLOGICAL STRATEGIES

Seasonal Variation in Food Production

There are important seasonal variations in the quantity and composition of food resources. This seasonality is very marked in tropical deciduous forests, and it is also apparent to a lesser extent in rain forests. For instance, if we consider the leaf production for two types of dry deciduous forests, measured after litter fall occurs in different seasons, the maximum variation of dry matter is 0.0–2.5 g/m^2 per day in Madagascar (in a forest near Morondava), and 0.5–1.5 g in Sri Lanka (Polonnaruwa Forest). For rain forests. on the other hand, the same measures of leaf production are 1.0–4.0 g in Panama (Barro Colorado) and 1.5–3.0 g in Gabon (Ipassa Forest, near Makokou). Such litter-fall data may seem irrelevant in the study of what is actually eaten by the resident primates, but when one considers that a flush of new growth generally follows leaf fall in rain forests (A. Hladik, 1978a), the data can be used to estimate variations in food availability for the following months. Measures of fruit production are more directly relevant and may also vary seasonally: 0.0–0.5 g of dry matter per m^2 per day in the dry forest of Sri Lanka; 0.1–0.5 g in the rain forest of Panama; and 0.1–0.6 g in Gabon, where large differences have also been recorded from year to year. Secondary production has even greater variability: the amount of invertebrates found in the litter collection baskets used in Gabon ranged from 0.17 g of dry matter per 100 m^2 per day during the major dry season to 1.50 g during the minor dry season.

These rough data, assembled from Leigh and Smythe (1978) and from the unpublished records of A. Hladik, give some idea of the seasonal oscillations in availability of primate foods.

Physiological Adaptations

Some primate species cope with extreme variations of food availability by means of specialized and unusual physiological adaptations. The Cheirogaleinae of Madagascar face a long dry period during which little food is available (C. M. Hladik, Charles-Dominique, and Petter, in press; Petter, 1978). During the preceding wet periods the dwarf lemur, *Cheirogaleus medius,* feeds heavily on abundant fruits and insects and accumulates fat deposits under the skin and inside the tail (the tail volume increases from 20 to 55 cm³). It then goes into hibernation for 7–9 months. The lesser mouse lemur, *Microcebus murinus,* does not truly hibernate but lives off accumulated fat in the tail and reduces basal metabolism by means of an internal cycle also found in other prosimians that do not have to face such drastic food shortages (Perret, 1974). The other two nocturnal prosimians inhabiting the same forest have adapted to seasonality by selective utilization of the few food resources available in the dry period. *Phaner furcifer* eats large amounts of gums, and *Microcebus coquereli* feeds mainly on the sweet secretions of homopterans. These dietary specializations involve physiological responses to extreme environmental conditions.

The fluctuation in the physiological cycle of *Cheirogaleus* is exceptional among primates; no other genus in this order has acquired an ability to store fats and then hibernate in direct relationship with seasonal variations. Nevertheless, in most (if not all) primate species there are less pronounced seasonal cycles of growth and fattening.[6] In the chimpanzees observed in Gabon (C. M. Hladik, 1973), the growth rate is highest when the production of fruit is at a seasonal peak between November and January, whereas body weight remains approximately constant during the months of low productivity, from February to June. Because of the important annual variations in food production in every type of habitat, the growth curves of all primate species normally are irregular.

Behavioral Adaptations

Despite important seasonal variations in food availability and consumption, primate species tend to maintain some level of constancy in their feeding habits throughout the year. This was clearly shown in a comparison of the food intakes of several sympatric species during successive seasons in Sri Lanka (C. M. Hladik, 1977a; C. M. Hladik and A. Hladik, 1972), where the diets of two *Presbytis* species follow seasonal variations in fruit and leaf production (figure 7.6). The variation in this case is so large, however, that interspecific comparisons cannot be made across seasons. Yet there is an underlying constancy when the two species are compared in any given calendar period. For instance, in the dry season (May–June) both species eat large amounts of fruits, which are very abundant then, but the more frugivorous species, *P. entellus,* continues to ingest proportionately more fruit while the more folivorous, *P. senex,* continues to eat a larger proportion of leaves. There is even more seasonal variation in the dietary intake of the toque macaque, *Macaca sinica,* but in all seasons it supplements a fruit–animal diet with a small quantity of leaves, in a combination that differs from the diets of the other sympatric primate species.

Seasonal fluctuations in invertebrate production are likely to cause

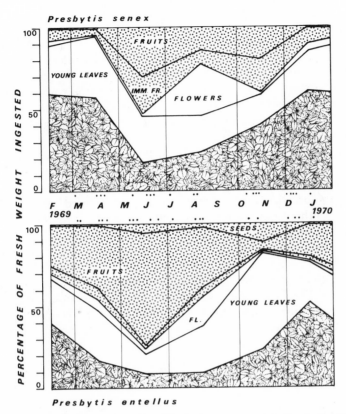

Figure 7.6. Annual variation of food intake in two sympatric *Presbytis* species of Sri Lanka, showing the relative proportions of mature leaves and immature leaves, flowers, and mature and immature fruits consumed each month, with dots along the time axis indicating the days of continuous observation used for calculations.

greater dietary variation in grade 1 and grade 2 primates, which utilize primary and secondary production (e.g., fruits and animals), than in grade 3 primates, which utilize only primary production (e.g., leaves). Capuchins, macaques, chimpanzees, and other primarily frugivorous primates that need a dietary complement of animal matter have the most seasonally variable diets. In the cercopithecid species of Gabon, which all have fairly similar diets (Gautier-Hion, 1978), the small interspecific differences are maintained throughout the year. The most folivorous among them, *Cercopithecus nictitans,* eats many insects during the period of maximum invertebrate production, but still less than the most carnivorous species, *Cercopithecus pogonias.*

This behavioral tendency to preserve a basic dietary pattern in the face of great seasonal variation in availability is a major factor in niche separation. In fact, it is probably related to physiological requirements and to sociological characteristics as well, as is discussed in the next two sections.

Dietary Flexibility and Specialization

The ranges of variation found in different primate diets must be a direct consequence of seasonality in food production, tempered by limits of what the animal can tolerate. Dietary flexibility appears to be greatest among grade 2 species, which supplement a largely frugivorous diet with considerable animal matter (see C. M. Hladik, 1979). This flexibility may account for the extensive geographical distribution of such grade 2 species as the chimpanzee, which lives in rain forests as well as savannah woodland habitats in much of equatorial Africa. By contrast, the most specialized primates in grade 3, which eat large amounts of leaves, are generally limited to more localized ranges by the availability of preferred plant species.

Dietary specialization can be approximately measured by the number of plants or other food categories utilized. In practice, only part of what is eaten can be accurately determined—usually between 50 and 90% of total intake, depending on field conditions. For instance, among the sympatric species of Panama (A. Hladik and C. M. Hladik, 1969), the howler, *Alouatta palliata,* is the most folivorous and has the least dietary flexibility; 12–15 plant species account for 80% of total food intake (table 7.1). In the spider monkey, *Ateles geoffroyi,* 18–25 plant species account for 80% of food intake during the same period of observation (table 7.2).

Table 7.1. Plant species eaten by *Alouatta palliata* on Barro Colorado Island (Panama)

Species eaten	Percentage of total food intake accounted for
Ficus insipida (Moraceae)	
F. yoponensis (Moraceae)	
F. tonduzii (Moraceae)	50
Cecropia spp. (Moraceae)	
Ceiba pentandra (Bombacaceae)	
Ficus obtusifolia (Moraceae)	
Spondias mombin (Anacardiaceae)	
Maquira costaricana (Moraceae)	>80
Dipteryx panamensis (Leguminosae)	
Anacardium excelsum (Anacardiaceae)	
Platypodium elegans (Leguminosae)	
Brosimum bernadetteae (Moraceae)	
Quararibea asterolepis (Bombacaceae)	
Virola nobilis (Myristicaceae)	
Inga spp. (Leguminosae)	

Note: Species are listed in decreasing order according to amount ingested during 46 days, in 1966/67/68 (A. Hladik and C. M. Hladik, 1969) and unpublished observations of 1977/78. Some changes in specific names follow a recent review of plant specimens by A. Hladik.

Table 7.2. Plant species eaten by *Ateles geoffroyi* on Barro Colorado Island (Panama)

Species eaten	Percentage of total food intake accounted for	
Cecropia spp. (Moraceae)		
Psidium guajava (Myrtaceae)		
Astrocaryon standleyanum (Palmaceae)		
Spondias mombin (Anacardiaceae)	50	
Socratea durissima (Palmaceae)		
Ficus insipida (Moraceae)		
F. yoponensis (Moraceae)		
Poulsenia armata (Moraceae)		
Chrysophyllum cainito (Sapotaceae)		
Ochroma pyramidale (Bombacaceae)		
Dipteryx panamensis (Leguminosae)		>80
Ficus tonduzii (Moraceae)		
F. obtusifolia (Moraceae)		
Annona spraguei (Annonaceae)		
Mangifera indica (Anacardiaceae)		
Citrus sp. (Rutaceae)		
Tocoyena pittieri (Rubiaceae)		
Doliocarpus major (Dilleniaceae)		
Quararibea asterolepis (Bombacaceae)		
Virola nobilis (Myristicaceae)		
Inga spp. (Leguminosae)		
Trichilia cipo (Meliaceae)		

Note: Species are listed in decreasing order according to amount ingested during 26 days, in 1966/67/68 (A. Hladik and C. M. Hladik, 1969) and unpublished observations of 1977/78. Some changes in specific names follow a recent review of plant specimens by A. Hladik.

The capuchin, *Cebus capucinus,* has the greatest dietary flexibility, with 36–42 plant species accounting for only 60% of the total food intake (table 7.3).

Similarly, primate species observed in Sri Lanka can be characterized by their choice of plant food (tables 7.4 and 7.5; see also fig. 7.6). There is a striking difference between the two *Presbytis* species at the 70% mark on each table: 3 plant species for *P. senex* and 10 species for *P. entellus*. This difference in dietary flexibility is maintained throughout the year, as are the relative proportions of ingested fruits, young leaves, and other plant parts. At all times of year *P. senex* utilizes a minimum number of plant species.

Other examples of sympatric primate species, such as the diurnal prosimian observed in Madagascar by Sussman (1974) and the monkeys of East Africa described by Struhsaker (1978), present a similar pattern of food selection. The most folivorous primates consistently include only a

Table 7.3. Plant species eaten by *Cebus capucinus* on Barro Colorado Island (Panama)

Species eaten	Percentage of total food intake accounted for
Scheelea zonensis (Palmaceae)	
Ficus insipida (Moraceae)	
F. yoponensis (Moraceae)	
F. obtusifolia (Moraceae)	
F. tonduzii (Moraceae)	
Cecropia spp. (Moraceae)	
Faramea occidentalis (Rubiaceae)	
Gustavia superba (Lecythidaceae)	
Dipteryx panamensis (Leguminosae)	≥50
Spondias mombin (Anacardiaceae)	
Miconia argentea (Melastomaceae)	
Psidium guajava (Myrtaceae)	
Rheedia edulis (Guttiferae)	
Hasseltia floribunda (Flacourtiaceae)	
Doliocarpus major (Dilleniaceae)	
Cordia lasiocalyx (Boraginaceae)	
Anacardium excelsum (Anacardiaceae)	
Mangifera indica (Anacardiaceae)	
Annona spraguei (Annonaceae)	
Olmedia aspera (Moraceae)	
Dendropanax arboreus (Araliaceae)	≥60
Ochroma pyramidale (Bombacaceae)	
Clitoria portobellensis (Leguminosae)	
Mouriri parvifolia (Melastomaceae)	
Apeiba membranacea (Tiliaceae)	
Hybanthus prunifolius (Violaceae)	
Rheedia madruno (Guttiferae)	
Lacistema aggregatum (Lacistemaceae)	
Virola nobilis (Myristicaceae)	
Desmoncus isthmius (Palmaceae)	
Tocoyena pittieri (Rubiaceae)	
Zanthoxyllum sp. (Rutaceae)	
Cupania latifolia (Sapindaceae)	
Alibertia edulis (Rubiaceae)	
Pentagonia macrophylla (Rubiaceae)	
Randia armata (Rubiaceae)	
Spondias radlkoferi (Anacardiaceae)	
Virola sebifera (Myristicaceae)	
Musa sapientum (Musaceae)	
Chrysophyllum cainito (Sapotaceae)	

Note: Species are listed in decreasing order according to amount ingested during 34 days, in 1966/67/68 (A. Hladik and C. M. Hladik, 1969) and unpublished observations of 1977/78. Some changes in specific names follow a recent review of plant specimens by A. Hladik.

Table 7.4. Plant species eaten by *Presbytis senex* at Polonnaruwa (Sri Lanka)

Species eaten	Percentage of total food intake accounted for		
Adina cordifolia (Rubiaceae)	⎤ 40	⎤ 70	⎤
Schleichera oleosa (Sapindaceae)			
Drypetes sepiaria (Euphorbiaceae)	⎦	⎦	
Alangium salvifolium (Alangiaceae)			
Elaeodendron glaucum (Celastraceae)			
Grewia polygama (Tiliaceae)			>90
Syzygium cumini (Myrtaceae)			
Holoptelea integrifolia (Ulmaceae)			
Garcinia spicata (Guttiferae)			
Walsura piscidia (Meliaceae)			
Ficus spp. (Moraceae)			
Sapindus trifoliatus (Sapindaceae)			⎦

Note: Species are listed in decreasing order according to amount ingested during 20 days, in 1969/70 (C. M. Hladik and A. Hladik, 1972).

small number of plant species in their diet. Accordingly, the dietary specialization amounts to a minimum level of flexibility, or a low tolerance for new food items. This characteristic is commonly encountered in the maintenance of captive primates: folivores are the least able to cope with new foods (C. M. Hladik, 1979).

One adaptive advantage of dietary specialization among primates is that overlap in resource exploitation by sympatric species is reduced or eliminated (C. M. Hladik, 1978). Furthermore, the range of dietary flexibility is probably related to the social characteristics of each primate. It is impossible with the data now at hand to determine whether food availability and choice determine social organization or whether sociological patterns lead to particular food choices. Nevertheless, we can state that different combinations of food choice and social organization are strategies of habitat utilization (C. M. Hladik, 1975), and that a limited number of possible combinations exist.

Social Organization and Resource Distribution

If we want to consider the way in which different food resources are partitioned among the individuals of a given primate group, social structure is a key factor. The simplest form of social organization is found in nocturnal prosimians such as *Lepilemur leucopus* and *Galago demidovii*. In these species, the food available within the range of any individual is cropped mainly by the resident. Taking overlap of ranges into account, the "supplying area" (C. M. Hladik, 1977a) provides approximately the same amount of food for each individual. This area is very small, less than 0.3 ha,

Table 7.5. Plant species eaten by *Presbytis entellus* at Polonnaruwa (Sri Lanka)

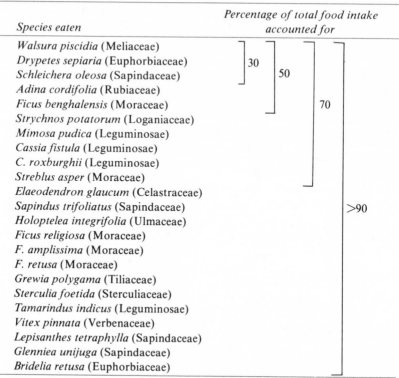

Species eaten	Percentage of total food intake accounted for
Walsura piscidia (Meliaceae)	
Drypetes sepiaria (Euphorbiaceae)	30
Schleichera oleosa (Sapindaceae)	50
Adina cordifolia (Rubiaceae)	
Ficus benghalensis (Moraceae)	70
Strychnos potatorum (Loganiaceae)	
Mimosa pudica (Leguminosae)	
Cassia fistula (Leguminosae)	
C. roxburghii (Leguminosae)	
Streblus asper (Moraceae)	
Elaeodendron glaucum (Celastraceae)	
Sapindus trifoliatus (Sapindaceae)	>90
Holoptelea integrifolia (Ulmaceae)	
Ficus religiosa (Moraceae)	
F. amplissima (Moraceae)	
F. retusa (Moraceae)	
Grewia polygama (Tiliaceae)	
Sterculia foetida (Sterculiaceae)	
Tamarindus indicus (Leguminosae)	
Vitex pinnata (Verbenaceae)	
Lepisanthes tetraphylla (Sapindaceae)	
Glenniea unijuga (Sapindaceae)	
Bridelia retusa (Euphorbiaceae)	

Note: Species are listed in decreasing order according to amount ingested during 20 days, in 1969/70 (C. M. Hladik and A. Hladik, 1972).

in the case of *Lepilemur leucopus* (Charles-Dominique and Hladik, 1971) and fairly large, about 3.0 ha, for *Galago demidovii* (Charles-Dominique, 1972). The size of the supplying area is obviously correlated with the production of the food type utilized, but dietary flexibility is also involved. The small territories established by *Lepilemur* are associated with a folivorous diet of limited diversity, in which one or two plant species may account for more than 50% of the total food ingested.

Food partitioning among neighboring social groups can be viewed in similar terms by considering home ranges and territories as the primary limiting factor for the supplying area used by each group. Our studies of the primates at Polonnaruwa, Sri Lanka, mentioned earlier as examples of behavioral adaptations to dietary diversity, were initially carried out to provide this kind of information about potential relationships between habitat and social structures (C. M. Hladik, and A. Hladik, 1972). *Presbytis senex,* which feeds mainly on a small number of plant species, lives in groups of 4–7 members on home ranges that rarely exceed 4 ha (Rudran, 1970). When the distribution of tree species used as food sources by this primate is plotted (C. M. Hladik and A. Hladik, 1972:175), it becomes apparent that the key resources (*Adina cordifolia* and *Schleichera oleosa*) are evenly distributed throughout each home range. Therefore every *P. senex* group has guaranteed access to a minimum number of food-bearing trees at any given time. Their feeding strategy may be based mainly on an abundance of leaves and flowers produced by the most common plant species, but their grouping strategy also allows exploitation of lower-quality resources with minimal energy expenditure (C. M. Hladik, 1977a).

The gray langur, *Presbytis entellus,* which feeds on a wider variety of plant species, forms larger groups of 20–30 members that use ranges of 10–15 ha (Ripley, 1967, 1970). This species uses about the same quantity of food as *P. senex,* but some more uncommon and unevenly distributed plant species are included regularly in the supplying areas of each group (C. M. Hladik and A. Hladik, 1972:190). In this case, the feeding strategy involves more energy expenditure on exploitation of a broader resource base (C.M. Hladik, 1977a), and the grouping strategy is correspondingly different.

The toque macaque, *Macaca sinica,* lives in groups of about a dozen members but utilizes very large ranges of 30–50 ha (Dittus, 1974, 1977). In this case the need for a large territory is essentially due to a diet that includes animal prey. Since this food resource requires extensive foraging, the plant species which have the most scattered distribution can also be used as food resources when necessary, and shared fairly evenly among the different groups of toque macaques (C. M. Hladik and A. Hladik, 1972:203).

Each plant species has a particular distribution that reflects competition with other plant species, seed dispersal by wind or animals, and so on. Conventional statistical methods classify the plant population in a supposedly homogeneous area into classes based on size (Greig-Smith, 1971), but what is needed in order to understand the feeding strategies of primates is an exact representation of the irregularities of plant distribution.

The theory of regionalized variables (Matheron, 1970) provides this type of information and can be applied without sophisticated mathematical tools. For instance, at the Polonnaruwa field station in Sri Lanka, the canopy size of every tree was measured to allow calculation of fruit and leaf production. The different tree species were then characterized by a "variogram" (A. Hladik, 1978b), which illustrates the variance in the increment of the total canopy size (adding all areas of individual tree canopies) of a given tree species (measured in successive quadrats) in relation to the distance traveled in any direction. In the practical case of a monkey starting to move after feeding in a tree, the profile of the variogram represents what the primate will actually discover along its arboreal path. A flat line means no change in the abundance of the canopy for a given tree species. This occurs in the case of *Adina cordifolia,* an evenly scattered tree used as a main food by *Presbytis senex* (fig. 7.7). A fluctuating line, on the contrary, indicates an irregular distribution of a tree and, accordingly, of food in the canopy. A good example is the irregular availability of *Strychnos potatorum* for *Macaca sinica.* The intermediate types of distribution are those of trees used by *Presbytis entellus.* The variograms of tree species at the Sri Lanka site can thus be grouped according to the specific ranges and activity patterns of the various primate species utilizing these resources. Of course, the seasonal production (phenology) of these plants is as important as their localization and must also be taken into account during such studies (A. Hladik, 1978b).

Group foraging involves a more sophisticated strategy for utilization of dispersed resources than does individual foraging of the type practiced by nocturnal prosimians. These group strategies probably evolved independently in different species but seem to have converged toward the model described above for the primates of Sri Lanka. The two diurnal *Lemur* species studied by Sussman (1974) exhibit ranges of dietary flexibility similar to those of the two *Presbytis* species I studied. These sympatric

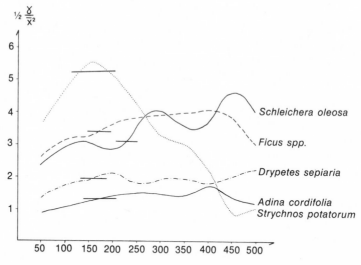

Figure 7.7. Distribution of some tree species in the deciduous dry forest of Sri Lanka in relation to their utilization as food by primates, showing variations in food availability in terms of total canopy area for each tree species and distance traveled to utilize the resource. These variogram functions (γ) have been related to the mean canopy area ($\overline{x}$) and its variance (horizontal lines), in order to permit comparisons with different areas (after A. Hladik, 1978b).

primates partition their habitats similarly: one species lives in small groups (but has a high population density) and feeds on the most common plants, while the other species lives in large groups and feeds on a larger set of more uncommon resources. Despite the absence of detailed information about vegetation structure in these habitats, the general adaptive pattern seems obvious (C. M. Hladik, 1978).

Similar relationships can be seen among the East African primate species studied for many years by Struhsaker (1975, 1978) and his associates. The feeding strategies of the two *Colobus* species, *C. guereza* and *C. badius,* parallel those of the two *Presbytis* species in Sri Lanka (C. M. Hladik, 1977a). However, the evolutionary relationship between feeding strategy and social organization has advanced to a new level of sophistication in *Colobus badius,* which lives in large groups and utilizes many tree species. The groups are so tolerant of each other that their homes ranges overlap considerably even though the resource density and the average supplying area are quite similar to those used by *Presbytis entellus.* Another sympatric species in this East African forest, *Cercocebus albigena,* has even larger home ranges and has specialized in feeding on widely scattered but clumped resources (e.g., fruiting trees).

The most complex systems are found in polyspecific associations of primates, such as those occurring in the rain forests of Gabon (Gautier and Gautier-Hion, 1969; Gautier-Hion and Gautier, 1974). There, several species of *Cercopithecus* have semi-independent groups that join to form large interspecific bands of 50 or more monkeys. These species, which live mainly in the nonflooded sections of primary rain forest (see fig. 7.4), reap the advantage of interspecific social bonds which enable them to exploit additional resources. Each species obtains invertebrate prey "at different heights" (actually in different structural parts of the forest, as discussed earlier), and there is little competition for animal food. The interindividual competition that would tend to occur in a large monospecific group whose members practiced the same feeding strategy is thereby lowered. Although the Gautiers use arguments involving agonistic behavior to account for the absence of large monospecific groups, I believe my ecological explanation is quite sufficient in itself.

At the same time, the different species all feed on the same sort of fruiting trees, which are extremely scattered but yield an abundant though localized crop. Thus, by increasing group size, the polyspecific grouping tendency necessarily leads to a very large supplying area. There may be several subtle explanations for the polyspecific primate groups now being investigated by the Gautiers, the most likely of which involves the complex dispersion of tree species in the rain forest. A somewhat similar phenomenon has been observed in New World rain forests, where many tree species utilized by primates are widely scattered. For example, subgroups of *Ateles* often form large foraging units (L. Klein and D. Klein, 1975) that are sometimes joined by *Cebus* (Carpenter, 1935).

Diversifying the food resources and extending the range of feeding units are ways of coping with the seasonal variations of food production, compensating in part for the lack of specific physiological specializations. These strategies are governed, however, by psychosensory adaptations that may be key factors in the evolution of social organization.

PSYCHOSENSORY ADAPTATIONS
TO DIET

Perception of the Chemical Environment

Teitelbaum and Epstein (1963) have demonstrated that motivation and regulation of the feeding response can depend exclusively on internal information. In their experiments, rats were fed by a tube directly connected to the esophagus, thus excluding input of information from the senses of taste and smell. The animals were trained to feed themselves by pressing a bar. Their responses were regular as long as the food mixture was held constant, but any change in the mixture was compensated for within a few hours by a change in the response. For example, when the food mixture was diluted by 50%, the rats responded by pressing the bar twice as often. This behavior can be interpreted as a response to satiation following the intake and intestinal absorption of food, and there is every reason to believe that this response exists in primates as well as other mammals.

Other experiments, however, have demonstrated further complexities in the regulating mechanism. Pfaffmann (1960) fed rats a diet with a controlled composition in order to eliminate differential biochemical reactions. But some rats received the food after it had been flavored with artificial substances that were nonnutritional. The rats receiving "varied" foods ate significantly more than the rats given the food with the standard taste.

This second type of feeding response has been called "hedonic" by Le Magnen (1966), because it involves only subjective taste. In this case, food intake is regulated by perception of "pleasant" taste or odor. It is possible, of course, that the two are intimately linked in most situations, taste being associated with internal requirements. Nevertheless, since taste thresholds differ among primate species (Glaser, 1972), the second mechanism will operate differently for each of them. This idea was initially developed into a hypothesis of feeding strategies by C. M. Hladik, A. Hladik, et al. (1971) and has since been corroborated by many observations. Thus, the different feeding strategies developed and maintained by various primate species may have their roots in the relative importance of the two types of reaction presented above, by which the chemical environment is perceived.

Food Composition and Behavior

From biochemical analyses of the foods utilized by wild primates, we can estimate what is likely to be detected by taste in terms of water-soluble substances, such as sugars and organic acids. There are significant differences in the diets of primates in Panama (A. Hladik and C. M. Hladik, 1969). The immature fruit (mainly wild figs) and leaves eaten by the howler, *Alouatta palliata,* have a minimum of these soluble substances (C. M. Hladik, A. Hladik, et al., 1971). Furthermore, howlers have been observed to feed for several days on the same, unvaried type of food. This suggests that their capability for a hedonic response is low, and so their feeding behavior may be governed mainly by the first mechanism described above.

By contrast, the spider monkey, *Ateles geoffroyi,* and especially the capuchin, *Cebus capucinus,* search for foods that are high in soluble sugars; this indicates a more highly developed hedonic response. One might expect that this response has been positively selected for in the evolution of these species, because a sensitivity for taste can improve feeding performance. The capuchin searches for widely scattered food resources that require large amounts of foraging time, and a high degree of motivation is necessary to maintain this particular strategy.

Detailed analysis of the relationships between feeding strategies and food composition has been attempted for two langur species in Sri Lanka (C. M. Hladik, 1977a). The dietary intake of each species was calculated in terms of the biochemical composition of the foods eaten at different seasons (fig. 7.8). Both species are even more folivorous than *Alouatta* and probably are not very sensitive to taste stimulation. There is a difference in food selection, however, so that their diets are not the same. For *Presbytis entellus* the nutrients are variable, and while proteins can be low for short periods, the average lipid and protein intake is much higher than for *P. senex.* For the latter species, the nutrients, especially proteins and lipids, are stable but low in concentration. Thus, one can infer that the feeding behavior of *P. senex* is mainly determined by the long-term response of the organism and is characterized by a minimum of energy expenditure to find the most abundant food resources of low-energy return. A relatively larger energy return is obtained by *P. entellus,* but this requires high motivation to find and utilize more scattered plant species; therefore a more highly developed hedonic response is probably operating in this species. In these anatomically similar species, the presence of such different feeding strategies can be explained most reasonably by differences in taste perception, either at the level of the taste buds and nerves or at a higher level of cognitive perception. For the macaques *(Macaca sinica),* which live sympatrically with the langurs, the level of taste stimulation must be even higher in order to provide motivation for feeding on the most scattered

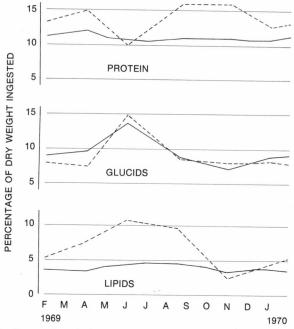

Figure 7.8. Seasonal variation in the diets of *Presbytis senex* (solid lines) and *Presbytis entellus* (dashed lines), based on analysis of food specimens collected in the field during different seasons (see fig. 7.6).

resources. This kind of adaptation would apply mainly to carnivorous and frugivorous forms, and might best represent the primitive condition for primates.

Some of the extant primates that are morphologically specialized to feed on very abundant resources (e.g., *Presbytis senex*) may have as a secondary adaptation a decreased sensitivity to taste, their primary adaptation remaining the long-term satiation response common to all primate species. Further psychosensory experiments would be necessary to confirm this hypothesis, but the recent work of Glaser and Hellekant (1977), demonstrating a relationship between level of stimulation and behavioral thresholds of taste in squirrel monkeys, is the beginning of such evidence.

Effects of Primary and Secondary Compounds

Food selection by primates is presumably related to the differential presence of nutrients and to specific physiological and morphological adaptations that contribute to long-term responses to food intake. Deviation from an adequate diet, resulting in illness when digestion was unsatisfactory, would be automatically corrected by what amounts to an aversive conditioning process, and dietary selection would be redirected toward foods containing the correct nutrients (or primary compounds).

Plants also contain secondary compounds, including chemicals such as alkaloids, tannins, and glucosides, which have no direct physiological function in plants and are not nutrients for primates. Some of these may actually be toxic to primates (Whittaker and Feeny, 1971). The role of these chemicals in preventing seed destruction by insects has been demonstrated (Janzen, 1971). The function of secondary compounds in leaves and other plant parts is not yet evident.

The food choices of forest primates might not be strongly affected by secondary compounds, which often occur in low concentrations in plants (A. Hladik, 1978a). A few toxic plants (and especially seeds such as those of *Strychnos*) cannot be eaten by primates, which are unable to detoxify such chemicals by rapid bacterial fermentation. These avoidance responses can be learned definitively in one trial with a sublethal dose (Garcia, Hankins, and Rusiniak, 1974), and form an important survival mechanism.

Recently there has been great interest among primatologists in the role of secondary compounds in diets and their potential toxicity, but very few data are available. We have screened for alkaloids in food samples collected in Sri Lanka (table 7.6) as well as in many specimens of foods eaten by the chimpanzees in Gabon (table 7.7). In Sri Lanka, only a few plant species are likely to contain large amounts of alkaloids. Some are eaten by the langurs and avoided by the macaques, but the latter nevertheless regularly eat the leaves of *Strychnos potatorum*. In Gabon the situation is different; there many plant species contain alkaloids or other secondary compounds. Of 382 plant species analyzed, 14% have significant amounts of alkaloid (A. Hladik and C. M. Hladik, 1977). Since the chimpanzees do not always avoid the species containing alklaoids (15% of the species eaten contain these compounds), many of the alkaloids are evidently harmless to these primates, or at least their detoxification is possible at a relatively low cost.

Accordingly, theories that relate primary food choices to the presence or absence of secondary compounds should only be accepted if there are supporting data. One field study of *Colobus* in the coastal forest of Cameroon does supply such data (Gartlan, McKey, and Waterman, 1978). In this particular habitat the primates select plant parts with a minimum of phenolic compounds, but they also rely on the seeds of many tree species selected according to the minimum of toxicity.

An alternative hypothesis concerning coevolution of animals and plants complements the evidence presented by Janzen (1971). Plants could avoid predation on their leaves by manufacturing minimal amounts of nutrients there (C. M. Hladik, 1978). Among primates, only specialized folivores, such as *Presbytis senex*, can rely on plants containing these small amounts of soluble sugars and smaller-than-average protein fractions, owing to their

Table 7.6. Results of screening tests for alkaloids in samples of the main foods ●
Presbytis senex, P. entellus, and *Macaca sinica* in Sri Lanka

Food samples	Alkaloid tests		Eaten by		
	Mayer's	Dragen-dorff's	P. senex	P. entellus	M. sinica
Adina cordifolia: young leaves	−	−	×	×	×
leaves	+	+	×	×	
flowers	+	+	×		
Drypetes sepiaria: young leaves	−	−	×	×	
leaves	+	+	×	×	
Walsura piscidia: young leaves	−	−	×	×	
leaves	−	−	×	×	
Schleichera oleosa: young leaves	−	−			
leaves	−	−			
Manilkara hexandra: young leaves	−	−	×	×	
leaves	−	−			
Grewia polygama: leaves	−	+	×	(×)	(×)
Ficus amplissima: leaves	−	−	×		
F. benghalensis: leaves	−	−	×		
F. mollis: leaves	+	+	(×)		
F. parasitica: leaves	−	−			
F. racemosa: leaves	−	−	×		
F. religiosa: young leaves	+	+		×	
leaves	+	−		×	
F. retusa: leaves	−	−			
Premna tomentosa: leaves	−	−		×	(×)
Lepisanthes tetraphylla: leaves	−	−	(×)	(×)	
Diospyros montana: young leaves	−	−		×	
leaves	±	±		×	×
D. ovalifolia: young leaves	−	−			×
leaves	±	±			
Ixora arborea: young leaves	−	−		×	
leaves	−	−			
Mimosa pudica: leaves	−	−		×	×
Alangium salvifolium: young leaves	+++	+++	×	×	×
leaves	+++	+++	×	×	
Strychnos potatorum: young leaves	++	++	×	×	
leaves	++	++	×	×	×
Elaeodendron glaucum: young leaves	+	+	×	×	
leaves	+	+	×	×	

Table 7.6 *(continued)*

Food samples	Alkaloid tests		Eaten by		
	Mayer's	Dragen-dorff's	P. senex	P. entellus	M. sinica
Cassia fistula: young leaves	+	++		×	×
leaves	±	+		×	
Streblus asper: young leaves	+	+		×	
leaves	+	+			
Glycosmis pentaphylla: leaves	+	+	×	×	
Sterculia foetida: leaves	−	−	(×)	(×)	
Vitex pinnata: leaves	+	+	×	×	
Syzygium cumini: young leaves	+	+	×	×	
leaves	−	−	×	×	
Feronia limonia: leaves	−	−			
Morinda tinctoria: leaves	+	+			
Pleiospermum alatum: leaves	++	+			
Atalantia sp.: leaves	+	+			
Mallotus eriocarpus: young leaves	+++	+++			
leaves	++	++			
Cassia occidentalis: leaves	+	+		×	
Crotalaria pallida: leaves	+++	+++		×	
Phyllanthus polyphyllus: leaves	+	+			
Micromelum ceylanicum: leaves	+	+			
Tarenna asiatica: leaves	−	+			
Allophyllus cobbe: leaves	−	−			
Randia malabarica: leaves	−	−			

Note: The positive results are generally due to alkaloids, but other compounds may interfere. By contrast, negative results are clear indications of the absence of alkaloids.

Key: × Mature leaves.
      (×) Young leaves.
      − No reaction.
      + Slight positive reaction.
      ++ Precipitate formed.
     +++ Large amount of precipitate formed.

low-cost, low-energy-return feeding strategies. Such strategies might be the ultimate stage of coevolution in this particular direction.

DISCUSSION AND CONCLUSIONS

Evolution of Predatory Behavior

Predatory behavior directed toward small invertebrates appears to be the basis from which primate feeding behaviors evolved, but some extant predatory species no longer reflect this primitive condition. Moreover,

Table 7.7. Results of screening tests for alkaloids in food samples of chimpanzees in Gabon.

Food samples	Alkaloid tests	
	Mayer's	Dragendorff's
Baphia leptobotrys: young leaves	++	++
leaves	±	−
flowers	++	++
Hypselodelphis violacea: stems	−	−
leaves (not eaten)	±	±
unripe seeds	−	+
Ongokea gore: leaves	+	+
Tetrapleura tetraptera: leaves	+	+
Dalhousiea africana: leaves	+	+
Roureopsis obliquifoliata: leaves	+	+
Newbouldia laevis: leaves	++	++
Neuropeltis acuminata: leaves	−	+
Cissus dinklagei: young leaves	−	−
Ficus sp., spec. no. 1906: leaves	−	−
Ficus sp., spec. no. 2193: leaves	−	−
Uapaca heudelotii: leaves	−	−
Dinophora spennerioides: leaves	−	+
Spec. no. 2034 (unidentified): young leaves	++	++
Spec. no. 2176 (unidentified): young leaves	+	+
Spec. no. 2178 (unidentified): young leaves	+	+
Symphonia globulifera: flowers	−	−
leaves (not eaten)	−	−
Musanga cecropioides: petioles	−	−
leaves (not eaten)	++	+++
Pseudospondias microcarpa: petioles	−	−
leaves	−	−

many insect species evolved toward unpalatability by developing secretions and glands in which plant secondary compounds are concentrated (Whittaker and Feeny, 1971). These invertebrate secretions are very efficient deterrents against most potential predators, as demonstrated by a series of tests made in Gabon (Bernardi and Charles-Dominique, personal communication; Bigot and Jouventin, 1974). The ultimate stage of coevolution, in this case, is an adaptation to feed on such "unpalatable" prey. This has happened with *Loris tardigradus* and *Arctocebus calabarensis*, which exhibit convergent adaptations evolved in Asia and in Africa. These species rely on an acute sense of smell to locate small invertebrates that are considered inedible by other local predators (Charles-Dominique, 1971, 1977; Petter and Hladik, 1970). It is noteworthy that the invertebrates' strong-smelling secretions, which normally function to repel

Table 7.7 (*continued*)

Food samples	Alkaloid tests	
	Mayer's	*Dragendorff's*
Pterygota bequaertii: leaves	−	−
seeds	−	−
bark	+	−
Hypselodelphis hirsuta: stems	−	−
Haumania dankelmaniana: stems	−	−
Scleria verrucosa: stems	−	−
Eremospatha wendenliana: stems and apex	−	−
Afromomum giganteum: stems	−	−
leaves (not eaten)	−	−
Garcinia polyantha: bark	−	−
leaves (not eaten)	−	−
Musa sapientum: banana skins	−	±
Tristemma leiocalyx: unripe fruits	+	+
Caloncoba glauca: unripe fruits	+	+
leaves (not eaten)	−	−
Dichostemma glaucescens: unripe seeds	±	±
leaves (not eaten)	+	±
Synsepalum letestui: seeds	++	++
leaves (not eaten)	−	−
Oubanguia africana: seeds	±	±
leaves (not eaten)	−	+

Note: These secondary compounds are absent or exceptional in the fleshy parts of fruits. When both seeds and fruits are eaten, positive results likely to show large amounts of alkaloids (++) were found in 15% of samples tested; some samples are listed by specimen number. Certain plant parts not eaten were analyzed for comparison. For key, see table 7.6.

predators, are the means by which *Loris* and *Arctocebus* find them. This strategy implies physiological as well as sensory adaptation (C. M. Hladik, 1979) and represents an evolutionary trend toward specialization. A primitive type of predatory behavior exists in the less specialized forms, such as *Galago* and *Microcebus* (Charles-Dominique and Martin, 1970), as well as in most simian primates of grade 2, which feed on fruits and insects.

Learning Capacities and Feeding Behavior

Increased intelligence, which is one of the most remarkable traits of the order Primates, plays a vital role in the adoption of complex feeding strategies. The prosimians that closely resemble the ancestral primate stock lack behavioral flexibility. Cooper (in press) demonstrated that the lesser mouse lemur (*Microcebus murinus*), a nocturnal, solitary species, can rapidly learn to make visual discriminations in order to gain a food reward, but afterward the animal experiences great difficulty in reversing this

Table 7.8. Relative percentages of essential amino acids in samples of the plant and animal foods accounting for most of the protein ingested by the chimpanzee, Pan troglodytes troglodytes, in Gabon

Amino acid	Stems of Hypselodelphis violacea	Leaves of Baphia lepto-botrys	Ants' nest of Macromiscoides aculeatus	Ants and grubs of Œcophylla longinoda	Average[a]	Protein of egg as reference
Cystine	4.6	7.7	2.7	1.8	5.9	4.8
Histidine	4.8	2.9	9.0	6.6	4.3	4.6
Isoleucine	11.0	11.5	11.3	12.4	11.6	10.4
Leucine	20.3	13.5	19.2	22.1	16.2	16.7
Lysine	10.5	8.7	12.9	15.0	10.4	13.9
Methionine	4.6	2.7	3.4	3.5	3.1	6.1
Phenylalanine	11.5	8.7	8.1	7.6	8.7	11.6
Threonine	11.8	7.9	11.3	10.2	9.0	9.3
Tyrosine	6.1	9.0	8.7	8.4	8.6	9.3
Valine	15.2	27.6	13.4	12.4	22.3	13.5

Note: Due to rounding, columns do not equal exactly 100%. Data are from C. M. Hladik and Viroben (1974).
[a] Calculated according to the proportions of the different items in the diet of the chimpanzee.

learned response. In a response comparable in many ways to the phenomenon of "imprinting," *Microcebus* displays a persistent attachment to the first object to be associated with a food reward. The aversive response to toxic substances, which primates and other mammalian species learn extremely rapidly (Garcia, Hankins, and Rusiniak, 1974), involves a similar persistence. The kind of positive learning which Cooper demonstrated in *Microcebus* is highly adaptive for this primate in the Madagascar forests, where it must utilize animal prey and fruiting trees that are available only for short periods.

Among gregarious diurnal prosimians and simian primates, behavioral responses to food items are much more flexible (Wilkerson and Rumbaugh, 1978). This greater flexibility may be made possible by the ability to "unlearn" the initial response [although Doyle (1979) and others have ignored this aspect of learning]. In intermediate forms such as *Phaner furcifer,* a semigregarious nocturnal prosimian (Charles-Dominique, 1978), the ability to "unlearn" an initial response is partly developed (Cooper, in press). This increased behavioral flexibility may be related to specific feeding strategy: for several days the animals use one itinerary through the forest to collect gums and other exudates on which they feed (Charles-Dominique and Petter, in press), but they shift to a different itinerary when some of the gums are no longer available.

For many simian primates, the ability to adjust behavior to the changing conditions of the environment obviously increases the efficiency of food exploitation. Tests demonstrating the presence of this ability have been applied in comparative studies of "intelligence" in various primate species (Rumbaugh, 1975), although such results are not directly applicable to food exploitation in the wild. Nonetheless, the evolution of cerebral structures that promote behavioral flexibility parallels the evolution of hand structures that allow accurate manipulatory movements (Bishop, 1964) and of eye structures that increase visual acuity and color vision (Pariente, 1976).

The talapoin, *Miopithecus talapoin,* observed in Gabon by Gautier-Hion (1971), has developed a sophisticated technique for approaching and capturing invertebrate prey, which involves moving behind a tree trunk or a large branch (being purposely deceptive?) and grabbing the prey after a sudden turning movement. A more unusual technique is employed by the toque macaque, *Macaca sinica,* in Sri Lanka (C. M. Hladik and A. Hladik, 1972). These monkeys feed on caterpillars that are abundant in *Adina* trees but escape from most predators by dropping down on a silk thread as soon as anything moves nearby. The macaques simply "fish" them back up again by this thread, pulling faster than the caterpillar is able to descend. A feeding technique of the barbary ape, *Macaca sylvana,* demonstrates even greater perfection in precise coordination of movement. When a scorpion is found by turning over a stone, it is grabbed in one hand and the part of the abdomen with the sting is broken off at once with the other hand (Deag, 1974). Chimpanzees in Gabon also feed on scorpions (C. M. Hladik, 1973), but these scorpions (*Opisthacanthus lecomtei*) have a less dangerous sting, and a rapid hand slap serves to immobilize them.

Most of these specialized feeding techniques can also be observed in other taxa, such as bats and birds. *Nycteris thebaica,* for example, can remove the stingers of scorpions (Brosset, 1966), and the bee-eaters (Meropidae) can deal with wasp stingers by rubbing them on tree bark. What may be characteristic of primates is a larger repertoire of such techniques and greater flexibility in applying them to changing conditions. In this sense, intelligence can be defined as an ability to cope with a high degree of informational complexity.

Feeding Strategies in Chimpanzees

The most advanced feeding strategy employed by nonhuman primates is the using and making of different kinds of tools for food-gathering purposes. Of these techniques, insect-fishing by chimpanzees has been well documented since it was first described by Goodall (1963b). The feeding habits of different populations of chimpanzees vary throughout their geographical range (C. M. Hladik, 1977b), as do their technological skills (Sabater Pi, 1974; Teleki, 1974). However, tool use has been observed in most places where these apes feed on termites or ants. In Gabon, the chimpanzees use their hands to collect ants and larvae from hollow trunks. If the hole is too narrow, the chimpanzee probes into it with a twig collected nearby and then eats the ants that bite the stick. The large Ponerine ants that burrow into the ground can be "fished" for hours to procure an abundant meal. As Teleki suggested (1974), tool use by chimpanzees considerably increases the efficiency of insect foraging.

The insect and other invertebrate prey eaten by chimpanzees balances the composition of the diet by providing an adequate proportion of different amino acids (C. M. Hladik, 1977b; C. M. Hladik and Viroben, 1974) (table 7.8). Given this ape's large size (up to 50 kg), and in accord with the principles developed earlier, techniques that improve the efficiency of food-gathering are one way of compensating for the large variation in composition which affects any frugivore/carnivore diet of grade 2. The chimpanzees in Gabon utilize many different fruiting trees during the annual cycle, yet no single type forms a large proportion of the total food intake. Predation on larger vertebrates, which has been documented by Teleki (1973a,b, 1975) and others, does not serve as a major source of animal protein for a chimpanzee population as a whole (C. M. Hladik, 1977b; C. M. Hladik and Viroben, 1974) because females and young do not benefit significantly from these prey. However, there is some evidence that females consume more insects than males do (McGrew, 1974, 1979), which may compensate for the uneven distribution of vertebrate meat (Teleki, in this volume). These facts do not support the hypothesis offered by Gaulin and Kurland (1976), who contend that large primates are inclined to feed on large prey because of the relatively smaller energy cost. Predation on small invertebrates and vertebrates is a primitive pattern in primates and survives in a more behaviorally sophisticated manner in chimpanzees, perhaps in tandem with an expansion into such varied habitats as dense forests and open "parkland" (Kortlandt, 1972). The large social units of chimpanzees (Suzuki, 1969) permit efficient utilization of a large supplying area and a very diversified environment, which includes many types of food resources with complementary cycles of availability.

Recent Evolutionary Trends

Although ancestral dietary patterns persisted in the forest-dwelling primates, the invasion of new habitats by the evolving hominids may have been facilitated by an emphasis on the trait I have termed dietary flexibility; that is, the addition of small prey to a primarily frugivorous diet, the utilization of varied and widely dispersed foods, and the ability to make and use tools. The subsequent migration of the hominids out of Africa and their colonization of new environments in much of the Old World may also have been made possible by dietary flexibility, as hominids peripheral to a group moved slowly away from its center, coping with new and varied foods and establishing new groups.

From Plio-Pleistocene times (Isaac and Crader, in this volume) to more modern ones (Gould, in this volume; Lee, 1968), gatherer/hunters have used broadly similar feeding strategies based on the harvesting of diverse and widely dispersed resources with high caloric returns. With the beginning of agriculture, humans began to utilize a large sector of primary production more efficiently by concentrating plant species that had originally been scattered. Their crops, in turn, may have attracted and locally increased small-mammal populations that could be captured and eaten (see Linares, 1976). In thus adding small prey to fruits and seeds obtained from their own crops, human populations continued the primitive primate trait of dietary flexibility.

Acknowledgments

The author is indebted to Professors F. Bourlière, A. Brosset, J. Dorst, P. Dreux, M. Lamotte, and J.-J. Petter for their valuable comments on the original version of this chapter, which was presented and discussed in French at the Museum d'Histoire Naturelle in June 1977. Further comments from Drs. M. Moynihan, O. Linares, M. Robinson, R. S. O. Harding, H. Cooper, A. Hladik, and the final editing work of G. Teleki contributed to the present version.

NOTES

1. Note that this representation does not differ from the classical system with three axes at 60° used by MacKinnon and MacKinnon (1978).

2. Perpendicular axes are more convenient for plotting diagrams, and they are used here to obtain dietary values that can be compared to the measures of gut differentiation discussed in the next section.

3. The mean values on axis $0x$ (+25, +12, and −5, respectively) provide a useful approximation of dietary divergence.

4. Similar but less precise correlations have been found after calculating the total area available for absorption in the small gut of different primate species: for folivorous forms, the index approaches +100, and it may reach as low as −100 for animalivores.

5. Similarly, no folivores were found among the primitive reptiles of the Permian (Halstead, 1969; Olson, 1966).

6. Other physiological changes, such as seasonal birth periods, are also known to occur in most species.

Shirley C. Strum

8.
Processes and Products of Change: Baboon Predatory Behavior at Gilgil, Kenya

As the search for hominid origins has intensified in the last two decades, so has the attempt to find an animal model for the predatory component of early hominid behavior. Various animals have been proposed as representative of the early hominid adaptation, including baboons (e.g., B. Campbell, 1966; Dart, 1963; DeVore and Washburn, 1963; R. Fox, 1967; C. J. Jolly, 1970; Oakley, 1961), social carnivores (e.g., Crook, 1966; Peters and Mech, 1975; Pfeiffer, 1969; Schaller and Lowther, 1969; P. Thompson, 1975), and chimpanzees (e.g., Crook and Gartlan, 1966; Kortlandt, 1972; Kortlandt and Kooij, 1963; Lancaster, 1968; Reynolds, 1966; Teleki, 1975).

These models have been inadequate because our understanding of the evolution of behavior has been rudimentary, the relevant data have been sparse, and we have tended to underestimate the behavioral variability of a predaceous species. Early hominids were at the same time primates, social predators, and anatomically transitional forms; therefore a precise analogue, whether animal or human, can never exist. Yet the study of nonhuman primates and social carnivores can illustrate the basic interplay between an organism and the complexity of its environment and help us to generate hypotheses about the evolution of the subsistence patterns which we now recognize as unique to humans. By understanding processes, we can better comprehend the products of evolutionary change.

Essential to such an understanding is knowledge about the behavior that led to the inclusion of large animals as prey, a significant difference from predatory behavior of living nonhuman primates. This article presents data on the predatory behavior of one baboon troop that had been under almost continuous observation for 7 years at the time of writing. These data provide specific areas of contrast with other primate predators, including human ones. More important, they illustrate how predation may be affected by the individual, social, and ecological contexts of a group-living primate species, as well as the processes that initiate, facilitate, or inhibit changes in this particular behavior.

255

THE STUDY SITE

The data presented here were collected on Kekopey Ranch near Gilgil, Kenya, roughly 115 km northwest of Nairobi in the Great Rift Valley, an area of high-altitude savannah with volcanic soils. Descriptions of this area and its climate have been published elsewhere (Blankenship and Field, 1972; Blankenship and Qvortrup, 1974; Harding, 1976). The ranch covers some 182 km^2, but the baboons under study live within a central area of about 73 km^2. About 52% of this area is grassland (40% preexisting, 12% the result of recent bush removal), while the remaining 48% is bush of varying densities, dominated in most areas by leleshwa (*Tarchonanthus camphoratus*). The volcanic soil, in combination with sufficient water, can produce good grassland, but relatively low rainfall between 1970 and 1977 resulted in periodic drought conditions and low grassland productivity.

During the past 20 years the area has been altered for cattle raising by bush clearing and construction of a system of cattle troughs that bring water into previously dry areas. A large biomass of wildlife coexists with the cattle. In addition to the baboon population, of interest to the present discussion is the abundance of several antelope species (Thomson's gazelle, impala, reedbuck, steenbok, dikdik, klipspringer, duiker), Cape hares, and numerous predatory and nonpredatory birds.

Large carnivores have been shot or trapped since the early part of this century, but despite their reduced numbers, hyena, lion, and cheetah have occasionally preyed on the cattle. A sizable leopard population still remains, along with three species of jackals, bat-eared fox, and feral domestic dogs that hunt in packs.

Baboon and ungulate populations have increased rapidly, probably as a result of ecological modifications at Kekopey (additional grassland and water plus lowered predator density). Although a rough estimate of 50 Thomson's gazelle in the central area in 1956 (A. and T. Cole, personal communication) is probably imprecise, the order of magnitude seems correct. By the middle of 1970 the population had expanded to 2,000 (Blankenship and Qvortrup, 1974). At this time, in the central area there also were approximately 1,400 impala, 1,000 reedbuck, 200 zebra, 100 buffalo, and 150 eland, in addition to the smaller antelope species.

In 1970, seven baboon troops were identified in this area, with group sizes ranging from 35 to 125 and a population density of 10.3 baboons/km^2 (Harding, 1973b), at the upper range for "savannah" baboons. Since 1970 most baboon troops have doubled in size, and many have split. In 1977 there were a minimum of 12 troops within the same area, yielding a density of roughly 19 baboons/km^2.

Although it was a cattle ranch, Kekopey remained "wild" in many respects. The human population was sparse and dispersed, consisting of a dozen cattle herders and their families, the ranch owners, and occasional groups of migrant charcoal burners, temporary residents when a new area was being cleared of bush. Harassment of wildlife or contact between wildlife and humans remained minimal, unlike in other areas in Kenya. Ecological modification was slight but critical because it opened up new opportunities for wildlife as well as cattle.

THE GROUP AND STUDY METHODS

One group of baboons in the Kekopey population has been under close observation since September 1970, when R. S. O. Harding began the initial study. This group (PHG) has been studied by a succession of 11 scientists with only one break in continuity, August 1974–March 1975. Between 1970 and 1977, the period covered by this report, the troop grew from an average of 49 individuals to 63 animals in 1973, 84 in 1975, and 91 in 1976 (table 8.1). This increase is the result of both an excess of births over deaths and some male immigration; the number of adult females has remained fairly constant.

Harding was the first to document extensive predatory behavior in PHG (1973a, 1974, 1975), and later researchers have extended his observations (Strum, 1975a,b, 1976a,b; N. Chalmers; H. Gilmore; L. Scott; D. Manzolillo; M. Demment, personal communications).

Predation has never been the focus of any PHG studies, but because of excellent observation conditions and the frequency of the behavior, data on baboon predation have been collected during each study. The differences in methodology, orientation of observers, and focus of projects have had an unavoidable effect on the predation data. As a result, my discussion of PHG predatory behavior relies most heavily on my own data collected

Table 8.1. Age–sex classes

	1970–1971	*1973*	*1975*	*1976–1977*
Adult males	4	7	10	10
Subadult males	2	—	2	5
Adult females	18	19	21	21
Juveniles	15	24	32	39
Infants	10	13	19	16
Total	49	63	84	91
Observation hours	1,032	1,200	250	792.5

Note: Figures given here represent mean numbers of animals for each observation period. Study periods are those of Harding (10/70–10/71) and Strum (12/72–1/74; 6–8/75; 8/76–4/77).

during three periods: December 1972 to January 1974 (referred to here as "1973"); June to September 1975; and a third period beginning in August 1976. I report here on data collected through April 1977.

Systematic sampling was used for the main topics during each of my three studies, but data on predatory behavior were collected in an *ad lib* manner (J. Altmann, 1974). Routine sampling was interrupted for any instance of predatory behavior, and potential episodes and factors thought to be important to this behavior were monitored continuously. Notes on predatory episodes were taken in narrative style, and individual sequences were photographed.

ELEMENTS OF
BABOON PREDATORY BEHAVIOR

Predation, like any complex behavior, is dynamic and varies over time, depending on the context and participants. Among PHG baboons this variability is quite marked. Although it is difficult to characterize the PHG predatory pattern for the entire period since 1970, some basic elements exist; I will briefly review them before discussing how this behavior has changed.

Prey Species

With minor exceptions, the species preyed on by PHG baboons have remained the same over the years, but the proportional representation of these animals (the prey profile) differs from year to year (table 8.2). Not all available prey species are captured, and baboon troops in the same population differ in their selection of prey. The PHG baboons capture the young of several antelope species (Thomson's gazelle, impala, dikdik, steenbok, reedbuck, klipspringer) plus individuals of all ages of the smaller antelopes, such as dikdik and steenbok. Cape hare and button quail, several smaller ground-nesting birds, and some tree-nesting bird species are also frequent prey.

Methods of Capture

Teleki (1973a) distinguishes opportunistic and systematic predation in primates, a classification based on the mode of pursuit employed by the predator. Dividing predatory episodes into three stages (pursuit, capture, and consumption), he also identifies three behaviorally distinct modes of pursuit: seizure, chase, and stalk. Opportunistic predation takes place when "no systematic searching or stalking activities precede the capture" (1973a:50). Nonhuman primate predation is said to include hunting when there is deliberate searching, or the presence of chase or stalk as modes of pursuit.

Table 8.2.   Prey species

	1970–1971		1973		1975		1976–1977	
	No.	%	No.	%	No.	%	No.	%
Thomson's gazelle	16	34	33	33	—		9	20
(*Gazella thomsoni*)								
Dikdik	8	17	7	7	2	13	5	11
(*Rhyncotragus kirki*)								
Steenbok	1	2	6	6	1	6	1	2
(*Raphicerus campestris*)								
Impala	1	2	1	1	—		—	
(*Aepyceros melampus*)								
Klipspringer	—		1	1	—		—	
(*Oreotragus oreotragus*)								
Antelope, *sp. indet.*	5	11	—		—		—	
Hare	12	25	41	41	9	56	24	53
(*Lepus capensis*)								
Bird	1	2	11	11	4	25	5	11
Small mammal, *sp. indet.*	3	6	—		—		1	2
Total	47	100	100	100	16	100	45	100

Note: These figures should be compared with caution, since different observation methods were used in 1970–1971 and the other three periods, and different numbers of observation hours were involved in each period (see table 8.1).

PHG baboons captured prey both opportunistically and systematically, although the ratio between these two approaches varied from year to year. Opportunistic capture consisted of simple seizure of exposed prey. Systematic capture exhibited varying degrees of sophistication, the extremes of which I have arbitrarily classified as *simple* and *complex* hunting (cf. "extended hunting"; Strum, 1976a). *Simple hunting* required active searching and either stalking or chasing of the prey. It involved only one baboon predator, pursuit lasted less than 10 minutes, and the distance the predator traveled from the troop was less than 300 m. *Complex hunting* involved more than one predator, the pursuit lasted more than 10 minutes (table 8.3), and the distance the predator traveled to contact the prey ranged from 300 to 1,600 m, although the predator might travel up to 4,000 m during the course of the hunt.

There are intermediate cases, and the assignment of such cases to the simple or complex category was based on variables such as predatory intent (e.g., watching prey or predatory activities of other animals) persistence over time or space, and comparison with the initial predatory pattern. Most of the significant deviations from the initial pattern were termed complex hunting for purposes of analysis. However, some episodes were classified as simple hunting although the baboon predator involved had traveled more than 300 m, because the prey was contacted only incidentally, in the course

Table 8.3. Duration of Thomson's gazelle hunts (1973)

	Successful (n = 24), minutes	Unsuccessful (n = 26), minutes
Total	1145	620
Range	10–120	5–85
Mean	—	24
Mode	60	10, 20
Median	50	30

Note: The sample of successful hunts includes 7 simple hunts, 13 complete complex hunts, and 4 lengthy complex hunts, the beginning of which could not be observed. The unsuccessful sample refers to complex hunts only (see text for definition of "simple" and "complex" hunts).

of a search for something else. In addition, many single-predator episodes were classified as complex hunting if the baboon hunter covered more than 450 m in order to contact a prey animal *and* spent more than 15 minutes in pursuit without any other feeding activity. If a stalk was followed by a sequential chase by several baboons, the episode was classified as complex hunting regardless of the time spent in pursuit. Finally, if the prey was contacted less than 300 m from the point where the predator first began to hunt but the pursuit involved more than one predator and lasted more than 10 minutes, the episode was designated a complex hunt.

It is difficult to distinguish between types of hunting that lie along a continuum of behavior, but the contrasts between types of hunting at either end of the continuum are clear. I suggest that one baboon moving 3 m to pursue a small animal for a few minutes and five male baboons moving synchronously over 1,600 m to contact a prey animal, then spending 2½ hours in following, scattering, searching, and chasing, represent different hunting patterns. Figure 8.1 provides basic data on complex hunting episodes observed in 1973.

Chances for opportunistic capture arose during the day, as the troop searched for vegetable foods. Because hares and infant antelopes attempted to avoid detection by remaining concealed and immobile, a baboon often fed as close as 10 cm to a potential prey before it ran away. However, concealment may not be as effective a defense against baboon predators as it is against predators that rely on movement cues.

Not all successful kills were the result of accidental discoveries. In simple hunting, two methods of active searching were employed. In the first, a baboon left the troop to approach a nearby herd of Thomson's gazelle, then moved through the herd and scrutinized the surrounding area. These searches sometimes resulted in the location and successful capture of infant gazelles. Since dikdik and steenbok prefer denser cover and are not clearly visible to the baboons during troop movement, searching also included

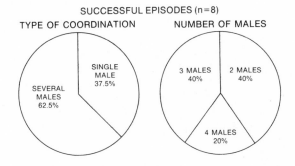

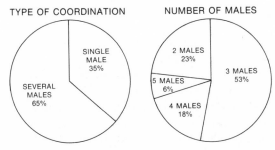

Figure 8.1. Complex hunting on Thomson's gazelle by Gilgil baboons (1973). Five episodes of complex hunting that were not observed in their entirety are omitted here.

detouring through thickets, with the result that prey was flushed, chased, and sometimes captured.

Active pursuit also characterized simple hunting, although it was not always successful. For example, male RD spotted a juvenile hare 225 m away and began to pursue it. As soon as RD had closed the distance to 150 m, the hare took off, with RD chasing it in a zigzag path at full speed for 4 minutes. As he was about to grab it, the hare dashed into a hole, some 450 m from the point where the chase had begun. RD tried to follow into the hole but lost the hare. He sat above the hole for 2 minutes, then tried probing it again, but gave up after 2 minutes more. RD was able to close the distance between himself and the hare and, had the hare not ducked into the hole, RD would have caught it.

At times, fortuitous episodes seemed to stimulate more systematic efforts:

A female baboon chases a hare that has raced out from among the bushes in which the baboons are feeding. Several females and juveniles take up the chase, all rushing at it from different directions. From 245 m away, male RD sees the commotion and runs to intercept the hare, chasing it over 400 m. In the chase, the hare runs past several other baboons who try for it but miss, and RD is the only one to really pursue. Ten minutes later RD gives up, having lost the hare in a thicket. The troop has moved quickly through the neighboring area and RD turns back to rejoin the troop. RD eyes several large herds of tommies as he walks very slowly toward the troop. RD then walks obliquely towards the troop and more directly towards a herd of tommies, glancing back at another herd as he goes. He has been searching through all the clumps of grass and low bushes as he doubles back. The hare has circled around and hidden itself out of RD's path. In this process of searching, RD walks past a very small tommy which is "freezing" in the grass. He doesn't see it but after he moves 30 m away, the tommy gets up and runs off. This catches RD's attention and he sits down, gazing at the baby. A female tommy runs after the baby, moving it even further away from the baboon. RD, standing bipedally to observe the infant, changes his direction and walks towards the tommy and away from the baboon troop.

RD devoted the next 20 minutes to tracking the baby, trying to close the distance between them, as Thomson's gazelle from two herds raced back and forth in front of him. He surveyed other herds as he moved past them, but persisted in following the small gazelle. He finally gave up.

RD's behavior at the end of this example verges on what I have termed complex hunting, for it was systematic hunting, sophisticated in its searching and chasing techniques, and pursuit was persistent and prolonged. Complex hunting could also involve more individuals, greater expenditure of time and effort, and more coordination and strategy, and was quantitatively, if not qualitatively, different from simple hunting. Complex hunting was directed only toward Thomson's gazelle. Two hours could be spent searching, stalking, and chasing, and the same prey animal could be pursued on several days, as the baboon troop revisited an area during its daily movements.

The involvement of many baboons in complex hunting was often accidental, as when several baboons, beginning independently, all converged on the same prey animal simultaneously. But at times activities were coordinated among hunters. For instance, since adult male baboons continually monitor the behavior of other troop members, particularly other adult males, behavior sequences on the following pattern occurred. An adult male baboon looks up from feeding and sees a herd of Thomson's gazelle at a distance. He stops foraging and sits with his gaze fixed at that distant point. Then, beginning either with the closest male or with the male who first observed the alert male's behavior, recognition spreads among the troop's males. When the first male walks off in the direction of the gazelle herd, the others watch him as he moves toward the prey. Once capture appears imminent, the other males might move out to join him. If the predatory event occurs far from the troop, the observing males often move to new positions that allow them a better view.

Sometimes, other males moved toward a distant herd only seconds after the first male had started in that direction. They concentrated on the same prey animal or on other prey, but they also used the presence of other hunters to their advantage by taking over a chase when the previous hunter tired, or by purposefully chasing their own target in the direction of other hunting baboons.

Timing of the chase was critical. Male baboons are rapid runners, but they seemed able to sustain top speed for only about 5 minutes. Sequential chases by several males enabled pursuit to be conducted at top speed for a much longer period, and initial errors in timing could often be overcome if more than one baboon were involved.

Kill and Consumption

The actual moment of capture was not always observable. However, in those instances for which there are data, baboons did not attempt to kill the prey before eating it. Usually, baboons grabbed an antelope and began eating on the soft underbelly, whether the animal was still alive or dead. The prey animal might remain alive for as long as 10 minutes after consumption began, but more often it died as it was being transported from the place it was seized to the first eating site. Although prey was captured with the hands, it was carried in the mouth, usually by the neck, and as a result a broken neck was often the cause of death. I have never observed what appeared to be a purposeful kill bite, although twice a killing bite was inflicted, seemingly accidentally.

Holding the antelope to the ground with both hands and feet, the consumer took the first bite from the underbelly. After the viscera were eaten, the meat on the ribs, the vertebral column, and the limbs was consumed. In the process of eating the limbs, the baboon often turned the skin inside out. The consumer alternated between these various parts of the body until only the limbs and head remained. Once the fleshy parts were gone, the consumer had to exert more and more effort to free the meat from bones and skin. Force was applied by using the incisors to pull in opposition to the hands and feet. The head was consumed last, although marrow eating often followed brain consumption and the carcass might be reexamined for further edible portions. Before the brain was attempted, the ears and eyes were eaten.

The brains of prey were not always eaten. Baboons consumed the brains of smaller species, such as Cape hares, as a matter of course, but they often left the brains of the larger antelopes intact. Two factors were influential: the age of the individual prey animal and the identity of the baboon consumer. The PHG baboons used several techniques to extract the brain from larger prey: crunching, cracking with canines, and entry through the upper palate. The crunching technique was primarily used on infant antelopes, whose thin bones were easily cracked. Their skulls fit easily between the baboons' molar teeth, while positioning of larger prey was more difficult and might be impossible. When the entire skull of the prey was placed between the molars of the consumer and pressure was applied, the braincase cracked into small pieces. Usually the brain was sucked out or licked off the pieces of bone to which it adhered, but fingers might be used to scoop out the remainder. Eating away at the bones of the face and upper palate also allowed the brain to be sucked out. Sometimes several techniques were tried if the first was unsuccessful. Most often, attempts at crunching the skull were followed by attempts to enter through the palate.

The condition of the carcass of an antelope eaten by a baboon was distinctive and possibly diagnostic: the pelt was split from underneath, with portions of limb bones still attached, but all other bones were no longer articulated. Sometimes the pelt appeared to have been turned inside out, the result of the baboons' attempts to break limb bones for their marrow without separating the tough skin from the bones. Around the pelt might be found fragments of skull and facial bones (often the mandible was broken into two segments), and limb bones, either whole or with ends broken off. Scattered throughout the area were bits of ribs and vertebrae.

Consumption of hares and birds was not so systematic. Baboons often crammed small items into their mouths in one movement, or, if they had been eating leisurely, bolted their prey when approached by another potential consumer. The remains of birds and hares were seldom more than a bit of fluff or feathers.

Some baboons apparently did not know how to dispatch prey once they had caught it. For example, having wounded a young Thomson's gazelle during capture, a subadult male licked the wounds as he held down the prey. When he picked up the gazelle and attempted to feed, he did so at the forelimb, then at the elbow, but with little success (baboon teeth and hands seem to have difficulty penetrating the hide of most ungulate prey except in the thin-skinned underbelly). When he next tried to bite into the back, he obtained only fur. The male then tried unsuccessfully to bite through the skin in several other regions, and returned to licking the wounds. At last he managed to break the skin and pull the shoulder joint through, using the incision his initial wounds had made, but even so, 10 minutes after he had begun, he still had obtained little from the carcass of his prey. After 20 minutes of consumption, the male finally bit into the underbelly and fed easily.

Prey Response

Hares. Cape hares employed two methods of escape from a baboon. Remaining immobile ("freezing") was the simplest method and occurred both in the open, where the hare was in plain view, and in denser cover, where the hare was partially concealed. Baboons often passed very close to a "freezing" hare without apparently noticing it. In these cases I could not determine whether the camouflage was effective or whether the baboon had no predatory interest at the time. Hares also escaped by running away either at high speed in a straight line or in a zigzag motion. Zigzagging occurred only during active and close pursuit by a baboon and appeared to be an effective means of predator avoidance.

Baboons never were observed engaging in complex hunting for hares, but long chases could follow an unsuccessful short lunge. If a hare disappeared from view during the pursuit, a baboon might search in bushes or clumps of grass over an area of about 0.5 ha, the longest search lasting 40 minutes but most averaging 5 minutes. Sequential chasing of a hare occurred once in 1973, when several males converged on the prey from different directions, each taking up the chase at appropriate intervals. As was often the case with Thomson's gazelle, the prey had outrun the first baboon that pursued it and probably would have escaped if additional baboons had not intervened.

Birds. The usual mode of pursuit for solitary birds was simple seizure, although one stalk was observed. Prey animals ranged from nestlings to fully adult members of several species. A bird being preyed upon did not actively defend itself, nor did conspecifics come to its aid; furthermore, birds did not obviously avoid baboons as hares did. Bird eggs are not considered under the category of predation in this study (although others have included eggs as prey; e.g., Hausfater, 1976), but baboons consistently and frequently searched for and obtained eggs. As a result they were mobbed by adult birds attempting to defend their nests (particularly crowned plovers, *Stephanibyx coronatus*). These maneuvers occurred regardless of whether the baboons were actively raiding a nest or not, but the behavior seldom deterred any but the smallest baboons.

Ungulates. The literature refers to the peaceful coexistence of and symbiotic relationship between baboons and ungulates (e.g., DeVore and Hall, 1965; Struhsaker, 1967). Predation on impala (*Aepyceros melampus*) was rare among PHG baboons, perhaps because capture of all but the youngest infants was so difficult. Young impala were defended by their mothers, occasionally successfully. In general, the two species intermingled and responded to each others' alarm signals, although not consistently.

Thomson's gazelle (*Gazella thomsoni*) have several methods of general predator avoidance, including simple running, doubling back, stotting (a form of stiff-legged prancing), jumping, and crossing (Walther, 1969). Vigilance, approach to the predator, coalescence into larger herds, concealment, and lying down (without complete immobility) are also employed. PHG baboons normally preyed on gazelle fawns approximately 1 week old or younger. Fawns usually lay concealed when left by their mothers during the first week of their life, which allowed the mother to move off to feed, either singly or with a female herd. The mother then returned to her fawn for nursing, leaving it hidden again in a place where it would stay until her return. Females sometimes defended their young once the baboons had captured them. This defense was rarely effective, but it sometimes delayed consumption of the prey for a few minutes, as the predator moved to avoid the charge of the female gazelle. Once the fawn stopped vocalizing, its mother's interest appeared to cease. For most of the study period, Thomson's gazelle herds did not show flight or avoidance of PHG baboons. Between June and December of 1973, however, when complex hunts were frequent, those herds in which baboons had hunted recently or frequently became vigilant, wary, and fled quickly. This behavioral change occurred as little as 1 week and as much as 4 weeks after an initial complex hunt.

Other species of antelope (dikdik, steenbok, reedbuck) did not usually avoid baboons. When not being preyed upon, these animals peacefully fed close to the baboons without signs of wariness or nervousness. Since these species were not objects of complex hunting and were infrequently preyed upon, they may not have regarded baboons as potentially dangerous predators.

Interactions With Other Predators

Lions have been eliminated and leopard numbers have been reduced at Kekopey; baboons were only seen in contact with smaller predatory species. Interactions with jackals, tawny eagles, Egyptian vultures, and ground hornbills resulted from competition around baboon kills. For example, jackals repeatedly tried to gain access to a Thomson's gazelle carcass while the baboons still possessed it. The baboons usually responded by avoidance but at times aggressively attacked the jackals. During these encounters, jackals had a better chance of getting the carcass because the baboon consumer temporarily abandoned it. Ground hornbills competed in a similar manner, but the only baboons they could intimidate were immatures (up to about 4 years of age).

Participants

The degree to which age–sex classes and individual baboons took part in predation has varied over the years at Kekopey (table 8.4). As a result, no one study period is representative of a general pattern. Trends in participation are discussed later, but the following general characteristics of PHG baboon predatory behavior are presented as an introduction.

Adult males, adult females, and juveniles (of both sexes) all captured prey animals; infants did not, although they did eat meat. Adult males made more kills than females, but during some periods juveniles captured nearly as many animals as adult males.

Table 8.4. Age–sex class of known captors

	Thomson's Gazelle	Dikdik	Other ungulates	Hares	Birds	Total No.	%
1970-1971							
Males	16	8	10	9	1	44	94
Females	—	—	—	3	—	3	6
Juveniles	—	—	—	—	—	0	
Total	16	8	10	12	1	47	
1973							
Males	24	4	8	22	3	61	67
Females	1	3	—	9	1	14	15
Juveniles	1	—	—	9	6	16	18
Total	26	7	8	40	10	91	
1975							
Males	—	1	1	2	—	4	29
Females	—	—	—	3	—	3	21
Juveniles	—	—	—	4	3	7	50
Total	—	1	1	9	3	14	
1976-1977							
Males	2	—	—	5	1	8	19
Females	1	1	—	4	1	7	25
Juveniles	3	2	—	6	2	13	46
Total	6	3	—	15	4	29	

Note: Predatory episodes in which the identity of the captor could not be determined are excluded here.

Male, female, and juvenile baboons[1] generally employed different modes of pursuit. Complex hunting was entirely an adult male activity, but for other age–sex classes, the type of pursuit (stalk, chase, or seizure) appeared to be consistent with the prey items taken most frequently by that class (fig. 8.2; table 8.5).

The adult males heavily involved in capturing prey were similarly involved in consumption. Only certain adult females showed definite interest in predation, but those who captured the most were not necessarily those who obtained meat captured by others. The range of individual participation in predatory behavior for adult males and adult females overlapped, with several females capturing and consuming more than some of the males.

Although the amount of meat that each individual obtained may have been quite small, meat-eating was widespread, particularly during 1973. In that year, for example, 58 members of the troop (76%) ate meat; participation ranged from individuals who ate in 63% of the predatory episodes to those who ate in only 1%. Interest in meat was even higher than

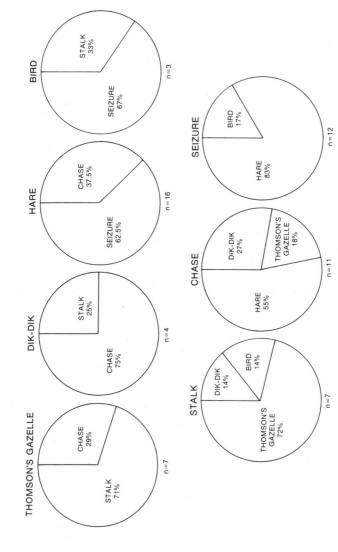

Figure 8.2. Modes of pursuit exhibited by Gilgil baboons (1973) when hunting various prey species. Figures for Thomson's gazelle are based on observed episodes that did not involve complex hunting.

Table 8.5. Mode of successful pursuit by different age–sex classes of captors (1973)

Age–sex class	Stalk No.	Stalk %	Chase No.	Chase %	Seizure No.	Seizure %	Total No.	Total %
Male	6	55	2	18	3	27	11	100
Female	—		6	67	3	33	9	100
Juvenile	1	10	3	30	6	60	10	100
Total	7		11		12		30	

Note: These data are based on the 30 episodes in which the entire pursuit was observed and which did *not* involve complex hunting.

this figure indicates, for when attendance at kills in 1973 is examined rather than success in obtaining meat, it is evident that 96% of the troop attended some predatory episode. (Attendance is defined here as visual orientation toward a kill and physical presence within 7.6 m of it.) Each of these troop members attended at least 2% of the episodes in 1973, but some individuals attended as many as 75%.

The data on capture and consumption show marked sexual differences. Adult males killed more frequently, and they alone practiced complex hunting. These differences did not stem from differential access to prey as the result of different locations within the troop (detailed in Strum, 1976a) but from significant differences in behavioral patterns. However, the dynamics of participation of individual males and females are not what might be predicted from the capture data.

The Male Pattern

Fluctuations in the predatory behavior of individual adult males were related to their interactions with other adults, male and female. For example, when a male was in sexual consort with a receptive female and then conflict occurred between maintaining proximity to the female and eating meat, the male chose to continue consortship. At times the male appeared to be deliberating, looking back and forth between the meat and the female, but finally chose to follow the female. In 1973, I observed 35 cases of conflict between consort and meat-eating behavior during predatory episodes. Resolution of such conflicts ranged from consort males entirely ignoring meat-eating opportunities to males allowing their consort females to have, keep, and eat the carcass. Even males with very high predatory scores chose estrous females over meat. Adult males following a consort pair also found themselves in situations where opportunities for consort behavior and meat-eating occurred simultaneously. Their response was similar to that of the consort male except for occasions when there was a large number of following males, when one might approach a kill site for a brief period; however, he quickly followed the consort group whenever it moved.

During unstable periods in a relationship between two adult males, their participation in predation dropped noticeably, resuming only after the uncertainty was resolved. This was particularly apparent after the arrival and subsequent integration of a new male in the troop, which involved resident males in a series of dyadic interactions.

Adult male participation in predatory behavior was clearly influenced by social factors. While male scores for all aspects of predation (capture, attendance, consumption) were highest as a class, males gave predatory behavior a lower priority than either sexual behavior with receptive females or social behavior with other males.

The Female Pattern

Individual PHG adult females can be characterized as having high, medium, or low interest in predatory behavior, based on their frequency of attendance at consumption episodes and amount of meat eaten. High-interest females were present at kills and obtained meat with a frequency that fell well within the range for adult males (fig. 8.3). Neither rank, sexual

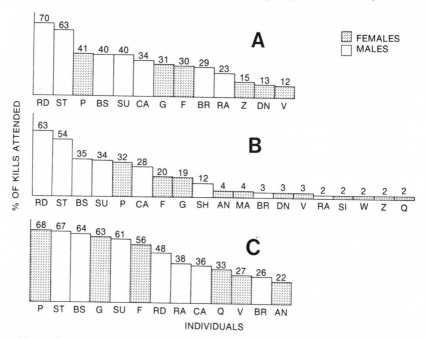

Figure 8.3. Attendance at kills by various members of PHG troop at Gilgil (1973). *A*, percentage of kills attended; *B*, percentage attended at which carcass or scraps were eaten; *C*, percentage attended at which only scraps were obtained. The top graph does not include individuals who attended less than 12% of the kills.

state, family size, nor the number of male or female associates appeared to influence a female's rank in predatory behavior (table 8.6).

For high-interest females, meat-eating took precedence over other behaviors, social or sexual. The interest of these females did not lessen when their own infants or the infants of female associates were born, or when they were in consort; indeed it was often the high-interest female who brought her consort to the kill. These females took advantage of opportunities passed up by their male partners, taking the carcass while the consort male threatened the previous consumer. The contrast between male and female behavior during consortships was exemplified by an incident in which the consort male copulated with and then groomed his female after an agonistic encounter with another male, while the female paid little attention to anything but the meat in her possession.

This suggests that the participation of high-interest females in predatory behavior is more constant than that of adult males. While a female may gain special access to meat through her social or sexual relationships, her interest in meat remains the same in varying social and sexual contexts. Meat ranks highest among incentives for these particular females, and their participation in predatory episodes contrasts markedly with that of males.

Duration of Bouts and Number of Participants

The behavior of the troop played an important role in determining the duration of consumption, the number and type of participants, and the timing of an individual's participation. Adult male PHG baboons were relatively mobile by comparison with adult females or immatures, but even males monitored the troop's behavior when beyond its periphery and responded accordingly. For instance, males who had no difficulty leaving the troop during a hunt showed signs of nervousness and vigilance after consumption had begun and time spent out of contact with the troop increased. Males abandoned a carcass prematurely to rejoin the troop. No captures by adult females and immatures occurred away from the troop, and these animals rarely joined in consumption until the meat was carried close to the periphery of the troop. When the troop moved, adult females and juveniles appeared more nervous than adult males, and attempted to keep the main group within sight. If they could not, then the prey was abandoned and the female or juvenile rejoined the troop.

A subgroup of adult males, adult females, and immatures often formed around the consumer of a carcass. If a sudden troop movement isolated the subgroup, females and immatures remained longer when an adult male was present than they did when one was not involved in consumption. The order of departure from the carcass indicated different distance thresholds for individual baboons and age–sex classes: first to leave were juveniles, then females, and finally males.

Aside from prey species differences (table 8.7), three factors influenced

Table 8.6. Participation of individual females in predation (1973)

	P	F	G	AN	MA	DN	V	SI	W	Z	Q
Consumption rank	1	2	3	4	4	5	5	6	6	6	6
Capture rank	3	3	—	—	3	3	—	—	2	1	—
Dominance rank	1	12	11	16	8	4	7	15	20	6	19
Family size (putative)	4	3	3	3	1	0	2	1	1	2	2
No. of male associates	5	1	0	2	2	0	4	0	0	2	1
No. of female associates	1	3	1	1	2	1	1	2	2	1	1
Sexual state	C/P	P/L	L	P/L	P/L	C	P/L	L/C/P	L/C/P	L/C/P	L/C/P

Note: Only the most interested female participants are listed in this table (11 of 21 adult females in the troop). Their sexual states are listed as C (cycling), P (pregnant), or L (lactating). Associates are defined by individual preference patterns in proximity and grooming. In case of ties in the capture and consumption scores, more than one individual was given the same rank. Dominance position rankings are consecutive and are based on the outcome of agonistic encounters (Strum, 1978).

Table 8.7. Participation in prey consumption (1973)

	Thomson's gazelle	Steenbok	Dikdik	Hare	Bird
Number of baboons attending					
Range	2–24	1–29	2–30	1–30	1–10
Mode	2, 8, 11	11	2, 20	2	3
Median	10	11	20	4	5
Total	312	74	112	252	41
Number of baboons fed					
Range	2–15	1–10	2–8	1–16	1–4
Mode	6	—	2	2	1, 2
Median	6	7	3	2	2
Total	184	34	29	129	16
Number of baboons feeding on carcass					
Range	1–6	1–7	1–4	1–5	1–2
Mode	3, 4	3	1	1	1
Median	4	3	1	1	1
Total	100	20	13	55	13
Time spent feeding on a carcass (min)					
Range	20–96	33–87	17–68	2–60	3–13
Mode	20			5	5
Median	51	37	33	10	7
Relative access to meat					
No. of episodes	28	6	7	39	9
Average attendance	11.1	12.3	16	6.5	4.6
Average no. fed	6.6	5.7	4.1	3.3	1.8
Average no. fed on carcass	3.6	3.3	1.9	1.4	1.4

Note: Of the 100 kills observed during 1973, 11 were not included because the data were incomplete. Of the 89 kills analyzed here, observations of 26 began after consumption was already under way. A total of 791 baboons attended these kills; 392 (49.6%) were able to feed on either carcass or scraps, and, of these, 201 (25.4%) got access to the carcass of the prey animal.

the duration of consumption: proximity to the troop, the troop's movements, and the number of participating baboons. Long consumptions took place close to the troop, with little troop movement, and with a large number of participants. Although the size of the prey limits the number of meat-eaters more obviously than it does the duration of consumption, the overlapping ranges of different prey species also reflect the influence of these social factors.

VARIATION IN PREDATORY BEHAVIOR,
1970–1974

Notable changes in the predatory behavior of PHG baboons have occurred over the years, as shown during my 1973 study and by a comparison of my 1973 data with a 1970–1971 study by Harding (1973a, 1975). Further modifications have taken place since 1973. Because some of these occurred either between my study periods or during a break in observation from August 1974 until March 1975, detailed data on the dynamics of change from 1974–1977 are lacking, and I can only describe the results of the later changes.

Changing Capture Techniques

The main type of predation during 1970–1971 was opportunistic capture of concealed prey, but techniques of active searching (simple hunting) were also employed, though infrequently. Harding also observed an unsuccessful sequential chase of an infant Thomson's gazelle by male baboons.

The basically opportunistic nature of predatory behavior was still evident at the beginning of the 1973 study, but simple hunting increased in sophistication and persistence during 1973, culminating in the development of elaborate searching, stalking, and chasing, or what I have termed complex hunting. From December 1972 until July 1973 there was a steady increase in hunting distance, from less than 300 m to 4,000 m ($n = 18$). From August 1973 until January 1974, there was no perceptible change in complex-hunting distance ($n = 23$).[2]

Complex hunting increased in frequency from January to June of 1973[3] and in number of simultaneous hunters (1–5) between January and September of 1973.[4] At first, single males were responsible for most complex hunting, especially RD, who increased the amount of time he spent in search and scatter, or stalk and chase, behavior from 5 minutes (January, February) to 120 minutes (April, July). At the same time he increased the distance covered during the hunt and distance traveled between the troop and the nearest herd of tommies from 400 m (March) to 4,000 m (July). While RD was the most frequent hunter and most instrumental in the elaboration of complex hunting patterns, other males were also involved in individual fortuitous captures, then in solitary hunting, and finally in multiple efforts.

The sequential chase of Thomson's gazelle observed by Harding was both unsuccessful and probably fortuitous; there was no evidence that the baboons were consciously acting together. Midway in the 1973 study, I observed another instance that succeeded. From that point onward, male baboons changed the orientation of their chases when other hunting baboons were near. Prior to this incident, the prey individual was chased in any direction, often out onto the open plain. Thereafter, baboon males chased Thomson's gazelles toward other hunters, and several kills resulted from sequential chases. Coordination of hunting activities between several males increased, as evidenced by the rise in the number of simultaneous hunters, from two in April to five in August. However, all incidents that ended with coordination still began with what appeared to me to be individual efforts.

Sometimes several male baboons stalked a herd of gazelles at the same time, often with different prey individuals as their objects. But once one baboon gained on his prey or was near success, others abandoned their individual efforts and converged on the prey. Sometimes this happened after the actual capture, and at other times sequential chases resulted (see "relay chases," Strum, 1975b). If the prey escaped and was not visible, then the assembled group of baboons searched simultaneously.

Whether these behaviors should be considered as "cooperation" (Strum, 1975b) rather than coordination depends both on the definition of the terms and on the degree to which one wishes to ascribe intention to the behavior of the individual baboons. Since social interactions among baboons, and between adult males in particular, are complex (e.g., their ability to ally against specific individuals or against a common threat from outside the group), the basis for strategy, coordination, and cooperation in behavior was already present. Normally these behaviors are used primarily in social situations, but I believe that the elaboration of hunting behavior by PHG males was simply an extension of their basic repertoire to a specific foraging situation.

Discrimination of Prey and Prey Response

Thomson's gazelle herds take three forms: all-male herds; mixed herds containing adult males, females, and young; and female herds with young. Initially the baboons did not distinguish between different types of herds during their complex hunting, and spent much time following, scattering, and searching through herds containing only adult males. As complex hunting developed, the baboons began to look briefly at all-male herds and then ignore them in favor of mixed herds or female herds. During the first 15 complex hunts, from March and May 1973, the baboon did not obviously discriminate between types of gazelle herds. During the sixteenth complex hunt in late May, one male did make this distinction, and at least one baboon hunter did so during the remaining 25 complex hunts observed, between June 1973 and January 1974. During this latter period, if a gazelle herd divided into subunits during a pursuit, the baboon hunter glanced quickly at each but followed only the group containing females and young.

Gazelle herds did not flee from or avoid PHG baboons in 1970–1971 or for the first 6 months of the 1973 study. But in May 1973, the month with the highest complex-hunting rate, herds that had been hunted most recently or most frequently changed their behavior. They began to show vigilance, and a flight distance of 20–25 m was established. This distance increased during the next few months to 45–275 m, the normal range distance from predators such as lions (Walther, 1969). The change in response of Thomson's gazelle toward baboons was a process of adjustment in which at least certain herds began to recognize baboons as potentially effective predators.

Participants in Capture

Adult male baboons were the main predators in 1970–1971, capturing 44 prey animals. Adult females caught three hares, but male harassment forced two females to relinquish their prey. In 1973 the adult males still captured prey more frequently than did other age–sex classes, and they alone participated in complex hunting. However, females captured prey more often in 1973 than they had during the earlier study, including prey of more varying sizes (see table 8.4).

A change in female response to male harrassment was also observed in 1973. Initially, females gave up their prey when approached or chased by males, as they had done in 1970–1971, but during the year they began to avoid adult male pursuers. In 1970–1971, females kept 33% of the prey they captured ($n = 3$), and in 1973 the figure rose to 43% ($n = 14$).[5] Females lost all antelope prey but kept 60% of the hares and birds they captured.

Juvenile participation in capture began during the 1973 study, and I observed its initial stages. In April 1973 I saw three unsuccessful attempts to capture prey by juveniles, and in May the fourth juvenile seen to try hunting made a successful capture. Two juvenile kills were recorded in June, July, September, and November, three in August and December, and one in October. At first the juveniles were interested only in eating meat, but the successful appropriation of meat appeared to stimulate their interest in capture. Thus juveniles, as a class, started capturing prey after they had been exposed to meat-eating. The same was true of individual juveniles: attendance at consumption episodes consistently preceded attempts by those individuals to capture their own prey. Thus there was a clear sequence of events in individual juvenile participation:

1. Exposure to meat.
2. Obtaining meat fortuitously.
3. Consistent attendance at kills.
4. Attempts to obtain meat against opposition.
5. Opportunistic capture of small prey.
6. Opportunistic capture of larger prey.

Participants in Consumption

Harding noted that males were the major captors and the major consumers in 1970–1971, actively excluding other baboons from their prey (although females gained access to carcasses after males had discarded them). In contrast, by the beginning of the 1973 study, females were frequently present at kills and actively consumed their own prey or that of others. Juveniles and infants began to eat meat during 1973, with infants preceding juveniles. After an initial spurt, infant participation leveled off, while juvenile attendance and meat-eating continued to increase through the 1973 study (fig. 8.4).

Distribution of Meat

Elsewhere in Africa, baboons have not been observed to share food of any kind, either between a mother and her offspring or among adults (e.g., Altmann and Altmann, 1970; DeVore and Hall, 1965; Kummer, 1968; Ransom, 1971; Rowell, 1966; Stolz and Saayman, 1970), although a single piece of food, such as meat, is often consumed in serial fashion by several individuals.

Changes in the pattern of attendance and consumption affected the distribution of meat within the troop. The amount that some individuals obtained during the year was relatively small, but the widespread nature of meat-eating within the troop in 1973 contrasted with the 1970–1971 period.

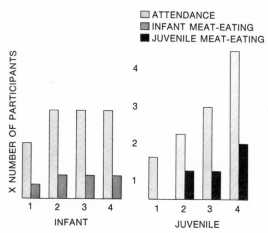

Figure 8.4. Infant and juvenile baboon participation in consumption of meat (1973). The 91 analyzed kills during 1973 are here divided into four groups; the first 22 are placed into quarter 1, and the remaining kills are divided into three groups of 23 each.

Two additional changes in behavior were seen midway in the 1973 study: first, individual baboons moved to one side, leaving a significant portion of meat and allowing other individuals (of the opposite sex) to approach and feed in proximity; second, individuals fed from the same carcass simultaneously. Because the distribution of meat between individuals during these episodes differed from the serial distribution of meat seen at other times and was more active in its form, I classify these interactions as "sharing."

A total of 27 instances of sharing were observed in 6 months, beginning with Thomson's gazelle and later including other ungulates and hares. Sharing among adult males and females occurred as frequently in consort situations as outside them. Females shared with males and vice versa; however, sharing between adult males and females occurring outside of consort relationships took place only between adults with a previously established affiliative bond (see Social Factors, below, and table 8.8).

Mechanisms for Change in Predatory Behavior

The PHG baboons offer an unusual opportunity to examine the influence of social, individual, and ecological factors upon predatory behavior in a group-living primate species. Social mechanisms of change are the easiest for me to identify and interpret, since the purpose of my main research project was to describe the troop's social networks. A simple description of ecological variables involved in the changes is possible with the data collected over the years at Kekopey, but since these data are not detailed, they must be interpreted using comparisons with other sites where baboon predation has been observed. Finally, identifying individual factors that influence change is difficult: overt changes in the behavior of individual baboons were easy to observe and record, but motivation or psychological variables can only be inferred.

Social Factors. Among the many affiliative social networks that exist, several have important implications for the social dynamics of the troop and for the dynamics of change in predatory behavior over time. Of particular interest are special relationships between animals known or believed to be related, between adult males and adult females, and between adult males and immatures. Individuals involved in these relationships spent more time together, sought each other's proximity for feeding, resting, and sleeping activities, showed preference for each other as grooming partners, and supported each other during agonistic encounters.

The acquisition of a new behavior requires some type of learning. Investigators have described special requirements for primate learning: the animal must feel safe and secure, it must have a model to imitate, it must be motivated to approach and observe, and it must be motivated to repeat the behavior a number of times (e.g., DeVore, 1963; Hall, 1963a, 1968; Jay, 1962, 1963). The special affiliative relationships which existed in PHG

Table 8.8. Episodes of sharing

Nonsexual			Consort			Mother-offspring			Male–Male		Presumed siblings		Total	
♂	♀	n	♂	♀	n	Mo.	Off.	n		n		n	n	Total
1973 (1,200 observation hours)														
BS→P		6	BS→P		4	F→FO		4	RD→CA	1				
RD→F		2	SU→P		4				ST→RD	1				
RD→P		2	CA→P		2				ST→PA	1				27
1975 (250 observation hours)														
SU→P		1				P→PA		1			TI(♂)→RO(♀)	1		
						F→IA		2						5
1976–1977 (792.5 observation hours)														
GA→F		1									HD(♂)→MI(♂)	1		2
Total		12			10			7		3		1	2	34
		(35%)			(29%)			(21%)		(9%)			(5%)	(100%)

Note: An episode is defined as one example of sharing between partners. There can be more than one sharing episode during a single predatory event if (1) different animals are involved, or (2) time and/or an interaction with other animals intervenes between two episodes. In all cases, *n* = number of episodes.

Male PA was an infant in 1973 and a juvenile in 1975, and the mother–offspring relationship between F and IA (1975) is inferred.

provided appropriate learning contexts and played an important role in the acquisition of certain aspects of predatory behavior by individuals.

Early in 1973 the participation of infants and juveniles in meat-eating was observed. The first infants observed attending kills were the offspring of females with a demonstrated interest in eating meat. These infants were there either because they were still dependent on their mothers or because they were attracted to the kill by their mother's presence, and thus their interest focused on their mother, not on the meat. But observation, investigation, and imitation resulted in meat-eating for infants of all ages.

Special relationships with adult males also influenced infant participation. These were especially important for infants whose mothers were not active participants in meat consumption but whose adult male associates were. An infant might approach when a male associate was attending a kill or when he actually had possession of some meat. Again, the primary attraction for the infant was the male associate, but proximity, observation, investigation, and imitation resulted in meat-eating here also.

A change in adult male possession of the carcass often had a marked effect on infant participation. For example, on one occasion several infants attended a kill with a male with whom they associated regularly. They had no special relationship with the male feeding on the carcass at the time and did not approach it or him. For over 45 minutes they stayed near their male associate, and when the previous consumer finally left and the second male took the carcass, the infants immediately rushed toward him and the meat, investigating the carcass and feeding on scraps that were nearby.

Similar changes occurred in juvenile participation in consumption. In general, juveniles first approached meat because an animal with which they maintained a special relationship was already eating. But juvenile play groups also approached a kill site *en masse,* stumbling across a meat-eating bout while chasing one another in play. They investigated as they would a novel object in the environment, but these investigations seemed to make little impression on a young baboon unless he or she actually obtained some meat. Once this happened, the successful juvenile appeared highly motivated, and meat became a high-priority incentive for juvenile after juvenile.[6]

During 1973, the different effects of adult male–adult female special relationships on female participation were observed. For example, of the two females with the greatest interest in meat, one had no special relationship with the most frequent male captor and consumer. Although she had a number of affiliative relationships with major male predators, her participation appeared relatively independent of them. On the other hand, the second female did have a strong affiliative bond with the major adult male predator, and her success in gaining proximity to meat appeared to be influenced by his presence.

Special relationships were less important in capture than in consumption, although such factors as degree of mobility and social facilitation played a definite role in adult male capture techniques. Male migration occurred frequently within the study population, and males wandered farther from the troop than did females during daily foraging, occasionally detaching themselves to visit distant food sources or another troop, although individuals varied in their day-to-day mobility from the troop. By contrast, females and immatures maintained continuous visual or auditory contact with the troop, and can be characterized as more attached to the troop than adult males, spatially, socially, and probably psychologically as well. The elaboration of hunting behavior during 1973 would not have been possible without this element of male mobility. At first, predatory opportunities were exploited only near the troop, but in time adult males wandered farther and farther. Predatory behavior did not initiate a totally new pattern of ranging for adult males, but existing patterns were modified in response to opportunities for predation.

Capture of prey was primarily a solitary activity, but predatory behavior of one male might stimulate the interest of others. In several cases, the efforts of one male to capture an animal appeared to set off additional attempts by the observing baboons. Overall, the increase in hunting by one male appeared to change the frequency of hunting in other PHG males.

While I could document the interactions through which these changes were accomplished, without controlled experiments I could not pinpoint the exact type of learning that might have been involved. Nevertheless, focusing of attention, communication of intent (predatory or otherwise), and facilitation of behavior were clearly operating within the existing social and motivational system of the adult male baboons. A different social milieu could have prevented or hindered the flow of information and the facilitation of behavior crucial to the elaboration of the baboon's pursuit behavior.

Individual Factors. Physiological and psychological developments occurring within individual animals can rarely be evaluated using field data. Yet our inability to detect these developments through field observations does not negate their importance. A change in primary predatory males that took place in PHG in 1973 provides some suggestion of the nature and role of individual variables in predatory behavior.

In 1970–1971, adult male CA was the most successful predator in PHG, and at the beginning of the 1973 study he maintained this position. RD was also an active predator at this time, but both his success and participation in capture and consumption were less than CA's. In meat-eating, CA appeared to directly limit RD's participation, as CA was able to actively displace RD from kills. Then CA suffered an injury to his hand that was serious enough to hamper his movement; for more than a month he had difficulty keeping up with the troop, and this curtailed all his activities. CA continued to show interest in predation, but his success was impaired; his chases of prey were too slow and too short. When meat was being eaten, CA waited at a distance, whereas earlier he would have supplanted other animals and obtained the carcass.

After CA's injury, RD was more successful in keeping the meat that he had captured and in obtaining meat that others had captured. Whatever inhibition CA's behavior might have placed on RD was now eliminated, and RD increased his capture and consumption of prey markedly.

The changed relationship between CA and RD had several consequences, the most important of which resulted from RD's predatory behavior and its influence on the predatory behavior of the troop. RD was an integrated member of the troop who formed consortships, had a number of female and immature associates, and had well-defined relationships with other adult males. But he occupied a unique position in the troop, spatially and behaviorally. He was often at the rear (less frequently at the front) of troop movements (cf. Harding, 1977) and at the periphery of the troop when it was stationary. In foraging, he was the widest ranging of the males and readily detached himself from the troop to follow his own route and exploit distant resources. He was out of sight of the troop more frequently than any other individual. Thus RD, while integrated socially into the troop, was at one end of the range of variation in foraging and movement. His predatory behavior also followed this pattern, so that soon he traveled farther and farther from the troop in pursuit of prey, covering more distance than any of the other males had done under similar circumstances. RD also seemed highly motivated in his predatory behavior after CA's change of status, and it probably was his behavior that stimulated complex hunting among PHG males.

RD's effect on PHG baboon predatory behavior resembles the influence exerted on a Japanese macaque troop by specific individuals (Frisch, 1968). CA and RD had the same opportunities for capture, but CA did not respond in the same manner. CA was more attached to the troop, spatially and behaviorally, and even after the initiation of complex hunting, he did not travel as far from the troop to hunt as did most of the other males.[7] The elaboration of hunting might not have occurred in PHG or might have taken a different form had RD, with his idiosyncratic behavior, not become the principal predatory male.

Ecological Factors. During the preceding 20 years, the study area had been altered for cattle raising by creation of additional grassland through bush-clearing, distribution of water to new areas, and destruction or removal of large predators. Largely as a result of these developments, much of the indigenous wildlife underwent a marked population expansion. For baboons this meant increased opportunities for predation, especially on

Thomson's gazelle. At the same time, baboons were less subject to attack by normal predators (other than man) and were also freer from competition with other predators that might prey on the same species and on the baboons as well.

The primate group, and especially the baboon troop, has been viewed by some as a basic adaptation to problems of defense against predation (A. Jolly, 1972; Simonds, 1974; Washburn and Hamburg, 1965). Animals living in groups are often thought to be in less danger because of the safety-in-numbers principle and because the combined defensive activity of several animals could act to deter a predator. The possibility of attack by large predators is irrelevant to opportunistic baboon hunting that occurs within or near the troop, but it is important in considering activities that take an individual away from and out of contact with the group. (In addition, of course, the presence of researchers reduced the exposure of PHG to attacks by humans.)

A bioenergetic approach to understanding predation, relying on time and energy considerations (e.g., Pianka, 1974; Schoener, 1971), requires that opportunistic predatory behavior be separated from that which involves systematic pursuit, since opportunistic capture costs the predator little in relation to the energy yielded by the prey, while systematic pursuit requires an investment of considerably more time and energy. Data on baboon time and energy budgets during foraging and prey pursuit are not currently available but are needed to determine the costs and benefits of different foraging strategies, a necessary step if baboon predation is ever to be understood in bioenergetic terms.

However, bioenergetic considerations can be applied to PHG baboon predation in another way. Since prolonged or systematic search and pursuit (complex hunting) requires an investment of time and energy, it is reasonable to assume that this effort would be directed toward situations where the likelihood of obtaining the benefits (energy, nutrients, social status, etc.) was increased. Extra effort devoted to hunting solitary animals or secretive animals that live in pairs might not sufficiently increase the chances of finding them to warrant the additional energy expenditure. Group-living prey could change the equation, however, for groups are easily visible and contain more individuals that might be suitable prey. The time and energy cost of hunting a group-living prey would be justified if it increased the chances of obtaining the benefits associated with meat.

PHG baboons take only prey that are smaller than themselves. This implies that baboons cannot easily solve the problems involved in capturing, killing, and consuming larger prey individuals. Since baboons have a generalized primate anatomy, they cannot match the speed of older antelopes, for example, and are limited to younger, less swift individuals. Animals that are small enough for a baboon to hold down do not need to be killed before being consumed, and immature animals can be dismembered more easily.

Hands are essential to baboon predatory behavior and appear to compensate in part for a lack of predatory specializations. Hands allow a baboon to catch, hold, and consume an animal, but they alone are insufficient to overcome the prey size limitation.

If bioenergetic constraints limit complex hunting to prey living in groups, and if baboons cannot prey on individuals above a certain size because of anatomical restrictions, Thomson's gazelle is the only species at Gilgil that is appropriate for complex hunting.

Why Complex Hunting?

Opportunistic predatory behavior appears to be part of the species repertoire for baboons and may have its origins in protein or nutrient requirements. Thus meat-eating per se does not require explanation, but the development of systematic and extended pursuit by baboon predators does. Complex hunting by baboons, as I have defined it here, has been observed only at Gilgil, although other populations eat meat and take part in simple hunting. A synthesis of the social, individual, and ecological aspects of complex hunting by PHG baboons may help us arrive at an understanding of the changes in predatory patterns from 1970 to 1974. The following assumptions are made:

1. Complex hunting has bioenergetic constraints in which expenditure of time and energy should be offset by an increase in the likelihood of prey capture.
2. Baboons are limited to prey of a certain size by their ability to solve the problems of capture, kill, and consumption with a generalized primate anatomy.
3. In areas with a normal complement of predators, it is hazardous for baboons to engage in behavior that takes them away from the troop.
4. Humans have killed baboons for over 1 million years (Isaac, 1968). In most areas where baboons are found today, possible human intervention must be considered in evaluating baboon safety and behavior.
5. The existence of an abundance of prey and an absence of their usual predators provides new exploitative opportunities for baboons.

Thus the necessary conditions for the development of complex hunting may be the presence of suitably sized, group-living prey in high density, the absence of indigenous natural predators for these prey, and the baboons' relative safety from predation or interference by large feline or human predators.

Usually prey and predator densities go hand in hand; where there is prey in abundance, there are also predators. But at Kekopey there has been a rare abundance of appropriate prey and absence of normal predators. In addition, the presence of researchers has provided some protection from human predation or interference in the general vicinity of the troop.

Although these may be the necessary conditions for elaboration of baboon hunting, they may not be both necessary *and* sufficient. Not all opportunities are exploited, even when they are obviously advantageous. What is ecologically possible must also mesh with what is socially and psychologically possible. Further conditions for the development of complex hunting behavior might include:

6. Presence of predatory behavior within the species repertoire and that of the group.
7. Individual mobility from the troop within foraging and social contexts.
8. Behavioral variability resulting in individual innovative behavior.
9. Social facilitative mechanisms.
10. Observational learning that allows the transmission of learned behavior from one individual to another.

Most of these conditions exist within any primate group, although the combination and degree of emphasis on each varies. It is apparent in examining PHG baboons that *all* of these conditions were met during 1973, including an especially important one: innovative behavior. The behavior of RD in particular appears to have provided a crucial impetus to the development of complex hunting, and for a time this type of pursuit became a pattern for other adult males as well.

This synthesis suggests that baboons would not practice complex hunting in areas where there are large predators, even when there are group-living prey species of appropriate size. This is the situation at Amboseli, Kenya (Altmann and Altmann, 1970; Hausfater, 1976), where baboons capture prey opportunistically and may pursue them over short distances but do not practice complex hunting [Altmann and Altmann (1970:41) described a male baboon who lagged behind during a predatory pursuit and became another's prey].

Elaboration of baboon hunting behavior could only be expected to occur in areas where group-living prey species the size of Thomson's gazelle or smaller exist in high densities and the usual large predators are absent. These conditions are very limited today in Africa. Group-living animals of appropriate size living in high densities include several species of antelope (Thomson's gazelle, Grant's gazelle, and their faunal equivalents in other parts of Africa), sympatric primate species, and domesticated animals, such as goats and sheep. Human intervention has resulted in widespread faunal destruction; thus the necessary combination of baboons, prey, and an absence of predators seldom occurs.

Appropriate conditions may exist in areas of South Africa where baboons are reported to prey frequently on the young of domesticated stock (Dart, 1963; Marais, 1939; Stoltz and Saayman, 1970), but it is unclear from these reports whether the South African baboons resemble PHG in their hunting behavior. If this pattern of predatory behavior is *not* found in baboon populations living under the appropriate ecological circumstances, some of the other social or individual variables are likely to be absent, especially the kind of innovative behavior reported here. However, PHG data from 1975–1977 also indicate that before predatory behavior can be incorporated into a group's repertoire over the long term, additional requirements must be met.

FURTHER CHANGES IN PREDATORY BEHAVIOR, 1975–1977

Changes that have taken place since 1975 are as marked as those occurring between 1970 and 1974. Unfortunately most of these changes began during a break in observation from August 1974 until March 1975, and therefore discussion of their cause must remain tentative.

Form of Predatory Behavior and Male Participation

Perhaps the most obvious change since 1975 is the cessation of complex hunting and the reduction in amount of simple hunting. Most predatory behavior has become accidental or opportunistic, and systematic searching for prey is rare, although once prey is encountered, pursuit may be systematic. The decline of complex hunting has been accompanied by a markedly decreased participation of adult males as a class in predatory behavior, as well as a striking change in individual male participation. In 1973, adult males were 14% of the troop (excluding infants, who are not potential predators) and accounted for 67% of those captures where the identity of the captor was known. In 1976–1977, adult males composed 20% of the troop, a slight increase, but were responsible for only 31% of all captures (table 8.9).

The participation of each individual male declined as well, particularly those males most involved in complex hunting during 1973. Although RD had been influential in initiating and elaborating complex hunting and was the primary predatory male in 1973, he was not observed to capture any prey during the short 1975 study, or during 1976–1977. The predatory behavior of the other three males (BS, BR, ST) declined similarly (table 8.10).

Although predatory behavior had already changed by the time of the 1975 study, major ecological factors can be excluded as explanations for the change. The drought continued through this period, and there were no

Table 8.9. Trends in prey capture by age-sex class

| | 1973 | | 1975 | | 1976–77 | |
	% of troop	% of captors	% of troop	% of captors	% of troop	% of captors
Males	14	67	19	29	20	31
Females	38	15	32	21	28	24
Juveniles	48	18	49	50	52	45
n	50	91	65	14	75	29

Note: Only instances where captors are known have been included here, and subadult males have been included under the "male" category. Since infants were not involved in prey capture, the numbers under "% of troop" refer to the troop size after infants had been subtracted.

Table 8.10. Participation in capture by adult males

	1970–1971 (1,032 hr)	1973 (1,200 hr)	1975 (250 hr)	1976–1977 (792.5 hr)
AL	3	—	—	—
MO	2	—	—	—
CA	18	13	—	—
SU	10	10	1	—
RD	5	18	0	0
BS	0	4	0	1
RA	—	1	—	—
BR	—	3	1	0
ST	—	9	1	2
GA	—	—	1	2
DR	—	—	0	0
MQ	—	—	0	0
RE	—	—	0	—
HD	—	0	0	1
TI	—	0	0	1
BL	—	0	0	1
SN	—	0	0	1

Note: Numbers in parentheses represent observation hours. Where no data appear, the male baboon either had not yet entered the troop or had already left it; a 0 means that the animal was present in the troop but was not observed to capture prey during that year. Male BS was a subadult in 1971 and an adult in 1973; RA entered at the end of 1972; ST and BR entered the troop midway through 1973; GA, DR, and MQ entered between July 1974 and March 1975; RE entered in June 1975; and HD, TI, BL, and SN were juveniles in 1973 and 1975 and subadult males in 1976–1977.

changes in rainfall pattern or in prey availabilty. Only social and demographic conditions changed, and since these factors were implicated in the previous modification of PHG predatory behavior, it seems reasonable that they influenced this second set of changes as well.

Males gave predatory behavior a low priority when it conflicted with social interactions with males and sexual behavior with receptive females. Major alterations had occurred in the male component of the troop between 1974 and 1975 with the immigration of four males, the emigration of three, and the maturation of seven. The instability caused by such flux and the increase in interactions among males which accompanied these events could account for some of the decline in male predatory interest.

Furthermore, the adult males who left PHG included two major predators: CA, followed shortly afterward by SU. The immigrating males tended to stay close to the troop, a behavior that conflicted with complex hunting. When one of these males had possession of a carcass and the troop departed, the male often abandoned the kill prematurely to keep up with the troop. During this period RD seemed unable to gain or retain possession of carcasses. He continued to attend consumptions but patiently waited his turn, which might come after some females and juveniles had already eaten. RD's inability to keep his kills may have lowered his motivation to capture prey and especially to expend considerable time and energy in complex hunting. This would be a reverse of the proposed process which stimulated his predatory interest and behavior in 1973. The predatory motivation of ST, the other complex-hunting male remaining in the troop, may have been similarly influenced.

Whatever the correct explanation may be, the behavior of males has changed, both in the type and the amount of predatory behavior they practice. This is more than a simple reversion to the earlier pattern, for the males are now killing less and doing it less systematically than they did during 1970–1971. Thus, while predatory behavior seems established in the troop and independent of any one individual, the *form* that the behavior will take may depend on the motivations and possibly the personalities of the individuals within the troop.

Other Developments in Capture and Consumption

Adult female and juvenile participation in capture seems to have continued the trend identified during 1973, despite the general decline in predatory behavior. Females have increased their participation in capture, although they represent a smaller proportion of the potential captors within the troop (table 8.9). As in 1973, the change in female behavior is less marked than the change in juvenile behavior. Although their proportion in the troop has remained approximately the same, juveniles' participation in capture has more than doubled. The processes identified in the development of juvenile participation (during 1973) continue to apply, and the offspring of high-interest females or the immatures who developed predatory interest early are the highest-scoring individuals in this later period.

Special relationships played an important role in the spread of predatory behavior and in the development of meat-sharing in 1973. Sharing between baboons coincided with already-existing relationships between mothers and infants and between males and females. More sharing was observed in 1973 than in 1975–1977 (table 8.8). The explanation probably involves changes in the nature of existing relationships. In 1973, most sharing took place between four males and two females with whom the males had special relationships, but by 1977 two of these males (CA and SU) had left the troop, one of the males (BS) had a less intense relationship with the same female (P), and the fourth male (RD) no longer got much meat. Males feeding on a carcass in 1977, under circumstances that would have led to sharing in 1973, did not seem inclined to share with females, including the ones with whom special relationships existed. This led one female (P) to try devious tactics to obtain meat from a new male (DR). First she tried to groom the male into a state of extreme relaxation and obtain some meat while he was not paying attention to her. The male soon realized the effectiveness of this tactic, however, and continued to allow her to groom him, but prevented her from actually seizing any meat. Her next tactic was to direct aggression at a female with whom the male was in association, thus creating for the male a situation of conflict between the meat and his sociosexual interests. The male then abandoned the meat and the female aggressor obtained it. Interested females such as the one described here took advantage of conflicts between males around kills to steal a temporarily neglected carcass.

The development of new special relationships did open opportunities for females whose access to meat had previously depended on other male affiliations that had waned. Thus, the second-highest-interest female (F) gained access to kills in 1973 as a result of her special relationship with RD. Both the decline in RD's predatory behavior and the decline in their special relationship decreased her opportunities for meat-eating, although she still attended kills frequently. However, a developing relationship with a new male (GA) increased her access to meat once more. Sharing between mothers and their offspring still occurred in 1977, and sharing between presumed siblings was documented.

Prey Species

There are differences in prey species profiles between the two periods. If the numbers of successful predations, complex hunts, and Thomson's gazelles captured in 1973 are compared by month, there is a significant correlation between complex hunts and Thomson's gazelles[8] and between complex hunts and successful predations,[9] but the correlation between successful predations and Thomson's gazelles captured is not significant. If these correlations were not chance events, then one would predict a decline in the proportion of Thomson's gazelles in the prey profile as complex hunting declined. The decline that occurred between 1975 and 1977 suggests that there is a causal link between complex hunting and Thomson's gazelles captured, and between complex hunting and the amount of successful predation.

If we compare the prey species taken in 1973 and in 1976–1977 (table 8.2), differences in the prey profile are largely due to an increase in the proportion of hares taken and a decrease in the proportion of Thomson's gazelles. Since there is no evidence that prey densities declined between the two periods, and since in 1976–1977 there were repeated examples of situations that would have elicited either simple or complex hunting during 1973 but were now ignored,[10] at least part of the difference in prey profile reflects preferences of different age–sex classes and their differential participation in capture (table 8.4). However, the type of prey taken by each age–sex class has changed as well. Of the animals caught by males, proportionately fewer were Thomson's gazelles and more were hares, while juveniles began to take more ungulate prey, a continuation of the behavior seen at the end of 1973. Therefore the decline in male participation, the disappearance of complex hunting, the increase in juvenile and female participation in capture, and shifts in prey preference of the various age–sex classes have all affected the PHG prey profile in 1976–1977.

Prey Response

As predatory techniques changed and complex hunting ceased, Thomson's gazelles changed their behavior toward baboon predators. In 1976–1977 herds were less wary of baboons than they were at the end of 1973, no longer fleeing when baboons approached or employing vigilance behavior. It became possible for a baboon to approach within 3–8 m of a gazelle, even a young one, without arousing suspicion. Gazelle mothers stopped herding infants away from the baboons, and the two species often fed peacefully in close proximity.

Scavenging

During a very tense and aggressive interaction between males in 1973, a male baboon briefly ate meat from the carcass of an animal which had not been seen to be captured by the baboons. Although this appeared to be a displacement activity rather than true feeding, it was still the first incident of its kind observed in this population of baboons; on other occasions, including experimental exposure of carcasses (Strum, 1976a), the baboons had investigated but ignored such opportunities when they had not witnessed the prey being captured or consumed by another baboon.

During 1976–1977 six cases were reported of baboons eating animals which they found already dead. Three times they ate a hare (personal observation with D. Manzolillo; J. Stone, D. Harding, personal communications), once they fed on the disarticulated leg of an impala (personal observation), once they ate a bird electrocuted by high-tension wires (M. Demment, personal communication), and once they ate a bird found dead in a trap (personal observation). One of the hares was decapitated and already stiff, and the impala leg and two birds were still warm. In the most recent hare incident, the carcass was treated as if the baboons had captured it themselves.

The PHG baboons have exploited more opportunities to eat dead animals during 1976–1977 than they have in the past: using my data only, in 1973 one case was seen during 1,200 hours of observation that could be classified as scavenging, compared to three cases in 792.5 hours during 1976–1977. Furthermore, opportunities to eat dead animals were ignored in previous years, whereas no such opportunity was missed in 1976–1977; interestingly, as more chances for predatory behavior have been ignored, scavenging has increased.

Rates of Predation

Predatory behavior and, by extension, rates of predation are obviously influenced by the demographic characteristics of the predatory species, their social behavior, and ecological considerations such as prey density and availability. Table 8.11 shows four different ways in which a rate of predation might be constructed, although each method is inadequate to some degree. Method 1 provides a rate uncorrected for any biases. Method 2 attempts to correct for number of animals in the troop (see Hausfater, 1976) but the rate is distorted to a greater or lesser degree, depending on the demographic structure of the troop, because infants are included in the figures. Method 3 corrects Method 2 by eliminating infants (who are not potential captors) from the calculation, but it does not correct for differential participation of age–sex classes in capture. Method 4, a first attempt at incorporating differential age–sex class participation into the construction of a predatory rate is based on the 1973 PHG baboon data. At that time it seemed appropriate to weight males more heavily as potential predators, the assumption being that the significant male proportion of participation in capture would remain relatively constant. However, the 1976–1977 PHG data contradict this assumption, further illustrating how difficult it is to make comparisons of rates. Whichever method is used, the predatory rate of PHG baboons has declined by one-half or more between

Table 8.11. Methods of estimating predation rates at Gilgil

	1970–1971	1973	1975	1976–1977
Method 1[a]	22	12	16	17
Method 2[b]	1076	756	1312	1534
Method 3[c]	856	600	1016	1265
Method 4[d]	747	425	739	927

Note: Figures are number of observation hours necessary to log one kill, calculated according to the following formulas:

a. $\dfrac{\text{observation hours}}{\text{number of kills}}$

b. $\dfrac{\text{observation hours} \times \text{troop size}}{\text{number of kills}}$

c. $\dfrac{\text{observation hours} \times \text{troop size (less infants)}}{\text{number of kills}}$

d. $\dfrac{\text{observation hours} \times [M + \frac{2}{3}(N - M)]}{\text{number of kills}}$

where N = troop size less infants, and M = adult and subadult males.

1973 and 1976–1977. The 1975 rate, although from a shorter time period, seems to be intermediate between the two.

It is difficult to attribute the changing rate to demographic changes, because there were more potential captors and also more male captors in the later period, and thus one would expect the predatory rate to increase rather than decrease. The decline in rate is not likely to be the result of reduced prey density, as we know of no reduction in prey populations. Although prey availability may have been different between the study periods because of the complex interaction between prey movements and predator ranging patterns, the baboons ignored too many potential opportunities each month to make that a convincing explanation.

In all probability, the change in rate reflects actual changes in the behavior (and motivation) of the baboon predators. The predatory behavior of adult males has changed, both in overall participation and in complex hunting of Thomson's gazelles, but there also seems to be a general decline in predatory behavior by all age–sex classes which requires explanation. There may be ecological or nutritional factors, in addition to the social ones already identified, that contributed to the decline in PHG predatory behavior; a simple ecological explanation is unlikely, however, as drought conditions persisted throughout this period.

Conclusions from the 1976–1977 Data

Although PHG baboons still captured prey and ate meat frequently, by 1976–1977 the form of this behavior had changed once again. They no longer hunted over long distances or used relatively sophisticated tactics to capture Thomson's gazelle. Gazelle herds were less wary of baboons than in 1973, perhaps because of the decline of complex hunting. Young baboons were still introduced to meat-eating as they had been in 1973, and the social interactions around the consumption of a carcass were similar although there was less sharing of meat. Females and juveniles continued their trend toward greater participation in capture whereas male participation declined significantly. Males took fewer Thomson's gazelle, while juveniles took proportionately more than they ever had. The overall predatory rate decreased by more than half, and opportunities for predatory behavior were routinely ignored. At the same time, scavenging, though still rare, was slightly more frequent than before.

The 1976–1977 data on predatory behavior in PHG may raise more issues than they settle, but they emphasize several important points. Social processes are influential in predatory behavior, and we cannot assume that this behavior will remain unchanged over time. The evolution of behavior cannot be seen in orthogenetic terms, for reversals in behavioral development may be the rule, rather than the exception, in dynamic and complex social systems.

Male predatory behavior may be more flexible and more subject to change than female predatory behavior. This hypothesis fits well with what is known about other aspects of baboon behavior: females appear to be the conservative and stable element while males' relationships are more fluid and dynamic (Hausfater, 1975; Strum, 1978, n.d.).

The 1976–1977 data on predatory behavior demonstrate the sometimes crucial role of individual motivation. Although the baboons had the same opportunities to hunt Thomson's gazelle in 1977, they no longer practiced complex hunting. Complex hunting appeared to be an effective predatory pattern, and it is thus all the more curious that it was so quickly extinguished. Why was there a decline in general predatory behavior, in particular among adult males, who had previously been the major predators? Why should the baboons scavenge more than before, while at the same time ignoring many chances to capture prey for themselves?

Finally, the recent changes in predatory behavior, although not documented as thoroughly as the changes that took place between 1970–1971 and 1973, raise the same important questions. How and why does a new behavior pattern develop, and how and why does the new pattern become incorporated into a group's permanent behavioral repertoire? The 1975–1977 data suggest that innovation, cultural transmission, and success and efficiency of a pattern, as seen in 1973, may be necessary for the initial incorporation of behaviors, but may not be sufficient to maintain them in a group over a longer period of time, even though ecological conditions remain constant.

DISCUSSION

Teleki's discussion of primate subsistence patterns (1975) emphasizes that subsistence behavior within the order Primates, and predatory behavior in particular, exists along a continuum. To interpret the evolution of human subsistence patterns, we must use a variety of information. Studies of baboon and chimpanzee behavior have identified a primate potential for predation. Comparison of this evidence with the behavior of living human hunters should provide insights into the way in which predatory behavior developed during the course of hominid evolution. The time scale of change and the sequence of events can be determined by the fossil evidence of hominid remains, both their bones and their cultural assemblages. Speculations about the mechanisms leading to change during hominid evolution should then derive from the evidence of the predatory behavior of human and nonhuman primates, as well as from the behavior of social carnivores.

As a starting point, I suggest that a crucial difference between nonhuman and human primate predators is that humans can hunt game as large as or larger than themselves. Given the difficulties faced by a small unspecialized primate in the capture, killing, and consumption of large prey, determining the means by which the early hominids overcame these limitations becomes a vital task if we are to understand the human position on the primate subsistence continuum.

The time when the transition from predation on small animals to hunting of large ones took place is uncertain and depends on interpretations of the fossil evidence. Which (if any) of the known early hominids made this transition is complicated by the number of different hominid species that coexisted during the Plio-Pleistocene (Day, Leakey, and Wood, 1975; Day et al., 1975; F. C. Howell, 1969; Johanson and Coppens, 1976; Johanson, Taieb, and Coppens, 1978; Johanson, White, and Coppens, 1978; R. E. Leakey, 1971, 1972, 1973, 1976), and by questions about the nature of the association between the hominids and the fauna found with them. New data have revived old issues about who were the hunters and who the hunted (e.g., Dart, 1949; Washburn, 1957), about which hominids and which cultural assemblages belong together (e.g., Dart, 1957; L. S. B. Leakey, Tobias, and Napier, 1964; Robinson, 1963), about the relationship between hunting behavior and hominid anatomy (e.g., Bartholomew and Birdsell, 1953; Laughlin, 1968; Dart, 1949; Washburn and Avis, 1958), and about the importance of technology, communication, and brain expansion to predation on large game (e.g., B. Campbell, 1966; Holloway, 1966; Oakley, 1961; Washburn and DeVore, 1961; Washburn and Lancaster, 1968).

If the fauna found in association with the australopithecines was killed and eaten by these hominids, then it is apparent that a small-brained, bipedal hominid with a relatively simple tool assemblage successfully solved the problems of predation on large game. If the newly found hominid forms with their larger brains were hunters and tool-makers, then past arguments about the relationship of increasing brain size and predation on large animals may still be valid. Yet the nonhuman predation data suggest the possibility that early hominids could have practiced a variety of subsistence patterns (e.g., Schaller and Lowther, 1969; Teleki, 1975) with different lineages or different populations possessing unique variations.

There is less controversy about the evolutionary status and behavior of Middle Pleistocene hominids, collectively referred to as *Homo erectus* (Howell, 1966, 1967; Howell and Clark, 1963; Howells, 1967; Isaac, 1968; Mann, 1971; Pilbeam, 1970, 1975). These hominids regularly hunted large game and had larger brains, more advanced toolkits, and knowledge and use of fire. The elaboration of their material culture may have been instrumental in the expansion of their distribution from the tropics to the temperate zones of the Old World. Isaac (1975) has argued that, given the current archaeological evidence, the contrast between Lower and Middle Pleistocene hominid predatory behavior was not marked, with only a slight increase in large mammalian prey and more remains of individuals of gregarious animal species.

Although there is disagreement over the interpretation of the fossil record, the contrast between hominid and nonhuman primate predator behavior indicates that there was a transition from a collector/predator pattern to a gatherer/hunter one, in which prey individuals larger than the primate predator were successfully captured, killed, dismembered, and consumed.

Study of the predatory behavior of the PHG baboons is useful to the interpretation of human evolution in two ways. First, it serves to establish a baseline for the subsistence behavior of nonhuman primates, and especially for the predatory component of this behavior. From this foundation, intelligent questions about the changes which had to occur during the course of human evolution can be formulated. But beyond that, assuming that the early hominids were at least as complex as the PHG baboons, we can make specific speculations about precursors to later human behaviors and about processes that facilitated or inhibited changes in the general pattern of behaviors.

Perhaps it is the multiplicity of factors contributing to changes in predatory behavior which is the most important new emphasis resulting from the PHG evidence. In particular, the elaboration of predatory pursuit to include complex hunting in PHG in 1973 can be seen as a response to the rare convergence of a number of factors: an abundance of group-living prey of appropriate size, the reduced numbers of natural predators, the innovative behavior of a specific baboon, and the influence of that individual's behavior on other group members.

These data suggest that explanation of adaptive shifts by hominid predators should take into account the importance of ecological, social, and individual variables, since no one of these would be sufficient to explain the exploitation of a new opportunity. Hooton's observation that "a cat does not become a walrus because of an inundation; it either drowns or scuttles away to dry land" (1931) is particularly relevant to those discussions of hominid evolutionary events which primarily emphasize ecological factors. Selective forces in the Plio-Pleistocene period were operating on a primate species which already had certain predispositions, and not on a *tabula rasa*. Obviously there was an interaction between predatory behavior, as performed by a primate, and those adaptations existing at the time the initial adaptive shift to a gatherer/hunter subsistence pattern occurred. It may be important to consider the susceptibility of these basic adaptive patterns to modification, their advantages and disadvantages for a hominid predator, and the compromises in behavior and social organization necessary and possible once a gatherer/hunter mode of subsistence became important to a group-living primate. Furthermore, as the 1975–1977 PHG data demonstrate, changes in predatory behavior can come without any major change in ecological conditions. This would suggest that predatory behavior, although part of a subsistence pattern, at times might change as a result of social or other stimuli not normally conceptually linked with subsistence.

Changes in predatory behavior among the PHG baboons depended on both elaboration of existing elements in their repertoire and on innovation, the creation of new elements. For example, the mobility of the adult males in general foraging and in group transfer made some aspects of their predatory behavior possible. Strategies and cognitive abilities necessary in nonpredatory contexts may have been preadaptive for more elaborate predation. Adult male baboons cooperate with each other in response to threats from within the group or outside of it, and this cooperative experience may have facilitated the coordination of male predatory behavior seen in 1973.

Innovation in the context of subsistence is not rare in nonhuman primates, and some of the changes in PHG baboon predation between 1970 and 1977 can probably be attributed to this factor alone. Variability in primate behavior and personality can be an important source of innovations (Frisch, 1968; Green, 1975; Itani and Nishimura, 1973). Once an innovation occurs, individuals acquire the new behavior through learning. How and from whom they learn depends on the type of behavior and the nature of communication and affiliation networks within the group (for other primate examples, see Beck, 1975; DeVore, 1963; Hall, 1962, 1963, 1968; Jay, 1963; Kawai, 1965; Kawamura, 1959; Rogers, 1973).

The initial success of the PHG male predators may have reflected the hitherto peaceful relationship between them and their prey. At first, it may have been relatively easy for baboons to get close to a Thomson's gazelle with a minimum of effort, time, and strategy. With increased hunting by baboons, gazelle herds modified their behavior, instituting and increasing flight distance, vigilance, and protective maneuvers. This increased wariness made approaching and stalking more difficult for baboon hunters, and the greater amount of time which baboons spent hunting in 1973 may reflect both their interest in predation and the newer difficulties involved in pursuit. Thus the success of the hunting behavior itself may have provided negative feedback in which initial elaboration of techniques increased prey avoidance and success simultaneously. Baboons then required more time and effort to be as successful as they had been; thus the conditions for further elaboration of hunting techniques were created but additional innovations may have been beyond baboon capabilities.

Although all the members of PHG troop (except infants) are potentially capable of certain kinds of predatory behavior and most have an interest in meat to motivate them in the performance of these behaviors, there are limits on participation even for very interested individuals. These include the existing group structure, established patterns of interaction, and underlying emotions. "Learning often involves the differential strengthening of existing behavioral tendencies rather than the establishment of entirely new ones" (Bitterman, 1975:699).

The most highly motivated female baboon, with or without a dependent infant, never took part in a complex hunt although she was physically capable of doing so. By contrast, when the potential victim was near the troop, she chased and captured prey animals equal in size to those hunted by the males. Male participation was also controlled by individual differences in mobility. The different priorities that PHG males and females gave to meat-eating suggests that male reproductive strategies may have strongly limited the degree of male involvement in predation while female reproductive strategies did not.

Let us apply the information on PHG baboon predation to make suggestions about human evolutionary events. Here I am not using baboons as a model for hominids but rather as an illustration of how a primate system operates and how behavior might change. The divergence of the hominids from the nonhuman primates in such areas as cooperation, strategy, division of labor, and certain cognitive abilities is widely discussed by authors concerned with human behavior. The PHG baboon data illustrate that these behaviors, which would be critical to a primate predator attempting to capture large game, have precursors among the nonhuman primates. Differences between human and nonhuman primates could have resulted from increasing selection for certain behaviors that differentially strengthened existing tendencies. For example, those writing about the role of hunting in human evolution (e.g., B. Campbell, 1966; Laughlin, 1968; Lee and DeVore, 1968a; Pfeiffer, 1969; Tiger, 1969; Washburn and Lancaster, 1968) have speculated that the origin of human sexual division of labor is to be found in hunting for prey that included large animals. But the PHG data suggest that even among collector/predators a difference in male and female predatory behavior exists that may reflect basic differences in the way male and female primates are integrated into the group, and perhaps differences in reproductive strategies for the two sexes as well. Chimpanzee predation, tool use, and insect exploitation (McGrew, 1974; Teleki, 1974, 1975) also support such a notion. Sexual differences may have originated before the shift from collector/predator to gatherer/hunter took place, while males but not females engaging in certain aspects of predatory behavior. The infant dependency argument which has been advanced as part of the hunting/sexual division of labor position may still be valid, for once hominids had larger brains, more helpless infants, and longer periods of infant dependency, the problems of infant care could have further contributed to whatever patterns already existed.

Sexual division of labor is intimately tied to reproductive strategies of males and females, for all mammals. For PHG baboons, reproductive strategies may limit a male's ability to participate in predatory behavior and place a ceiling on the development of predation as an important subsistence activity. If a similar system existed among early hominids, a major change in reproductive strategies would have been necessary before males could give predation the priority it needed as a prelude to further division of labor between the sexes. This is not a novel suggestion but is a more plausible one now that there are some data demonstrating the limitations that the nonhuman primate pattern places on elaboration of a subsistence economy based on hunting and gathering.

How did changes occur? As was the case with the PHG baboons, changes in hominid behaviors could have resulted from innovation; the behavior of one hominid could have provided an initial impetus for the group (and population). I am not implying that such a possibility existed only once, in one individual of one group at a particular time. Rather, I suggest that the potential for innovation and exploitation of new opportunities could have existed in many groups, under suitable conditions.

Once an innovation occurs, its development and elaboration may be quite rapid, if the PHG baboon data provide a reasonable model. In the past, theories about human evolution have often assumed that adaptive changes occurred slowly and were irreversible, but the PHG data show that rates of change can be more variable when the behaviors involve learning. Once a new behavior pattern is introduced, its acquisition and elaboration may proceed rapidly, among hominids as well as baboons. Since some behaviors are appropriate only under a complex set of conditions, changes in those conditions will affect such behaviors. As the more recent PHG baboon data illustrate, behaviors can become extinct as rapidly as they are elaborated, and reversals or rapid alternations may have been common in human evolution. As I have speculated was the case with baboon predators, the initial stages of the hominid adaptive shift to predation on large game may have been facilitated by the newness of the predatory behavior and the consequent lack of effective prey response. When predation became successful, prey wariness may have increased as well, producing a situation that required improved hunting techniques to achieve essentially the same results. If the members of a hominid group were not capable of further innovations (as may have been the case with the PHG baboon predators), the development of predatory behavior would not have proceeded any farther.

Burton and Bick discuss the phenomenon of a deme-wide shift in behavior following an innovation by an individual, and label it "tradition drift." They raise important questions about "when, how, and how frequently do behavioral innovations occur, who are the innovators, what are the conditions for the spread of such innovations within a deme, how rapidly do such innovations spread, how much innovation loss occurs, when can we say that such innovations have become fixed in the behavioral/pool-repertoire, etc.?" (1972:58). These questions are particularly relevant to the development of primate and hominid predatory behavior over both short and long terms. The PHG data show that many conditions are necessary for the initial incorporation of behaviors into a group's repertoire but these same conditions may not be sufficient to maintain the behaviors over a longer period of time.

The PHG baboon data (along with evidence from other baboon and chimpanzee predator populations) suggest that primate predatory habits could have occurred and developed in a variety of habitats, given the appropriate ecological, social, and individual opportunities. But if elaborate hunting behavior has important bioenergetic determinants, then some habitats would be especially suitable for the hominid development of large-game hunting. For example, a forest habitat has few species of large animals and few communal species; prey exist there in low density and wide distribution, and visibility is poor. These conditions would make the development of predation on large animals unlikely. By contrast, the savannah, with its great numbers of large, group-living prey, would provide frequent opportunities for this type of hunting to develop. Thus, if the evolution of predation within the primate order was a graded process, the adaptive shift that included large animals as prey probably occurred in open savannah or open woodland. Once predation on large animals became an established pattern, improved techniques or special ecological conditions could have made hunting the larger forest species feasible, or necessary.

The PHG baboon data also argue against single-origin explanations of hominid hunting behavior (see Teleki, 1975, for chimpanzee evidence). Population variability in predatory behavior appears to be the norm, not only among baboons but also among chimpanzees (J. Goodall, 1963b; Suzuki, 1969; Teleki, 1973a,b; Wrangham, 1975) and social carnivores (Kleiman and Eisenberg, 1973; Kruuk, 1972).

Just where and how scavenging fits into the evolution of human predatory behavior is still debated (Bartholomew and Birdsell, 1953; W. E. L. Clark, 1967; Reynolds, 1966; Schaller and Lowther, 1969). Whether scavenging played an important role cannot be decided by the data now available on nonhuman primates. However, the complexity of the relationship between hunting and scavenging was demonstrated in 1976, when the PHG baboons ignored usual opportunities to capture prey while eating more dead animals than in the previous years. The PHG material does sound a note of caution—the relationship of scavenging to hunting may not be as simple as often conceived of in discussions of hominid evolution.

The primate potential for predatory behavior is well illustrated by the data on PHG baboons, which add to our understanding of the continuum of predatory behavior within the order Primates and clarify some of the issues in the evolution of human behavior. In particular, they provide an example of how a predatory potential can be elaborated, and how complex the adaptive shifts in primate groups can be. As a result we have a better, albeit only partial, understanding of the multiple factors at work and how these can interact.

The predatory behavior of the earliest hominids may have been similar to that of today's baboons or chimpanzees, and could have originated many times, among groups in different populations living under differing ecological conditions. But there was an additional transition that involved a shift from a "collector/predator" mode of subsistence to a "gatherer/hunter" mode including predation on large animals. The fact that nonhuman primates can be sophisticated and successful hunters of small animals, without elaborate tools or more advanced systems of communication, does not repudiate ideas about the importance of (large-game) hunting in human evolution. Instead, the comparison clarifies the limitations of nonhuman primate predatory behavior and the unique aspects of the human predatory pattern. What baboon and human hunters do *is* different: to hunt just one large animal requires solutions to specific problems which, based on the current evidence, appear to be outside the reach of nonhuman primates. Artificial barriers in the evolutionary continuum should not be constructed to assure the unique status of hominid behavior, but at the same time we must recognize the crucial difference between similarity and identity.

Acknowledgments

I would like to thank Arthur and Tobina Cole for their hospitality and for their support of baboon research at Kekopey. The Government of Kenya kindly granted permission for this research, and the University of Nairobi and the National Museums of Kenya provided local sponsorship. The research was funded by National Science Foundation grant GS 35180 and grants from the University of California Academic Senate and the L. S. B. Leakey Foundation. R. H. Byles provided statistical analysis.

NOTES

1. Age–sex classifications used in both text and tables are: infant, 0–12 months; juvenile female, 1–4 years; juvenile male, 1–5 years; subadult male, 5–8 years; subadult female, 4–5 years; adult female, >5 years; adult male, >8 years. Where subadult is not a separate category

in text or tables, these individuals are included in the adult category. Juvenile males and females are usually combined.

2. The best fit line calculated for these data has the characteristics: $y = 0.06x - 0.23$. Regression analysis shows that $F = 11.602$, where rejection at the .005 level takes place at $F = 10.64$.

3. Using a runs test for trend data, analysis of change in complex hunting rate from January through May of 1973 yields a t_s of 3.51, where rejection at the .001 level is 3.29 for departure from a random trend.

4. Using a runs test for trend data, analysis of change in number of simultaneous hunters in complex hunts from March through August of 1973 yields a t_s of 3.51, where rejection at the .001 level is 3.29 for departure from a random trend. The trend is for an increase in the average number of simultaneous hunters (1 to 3) and the greatest number of simultaneous hunters (1 to 5) in hunts per month.

5. A χ^2 test with a Yates correction for continuity comparing the ability of females to retain captured prey in 1973 with that in 1970–1971 shows a significant difference: $\chi^2 = 3.85$, with 1 d.f., $p = .05$.

6. In comparing the monthly attendance of 12 juveniles at predatory episodes before and after they first gained access to meat, the hypothesis that these two sets of data had the same distribution can be rejected using a χ^2 evaluation for goodness of fit: $\chi^2 = 70.63$, with 11 d.f., where rejection at the $p = .001$ level is at 31.2.

7. The average distance traveled from the troop during complex hunts from March 1973 through January 1974 was as follows: RD, 1200 m; ST, 1060 m; SU, 800 m; BS, 800 m; BR, 645 m; RA, 645 m; CA, 530 m.

8. $r = .593$, $\alpha = .01$.

9. $r = .75$, $\alpha = .001$.

10. In 1976–1977, the PHG baboons failed to take advantage of opportunities to prey on Thomson's gazelle at a rate of one case every 21 hours of observation. This contrasts with a rate of one case every 226 hours from May 1973 until January 1974, when the same scan sampling technique was used.

Geza Teleki

9.
The Omnivorous Diet and Eclectic Feeding Habits of Chimpanzees in Gombe National Park, Tanzania

A century ago, long before accurate information on the dietary patterns and feeding habits of wild primates was available, some naturalists were open-minded enough to speculate that faunal resources, including vertebrate meat, were occasionally exploited by the nonhuman members of the order Primates (e.g., Hartmann, 1886). Between the 1880s and the 1960s (when firm data on primate feeding habits began to accumulate from numerous field studies), many eminent scientists concerned with human evolution adopted the notion that all nonhuman primates are, and always were, plant-eating mammals, that monkeys and apes do not hunt prey or share food (e.g., Spuhler, 1965). Even those professionals who presumably knew of Jane Goodall's preliminary observations (1963b) on chimpanzee hunting behavior had become so locked into viewing primates as vegetarians that they described these predatory apes as "unusual" and "atypical" of the species (e.g., Morris and Morris, 1966) or as "deviant" in their behavior (Thompson, 1975).

How this shift of opinion occurred when no additional evidence was obtained during those years is baffling, for it is widely claimed that scientific thought progresses in tandem with accumulation of reliable information. I would venture, in retrospect, that changing perceptions in the arena of paleoanthropology, especially among those bent on promoting a "man-the-hunter" interpretation of human evolution, played a basic role in establishing belief in the existence of a vegetarian primate prototype. It was vital, given the nature of the hypothesis, to have a plant-eating, tree-living, forest dweller as ancestor to the emergent primate novelty—a meat-eating, ground-living, savannah-dwelling hominid.

Launched in the 1920s, this view continues to lead a robust and healthy life (Wood Jones, 1926; Pfeiffer, 1978). Indeed, the premise that hunting behavior was a unique development—a pivotal adaptation—of the hominid line has become the prevailing doctrine, stated and restated in most of our textbooks (e.g., B. Campbell, 1974; Fagan, 1974) and in popular literature (e.g., Ardrey, 1976). One result is the dogmatic perpetuation of an unverified theory. Another is that new evidence on active predation by nonhuman primates, notably baboons and chimpanzees (Teleki, 1975), and on widespread omnivory among living primate species (Harding, in this volume), is greeted with skepticism and debate no matter what the quality or quantity of that evidence. For instance, the concept of food-sharing by nonhuman primates continues to be rejected by some anthropologists (e.g., Lancaster, 1978; Swartz and Jordan, 1976) despite publication of numerous reports documenting meat-sharing *and* plant-sharing by chimpanzees and other primates (e.g., Kavanagh, 1972; McGrew, 1975, 1979; Teleki, 1973a,b). Similarly, the predatory status of Gombe chimpanzees is still questioned (Gaulin and Kurland, 1976; Reynolds, 1975) even though predatory behavior occurs in widely dispersed populations, some of which have not been provisioned by humans (Teleki, 1973a, 1975).

Thus, many anthropologists continue to build models of hominid emergence based on the premise that other primates do not possess the behavioral, social, and psychological equipment to truly resemble humans, maintaining at the same time, however, that biological and morphological affinities between nonhuman and human primates are strong. I believe this amounts to an error in logic that derives from indiscriminate mixing of evolutionary continuities and discontinuities.

In this article I intend, at one level, to focus attention on the diversity and sophistication of hunting and meat-eating activities within one nonhuman primate species, the African chimpanzee (*Pan troglodytes*). This ape exhibits many traits that we have until now attributed only to humans and their direct hominid ancestors. Reviews of omnivory in primates have been supplied by others (Gaulin and Konner, 1977; Harding, in this volume; C. Jones, 1972); my account is a case study of predation by chimpanzees in the Gombe National Park of Tanzania. In addition to my own reports on predatory behavior (Teleki, 1973a,b, 1975, 1977a), I include more recent data collected by several Gombe investigators.

At another level, I intend to raise questions about the plausibility of traditional reconstructions of hominid emergence and evolution, as sketched by S. Washburn and C. Lancaster (1968), J. D. Clark (1970), J. Lancaster (1975), J. Pfeiffer (1977, 1978), and many others who still perceive hunting as the key adaptation of early hominids.

CHIMPANZEES AS OMNIVORES

Like many of the nonhuman primates surveyed by Harding (in this volume), wild chimpanzees have eclectic feeding habits and consume a wide assortment of foods in yearly, monthly, daily, and even hourly periods. According to reports from several field studies conducted since 1959 in

Tanzania, Uganda, Rio Muni, and Senegal, and from a study of captive chimpanzees reintroduced to a natural habitat in Gabon,[1] the omnivorous diet of these apes includes the following broad categories of food: leaves and shoots, buds and blossoms, fruits and berries, grains and seeds, husks and pods, nuts, reeds and grasses, vine stems, barks and resins, lichens, galls and larvae, ants and termites, caterpillars and cocoons, birds and eggs, honey, various mammals, minerals, and water. An itemized list would include hundreds of floral and faunal species known to be exploited by wild chimpanzees and, as additional items are continuously being observed, the final list may turn out to be considerably longer.

If we narrow the focus to vertebrate foods, the list still includes 10, possibly 11, other species of primates; 4 species of ungulates; and at least 3, but possibly 4, species of small mammals. In addition to these, 9 avian species are consumed, but aside from the guinea fowl most of these are fledglings collected from nests rather than actively hunted.[2] Moreover, predatory behavior involving vertebrate prey has now been recorded at all major study sites in equatorial Africa, from Uganda and Tanzania to Sierra Leone and Senegal.[3] I expect that the known geographical distribution of predatory behavior will continue to expand as new chimpanzee projects are launched, though it is probable that some populations practice this behavior little or not at all while others do so regularly and systematically (Teleki, 1975). Technological skills also vary regionally, with each chimpanzee population exhibiting somewhat different patterns of tool-using and tool-making behavior in its subsistence activities (Sabater Pi, 1974; Teleki, 1974). Performance variations across populations, and probably also across social communities, may result partly from differences in environmental conditions, but behavioral, social, and psychological factors may be equally or even more influential in the differential formation and dissemination of activity patterns or social customs (McGrew and Tutin, 1978; Teleki, 1974, 1975). If technological skills, predatory habits, and other traits are so variable in chimpanzees, the adaptive potential of this genus may be greater than anyone has hitherto suspected.

Food lists are, of course, not the best indicators of chimpanzee dietary patterns or feeding habits (see Harding, in this volume), yet they can be useful in formulating a rough index of dietary diversity, which can then be used to compare results obtained from other species. On such a scale, chimpanzees are not exceptional among nonhuman primates in terms of dietary diversity, falling within the omnivorous spectrum. Moreover, chimpanzees are at least as eclectic in their feeding habits as any human gatherer/hunter band now living outside the high latitudes. (Comparisons with other mammalian omnivores, such as pigs and bears, would be enlightening, but the dietary data are not available.)

Excellent dietary information has been obtained in recent studies of

Kalahari gatherer/hunter bands. Lee (1968) notes that the !Kung Bushmen consider 85 plant species and 54 animal species to be food, and Tanaka (1976) points out that the ≠Kade Bushmen regard 79 plant species and over 50 animal species as edible. In both cases, however, only a small proportion of these serve as staple resources. Lee (1968:35) comments that "about 90 per cent of the vegetable diet by weight is drawn from only 23 species" of plants, and Tanaka (1976:105) cites only 3 plant species as "major foods." These findings underscore the omnivory of chimpanzees, which have been observed to eat 201 plant food types and 41 animal food types in Gombe National Park; almost all of the total feeding time (93–95%) is devoted to exploitation of only 50% of the edible resources available in a given month (Wrangham, 1977). Dietary diversity is similarly broad at other research sites. At least 330 food types are consumed in the Mahali Mountains area of Tanzania (Nishida, in press), and even the chimpanzees reintroduced to a forest in Gabon utilized 141 food types within a 12-month study period (C. M. Hladik, 1973). Based on these data, I see no reason to rank chimpanzee communities and human bands on different scales of omnivory.

There are, of course, some differences hidden within these crude measures of dietary diversity. Critics of this comparative approach often point out that the types of prey hunted by apes and humans are radically different, particularly in size, and that hunting of large prey calls for special techniques which only humans possess (e.g., King, 1975). It is undoubtedly true that chimpanzees and other nonhuman primates prey only on species smaller than themselves while humans prey on more kinds of game, including some larger than the hunters (Teleki, 1975:138); nonetheless, collector/predator chimpanzees and gatherer/hunter humans are quite similar in other dietary parameters, including exploitation of small vertebrates and invertebrates. As Silberbauer and Harako (both in this volume), and others have shown, most of the fauna consumed in band societies consists of small game.

More penetrating comparisons of diets among nonhuman and human primates would be enlightening but are not feasible at present. Nutritional analysis of natural foods is both complicated and expensive when samples must be sent to properly equipped laboratories. C. M. Hladik and his colleagues stand nearly alone in applying these sophisticated techniques to the study of primates in the wild; unfortunately, few populations have been adequately sampled to date. Their work does cover chimpanzee nutrition (C. M. Hladik, 1973, 1974, and in this volume; C. M. Hladik and Gueguen, 1974; C. M. Hladik and Viroben, 1974), though not in a completely natural context. Valuable as it is in showing how young chimpanzees learn to exploit a new environment, the approach needs to be more extensively applied to truly wild populations.

A related technique, estimation of food weights and volumes, has also been attempted by some field primatologists and ethnographers, with varying degrees of success. In studies of human band societies, where food items can often be weighed and sized before they are consumed at campsites, reasonably accurate measures of food intake can be obtained (e.g., Lee, 1969; Tanaka, 1976). One problem with this technique is that many foods, and especially edible plants that require little or no preparation, are consumed during foraging expeditions on a hand-to-mouth basis (Hayden, Mann, in this volume). My guess is that even the most meticulous estimates of food intake among gatherer/hunters have in the past inflated the faunal component of the diet because plant foods, particularly small items such as berries, are less likely to be brought to the camp for distribution. Also, the social customs that regulate meat-sharing tend to be more stringent than those regulating plant-sharing in both nonhuman and human primate groups (e.g., McGrew, 1975, 1979; Marshall, 1961), which indicates that fauna are the more attractive foods for all omnivorous primates.

Many field researchers have offered percentage estimates of food intake in order to draw attention to special components in the diets of monkey, ape, and human groups. In both ethnographic and primatological literature, these estimates commonly derive from intuitive evaluations of feeding budgets (see Hayden, in this volume) and therefore are questionably useful for intergroup and interspecies comparisons. Reynolds and Reynolds (1965), for instance, viewed Budongo chimpanzees as "frugivorous" because 90% of their bulk food intake purportedly consisted of fruits, while only 5% consisted of leaves, 4% of bark and stems, and 1% of insects. Similarly, Gombe chimpanzees supposedly rely on mammalian prey for about 1–3% of their total annual food intake (Busse, 1977:908). Neither in these cases nor in many others encountered in the primatological literature do the authors specify how such figures were obtained, yet the numbers tend to be widely quoted. It is particularly unclear in many instances whether actual food intake or time spent feeding is the element being measured.

In view of these problems, comparisons of dietary patterns among populations of omnivorous primates, both nonhuman and human, are perhaps premature as well as misleading. But it is impractical to dismiss all studies of dietary patterns simply because additional refinements in data collecting and processing would be advantageous. There are many projects in which primatologists have attempted to assess dietary patterns quantitatively by tabulating the relative amounts of time allotted to routine activities such as feeding, traveling, resting, and interacting (reviewed by Teleki, 1977a). Several of these projects have focused on the feeding schedules of wild chimpanzees (Nishida, 1974; Teleki, 1977a; Wrangham, 1975, 1977), and the results can yield some valuable insights about resource exploitation. A summary of my own research on chimpanzee activity rhythms, based on data collected at the Gombe Stream Research Centre (4°41'S, 29°38'E) between 26 August 1968 and 28 February 1971, is presented here with this purpose in mind, for it provides a broad subsistence context within which to view predation on mammals.

Before presenting such a summary, however, I must draw attention to certain problems associated with time–motion studies of feeding habits. First, duration measures of behavior can and do vary considerably, depending on the criteria used to classify and clock various activities (see Teleki, 1977a:15–22). As A. Jolly has dramatically shown (1972:111), inconsistent tabulation methods can lead to wide discrepancies in results even when all other factors are reasonably stable: four studies of the same howler monkey population in Panama yielded figures of 24.5, 21.5, 13.3, and 9.9% for relative amounts of time spent on feeding activities. Second, the proportions of time devoted to feeding on one resource or another are not necessarily equivalent to the proportions of each food within the total diet. Many small items such as seeds or insects may require unusually large amounts of time for collection, preparation, and ingestion, whereas large items such as fruits or leaves can be rapidly picked and eaten in bulk (Teleki, 1977a).

The chief drawback, however, in trying to compare the feeding schedules of chimpanzees and humans is simply that time–motion data on food search, acquisition, preparation, and consumption activities can rarely be extracted from the available ethnographic literature (Hayden, in this volume).

FEEDING RHYTHMS OF GOMBE CHIMPANZEES

My study of chimpanzee activity rhythms was designed to complement other projects focusing on the nutritional and ecological parameters of chimpanzee omnivory (C.M. Hladik, 1973, 1977b; Nishida, 1974; Suzuki, 1969, 1971; Wrangham, 1975, 1977). It concentrated on the temporal and spatial dimensions of all routine activities performed during 786.3 hours of observation of 31 target chimpanzees in the Gombe study population (Teleki, 1977a).[4] All activities were timed to the minute and logged on maps as the individuals under observation moved freely through the mosaic grassland–woodland–forest habitat in a centrally located study area (about 8 km^2) within Gombe National Park (approximately 32 km^2).

The temporal breakdown of feeding, traveling, resting, and interacting activities appears in table 9.1, providing a general impression of how Gombe chimpanzees distribute their time on an average day and year. Note that the feeding budget (42.8%) is nearly double that of any other routine activity, and that the subsistence budget (feeding time + traveling time) accounts

Table 9.1. Percentages of time allotted by Gombe chimpanzees to four basic routine activities

Routine activities	Diurnal span (15 hr)	Diel span (24 hr)[a]	Annual span		
			Dry season (no rains)	Wet season 1 (short rains)	Wet season 2 (long rains)
Feeding	42.8	27.1	44.4	44.0	40.2
Traveling	13.4	9.4	14.1	15.6	9.3
Resting	18.9	47.7	15.7	21.3	18.8
Interacting	24.9	15.8	25.8	19.1	31.7

Note: These percentages are based on a total observation sample of 47,177 minutes (786.3 hours) (after Teleki, 1977a).
[a] Estimated figures, assuming that 8 hours per night are devoted to resting in night nests, based on irregular all-night observations.

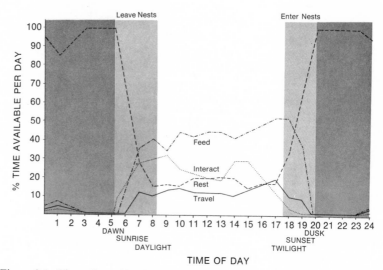

Figure 9.1. Time allotted by Gombe chimpanzees to four basic routine activities during the 24-hour day, with diurnal rhythms (covering 15 hours) computed from 47,177 minutes (786.3 hours) of observation and nocturnal rhythms (covering 9 hours) estimated from 2,615 minutes (43.6 hours) of incidental observation.

for 56.2% of the total available time on a daily basis. Moreover, feeding budgets vary little across the seasons even though radical changes occur in the vegetation cover (Teleiki, 1977a) and the distribution and availability of certain food resources over the year (Wrangham, 1975, 1977).

For present purposes, a more interesting profile of diurnal activity rhythms is provided in figure 9.1, which traces the hourly distributions of all routine activities across an average day. In contrast to other reports that refer to two or even three sharp feeding peaks during the day (Nishida, 1974; van Lawick–Goodall, 1968; Wrangham, 1977), the hourly feeding budgets in figure 9.1 show a relatively steady rate of feeding from sunrise to sunset. The slight slumps observable at 0900 and 1400 hours apparently coincide with peaks of social interaction and may be due to slight increases in grooming (Wrangham, 1977)—grooming tends to increase as groups form in the morning hours (Bauer, 1975; Teleki, 1977a). More importantly, statistical analysis of the temporal relationships among different routine activity budgets indicates that feeding and traveling profiles are closely linked, and that the resting profile is inversely related to the total subsistence profile. As set forth elsewhere (Teleki, 1977a), the implications are that most traveling occurs in conjunction with feeding, and that most daytime resting is a response to energy expended on subsistence activities. Moreover, when routine activity budgets are tested for correlations with environmental variables such as temperature, rainfall, and vegetation cover, the feeding profile is more closely linked to these extrinsic factors than is any other activity. Conversely, the interacting profile is at best weakly linked to other routine activities and to environmental variables, suggesting that social behavior is a "residual" activity that may be essential to group solidarity but is superseded by the maintenance requirements of individual survival. In other words, Gombe chimpanzees must feed to stay alive, must travel to locate food, must rest to restore energy depleted by foraging, and can then apply surplus time to social interaction. This is of course a grossly simplified model of chimpanzee adaptation and of the balance between subsistence and social requirements (see Teleki, 1977a, for more details), but it makes clear the fundamental role of feeding behavior in a nonhuman primate population.

Closer examination of the diurnal and annual feeding profiles yields additional insights about chimpanzee omnivory. As shown in table 9.2, where the total feeding budget has been segmented into units according to the relative amounts of time spent exploiting different food resources, Gombe chimpanzees subsist primarily on plant parts and products. Since nearly 80% of their feeding budget consists of time spent collecting plant foods, it might be reasonable initially to classify these apes as vegetarians. But in that case most mammals, including most human populations, must also be classified as vegetarians. Only the true carnivores might fall outside this category, though that exclusion would also be inaccurate for some carnivorous species. The coyote (*Canis latrans*), for instance, incorporates substantial amounts of plant food in its annual diet, including blackberries, blueberries, prickly pear fruits, chapotes, grasses, and many kinds of cultivated fruits and vegetables (Gier, 1975). Construction of an empirical

Table 9.2. Percentages of time allotted by Gombe chimpanzees to feeding on four broad categories of food items

Food categories[a]	Diurnal span (15 hr)	Annual span		
		Dry season (no rains)	Wet season 1 (short rains)	Wet season 2 (long rains)
Fauna	20.4	18.5	32.9	1.7
Flora 1	32.0	36.3	17.6	51.5
Flora 2	47.1	44.5	49.3	45.8
Miscellaneous	0.5	0.7	0.2	1.0

Note: These percentages are based on a total observation sample of 20,204 minutes (336.7 hours) (after Teleki, 1977a).

[a]Category components: *fauna*, animal parts (insects, mammals, etc.) and products (eggs, honey, etc.); *flora 1*, plant parts (mainly foliage); *flora 2*, plant products (mainly fruits and nuts); *miscellaneous items*, minerals (salt, water, etc.) and some rarely exploited materials (resin, cocoons, etc.).

scale of dietary patterns, ranging from monophagous plant-eaters to monophagous meat-eaters, should have the highest priority if comparisons across taxa are to achieve real validity in the future.

The charting of chimpanzee feeding activities across hours of the day and months of the year highlights several interesting features, or trends, in their food intake. For example, the diurnal feeding schedule (fig. 9.2, top) shows that plant products are most heavily exploited in the morning hours, while plant parts are mainly eaten in the evening hours. Also, feeding activities are most eclectic in the late morning and midday hours, when both flora and fauna are exploited, although it should be noted that most of the time spent on exploiting fauna, as depicted in figure 9.2, involves only collection of insects.

According to Wrangham (1977:517), "changes in feeding time on the major foods appeared largely related to availability." From the annual feeding schedule (fig. 9.2, bottom), it is apparent that Gombe chimpanzees exploit flora heavily during half the year, from January through July. That

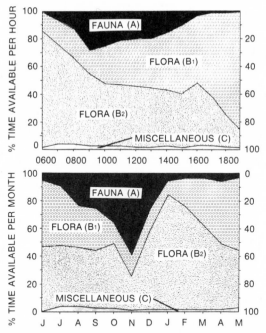

Figure 9.2. Diurnal and annual rhythms of feeding activity, based on 20,204 minutes (336.7 hours) of observation, showing the proportions of time (percentages on the vertical axis being cumulative) allotted by Gombe chimpanzees to exploitation of: *A*, fauna; *B1*, foliage; *B2*, fruits and nuts; *C*, miscellaneous items. (Categories are described more fully in notes to table 9.2.)

period covers the second wet season and the onset of dry season, at which time the vegetation cover is exceptionally dense and lush throughout the park, with foliage and fruits at high productivity levels (Teleki, 1977a). Some fauna are exploited in all months of the year, but this resource is used most heavily during the first wet season, between August and December, when termites, safari ants, galls, and other insect foods are plentiful (McGrew, 1974; Teleki, 1974; Wrangham, 1977). There is some indication that predation on mammals decreases during the insect-collecting season (Teleki, 1973a; Wrangham, 1975), and so hunting may be partly a response to shortage of invertebrate foods between February and August.

Together with Wrangham's work on the ecology of resource exploitation (1975, 1977), my observations on the temporal distributions of feeding habits firmly establish the omnivory of Gombe chimpanzees, who consume an eclectic assortment of foods within diurnal, seasonal, and annual intervals. Patterns of food exploitation during the day are particularly indicative of omnivory, because they demonstrate that Gombe chimpanzees feed selectively on a number of resources even when availability does not vary from hour to hour. For this reason I do not yet concur with Wrangham (1977) that diet variability is geared mainly to resource availability on a month-to-month basis; until conclusive evidence is marshaled, I prefer to leave open the possibility that chimpanzees maintain a maximum level of omnivory at all times of year by selective utilization of as many different resources as is feasible, with both extrinsic and intrinsic factors modulating their choices (Teleki, 1977a).

It is perhaps significant, in this light, that exploitation of fauna accounts for more than 20% of the total feeding budget during 4 months of the year, and for more than 50% during 1 month. Even if the bulk intake of faunal resources remains low compared to intake of floral resources, these figures indicate that motivation to consume invertebrates (and to a lesser extent vertebrates) is consistently high among Gombe chimpanzees.

GOMBE CHIMPANZEES AS PREDATORS

Much has been written about the predatory proclivities of Gombe chimpanzees since their hunting and meat-eating activities were first observed in the early 1960s (J. Goodall, 1963a,b, 1965; van Lawick-Goodall, 1968, 1971). Systematic studies of the behavioral and ecological aspects of predation on vertebrates (Teleki, 1973a,b, 1975, 1977b; Wrangham, 1975, 1977) have recently been supplemented by numerous special reports covering an array of topics (Busse, 1977, 1978; J. Goodall and Hamburg, 1975; Morris and Goodall, 1977; Plooij, 1978; van Lawick-Goodall, 1973). The cannibalistic tendencies of Gombe chimpanzees have also been documented and discussed (Bygott, 1972; J. Goodall, 1977;

Teleki, 1975), as have the relations between chimpanzees and other predators living in Gombe National Park (Teleki, 1973c). Accordingly, I shall draw upon this rich literature to update, and in some instances to correct, the conclusions and speculations I developed from my own study of predatory behavior in 1968–1969.

The Gombe Data Base

In 1973, when I collated the available data on predatory events documented at different chimpanzee study sites (Teleki, 1975:133), the total number of *kills* made by wild chimpanzees stood at 143, with 130 of them (91%) logged at Gombe alone.[5] The total number of kills recorded at all sites in equatorial Africa, including those in Senegal and the Ivory Coast, now exceeds 200.[6]

The species of prey captured by chimpanzees (table 9.3) cannot always be surely identified, and the percentage breakdowns by prey types do not necessarily portray actual predation frequencies or rates, since many variables can affect observations of predatory behavior (Teleki, 1973a; Wrangham, 1975). Some of these parameters are discussed later. Suffice it to note here that when banana provisioning was dramatically reduced at Gombe in the middle of 1969, causing numerous changes in behavior, social structure, and population dynamics (Teleki, Hunt, and Pfifferling, 1976; Wrangham, 1974), baboons and chimpanzees were no longer strongly attracted to the provisioning area, and as a result, chimpanzee predation on baboons declined sharply. This shift was predictable some years ago (Teleki, 1973a), although it was not known then that colobus

Table 9.3. Mammalian prey killed by Gombe chimpanzees, 1960–1973

Prey types	No. of kills	% of subtotal	
Red colobus, *Colobus badius*	53	43	
Olive baboon, *Papio anubis*	25	21	68% primates
Blue monkey, *Cercopithecus mitis*	3	2	
Redtail monkey, *Cercopithecus ascanius*	3	2	
Bush pig, *Potamochoerus porcus*	21	17	32% other
Bushbuck, *Tragelaphus scriptus*	18	15	
Subtotal	123	100	
Unidentified prey	39		
Total	162		

monkeys would become the primary targets in subsequent years, from 1970 to 1974 (Wrangham, 1975; Busse, 1978).

The range of small-game species listed in table 9.3 not only represents a fair cross section of the mammalian prey available in the park but also compares favorably with the small-game lists compiled from studies of collector/predator baboons and gatherer/hunter humans (Teleki, 1975). Each predatory primate must, of course, operate within set limits of prey availability at any given locality, so variation in prey emphasis is to be expected across habitats. In the Gombe National Park, few potential mammalian prey species remain unexploited by the chimpanzees.[7] Heavy predatory emphasis on the other nonhuman primates (68% of 123 cases) is probably related to prey distributions and densities (Wrangham, 1975) and to the multidimensional mobility of chimpanzees (Teleki, 1973a, 1975, 1977a).

One interesting distinction in the predatory habits of Gombe chimpanzees is that they have not been observed to exploit any of the numerous fish, amphibian, or reptile species available in the park (Wrangham, 1977). The fish (*Stolothrissa* sp.) being dried on the beaches by humans are frequently bypassed, as are skinks (*Mabuya* sp.) and monitor lizards (*Varanus* sp.). These resources are not ignored by collector/predator baboons at Gombe and elsewhere (e.g., Ransom, 1971) and are commonly exploited by gatherer/hunter humans when available (see e.g., Silberbauer, in this volume). Since I cannot account for this difference in ecological terms, I can only speculate that it relates to some form of dietary conservatism or to a lack of recognition that these species are edible.[8]

Environmental Parameters of Predation

The ensuing synopsis focuses on new developments, and to some extent revision of old ones, that pertain to the environmental underpinnings of predatory behavior. Many of the results presented here stem from Richard Wrangham's 12-month study of the behavioral ecology of Gombe chimpanzees in 1972–1973 (Wrangham, 1975, 1977).

Temporal Patterns. Two aspects of predation—diurnal and seasonal variations—can now be outlined on the basis of larger event samples than were previously available.

Graphing of the 30 predatory episodes (12 kills plus 18 attempts) that I observed in 1968–1969 originally led me to speculate that initiation of this activity tends to coincide with a morning peak in other feeding activities (Teleki, 1973a:115–16). Since then it has become apparent that feeding activities on the whole may not peak in the morning hours (Teleki, 1977a), and that this small sample of episodes may have been skewed by the fact that baboons, which were the most common prey in 1968–1969, congregated at the provisioning station in the morning hours when bananas were being distributed to chimpanzees (Wrangham, 1974). Using a later sample of 25 kills, Wrangham (1975) concluded that predatory events are rather evenly distributed throughout the morning, midday, and afternoon periods.

When the two samples are combined for a total of 37 kills, however, the diurnal pattern depicted in figure 9.3 does include a distinct morning peak followed by a gradual tapering off during the midday and afternoon hours. Moreover, when the percentages of time spent feeding on insect resources are added to the graph, it becomes clear that the diurnal distributions of mammal-hunting and insect-collecting activities show considerable overlap.[9] This may be coincidental, or perhaps even an artifact of observing methods, yet I strongly suspect that it is rooted in, and currently related to, more fundamental patterns of resource exploitation. For instance, I lean toward the premise that invertebrate-collecting is the more ancient subsistence pattern from which vertebrate-hunting developed some millions of years ago in the course of chimpanzee (and human?) evolution, and that the temporal overlap exists now because insect-collecting was originally locked into that segment of the diurnal schedule by underlying plant-collecting cycles.

There is already some evidence that diurnal variations in the utilization of faunal resources by chimpanzees are related to fluctuations in the exploitation of floral resources. Wrangham (1977:520–22), for instance,

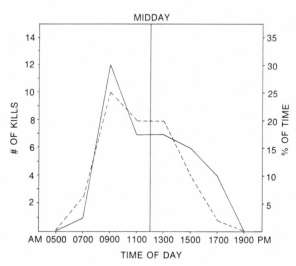

Figure 9.3. Composite graph of diurnal variations in the initiation of predatory episodes (solid line) and in the proportions of time spent feeding on insects (dashed line) by Gombe chimpanzees. Data on 37 kills include 12 from Teleki (1973a) and 25 from Wrangham (1975). Percentage of time spent feeding on insects is from figure 9.2 (*top*, "fauna").

has suggested that "diurnal variation in item quality" might explain some of the fluctuation observed in feeding activities, because alkaloids and other compounds can vary markedly during the day and this is known to affect food selection in other mammals. Alternatively, I have suggested (Teleki, 1977a) that diurnal feeding rhythms may be related to digestive processes, in that moist, fleshy foods with a high sugar content are consumed mainly at the start of an active day when energy requirements are high, while more fibrous foods that are less easily digested and retained longer in the stomach and intestinal tract are eaten mainly in the afternoon and evening, before chimpanzees retire into night nests. Given that plant foods are dietary staples for these apes, exploitation of fauna might be expected to peak at a time when energy requirements are still high but some basic level of satiation has been achieved, i.e., the late morning and midday periods (see fig. 9.2).

Speculative as these interpretations are, they offer promising lines of investigation that might eventually yield specific hypotheses about the origins of primate predatory behavior, supplementing studies that outline behavioral developments (e.g., Teleki, 1975; Rose, 1978) with more concrete ecological/physiological investigations.

Several attempts to link the incidence of predation with seasonal variations in the availability of other resources, at Gombe and elsewhere (Suzuki, 1969, 1971; Teleki, 1973a; Wrangham, 1975), have had little success. The variables involved are numerous and therefore difficult to tease apart when event samples are small.

Seasonal changes in plant productivity are known to influence monthly patterns of food exploitation (Wrangham, 1977), yet predation on mammals apparently is not directly regulated by such environmental factors as temperature, rainfall, or growth rate of vegetation (Teleki, 1977a). But the lack of distinct seasonal cyclicity does not prove that predatory behavior is uninfluenced by ecological factors. It may simply mean that no one has yet managed to pinpoint the regulatory mechanisms. Having conducted thorough tests for relationships between monthly predation rates and such variables as male body weights, salt-licking tendencies, and prey availability, Wrangham was able to conclude only that "the ecological factors affecting predation were therefore apparently not food availability alone" (1975:4.9). He was also unable to show that kills are nonrandomly high in particular months, which is surprising because kills do sometimes occur in runs, with several consecutive episodes falling within hours or days.

My own manipulations of the data have also been largely inconclusive in this regard. Of the kills made by Gombe chimpanzees between 1968 and 1973, 68 cases can be charted according to month of occurrence (fig. 9.4). No clear pattern of seasonal cyclicity is apparent when all kills are lumped,

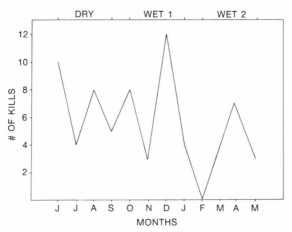

Figure 9.4. Monthly and seasonal distributions of 68 kills made by Gombe chimpanzees between March 1968 and August 1973 (after Teleki, 1973a, and Wrangham, 1975).

nor is it more enlightening to break down the kills by prey species or type. The only pattern I can identify is that mammal-hunting tends to be higher when insect-collecting is a substantial component of the feeding schedule. Between August and December, when a lot of time is devoted to exploiting insect resources, 7.2 kills occurred per month; between January and July, on the other hand, only 4.6 kills occurred per month. As mentioned previously, the significance of this shift is not yet clear. Only a thorough study of the Gombe ecosystem can provide the detailed information needed to decipher what goes on in such a complex situation. Data on prey distributions and densities for different months are particularly desirable.

Spatial Patterns. Most of the 12 kills recorded in my 1968–1969 study occurred at or near the provisioning station in Kakombe Valley (fig. 9.5), and quite likely their spatial distribution was influenced by human activities in that small area (Teleki, 1973a; Wrangham, 1974, 1975). Locations of the 35 kills documented between 1960 and early 1968 are so uncertain that mapping of those data is impossible. However, Wrangham was able to pinpoint 33 kills observed between 1971 and 1973; he concluded that "all predations in Gombe have been seen in or close to forest, where prey species were most often encountered" (1975:4.10). I would add that all kills occurring in canopy forest also occur in valley bottoms because the forest zone tends to follow land contours established by stream watersheds, and there is some possibility that terrain may be as much of a factor in successful predation as are vegetation cover and prey distributions. Other environmental contingencies to success or failure in predation have been discussed elsewhere (Teleki, 1973a; Wrangham, 1975).

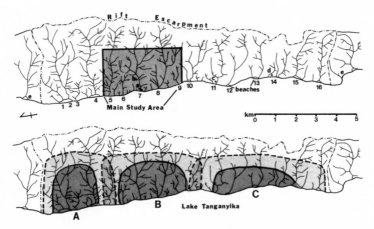

Figure 9.5. Physiographic sketch maps of Gombe National Park, drawn to scale from an aerial photographic mosaic prepared by L. Baldwin and G. Teleki, showing locations of important landmarks and human settlements (*top*) as well as the approximate home ranges and core areas of three chimpanzee communities (*bottom*) as they existed up to 1971 (after Teleki, 1977a).

TOP MAP:

Valley and Streams	*Human Settlements*
1. Mitumba	a. Gombe Stream Research Centre, headquarters
2. Kavusindi	
3. Busindi	**b. Gombe Stream Research Centre,**
4. Rutanga	provisioning station
5. Linda	c. Tanzania National Parks Station,
6. Kasakela	ranger headquarters
7. Kakombe	d. Gombe Valley Research site, pro-
8. Mkenke	posed tourist station
9. Busambo	e. Fishermen's villages, permanent
10. Kahama	settlements
11. Nyasanga	
12. Kalande	
13. Kitwe	
14. Gombe	
15. Bwavi	
16. Nyamagama	

BOTTOM MAP:

Chimpanzee Communities
A. Kavusindi community, 40–50 members
B. Kakombe community, 40–50 members
C. Gombe community, 20–30 members

Range Utilization
Broken lines: Home ranges
Solid lines: Core areas

Primate species are most heavily preyed upon by Gombe chimpanzees, and most of these species utilize the forest zone on a regular basis. Red colobus monkeys, which composed 44% of the kills logged in 1970–1974 (after banana provisioning was reduced to a minimum level), live almost exclusively in the forest component of the Gombe habitat (Clutton-Brock, 1975b). Less is known about the ranging habits of bushbucks and bush pigs, but these mammals have usually been observed in the forest and woodland zones. Only baboons, a mere 8% of the kills logged in 1970–1974, range habitually throughout the grassland–woodland–forest mosaic of the park (Ransom, 1971). Hence, there is nothing remarkable in the fact that Gombe chimpanzees kill most of their prey in or near the forest zone.

Two tangential sources of information are also pertinent here. Gombe chimpanzees do not habitually travel in areas of canopy forest; rather, they are most likely to travel across open grassland or sparse woodland, moving over level or gradually sloping terrain on worn trails (table 9.4).[10] Also, they are more arboreal than terrestrial in only one activity: feeding on plant resources, especially the fruits and nuts that grow mostly on trees and clinging vines (table 9.5).[11] Accordingly, these apes should not be categorized as arboreal, forest-dwelling, brachiating primates (see Napier and Napier, 1967).

When these new perspectives are added to Wrangham's observations (1975) on the spatial distribution of kills, it becomes evident that Gombe

Table 9.4. Proportions of time spent by traveling Gombe chimpanzees in various environmental conditions

Categories	Conditions	%[a]
Route type	Worn trails	82.2
	Cross country	13.4
	Ravines and cliffs	3.4
	Above ground level	1.0
Terrain gradient	Level ground	39.6
	Gradual slope (<30°)	42.0
	Steep slope (>30°)	17.5
	Above ground level	0.9
Vegetation cover	Open grassland	31.4
	Sparse woodland	35.2
	Woodland	6.5
	Canopy forest (open floor)	8.3
	Canopy forest (dense undergrowth)	9.6
	Thicket	9.0

Note: These percentages are based on 6,314 minutes (105.2 hours) of observing traveling activities in each set of conditions (for details, see Teleki, 1977a).
[a]Each category totals 100%.

Table 9.5. Proportions of time spent by Gombe chimpanzees in performing various routine activities in terrestrial versus arboreal settings

Activity categories			% Terrestrial	% Arboreal
Feeding			38.7	61.3
Traveling			99.2	0.8
Resting			65.8	34.2
Interacting			84.5	15.5
Feeding	A.	Fauna	93.7	6.3
	B1.	Foliage	72.1	27.9
	B2.	Fruits & nuts	7.8	92.2
	C.	Miscellaneous	100.0	0.0
Traveling	D.	Climbing	67.9	32.1
	E.	Walking	99.9	0.2
	F.	Running	100.0	0.0
Resting	G.	Sitting upright	59.2	40.8
	H.	Lying supine	85.8	14.2
Interacting	I.	Grooming	83.2	16.8
	J.	Playing	98.1	1.9
	K.	Other	82.9	17.1
Subsistence (feeding + traveling)			56.1	43.9
Maintenance (feeding + traveling + resting)			59.5	40.5
Average diurnal pattern (15-hour span)			63.1	36.9
Average diel pattern (24-hour span)			58.6	41.4

Note: These percentages are based on 47,177 minutes (786.3 hours) of observations in 1968–1971 (details given in Teleki, 1977a).

chimpanzees are (1) competent predators in the forest zone despite their preference for traveling through open grassland and woodland zones, and (2) morphologically and behaviorally equipped to utilize all dimensions of their habitat with equal ease, no matter where prey may be located, despite their tendency to perform nearly all routine activities on the ground. It is difficult for me to envision how such a primate would be deterred from colonizing a fringe woodland habitat or even a savannah habitat comparable to that characterizing much of eastern Africa at the time the earliest hominids emerged (see Isaac and McCown, 1976), or what major adaptive changes would be required for it to become an adept predator on larger game, supplementing an omnivorous diet with meat from regular hunting expeditions.

Sketchy as this picture of chimpanzee life still is, it lends considerable support to the proposition of Mann (1972) and others that chimpanzees are ecologically, behaviorally, socially, and psychologically best suited to serve as a model for reconstructing hominid origins. No other extant nonhuman primate species has equivalent tendencies and talents to exploit an array of resources (leaves, fruits, vertebrates, etc.) in mosaic habitat conditions with complete multidimensional mobility.

Prey Selection. At Gombe, and probably other sites as well, chimpanzees exploit various prey species differentially; therefore numerous questions arise about what factors, aside from the acknowledged observational ones (Teleki, 1973a; Wrangham, 1975), underlie the discrepancies.

One such factor is prey size or, more precisely, the relative sizes of prey and predator. In marked contrast to human hunters, some of whom can individually track down and kill mammals as large as elephants (Harako, in this volume), nonhuman primate predators do not try to capture and kill prey larger than themselves (Teleki, 1973a, 1975). The Gombe chimpanzees (weighing about 40–45 kg) are no exception to this rule even though they exhibit cooperative hunting tactics, technological skills, and other capabilities that might be advantageously applied to killing larger prey. Although Gombe National Park contains few large mammals on which chimpanzees could test their skills, other study areas where predation has been observed are much richer in large game species (see, e.g., Kano, 1971a). Nevertheless, the prey taken by chimpanzees at all sites commonly weighs between 3 and 5 kg, and probably never exceeds 9–10 kg.

In Gombe National Park, the only adult prey taken by chimpanzees is blue, redtail, and colobus monkeys, all of which weigh less than 7 kg. Baboons are commonly taken when less than 6 months of age, though some infants are killed after the color transition from black to buff (about 6 months). Bushbucks and bush pigs are only taken when very young. None of these prey have been weighed in the field, but estimates based on other sources for prey species and on actual weights of chimpanzees at the Gombe Stream Research Centre (L. S. B. Leakey, 1969; van Lawick-Goodall, 1975) indicate that a ratio of 1 kg of prey to 8 kg of predator is representative. This ratio is fairly standard for known omnivorous nonhuman primates (Teleki, 1975:158), and it may hold true for most predatory members of the order, from prosimians that actively prey on insects to chimpanzees that actively prey on mammals. Human gatherer/ hunters are also known to operate within this ratio of body weights, exploiting many kinds of small game, but the ratio reverses for bands that hunt large game such as giraffe and elephant, in which case it may reach 20–25 kg of prey to 1 kg of hunter. Several authors have taken note of this trend (Teleki, 1975; Zihlman and Tanner, in press) in reconstructing early hominid subsistence habits, emphasizing the probable role played by technological materials and skills in the transition from small- to large-game hunting, but no one can be sure how the shift actually occurred.

Prey habits are also likely to influence chimpanzee predation, for each species—indeed, each individual—is vulnerable to a different degree. Among the more important variables discussed in earlier reports (Teleki, 1973a; Wrangham, 1975) are the following: overall distribution and density of prey; exact location of prey at the time predation occurs; environmental conditions at predation sites; prey flight tactics and options during predation; prey defense tactics before, during, and after predation occurs; hunger/satiation levels of the predator; and general resource availability in the habitat.

A brief discussion of predation on red colobus monkeys, drawn mainly from reports by Clutton-Brock (1975a,b), Wrangham (1975) and Busse (1977, 1978), illustrates some of these points with a prey species other than the baboon (Teleki, 1973a,b). Colobus are particularly relevant here because some of the best cases of predatory cooperation at Gombe have involved this species (van Lawick–Goodall, 1968; Wrangham, 1975).

In Gombe National Park, red colobus monkeys normally move around their home range area (about 1 km^2 of evergreen and semideciduous forest) in social units numbering 40–80 individuals. Troop members may be clumped or dispersed, sometimes covering an area as large as 0.2 km^2, and solitary adults are also encountered. I originally hypothesized that colobus monkeys—in fact, all prey of suitable body size living in large social units—are especially vulnerable to chimpanzee predation because their movements and vocalizations tend to act as beacons. Solitary prey, on the other hand, are much more difficult to locate and are encountered largely by chance. Based on the ease with which chimpanzees wade into large baboon troops to capture infants, I also surmised that chimpanzees working singly or collectively run little risk of harm in confrontations with monkey troops.

The more than 50 cases of predation on colobus monkeys observed since 1970 add considerably to these initial speculations. It now appears, for example, that canopy discontinuity is a basic requirement for predation. As Wrangham states, "in continuous canopy the monkeys were usually ignored, in broken canopy they were not" (1975:4.11). Dispersed trees, or emergent trees reaching well above the canopy layer, often become traps for the colobus, limiting its opportunities to escape pursuing chimpanzees. Certain types of trees (e.g., *Albizia* spp.) are especially dangerous for monkeys because of their structural features: stable, spreading boughs on which chimpanzees can move easily and swiftly, and tapering end branches that tend to sag when a fleeing colobus tries to leap away. If several adult chimpanzees surround a lone monkey in this situation, or manage to isolate one from a troop, with one or two chimpanzees climbing up to start pursuit as others disperse on the ground below to cut off potential escape routes, the prey has little chance of evading the predators. The risk of capture in broken canopy is also higher because retaliatory attacks by adult colobus monkeys attempting to defend a troop member are hampered in this situation. Mobbing tactics, for instance, are probably most effective in continuous canopy.[12] Defensive action may add some risk, however, in that adult females protecting infants are themselves killed and eaten on occasion (Wrangham, 1975). Multiple kills of colobus have been observed several times, yet adult males are apparently exempt from the risk of being killed during troop defense maneuvers, possibly because they are larger and more formidable: adult males successfully defended their troops on at least 12 occasions, and so far none have been killed and eaten by Gombe chimpanzees (Busse, 1977). Finally, lone adult monkeys may suffer higher casualties than adults attached to troops (Wrangham, 1975).[13]

In sum, the optimum conditions for chimpanzee predation on colobus monkeys, and probably on other arboreal mammals, would include: discontinuous tree canopy that inhibits escape; presence of prey that is solitary or at least isolated from the troop, such that risk of retaliation is low; trees of suitable size and structure to enable chimpanzees to move with speed and coordination. Optimum conditions on the ground have been discussed elsewhere (Teleki, 1973a).

Primate prey usually gives alarm calls and flees when confronted by predatory chimpanzees (Busse, 1977; Teleki, 1973a). Evasive and defensive tactics are known to all prey species at Gombe, and some tactics are very successful, such as an attack by baboons on a serval (Teleki, 1973a), while others seem to have no effect. When infant bushbucks react by becoming immobile (the classic "freezing" response), the chimpanzees may counter by climbing into trees for a better view. In contrast to primates whose diurnal habits add to their vulnerability, bushbucks and bush pigs have the advantage of being crepuscular. Yet Gombe chimpanzees are highly successful predators despite all these factors, even though they are basically omnivores.

Gombe chimpanzees exploit various prey species at different rates, although the figures in table 9.3 are not necessarily representative of natural selectivity. For instance, the baboon figure is probably high, owing to banana provisioning, while the blue and redtail figures may be low, because observers did not notice small monkeys in dense vegetation. Wrangham's more detailed picture (1975) based on 82 of the most reliable predation records in the Gombe Stream Research Centre files, covering four different periods of investigation between 1960 and 1973 and excluding all kills made at the provisioning station, implies that there is a kill rate of 33 colobus monkeys, 23 bush pigs, 14 bushbucks, 2 redtail monkeys, 2 blue monkeys, and 1 baboon per year by the 48 chimpanzees exploiting a home range area of about 8 km^2 in the central study area. Since the variation among these estimated rates does not appear to be related to relative frequencies of contacts between chimpanzees and various prey species (Wrangham, 1975), it is more plausible that the differential emphasis is related to prey population parameters. Formal censusing of mammal populations in Gombe National Park, or even in the central study area, has not yet been attempted, and so this hypothesis cannot be confirmed. Consequently, it is not clear which extrinsic factors (such as prey distribution or density) or which intrinsic factors (such as hunting tactics or even taste) are likely to be the key regulators of prey selection.

One other point warrants attention. Some mammals present but not preyed upon in Gombe National Park (e.g., the giant rat, *Cricetomys* and the bush baby, *Galago*) are killed and eaten at other chimpanzee study sites, and some mammals that do occur in Gombe National Park and would seem to be suitable as prey (e.g., the duiker, *Sylvicapra*) have not been listed as known chimpanzee prey species for the area. If the fact that chimpanzees at Gombe do not eat these animals can be confirmed in future studies, the implication is that prey selection varies from one chimpanzee population to another, perhaps in line with variations in other subsistence activities (see C. M. Hladik, 1977b; Nishida, 1974; Suzuki, 1971; Wrangham, 1977). Differences among neighboring regional populations may also be recognized eventually, thereby adding considerable weight to the notion that chimpanzees have some cultural propensities (J. Goodall, 1976; McGrew and Tutin, 1978; Teleki, 1973d, 1974; van Lawick–Goodall, 1973).

Rates of Predation. Omnivorous primates need not and do not practice predation regularly, as must the carnivores; it is to be expected that performance of this subsistence activity varies across time and space in both nonhuman and human primate species. But this irregularity presents researchers with a special problem, quite unlike the routine logging of kills among other predatory mammals (Eaton, 1974; Kruuk, 1972; Schaller, 1972). In primate studies, kill (and attempt) frequencies must often be inferred from indirect evidence, always taking account of variations in observation time, and predation rates can be estimated only by juggling various kinds of data until the most reasonable, and preferably most conservative, results are obtained. The complexity of this analytical process has been discussed by Wrangham (1975), Strum (1976a), and Hausfater (1976).

The simplest, most direct measure of predation rate within a single primate social unit is tabulation of the number of episodes logged within a given span of observation time. The crude estimates derived from my 1968–1969 study in Gombe National Park, where I surmised that a total of 150 chimpanzees make about 30 kills and 45 attempts per year, did not include the variable of observation time because research in the park was neither continuous nor methodical in the early years (Teleki, 1973a:57). Predation data collected at other chimpanzee research sites have also been largely incidental and anecdotal, precluding any attempt to estimate rates in a meaningful way. Even the fecal analysis conducted by Suzuki (1969), and later used quite erroneously by Gaulin and Kurland (1976) to develop a bioenergetic model of predation in baboons and chimpanzees,[14] falls far short of desirable levels of precision.

According to Wrangham (1975), who collated all kills observed in a 3-year period except those involving baboons habituated to human observers, predation by Gombe chimpanzees occurs at a rate of 0.5 kills/100 hours of observation. Focusing only on kills of colobus, Busse (1977) estimates a rate of 1 kill/100 hours of observation. Several skeptics have recently argued that all such estimates, including the more conservative one offered in my earlier reports, are exceptionally high and out of line with other nonhuman primate populations (see Gaulin and Kurland, 1976; Reynolds, 1975) even though similarly complete figures are not available from other chimpanzee sites for comparison (Wrangham, 1975). These authors also neglect the even higher estimates of predation rates by baboon populations: 1.8 kills/100 hours of observation at Amboseli (Hausfater, 1976); 4.5 kills/100 hours at Gilgil in 1970–1971 (Harding, 1973a); 8.3 kills/100 hours at Gilgil in 1972–1974 (Strum, 1975a). I am neither informed enough nor naive enough to debate whether these figures are representative of "normal" predation rates for the species in question, which seems to be a rather minor point in any case, given that variability among individuals, social units, and regional populations is not only expectable but completely in line with the basic tenets of Darwinian evolution. Of far greater significance, I believe, is the demonstration of the degree to which collector/predator primates such as baboons and chimpanzees can expand their subsistence economies, given appropriately conducive conditions, in an omnivorous direction. Be they latent or overt, the capabilities needed for practicing regular predation on mammals are an evolutionary legacy shared by monkeys, apes, and humans.

From data covering all kills observed between August 1970 and August 1973, excluding those involving habituated baboons near the Gombe station, Wrangham (1975) estimates that a chimpanzee community kills some 75 mammalian prey (minimum = 50, maximum = 76) per year, comprising about 44% colobus, 31% bush pig, 18% bushbuck, 3% redtail, 3% blue monkey, and 1% baboon. If there are 3–4 communities in Gombe National Park (Teleki, Hunt, and Pfifferling, 1976), the resident chimpanzees would kill about 225–300 mammals per year. According to Wrangham 1975:4.32), each prey species would, on this basis, incur a substantial loss to predation by chimpanzees. Focusing again on colobus prey, Busse (1977:908) calculates that 8–13% of the local colobus population is lost each year to predatory chimpanzees. Similar estimates are not yet available for other nonhuman primate populations, but these figures are in line with the kill rates of some large carnivores: 11% of the wildebeest population and 9% of the zebra population were killed by hyenas in Ngorongoro Crater (Kruuk, 1972), and 5.2–5.9% of the zebra population was killed by lions in the Serengeti (Schaller, 1972). Whether we postulate that internal psychological or social motivations underlie their predatory proclivities, or hypothesize that a vacant niche lacking competitive large carnivores (except the occasional leopard) is being filled by these omnivorous apes, Gombe chimpanzees emerge as competent, skilled predators whose impact on the local fauna is greater than anyone expected. Given comparable data on prey exploitation by human band societies, and keeping in mind differences in utilization of small versus large game by apes and humans, one should eventually be able to combine information on the impact of each upon local fauna and then to construct a reasonably accurate model of early hominid subsistence economy. Explorations of demographic homologies (Teleki, Hunt, and Pfifferling, 1976) and behavioral homologies (McGrew and Tutin, 1978) have already been initiated, and a similar approach to the study of subsistence habits should be equally productive.

Meat Intake. My 1968–1969 study of predatory behavior did not yield data suitable for estimating meat intake over hourly, daily, or yearly intervals. Tentative suggestions that mammalian meat constitutes less than 1% (Teleki, 1973a:58) or 1–3% (Busse, 1977:908) of the total annual diet can now be reexamined in the light of more complete evidence compiled since 1970 at the Gombe Stream Research Centre.

Basing his calculations on an estimated predation rate of 75 kills per year by a chimpanzee community, and on rough estimates of 3–5 kg per prey individual, Wrangham (1975:4.34) proposes that 321 kg of mammalian meat are consumed by 31 adult chimpanzees, for an average intake of 10 kg per chimpanzee per year. Speculative though it is, this figure provides an order of magnitude with some comparative value. Lee (1969), for example, estimates meat intake among the !Kung Bushmen at about 256 g per person per day. That is about 9.5 times the estimated figure of 27 g per chimpanzee per day, but even this amount is hardly what one would expect from a "frugivorous" ape.

During my 12-month study, the 12 observed kills accounted for a net 43 hours of time spent eating meat in a single chimpanzee community (Teleki, 1973a). Extrapolation to 75 kills would therefore yield about 270 hours of predatory activity per year (or 0.74 hours per day). If in a given year the average adult chimpanzee spends 42.8% of his/her time on feeding, about 10% of the total annual feeding budget is devoted to predation on mammals. For obvious reasons, this figure is not equivalent to meat intake, but it does indicate a high level of interest. Moreover, as the average duration of meat-eating episodes is 3.5 hours, with about 8 chimpanzees obtaining meat in each consumption period (Teleki, 1973a,b), Gombe chimpanzees can consume meat at the rate of about 110–180 g per chimpanzee per hour.[15] According to McGrew (1974), ant-collecting yields about 70 g per chimpanzee per hour. Thus, predation on mammals seems to be a higher-yield activity than collection of safari ants, which may explain in part why chimpanzees accept the higher risk and greater energy output involved in predatory behavior. It may also be significant that pursuit, capture, and consumption of animals are primarily male activities (Teleki, 1973a; Wrangham, 1975), while collection of insects such as weaver ants, safari ants, and termites is primarily a female activity (McGrew, 1974, 1979). As a result, adult male chimpanzees benefit most from actively seeking mobile prey and adult female chimpanzees benefit most from leisurely exploitation of invertebrate resources. The evolutionary implications of these observations are extensively discussed by McGrew (1979), and I concur with his points.

In my earlier reports on chimpanzee predatory behavior, I presented various kinds of evidence supporting the premise that predation on vertebrates has more social than nutritional benefits (Teleki, 1973a, 1975). Both erroneous and legitimate objections have since been raised against this viewpoint (de Pelham and Burton, 1976, 1977; Wrangham, 1975), objections to which I have replied (Teleki, 1977b), but the debate has unfolded in what amounts to an information vacuum. I did not and do not reject nutritional value as one consequence of predation, but I believe that an ape as complex as the chimpanzee can operate at different levels of benefit and is quite capable of performing actions that are energetically costly when there are social advantages to be gained. As Wrangham (1975) has aptly noted, however, only when we discover what nutrients are essential to wild chimpanzees, and what nutrients are obtained from fauna versus flora, will the biochemical benefits of predatory behavior become clearer.

Scavenging for Meat. With the exception of a few baboon cases observed at Gilgil in recent years (Strum, in this volume), nonhuman primates that actively prey on mammals do not seem highly motivated to eat carrion (Teleki, 1975:159). All experiments conducted with collector/predator baboons and chimpanzees at sites where predatory behavior is frequent— experiments in which various kinds of meat, including carcasses of species normally preyed upon, were offered for examination—have thus far failed to stimulate a meat-eating response (van Lawick–Goodall, 1968). Among chimpanzees, the dietary conservatism of adults extends to numerous types of flora, fauna, and novel objects placed in clearings and along trails by humans (Kortlandt, 1967; van Lawick–Goodall, 1968). Moreover, foods that are naturally available on a particular day or week are not always exploited (Wrangham, 1975). There have even been cases where chimpanzees, upon discovering the corpse of a species normally preyed upon, have responded as though it were a dead conspecific (Ransom, 1971; Teleki, 1973d).

The only behavior in chimpanzees that resembles scavenging is the appropriation of bushbuck carcasses from Gombe baboons (Morris and Goodall, 1977). The meat is always quite fresh, however, because such pirating occurs within seconds or minutes of capture by the baboons. These cases certainly demonstrate that direct competition for favored foods sometimes occurs between two omnivorous primate species exploiting the same habitat, but they are questionably definable as authentic scavenging. My impression is that this appropriative behavior is unlike the classic scavenging described by Kruuk (1972), Schaller (1972), and others studying large carnivores, and is instead deeply embedded in a special set of affinitive/aggressive relationships that exist between baboons and chimpanzees living in Gombe National Park. Other elements of that special relationship run a gamut from play to predation (Morris and Goodall, 1977; Teleki, 1973a; van Lawick–Goodall, 1968, 1975).

In view of these observations, I am puzzled that the original notion of a "scavenger phase" in hominid evolution (L. S. B. Leakey, 1967a; F. C. Howell, 1968; Pfeiffer, 1969) has recently regained popularity among scholars concerned with the hominid fossil record (Read-Martin and Read, 1975), with primate evolution (Szalay, 1975), and with carnivore behavior (King, 1975; Peters and Mech, 1975). Evidence to the contrary has been appearing regularly over the same span of years (J. Goodall and Hamburg, 1975; Harding, 1973a; Shipman and Phillips, 1976; Strum, 1976a; Teleki, 1975), but with little apparent effect.

The power of the scavenger hypothesis seems to be linked closely to propositions initially developed by Schaller and Lowther (1969); in a paper widely quoted by proponents of the hypothesis, they argued that a comprehensive model of early hominid subsistence and society must be based on data from contemporary band societies, living nonhuman primates, and extant social carnivores. Ironically, Schaller and Lowther themselves rejected the scavenger hypothesis (1969:326) on the grounds that scavenging is not a separate evolutionary stage of subsistence activity among carnivorous mammals but merely an adjunct to predatory adaptations. To emphasize their conclusion, they quoted DeVore and Washburn's comment that "the hunting of small animals and defenseless young is much more likely to lie at the root of the human hunting habit" (1963:365).

Predator–Prey Relations. Relations between chimpanzees and some prey species, such as bush pigs, are quite normal—there are no interspecific social interactions, the chimpanzees consistently show predatory interest upon encountering pigs, and the pigs exhibit standard prey responses when discovered by roving chimpanzees. This pattern is common in most predator–prey systems (see e.g., M. Fox, 1975).

Relations between chimpanzees and other prey species, however, are far more unusual and enigmatic. To begin with, Gombe chimpanzees interact amicably with many of the primates upon which they also prey (Morris and Goodall, 1977; Teleki, 1973a; van Lawick–Goodall, 1971, 1975). The range of interactions observed between chimpanzees and baboons, for example, includes playing and grooming as well as aggression, submission, and even copulation. In addition, some communicative signals are mutually understood and may be used to elicit specific social responses.

There is also considerable niche overlap between chimpanzees and various monkeys, providing frequent opportunities for encounters while traveling and feeding. These encounters range from complete tolerance to mutual avoidance, and from sociable interplay to aggressive displacement (Teleki, 1973a; van Lawick–Goodall, 1968). The maturation and socialization of chimpanzees is not a purely intraspecific process, for youngsters of different species are particularly likely to interact in a variety of ways. In some instances, these relations are apparently so firmly established that adults exhibit special affiliative bonds.

This aspect of the predatory behavior of Gombe chimpanzees intrigues human observers, who often find it difficult to understand how socialization and predation can coexist. One is at first inclined to reject the dilemma as being a phenomenon peculiar to Gombe chimpanzees, whose behavior has admittedly been modified in many ways by some of the research techniques employed in the 1960s (Teleki, Hunt, and Pfifferling, 1976; Wrangham, 1974). This is not an acceptable solution, however, because the entire predator–prey system in Gombe National Park has not been uniformly altered by research protocols, and also because a similar set of relations occurs elsewhere. In the Amboseli Game Reserve, for instance, baboons socialize with and prey upon vervet monkeys (Altmann and Altmann, 1970). It is possible, therefore, that this situation occurs in many other predator–prey systems involving two kinds of primates. If so, then problems arise with the premise that the arboreal adaptations of primates were in part a response to predator pressures on small ground-dwelling mammals some millions of years ago (see Wood Jones, 1926). When these observations are coupled with the omnivorous habits and multidimensional mobility characterizing the order (Teleki, in press), they imply that primates may long have been the chief prey of other primates, which in turn implies that the arboreal niche would hardly have served as a refuge from predator pressure.

No less interesting is the fact that 75% of the bushbucks eaten by Gombe chimpanzees were appropriated from baboons (McGrew, 1979). Several of these pirating cases were described by Morris and Goodall (1977), who stress the anomalous nature of an interspecific relationship that includes play with baboons, consumption of baboons, and competition with baboons for at least one kind of prey.

Frankly, I am no closer to a satisfactory explanation of this puzzling phenomenon than I was 10 years ago, when I first saw chimpanzees eat a young baboon who was a regular play partner of several infant chimpanzees (Teleki, 1973a). It is particularly intriguing to me that predatory chimpanzees have not been injured in any of these interactions. The working hypothesis I advanced to account for some aspects of these interspecific relationships—namely, that interspecific socialization somehow inhibits the normal retaliatory responses of baboons (Teleki, 1973a:154)—is now even less tenable because relations between chimpanzees and colobus monkeys, which have since become the major prey species, are somewhat different. According to Busse (1977:908), adult male colobus monkeys frequently and successfully attack chimpanzees in both predatory and nonpredatory situations, sometimes sending them into precipitious flight. Moreover, active defensive tactics can clearly be functional, for 12 out of 33 unsuccessful attempts involved several male colobus chasing chimpanzees through the forest canopy. Gombe chimpanzees nevertheless continue to prey, with considerable skill and efficiency, and with little risk of injury, on large troops of primates. The impact of such predation is not negligible: the Gombe chimpanzees removed 8% of the local baboon population in 1968–1969 (Teleki, 1973a), and 8–13% of the local colobus population in 1973–1974 (Busse, 1977). How is it possible, then, that the primates serving as prey to chimpanzees in Gombe National Park, and possibly also at other sites, have not developed more successful defensive tactics? Any answer other than the proposition that chimpanzees have only recently acquired predatory inclinations, for which there is no supportive evidence at all (Teleki, 1973a), would be welcome.

Behavioral Parameters of Predation

The basic elements of chimpanzee predatory behavior have been described and analyzed extensively by several authors who worked at different research sites.[16] At the Gombe Stream Research Centre, the behavioral aspects of this subsistence activity have been documented mainly by van Lawick–Goodall (1968), Teleki (1973a,b, 1975), Wrangham (1975), and Busse (1977). These and other special reports dealing with specific topics, such as tool use in connection with predation, are briefly reviewed here in order to survey new developments and to highlight points of debate.

Cooperation in Pursuing Prey. When ethnographers write about cooperative hunting in band societies, few are inclined to question their use of the term "cooperation" because we automatically assume that this is a standard procedure in human hunting ventures (see Bicchieri, 1972; Lee and DeVore, 1968a). Yet humans sometimes hunt alone and sometimes in groups (see, e.g., Harako, in this volume), practicing cooperation in some situations but not in others (see e.g., Woodburn, 1968a). Moreover, the widespread assumption that cooperation is the basis of human hunting activities is rarely substantiated by empirical data, for ethnographers usually do not provide detailed descriptions of subsistence activities. An action-by-action comparison of hunting behavior in baboons, chimpanzees, and humans is therefore impossible. And, since we lack an operational definition of cooperative hunting among humans, it is equally difficult to determine what degree of overlap exists in these species.

Another problem is that even the most detailed descriptions of cooperative behavior among nonhuman primates are based in part on the human observer's intuitive judgment, because the actions themselves are not always obviously different from noncooperative behavior. The total context can be a decisive factor in correctly identifying cooperative behavior, but that requires very close observation of predator as well as prey maneuvers. No single action can be labeled as diagnostic of cooperation. Many cases of cooperative predatory behavior have been logged by Gombe researchers (Teleki, 1973a; van Lawick–Goodall, 1968; Wrangham, 1975), yet some authors still harbor reservations about "the extent to which chimpanzee predatory behavior can be termed cooperative" (Busse, 1978:767).

The issue warrants further consideration and field study, not because these doubts threaten to refute the presence of cooperative behavior among wild chimpanzees, but rather because they illustrate the absence of an operational definition based on empirical evidence. Although I reject Busse's premise that successful predation by a lone chimpanzee demonstrates that collective action is not necessary,[17] I fully agree that "data are unavailable to determine whether group hunting in fact offers any advantage to chimpanzees preying upon infant baboons" (Busse, 1978:767). As I noted some years ago, it is very puzzling that cooperative chasing and stalking of prey are practiced at all if these tactics often fail (Teleki, 1973a:132). The fact remains, however, that Gombe chimpanzees do pursue various prey species, including baboons and colobus monkeys (Teleki, 1973a; van Lawick–Goodall, 1968, 1971), in a coordinated manner, with 2–9 adults positioning and repositioning themselves to maintain an enclosure, sometimes for an hour or more, to effectively anticipate and cut off all potential escape routes of the prey.

A more telling point raised by Busse (1978) is that predatory group size is inversely proportional to the rate of success in capturing colobus prey, with lone individuals being the most successful (31%) and groups of 5 or more being the least successful (15%). Yet these data do not justify concluding that cooperation is counterproductive when no empirical measure of cooperative behavior is given. It is not cooperative action merely because many individuals are present when pursuit begins (Teleki, 1973a); the real question is whether cooperation increases the probability of making captures when a large chimpanzee group encounters prey. If a 15% success rate drops to 5% in the absence of cooperative behavior, then cooperation is advantageous.

Given the information now on record, I submit that cooperative behavior is performed by wild chimpanzees, in predatory and perhaps other contexts, but that its functions remain unclear. Moreover, bioenergetic models of predatory behavior, such as the one outlined by Busse (1977, 1978), may fail to uncover solid explanations because they exclude social motivations for acting cooperatively. As in the case of human hunting behavior, chimpanzee predatory behavior is a complex subsistence activity in which success depends on multiple factors, among them terrain and vegetation cover, location and behavior of the prey , and individual predatory skills, and in which motivation derives from both social and nutritional rewards (Busse, 1977; Teleki 1973a; Wrangham, 1975). It is no easy task to define the role of cooperative behavior within this complex system, yet there is no reason to reject the occurrence of cooperative behavior (among chimpanzees or humans) on the grounds that individuals are more apt to be successful than groups. As Harako (in this volume) and others have noted, there may be optimum numbers of participants for different forms of group hunting, with failure more likely when these optimum levels are not met.

Distribution of Meat. During 43 hours of meat-eating activity observed during 1968–1969, segments of carcasses, ranging in size from small slivers to entire haunches, were widely distributed among 4–15 participants in predatory episodes, with consumption time being directly proportional to attendance numbers, regardless of prey weight (Teleki, 1973a). Meat is distributed in several ways: by removing pieces (without asking permission) from an owner's portion, by overtly requesting shares from owners, or by simply recovering dropped fragments. Excluding the third method, which by definition is always successful, Gombe chimpanzees share meat at an average rate of once every 8.6 minutes. Requests, which involve active solicitation with postures, gestures, and vocalizations, occur every 6.5 minutes and are successful every 22.5 minutes (Teleki, 1975). Voluntary offers of small and sometimes large portions have also been observed. Sharing of plant foods is perhaps less common and less intense but does occur with some regularity in Gombe National Park (McGrew, 1975, 1979; Wrangham, 1975).

The fact that a 3-kg carcass can be distributed among as many as 15 chimpanzees who spend up to 9 hours sharing and consuming the meat contributed greatly to the premise that predatory behavior among these apes has a social as well as a nutritional basis (Teleki, 1973a:171–73). Assuming maximum and even distribution among participants, this would amount to about 200 g of meat (muscles, viscera, bones, teeth, skin, etc., all of which are consumed) per chimpanzee over nearly a day of active participation.[18] This is not much by any standard, but perhaps enough to add important supplements to the diet if 75 or more prey are taken annually (Wrangham, 1975). The question of social versus nutritional benefits must remain open until more detailed investigations can be conducted at Gombe or other sites.

Whatever the motivations that prompt chimpanzees to prey on various fauna, their sharing of meat and to some extent other resources has been firmly established at several research sites. As yet there are no indications that predatory behavior varies significantly from one area to another, but that view may well change when more systematic observations accumulate in several localities. There is already some evidence, however, that factors such as sexual receptivity in females, kinship ties within matrifocal units, relative age, and perhaps social status are important in regulating meat distribution (Teleki, 1973a; Wrangham, 1975). That these and other factors have also been identified as regulators of meat-sharing in several band societies (Bicchieri, 1972; Lee and DeVore, 1968a; Marshall, 1976) is of some significance, indicating a common ancestral source for the subsistence habits exhibited today by these genera.

In view of this evidence, I am surprised that efforts continue, in some circles, to downplay the presence of sharing behavior among nonhuman primates (Isaac and Crader, in this volume; Lancaster, 1978) or to altogether deny its presence outside the hominid line (Pilbeam, 1972). Data on nonhuman primate sharing behavior are a matter of record for several species, in both captive and wilderness settings (Dare, 1974), and more evidence accumulates each year. At what point can we expect the data to reach a critical mass sufficient to dispel the notion that human sharing behavior is unique within this mammalian order? Is it so unbelievable that the hourly rate of meat-sharing behavior might be similar for collector/predator chimpanzees and gatherer/hunter humans? And if that turns out to be the case, what arbitrary criteria will we then apply to distinguish between the sharing behavior of Gombe chimpanzees and, let us say, Kalahari Bushmen? My own view is that in this instance frequency is less diagnostic than form, and that chimpanzee meat-sharing clusters exhibit all the basic behavioral and social forms of human meat-sharing interactions, though the absence of language in monkeys and apes probably limits the complexity of the exchange system to some degree.

Competition over Meat. After a carcass is divided among those adults (usually males) who participated in pursuing or capturing the prey, other chimpanzees assemble around the owners of large meat portions. Once the sharing clusters form and the participants settle down to consuming and distributing meat, aggressive competition is rare in comparison to other social interactions. Only 68 instances of mild aggression and 17 instances of violent aggression[19] were logged during 43 hours of meat-eating activity in 1968-1969, while 579 instances of meat-exchange interactions occurred in the same span of time (Teleki, 1973a). Other amicable interactions, ranging from copulation to grooming, are also common at predatory episodes involving many chimpanzees, so the overall rate of interaction is even higher than these figures indicate. Aggressive behavior during meat-eating does not appear to have a disruptive influence on chimpanzee society, contrary to what occurs among some social carnivores (Schaller, 1972:132), although there is some indication that success in establishing control of meat distribution enhances chimpanzee social status in the long run (Teleki, 1973a). Comparative data on competition over meat among human gatherer/hunters are unfortunately not available.

My conclusions about the low incidence of aggressive competition at predatory episodes have since been questioned by Wrangham (1975) and others, who claim that aggression is more common in this context than in other social situations. Detailed analysis of long-term rates of aggression, obtained by Wrangham (1974) from records of chimpanzee attendance at the Kakombe Valley station on nonprovisioning days, indicate that the frequency of aggressive attacks is generally low among Gombe chimpanzees, averaging 0.2 attacks per day, and that the number of attacks does not rise with increase of group size. In this light, competition is certainly greater at predatory events, where 4–5 severe attacks occur per observation day (12 hours) according to my estimates. It is also true, however, that overt competition for meat is rarely productive—only 15% of attacks on owners resulted in meat appropriation (Wrangham, 1975).

Participation by Sex and Age. Less than 4% of the chimpanzee kills documented in Gombe National Park have been made by adult females and adolescent males (McGrew, 1979). Exceptions include 3 adult females killing bush pigs and 2 adolescent males killing monkeys (Wrangham, 1975). Predation on mammals is, in effect, an adult male domain, with males performing most pursuing, capturing, and consuming activities, and with *control* males presiding over meat distribution (Teleki, 1973a). Since pursuit is undertaken almost exclusively by adult males, who then become the owners of major portions and play key roles in cluster formation and meat distribution, adult females depend almost entirely on mature males for their meat intake. In my 1968–1969 study, 80% of the observed taking and requesting interactions consisted of adult male owners being approached by adult females or adult males seeking shares, and the adult females accounted for 41% of all interactions in 9 combinations of age–sex classes (Teleki, 1973a, 1975).

As mentioned earlier, high social status does not guarantee a key position in group pursuit or capture of prey, nor does it necessarily lead to control of meat distribution. Wrangham's analysis (1975) of a different sample of events has confirmed this point and added the conclusion that success in obtaining meat has a strong positive correlation with age.[20] Thus, seniority (i.e., experience?) as well as sexual attractiveness and kinship ties are important prerequisites in obtaining meat at predatory episodes.

The relevance of these observations to reconstructing the origins of labor division—which is perceived by many as a cornerstone of hominid social organization (e.g., Watanabe, 1968)—has recently been enhanced by studies of the insect-collecting habits of wild chimpanzees (McGrew, 1974; Nishida, 1972a; Teleki, 1974). Of greatest interest is McGrew's discovery (1979) that insect-eating is primarily an adult female domain. Using information gleaned from 7,461 observation hours logged at the Gombe Stream Research Centre in 1972–1974, McGrew clearly demonstrates that female chimpanzees exploit various invertebrates (such as termites, weaver ants, and safari ants) up to twice as much as males do. Moreover, since females benefit to some extent from male predatory activities while males do not benefit directly from female collecting activities, it is possible that the annual intake of fauna is greater among females than among males. That is, community exploitation of faunal resources may yield the greatest net benefit to female chimpanzees.

In complete agreement with McGrew (1979), I suggest that these sex differences are an incipient form of labor division that evolved, in the hominid line (perhaps in tandem with a shift toward hunting larger game), toward the more rigidly patterned forms of labor division observable today among gatherer/hunter band societies (Galdikas and Teleki, 1981).

Technological Skills. The technological skills of wild chimpanzees have been widely publicized since J. Goodall (1964) first observed termite-collecting behavior in Gombe National Park. Since then, information about these skills has been obtained at many sites in equatorial Africa, permitting some tentative generalization about technological *complexes* that vary from region to region (Teleki, 1974). Gombe chimpanzees exhibit a technological repertoire that includes most but not all of the skills and materials that occur elsewhere (J. Goodall, 1964; McGrew, 1974, 1977, 1979; Teleki, 1974; van Lawick–Goodall, 1970).

Given the varied technological skills of wild chimpanzees, I am surprised that only two cases of tool use in a predatory context have been recorded at any research site. The first was an adult male wiping brain tissue from a baboon skull with a crumpled wad of leaves (Teleki, 1973a:144). And on 26 October 1972, Frans Plooij (1978) observed an adult male chimpanzee throw a large stone, measuring $25 \times 10 \times 10$ cm, at an adult bush pig during a cooperative predation on a group of pigs. The stone hit but did not visibly injure the pig, yet it retreated sufficiently from its protective stance over a small piglet for another chimpanzee to make the capture. This represents only one case of weapon use in over 200 observations of predatory behavior, but I predict that more such incidents will be reported in time.

It is instructive that the chimpanzee, a species noted for its technological skills in other contexts, rarely use tools in predation. Many authors have assumed that early hominids required a toolkit in order to become effective hunters (e.g., Tiger and Fox, 1971), yet it is clear that chimpanzees can prey efficiently upon mammals without recourse to tools; this in turn implies that early hominids may not have applied technological skills in the hunting context until big-game hunting tactics emerged over a million years ago.

My impression, based on these and other observations reported by field primatologists, is that technological skills may well have been applied initially in plant- and invertebrate-collecting activities. The grasses, vines, and sticks used by chimpanzees for so many purposes are excellent prototypes for the digging sticks carried by many gatherer/hunters. These simplest of implements are useful in exploiting various subsurface fauna and flora (see also Mann, 1972; Coursey, 1973). Use of projectiles in a predatory context, as observed among Gombe chimpanzees, may actually have emerged as an aid in threatening and scaring away, or even stampeding, prey animals attempting to protect their young from capture. Once successfully applied to such a purpose, however, the further use of tools in killing and butchering large prey would be a small step toward hominization.

Transporting Meat. Wild chimpanzees carry many kinds of objects, especially prized food items, in a variety of situations (Teleki, 1975; McGrew, 1979), and can do so while traveling quadrupedally, tripedally, or bipedally (Teleki, 1977a, 1978). That chimpanzee carrying behavior is less efficient than human methods of transporting objects while striding bipedally (Hewes, 1961) cannot be denied. But that discrepancy is not enough to justify the claim that nonhuman primates "neither share nor carry" (Lancaster, 1978:86), for chimpanzees, baboons, and other non-human primates are known to carry objects from one place to another (e.g., Bauer, 1977; Rose, 1976, 1977). Adult chimpanzees carry some items, such as termite-collecting tools, for considerable distances (several hundred meters, or more) when there is motivation to do so (Teleki, 1974).

Although most food is processed and consumed where it is collected or killed, Gombe chimpanzees do transport prey, or at least carcass sections, for distances of several kilometers, sometimes keeping bones or skins for 2–3 days of routine travel within the home range (Teleki, 1975; McGrew, 1979). However, because these chimpanzees forage and nest in different locations nearly every day, rarely using the same sites on consecutive days unless there happens to be a concentration of food nearby, they have little incentive to carry objects repeatedly to a particular spot in the home range area. To be sure, there are preferred zones of activity for both males and females (Teleki, 1977a; Wrangham, 1975), but nothing that corresponds to a settlement or encampment such as we commonly find among human band societies. Transportation of food and other objects may therefore have developed largely in conjunction with the advent of temporary group settlement at favorable sites (see Speth and Davis, 1976). A strong impetus toward labor division may also have appeared in connection with these developments. But neither object transportation nor labor division was devised by early hominds; both must have been inherited, in rudimentary if not complex forms, from common ancestors of apes and humans.

CONCLUDING REMARKS

No one person can sketch a scenario of hominid origins and evolution that is both accurate and appealing to the many scholars concerned with tracing human ancestry. Yet that is precisely what we all—as ethnographers, paleoanthropologists, primatologists, and so on—strive to do when we conduct research or write articles and books. Indeed, the motivation to enter this arena of theorizing is often the hope that *the* significant insight will come from a particular line of investigation. In the process, we run through evolutionary models of various kinds, from savannah baboons (DeVore and Washburn, 1963) to chimpanzees (Teleki, 1975), and from social carnivores (Schaller and Lowther, 1969) to human gatherer/hunter societies (Washburn and Lancaster, 1968), finding that each yields only a temporarily popular explication of our ancestral wanderings. And so we leap from a "killer ape" hypothesis (Ardrey, 1976) to a "benevolent ape" hypothesis (R. E. Leakey and Lewin, 1977), and perhaps back again through the same hoop (Wilson, 1978), depending largely on what lines of thinking happen to be in vogue in our own society at the time, only to discover in the coming years that nothing we have concluded is quite satisfactory. The debates intensify and the convictions solidify, marching in and out of our texts even as the chief proponents of each popular model march in and out of life. But all that seems certain about human origins is that they always remain enigmatic, no matter how much we pressure and posture in favor of one scenario or another.

Ultimately the paleoanthropologists are better equipped than I to reconstruct prehistoric conditions and to speculate about the possible activities of early hominids (e.g., Isaac, 1976a; Mann, 1972; Tanner and Zihlman, 1976). Primatologists, on the other hand, are sometimes in a better position to test these propositions through their knowledge of living prosimians, monkeys, and apes; some of the ideas presented in all seriousness by paleoanthropologists are simply not supported by field observations of nonhuman primates. Classification of the chimpanzee as a arboreal brachiator is a clear example.

As I see it, my role in writing this article—and in studying wild chimpanzees—is that of a devil's advocate, to probe and test for reasonability and validity in the interpretations proposed by my colleagues, and to point out where their ideas stray most radically from probability. Human behaviors are often attributed to early hominid innovation simply because we lack or ignore first-hand knowledge of what other primates actually do when left to their own devices in their native habitats. Many cases of this kind are on record in our literature, but I refer here specifically to the common habit of elevating hominid accomplishments by denying that other primate species evolved a given trait or set of traits. Insofar as I can determine, this habit accounts for the notions that nonhuman primates do not perform or possess an entire array of "human" characteristics: hunting game, sharing food, cooperating, carrying objects, having lifelong kinship ties, practicing labor division by sex, having incest prohibitions, making tools, exhibiting linguistic capability, possessing long-term memory, and so on. Whether or not we wish to accept it, the fact is that some nonhuman primates *do* have all these attributes at some level of simplicity or complexity (Teleki, in press). Some may reply that humans are unique precisely because they are in all ways more complicated than their primate cousins. However, the relative differences I see in comparing collector/predator chimpanzees with gatherer/hunter humans are not the broad abyss described by many other authors. Instead of struggling to identify absolute differences that often merely cater to our desire for human uniqueness, we must collectively seek to outline continuities as well as discontinuities in biological, behavioral, social, and psychological qualities within the order Primates. Since many of these continuities have already been perceived by field primatologists, part of the problem now is to win acceptance for them in related scientific disciplines. Rejection of the existing affinities between nonhuman and human primates can add nothing valuable to our search for human evolutionary roots.

Insofar as field study of nonhuman primates has something to offer in this regard, its greatest potential lies in providing a template against which to measure the validity of hypotheses developed in other branches of scientific research. Separation of the most probable from the most improbable speculations about early hominid behavior and society would be a practical step toward sketching a reasonable scenario of hominid divergence and evolution, but that cannot be accomplished so long as artificial distinctions continue to be drawn between "us" and "them." The material summarized here has been presented with the intention of refocusing attention on evolutionary continuities, stressing how like humans chimpanzees can be without being entirely human.

By way of conclusion, I submit the following general points for consideration.

1. Despite the availability of an array of niches within a mosaic habitat

that encompasses grassland, woodland, and forest zones, Gombe chimpanzees travel mainly through the flatter, more open areas on a network of permanent trails. Cross-country travel is rare, and dense vegetation is often avoided during movement through the home range. Gombe chimpanzees are clearly adapted, both morphologically and behaviorally, to utilize different vegetation zones and terrain types; I find it difficult to conceive how such a generalized primate would be deterred from quickly colonizing a transitional, fringe woodland habitat or a savannah–woodland biome comparable to that which supposedly launched early hominids in a unique evolutionary direction.

2. Gombe chimpanzees are adapted for multidimensional mobility and are capable of utilizing all spatial dimensions of their habitat while performing routine activities such as feeding, traveling, and resting. Far from being specialists in one form of locomotion, they can move with remarkable agility and speed in both terrestrial and arboreal environs, using quadrupedal, tripedal, bipedal, as well as suspensory modes of locomotion as the conditions dictate. Given these generalized capabilities, I again find it difficult to envision what great modifications would be required to colonize an array of biomes, including the open grasslands that supposedly characterized much of eastern Africa at the time of the earliest hominids.

3. Gombe chimpanzees qualify as true omnivores, subsisting on an eclectic assortment of flora and fauna. They have even developed appropriate technological skills for exploiting some resources that cannot simply be picked and eaten. This condition, too, is diagnostic of generalized adaptations for surviving in a variety of environmental conditions. Equipped with such omnivorous propensities, chimpanzees can probably absorb short-term environmental changes (e.g., seasonal resource fluctuations) and also long-term environmental modifications (e.g., gradual deforestation), as long as basic nutritional requirements can be met. A gradual shift from forest to woodland and eventually to grassland would, in my mind, not be a serious limiting factor to chimpanzee survival, and would not require major adaptive changes.

4. Gombe chimpanzees possess a variety of behavioral, social, and psychological attributes that fulfill many of the conditions used in previous years to define human uniqueness. Cooperative hunting, food sharing, and incipient labor division are merely three of the more obvious instances. Many additional ones are already known, and some undoubtedly remain to be discovered. Few, if any, major innovations would be required to develop from this generalized prototype the qualities that we consider to be so human.

To paraphrase the late Louis Leakey, we are now faced with the choice of reconsidering our views on the origins and evolution of humans or expanding the hominid category to include at least one pongid. Since chimpanzees are probably no more unique, when compared to other nonhuman primates, than humans are when compared to chimpanzees, I would favor the former approach as the more revealing and productive.

NOTES

1. Incidental comments on foods eaten by chimpanzees appear in numerous reports reviewed by Baldwin and Teleki (1973), but a list of typical foods can best be compiled from the following reports: J. Goodall (1963b, 1965), C. M. Hladik (1973, 1974, 1977b), C. M. Hladik and Gueguen (1974), C. M. Hladik and Viroben (1974), Izawa and Itani (1966), C. Jones and Sabater Pi (1971), McGrew (1974), Nishida (1972a, 1974, 1976), Reynolds and Reynolds (1965), Sabater Pi (1974, 1978), Suzuki (1966, 1969, 1971), Teleki (1973a,b, 1974), 1975), van Lawick-Goodall (1968), Wrangham (1975, 1977).

2. The prey species list I compiled several years ago (Teleki, 1975:134) can now be expanded to include the following mammals.

Primates: black and white colobus (*Colobus polykomos*), red colobus (*C. badius*), olive baboon (*Papio anubis*), redtail monkey (*Cercopithecus ascanius*), blue monkey (*C. mitis*), green monkey (*C. sabaeus*), vervet monkey (*C. aethiops*), potto (*Perodicticus potto*), greater galago (*Galago crassicaudatus*), and dwarf galago (*G. demidovii*) or bushbaby (*G. senegalensis*).

Ungulates: bushbuck (*Tragelaphus scriptus*), bush pig (*Potamochoerus porcus*), suni (*Nesotragus moschatus*), and klipspringer (*Oreotragus oreotragus*).

Small mammals: white-tailed mongoose (*Ichneumia albicauda*), giant forest squirrel (*Protoxerus stangeri*), and giant rat (*Cricetomys eminii*).

The guinea fowl (*Francolinus squamatus*) should perhaps be listed as well, although I have previously limited discussions of predatory behavior to mammalian prey (Teleki, 1973a, 1975) and do so here.

3. The following reports provide original information on chimpanzee predatory behavior: Boesch (1978), Brewer (1978), Busse (1977, 1978), J. Goodall (1963a,b, 1965), Izawa and Itani (1966), Kano (1971a), Kawabe (1966), McGrew et al. (in press), Morris and Goodall (1977), Nishida (1969, 1972b), Nishida, Uehara, and Nyundo (1978), Plooij (1978), Riss and Busse (1977), Suzuki (1966, 1968, 1971, 1975, 1976), Teleki (1973a,b, 1975), van Lawick-Goodall (1968), Wrangham (1975, 1977). I observed a red colobus kill in central Sierra Leone during a 6-month nationwide survey of primate populations in early 1980.

4. The sample excludes all dependent offspring whose behavioral rhythms are linked to those of mothers or siblings. For additional demographic details, see Teleki, Hunt, and Pfifferling (1976).

5. These figures differ from totals given in earlier reports (Teleki, 1973a, 1975), in which unsuccessful attempts to capture prey were also tabulated. Only successful kills are summarized here because records of attempts are not consistently kept by all investigators, and not even reported by some authors.

6. None of the figures listed here include observations on cannibalism or infanticide, which have now been recorded at all three East African sites (Bygott, 1972; J. Goodall, 1977; Nishida, Uehara, and Nyundo, 1978; Suzuki, 1971). These cases differ from normal predation on vertebrates in many ways, and warrant separate consideration (Teleki, 1975). See note 3 for sources.

7. Gombe National Park is singularly deficient in large mammals other than buffalo

(*Syncerus caffer*) and an occasional leopard (*Panthera pardus*), both of which are avoided by chimpanzees (Teleki, 1973c; van Lawick-Goodall, 1968). Wrangham (1975) discusses the vulnerability of five small game species not utilized by chimpanzees, concluding that these are seldom encountered owing to their specialized habits, such as being nocturnal or holing up in subterranean or arboreal dens.

8. Many instances of feeding conservatism are recorded for wild chimpanzees, especially among adults presented with new foods by experimenting researchers (Kortlandt, 1967; Teleki, 1975; van Lawick-Goodall, 1968). Conversely, once a new resource is discovered and exploitation is initiated, the habit can spread rapidly through the social unit, among chimpanzees and other nonhuman primates (McGrew and Tutin, 1978; Strum, 1975a; van Lawick-Goodall, 1968), though permanence of the habit is not always assured.

9. Pearson $r = +.99$, $p < .01$, $N = 8$ hourly intervals.

10. This refers only to travel activity, not to the performance of all routine activities in different environmental conditions (see Teleki, 1977a, for elaboration).

11. The only extrinsic factor that clearly affected arboreality was precipitation: Gombe chimpanzees are more arboreal in wet months (Pearson $r = +.93$, $p < .01$, $N = 12$ monthly intervals).

12. High grass and underbrush may inhibit mobbing on the ground (Teleki, 1973a). The mobbing defense tactic has been noted in other field studies (e.g., L. Brown, 1971; Galef, Mittermeier, and Bailey, 1976).

13. Possibly conflicting information has been offered by Busse (1977), who claims that solitary colobus are rarely encountered (3.5% of 85 encounters where chimpanzees approached within 90 m), but there is some chance that human observers are less adept at noticing lone monkeys, thereby skewing the sample toward troop sightings.

14. Responding to Strum's (1975a) preliminary description of baboon predation, Gaulin and Kurland (1976) propose a laudable but completely impractical avenue of investigating primate predatory behavior. They begin by predicting that chimpanzees outside Gombe will engage in little predation, then confirm their hypothesis by selecting for analysis a field study in which only one item, "presumed to be the bone of some animal" (Suzuki, 1969:121), was recovered from 174 fecal samples collected in a 201-km² area over 15 months. Subsequent studies in the same area and at other sites, all of which did yield data on chimpanzee predation, are ignored. Since the only animal matter found in the fecal samples consisted of one bone, plus insect remains in 5 out of 15 months of collecting dung, there appears to be some confusion in Gaulin and Kurland's minds between predatory behavior and collection of animal products and parts, including insects. The point is not simply a semantic one, for if insects are to be ranked as prey in such a bioenergetic model, then virtually all primates would be heavily predatory. Moreover, since Suzuki did not collect the fecal samples systematically (monthly samples range from 3 to 22 pieces of dung), they cannot be representative of a chimpanzee population's dung production or, by implication, of its diet. It is difficult enough to see how the "foraging efficiency" of a primate population can be estimated from such data, let alone to accept a bioenergetic model that is closely tied to production and collection of fecal matter yet not based on known relationships between ingestion and excretion. Given the selectivity of the data used by Gaulin and Kurland to construct and test their hypothesis, the incomplete and ambiguous information available about causal mechanisms underlying primate predatory behavior at different sites, the wide range of species and habitats involved, and the dubious assumption that food input can be accurately deduced from dung output, I submit that bioenergetic models of this kind are at present both premature and prone to error.

15. The range of grams results from using two estimates of prey weights, a minimum of 3 kg (e.g., baboon infants) and a maximum of 5 kg (e.g., colobus adults).

16. See note 3 for sources.

17. To illustrate this point, Busse (1978:767) states that "a recent observation of a lone male chimpanzee stalking and coming to within a meter of capturing an infant baboon (personal

observation) indicates that collective action is not required for successful predation upon baboons, contrary to Teleki's earlier tentative conclusion." Not only are there explicit descriptions of lone adult males (and even a crippled one) capturing and killing young baboons in my monograph, but I never have concluded, tentatively or otherwise, that collective action is required for successful predation on any species (Teleki, 1973a,b, 1975). What purpose is served when pertinent original data and conclusions are considered malleable or ignored altogether? (See also Teleki, 1977b.)

18. In terms of a practical comparison, a typical pork chop weighs about 225g these days.

19. "Mild aggression" refers to vocal and gestural threats by meat owners toward those attempting to take or request portions, and "violent aggression" to pushing, hitting, kicking, dragging attacks between bystanders, mainly those who were unsuccessful in gaining access to carcass portions.

20. Data on females are too limited to permit testing of correlations with other factors, but only two males were less successful in obtaining meat than some of the females (Wrangham, 1975).

Brian Hayden

10.
Subsistence and Ecological Adaptations of Modern Hunter/Gatherers

This survey of hunter/gatherer[1] subsistence habits is not exhaustive, for such an undertaking would be monumental; I hope, however, that what follows is generally representative of hunter/gatherers in their major types of habitats at various levels of technological development. Nor is this survey just an inventory of facts. Rather, it is designed as an exploration of possible relationships and principles. In some cases one can do little more than present data in catalog fashion; in others, relationships can be guessed at; and in still others, explanation of the data appears to be relatively sound. Definite confirmation of many features may never materialize, since hunter/gatherer societies are passing rapidly into the province of the archaeologist and the prehistorian.

Because of the exploratory nature of this review, groups were not selected by rigidly systematic or random sampling. Comprehensive coverage of the world's hunter/gatherers was impossible, so the sample cuts across several major cultural areas, geographical zones, and environmental regions (fig. 10.1). A major problem was that data in the various ethnographies were seldom directly comparable. Observations ranged from passing mention of the presence or absence of a trait to unsubstantiated quantifications such as: "$x\%$ of the time women obtained $y\%$ of food." Measurements were reported in varying ways (in terms of distance, time, calories, etc.), often with little indication of even the range of variation involved. Still more serious was the lack of comparable descriptions of data-gathering techniques. Some ethnographies were compiled from the front porch on mission or cattle stations by talking with natives about traditional activities. Other reports were written by field-workers who lived at contemporary campsites but obtained only verbal information about subsistence forays. Very few ethnographers actually accompanied natives on such forays. (It is remarkable how often the statement appears that natives ate "undetermined" amounts of food as snacks while foraging.) Some authors give no indication as to how their information was obtained (e.g., Clastres, 1972; Roth, 1901).

344

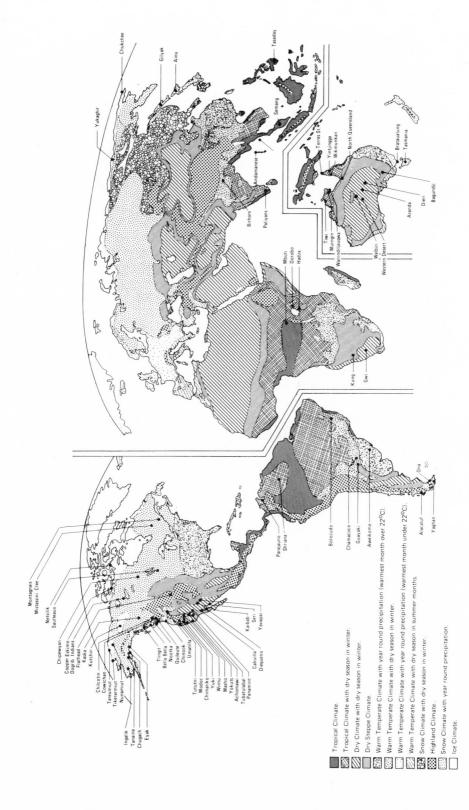

Figure 10.1. Hunter/gatherers of the world, related to the Koppen-Geiger system of climate classifications.

Montagnais
Mistassini Cree
Netsilik
Saulteaux
Chipewyan
Copper Eskimo
Dogrib Indians
Flathead
Kaska
Kutchin
Chilcotin
Cowichan
Tareumiut
Tikeramiut
Nunamiut
Ingalik
Tanana
Chugach
Eyak
Tlingit
Bella Bella
Nootka
Quileute
Chinook
Umatilla
Tutuni
Modoc
Chumario
Yuki
Wintu
Washo
Yokuts
Achomawi
Tubatulabal
Panamint
Cahuilla
Seri
Yavapai
Kalab
Diegueno

Yukaghir
Chukchee
Gilyak
Ainu

Semang
Andamanese
Birhors
Paliyans
Torres St.
Tasaday
Yintjungga
Wikmunkan
North Queensland
Brataualung
Tasmania
Tiwi
Murngin
Wanindiljaugwa
Walbiri
Western Desert
Aranda
Dieri
Bagundji

Mbuti
Dorobo
Hadza

Kung
Gwi

Parajauno
Shriana
Botocudo
Chamacoco
Guayaki
Aweikoma
Alacaluf
Yaghan
Ona

Tropical Climate.

Tropical Climate with dry season in winter.

Dry Climate with dry season in winter.

Dry Steppe Climate

Warm Temperate Climate with year round precipitation (warmest month over 22°C).

Warm Temperate Climate with dry season in winter.

Warm Temperate Climate with year round precipitation (warmest month under 22°C).

Warm Temperate Climate with dry season in summer months.

Snow Climate with dry season in winter.

Highland Climate.

Snow Climate with year round precipitation.

Ice Climate.

Given this state of affairs, a considerable amount of intuitive extrapolation was required to make the data at all useful for comparative purposes. In this, I must beg the reader's indulgence and state that I have attempted to avoid distortions and improbable conclusions, even though some errors must inevitably occur.

The tables in this article include all available information on the various topics which I covered during the literature survey. Different groups are represented in various tables because no ethnographer covered the full range of topics treated here. Thus, sample sizes for a topic vary from 1 to 65 groups. Owing to limitations in the quality and quantity of the data, many of these tables are exploratory.

SCOPE AND ORGANIZATION

If we are to take cultural materialists at their word, subsistence activities are inextricably bound up with every facet of culture and social organization, and the scope of this review should be coterminous with almost all cultural manifestations of hunter/gatherers. In fact the scope is much less ambitious and is limited to the organization of the subsistence activities themselves (e.g., division of labor, work, food preparation), and to some immediately related social phenomena (e.g., sharing, group size). I have not listed individual species exploited by groups; in a comparative study this would be useless. Nor have I attempted to deal with all topics that might be relevant to subsistence activities. Some topics, though relevant, are difficult to treat because of their complexity and the lack of good data. For instance, residence patterns are not considered in terms of the relative importance of hunting versus gathering activities (those familiar with the literature will realize the treacherous nature of the topic). Likewise, information on territoriality was either equivocal or contradictory, and so meaningful comparisons were not feasible. This problem is particularly apparent in regard to Australia (see Berndt, 1959; Blundell, 1975; Gould, 1969a; L. Hiatt, 1962; Myers, 1976).

Finally, I found it necessary to make a distinction between "commercial" and traditional hunter/gatherers. Commercial groups rely to a *large extent* on bought or bartered foodstuffs, usually trading meat, furs, or other forest products for calorie-rich foods such as starches and sugars. The distinction becomes very important in explaining variability in several key subsistence-related areas, such as the amount of work per capita expended for subsistence, the hunting techniques employed, the game size exploited, and the frequency and magnitude of environmental stress. Typical commercial hunter/gatherers include the Mbuti and Birhor. A lack of quantified or relative statements makes it difficult to classify other groups such as the Dogrib or Mistassini, which are known to do some trading.

HABITATS AND SUBSISTENCE HABITS

Since the environmental setting is so basic to subsistence habits at the hunter/gatherer level, it merits a few preliminary remarks. The aims of this paper are better served by a general theoretical, rather than a particularist, approach, and contemporary ecological theory provides a number of principles that can be used profitably in explaining variation in hunter/gatherer subsistence habits.

In general, low temperatures and/or low precipitation in nonlittoral and nonriparian environments result not only in reduced quantities of food for humans but, more importantly, in reduced diversity of food items (Odum, 1971:70). Thus, an exhaustive list of 40 edible plant species and 47 edible animal species characterizes the Australian Western Desert, while a rather incomplete list of 240 plant species and 120 animal species (including mollusks) characterizes Northern Queensland, where rainfall and heat are both moderately high (table 10.1).

Subsistence in areas with little diversity in edible items tends to be precarious (especially with pronounced seasonality), since overexploitation by humans of even one resource may result in disastrous effects for local groups, and naturally occurring fluctuations in even one of the resources may lead to famine and starvation. In areas of greater resource diversity, natural plant failure or human overexploitation of one or several edible species can often be countered by switching to other species, and such areas are therefore considered more stable.

Without detailed field data from specific groups, characterizing general habitats in terms of resource density and diversity presents some problems. The relationship between overall biological productivity and the edible resource base for humans has not been clearly established. Nevertheless, gross biological productivity is probably more important than any other factor in predicting resource availability, although the regression line may be complex. Similarly, the relation between climate and resource diversity (and density) cannot be plotted as a simple regression line, or by using only two dimensions. For instance, while there is a positive correlation between precipitation and resource availability in Australia for dry to moderately wet areas (Birdsell, 1953, 1975), this relationship begins to reverse itself with high precipitation values, to the point that in rain forests the terrestrial fauna available to hunter/gatherer groups is negligible. Butzer (1971a:151), in particular, draws attention to these ecological variables and classifies resources in terms of the following vegetation types:

1. *High animal biomass areas:* grassy, tropical, deciduous woodland and savannahs; mid-latitude grasslands; low-latitude Pleistocene tundras.
2. *Moderate animal biomass areas:* temperate and subtropical deciduous and mixed woodland; high-latitude tundras.

Table 10.1. Diversity of food resources utilized in various habitats

Groups	Temperature	Precipitation (cm)	Flora (no. of species)	Fauna (no. of species)	References
Australian Western Desert Aborigines	high	low, 25	40	47 (includes mammals, insects, reptiles, birds)	Gould, 1969a:260
Dogrib	low	low, 38	10	33 (includes mammals, fish, birds)	Helm, 1972:61
G/wi Bushmen	high	low, 30–35	30	>20 (includes mammals, birds, reptiles, insects)	Silberbauer, 1972:283, 287
!Kung Bushmen	high	low–moderate, 48	100	144 (includes mammals, birds, insects, reptiles; only 53 sp. used regularly)	Lee, 1972a:341–42
Australian North Queensland Aborigines	high	moderate, 38–63	240	120 (includes mollusks & birds; minimal listing of mammals)	W. Roth, 1901:16–18
Tasaday	high	high	52	traditionally included only tadpoles, crabs, grubs, frogs, and small fish; now includes some land mammals	Yen, 1976:110

3. *Low animal biomass areas:* tropical rain forest; boreal forest; semi-deserts and deserts.

In support of this classification, we find that the rain forest of Tasmania has been virtually uninhabited (B. Hiatt, 1967:193; R. Jones, 1968:207–10), and there is no evidence that the densest rain forests of the Congo Basin, the Amazon Basin, and Borneo were occupied before the advent of fishing and horticultural technology. On the other hand, some rain forests do seem to adequately support technologically simple hunter/gatherers such as the Tasaday and the prehistoric Hoabinhians. Certainly one issue that merits detailed scrutiny is the general and specific limitations of rain-forest habitats for hunter/gatherer groups. In the literature there are conflicting claims on the ease of travel in rain forests, the ease of obtaining food, and characteristic population densities (e.g., the Tasaday and the Guayaki *may* have had relatively high densities).

We are on firmer ground in considering the other extreme: areas with low temperatures or precipitation, or both. Given that species diversity is comparatively lower in these conditions, resource stability is expected to be less, especially in regions with pronounced seasonality.[2] Fitzhugh (1972:165–67) has documented archaeological examples of this instability for the Subarctic.

Resource Conservation

Under conditions of resource instability, greater emphasis on resource conservation behavior would be expected. Unfortunately, information on conservation practices is sparse in the literature, much of it being conjectural. Two main types of resource conservation might be expected: avoidance of overexploitation during normal periods or during critical periods of environmental stress; and selective cropping of animal herds during periods of abundance. The latter behavior might prevent severe oscillations in prey populations caused by Malthusian overexploitation of their own resource base and subsequent population crashes—a feature observed in ungulate herds that are not hunted (Caughley, 1966, 1970; Lack, 1954).

Inferential as they are, the data on conservation practices (table 10.2) do tend to support the concept that environments with low resource diversity and pronounced seasonality are inherently more unstable in terms of human subsistence. Residents in such areas will be the most affected by overexploitation as well as by natural food failures, and are therefore expected to exhibit the most pronounced resource conservation behavior.

Two of the most aberrant groups appear at the bottom of the table because of their special relationships with commercial economies where meat is traded for other goods. Neither the Birhor nor the Mbuti are self-sufficient, and certainly the argument can be advanced that they are

Table 10.2. Conservation practices and resource variability

Groups ranked by resource diversity	Resource diversity	Seasonality	Conservation practices	References
Western Desert Aborigines	very low	pronounced	Consistent use of peripheral areas whenever possible; use of major waterholes last	Gould, 1969a:266
G/wi Bushmen	very low	pronounced	Cannot kill more or gather more than needed without angering Supreme Being	Silberbauer, 1972:292, 321; in this volume
Great Basin Numa	very low (13–38 cm precipitation)	pronounced	Dislike using fire drives because brush requires many years to regenerate; antelope drives held only every 12 years to permit animals time to reproduce	Steward, 1938:35–39
Montagnais	very low	pronounced	Randomization of kill areas via divination practices, preventing overexploitation	Moore, 1965
Aranda	low–moderate	pronounced	Sacred nature of major sites precluded hunting within 1-mile radius and provided game refuges in time of environmental stress, thus preventing overexploitation; totemic prohibitions may have also provided differential refuge areas for particular species; compassion for animals	Strehlow, 1965:140, 143; Spencer and Gillen, 1927:17

Tasaday	low–moderate	negligible	Conscious perpetuation of yams by leaving stems; possible rotational system of area exploitation; no conservation of newly introduced resources (palm, land mammals)	Yen, 1976:160–62
!Kung Bushmen	moderate	pronounced	Use of peripheral areas whenever rainfall permits; conservation of water by using seasonal sources rather than permanent ones when possible	Lee, 1972a:339–40
Hadza	moderate–high (56 cm precipitation)	pronounced	No vegetable or animal conservation; kill as much as possible	Woodburn, 1968a:53
Tanaina	high (ecotone)	pronounced	Pregnant animals not killed, to conserve population levels	Osgood, 1937:32
Tlingit	very high (ecotone) (150–200 cm to 100–150 cm precipitation)	pronounced	Competition over resources	Oberg, 1973:55–56
Birhor	high	moderate	Allow areas to lie "fallow" for 1–4 years; prefer not to join groups in order to conserve limited game; conscious of needing conservation for long-term productivity	Sinha, 1972:375, 377, 385
Mbuti	high	negligible	Conscious effort to use every part of animal; never kill more than necessary for the day	Turnbull, 1965b:161; Harako, in this volume

encouraged to exploit their environment (especially for choice game) much more intensively than they would under more "pristine" hunter/gatherer conditions, thereby necessitating more careful conservation of their resources.

Resource diversity and availability in the Northwest Coast area are legendary, despite the many qualifications voiced by Suttles (1968) and others, and there seems to be a distinct lack of conservation practices in this area. Indeed, the Northwest Coast is the only region where competition—the antithesis of conservation (Wynne-Edwards, 1962)—seems to have overridden it. Groups habitually quarreled over resource wealth in status disputes, and even drove weaker clans from coveted areas (Oberg, 1973:55, 59). This pattern is extremely rare among hunter/gatherers anywhere else in the world.

All of the remaining groups in table 10.2 exemplify the avoidance of overexploitation in environments with low resource diversity. There are a few accounts from poor areas which refer to slaughter of herd animals in numbers which the hunters could never use (Fitzhugh, 1972:182). These latter cases appear to be anomalous, and it can only be surmised that some hunting groups used intensive cropping techniques when herds appeared to be getting too large. In some instances such "overkill" might have served to prevent herd overpopulation and subsequent disastrous declines in prey numbers; fluctuations of great amplitude can even lead to extinction (MacArthur and Connell, 1966). Thus, cropping of prey populations would presumably be found most often in environments that naturally generate large fluctuations. Unfortunately, the ethnographic literature does not provide a clear picture of such processes.

Several additional points can be made about environmental aspects of subsistence. First, where seasonality is pronounced, the season of lowest temperature or lowest precipitation is characteristically the season of least resource variability (Poiner, 1971:89; Silberbauer, 1972:283). However, mitigating circumstances sometimes make certain resources highly accessible at times when resource availability is generally low. For example, snow and ice can make tracking, hunting, and transport easier during winter months.

Second, despite the widespread use of the concept of carrying capacity, it is operationally unfeasible to determine what this balance might be for any given region or human group (Birdsell, 1968a; Hayden, 1975). This does not imply that gross estimates of the population densities which a habitat can efficiently accommodate are unattainable or useless. However, these estimates should not be translated into a mythical maximum density that an area can sustain. By definition, *all* human groups that survive are living below the carrying capacity of their environments, and it is therefore impossible to assign a concrete maximum value to carrying capacity.

A third point meriting attention is that all hunter/gatherers for which we have reasonable data are often viewed as unrepresentative because they live in "marginal" or "peripheral" habitats (e.g., Tanaka, 1976:114). This position is clearly untenable. Observations indicate that some coastal Australian and West Coast North American groups lived in what can only be described as ideal hunting/gathering conditions into the late nineteenth or mid-twentieth century, and information on these groups is often useful for studies such as this. Moreover, areas where dry farming is entirely marginal, because of low precipitation or difficulty in tilling, often have the highest animal biomass and high plant productivity (e.g., savannahs), and can thus support thriving hunter/gatherer populations. These are in many respects optimal environments for hunter/gatherers, even though agriculturalists tend to live there only when all other options are exhausted (Butzer, 1971a). Allen (1974) fully documents this situation for the Bagundji of western New South Wales, Australia.

The Subsistence Base

Reviews of hunter/gatherer subsistence habits have been compiled by R. Lee (1968) and B. Hiatt (1970). Hiatt's presentation appears in table 10.3, while Lee's data plus information obtained from my literature review appear in table 10.4. The estimates in these reviews are, in my opinion, often highly subjective. Reports that give relative percentages or actual weights of edibles consumed are exceedingly rare (e.g., Lee, 1969; E. Rogers, 1972), and even in these cases no consideration is given to the often substantial "snacks" eaten while people forage. Other problems also arise. For instance, Woodburn (1968a) estimates the relative contribution of various foods but fails to take into account the fact that the Hadza themselves have noted dwindling game reserves over the past 50 years because of encroaching cattle stations (Tomita, 1966:165) and a 60% reduction in hunting and foraging ranges (Eibl-Eibesfeldt, 1974:437), while Clastres' views (1972:153) on the importance of hunting conflict with those of other ethnographers who did earlier work among the Guayaki (Baldus, 1943; Vellard, 1939). Then again, Gould (1966c, 1969a:256) estimates that Australian Western Desert Aborigines consumed about 1.2 pounds (0.5 kg) of meat per day, but on actual trips into the bush he noted only a "few ounces" of lizard meat consumed per person per day (Gould, 1969a: 262).[3] To these specific problems can be added the inconsistency with which various authors attend to seasonality of food availability and intake. Most studies do not cover a complete annual cycle, yet food intake might well vary greatly, in both total amounts and relative proportions, for different seasons of the year.

Another major shortcoming in many ethnographic reports is lack of precision about whether the figures provided are based on weights, caloric

Table 10.3. Diet, latitude and the division of labor

1	2	3	4	5	6	7	8	9	10	11	12
			G	H	F	G	H	F	F	M	M
N. Amer.	Copper Eskimo*	69N	0	55	45	F	M	N	10	90	M
"	Nunamuit	68N	10	70	20	F	M	N	15	85	M
"	Ingalik	62N	10	40	50	F	M	N	20	80	M
"	Chugach*	60N	10	60	30	G	M	N	15	85	M
"	Chipewyan	60N	0	60	40	O	M	M	0	100	M
"	Eyak*	60N	20	45	35	F	M	M	20	80	M
"	Kaska	59N	10	40	50	F	M	E	35	65	M
"	Tlingit*	58N	10	40	50	F	M	M	10	90	M
S. Amer.	Yahgan*	55S	30	20	50	F	M	D	55	45	F
N. Amer.	Tsimshian*	55N	20	30	50	F	M	N	30	70	M
S. Amer.	Ona	54S	20	60	20	F	M	N	25	75	M
Asia	Gilyak*	53N	30	30	40	F	M	M	30	70	M
N. Amer.	Northern Saulteaux	52N	20	35	45	F	M	N	30	70	M
"	Chilcotin	52N	20	30	50	G	N	N	35	65	M
"	Cowichan*	49N	40	30	30	F	M	M	40	60	M
"	Montagais	48N	20	60	20	F	M	E	30	70	M
"	Quileute*	48N	30	30	40	F	M	M	30	70	M
"	Chinook*	46N	30	20	50	F	M	M	30	70	M
"	Flathead	46N	30	40	30	F	M	N	40	60	M
"	Umatilla	46N	30	30	40	F	M	M	30	70	M
Asia	Ainu*	44N	30	30	40	F	M	D	50	50	F/M
N. Amer.	Moduc	43N	50	30	20	F	M	M	50	50	F/M
"	Chimariko	41N	40	30	30	E	M	M	20	80	M
"	Achomawi	41N	30	40	30	F	M	N	40	60	M
"	Wintu	41N	30	30	40	G	M	M	20	80	M
"	Coast Yuki*	39N	60	20	20	G	M	N	50	50	F/M
"	Washo	39N	40	30	30	G	M	E	45	55	M

Region	Group	Lat.	G%	H%	F%	G labor	H labor	F labor	Female %	Male %	Sex
N. Amer.	Tubatulabal	36N	50	30	20	G	M	N	40	60	M
"	Panamint	36N	60	40	0	F	M	O	60	40	F
"	Kaibab	36N	70	30	0	G	M	O	50	50	F/M
"	Yavapai	35N	60	40	0	G	M	O	45	55	M
"	Diegueno	32N	50	40	10	F	M	M	50	50	F/M
Aust.	Dieri	28S	70	30	0	F	M	O	70	30	F
S. Amer.	Aweikoma*	28S	60	40	0	G	M	O	45	55	M
Aust.	Aranda*	24S	70	30	0	F	M	O	70	30	F
Africa	Gwi Bushmen	22S	70	30	0	F	M	O	70	30	F
Aust.	Walbiri	22S	70	30	0	F	M	O	70	30	F
Africa	!Kung*	20S	70	30	0	G	M	O	50	50	F/M
S. Amer.	Chamacoco	20S	60	40	0	E	M	O	30	70	M
"	Botocudo	18S	50	40	10	F	M	M	50	50	F/M
Aust.	Wikmunkan*	14S	60	30	10	F	M	D	65	35	F
Asia	Andamanese*	12N	50	20	30	G	M	D	50	50	F/M
Aust.	Murngin*	12S	60	30	10	G	M	N	50	50	F/M
"	Tiwi*	12S	60	30	10	F	M	D	65	35	F
Asia	Semang	6N	40	30	30	D	M	M	20	80	M
S. Amer.	Shiriana	4N	30	40	30	F	M	M	30	70	M
Africa	Hadza*	3S	80	20	0	F	M	O	80	20	F
"	Dorobo*	2S	60	40	0	G	M	O	45	55	M
"	Mbuti Pygmies	2N	60	30	10	G	N	E	60	40	F

Source: B. Hiatt (1970), reproduced with permission.

Note: Asterisks indicate groups for which Lee changed the estimates on percentage of hunting in his review (Lee, 1968).

Key:

Column 3: Latitude.

Columns 4, 5, 6: Percentage importance of gathering (*G*), hunting (*H*), and fishing (*F*).

Columns 7, 8, 9: Division of labor associated with gathering, hunting and fishing: *F*, women alone active; *M*, males alone; *G*, both sexes participate but females predominate; *N*, both sexes participate but males dominate; *E*, equal participation; *D*, sexual differences in component tasks, but overall equal participation; 0, activity absent or not important.

Columns 10, 11: Approximate percentage of subsistence provided by females and males.

Column 12: Sex which provides the larger amount of subsistence.

Table 10.4. Proportional importance of food types in the total diet

Groups	Gathering	Hunting	Fishing	Insects	References
Great Basin Numa	75	15	0	10	Fowler and Fowler, 1971:48; Steward, 1938:33
Nootka	5	55	40	0	Jewitt, 1974
Western Desert	75	15	0	10	Gould, 1969a:258, 260
Aborigines	60	30	0	10	Tindale, 1972:249–53
Mistassini	+	75	25	?	E. Rogers, 1972:104
Guayaki[a]	15	50	?	30	Clastres, 1972:156–66
Paliyans	75	18	5	0	Gardner, 1972:413
Tasaday					Yen, 1976:177;
Traditional	75	0	25	+	Fernandez and Lynch, 1972:311
Present	60	20	20	+	
≠Kade Bushmen	81	19	0	?	Tanaka, 1976:112
Alacaluf	30	20	50	?	
Paraujano	40	10	50	?	
Yukaghir	10	60	30	?	
Kutchin	10	40	50	?	Lee, 1968
Bellabella	20	30	50	?	
Seri	30	20	50	?	
Cahuilla	60	40	0	?	
Lake Yokuts	50	20	30	?	
Tututni	45	20	35	?	

Note: + means that some was recorded.

[a] Considerable disagreement exists between Clastres' estimate and estimates of previous ethnographers; see text.

values, or other measures of food intake. Most estimates appear to be based on raw weights, and occasionally on processed weights. As dieticians are wont to note, however, the net weight of food is a very poor indicator of nutritional value; not all ingested materials can be digested (rinds, pits, bones, etc.), and different food items contain highly variable amounts of water, sugar, fat, and protein. Thus, while it may be true that most hunter/gatherers consume more vegetable matter than meat by *weight,* it is not at all certain that they derive the majority of their *calories* from vegetable matter. Since there are virtually no comparative data on the caloric contributions of the various wild plant and animal foods, such problems cannot be resolved at present. However, since meat is generally much higher in calories per gram than most vegetable foods, my impression is that meat probably contributes more than vegetable resources to the total calorie needs of groups, or at least an equal amount.

Despite shortcomings in the quality of the data base, several basic principles of subsistence have been proposed by Lee and others. These can be summarized as follows, with the reservation that major modifications may be necessary when nutritional values are eventually recalculated on the basis of caloric intake.

1. Hunter/gatherers can be expected to place primary emphasis on exploiting the most reliable resource whenever possible. Gathered vegetable foods provide the most reliable resource base (Woodburn, 1968a; Tanaka, 1976), followed by shellfish and fish, and then by mammals, which are unpredictable because of their high mobility. Although meat may be highly desired, Lee (1968) maintains that it is obtained opportunistically and is not counted upon for subsistence needs where other resources are available.
2. In the ethnographic sample covered in table 10.4, hunting is of least importance (by weight) to most hunter/gatherer groups.
3. At high latitudes, where plant foods are exceedingly scarce, fishing and hunting must, by default, contribute more to the total diet (see tables 10.3, 10.5). Among Arctic and Subarctic hunter/gatherers, animal foods are clearly the primary resource base, with mammals and fish providing as much as 90–100% of the total diet. This observation serves to distinguish between "generalized" hunter/gatherers, who have access to the many plant resources available in temperate and tropical zones, and "specialized" hunter/gatherers, who exploit limited varieties of resources (mainly animals) in Arctic and Subarctic zones.
4. On the basis of relative weights (or other unspecified criteria), hunting among generalized hunter/gatherers of the temperate and tropical zones provides anywhere from 10% to 60% of the total diet, with modal, mean, and median values for all the sampled societies converging at about 35%.

Table 10.5. Primary subsistence source by latitude for 58 groups

| Degrees from equator | Primary Subsistence Source | | | Total |
	Gathering	Hunting	Fishing	
>60°	—	6	2	8
50°–59°	—	1	9	10
40°–49°	4	3	5	12
30°–39°	9	—	—	9
20°–29°	7	—	1	8
10°–19°	5	—	1	6
0°–9°	4	1	—	5
World	29	11	18	58

Source: After Lee (1968:43).

Finally, in addition to the usual categories of foods consumed by humans, there are two habitually neglected categories: insects and earth. Tacit assumptions, perhaps stemming from dietary ethnocentrism, seem to relegate these items to insignificant roles in descriptions of hunter/gatherer subsistence. Among a number of known groups, however, insects and insect products are major seasonal staples. In the Southeastern Highlands of Australia, the seasonal emphasis on the fatty, nutritious bodies of the Bogong moth has resulted in labeling of their human consumers as "moth hunters" (Flood, 1973). Intensive exploitation of insects or insect products appears to be confined largely to tropical and subtropical regions and is perhaps most pronounced in the dry areas of these regions [table 10.6; for an expanded but largely anecdotal discussion, see Bodenheimer (1951)]. None of the Arctic and Subarctic ethnographies even mention the use of this resource. In the literature there are no observations of any marked sexual division of labor associated with obtaining insects. Occasional notes appear to the effect that males generally obtain honey because of the usually arduous work involved in opening or felling trees.

Also surprising is that some groups apparently consume large amounts of clay which has been carefully ground, dried, made into "cakes," and baked. Kaolin appears to be the preferred material. Considered delicacies, clay cakes are consumed regularly after meals by Queensland hunter/gatherers (Roth, 1901:9). The use of clay as a dietary supplement has also been recorded for Western Australian Aborigines (Grey, 1841), for the Aranda (Spencer and Gillen, 1927:17), and for the Pomo (Barrett, 1964).

Anthropophagy is also unexpectedly widespread among hunter/gatherers, at least in Australia and probably other areas as well (e.g., Schultz, 1891:234; Forrest, 1875:44; Basedow, 1925; Spencer and Gillen, 1899:474–75; Davidson, 1935:153; Steward, 1938:20; Osgood, 1936:31). This behavior seems to have been associated in most cases with the ritual

Table 10.6. Recorded use of insects or insect products by hunter/gatherers

Groups	Use of insects	References
Andamanese	>50% of diet seasonally (largely honey)	Radcliffe-Brown, 1922:40
Semang	dislike insects, but honey is important	Bodenheimer, 1951:245
Ceylonese Veddas	depend largely on honey for 6 months	Bodenheimer, 1951:251
Western Desert Aborigines	>50% seasonally	Gould, 1969a:258, 260
	10–15% yearly[a]	Tindale, 1972:249–253
Guayaki	>30% (largely honey) yearly	Clastres, 1972:156–166
Hadza	some use	Woodburn, 1968a:51
	seasonally important	Tomita, 1966:169
!Kung Bushmen	2 days of ant harvest	Yellen and Lee, 1976:42
G/wi Bushmen	>3%	Silberbauer, 1972:413
Mbuti	some use	Turnbull, 1965b:168
	honey and termites both important	Bodenheimer, 1951:145
Great Basin Numa	seasonally very important	Fowler and Fowler, 1971:48; Steward, 1938:33
Paiute (Mono Lake, Calif.)	caterpillars eaten in great quantities	Bodenheimer, 1951:289
Modoc (N. Calif.)	hundreds of bushels per day of flies gathered seasonally for food	Bodenheimer, 1951:289
Snake (Northern Paiute), Utes, Cheyenne, Assiniboine, Shoshoco—various locations	communal grasshopper hunts	Bodenheimer, 1951:288–9
Tasaday	some use	Yen, 1976

[a]Present reviewer's impression.

killing and consuming of close relatives or enemies, but sometimes it occurred at times of extreme starvation. The extent to which such activities contributed to subsistence remains unknown.

GROUPING TENDENCIES

Group size

Extraordinarily little attention has been devoted to discovering the determinants of group size, in any branch of anthropology or archaeology. Some authors are content with the explanation that humans are and have been innately gregarious, while others seem to assume that variation in group size has no theoretical interest. Yet few characteristics play a more important role in directly determining major aspects of culture and few lend themselves as readily to modeling in terms of subsistence, economics, and environment.

According to the anthropological and ecological literature, several factors may explain the relationship between group size and subsistence behavior. Briefly, the most important parameters are: resource density, resource nucleation, resource reliability, the importance of hunting, techniques of hunting, the nature of game hunted, and food-sharing practices. Other, nonsubsistence factors have also been advanced to explain grouping tendencies, such as trade (Irwin, 1974) and group selection (Wynne-Edwards, 1962), but only the subsistence-related factors are covered here.

Important reasons lead me to expect that the most efficient subsistence economy occurs in groups of *minimum* size (Hayden, 1978). Because substantial energy is used in travel and transportation of food (see the section on Economics of Subsistence), *large* aggregations of people are likely to *rapidly* exhaust food resources within the foraging range of campsites, thereby forcing the entire group to move frequently. The smaller the group, the less often it must move, and the less travel and transport work it must perform. Settlement stability is particularly important for women, who usually carry children and household materials during camp moves and must erect shelters. Lee (1972b:334) estimates that the average yearly walking distance for !Kung women is about 2,400 km, which represents a considerable energy expenditure, especially when a child, food, or equipment is being carried. In terms of the principle of least effort (Zipf, 1949), as well as the greater risk of disease, the increased competition for resources, and the geometrically increasing potential for conflict and dispute as groups grow larger (Alexander, 1974:328; M. Harris, 1971:224, 227; Rappaport, 1968:8), we are logically led to expect a grouping tendency that hovers around the smallest self-sufficient reproductive unit—i.e., the nuclear family. That this is perfectly feasible even in poor areas is demonstrated by Silberbauer's observations that the G/wi disperse into nuclear-family foraging units both seasonally and in times of stress in order to make more economical use of scarce resources (1972:297). In the Great Basin of western North America, the sexual division of labor made the nuclear family the smallest efficient exploitation unit, and groups existed for large parts of the year at these minimum numbers when resources were scarce (Steward, 1938:2-3). Among the Hadza of Tanzania, individuals were not only capable of providing all their own subsistence needs, but even lived in solitude for periods of years (Woodburn, 1972:198).

Since living in nuclear family groups is feasible, and since many groups spend at least part of their annual cycle in this state, it comes as a surprise that groups of 25–50 are characteristic for hunter/gatherers (table 10.7). What factors can account for such unexpectedly large group sizes?

Resource Density, Sharing, and the Importance of Hunting

Several recent articles have dealt with the influence of the resource base on grouping tendencies among humans and other species. For example, Horn (1968) showed that when blackbird resources are unevenly distributed in space and time, the optimum exploitation strategy is to forage in groups and to abandon defense of individual territory, since the individual is then able to utilize the knowledge of the entire group. Wilmsen (1973) has applied this principle to hunter/gatherers and suggests that the most effective strategies for hunting game are not efficient for collecting edibles, because the temporal and spatial distribution of large game is less predictable than that of collected foods, and hence game is much more difficult to locate. This situation is explicitly described for the !Kung (Yellen and Lee, 1976:39), and is perhaps a universal condition of hunter/gatherer subsistence. Even caribou migration routes and herd sizes are much more variable than many ethnographies and popular accounts indicate (Burch, 1972). The importance of hunting to those who practice it is evident from both the major caloric contribution made by hunted foods to human diets (see section on the Economics of Subsistence) and the high value placed on meat (see Diet Selectivity). But whatever the reasons for the importance of hunting, Horn and Wilmsen's arguments lead us to expect *hunter*/gatherers to live in groups, while there is no apparent ecological reason why the gathering of plants and other stable foods should result in significant grouping behavior.

Group size among lions appears to be dependent on the density of the prey (Caraco and Wolf, 1975). Similarly, for omnivorous humans, group size may be partially related to overall resource density; a number of ethnographers have noted a positive relationship between density of food resources and group size (Gould, 1968b:119; Tobias, 1964:80; Warner, 1958:128). Thus, both theoretical and empirical considerations suggest that

Table 10.7. Group size, hunting, and resource density

Group	Group size[a]	Population density (per 100 mi²)	Ratio of group size to pop. density	Percentage of food hunted[b]	References
Nootka	1,500[c]	200	7.5	55	Jewitt, 1974
Western Desert Aborigines	20	3	6.7	20	Gould, 1969a:256
Mistassini	15	1	15.0	75	E. Rogers, 1972:91, 121
G/wi Bushmen	55	16	3.4	30	Silberbauer, 1972:295, 297
Guayaki	16	7	2.3	50	Clastres, 1972:163, 165
!Kung Bushmen	20	41	0.5	30	Lee, 1972a:334, 350
Tasaday	26[c]	50	0.5	0	Yen, 1976:176
Andamanese	45	200	0.2	20	Radcliffe-Brown, 1922:28, 46
Hadza	9 (8)	40	0.3	20	Tomita, 1966:147
Paliyans	18–30 (24)	200	0.1	18	Woodburn, 1968a:49, 1972:193; Gardner, 1972:41

[a]Figures used in computation are given in parentheses.
[b]From tables 10.3 and 10.4.
[c]Estimates based on Suttles' comments on the high densities on the Northwest Coast, and on Yen's statement that previous densities of 1/km² for the Tasaday were untenable.

group sizes tend to vary in direct proportion to two variables: the importance of hunted food in the diet, and the overall resource density (fig. 10.2).

Assuming that hunter/gatherers generally increased in numbers until some optimal balance with their resource base was reached [a concept explored theoretically by Wynne-Edwards (1962) and empirically by Birdsell (1975)], human population density may be the most readily available indicator of resource density. Although this assumption may be susceptible to some error (considering especially the depopulation during European contact and attendant epidemics), I believe that population density provides at least a rough degree of resource ranking appropriate for testing relationships among some of the variables listed in table 10.7.

Unfortunately, all but 10 ethnographies lack even gross estimates of the critical variables: group size, population density, and degree of reliance on hunting. To examine the relationship of these three variables in a two-dimensional graph, I have transformed the first two into a ratio. Figure 10.1 thus displays the relationship between the group size/population density ratio (from table 10.7) and the percentage of reliance on hunted food (from tables 10.3 and 10.4). Theoretically, if resource density (represented here by population density) and degree of reliance on hunting were the only variables determining group size, a perfect regression line would result, with all points falling on a single line. Granted that the data are equivocal and the sample size is small, the relationship is nevertheless quite strong ($r = .79, p < .01$).

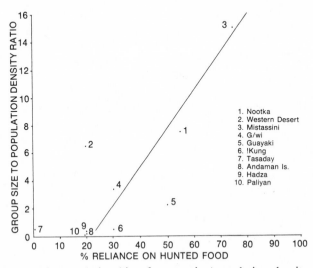

Figure 10.2. Linear relationship of group size/population density ratio and percentage of reliance on hunted food.

Moreover, the two groups that fall farthest from the regression line—the Western Desert Aborigines and the Guayaki—may not be nearly as anomalous as they appear. Gould (1969a:256) notes that the population density for the Western Desert area is probably lower now than it was prehistorically, having been recently reduced by the arrival of European diseases and the opportunity to migrate to government settlements and ranching stations. So the current population density probably does not accurately reflect the resource density. If a density of about 10/100 mi^2 were assumed for the Western Desert—which is reasonable for this habitat— these Aborigines would fall much closer to the regression line. As noted, Clastres (1972) estimates a much greater reliance on hunting among the Guayaki than did earlier ethnographers. In addition, the Guayaki live in a rain forest, where one would ordinarily expect a low animal biomass. If they actually obtained about 30% of their subsistence needs (by weight) from hunting, as do most tropical forest groups, then they too would fall much nearer to the regression line.

It is difficult to take into account the seasonal fluctuations in game availability and group sizes in this review because of the complexity of the subject and a total lack of quantitative data. It is interesting, however, that some anecdotal cases of seasonal group-size changes conform to the hypothesis that group size is a function of resource density and reliance on hunted game. The response of the G/wi and Great Basin hunter/gatherers to seasons of extreme scarcity has already been mentioned (see section on Group Size and Foraging Area). Conversely, Gould (1969a:256) stresses that the Western Desert Aborigines only congregate for their major ceremonial feasts at times when game is unusually abundant. Such gatherings are often 100–200 strong and are the largest aggregates recorded in the Western Desert. Woodburn remarks that Hadza camp sizes vary in relation to seasonal fluctuations in the availability of faunal resources: "The most important single factor creating the larger camps of the dry season is that at this time of the year more large game is being killed" (1968b:106). He then discusses the emic values that draw individuals together, all of which, not surprisingly, center on meat-eating. Sinha (1972:377) claims that large settlements are not feasible for the Birhor because of the scarcity of game.

There are strong reasons, then, for viewing most of the observed variability in group size as a function of the relative importance of meat in the diet and of the local resource density, yet some ethnographers claim that hunting practices and resource density are not primary determinants of group size. The Mbuti aggregate during the rainy season when there is an official prohibition on hunting but when honey is abundant, according to Harako (in this volume); he concludes that social factors, in particular festive occasions, are the main causes of aggregation, and that environmental variables play only a secondary role. However, the Mbuti are dependent on the Bantu for many of their plant foods, and they cash in on food obligations mainly during Bantu festivals. Given the economic interdependence of the two groups, Mbuti aggregations may well take place at the time of the most reliable and abundant food availability, which Harako implies coincides with and derives from Bantu festivals. Grouping behavior thus is still consistent with the principle relating large group size to high resource densities. In this particular case, resource nucleation within Bantu villages might also be an important factor in promoting Mbuti aggregation.

A more difficult problem is raised by Damas' observation (1972:24) that Copper Eskimo groups aggregate in autumn only for social benefits, because virtually no economic activities occur then. The same applies to many Northwest Coast winter settlements, although defense (Drucker, 1951) and the attraction of wealth might have promoted aggregation even in the absence of specific environmental influences. Williams (1969:148) also maintains that Birhor bands do not aggregate for economic reasons, but he does not present any alternative mechanisms. Like other authors, such as Silberbauer (1972:295) and Gardner (1972:417), Williams seems to assume the presence of an innate human gregariousness that can regulate grouping habits in the absence of other factors.

Communal Hunting Tactics

Another theory that purports to explain contemporary and prehistoric human grouping tendencies involves the popular concept that humans—and especially early hominids—have had to hunt cooperatively in groups to be able to bring down large game. Washburn and Lancaster (1968), Schaller and Lowther (1969:314), and others have suggested that hominids banded together to increase hunting (and gathering) efficiency and that this condition promoted the emergence of cooperation, food-sharing, language, and many other traits supposedly not shared with nonhuman primates. Hunting practices are interesting, therefore, not only as forms of subsistence behavior but also because of their possible relevance to grouping tendencies and other major trends in human evolution.

As mentioned, humans need not hunt in groups in order to capture game. Lone Hadza hunters are one case in point (Woodburn, 1972:198), and solitary Ainu families can be totally self-sufficient (Watanabe, 1972:456–59). Even the largest extant land mammal, the elephant, can be killed by lone Pygmy hunters using the crudest of weapons—wooden-tipped spears (Turnbull, 1965b:153; 164). Nevertheless, as table 10.8 shows, communal hunting does occur in numerous hunter/gatherer societies. Under what conditions is it more adaptive than individual hunting?

Bicchieri (1969:176) assumes that individual and communal subsistence

Table 10.8. Importance and characteristics of group hunting

Groups	Dependence on group hunting vs. individualistic hunting	Prey species	Seasons	Participants	References
Caribou hunters					
Mistassini	high	woodland caribou		3–5 adult men per hunting group	E. Rogers, 1972:111
Kutchin	high	caribou	late fall, early winter	communal encircling technique	Osgood, 1936:25; Vanstone, 1974:24
Netsilik	moderate	caribou	late summer		Damas, 1972:13
Cooper Eskimo	moderate	caribou	July	women & children are beaters; adult men are hunters	
Tanaina	moderate	caribou, bear, sea otter		communal drives by several adult men	Osgood, 1937:31–38
Net hunters					
Mbuti	high	most game	year-round	women & children are beaters; adult men are hunters	Harako, in this volume
Birhor	high	all game	year-round	entire community involved	Sinha, 1972:376
Great Basin Numa	moderate to high	rabbits		women and children are beaters	Fowler and Fowler, 1971:47, 48; Steward, 1938:34 ff.
		antelope (rare)		women and children are beaters	
		deer (very rare)		women and children are beaters	
		bear		adult males	

Group		Game	Season	Participants	Reference
Northwest Central Queensland Aborigines	moderate	kangaroos, emus		adult men operate net traps or all men & women in drives; 9–10 men	W. Roth, 1897:97–100, 1901:24–29
Others					
Guayaki	high	all	year-round	2 or more men	Clastres, 1972:171–72
Andamanese	high–moderate	all?		2–5 adult men	Radcliffe-Brown, 1922:36
Tlingit	moderate–high	bear, deer mountain goat		many adult men adults	Oberg, 1973
Ainu	moderate	bear, deer	spring & autumn	adult males from 3 houses	Watanabe, 1972:456–59
Murngin	moderate–low	kangaroos turtles, crocodiles		adult men & boys adult men	Warner, 1958:129, 131
Nootka	low–moderate	whales seal, porpoise, sea otter (traditionally)		many 7–8 adult men per boat & several boats; or 2 adult men	Drucker, 1951:45–46, 49
Archer Mbuti	moderate–low				Harako, in this volume
Western Desert Aborigines	low	kangaroo firedrives			Gould, 1966c:44, 1969a:262
!Kung Bushmen	very low				Lee, 1972a:346
G/wi Bushmen	very low				Silberbauer, 1972:290–91
Hadza	very low				Woodburn, 1968a:51
Alacaluf	very low				Bird, 1963:58–59
Paliyans	very low				Gardner, 1972:414–16

techniques are functionally related to specific habitat conditions, although he does not explain which habitat features are relevant. One possibility is that group hunting is most adaptive under conditions of high game density. However, when we turn to the Hadza, who inhabit one of the richest hunting areas in the world, there is an almost total lack of group hunting. It might therefore be more reasonable to assume that group hunting is characteristic of areas where game is unusually scarce.

A review of hunting tactics reveals that there are at least two types of group hunt: communal hunts involving large numbers of people, often including women and sometimes children; and small-scale cooperative ventures involving only a few men.[4] Regular communal game drives appear to be largely restricted to areas with limited resources. In northern latitudes, it is essential for groups to procure large amounts of meat in order to survive lean seasons, and among "commercial hunters" such as the Birhor and Mbuti, it is economically imperative to obtain large amounts of game for trade or sale, in addition to subsistence needs.

Based on these observations, I submit that communal hunting occurs predominantly in areas where meat is an absolute survival necessity, because this tactic is more *reliable* than individual hunting and probably yields more meat per day per group. Most likely, communal hunting is not practiced otherwise because of its high cost in time and effort (table 10.9). I would suggest that this type of interaction between work effort, yield, and exploitation technique is not unique to hunter/gatherers. An analogous situation exists between extensive cultivation (with high yield per man hour, as with individual hunting) versus intensive cultivation (lower yield per man hour, but higher total yields, as with communal hunting). Commercial net hunters, such as the Mbuti and Birhor, must work hard and long during communal hunts. The Mbuti sometimes work so hard that they may not have time to visit relatives or gather enough vegetable foods for their own needs (Harako, in this volume). Yet communal net hunting can result in large and consistent game captures and provide stable and

Table 10.9. General characteristics of individual versus communal hunting

Individual Hunting	Communal Hunting
Fewer people needed	many people required
Higher yield/work hours/person	lower yield/work hours/person
Low total number of hours work per group	higher total number hours work per group
Lower total yield/day/group	higher total yield/day/group
Less certain results per day	more certain results per day
Extensive area covered	small area covered intensively

reliable returns (Fowler and Fowler, 1971:48; Harako, in this volume; Turnbull, 1965b).

If the reports of greater and more reliable yields in communal hunts are accurate and if communal hunting had no disadvantages, every hunting group in the world presumably would practice communal hunting on a regular basis. Since only groups that inhabit resource-poor areas do so, there must be some disadvantage to the technique. This disadvantage may well be the *intensive* nature of exploitation, which requires far more work per capita than individual hunting. To obtain the highest return per unit of time and energy expended on searching for a mobile resource, the best strategy would seem to be to cover as much area as possible per person. If other resources such as vegetable foods are plentiful, it is relatively unimportant that game be procured at every outing. The most energetically efficient hunting technique can then be employed. Groups that must depend on regular procurement of game (because of the absence or periodic scarcity of other resources) cannot afford that luxury. Thus, groups will hunt individually when they can and communally when they have to. (See also Ross, 1978.)

Of special interest here is Drucker's account (1951:48–49) of the introduction of communal hunting tactics among the Nootka, who in historical times developed the technique of capturing rare quarry by thorough coverage of large areas. For example, the hunting of sea otters was transformed from a traditional quest by two men (a steersman and a harpooner) to a prolonged quest involving 20 or more boats. The effort involved in securing prey in this manner was worthwhile because pelts retailed in China for as much as $1,000 apiece. Heizer (in Drucker, 1951) notes the same development among the Aleuts. Drucker also characterizes whale hunting among the Nootka as a largely sportive, or luxury, activity that contributed to the prestige of the clan heads, even though whale hunting produced notoriously poor returns in relation to the time and energy invested. That whaling should be, by contrast, an important subsistence activity among coastal Eskimo groups with scarce resources is consistent with the arguments made above.

Other examples indicate, however, that additional factors may stimulate communal hunting tactics. Game drives occurred in the Australian Western Desert only after rains, when prey were both numerous and clustered (Gould, 1966c:44; 1969:262). Boas (1964:101) noted that the central Eskimo resorted to individual stalking only when deer were scattered; and when game is highly dispersed, as in the Kalahari area, it usually cannot be hunted by communal drives (Silberbauer, 1972:290–91). In the case of caribou hunting, large amounts of meat must be obtained, prepared, and stored within a short time (Brolly, n.d.), requiring many participants.

The pattern which seems to emerge here is an inverse relationship between prey density and work effort. Increasing density and aggregation of prey compensate for the excessive work per pound yield involved in communal drives (figure 10.3), whereas at the other extreme of very low game density, the work effort involved in communal hunting becomes so excessive that the result is greater energy expended than energy captured. Thus, it may be appropriate to use communal techniques only within certain limits of game density, and when obtaining a given quantity of meat per day per group is more important than the attendant increase in work effort per pound of meat yielded. Such conditions are most frequently encountered in areas where plant resources are scarce and where game is at least periodically above a certain density threshold (as well as under "commercial" hunting/gathering conditions).

Still other considerations may be important. For example, Steward (1938:34–38) explained the communal drives for antelope on the basis of the extreme speed and wariness of these animals, and pointed out that these drives so severely depleted the antelope herds that they could only be held every 12 years. In addition, small-scale group hunting may be more functional than individual stalking when there is high risk associated with pursuit—notably in the case of large and aggressive prey, such as bears. Among the Tlingit, for instance, injuries were frequent when hunters went

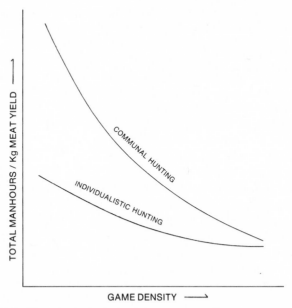

Figure 10.3. Hypothetical relation between work effort expended and kilogram of meat yield, for two hunting tactics.

after bear (Oberg, 1973:67). The Ainu went in small groups to hunt bears for this reason (Watanabe, 1972).

In the remaining groups in table 10.8, most hunting is done by individuals or in small cooperative groups of 2–4 persons. It is not clear whether these small hunting units are more efficient than individual hunters. Much of the foraging done by small groups of hunter/gatherers probably includes little or no cooperative behavior, especially in the case of plant-gathering by women (table 10.10). Indeed, there is no good indication in the literature that hunting and gathering in small groups occurs for any reasons other than companionship and safety.

In summary, it seems that communal hunting is most practical when obtaining a given amount of meat per day is more crucial than the increased work effort associated with communal hunting (i.e., under resource-poor or commercial hunting conditions), when prey are at least periodically dense enough to warrant group tactics, or when there is a high risk of injury to individual hunters. Based on these observations of contemporary hunter/gatherers, it is unlikely that prehistoric human groups needed to form communal or even small cooperative hunting units to acquire prey. In fact, under most conditions, communal hunting may have been the least efficient mode of capturing prey.

Pooling Resources

The arguments just discussed beg the question of why peoples who hunt most efficiently as individuals nonetheless live in groups. If the degree of reliance on hunting is a major determinant of group size, and if communal hunting is *not* responsible for grouping tendencies, what is? In contrast to group hunting, which involves active coordination and cooperation by participants, there is another type of "cooperation" in which each individual hunts alone (or with a companion) and pools his yield with other group members on his return. This has the advantage of yielding the highest poundage per man-hour of work and ensuring fairly regular provisioning of meat for all or most group members. Indeed, if we assume that game is a desirable commodity, we can also surmise that living in groups in order to pool individual hunting efforts is highly functional. A pattern consisting of individuals dispersing from a campsite in different directions and covering large areas is probably the most work-efficient method of procuring mobile prey. Even at this relatively efficient level, however, failure is more frequent than success. Lee (1972a:342) calculates that on the average, only one in four days is productive for individual !Kung hunters. It makes sense to maintain groups that can field enough hunters to make at least one kill per day highly probable. Both Damas (1972:14) and Balikci (1968:80) have emphasized this aspect of subsistence. During the winter, lone Copper Eskimo and Netsilik hunters had little hope of encountering seals with

Table 10.10. Group resource exploitation that is not cooperative

Group	Comments	References
Nootka	Women went in groups or "parties" to gather berries, a noncooperative endeavor	Drucker, 1951:39, 57; Jewitt, 1974:81
!Kung Bushmen	Women forage in groups of 3–5 but gather their own food items	Lee, 1972a:345
Aborigines, Murngin	Women of different clans often forage together; no evident economic reason	Warner, 1958:129
Aborigines, Arnhem Land	Women work as individuals even if there are a number in the party	Bowdler, 1976; Thomson, 1949
Ainu	Women went in groups to gather plants, although they did not engage in cooperative tasks	Watanabe, 1972:471
Paliyans	Subsistence work was often done in groups of families; but work is parallel, not cooperative	Gardner, 1972:417
Tlingit	Fishing was usually done in groups, although it could be done by individuals	Oberg, 1973:66
Birhor	Most male commercial activities were cooperative, although there was no economic need	Sinha, 1972:379
Andamanese	Men hunt in pairs for fear of forest animals	Sen, 1962
Mistassini	Men hunt and trap in groups for companionship and to educate the young	E. Rogers, 1972:120

much predictability, but numerous individuals acting on the basis of a coordinated plan of dispersal were assured of daily kills. In fact, these were the times of maximum aggregation for these Eskimo groups.

Understandably, then, the *pooling of individual hunting efforts* is viewed favorably by most hunters. Woodburn (1972:199) certainly emphasizes this, as does Clastres (1972:164), who claims that Guayaki groups numbering less than 15 individuals would have great difficulty surviving because of the irregularity of game capture. Pooling of individual efforts also leads to more efficient use of meat, in that all or most of it can be consumed before it begins to spoil [see Mackey (1976:61, 69) for similar behavior in social carnivores.] Accordingly, one expects group size to be positively related to an increasing dependence on hunting, as indicated in figure 10.2.

Discussion

Several conclusions emerge from this evidence: (a) group size is strongly influenced by dependence on hunting and by resource density; (b) communal hunting is also dependent on the importance of hunting plus resource density; and, (c) one of the major reasons why individuals and families aggregate is to pool resources.

There is still a considerable amount of residual data that does not fit comfortably into these conclusions. Certainly some groups aggregate, at least temporarily, in order to exploit extremely localized resources, such as salmon runs. Such intensive localization may be rare in tropical regions, where food resources tend to be more dispersed than in the Arctic and Subarctic zones, but it might apply to resources such as water in arid habitats. For instance, Australian Western Desert Aboriginal groups cluster around water holes in times of drought (Long, 1971:265). The same phenomenon occurs among some Kalahari Bushmen (Lee, 1972d:134-40), as well as the horticulturalists of the southwestern United States (Hill, 1966). Moreover, I have not addressed the question of why high resource density should lead to large group sizes. Such densities certainly permit large group sizes, but they hardly compel them. It is therefore necessary to assume that other factors are also important. The problem is too complex to deal with here.

The review does indicate, however, that fundamental relationships exist between group size, group movement, and the reliance on hunting. Although I do not pretend to have described these relationships fully, we are in a somewhat better position to propose a reason for the tendency of hunter/gatherers throughout the world to maintain group sizes in the "magical" range of 25-50 members (Lee and DeVore, 1968b). First, I and others have postulated that it is uneconomical to exist in large groups, since work as well as the potential for conflict increase exponentially as group size increases. By contrast, the pooling of individual hunting efforts ensures that a highly valued resource (meat) is regularly available to all. If it is assumed that the !Kung rate of hunting success (one out of four days) is typical for other hunter/gatherers, then we may expect about 4–8 families to constitute hunter/gatherer groups, thereby making fresh meat probably available every day. An estimate of 8 families is based on the presence of one hunter per family in 6 families, plus 2 family heads too old to hunt, and allows for 2 adults not going hunting every day. If there were less than 4 families in a group, pressure would be much higher on all adult members to hunt every day. At 5 persons per family, these estimates yield group sizes of 20–40 members. A slightly lower success rate in hunting (e.g., once every 6 or even 10 days per hunter) owing to simpler technology (e.g., lack of bows) or other factors could account for slightly larger groups of about 50 members. Because of the economic disadvantages of large groups and the difficulty in maintaining cohesion, groups larger than 50 are not expected to occur except in special circumstances (e.g., water shortages). Groups smaller than 25–50 are probably characteristic of greatly impoverished areas such as boreal forests and deserts, where large numbers would tend to overstrain group members' physical capacities and the thinly dispersed resources on which they depend. When small groups do occur, it appears that generally all able adult males hunt every day—a situation not characteristic of richer environments.

RANGE UTILIZATION, NOMADISM AND SEDENTISM

Anthropologists commonly assume that hunter/gatherers must rely on resources that are widely dispersed and relatively scarce (i.e., low-density resources) in comparison to the resource base available to agriculturalists and horticulturalists, and that efficient exploitation of the large home ranges[5] occupied by hunter/gatherer groups must necessarily involve considerable nomadism (e.g., Drucker, 1951; Lee, 1976b:95; Silberbauer, 1972; Tanaka, 1976).

Some of the important postulated effects of a nomadic life include a tendency toward minimal accumulation of material items, natural restraints on population increase (Binford and Chasko, 1976; Lee, 1972b:342; but see Hayden, 1972:206), an absence of crop domestication (M. Harris, 1975:193; Sauer, 1969:22), and limited group size. I shall discuss three major variables as they relate to nomadism: environmental constraints, group sizes, and foraging distances.

Environmental Constraints

It is not universally agreed that low resource density is the major determinant of nomadism. Some ethnographers postulate that other emic or innate factors determine group movement. For example, according to Woodburn, the Hadza "move to satisfy the slightest whim," because possessions are few and relocation of camps is simple (1968b:106). Yet the regular movement of entire groups within large home ranges, with members carrying all their material possessions including dependent infants, and often water and food supplies, is more realistically viewed as work, not simply as a psychologically or emotionally regulated wanderlust. Drucker, for instance, notes that shifting residence for the Nootka was "awkward, and involved a good deal of wasted effort" (1951:59). Silberbauer also comments on causes of nomadism among the G/wi Bushmen, and ascribes their movements to the seasonal scarcity of resources (1972:297). The G/wi may be reluctant to move campsites until necessity dictates relocation, but in some areas of the Kalahari this necessity occurs with fair regularity. Silberbauer notes that plant supplies begin to dwindle and game animals learn to avoid hunting zones within about four weeks.

Although other hunter/gatherers also view camp relocation as work to be avoided whenever possible (see Lee, 1969), this does not mean that all available resources must be depleted before a group moves on to a new site. Limiting factors—such as water shortages—can immediately stimulate nomadism, but discovery of favorite foods, such as concentrations of insects, can also attract groups to new locations. The Guayaki, for instance, plan their movements to coincide with the emergence of insect larvae (Clastres, 1972), and the G/wi have been observed hastening across the countryside to exploit caterpillar infestations (Silberbauer, 1972). News of renewed or shifting resources can travel swiftly among the bands composing a hunter/gatherer population. Mobility of individuals and groups is therefore doubly functional, serving to transmit information and to enhance exploitation. Departure before complete depletion of local resources around *regularly* visited campsites also reduces the risk of creating shortages on subsequent visits. In sum, nomadism can be viewed as a balancing mechanism for maintaining and conserving the resource base while exploiting it at an optimum level. Therefore, it seems plausible that readiness to change camps, whatever the emic reason, would also have a latent economic function, and has been of general adaptive advantage among band societies throughout the Pleistocene and Holocene.

Most authors who supply information about nomadism cite the differential availability of resources in both time and space. It is also important to note that other proximate factors—such as defense or avoidance of conflict, sanitary conditions, and deaths—can influence group movements. Australian hunter/gatherers are a case in point, for Aboriginal camps are frequently moved for any or all of these reasons. However, since the new campsite may be only a few hundred meters away, and since other groups carry on intensive conflict under sedentary

Table 10.11. Patterns of nomadic movement among groups approximately ranked progressively from the most sedentary to the most nomadic

Groups[a]	Frequency of moves (months)	Distance moved (km)	Reasons	References
Ainu	23	?	seasonal movement of males only for hunting	Watanabe, 1968:72
Tlingit	?	?	seasonal for economic exploitation	Oberg, 1973:57
Nootka	?	?	seasonal for economic exploitation	Drucker, 1951:59
Birhor	18	?	resource depletion (with storage & preservation, could be sedentary)	Sinha, 1972:375
Andamanese	2–6	?	for better hunting, fishing, & shelter; due to garbage accumulation & deaths	Radcliffe-Brown, 1922:30–33
!Kung Bushmen	2–3	16–20	for food and water; go to range limits after good rains	Lee, 1968:32–35
N. Queensland Aborigines	?	?	due to change in season, food supplies, & sanitary conditions	W. Roth, 1901:7
Paliyans	?	?	partly economic; partly danger from agriculturalists	Gardner, 1972:418
Netsilik	?	?	seasonal moves due to changes in resource availability	Balikci, 1968:80

Great Basin Numa	<1 (weekly in summer, none in winter)	?	due to differential plant availability & storage	Steward, 1938:19
Mbuti	1	?	—	Turnbull, 1965b:22
Copper Eskimo	1 (in winter)	16	to exploit new sealing area	Damas, 1972:23
Hadza	<1 (2 weeks)	8	primarily because food and water not conveniently available; also: to get raw materials, to escape illness, to trade, to gamble, to avoid disputes	Woodburn, 1968a:52; 1968b:106; 1972:201
Western Desert Aborigines	<1 (1–2 weeks)	?	for food and water; follow rain storms; go to limits of ranges after good rains	Tindale, 1972:234, 248; Gould, 1969a:267
G/wi Bushmen	<1 (3 weeks)	13–20	move "when local resources exhausted," go to limits of range after good rains	Silberbauer, 1972:280, 296–97
Mistassini	"short periods"	?	move if no kills, or to seasonally productive areas	E. Rogers, 1972:109
Kutchin	?	?	economic availability of resources	Osgood, 1936:23
Guayaki	<1 (3 days)	?	moves "determined by economic factors"; also implies that defense determines frequency of moves	Clastres, 1972:145, 160, 163

[a] Ranking is, in many cases, a subjective estimate.

conditions, regional nomadism must be viewed primarily as a result of economic constraints. The popular notion of an "innate walkabout" urge among Australian or other hunter/gatherers is clearly not substantiated.

In table 10.11, groups are listed in terms of increasing nomadism. Mobility is universal, but the Ainu move approximately every two years whereas the Guayaki often move every 2–3 days (Clastres, 1972; Watanabe, 1968). Determining the conditions under which groups become highly sedentary is more difficult than accounting for group nomadism. The overall availability of resources does not fully account for the high degree of sedentism represented in the sample. Several authors maintain that resource patterning is equally important, and group size may also play a role. Watanabe (1968), for example, in comparing the Ainu of Hokkaido and the Northern Paiutes of Owens Valley, suggests that high degrees of sedentism occur only in narrow, temperate mountain valleys, presumably because many distinct ecological zones exist within these valleys; they are, in effect, mosaic habitats. Narrow mountain valleys, although possibly conducive to sedentism in this case, probably do not constitute a prerequisite for sedentism in most band societies. There are too many major exceptions, such as the highly sedentary groups in coastal and estuarine ecotones, including those inhabited by Aboriginal groups in Arnhem Land, South Australia, northern Queensland (Mulvaney, 1969), West Coast North America (Drucker, 1951), and coastal Florida (Goggin and Sturtevant, 1964). Watanabe also doubts that hunter/gatherers in tropical and subtropical ecosystems have much potential for sedentism. The examples just given indicate that this proposition too is dubious, although others have suggested that pronounced *seasonality* may be a major factor in determining sedentism among hunter/gatherers, and seasonality is usually (but not always) more pronounced in temperate regions.

The importance of seasonality as a regulator of nomadism has been outlined by Poiner (1971:47–50, 150), who postulates that nomadism increases in relation to the increasing scarcity, limited diversity, and greater unpredictability of resources. Conversely, sedentism is likely to occur with the increasing abundance, diversity, and predictability of resources, together with the increasing ability of groups to preserve and store essential foods. She maintains that most sedentary groups live in regions with marked seasonal variability.

It may not be immediately apparent why pronounced seasonality should strongly influence hunter/gatherer sedentism. Seasonally fluctuating animal and plant species yield high concentrations of edible matter for relatively short spans of time, often in enormous quantities, but provide poor fare for the rest of the year; in contrast, nonseasonal environments produce a relatively constant supply of food. If seasonality is readily predictable, the advantage of *storing* superabundant resources for use in subsequent periods of scarcity is obvious, and if storage techniques are adopted, then larger populations can be supported in higher local concentrations with more residential stability.

Efficient storage techniques would thus be a necessary condition for a high degree of sedentism, along with the complicated technology needed to exploit seasonally superabundant resources, the high resource diversity needed to create stability, high resource abundance, and a certain amount of synchronous production among food species. Hunter/gatherer groups living in areas without pronounced seasonality are not expected to exhibit significant storage behavior because of the economic disadvantages this technique may involve (see section on Storage of Food).

Group Size and Foraging Area

Group size may also influence the relative position of a hunter/gatherer group on a general scale of mobility. As Silberbauer has noted (1972), G/wi sedentism increases as bands shrink in size. If a group is small enough, it can remain sedentary for long periods even in very harsh environments. Lee (1972c) has explored the mechanisms of this relationship: since the energy cost of foraging becomes excessive in comparison with energy yield when individuals must travel more than a certain distance from a campsite, it is more economical to move the camp when foragers are obliged to travel beyond this "threshold distance" to procure food. Naturally, this distance will vary from group to group, season to season, and habitat to habitat. With large groups, this "economical foraging area" tends to become exhausted relatively quickly, whereas with smaller groups the same resources will last proportionately longer. Thus, degree of nomadism is a partial function of both group size and optimal foraging distances. It is important, therefore, to determine the most economical and efficient foraging distances, including the range of variability.

Optimum foraging distances are rarely reported in ethnographies, but the maximum convenient distance for plant-gathering seems to hover around 8 km. Lee (1972b) has observed that gathering forays of more than 8 km tend to increase sharply the energy cost of procuring food, whereas the amount of food that can be brought back to a campsite remains fairly constant. Thus, few !Kung individuals travel beyond distances that can be covered easily within a single day. In Australia, Tindale (1972) has recorded similar behavior among the Western Desert Aborigines, where women resist going more than 5 km for food and attempt to instigate camp relocation if foraging trips exceed 6–7 km. Additional information in table 10.12 confirms this picture of foraging ranges.[6]

Such observations were used by Higgs and Vita-Finzi (1972:31) in the reconstruction of subsistence economies at hunter/gatherer archaeological

Table 10.12. Comparative foray distances for hunting and gathering

Groups	Foray distances (km)	Comments	References
Tasaday	?	women gathered within 1-hour walk of camp	Fernandez and Lynch, 1972:308
Hadza	5–6	foraging radius for women	Woodburn, 1972:202
Birhor	5–8	forays for gatherers and hunters	Sinha, 1972:377
Copper Eskimo	8	radius exploited around winter camps	Damas, 1972:23
G/wi Bushmen	8	radius for gathering by women and children	Siblerbauer, 1972:280, 287, 290
	24	radius for normal 1-day hunting trips, with 2–3 extended hunts per year	
Australian Aborigines (general)	6–8	radius for gathering by women	Yengoyan, 1968:187
	11–13	radius for hunting	
!Kung Bushmen	10	general radius; women return by mid-day or late afternoon, never stay overnight	Lee, 1968:31, 33; 1972a:345, 346
	13–24	the distance men must go for fresh tracks (rarely stay overnight)	
	16–24	nut forays	
≠Kade Bushmen	16–48	distance hunters cover	Tanaka, 1976:102

Western Desert Aborigines	8–16 5–6	forays for gathering 1 day's travel for most hunting; long-distance hunting trips when game scarce; food caches in trees for men on long hunting trips	Gould, 1969a:261, 266 Tindale, 1972:242, 245 personal data
Mistassini	?	hunting trips: 1–several days; trapping trips, 7–10 days	E. Rogers, 1972:109
Dogrib	320	fall caribou hunt, including travel and transport one way	Helm, 1972:68
Ainu	?	resources within 1 day's trip; usually unnecessary to go far	Watanabe, 1972:473–75
Guayaki	?	"daily" forays (always less than 1 day)	Clastres, 1972:164
Mbuti Pygmies	?	net hunting a "daily" activity; early morning to midday or dusk	Harako, in this volume; Turnbull, 1965b:119
Andamanese	?	when game scarce, long-distance hunting trips	Radcliffe-Brown, 1922:33–39
Tanaina	?	hunting trips often so long that wives are taken	Osgood, 1937:31, 38
Kutchin	?	using sleds and canoes, travel long distances; hunters cover large ranges (greater than women's ranges); hunters are generally out "all day" looking for food	Osgood, 1936:57–60

sites. In a quantitative approach, they argued that the decline in net energy becomes significant beyond a 1-km radius for sedentary groups, and that it becomes oppressive at more than 3–4 km. They adopt a 5-km radius as a normal working limit and a 10-km radius as an absolute limit for efficient exploitation. These estimates undervalue the distance traveled in gathering forays, and hunting forays too are generally longer than portrayed. Hunting trips with a radius of 13–24 km or more (table 10.12) were probably common for both prehistoric and modern hunter/gatherers, although forays lasting more than a day were probably infrequent, occurring mainly in conditions of scarcity. However, groups with transportation aids (dogs, sleds, canoes), such as the Dogrib, Tanaina, and Kutchin, could embark on hunting forays of as much as several hundred kilometers and still return with substantial amounts of food (Helm, 1972; Osgood, 1936, 1937). Such aids are limited to specific regions, and the groups using them cannot be compared with the foot-traveling hunter/gatherers who lived or now live in many temperate and tropical habitats.

That hunting forays are commonly longer than gathering forays may be related to the fact that many band societies living in temperate and tropical regions depend heavily on plant resources that are depleted around campsites less rapidly than the local fauna. Settlement stability therefore may be more closely related to plant food availability (see, e.g., Lee, 1969). Alternatively, the foray distances may simply reflect the different requirements of the two exploitation strategies, or the limited mobility of women who are periodically infant-burdened.

Given the energy-expenditure limits of foot travel and food transport, we may expect that the annual ranging habits of bands will also be limited. In the Australian Western Desert, Gould (1969a) reports that one band covered an area of about 2,500 km^2 over a span of four months, and the Pintupi group I studied in the same region used a yearly area of about 1,000 km^2. Silberbauer (1972) observed that a G/wi group used about 1,900 km^2 during four months, and it is likely that the annual range of Kalahari groups is close to this figure. These examples are drawn from groups living in rather harsh environments; groups living in wetter regions would most likely have smaller home ranges. The maximum range utilized by generalized hunter/gatherers having no transportation aids is probably in the neighborhood of 2,500 km^2. If resources are so dispersed that not enough food can be obtained in an area of this size, especially if the home ranges of several bands overlap, it is likely that groups would have to expend more energy acquiring food than they could derive from consuming it. For this reason, vast areas of boreal North America may have been uninhabitable by hunter/gatherers until transportation aids became available. It is clear that foraging distances vary little throughout the world, except where aided transport is available, and so they need not be considered as a major factor in explaining the *variability* in nomadic behavior.[7]

ECONOMICS OF SUBSISTENCE

An array of topics could be discussed under this heading, since ethnographers often report on the economic aspects of hunter/gatherer societies. In this review, attention focuses on the basic elements of the subsistence economy, namely: subsistence technology and the preparation, distribution, and storage of food.

Subsistence Technology

Aside from groups that rely on specialized techniques for obtaining food, such as the sea mammal hunters in Arctic regions and the net hunters in Central Africa, most contemporary hunter/gatherers rely on a small toolkit for their subsistence activities (see Bicchieri, 1972; Lee and DeVore, 1968a). Implements for killing and butchering animals and digging up tubers compose a basic toolkit that has probably persisted with various additions since the time of the early hominids described by Isaac and Crader (in this volume). Possession of such equipment can markedly affect access to various resources and serves to increase the resource base as well as to encourage sedentism.

A single all-purpose tool, such as a digging stick, can be used to add tubers and other subsurface flora, small burrowing fauna, and underground water to the larder; these activities are well beyond the capability of any nonhuman primate species (Tanaka, 1976:101).[8] When more complex technology related to roasting, boiling, leaching, fishing, seed harvesting, and other types of food processing is added to the repertoire, the exploitable resource base further increases in diversity and stability, and the vagaries of lean periods are commensurately offset. Thus technology is an essential factor in accounting for resource diversity and abundance.

Where technology is sufficiently developed to harvest, store, and prepare large amounts of food, we can expect changes in ranging habits and population density, with a tendence for groups to become larger and more sedentary than groups that have simpler technologies in the same environment. Examples of relatively sedentary groups are the Ainu (Watanabe, 1968), the Bering Straits Eskimo (Nelson, 1899; Spencer, 1959), the Owens Valley Paiute (Steward, 1938), and many Northwest Coast groups (Suttles, 1968). In some cases the main settlement sites are permanently occupied even when some group members go on extended hunting expeditions.

Preparation of Food

The technology of food preparation is too varied to catalog here. I shall treat only those basic aspects which tend to increase the resource base above what is naturally available via foraging and feeding on raw substances.

The main types of preparation techniques are listed in table 10.13, which is based on 17 groups for which some information exists. Of the seven techniques shown in the table, the use of fire for boiling or steaming is clearly the most widespread. However, even though fire may have been under control for a million years or more (Chard, 1969:85) and may well have been used for roasting various foods throughout much of human prehistory, most of the techniques listed in table 10.13 probably came into use among hunter/gatherers only in the latter part of the Upper Paleolithic (about 20,000 years ago). Boiling, by which juices and fats can be extracted in the form of soups from animal, fish, and plant materials that might otherwise be inedible, and by which some toxic substances can be removed from the raw foodstuffs, was entirely absent even in the ethnographic present from the largest population of generalized hunter/gatherers in the world—the Australian Aborigines. Most of the groups that today rely heavily on boiling food have either been in close contact with neighboring cultivators or pastoralists or live in Arctic and Subarctic zones, where every calorie is prized. Thus, observations from ethnology seem to confirm the archaeological evidence that boiling and steaming techniques are rather recent innovations, perhaps because suitable procedures and containers were not developed until other technological advances occurred.

The hypothesis introduced recently by Leopold and Ardrey (1974)—that early hominid hunter/gatherers must have relied heavily on meat because they did not yet have the preparation techniques needed to remove the toxins that occur in many plant foods—is not tenable. Some potential plant resources certainly have toxic properties, and discovery of any means of removing toxins (boiling, grating, pounding, leaching; see table 10.13) would increase the usable resource base, but there is neither ethnological nor ecological evidence to support the assumption that large numbers of plant species contain easily removable substances toxic to humans. The vast majority of plant foods used by modern hunter/gatherers are simply not toxic in either their raw or roasted forms. Coursey (1973) argues, for instance, that the use of a simple digging stick had much more profound effects on the ability of humans to make use of plant resources than did the controlled use of fire. Among the hunter/gatherer groups listed in table 10.13, only three use preparation techniques to remove toxins; many such groups who subsist mainly on plant resources probably survive quite well without using any toxic plants.

Although in the literature surveyed there are a number of quantitative

Table 10.13. Food preparation techniques

Groups, by geographic areas	Boiling	Steaming	Soaking	Grinding/Grating(g)	Pounding	Putrefaction	References
Nootka	X	X	—	—	X	X	Jewitt, 1974:53, 83; Drucker, 1951:61, 62
Tlingit	X	X	—	—	—	—	Oberg, 1973:57
Tanaina	X	—	X	—	X	—	Osgood, 1937:41–45
Kutchin	X	—	—	—	X	—	Osgood, 1936:29–31
Great Basin Numa	X	—	—	X	—	—	Fowler and Fowler, 1971: 39, 42
Guayaki	X	—	—	—	—	—	Clastres, 1972:152
Chono	X	—	—	X	—	—	J. Cooper, 1917:187
Other Tierra del Fuego groups	0	—	—	—	—	—	J. Cooper, 1917:189
G/wi Bushmen	X[t]	—	—	X	X	—	Silberbauer, 1972:288
Hadza	X	—	—	X	—	—	Tomita, 1966:163, 166
Western Desert Aborigines	0	X	—	X	X	—	Gould, 1969a:261–62; Tindale, 1972:250–51
Aranda	0	—	—	X	—	—	Spencer and Gillen, 1927: 17–18
Murngin	0	X	X[t]	—	—	—	Warner, 1958:129–33
Northern Queensland Aborigines	X[1]	—	—	X	X[t]	—	W. Roth, 1901:7, 8
Tasaday	0	—	—	—	—	—	Yen, 1976:166; Fernandez and Lynch, 1972:298
Semang	X	—	X[t]	X[t](g)	X[t]	—	Evans, 1937:57–60
Paliyans	X	—	—	—	—	—	Gardner, 1972:413
Birhor	X	—	—	—	—	—	Sinha, 1972:387

Note: ×, present; 0, absent; —, no information; t, technique used to remove toxins.

[1] Princess Charlotte Bay only.

estimates of the amount of work necessary to procure food (see table 10.20), only two studies provide estimates of time spent per day in food preparation. Lee (1968:37) reports that !Kung women devote 1.0–3.0 hours to fire tending and food preparation per day, and Gould (1969a) estimates that Western Desert Aborigine women spend about 2.5 hours per day in parching, grinding, and otherwise preparing various staples. In both cases the preparation budget is equal to about 50% of the total time devoted to finding, harvesting, and transporting food. If this ratio holds for other groups, then reports that hunter/gatherers spend a relatively small amount of time in subsistence activity are somewhat misleading.

Distribution of Food

Most nonhuman primates are gregarious, living in social groups that include a mixture of age grades and sex classes (A. Jolly, 1972). Only among chimpanzees and baboons, however, has any indication of regular food-sharing and an incipient division of labor in subsistence activities been reported. In both species, adult males are the main predators on other mammals and regulate meat distribution to other group members (Strum, in this volume; Teleki, 1975). Among contemporary hunter/gatherers the division of labor is more marked, and the pooling of resources more extensive. In fact, sharing is such a definite criterion of group membership that refusal to share generally precipitates band fissioning (Lee, 1972a).

If group living is to be adaptive for individual hunters, the pooling of game resources must be encouraged and codified. We might therefore expect to find the most extensive and intensive sharing patterns in groups that exploit large game. This is certainly not a new concept, but it nevertheless concerns one of the most pronounced and widespread characteristics of the hunter/gatherers sampled here (table 10.14). The only real exception is the Paliyans, who live in an area with abundant resources and chose not to exploit big game. It is interesting how frequently hunters in band societies are prevented by strict codes of conduct from eating their own kills, or end up with nominal portions. This can best be interpreted as a method of rigidly reinforcing the pooling of individual subsistence efforts.

Although it is often assumed that *all* food is shared among the members of hunter/gatherer bands (e.g., Yengoyan, 1968), the actual extent of sharing has rarely been investigated. It is quite probable, as B. Hiatt (1970) and Bowdler (1976) point out, that most group members eat non-shared food during gathering and hunting expeditions. Such "snacks"—which may at times amount to substantial meals—have been documented in Australia (e.g., McCarthy and McArthur, 1960), and are also apparent in several documentary films on subsistence activity.[9] This behavior makes a great deal of sense, because additional food can then be carried back to base camps, and the total yield of each foraging trip is increased (see also Mann, in this volume).

Despite the scarcity of data, it is my impression that individual gatherers and hunters commonly consume a significant proportion of their diets in the form of snacks during foraging expeditions except in situations where food cannot be eaten without processing or where climatic conditions render such feeding impractical. The problem, of course, is that no field reports provide accurate measures of the amount of food eaten in this manner. Nutritional studies of food intake at campsites are therefore likely to underestimate total intake per season or year. While McArthur (1960), Yen (1976), and others consider hunter/gatherer diets to be of lower nutritional quality (including calorie intake) than the norm for our society. such generalizations may not hold up when systematic nutritional studies become available.[10]

Further insight into the factors controlling personal gratification as opposed to group welfare, which can be viewed in terms of proximate versus ultimate effects on the subsistence economy of a band society, might lead to an understanding of some of the behavioral and the nutritional variability observed among hunter/gatherer populations. Extensive sharing is habitual in some societies, such as the Kalahari Bushmen (Marshall, 1976), while in others, such as the Australian groups listed by Bowdler (1976) and the Paliyans of India (Gardner, 1972), sharing appears to be much more irregular. Based on observations that meat is often not shared with women, Bowdler (1976) and Mackey (1976) infer that dietary regimes among male and female members of hunter/gatherer societies differ markedly, and then speculate about the potential effect of these dietary differences on social bonding among males and on other intragroup phenomena.

Finally, food-sharing between groups was probably important during periods of low resource availability, at which time intergroup visiting tended to increase in some populations (see, e.g., Strehlow, 1965). Kinship rituals and other social ties among the bands composing a social nexus, as described by Heinz (1972) for the !ko Bushmen and Strehlow (1965) for Western Desert Aborigines, facilitate exchange of food and water in conditions of shortage and stress. The adaptive advantage of this behavior is such that it was probably widespread throughout most of the Pleistocene.

Storage of Food

The advantages of preserving and storing food by groups whose exploitation activities are subject to the vicissitudes of the environment seem intuitively obvious, yet these advantages must be weighed against other factors, including increased work efforts and the restrictions on

Table 10.14. Sharing practices among hunter/gatherers grouped by culture areas

Groups	Meat	Vegetable	Snacking	References
Nootka	Whale shared according to rank order (as in potlatch)	Gave food to guests even if short of food, and at feasts		Jewitt, 1974:46, 73; Drucker, 1951:55–57
Tlingit	Within households, food communally produced and consumed; elders and house chief took best portions; everyone had to contribute; during periods of shortage anyone in village with food gave to others; feasts and reciprocal sharing			Oberg, 1973:92, 96, 98
Tanaina	Game given to hunting partners who distributed it in village; sea otters (commercial) were personal property	Communal meals occurred primarily in rich areas		Osgood, 1937:32, 38, 135
Netsilik	All hunters in residence had right to portions; much casual gift giving			Balikci, 1968:81
Copper Eskimo	Rigid sharing partnerships (not necessarily close kin); hunter often kept only skin and fat; many communal meals and gift giving; expected sharing of cached food			Damas, 1972:24, 25
Kutchin	Large game always given to individual in wife's clan who made a feast for all; visitors always given food			Osgood, 1936:28, 31
Mistassini	Mutual aid within hunting groups; men gave food to those without and gave feasts; widows helped by those with food	No sharing of berries by women		E. Rogers, 1972:120–21
Dogrib	Caribou shared with anyone present; hunting parties shared without reservation; fish requested from kinsmen and neighbors when stores were low			Helm, 1972:67, 68, 69, 71

Group	Sharing rules		Foraging/eating behavior	References
Guayaki	Hunters and parents could not eat game, but had to distribute meat in successive order to: wife and children, close kin, ritually close persons, all others; small game went only to wife and children	Insect larvae shared and eaten collectively; expect sharing of other foods		Clastres, 1972:160, 168, 170, 171
Tierra del Fuego	Game habitually divided among friends even if hunter gets nothing			J. Cooper, 1917:177
!Kung Bushmen	Formalized sharing; small game eaten only by hunter's family			Lee, 1968:31; 1972a:348, 350
G/wi Bushmen			Men gather foods for themselves while hunting	Silberbauer, 1972:288
Hadza	Small animals eaten only by hunter's family; large game shared with those who transported game, or request meat; sacred portions reserved for initiated men	Only 50% of food brought back to camp likely to go to males	Men, women and children eat a lot while foraging; hunting trips often only an excuse to gather vegetable foods	Woodburn, 1968a:51, 53; Tomita, 1966:162, 163, 167, 168
Western Desert Aborigines	Hunter gave to in-laws and brothers; everyone with food had to share with relatives present who lacked food		Women ate fruits and berries while foraging; brought staples that needed processing back to camp; men ate while hunting	Gould, 1966c:55–56; 1969a:261–62; Tindale, 1972:248
Australian (various)	Men generally share among themselves and offspring, and only if enough with wives; game brought to camp shared according to strict kinship rules	Shared with husband and offspring	Men often eat all game in bush; women usually snacked while foraging, even consuming more than brought back to camp	Bowdler, 1976

Table 10.14 (Continued)

Groups	Meat	Vegetable	Snacking	References
Great Basin Numa	Hunters kept skin; flesh divided equally among all others	Food in camp considered common property		Fowler and Fowler 1971: 48, 49
North Queensland Aborigines	Communal sharing, even with people who did not work			W. Roth, 1901:7
Murngin	Large game eaten according to strict sharing rules by all group members		Women eat much shellfish where gathered; men gather and eat yams and bulbs for themselves when hungry; honey eaten where obtained	Warner, 1958:129, 133
Andamanese	Meat given to all group members; sharing determined by age and status (not kinship) after hunter's family provided for	Evenly distributed at campsite; those with food expected to give to those lacking		Radcliffe-Brown, 1922: 38, 43, 81
Semang	Communal food supply	Shared with visitors	Large amounts of food eaten while foraging; only foods abundant enough to be brought back in quantity are shared	Evans, 1937:59, 62
Tasaday	Meticulous sharing	Shared at base camp		Yen, 1976:163, 166, 174
Mbuti	Methodically shared by everyone, with special consideration for hunter and helpers	Individual property rights respected, although some sharing occurred		Turnbull, 1965b:158, 167
Paliyans	All had to demonstrate individual self-sufficiency; if no surplus, food could not be shared outside nuclear family			Gardner, 1972:416, 422, 432

cartage imposed by a nomadic life. Some hunter/gatherers store foodstuffs on a massive scale, while others do not practice food storage to an extent that noticeably affects their subsistence economy. Explaining this variation in storage behavior is important to our understanding of other phenomena such as the emergence of sedentism and plant domestication.

Many of the reports examined for this review contained no information about food storage techniques, and so table 10.15 provides only a general impression of these practices. But the reports mentioning storage techniques tend to emphasize that much extra labor is involved in preparing foods for storage. In addition to the effort and time expended on smoking, drying, pounding, grinding, and other preparation techniques, considerable work must be put into building storage facilities such as pits, containers, and houses. Writing about Northwest Coast groups such as the Salish, Suttles points out that some foods "required far more effort in storing than in the taking" (1968:63) and suggests that the limiting factor in exploitation of available resources was more the finite amount of time and energy available for storage processing than the amount available for acquisition. He suggests that drying and storage facilities may have been just as important as the resource itself. Woodburn also notes the Hadza's dislike of preserving meat, "which is tedious, time-consuming, and renders the meat less palatable" (1972:199).

Unfortunately, time–motion data on this subject hardly exist in the literature. Helm (1972) mentions that Dogrib women spent about 4 hours per day preparing fish for storage, while caribou had to be dried and smoked over open fires for several hours. Among the Kutchin, the drying and smoking of a fish catch took 3 or more days, although Osgood (1936) does not specify how many hours of actual labor were involved. Despite the lack of detailed data, it is clear that these storage practices must have involved substantial additional expenditure of energy and time. It thus is likely that most band societies avoided food storage except in the most stringent circumstances. As Lee remarks (1972a), the environment was a sufficient "storehouse" in most cases. Neither environmental nor technological limitations are likely to have prevented the storage of food if the motivation to do so were strong enough, although it was undoubtedly more feasible to store perishable food in Arctic or temperate habitats than in wet equatorial habitats, where heat and humidity promote decay. Nevertheless, nuts and seeds, as well as sun-dried fruit and meat, could be stored in most climates without sophisticated technology. In some areas, relatively complex technology may have been necessary to harvest vast amounts of food (e.g., cereals).

It is often assumed that food storage is strictly a response to anticipation of famine. Poiner (1971), for example, argues that storage behavior is most likely in habitats where the resource base fluctuates strongly from periods

Table 10.15. Food storage techniques among hunter/gatherers, grouped by culture areas

Groups	Storage techniques	References
Nootka	Dried fish, eggs, berries	Jewitt, 1974:76, 81; Drucker, 1951:63–66
Tlingit	Dried (and/or smoked) fish, clams, mussels, berries, chopped seaweed; boiled and dried roots, inner bark; oil as preservative; cached in boxes	Oberg, 1973:66–73
Tanaina	Dried clams, groundhogs, (and smoked) fish, seaweed, inner bark, oil preservative; made meat and fat into intestine sausages; cached in pits in permafrost	Osgood, 1937:41–44
Kutchin	Most fish dried and smoked; dried meat and fish eggs; preserved berries; fish fat and animal marrow boiled and preserved	Osgood, 1936:23, 28, 30
Dogrib	Fish dried and stored for months; caribou dried and smoked, but consumed within a few days	Helm, 1972:63, 68
Netsilik	Elaborate caching techniques for meat and fish	Balikci, 1968:80–81
Cooper Eskimo	Lived off dried or frozen caribou and fish for 2–4 weeks in winter; food in excess of immediate needs cached	Damas, 1972:13, 25
Montagnais-Naskapi Mistassini	Caribou meat dried and stored in fall for winter	Fitzhugh, 1972; E. Rogers, 1972:109

Group	Storage	References
Great Basin Numa	Stored seeds, berries, roots, nut meal cakes; dried and stored lizard and earthworm flour for winter consumption; seeds and berries kept in earth pits	Steward, 1938:19, 20, 32; Fowler and Fowler, 1971:39, 48
Guayaki	No storage of any foods	Clastres, 1972:152
Onas and Yahgans, Tierra del Fuego	Short term irregular storage of dried fungi and meat (or blubber)	J. Cooper, 1917:187
Western Desert Aborigines	Storage only in lean periods; tree caches left for men on long distance hunts; stored food *not* used for large gatherings (too much work); dried fruits; no meat storage	Gould, 1969a:260–65; Carnegie, 1898:2301; Thomson, 1962:12; Finlayson, 1935:84
!Kung Bushmen	Minimal storage of flora (2–3 days only); no meat storage	Lee, 1968:31
Hadza	No storage beyond a few days; fat melted and stored in gourds; dried meat kept up to 5 days	Tomita, 1966:161, 163
Ainu	Lived on stored salmon and venison and plants during winter; extra stores in case of shortage	Watanabe, 1968:72; 1972:467, 471
Tasaday	Short term smoking of excess meat; palm starch storage	Yen, 1976:166, 175
Birhor	No storage of any foods	Sinha, 1972:376
Aranda	No storage of any foods	Schultz 1891:233; Chewings, 1936:3

of great abundance to periods of scarcity. As mentioned earlier, these are also the conditions in which sedentism probably tends to increase. Following this line of reasoning, Brolly (n.d.) has suggested that only two subsistence strategies are available to groups that rely heavily on a single, mobile, seasonally available resource, such as the caribou exploited by Arctic Athapaskans: to follow the mobile resource throughout the year, or to harvest large amounts of the resource in a limited time in work-intensive communal hunts and then to store the surplus for use during the rest of the year. Brolly feels that the first alternative would tend to consume more energy than it would provide, and hence the Athapaskans choose the second.

The data presented in table 10.15 indicate that food storage techniques are more common and more sophisticated in higher latitudes, with little or no storage occurring in equatorial regions where seasonality is less pronounced, the need for storage is correspondingly less, and stored food spoils easily. In Australia, storage is especially infrequent [see Allen (1974) for a useful review of seed use and storage]. Given these limiting aspects, storage techniques must have conferred a major advantage to have persisted. Since we can say with some confidence that in all cases of regular storage, groups could not exist at their recorded densities without storing substantial amounts of food, the advantages of storage may be related to the frequency and magnitude with which resource stress occurred in specific habitats. Alternatively, it may be that in stable environments (i.e., highly diversified habitats with highly predictable seasonal changes) the enormous seasonal differences in resource availability are more easily anticipated, so that groups in these habitats have developed levels of technology in sedentism which make seasonally lean periods more secure. A subsequent rise in population density could then be viewed as a by-product of these subsistence activities.

DIET SELECTIVITY

Emic Value of Meat and Fat

The emic value of meat has often been noted in the literature describing hunter/gatherer subsistence, although I found only seven explicit statements that a particular group valued meat more than any other food, or at least much more than vegetable foods (Clastres, 1972:153–55; Gould, 1969a:260; Lee, 1968:40; E. Rogers, 1972:91; Warner, 1958:129; Woodburn, 1968a:52). Several reasons for this preference can be suggested.

1. Meat is a nutritionally rich resource, high in protein and caloric value.
2. Consumption of meat might provide more leisure time.
3. Capture of big game results in extensive sharing and feasting, which

involve major social as well as nutritional rewards (Lee, 1968:41; Silberbauer, in this volume).

Since data are few, however, the actual reasons for the high value placed on meat-eating by contemporary hunter/gatherers cannot yet be identified.

Given the ethnographic interest in emic values associated with meat, it is curious that equally abundant and explicit observations on preferences for fats have gone virtually unnoticed. This concern for edible fat is widespread among hunter/gatherer groups living in a variety of ecological zones (table 10.16).[11] Aside from being favorite foods, oils and fats are also significant trade items in some regions (e.g., Eskimo and Athapaskan groups in the Arctic and Subarctic, and American Northwest Coast Indian groups). To my knowledge, no definite explanation for this phenomenon has been offered, although the following hypotheses seem plausible.

1. Lipids act as an energy subsitute for sugars and starch in human metabolism (Drucker, 1951:62; Guyton, 1966:1002).
2. Some dieticians have suggested that in order to metabolize a given quantity of meat protein, a given amount of lipids (or carbohydrates) is necessary (one rationale behind lean-meat diets for removing excess body weight).
3. Lipids are necessary for synthesizing lipoproteins, lack of which results in malnutrition, ataxia, and retinal degeneration (Wintrobe, 1970:392, 635).
4. Lipids are essential for the absorption of many fat-soluble nutrients, especially vitamin A and carotenes (Wintrobe, 1970:392).
5. Two fats are known to be essential nutrients for children (Wintrobe, 1970).
6. Lipids are important in regulating oxygen absorption in biological systems, with deficiencies possibly leading to cystic fibrosis (Campbell, Crozier, and Caton, 1976).

Thus, the emic preoccupation with lipids may represent a very practical need among hunter/gatherers for a crucial scarce resource, rather than just an innate preference for rich food. A phenomenon called "rabbit starvation" in eastern North America is a type of malnutrition among hunter/gatherers who starve despite killing and eating a large number of rabbits, presumably because of lack of lipids in these animals in certain seasons. I have also heard a popular account of a similar situation occurring among an Inuit group that had more than enough lean whitefish but apparently could not metabolize the fish for lack of other nutrients. Stefansson (1962:143–44) documented a similar situation, regarding lean caribou:

Doing hard work in cold weather on a diet nearly devoid of fat is a most interesting and uncommon experiment in dietetics. . . . The symptoms that result from a diet of lean meat are practically those of starvation. The caribou on which we had to live

Table 10.16. Emic values placed by contemporary hunter/gatherers on consuming fats

Groups		References
Nootka	Parts with fat considered choice, delicious, and delicacies; heavy emphasis on fats	Drucker, 1951:62
Tlingit	Fish oil consumed in large quantities at feasts; large gatherings to obtain oil-bearing fish	Oberg, 1973:69
Hadza	Fat rare on game animals, thus fatty animals were precious and marrow was extracted	Tomita, 1966:160
!Kung	Fats were scarce and sought	Lee, 1972a:344 Yellen and Lee, 1976:39
Aranda	Intestinal fat "esteemed a great delicacy"	Spencer and Gillen, 1927:18
Western Desert Aborigines	Lean carcasses often abandoned	Tindale, 1972:248
Murngin	Lean emus considered poor eating; melted intestinal fat considered a great delicacy	Warner, 1958:130–31
Andamanese	Pigs often abandoned in hot season (because of lean condition?)	Radcliffe-Brown, 1922:39
Kutchin	Fat very important; excess boiled, preserved, and traded	Osgood, 1936:30, 37
Mistassini	Hare were "starvation food, since they possess very little fat"	E. Rogers, 1972:111
Tasaday	All observed animals were lean, possibly explaining "delicacy" status of fatty, bad-tasting palm grubs	Yen, personal communication

had marrow in their bones that was as blood, and in most of them no fat was discernible even behind the eyes or in the tongue. . . . We had an abundance of lean meat and we would boil up huge quantities and stuff ourselves with it. We ate so much that our stomachs were actually distended much beyond their usual size . . . but with all this gorging we felt continually hungry. Simultaneously we felt like unto bursting and also as if we had not had enough to eat. One by one the six Eskimo of the party were taken with diarrhoea.

Mowat (1963:83) also recorded a "craving" for fat when he was on a diet of disemboweled mice; this was remedied by inclusion of the intestinal fat in his mouse meals.

These incidental cases do not provide a solid basis for theorizing about the emic value of meat and fat. When combined with table 10.16, however, the evidence is provocative enough to warrant further study. Many aspects of hunting and resource exchange between groups, particularly hunter/ gatherer relations with horticulturalists and agriculturalists, might be clarified by research in this area.

It is widely recognized among hunter/gatherers that game animals are generally low in fat content, at least on a seasonal basis if not all year around. Gould (1966c), for example, observed that a 97-lb (44-kg) kangaroo yielded only 4 ounces (114 g) of removable fat. Tomita (1966:160) also noted that the Hadzapi prized eland above all other game species because this large animal had the highest fat content, and its fat was also used in ceremonial rites and as seasoning. Based on these observations, I suspect that an interest in lipids is a widespread phenomenon linked to specific nutritional requirements, especially in lean seasons or years. Such conditions probably prevailed during most of the Pleistocene, and the emic value attached to hunting game species among the modern hunter/gatherers may constitute an adaptation to the need for lipids.

Whatever the physiological basis for this phenomenon, it is tempting to ask whether a genetically determined "taste" for lipids might not have been adaptive in the lipid-deficient prehistoric environments, and whether the current penchant for "rich" foods might not be a consequence. Equally interesting is the possibility that the high emic value associated with meat is actually a misconception fostered by ethnographers. Could it be that the meat was actually valued little, whereas the fat contained in the prey was the real prize? This might explain the anomalous cases where "valuable" carcasses are abandoned after the kill because of inadequate fat content (Tindale, 1972:248), and other cases where normally shunned animals (e.g., cougars and eagles) are eaten when sufficiently fat (Drucker, 1951).

Another open question is whether plant foods that are rich in oils were as highly prized as fatty meat. Ethnographic observations lend no support to this premise, but emphasis on hunting may be so common among ethnographers that attitudes about plant resources are rarely recorded. In agricultural societies the emic value of oil-bearing plants tends to be high, and the fondness of Iron Age Danish peasants for oil-bearing seeds has been archaeologically demonstrated (G. Clark, 1953).

Dietary Preferences

Aside from the special, rare, or relatively inaccessible food items chosen to fill specific physiological requirements,[12] several principles of food selectivity have been described in the literature, which probably apply to most or all hunter/gatherers. Decisions about priorities of food collection are generally based on the following criteria.

1. Thirst or hunger-allaying properties (Silberbauer, 1972).
2. Ease and efficiency of exploitation of the resource, including travel and preparation time (Fernandez and Lynch, 1972; Lee, 1972a; Poiner, 1971; E. Rogers and Black, 1976).
3. Abundance of the resource (Fernandez and Lynch 1972; E. Rogers and Black, 1976).
4. Reliability or stability of the resource (Fernandez and Lynch, 1972; Poiner, 1971).
5. Taste and variety (Fernandez and Lynch, 1972; Lee, 1972a; Silberbauer 1972).

This list of criteria concerns mainly the choice of staple foods, and the ranking of priorities is approximate. Selection of foods to alleviate nutritional deficiency should probably also be considered [e.g., Tindale (1972:252) on the use of the curative, antiscorbutic plants of the Asclepiadaceae family], but ethnographic data are sparse. Another factor—scheduling of conflicting options—is important in some areas (Flannery, 1968), and an excellent example occurs in Drucker's ethnography of the Nootka (1951:60); these people ignored the extremely abundant and easily procured runs of pilchard fish because exploitation conflicted with other economic tasks in that season.

Regarding estimated proportions of food obtained by hunting, fishing, and gathering, Poiner (1971) maintains that marine resources rate highest in terms of reliability, quantity, and accessibility along the southeastern coast of Australia, and Woodburn (1968a) concludes that emphasis on plant foods by the Hadza (and by inference, other generalized hunter/gatherers) is due to their high reliability (see also Tanaka, 1976). Combining this notion with the high emic value of meat in most societies, we arrive at Lee's principle that Bushmen, and presumably others, "eat as much vegetable food as they need, and as much meat as they can" (1968:41).

Resource Selection

In general, one might logically expect that opportunities for selection are rather limited in areas that are low in resource diversity and density, while greater selectivity can presumably be exercised in environments that offer abundance and diversity. At high latitudes and in desert regions, groups probably had to exploit a higher proportion of available edible items in order to survive and probably had to exploit virtually all edible resources during regularly recurring periods of instability. In rain-forest habitats, where seasonal variation is less pronounced, the picture is much less clear.

The range of items that are avoided tends to grow as resource diversity increases (table 10.17). There may be occasional exceptions, such as the Guayaki, but resource availability in a rain-forest habitat is in any case far more difficult to evaluate. Other "rain forest" groups, such as the Birhor, contrast sharply with the Guayaki, having access to wide varieties of animals but being very selective (Sinha, 1972). An additional consideration is that groups described as living in "rain forests" may actually occupy drier or montane zones (e.g., the Mbuti described by Harako, in this volume). The last 4 groups in table 10.17 are somewhat anomalous. As commercial hunters with special symbiotic relationships with neighboring agricultural societies, these groups do not conform to the patterns characterizing the other 12 groups.

One of the more remarkable features of hunter/gatherer subsistence is the uniformly low priority of carnivores and raptors as a human food resource. This avoidance may be due to their "foul" taste, often mentioned in ethnographies; the difficulty and danger involved in capturing them; their relatively small numbers, since they are at the top of the food chain; and a feeling of respect and affiliation, noted by some ethnographers, between human hunters and other predators.

In some cases, the absence of large-game hunting has been explained in terms of an inadequate technology (e.g., the Birhor of India; Sinha, 1972:375). Such reasoning cannot be accepted at face value because large- and medium-sized game were efficiently hunted in other places where the available technology was even simpler, such as Tasmania and the Congo Basin. Moreover, the technology available to Lower Paleolithic big-game hunters was presumably just as or even more primitive.

Many of the societies sampled here preferred small game, and presumably some terminal Palaeolithic hunter/gatherers did too. This general emphasis on small animals, including rats, lizards, bats, mice, toads, and other choice morsels, raises numerous questions about the evolution of subsistence patterns and about the relative importance of small- versus large-game exploitation (see Teleki, 1975). Steward (1938:33) has suggested a number of advantages associated with small game exploitation: small game do not range far and need not be pursued over long distances; some species occur in colonies and can be exploited in large numbers; small game reproduce rapidly, making overexploitation unlikely; some species also store quantities of seeds and other foods that can be raided and used.

Table 10.17. Diet selectivity in relation to resource variability

Groups ranked by resource diversity	Resource diversity	Seasonality	No. of staples	Animal/vegetal selectivity	References
Western Desert Aborigines	very low	pronounced	8 flora 16 fauna	dingo and crow shunned, but eaten in need	Gould, 1969a:259–61
Great Basin Numa	very low	pronounced	—	when hungry, eat all kinds of meat; carnivores generally avoided (capture is difficult); eat all animal parts (blood, skin, stomach, intestines, brain, marrow, etc.); also eat insects, earthworms, toads	Steward, 1938:34–40 Fowler and Fowler, 1971: 47–48
Mistassini	very low	pronounced	—	utilize almost everything possible	E. Rogers, 1972:104
Kutchin	low	pronounced	—	puffballs, wolves, dogs, eagles, ravens, woodpeckers never eaten; small fur-bearers & whisky-jack (Canada jay) only eaten when starving	Osgood, 1936:24–29
G/wi Bushmen	low	pronounced	13 flora	—	Silberbauer, 1972:283, 284
≠Kade Bushmen	low-moderate	pronounced	13 flora	never eat vultures, dogs, or hyena; lion eaten rarely	Tanaka, 1976:112
Aranda	low-moderate	pronounced	—	everything eaten, including grubs, snakes, rats, frogs, flies, clay	Spencer and Gillen, 1927: 14, 17
!Kung Bushmen	moderate	pronounced	23 flora	of 223 animal species, only 54 considered edible; shun rodents, snakes, lizards, grasshoppers, termites; of 100 edible plant species, the most culturally unacceptable eaten only when nothing else available	Lee, 1968:35
Guayaki	rain forest	low		eat all available animals; seem to eat all available vegetable foods	Clastres, 1972:154–56

				Description	Reference
Hadza	moderate-high	pronounced	10 flora	high proportion of available animals eaten; no observations of snake, lizard, hyena, or buzzards being eaten	Woodburn, 1968a:51–52; Tomita, 1966:160, 165
Tanaina	high	pronounced	—	no shark, jellyfish, mink, wolverines, dogs, wolves, hawks, ravens, or mushrooms are consumed; others are shunned; herring not eaten in large amounts because bones are too numerous	Osgood, 1937:29–41
Nootka	high	pronounced	—	avoid eating sea snails, rock borers, barnacles, spider-crabs, pilchard fish, seaweed, conifer inner bark, sea gull eggs or flesh, ravens, crows, frogs, snakes, squirrels, dogs, wolves; deer and elk are nearly neglected; mink, marten, otter shunned; only fattest cougars and eagles are eaten	Drucker, 1951:39–61
Mbuti Semang	rain forest rain forest	low low	—	almost all animals considered edible consume almost every kind of edible, but some do not eat bear, elephant, or tiger (and eat little meat as a result)	Harako, in this volume Evans, 1937:58
Birhor	rain forest	moderate	—	no animals larger than monkeys are exploited (i.e., elephants, wild cattle, deer, bears, and large carnivores not used)	Sinha, 1972:375
Paliyans	high	moderate	—	exploit only a fraction of the available resources, ignoring plants and animals they do not prefer; generally ignore big game	Gardner, 1972:412–14

Deevey, too, stresses that small game have a very high potential for productivity and thus can be harvested at high levels and frequent intervals (1968:95). In fact, he speculates that efficient exploitation of mice, rather than deer, by humans living in temperate deciduous forests would permit a hundredfold increase in hunter/gatherer population density. Efficiency is the problem: capturing smaller animals may require much more effort in order to obtain an amount of meat equivalent to the yield from a single large animal—unless, of course, special technological harvesting techniques are available. It is likely that reliance on small game is adaptive primarily in situations where human populations are exerting considerable pressure on their resource base, where the resource base is initially limited, or where the technology already exists to "harvest" small game in large quantities (see also Ross, 1978). In the latter case, small game may supply such an important supplement to the total larder that a comparatively dense human population can be supported even in lean periods.

This interpretation accords reasonably well with the data presented in table 10.17. Both the Birhor and the Paliyans are being forced into more restricted habitats by extrinsic pressures, such as expanding populations in neighboring areas. But the widespread exploitation of small animals has additional implications for understanding the evolution of human subsistence patterns during the Pleistocene—a point to which I shall return later.

DIVISION OF LABOR

Sex Classes

The traditional view of labor division is that women gather plant foods whereas men hunt animal foods. In reality, this dichotomy is far too simplistic. Women gather small animals as well as plants, and in some instances even participate in capturing various prey; men, despite devoting most of their attention to hunting, may also gather plant foods to be eaten on the spot on hunting trips. Although Lee (1968), B. Hiatt (1970), and others have attempted to estimate the relative contributions of males and females to the total diet, time–motion studies of subsistence activities are so rare that precise comparisons cannot be made at present. Another complication is that division of labor is highly variable across societies, with some groups being extremely rigid in this regard while others are relatively casual. For the kinds of interpretations proposed by Tanner and Zihlman (1976), for example, much more refined data need to be obtained.

Table 10.3 (columns 7–12) provides an approximate analysis of the relative proportions of subsistence activities carried out by males and females in 49 groups (see B. Hiatt, 1970). Exactly how the compilers of the ethnographic atlas arrived at the proportions used by Hiatt is something of a mystery, inasmuch as the original sources often fail to provide such data altogether or do not specify what measures (weights, calories, etc.) were used to calculate the estimates and by what methods the data were tabulated. Discussion of this component of hunter/gatherer subsistence economy is therefore highly tentative.

Three basic hypotheses have been offered for the prevalence of division of labor by sex. First, some division of labor may be needed to exploit efficiently any highly diverse resource base. As noted earlier, the greater the diversity in the subsistence base, the more stable it is likely to be from the human standpoint. The problems inherent in the exploitation of widely different resources by omnivorous humans are aptly summarized by Flannery:

> So many possibilities for exploitative activity were open to these ancient Mesoamericans that it would have been impossible to engage in all of them even seasonally. It happens that there are times of the year when a number of resources are available simultaneously, producing a situation in which there is conflict for the time and labor of the group. Division of labor along the lines of sex, with men hunting and women collecting, is one common solution to these conflicts. (1968:75)

The same point is emphasized by Watanabe (1968), who stresses that hunting requires long-distance travel and active pursuit, and such mobility would be inhibited by the gathering and transporting of many small items.

Second, men may be innately more predisposed to hunting, while women may be behaviorally more predisposed to gathering. The contention here is that psychological and physiological differences orient females toward gathering and males toward hunting (e.g., Watanabe, 1968). Women are often regarded as more sedentary and less aggressive partly because they must expend more time and energy in child care (e.g., B. Hiatt, 1970:2). Moreover, female body odors may at times constitute a major handicap under primitive hunting conditions that generally require approaches to within 25 m of the prey (Dobkin de Rios, 1976). For these and other reasons, women would be handicapped in hunting excursions. Hunting forays would be seriously impaired by the need to nurse, care for, and carry children. Gathering requires less mobility and also involves less risk to fertile females and their young.

Third, as I have suggested elsewhere (Hayden, 1972), since women produce children and maintain infanticide practices, sexual division of labor may function primarily as a population control mechanism, in which the differential allocation of tasks ensures that, on the average, women cannot cope with more than one dependent offspring at a time no matter what the degree of sedentism or the richness of the environment. Thus, we expect fertile women in some groups to have very high work loads, reducing their ability and willingness to have offspring. This would partly account for the apparent life of ease that males sometimes enjoy in comparison to females. Both Tindale (1972) and Gould (1969a, 1970b) note that Western Desert women perform the most strenuous and tedious tasks. Other studies on the Aranda (Chewings, 1936), the Bangerang (Malinowski, cited by Bowdler, 1976), and the Gilgandra (Gaynon, cited by Bowdler, 1976) indicate that males often lead a comparatively leisurely existence. Referring to Tasmanian and Australian hunter/gatherers, B. Hiatt states that

> the men's tasks, by comparison, were light . . . they probably spent less time procuring food than the women and for the same reasons as the male Australians spent less time on food production than their women. The Tasmanian woman's tasks were time consuming and provided the reliable food supply. The men's tasks were less time consuming and provided the less reliable elements in the diet though their jobs at times demanded sudden expenditure of strength and energy. (1967:215)

These observations tend to support, in my opinion, the premise that division of labor is an important regulator of population growth in hunter/gatherer societies. From a cross-cultural survey of fertility and women's work loads, Dahlberg (1976) comes to much the same conclusion.

These hypotheses are not mutually exclusive; on the contrary, all three may be mutually reinforcing. The first two, in particular, are complementary, as Watanabe has noted (1968). Observations about other sexual differences in activities are also consistent with the premise that females are not as well adapted to hunting and tend to chose other alternatives when they are available. For instance, female members of hunter/gatherer bands do not own weapons designed specifically to hunt large game, are usually excluded from the mythology and folklore associated with hunting forays, and frequently serve as mere porters of household effects when groups relocate. Males, on the other hand, make and own the requisite technology for big-game hunting, learn all the appropriate skills at an early age, and rarely carry more than their hunting paraphernalia on long treks.

Indeed, it is fundamental that large prey require long and active pursuit, whether hunters operate alone or in small teams; Watanabe argues (1968:77) that big-game hunting by males is the only universal element in the sexual division of labor among hunter/gatherers, all other features varying in relation to local conditions and traditions. The Netsilik's evaluation of the relative hunting merits of males and females was clearly expressed in their practice of female infanticide (Balikci, 1968:81). Table 10.3 reveals only two potential exceptions to this rule (the Chilcotin and the Mbuti), and both cases may refer to female participation in communal drives. Landes (1938) provides several accounts of Ojibwa women who hunted for themselves in the absence of males in the family,[13] and Watanabe (1968:74) refers to occasional cases of Ainu women bringing down large game even though this was not a socially accepted occupation for females.

One important implication of these observations is that the division of labor between the sexes should be most apparent among groups that regularly hunt big game, and least pronounced among groups that exploit mainly small species. Similarly, if the sexual division of labor did function to restrict population by increasing the work load of women of childbearing age, the work differential between the sexes ought to be greatest in the richest habitats and least pronounced in the harshest habitats, where more work is required of everyone (see table 10.18). The problem remains unsolved because ethnographers have not supplied the data needed to evaluate the extent and intensity of labor division within and across many hunter/gatherer societies.

It is similarly difficult to evaluate the relative importance of individually versus communally procured large game. If we assume that all estimates shown in table 10.3 reflect the activities of single hunters or small teams,

Table 10.18. Intensity of sexual division of labor as a function of the importance of hunting

Groups	% of Hunting[a]	Sexual division of labor[b]	References
Mistassini	70	moderate-pronounced	E. Rogers, 1972:104, 109, 120, 126, 127
Copper Eskimo	55	pronounced-moderate	Damas, 1972:43
Nootka	50	pronounced	Jewitt, 1974:76, 109
Guayaki	50	pronounced	Clastres, 1972
Tlingit	40	pronounced	Oberg, 1973:80, 85
Kutchin	40	pronounced	Osgood, 1936:26, 29, 31, 59, 112
Ainu	30	pronounced	Watanabe, 1968:75
Murngin	30	pronounced-moderate	Warner, 1958:129
Net-hunting Mbuti	30	low	Harako, in this volume
!Kung Bushmen	30	low-moderate	Lee, 1972a:345–46
G/wi Bushmen	30	low	Silberbauer, 1972:304
Western Desert Aborigines	20	pronounced	Gould, 1969a:258, 260; Tindale, 1972:245, 249–53
Hadza	20	moderate-low	Woodburn, 1968a:51, 53; Tomita, 1966:164, 168, 169
Andamanese	20	moderate-low	Radcliffe-Brown, 1922: 37–44
Semang	20	low	Forde, 1934, 1954
Paliyans	15–20	low	Gardner, 1972:413, 416, 417, 424, 431, 435
Great Basin Numa	15	low-moderate	Steward, 1938:44
Tasaday			
traditional	0	low	Yen, personal
present	20	moderate	communication

[a]From tables 10.3 and 10.4.
[b]Combinations indicate uncertainty, with the first category being the most likely.

and then combine these estimates with inferences about the relative intensity of labor division in various groups, the results seem to support the hypothesis that sexual division of labor varies directly with the importance of hunting (table 10.18). There seems to be a consistent relationship between minimal division of labor by sex and high economic independence of *individuals* in hunter/gatherer groups—most notably among the Paliyans, the Hadza, and the G/wi.

Age Grades

The labor invested in subsistence activities can also be partitioned according to age grade in hunter/gatherer societies. Data on this topic (table 10.19) are even less detailed than for sexual division of labor, but a few hypotheses have been offered to account for variations across groups. Lee (1968:36–40) suggests that the degree to which subadults participate in subsistence activities reflects the exploitation pressure being placed on the resource base (see also P. Draper, 1976). The groups that enlist children most heavily in the work force are the Paliyans, the Mistassini, the Mbuti, and the G/wi Bushmen—all of whom either live in habitats characterized by low resource densities or function as commercial hunters.

As Watanabe has noted (1968), the most strenuous work burdens tend to fall on people between 15 and 35 years of age. Younger individuals usually contribute work on a sporadic basis, participating in gathering and preparing activities at the request of their elders, while older individuals perform various lighter, less strenuous activities near campsites.

In most hunter/gatherer societies the individuals responsible for specific subsistence activities are also responsible for producing and maintaining the requisite equipment. Technological specialization is rare, although elders who have retired from intensive subsistence work may contribute services in other ways, such as maintaining equipment, caring for ceremonial paraphernalia, teaching subsistence techniques, and so on. In some groups, such as the Inuit and the Guayaki, individuals not engaged in subsistence activities play important roles in the production and maintenance of equipment, and thus contribute indirectly to the subsistence effort.

If division of labor by age is related to differential physical capabilities, it may also be important in maintaining pressure on fecund women not to raise too many children. This is supported by Chewings' observations on the Aranda (1936), and by Gould's data from the Western Desert of Australia (1969a), in the sense that heavy work loads on females in the reproductive age grade may provide mothers with a strong incentive for infanticide (Hayden, 1972).

Two additional factors that influence the age at which individuals become food contributors are the amount of labor required for subsistence, and the percentage of the group that constitutes the work force (Balikci, 1968; Lee, 1968). Table 10.20 presents estimates of time spent in subsistence activities, made by various ethnographers. The data are not strictly comparable, because some estimates include only exploitation time, others exploitation and preparation time, or all work related to subsistence, and still others do not specify what is included. Nevertheless, there is some indication that time spent in subsistence activities is broadly related to environmental conditions. Groups that clearly work the hardest are either located in limited resource areas (e.g., the Netsilik) or operate as commercial hunters (e.g., the Mbuti).

The common claim that generalized hunter/gatherers spend, on the average, about 2–5 hours per day obtaining food seems to be an accurate statement. No allowance is made in these estimates, however, for other factors that might influence energy expenditure, such as food preparation, storage, and equipment maintenance. Moreover, few ethnographies supply the ecological and demographic information needed to place these data into a broader perspective. Only Lee (1968) and Peterson (1972) attempt to evaluate how many workers contribute subsistence labor, and their figures indicate that about 40% of each population (!Kung Bushmen in the Kalahari and Arnhem Land Aborigines in Australia) are nonproducers who contribute little or nothing to group larders. More anecdotal statements about the Hadza (Woodburn, 1968a:54) and the North Central Queensland Aborigines of Australia (W. Roth, 1897:124) also support such claims. These figures seem to contrast with the descriptions of Harako (in this volume), Gould (1969a), Clastres (1972), and others, who mention that most adults gather and/or hunt. These two sets of estimates probably represent the extreme of variation, and although the data base is extremely small, it is nevertheless consistent with the notion that more work is done by more people in harsher environments.

Communal Activity and Social Status

Communal hunting is an occasional or seasonal activity in several hunter/gatherer societies, but the women and children who participate in these activities are mainly "beaters" and are not formally involved in killing game, which is reserved for adult males (e.g., Damas, 1972:43; Harako, in this volume; Turnbull, 1965b:151). Watanabe's generalization (1968) that women are not accorded hunting roles appears valid, even in cases where women are more than peripherally involved. Bicchieri (1969:176) has proposed that division of labor becomes less pronounced when the importance of communal hunting increases—an interesting idea but one that is currently untestable, given the nature of the data and is highly dependent on the definitions used, as it can come close to a tautology. The Paiute, at least, do not fit readily into Bicchieri's proposition.

Table 10.19. Division of labor by age

Groups ranked from high to low resource density	Infants and children	Adults and elders	References
Tlingit	young are trained	young adults do hard work; the old direct activities	Oberg, 1973:86
Ainu	—	young men hunt bear, spear fish in winter; older men hunt deer, fish via peep-huts	Watanabe, 1968:76; 1972:469
Tanaina	boys get wood	older men keep camp and tell stories on hunting trips	Osgood, 1937:31, 135
Hadza	children help attack bird flocks and gather food	hunters are 18–35 years old	Tomita, 1966:161; Woodburn, 1968a:3, 54
Andamanese	children 5–6 imitate parents, by 10 make significant contributions	—	Radcliffe-Brown, 1922:76–78
!Kung Bushmen	no significant food contributions until 15–20; girls are 14 before beginning regular gathering; boys are 16 before beginning serious hunting	only after marriage expected to provide significant amount of food, continue contributing until after 60	Lee, 1968:36–38; 1972a:335–45; P. Draper, 1976:210
Paliyans	children economically independent by 13–14 at latest	all, including elderly, expected to be economically independent	Gardner, 1972:417–31
Murngin	young girls imitate mothers, young boys practice spearing	—	Warner, 1958
Guayaki	children help in fish drives	—	Clastres, 1972
Mbuti	from childhood to puberty, take part in all economic activities; over 10, act as game drive beaters, and get and prepare own food.	age is most important principle in division of labor; young married persons and older youths provide almost all food; elders prepare food and occasionally procure; few elders participate in hunt	Harako, in this volume Turnbull, 1965b:151, 152

Group	Children	Adults	References
Aranda	children imitate mother	—	Spencer and Gillen, 1927:24
Western Desert Aborigines	start as soon as possible, by 10 get ¼ of own food with mother	young males active in hunting; elder males no hunting	Tindale, 1972:247
Great Basin Numa	children help in game drives	young men drive game, older men shoot deer by game trails and butcher buffalo	Fowler and Fowler, 1971:48; Steward, 1938
G/wi Bushmen	early instruction for boys; girls help mother when able to walk; set traps for small game and birds; help as soon as able; girls self-sufficient by 7–8; boys by 14–15	men hunt to mid-30's, trap and procure small game after; women contribute all their lives	Silberbauer, 1972:292, 305, 316
Copper Eskimo	—	economically active from teens to 60	Damas, 1972:42
Mistassini	young children & girls help mother, older boys help father; teenage girls tend fires; full workdays by 10 for girls, by 13 for boys	—	E. Rogers, 1972:120, 122
Chukchee	children intercept wounded animals	young males go on long sea-mammal expeditions and kill animals from canoes; older hunt sea mammals on shorter trips and help women and children intercept wounded animals in streams	Watanabe, 1968:76
Tikerarmiut	children fish crabs	old people and children fish crabs from ice holes; younger men hunt seals in winter	
Nunatarmiut	—	younger men hunt in mountains during winter; aged stay in winter villages	
Iglulimiut	—	young men follow caribou; older men hunt sea mammals	
Dogrib and Yellowknife	children pick berries (& fish?)	young men: long distance trapping; older men, women & children: pick berries & fish	

Table 10.20. Time spent on subsistence activities, with groups ranked by increasing work expenditure

Groups	Average work expenditure	References
Hadza	2 hr/day per adult	Woodburn, 1968a:54
!Kung Bushmen	2–3 days/week per woman	Lee, 1968:33, 37, 38
	12–19 hr/week per adult (2.5 days)	
South Australian Aborigines	2–4 hr/day (general subsistence activities)	Eyre, 1845:2:252, 255
Tanaina	"a few minutes per day"	Osgood, 1937:26n
Tasaday	3 hr/day per adult (Yen argues that this is an underestimate)	Fernandez and Lynch, 1972:309; Yen, 1976:174
Paliyan	3–4 hr/day per adult	Gardner, 1972:309
Western Australian Aborigines	2–3 hr/day (general subsistence activities)	Grey, 1841:2:261–63
Arnhem Land (coastal) Aborigines	4 hr/day per male (all food activities)	McCarthy and McArthur, 1960:190, 191
	4 hr/day per female (all food activities)	
Arnhem Land (inland) Aborigines	5 hr/day per male (all food activities)	McCarthy and McArthur, 1960
	5 hr/day per female (all food activities)	
≠Kade Bushmen	5 hr/day to procure food	Tanaka, 1976:100

Western Desert Aborigines	4½ hr/day per female in gathering even during droughts	Gould, 1969a:262, 264; 1970:64
	2½ hr/day per female in food preparation; males spend more time in gathering and get less[a] than females (although women work ⅓ more if preparation work is included)	
Tlingit	4–6 hr/day per adult woman (all women work)	Tindale, 1972:261
Birhor	6–7 hr/day but not all subsistence so busy that visiting relatives is difficult	Oberg, 1973:89
Mbuti	8½ hr = adult workday	Sinha, 1972:386, 390
Netsilik	little leisure; males stayed out until they captured game	Harako, in this volume Balikci, 1968:82
Kutchin	hunters stay out all day in food quest, return at evening	Osgood, 1936:113
Great Basin Numa	1 day's work by a woman produced 3–4 pecks of processed seeds	Fowler and Fowler, 1971:42

[a]This may not be accurate, since Gould notes that men sometimes say they are going hunting but in reality just go to perform rituals and work on sacred boards. A similar situation is documented for the Hadza by Woodburn.

Division of labor according to relative social status has received scant attention in the literature covering hunter/gatherers, perhaps because status is often viewed as a function of sex and age in these societies or because relative social rank is not rigidly codified in most such groups. The hunter/gatherers of the American Northwest Coast were exceptional, however, in that clan leaders received "tribute" from others who exploited privately owned resources. Among the Tlingit, for example, nobles did not work, while members of a slave class carried out all the hard and menial tasks, including fishing and oil processing (Jewitt, 1974:65; Oberg, 1973:87, 102). Division of labor along class lines may have developed as a result of the extreme richness of the resource base available to these groups and the competition made possible by Northwest Coast technology. Under such special conditions, it is possible that social stratification and institutionalized competition become major factors in their own right, determining the status of women and the rigidity of the sexual division of labor.

HUMAN–ENVIRONMENTAL RELATIONSHIPS: THE FREQUENCY OF STRESS

Popular views of hunter/gatherer subsistence and society have swung, pendulumlike, from the "noble savage" of Rousseau's time, to the brutish, short-lived, and ill-nourished savage described during the Industrial Revolution, and back again to the modern image of affluent and leisurely primitives living in harmony with nature. To the extent that all of these views reflect changes in the social and psychological milieus of the various historical periods, none portrays hunter/gatherers accurately.

The scope of this problem is readily illustrated by the concept of "carrying capacity," which, in studies of human populations, refers to the upper limit of human population growth that can be achieved in a given habitat without eventual degradation of the resource base. The concept unfortunately is not operational, because the data needed to calculate carrying-capacity values for hunter/gatherer populations are simply not available in the ethnographic literature, and it is improbable that adequate data could be obtained even with the most sophisticated environmental approaches (Hayden, 1975). Alternative indicators of a human population's relation to its subsistence base can be used, however, such a nutritional status, work load, and resource selection (Balikci, 1968; Hayden, 1975; Lee, 1968). The proportion of a group engaged in productive subsistence activity might also indicate the degree of pressure on resources.

Table 10.21 lists those groups for which some information exists about human–environmental relationships; it provides at least a qualitative basis for generalizing. Examination of the table reveals, first, that high work load and low resource selection are broadly related to nutritional deprivation; second, that nearly all groups encounter periods of severe stress, although the data are inadequate for determining the regularity and ubiquity of starvation; and third, that the frequency and severity of these periods of stress seem to increase as resource diversity, density, and stability decrease.

The special position occupied by commercial hunter/gatherers needs further attention. One might expect that groups which barter or sell food resources to their neighbors would be located on the same part of the subsistence spectrum as groups which exploit low-diversity and low-density areas. In these circumstances there should be greater competition over and pressure on resources, leading to their degradation. This is certainly true of the Birhor, whose commercial base has only recently been undermined (Sinha, 1972). The Mbuti, whose symbiotic trade relationship with the Bantu is now an essential component of their way of life (Harako, in this volume), do not appear to fit this pattern, however, in that they apparently experience hunger quite rarely. This is surprising, given other indicators of stress among them, such as high work loads and limited opportunity for resource selection. It may be that one advantage of a commercial relationship is the ability to obtain staple foods on credit during lean periods, which might in turn cause population density and stability to increase markedly, at the cost of harder work and potential overexploitation of the environment. These issues are somewhat peripheral here, and the reader is referred to Hutterer (1976) and Hayden (1976) for additional details.

There is, in general terms, a substantial range of relationships between band societies and their resource bases. The subsistence level of most hunter/gatherers lies somewhere between extreme affluence and starvation. It appears that the hunter/gatherer way of life is not overly demanding most of the time but is punctuated with irregular periods of severe stress. These observations pertain primarily to food, although water can be the main limiting factor in arid regions (Gould, 1969a; Silberbauer, 1972; Tindale, 1972). Other related activities, such as food preparation, equipment manufacture, and equipment maintenance, can add considerably to the total work load. Thus, consideration of the effects of only food resource exploitation on population density, ranging habits, work loads, and other aspects of subsistence may be misleading. The central problem is that, until very recently, ethnographic research has not been oriented toward environmental phenomena. This omission may not hamper studies of kinship and technology, but it severely limits our understanding of subsistence economy and the effects that subsistence considerations may have on other aspects of culture. Fortunately, enough observations have been made so that the broad outlines of variability can at least be sketched in, with a few projects providing excellent detail.

Table 10.21. Human-resource relationships, with groups ranked by increasingly favorable relationships as determined by work loads, diet selectivity, and nutritional conditions

Group	Work load[a]	Diet selectivity[b]	Nutritional condition	References
Netsilik Eskimo	high	—	very harsh, 10% mortality from starvation every 2 yrs	Balikci, 1968:81, 82
Copper Eskimo	—	—	famine not uncommon	Damas, 1972:23
Mistassini	—	low	food a constant problem; many starvation cases	E. Rogers, 1972:104
Kutchin	high	moderate	near starvation in spring; sometimes cannibalism	Osgood, 1936:24, 28, 31
Great Basin Numa	—	low	starvation common according to informants & 19th-century observers	Steward, 1938:9, 19, 20, 46
G/wi Bushmen	—	—	early summer, hunger & thirst common; near famine after series of drought years	Silberbauer, 1972:278, 279, 282, 301
Western Desert Aborigines	low-moderate	low	semi-starvation at times of first rains; informants point to bad years	Gould, 1969a:259-65; Tindale, 1972:236-37
Birhor	high	high	scarce periods; starvation uncommon; semi-starvation due primarily to commercial situation	Sinha, 1972:377, 387
Aranda	—	—	in long droughts, privation and scarce food; ordinarily, life neither miserable nor hard	Spencer and Gillen, 1927:14

	Work load[a]	Diet selectivity[b]		
Yahgans, Alacaluf, and Chono of Tierra del Fuego	—	—	times of famine, although food usually abundant	J. Cooper, 1917:187
Tanaina	low	high	bay groups were only ones with enough food in all N. Athapaskan territory	Osgood, 1937:26, 27, 46
Nootka	—	high	often short of food, especially at end of summer; infrequent but severe shortages	Jewitt, 1974:46, 73, 96; Drucker, 1951:37
Mbuti	high	low	occasional times of scarcity, but hunger largely a result of laziness	Turnbull, 1965b:28, 128, 149
Paliyans	low	low	infrequent difficult times, resulting in interregional migration	Gardner, 1972:414
Tlingit	low-moderate	—	times of shortage, but usually so much free time that did not know how to use it	Oberg, 1973:89, 90
Tasaday	low-moderate	—	no overall food shortage, but low on starches; generally below ideal nutrition and must have had lower nutritional level before contact	Yen, 1976:182–83, 194–98
!Kung Bushmen	low	moderate/high	no evidence of nutrition problems even in droughts	Lee, 1968, 1972a
Hadza	low	moderate	no starvation or hunger, although critical times of year when eat nothing but roots and stalks; more difficult now since pastoralists reduced wild game	Tomita, 1966:160, 169; Woodburn, 1968a

[a]Work load is based on table 10.20.
[b]Diet selectivity is based on table 10.17.

EVOLUTIONARY TRENDS

Given the orientation of this volume, it is pertinent to consider how far into the past various aspects of hunter/gatherer subsistence activities can be extended by the use of analogy. As a start, we must assume that human subsistence patterns were susceptible to and modified by several kinds of selective pressure throughout the Pleistocene. When humans learned to modify their subsistence opportunities by cultural means—and the timing of this change is by no means clear (see Isaac and Crader, in this volume)—they acquired the potential for reducing some of the more undesirable constraints imposed by the environment. To the extent that this was possible we can expect trends toward increasing the *reliability* of the resource base, thereby decreasing the danger of periodic starvation or chronic malnutrition, and toward decreasing the work load.

Increasing resource reliability can be achieved in three ways, all dependent on technological innovation. First, utilizing more and more of the various species occurring in a given habitat can increase reliability. The number of potential food resources can be augmented by the use of fire, boiling, containers for carrying and cooking, tools for grinding and pounding, etc.[14]

Second, reliability can be enhanced by increasing exploitation of microedibles (such as insects and seeds) that have high rates of productivity, are more predictable, and are least susceptible to overexploitation. Exploitation of mice, as suggested earlier, could conceivably lead to a considerable rise in hunter/gatherer population density (Deevey, 1968). Thus, while reliance on long-maturing macroedibles may result in more energy in relation to the work invested, incorporation of microedibles would provide a relatively inexhaustible resource base. However, harvesting and processing small items *en masse* usually requires technology of a quite sophisticated nature.[15] Containers, beaters and grindstones or pounders are needed for seed collection and preparation; sophisticated traps, weirs, nets, or other paraphernalia are needed for obtaining fish and small animals in large amounts, and so on. There is no evidence for most of these technological innovations until the end of the Pleistocene, and they only became widespread in post-Pleistocene times throughout most of the world.

Yet there is a slow, persistent trend toward increasing technological complexity throughout the Pleistocene (Hayden, 1977; Leroi-Gourhan, 1964:93–197). I submit that this technological trend reflects a gradual expansion in the diversity of resources being exploited and is related to a continuing (although probably episodic) pressure for greater subsistence reliability. The trend culminates with the development of horticulture, where exploitation of introduced and cultivated resources supplements naturally occurring flora and fauna. Conklin (1954) reports that an incredible 2,000+ species are used by the Hanunoo of the Philippines, a figure far beyond those listed in table 10.1. In this respect, domestication of plants and animals can be viewed as an extension of a much more fundamental trend toward dietary stability through diversification of dietary habits (i.e., increasing omnivory). Thus, where it was not adopted through diffusion, we might expect domestication of plants and animals eventually to appear spontaneously in most areas of the world where climate and species were suitable.

If we assume that environmental stress is directly related to the emergence (or rate of emergence) of innovations and the adoption of technological subsistence aids, it follows that areas of low resource diversity would be primary centers of subsistence innovation, although for some innovations, such as cultivation, very extreme conditions would be inhibitory. The sedentary requirements of cultivation further tend to limit the range of habitats where we would expect cultivation to first appear. Thus, only highly seasonal areas with moderate to low *year-round* resource availability (although perhaps seasonally abundant resources) would be likely locales for the beginnings of cultivation—very unlike Sauer's tropical forests (1969).

Third, resource reliability can be increased by the development of storage techniques and facilities. Any trend toward dietary stability involving storage would also have produced a rather high degree of sedentism, yet most current band societies are quite mobile. Sedentism may not have occurred until groups attained high resource diversity in subsistence and began to exploit microedibles efficiently—probably as recently as the late Upper Paleolithic or Mesolithic.

On the basis of the principle of least effort, we should also expect trends toward decreasing work loads over time. Since one of the main types of work at the hunter/gatherer level is traveling, including the transport of goods, and since this kind of work can be reduced by increasing access to resources through technological innovation, relative increases in sedentism should characterize hunter/gatherers in any given area over long periods of time. High degrees of sedentism most likely depended on the development of technological skills for intensive exploitation of small-sized resources, and these skills do not appear in the archaeological record until the Mesolithic of the Old World and Late Archaic of the New World.

It is probably not coincidental that the technological innovations adopted by hunter/gatherers resulted in increased reliability of resources *and* decreased effort expended on nomadic movement. Both types of development appear to characterize the evolution of hunter/gatherer cultures, and it is clear that evolutionary trends toward a gradual decrease in the work loads required for survival and a simultaneous increase in subsistence diversification could not have continued indefinitely without reaching a threshold at which restructuring of fundamental environmental and behavioral relationships had to occur. When these thresholds were crossed, profound changes must have taken place in social ranking, stratification, wealth accumulation, sedentism, food domestication, and other aspects of the human condition. Prior to the attainment of this threshold, it is likely that environmental and cultural mechanisms maintained some control over population densities so that, through the Pleistocene, nutritional levels remained reasonably high in most habitats occupied by hunter/gatherers.

If the assumption is tenable that division of labor stemmed originally from the differential aptitude (physical and psychological) of men and women for hunting mobile game as opposed to gathering plant foods, and if division of labor has ancient prehistoric roots, then it is also reasonable to view the origins of human hunting behavior in terms of predation by individuals or by small cooperative groups. The appearance of labor-intensive communal drives would then be a relatively late evolutionary development.

Given the enormous flexibility and adaptability of the culture-information systems observable today, it is difficult to understand why many of the trends discussed above took so long to develop. The rate of technological change was incredibly slow during the first 2 million years of human evolution. It can only be suggested that the rate at which culture evolved in the Pleistocene was limited by biological capabilities; and by biological standards, of course, human evolution was very rapid.

SUMMARY

Low precipitation and temperatures result in low diversity, high instability, and wide fluctuations in the resource base. As a result, conservation practices are found most often in adverse environments. Many contemporary hunter/gatherers, such as the !Kung, do not occupy marginal environments and may, in fact, live in conditions close to the "ideal" hunting and gathering environment; they are probably not atypical of prehistoric groups.

Hunted meat may play a much more important role in all hunter/gatherer subsistence than current views hold; it may even be the major source of calories. Assumptions about the importance of vegetable food may require revision. Consumption of insects and earth is unexpectedly frequent. Meat is highly prized, but more importantly, so are fats. Circumstantial evidence suggests that limited fat availability is a serious and widespread nutritional bottleneck for hunter/gatherers.

Choice of resources is based on common-sense criteria such as efficiency and food value, while the degree of dietary selectivity possible is largely a function of environmental diversity and stability. The use of small game as opposed to large game would be adaptive in areas with high population densities, population pressure, or scant resource bases; however, in most cases, appropriate technology is a prerequisite.

The only form of division of labor by sex found universally is that women do not have established roles or equipment for hunting. This most likely reflects the different requirements of hunting and foraging strategies and the different aptitudes of males and females. The rigidity with which the division of labor- and age-specific work structures are enforced among females may serve to limit population size in various habitats. Division of labor along age lines is roughly correlated with environmental pressure.

Generalized hunter/gatherers normally spend 2–5 hours per day in subsistence activities. Moreover, in richer habitats 40% or more of the group may not produce food.

Nomadic movement is generally undesirable work, and pronounced seasonality, resource abundance, and resource diversity lead to increased sedentism. The efficient foraging distance from base camps is less than 8 km for gatherers and less than 16–24 km for hunters because travel and transportation costs increase while food return remains the same. This cost relationship also appears to limit the maximum range size to about 2,500 km^2 for hunter/gatherer groups without transportation aids.

Most variation in group size is attributable to resource density and the degree of dependence on hunting (assuming constant transportation costs and an egalitarian economic structure). The advantages of pooling hunted resources accounts for the formation of most groups with 25–50 members. Nevertheless, these factors do not explain all the variability in group size.

Communal hunting is a work-intensive method of procuring food and is regularly found only in areas of low resource diversity and reliability (where meat intake is critical) and among commercial hunters. Communal hunting is probably a late evolutionary development. Small cooperative groups of hunters, on the other hand, may form when unusually high risks are involved in hunting and when there are temporary very high densities of game.

Eating while foraging is much more prevalent among generalized hunter/gatherers than has usually been assumed. This probably has had an important skewing effect on most assessments of nutritional adequacy and food preferences in the literature.

Regular and long-term storage of food involves a considerable outlay of effort and time, and occurs only where the environment and population density absolutely require it. Highly seasonal areas and periodically dense resources constitute the major prerequisites.

Times of hardship are most frequent, most severe, and most often result in starvation in areas of low resource density and diversity. Nevertheless, almost all hunter/gatherers experience periodic subsistence stress.

Commercial hunters may achieve increased subsistence stability through their relations with cultivators, but at the cost of increased work effort and at the risk of overexploiting their own resource base.

The archaeological record shows that humans have consistently increased the diversity, and density, and stability of their resource base by cultural means, especially technological aids. This increase has been dramatic in the last 30,000 years, and culminated about 10,000 years ago in the crossing of several important systemic thresholds, including major behavioral changes in sedentism, ranking and stratification, the accumulation of wealth, and cultivation.

The points summarized here are presented as guiding principles only and are not to be considered as immutable facts. A number of interesting problems in the interpretation of hunter/gatherer subsistence remain to be investigated. For instance, we need to know more about the relationship between rain-forest environments and hunter/gatherer subsistence. The reason why meat is so highly valued also awaits detailed investigation, and the postulated role of lipids in human diets may contribute greatly to our understanding of hunter/gatherer nutrition, evolution, and behavior.

Acknowledgments

My appreciation to Geza Teleki for this opportunity to pursue some dormant theoretical musings (albeit at a high energy cost) and for his and Bob Harding's very generous editorial help; to Doug Yen for his interest and contributions; to Cathy Carlson for basic research on communal hunting; to Richard Brolly for unwitting collusion via his excellent manuscript; to Brian Spurling for reading the chapter; to Gayle Horsfall for her new nutrition; to Len Ham, Mike Blake, and others at the University of British Columbia for their many suggestions; to Doug Tait for his illustrations; and to Lynn Hill for her typing.

NOTES

1. Definitions of hunting and gathering vary considerably. After much discussion, participants in the 1966 symposium on "Man the Hunter" agreed that *gathering* is the collection of wild plants, small land fauna, and shellfish; *hunting* is the pursuit of land and sea mammals; and *fishing* is the obtaining of fish by any technique. They also agreed to retain "the term 'hunters' as a convenience shorthand despite the fact that the majority of people considered subsisted primarily on sources other than *meat*—mainly wild plants and fish" (Lee and DeVore, 1968a:4, 41–42). These same criteria apply in this chapter, where I examine the range of groups that are behaviorally hunter/gatherers and are not necessarily dependent nutritionally to any major extent on hunting.

2. Ecologists have noted that generally adverse climates often result in greater fluctuations of standing crop, and that environmental diversity is crucial for maintaining the viability of an ecosystem as well as the evolutionary potential of a species (Odum, 1971). MacArthur and

Connell (1966) have also shown that if the magnitude of population changes in relation to population size exceeds a certain threshold, deviation-amplifying processes dominate over deviation-reducing processes, such that extinction becomes highly probable. More recently, Hollings (1973) has argued that some stable ecosystems require only homogeneous environmental conditions, which adverse climates certainly do not provide in the long run, while Ames (1976) has expanded the argument to include a high diversity index as a requirement of ecosytem stability. Thus, low diversity, high temporal fluctuations in standing crop, and the resulting high probabilities of species extinction would all create a very unstable environment, which humans living in such areas would have to deal with in order to survive.

3. The only other quantitative measures of meat consumption I encountered in this survey were 0.14 kg/person per day for the G/wi Bushmen (Silberbauer, 1972) and 0.147 kg of processed meat per person per day for the ≠Kade Bushmen (Tanaka, 1976:112).

4. In this paper, large-scale "communal hunting" refers to hunts in which 5 or more persons act as a coordinated, cooperative group. Hunting by 2–4 people is referred to as small-scale "cooperative hunting."

5. By "home range" I refer to what Stanner (1965:2) has defined as the "range"—i.e., the total area regularly used for subsistence exploitation by a group (see also Peterson, 1975). A home range may overlap with those of neighboring groups, in contrast with the group "estate" or "territory," which is a nonoverlapping nuclear area to which a group retains exclusive rights.

6. Describing New Guinea horticulturalists (who are peripheral to this review), Rappaport (1968:52) notes that 20% of the energy intake from crops is consumed immediately in travel and food transportation to and from a village located in a total foraging area of only 8.3 km^2.

7. Note that these ranges are many times larger than the home ranges of nonhuman primate groups (Milton and May, 1976), and so an increase in home range size may be an important adaptation in hominid evolution.

8. The comparison holds even in the case of the chimpanzee, whose technological skills outstrip those of other living monkeys and apes (Teleki, 1974).

9. Prime examples are John Marshall's films on the Kalahari: *The Hunters, The Wasp Nest,* and *Debe's Tantrum.*

10. For those interested in cross-cultural comparisons of dietary habits, the surveys by Whiting (1958) and by Gaulin and Konner (1977) provide much useful information, although the societies sampled in these reports are not specifically hunter/gatherer groups. At the band society level, the most complete documentation of dietary habits occurs in studies of Kalahari Bushmen (Gaulin and Konner, 1977; Lee, 1968, 1969; Tanaka, 1976) and Australian Aborigines (Gould, 1969a; McCarthy and McArthur, 1960).

11. I was astounded the first time I saw Western Desert Aborigines (who had recently settled on government stations) kill a kangaroo, examine the intestines for fat, and abandon the carcass where it lay because it was too lean. Upon making a kill, Aborigine hunters always open the intestinal cavity and check the fat content. Virtually every ethnographer with whom I have discussed this observation confirms it, yet such details are seldom reported in the literature.

12. For example, Rolf Knight (personal communication) points out that collection of some berries in Subarctic regions involves greater energy expenditure than energy gain for the gatherer, but the berries provide essential minerals and vitamins.

13. Hickerson (1962:42) claims that Landes grossly distorted the picture in her attempt to sustain a notion of individualism among Ojibwa women.

14. This trend continues today among the Inuit, who are adopting many modern technological skills to diversify their resource base (Damas, 1972:19).

15. An interspecific example of this has been provided by Teleki (1974), who describes differences in the technological skills used by baboons, chimpanzees, and humans in the exploitation of termites.

Richard A. Gould

11.
Comparative Ecology of Food-Sharing in Australia and Northwest California

The argument that ecological conditions strongly influence primate social systems (Schaller and Lowther, 1969:307) has its counterpart in the study of both contemporary hunter/gatherers and early hominids. Nowhere is this relationship more apparent than in behavior related to the sharing of food and access to resources. Food-sharing behavior has traditionally interested anthropologists, but the literature on this subject has been concerned mainly with social and symbolic aspects of exchange (Lebra, 1975; Mauss, 1954; Sahlins, 1965, 1972). Even in cases where the question of food-sharing in hunting/gathering societies has been dealt with, there has been a tendency to reflect upon the role these exchanges play in fostering group cohesion (Dowling, 1968). However, most of the propositions arising from these studies cannot be related directly to the problem of discovering how early hominids organized their behavior with respect to food-sharing and resource access. To do this, we would first have to assume that early hominids behaved socially in a manner analogous to contemporary hunter/gatherers, thus assuming the very thing we were trying to discover. In other words, how can we be sure that early hominids' social behavior was at all like that of any living human society? Second, we cannot test these propositions as they presently exist, since the archaeological evidence available on early hominids is not sufficient for such detailed testing. Or, as Isaac has said, "Kinship systems and marriage arrangements . . . can scarcely be considered in relation to the archaeological evidence for the Pleistocene" (1968:254). Considering these strictures, is it possible for anthropologists to do more than simply speculate about the social life of early hominids?

In this paper I focus on the question of food-sharing behavior and access to resources, because of the ecological relationships implicit in these kinds of behavior. In contrast to the literature cited above, I concentrate on its adaptiveness in the context of particular physical and biotic habitats. First, however, I wish to note a few assumptions about the food-sharing behavior of living and ancient hunter/gatherers that are widespread in the literature.

1. Food-sharing is really meat-sharing. That is, food-sharing behavior is generally considered in the context of hunting, especially cooperative big-game hunting. The argument is that hunting is a risky business, and sharing helps to overcome the risks while at the same time fostering the group cohesion needed for successful hunts.

2. All current and historic hunter/gatherers share food above the level of the nuclear family. This idea is so deeply embedded in the anthropological view of hunters and gatherers that it seems almost wicked to suggest that some societies of this kind may not share food.

3. Simple abundance of food and other basic resources will eliminate the need for hunters and gatherers to share food.

These assumptions are challenged in this discussion, with the aim of specifying when and under what ecological conditions sharing of food and access to basic resources is likely to occur in hunter/gatherer societies. I look closely at two ethnographic examples of contemporary hunting and gathering in order to determine the ecological requirements for successful adaptation in each of these sharply contrasting habitats, and the extent to which particular modes of food-sharing behavior represent responses to these requirements. The two societies analyzed here are the Western Desert Aborigines of Australia (Ngatatjara and other Pitjantjatjara-speaking groups) and the Indians of the northwestern California coast (Tolowa, Tututni, and Coast Yurok). In many ways these two societies represent the extreme ends of the hunter/gatherer spectrum, and the contrast between their modes of adaptation should make it possible to posit general principles about food-sharing behavior.

APPLYING ETHNOGRAPHIC EVIDENCE TO EARLY HOMINIDS

Before embarking on this comparison, we must consider an important methodological point. As suggested earlier, a simple use of analogy from current to past behavior is not adequate, especially when dealing with the behavior of the earliest hominids. Although the ambiguities and errors inherent in such analogies may appear obvious, an example is worth discussing here. Schaller recently pointed out that no living social carnivores (lions, wolves, hyenas, hunting dogs, etc.) actually take the kill back to their lairs. The meat is always eaten at or near the site of the kill except in the unusual case of African hunting dogs, which carry chunks of meat back to the lair in their stomachs and regurgitate them for the adults that have remained there with the pups. Even in this case, the regurgitated meat is consumed immediately and completely, and no offal is left near the lair. Schaller argues that bringing a carcass to the lair would endanger the young by attracting other carnivores and scavengers. From an ecological and evolutionary point of view, such behavior would be maladaptive because it would threaten the survival of the offspring and thus the reproductive survival of the species (Schaller, 1973:275).

These same ecological constraints would have applied to early hominids. Before the use of fire, they could not have effectively defended their lair or home base from predation, especially at night, when considerable predation occurs. The use of fire changed the ground rules for survival, enabling early humans for the first time to bring their kill to camp and share it there without undue risk from predation. Current hunter/gatherers all use fire and are relatively free of this particular constraint. Thus, drawing analogies directly from modern or historic hunter/gatherers in order to understand early hominid behavior is risky, since early humans probably treated kills quite differently before and after the advent of controlled fire.

This cautionary example suggests, however, an alternative way of using ethnographic observations in the study of early hominids. Perhaps the relationship between ecological requirements and behavioral responses among particular hunter/gatherer societies can be modeled in such a way as to express general systemic interactions that can be compared with reconstructed ecosystems of which early hominids were a part. Each model can serve as a basis for specifying relationships between behavioral and ecological variables that can be posited as invariant in time and space. Each of these posited relationships could be generated by a single, well documented case but would need to be compared with and tested against other cases before it could be fully accepted. The main purpose of this paper is to provide descriptive models of adaptive behavior in two ethnographic cases, in order to generate propositions regarding the relationships between specific resources and other ecological factors on the one hand and particular kinds of behavior related to the sharing of food and access to resources on the other. Once such propositions have been posited, anthropologists should be able to consider them in relation to the paleo-ecology of early hominids in order to determine the most likely behavioral responses, given the conditions under which the hominids lived.

THE WESTERN DESERT ABORIGINES OF AUSTRALIA

In the Western Desert of Australia, isolated family groups of Aborigines that had not been contacted directly by Europeans still existed in 1966–1970, along with some families that had returned to the desert after varying periods of living in or near European settlements. These Aborigines lived entirely by hunting and gathering in a traditional manner but did not constitute a demographically viable society. Most desert Aborigines had gathered at or near missions, stations, or other kinds of settlements and had adopted a semi- or fully sedentary mode of existence in which traditional hunting and gathering played a diminishing role.

Nonseasonality of Water Resources

Some parts of Australia exhibit extreme annual seasonality of rainfall and resources following rains. A classic example is the Cape York Peninsula, where Donald Thomson described the seasonally transhumant subsistence pattern of the Wik-Munkan Aborigines as follows:

an onlooker, seeing these people engaged at different times of the year, would find them engaged in occupations so diverse, and with weapons and utensils differing so much in character, that if he were unaware of the seasonal influence on food supply, and consequently upon occupation, he would be led to conclude that they were different groups. (1939:209)

Similar effects of extreme wet and dry seasons on human subsistence behavior have been described for other parts of the Australian tropics, most notably Arnhem Land. But as one approaches the arid center of Australia, the annual average rainfall declines drastically, and so does the probability that one will be able to predict when and where rains are likely to fall (Fitzpatrick and Nix, 1973; Gentilli, 1972:219–47; Gibbs, 1969). Thus, in what I shall term the "core" desert of Australia, rainfall is extremely unpredictable from year to year and place to place. Almost the only possible generalization is that when heavy rains occur, they are likely to be offshoots of tropical monsoons from the north which appear during December, January, or February, in the hottest part of the Australian summer. The core desert is also characterized by large areas of uncoordinated drainage with no permanent rivers, freshwater lakes, or springs. There are many creek beds, but these rarely contain water except after torrential rains, which are infrequent and unpredictable. Runoff from these rains flows into depressions between the sand hills or into salt lakes. In other words, all water supplies for humans, flora, and fauna depend directly on rainfall. The only water sources are catchments of rainwater, usually in the form of shaded pools in rocky areas, claypans, and localized subsurface water tables ("native wells") where Aborigines can dig down to the water.

Since virtually all water supplies result directly from rainfall, and since that rainfall is irregular and unpredictable both from month to month and from year to year, it is hard to speak of seasons at all in the Western and Central Deserts. Temperature varies seasonally, but water is unquestionably the primary variable, and as such it is the essential limiting factor for human settlement in the Western Desert.

Geography and Food Resources

Most of the core desert is covered with sand hills—low dunes of red sand running parallel for many miles—separated by interdunal corridors ranging from a few hundred feet to many miles in width. There are also large areas covered by broad, undulating knolls of gravel, called *rira* by the Aborigines. Toward the center of Australia there are prominent mountain ranges, which are conspicuous landmarks in an area of otherwise monotonous relief. The sandhill and *rira* areas are dominated by various species of spinifex, a spiny, grasslike plant. Throughout the region, especially in rocky areas, there are concentrations of acacia scrub and various eucalypts. The Western Desert Aborigines distinguish 38 edible plant species, and they hunt and collect 47 named varieties of meat and fleshy food, most of which are small game such as goanna lizards, mice, birds, grubs and, today, rabbits and feral cats. When compared with other deserts such as the Kalahari or the Great Basin of North America, the Western or core desert of Australia is exceedingly poor, not only in numbers of edible plant and animal species but also in amounts of those particular species. In terms of water supplies and plant and animal resources, this is the most unreliable and impoverished physical environment in the world where people now live or are known to have lived directly off the land.

Aboriginal Subsistence Strategies

Table 11.1 lists staple foods on which nomadic desert Aborigines depended for their livelihood during the 2 years my wife and I spent carrying out fieldwork and observing hunting and gathering patterns directly. The following general comments about Aborigine subsistence behavior are based in part on this figure.

1. The diet is primarily vegetarian. Women forage for seven staple species and thus provide the bulk of the diet. (As used here, a "staple species" is any food that constitutes at least 30% of the total diet by weight at the time it is collected.) Although longer-term observations are needed before precise figures can be given, it is safe to say that about 90% of the time women furnish at least 80% of the food available to the group as a whole.

2. From year to year and place to place, the same staple may become available at widely different times (for example, wild figs were available in October–November in the wet year of 1966, and in November–December and April–May in the drought year of 1969–1970). This is the result of localized conditions of rainfall or drought. There is no regular seasonal pattern of food-collecting, since there are no predictable seasons in the desert when plants may be expected to ripen.

3. Although the number of edible plant species is reduced during

droughts, there are generally larger *quantities* of the drought staples in dry years. In the case of quandong (*Santalum acuminatum*), the dessicated fruits are naturally preserved while the weather remains dry, but larger yields of the other drought staples seem to be stimulated by the prolonged dry weather. Thus foraging in drought years may not be as hard as one supposes.

4. Men hunt constantly but with generally poor success. Both men and women collect small game, which provides the only protein available most of the time. Only on relatively rare occasions when there is sustained and heavy rainfall in areas of predominantly acacia-scrub cover does game become abundant enough for the men's hunting efforts to provide the bulk of the diet, and these periods are short. In a sense, it is the dependable efforts of the women in gathering that frees the men for more chancy hunting activities. In terms of food quantities obtained, the Western Desert Aborigines could be described as gatherer/hunters, since the bulk of their diet on most occasions consists of plant foods. Yet the amount of time and energy expended makes hunting a major subsistence activity. In behavioral terms, the idea of calling these people hunter/gatherers may not be too far off.

5. The largest groups, usually 100–150 individuals, come together on the rare occasions when hunting is good; ceremonies are also most likely to occur at these times. Mid-December 1966 to mid-January 1967 was one such occasion in an area of the Western Desert east of the Warburton Ranges Mission. Such groupings are the result of natural rather than man-made food surpluses, even though the Aborigines are able to prepare and store some vegetable foods. There is some evidence that these food-storage practices may be used mainly in emergency situations such as times of extremely prolonged drought.

6. As drought conditions worsen and hunting becomes more difficult, groups tend to fragment and move to areas near one or more relatively dependable water sources. No water sources are totally reliable or permanent, but some are better than others; these are used by minimal groups of 10–30 individuals during drought periods.

7. The search for food does not require more than 4–5 hours of work for each woman each day, and generally requires less. Even in times of drought, 2–3 hours' collecting by the women can provide sufficient food for the group for that day. Much more time is expended by the men in their hunting, for much poorer returns. On most occasions there is ample leisure time in which people can rest, gossip, make tools, and engage in other activities.

8. Aborigines must move frequently and travel long distances in order to maintain themselves. Journeys of 400–560 km are not unusual, particularly during droughts. Groups observed in this study moved as many as 9 times

Table 11.1. Staple food procurement systems of the Western Desert Aborigines of Australia

Wet Year (April 1966–April 1967)

Procurement systems	Staple foods	J	F	M	A	M	J	J	A	S	O	N	D
1. Ground and tree fruits	kampurarpa (fresh) (Solanum centrale)					▓	▓	▓	▓				
	kampurarpa (sun-dried) (Solanum centrale)	▓	▓	▓									
	ngaru (Solanum chippendalei)	▓	▓	▓									
	yawalyuru (Canthium latifolium)		▓	▓	▓	▓							
	wayanu, "quandong" (fresh) (Santalum acuminatum)												
	yili, "wild fig" (Ficus sp.)												
2. Edible seeds	wangunu (Eragrostis eriopoda)				▓	▓	▓						
	kalpari (Chenopodium rhadinostachyum)			▓	▓	▓	▓						
3. Large game	mainly large macropodids (kangaroo, euro, wallaby), emu	▓											▓

Drought Year (September 1969–September 1970)

Procurement systems	Staple foods	J	F	M	A	M	J	J	A	S	O	N	D
1. Ground and tree fruits	ngaru (*Solanum chippendalei*)	▓								▓	▓	▓	▓
	yili, "wild fig" (*Ficus* sp.)	▓			▓	▓	▓				▓	▓	▓
	wayanu, "quandong" (sun-dried) (*Santalum acuminatum*)				▓	▓	▓	▓					

|— Inadequate opportunity to observe —| |— Inadequate opportunity to observe —|

in a period of 3 months, living in a different camp each time and foraging over an area of roughly 2,600 km^2 during that period. This is perhaps the greatest amount of nomadism reported for any known hunting/gathering society. Along with this, there is evidence for extremely low population densities, on the order of one person per 90–100 km.^{2} Of course, local concentrations of population were much greater than this figure would indicate.

9. A campsite may be occupied more than once in the course of a single year, as different staples are exploited in the same area; or conversely, a camp may not be revisited for several years in succession if no rains happen to fill nearby waterholes during that period.

The grouping of food staples into "procurement systems" in table 11.1 reflects a modified use of Flannery's approach (1968). These groupings arrange the important edible resources in this region according to the way human beings must organize their movements, technology, and social groups to collect them effectively. Grouping resources according to exploitation technique permits the identification of interactions between aspects of human behavior and particular ecological variables, and leads eventually to a view of the total cultural system that operated aboriginally in the core desert region of Australia.

Western Desert Aborigine subsistence is characterized by opportunistic movement in response to assessment of uncertainties of food and water resources, based in turn on observations of specific situations on the ground. Truly the desert Aborigines "chase rain," in the sense that the primary determinants in planning any move are the observance of rainfall and Aborigine knowledge of water catchment locations and availability of plant staples nearby. In the desert rainfalls are visible for 80 km and more, and the Aborigines relate these rains to visible landmarks (often localities of totemic or sacred significance) that lie at or near waterholes.

In these cases, traditional geographical knowledge of the exact location of water catchments minimizes uncertainties. For example, it is always a tempting but high-risk proposition to move into an area where rain has been seen falling, staple food plants are known to abound, but few good catchments exist. Families are known to have become trapped and to have perished in such areas, where there may be plenty of food but no water. Aborigines tend to avoid these areas except when the rains are so extensive that even the smallest and most widely scattered catchments will be full. To avoid arriving at a key water source after several days' travel only to find that the rains (seen at a distance) just missed the catchment and failed to fill it, members of a group sometimes fan out while on the move and approach the water source by different routes, visiting other potential sources on the way. In such cases, whoever finds water lets the others know by a prearranged smoke signal, and they gather there. Aborigines generally avoid moving directly to the most reliable water source, preferring instead to collect food near smaller waterholes first and reserving the food near the better waterholes for the time when smaller sources have dried up.

None of the three food procurement systems in table 11.1 requires a high level of technological specialization or cooperative social organization. By looking at the tasks performed by Aborigines with traditional tools, perhaps we can understand more clearly the relationships that exist between material culture and social organization on the one hand and adaptive behavior in a core desert environment on the other. Aboriginal nomadism puts a premium on portability in material culture. Since these people lack horses or dogs, they cannot carry a large array of tools in their travels, particularly if these tools are bulky or heavy. They solve this problem in three ways. First, they use *multipurpose tools* that are lightweight and easy to carry, such as the spearthrower, which is used not only for throwing spears but also for starting fires, woodworking, mixing tobacco and pigments, and a variety of other tasks (Gould, 1970a). Second, they use tools (mainly of stone) that can be left where they are needed and reused whenever that particular place is visited—in other words, *appliances.* Grinding stones are the most common class of appliance in the Western Desert, where they are used to process all edible grass seeds (procurement system no. 2) and also sun-dried *kampurarpa.* Third, Aborigines take the knowledge of tool-making with them and make tools from raw materials immediately at hand when the need arises; I call these items "*instant tools.*" In most cases they are discarded immediately after use. For example, a naturally sharp stone may be picked up and used to slit a kangaroo's stomach in order to gut it, or a twist of grass may be made into an impromptu pad to cushion a large wooden bowl of fruit that a woman is carrying on her head. None of the tools in these categories requires more than a single individual to make, use, or maintain it.

The quantitative definition of a staple food given earlier does not fully describe the relationship between natural food resources and human adaptive responses in the Western Desert. Staple foods can also be viewed in behavioral terms. All the staples listed in table 11.1 are harvested in large quantities and are transported to camp for further processing and for division and sharing among kin. By contrast, supplemental plant foods are collected in small quantities and are usually eaten where found, as snacks, during the search for large game or staple plants. Behavioral observations and quantitative measurements discriminate equally well between staple and supplemental foods.

However, observations of procurement behavior also reveal an important variation that quantitative considerations alone might not. There is a low-level but steady intake of small game, such as goanna lizards (*Varanus gouldii,* hunted mainly in the sandhill country, and *V. giganteus,* more commonly found in rocky country), "bush turkeys" (*Ardeotis australis*), various small marsupials and birds, and feral cats and rabbits (introduced by Europeans and now widespread throughout the desert). Like the staples, these small animals are always carried back to camp for further division and sharing, despite the relatively small contribution they make to the total Aboriginal diet. Almost every day at least a few of these animals are brought into camp for consumption by the whole group. Although individual portions tend to be small—sometimes only a single mouthful— everyone in camp gets a share, just as they do with the staples. Given the fluctuating and undependable yields from hunting large macropodids (kangaroos, wallabies, etc.) and emus, small game is more important than large game as day-to-day source of protein. Small game is collected by everyone, without regard for the sexual division of labor that is such a conspicuous part of staple procurement. Even children contribute significantly by digging up small lizards and extracting grubs. Flavor is also a consideration, for meat of any kind, including small game, is consistently rated by the Aborigines as tastier than the available plant foods (which, I agree, are rather uninteresting to the palate). Any amount of meat is welcome for the variety it gives to the diet. Thus small game can be regarded as a fourth Aboriginal procurement system because of its nutritive value and the variety it provides, even though the quantity is not great.

In Australia, unlike other continents, humans are the only large predators. The scarcity of large gregarious mammals in Australia may have something to do with this unique condition, since the evolution of large predators is related to the presence of large prey that can be hunted efficiently, which in most cases means herd animals of some kind. There are both benefits and costs for the Aborigines in this situation. The principal benefit is that they do not have to compete with or defend themselves against predation. The principal cost is that they cannot become efficient predators themselves, since there are no herds to exploit.

Another unique characteristic of Aboriginal hunting is the total absence of traps or snares in the hunting technology. Although traps and snares may not be the most effective way to hunt the indigenous small marsupials, birds, and lizards (this point requires further research), it is clear from existing observations that the desert Aborigines expend extraordinary amounts of energy in their pursuit of game, both large and small. This is most evident in the taking of small mammals and lizards, where the animals are tracked to their burrows and dug out of the ground. Even European-introduced rabbits are obtained in this way, although mechanical traps are available that would accomplish the task with far less effort. A woman may dig continuously for 3–4 hours to obtain a single rabbit or rabbit-eared bandicoot (*Macrotis lagotis*), but, given Aboriginal skills in tracking and in digging out animal burrows, this method of hunting small animals is almost completely reliable. On only 4 out of 220 occasions when I observed Aboriginal men or women digging into burrows did they fail to obtain at least one animal for their efforts. From a behavioral standpoint, this reliability appears to justify the extra effort. To the desert Aborigines it is vital to maintain a steady, if sometimes low-level, supply of protein, and to this end low-risk, energy-expensive techniques are consistently applied.

While men often hunt in small groups (the largest observed was 11, but groups of 3 and 4 are more common), there is little planned, cooperative effort. Most hunting is done by stealth, from behind simple brush blinds, rock crevices, or tree platforms close to a water source. It is frequently a night-time activity, because most of the marsupial prey is nocturnal. Dogs are not used in hunting at all, since they would tend to frighten game away, and there is little hunting by direct pursuit unless an ideal opportunity presents itself. If a hunter can see a kangaroo before it notices him, he may be able to stalk it from a considerable distance. Once alerted, large macropodids are virtually impossible to catch, owing to their speed and bobbing movement. Sometimes, however, groups of men trap emus in natural defiles where there is water to attract the animals. While one or two men try to spear the emus from blinds close to the waterhole, a few position themselves near the entrance to the defile, hoping to block the birds' escape and get close enough for a good spear throw.

Western Desert Aborigines are also known to have used fire drives to flush game of all kinds, such hunts generally involving several men (Finlayson, 1935). In 1934 in the Warburton Ranges, a large hunt was observed that suggests a higher degree of cooperation than normally found in Aborigine hunting. The Warburton area contains numerous small, pointed or flat-topped knolls, many of them less than 30 m high. Both men and women surrounded the base of each knoll completely, then walked together toward the top while shouting and beating the bushes with sticks. Game fleeing to the top was trapped, whereupon the men administered the *coup de grâce* (H. Lupton, personal communication). Other early observers, such as Helms (1896:256, 295), Basedow (1925:143–44), and Finlayson (1935:62), have seen brush fences, which suggest some form of communal hunting. But all large game in the Australian Desert is basically solitary and cannot be hunted effectively *en masse*; even "mobs" of kangaroos or emus tend to disperse when pursued. Therefore the role of communal or cooperative hunting in the Western Desert would have been limited.

Both the Aboriginal staple food procurement systems and the hunting of small game are carried out efficiently by individuals or by small groups of relatives. Task-groups are fluid and are formed by personal preference and sentiment as much as by the rules of kinship. If they get along well, co-wives will forage together for staples and look after each other's children, but antagonistic co-wives prefer to forage with other women with whom they are friendly, even if they are more distantly related. Brothers and classificatory brothers tend to hunt together, as do fathers and sons, but only if there are friendly relations between them. Interpersonal relationships in food procurement are essentially egalitarian, with none of the seniority of age and knowledge that characterizes Aboriginal sacred affairs. Task-groups are always small. Even when a relatively large number of men go out from camp to hunt, they do not stay together as a single group but disperse into smaller groups to hunt in different localities and rendezvous later (usually in response to a prearranged smoke signal). It is rare to find a food procurement task-group of any kind which exceeds four individuals.

Kin-Based Sharing Behavior

Perhaps the most complex social behavior that can be related to uncertainties in resource availability is kin-based sharing of food and access to resources. Most anthropological discussions of Aboriginal kinship center on marriage, but they also make clear the obligatory nature and importance of sharing food with in-laws and other classes of affinal kin (e.g., Berndt and Berndt, 1964:82). In other words, food-sharing is not limited to the immediate family but ramifies widely. Second cross-cousin marriage is preferred among the Western Desert Aborigines [similar to the Aranda system described by Elkin (1964:72–84)], so that a man is expected to marry his mother's mother's brother's daughter's daughter. Whenever possible, marriages are arranged along these lines, and this system is correlated with and supported by the subsection system, which includes eight named categories of kin. A spouse may be sought from only one of these subsections—that containing one's second cross-cousins. The cumulative effect of these rules is a shortage of potential marriage partners where one normally lives and forages, since there will be very few people standing in this relationship in any local group, and most of those will already be married or betrothed. Thus a marriage partner must be sought farther afield, often hundreds of kilometers away. But a long-distance marriage of this sort can be viewed as adaptive, since it creates obligatory kin-sharing ties between people in widely distant areas. A drought or food shortage in one area can be overcome by moving into a better-favored region where food and access to resources can be shared with in-laws. Since the Aborigines are polygynous, multiple long-distance marriages may be arranged in several directions, and, in fact, widely ramified and interconnected kin-sharing networks exist throughout the Western Desert, serving to mitigate the uncertainties of rainfall and food. Such obligatory kin-based sharing has been widely observed among hunter/gatherer societies, although nowhere is it more elaborate or extensive than among the people of the Western Desert, where the uncertainties and risks in the physical environment are the greatest and the limiting factor of water presses most directly.

In everyday behavior, any extra food or goods such as spears and hairstring is given to one's relatives whenever the opportunity arises. Security consists of having as many kin as possible who are obliged to share what they have with you whenever you and your family have real need. Any individual accumulation of surplus in anticipation of future shortage negates this sharing ethic and engenders a revulsion more extreme than any European or American reaction to hoarding during times of scarcity.

All kinds of food are shared regularly among kin, but the division of the meat of large game involves the most formal rules and reveals several important principles. When a group of men hunts a kangaroo or other large animal, the man who kills the animal is the last to share, and he sometimes receives only the innards. A kangaroo is divided into a fixed number of named portions immediately after it has been roasted not far from the kill site. The desert Aborigines do not have any techniques for storing meat, so it must be shared as widely as possible and eaten before it rots. Certain classes of the hunter's kin, such as his father-in-law and brothers-in-law, have first choice of the portions, followed by other classes of kin, such as elder and younger brothers, and, last of all, the hunter himself. These shares are transported back to camp and, in turn, divided by each sharer among his own parents, wives, and children.

Since the hunter is related to the men he hunts with, these rules will entitle him, in the long run, to a share in someone else's kill. Thus meat is ultimately available more or less equally to all who hunt, and, through them, to the rest of the group; a remarkably even distribution of meat takes place regardless of the number or size of animals killed. But this arrangement does more than simply distribute the catch. It also doubles the rewards to the hunter by giving him social prestige as a good kinsman and later giving him meat, when he receives his share of someone else's catch. The Western Desert Aborigines have evolved a system that compels people to share food, even when such sharing might not be strictly necessary, in order to assure that when an emergency arises—such as drought or localized shortages of game—the relationships that require sharing between kin are strong. In short, food-sharing relationships are too important to be left to whim or sentiment.

THE AUSTRALIAN DESERT CULTURE ADAPTATION: A DESCRIPTIVE MODEL

Ethnographic observations show that the Western Desert Aborigines have no annual seasonal round; this lack is probably caused by the absence of seasonal rainfall patterns in the core desert regions of Australia. The desert Aborigines have adapted by combining their traditional knowledge of the local geography and the occurrences of edible staples with their observations of actual falls of rain. These are essentially random events that require an opportunistic response. All decisions and behaviors involved in subsistence tend to minimize uncertainty, even at the cost of passing up increased yields of food if areas do not also have reliable waterholes. Movement by groups is frequent, far-reaching, and basically random with respect to areas that contain usable waterholes. Group size also fluctuates in direct response to the local availability of rainwater. As long as the location of key water and food resources in the desert is known and this knowledge can be correlated with the actual occurrence of rains, life there is fairly comfortable. But virtually no other options exist, and a hunting/gathering life based on any other approach, including a seasonal one, would surely fail.

The Australian desert culture is a risk-minimizing adaptive system, in which technological, economic, and social behavior can be seen as responding to and interacting with ecological variables. This is not to say that all aspects of Aboriginal behavior are determined by ecological requirements. It would be difficult indeed to demonstrate that most of the stylistic complexities of Aboriginal mythology and ritual or the subtleties of belief concerning the sacred life are determined by environmental considerations. Rather, I am arguing for a kind of negative determinism and proposing that although style, belief, and other cultural elaborations follow rules of their own, they must be consistent with the essential requirements of living in a stressful habitat like the Western Desert. Any cultural elaborations that violate these requirements to an extreme degree will be selected against and will either change or disappear. My intention here is simply to show to what extent various characteristic kinds of Aborigine behavior conform to the requirements of life in a core desert. In particular, I have argued that ramified kin–sharing networks are an adaptive mechanism for minimizing risks in this risky habitat, and that elaborations of this pattern (e.g., second cross-cousin marriage, the eight-subsection system, division and sharing of meat) indirectly support or at least are consistent with this risk-minimizing mode of adaptation. The Australian desert culture is an extreme case of human behavioral response to particular ecological stresses and requirements, most notably the limiting factor of water and the related problems of food procurement. It is no coincidence that this region, which is extremely marginal for human settlement, contains the most elaborated and geographically expanded example of kin-based food-sharing and resource access so far documented in the ethnographic literature.

THE INDIANS OF THE NORTHWESTERN
CALIFORNIA COAST

As a result of a much longer history of European contact, the subsistence patterns of the Indians of California's northwestern coast require a greater degree of reconstruction than was necessary for the Western Desert Aborigines. By the late nineteenth century the Tolowa, Tututni, and Coast Yurok Indians of this region no longer relied completely on traditional hunting and gathering, although as late as 1910 some individuals still lived in this way. Some traditional food-collecting occurs here today—in particular some limited acorn collecting, smelt fishing, and seaweed gathering—but these are isolated vestiges of the former adaptive system, and in some cases they, too, have been altered. As a result, this study, carried out intermittently from 1962 to 1965 and in 1972, made extensive use of archaeological and archival sources in addition to the more usual means of direct observation and informant interviews.

The Northwestern California Ecosystem

The geography and ecology of northwestern California contrast about as sharply as is possible with the Western Desert of Australia, yet this, too, was the setting for a successful human adaptation based solely on hunting and gathering. This region has a rugged topography and heavy annual rainfall. The coastline alternates between stretches of sandy beach and rocky headlands, and offshore there are numerous rocks and islets. There is a narrow coastal plain composed of Pleistocene and Pliocene sand deposits, and a short distance inland are low but steep hills that increase in height until they merge with the foothills of the Siskiyou Mountains about 30–40 km inland, ultimately reaching heights up to 2,100 m. These hills are cut by the North, Middle, and South Forks of the Smith River and the lower Klamath River and their tributaries, which form deep gorges in some places. Except for the coastal plain and a number of small flats along the bottoms of these gorges, there is little level ground anywhere in this region.

Along the coast, annual rainfall averages 2,500 mm, and annual averages of 3,000 mm are recorded for some areas slightly inland. This rainfall is augmented throughout the year by frequent and heavy coastal fogs that completely cover the coastal plain and ocean-facing gorges. Rains are strictly seasonal, with about 80% of recorded rain falling between early October and late March. Temperatures are mild but cool during most of the year, with strong, cold northwesterly winds prevailing along the coast during the summer months. Snow rarely falls on the coastal plain or in the nearby gorges but is common during winter at elevations above 600 m.

Much of the coastal plain is subject to the effects of wind-borne salt spray and is thus treeless and covered only by assorted grasses and low shrubs. At various distances inland, beyond the reach of salt spray, there is a belt of low spruce and pine, and on the Smith River coastal plain there was once a dense stand of redwood, which has been destroyed by logging. The redwood belt extends 13–19 km inland, wherever the coastal fog can penetrate and wherever there is protection from coastal winds. The redwood trees were important to the Indians as a source of canoes and lumber for building houses; the forest also contained ferns used in making baskets and was frequented by game animals such as deer and elk, but on the whole it was poor in food resources. Still farther inland, where the hills reach more than 600 m, are large forests dominated by Douglas fir, which extend continuously, in some cases, from the tops of the hills to the edges of the river. On scattered flats along the east edge of the redwood belt and in the gorges in the Douglas fir area are grassy, parklike openings containing small oak groves. Just inland from the redwood belt there is also an isolated but distinct area of chaparral vegetation covering mainly the steep hills along the drainage of the North Fork of the Smith River. This is a mixed chaparral containing various species of manzanita and madrone along with open stands of ponderosa pine, sometimes merging with south-facing slopes containing tanbark oak and madrone as well as the usual dense cover of Douglas fir.

The marine and riverine components of the ecosystem have their own distinctive vegetation types. Along the lower course of the Smith River where it emerges onto the coastal plain, and along the margins of Lake Earl, Lake Talawa, and Dead Lake, there are swales containing tule and camas lilies. Camas, thought not abundant in this area, were eaten by the Indians, and tule rushes were used in fashioning mats. These marshy areas also sheltered various ducks and geese, of secondary importance compared to other food resources in the region. Large amounts of seaweed accumulate along the coast, particularly in rocky inlets. The Indians collected this seaweed, dried it, and ate it as a condiment; it also served as a moisture-absorbent packing material in storage baskets, especially for storing food.

Thus within a relatively small area of rugged terrain there are complex microhabitats of varying richness as far as resources available for humans are concerned. Although logging, mining, and other historic activities have done much to alter some of these microhabitats, there is a remarkably detailed literature covering indigenous food resources in this region and their ecological associations. In addition to authors mentioned later, sources such as Smith (1929), Hewes (1942), Schaeffer (1958), and Hedgepeth (1962) provide useful accounts of different basic resources.

Food Procurement in Aboriginal Northwestern California

Traditional food-getting behavior among the northwestern California Indians can be considered in terms of primary food-procurement systems. Ideally, staple foods should be identified by direct observation and weighing at the time of collection but, as this is plainly impossible with California Indians today, we must rely on estimates taken from data on the availability of various resources and existing reconstructions of the traditional subsistence economy. The primary foods listed here are so overwhelming in their natural abundance (as measured by recent studies) and were described as so important by historic sources that they may confidently be designated as staples, even without comprehensive, quantified observations. Supplemental foods never attained the quantitative importance of staples, although their importance in varying the diet and occasionally providing much-needed nutritional elements should not be overlooked.

Procurement System No. 1: Large Sea Mammals. The Steller sea lion, *Eumetopias jubata,* dominated this procurement system, mainly because the larger islets off this part of the Pacific coast are among the largest summer rookeries for this gregarious species. Steller bulls can weigh as much as 900 kg, although the females are smaller. The smaller California sea lion, *Zalophus californianus,* also occurs on this coast during the summer and was hunted by the Indians, but this species does not breed there and was less common than the Steller. Other prey included the sea otter, *Enhydra lutris;* the Northern fur seal, *Callorhinus ursinus;* and the harbor seal, *Phoca vitulina.* Whales were not actively hunted but were consumed whenever found stranded on the beaches.

Sea-mammal hunting required a more complex technology and a higher level of group organization than any other activity in northwestern California Indian culture. Sea lions were hunted from large redwood dugout canoes up to 12 m long (Gould, 1968c; Powers, 1877:69). These canoes were seaworthy in the unprotected waters off the northwestern California coast and were used for hunting on the rookeries that were farthest out to sea, 10 km offshore. The preferred method for killing sea lions was to land on the rookeries and club the animals to death, although animals were often harpooned in the water. The coastal Indians used sophisticated composite harpoons for this task as well as for hunting other swimming sea mammals. Late each summer there was a first sea lion hunt, akin to the first salmon ceremony and other "first fruits" ceremonies seen elsewhere on the northern Pacific coast (Gunther, 1926), which involved the lifting of ritual prohibitions and restrictions on individual hunting when the "season" was officially opened. Each Tolowa coastal village had one of the large canoes, and most sea lion hunts were carried out in these canoes under the leadership of a single individual (Gould, 1968c:27; Hewes, in Kroeber and Barrett, 1960:118). The annual first sea lion hunt represented an even higher degree of unification, in that all the participating canoes from the different villages traveled together to the rookeries before the actual hunt started (Gould, 1968c:26–28). Once the killing of the animals began, however, the men in each canoe hunted on their own, and each boat independently brought its catch back to its own village. No doubt many sea lions also were taken by individual hunters or small groups of men on the rookeries that lay close inshore. All that was needed for this was the small river dugout canoe (about 4.5 m long), clubs, and harpoons, but serious offshore sea lion hunting required a level of technology and group interaction well above that of most northwestern California Indian procurement activities.

In the seagoing canoe, the Tolowa Indians possessed a type of extractive technology requiring a wider social context than any found among the desert Aborigines of Australia—what may be termed a *facility*. [A facility is here defined as an artifact that is built, used, and in some cases maintained by a task-group larger than the minimal social unit, and should not be confused with Binford's earlier and quite different concept (1968a:272).] The Tolowa ocean-going canoe and its accouterments may be regarded as a type of facility, in the same way as, for example, the Kepel fish weir of the Yurok (Waterman and Kroeber, 1938).

Sea lions were valued for their meat and oil, and the amounts of both provided by a successful hunt were prodigious. A single large canoe could be counted on to bring in at least 1,800 kg of sea lion meat after one offshore hunt. Since the animals are reliable in their annual appearance in large numbers at the rookeries, this was an exceptional resource. The Tolowa had access to more extensive rookeries than their coastal neighbors, although the Coast Yurok, too, were known for their effectiveness at sea lion hunting, especially at Redding Rock (Kroeber and Barrett, 1960:117).

Procurement System No. 2: Marine Shellfish. The principal bivalve collected by northwestern California Indians was the sea mussel, *Mytilus californianus.* Mussels are abundant along rocky shores at the mid-tide zone where there is strong surf action to sweep in nutrients. This species was favored for its abundance, the relatively large amount of edible muscle and other tissue of the individual bivalves, and its generally good flavor (Greengo, 1952:65). Mussels are available in large numbers all year long, but during the late summer months they may ingest a marine dinoflagellate, *Conyaulax catenella,* which is harmless to the mussels but can cause severe and even fatal poisoning to people who eat infected shellfish. The Indians were aware of the risk of mussel poisoning, but informant testimony indicates nevertheless that people sometimes became ill and died from eating poisoned mussels.

Nutritional tables in Greengo (1952:83) provide a rough but useful estimate of food value for sea mussels based on figures for the closely related *Mytilus edulis* of the east coast of North America. 100 g of cooked mussel meat can provide 18.2 g of protein, or about half the adult daily requirement; therefore the daily protein needs of an active adult man could be met by only 50 sea mussels. In addition, mussels are rich in vitamins B_1, B_2, and C. Mussels were generally placed directly in the fire and allowed to cook in the shell, although mussels and other shellfish were often sun-dried or fire-dried.

Sea mussels were collected by individuals, usually women. Collection was easy and rapid, and was limited only by unusually heavy surf. Fifty mussels, the amount posited for an adult male's daily protein needs, could have been collected in about half an hour under optimal conditions, with the only strenuous work being the effort of carrying large baskets full of shellfish back to the village. Many other species of shellfish were collected as well, including the common littleneck clam, *Protothaca staminea;* rock scallop, *Hinnites multrugosa;* northern razor clam, *Siliqua patula;* Washington clam, *Saxidomus* sp.; giant chiton, *Cryptochiton stelleri;* shortspine sea urchin, *Strongilo sintrodus;* and various large barnacles. Like mussels, these could all be collected efficiently by individuals, although many of the clams are found in the sandy beaches and required more effort to locate and transport than mussels and other shellfish, which tend to be concentrated on the rocky parts of the shoreline.

Procurement System No. 3: Acorns. Although relatively poor in acorn-bearing oak trees compared to other parts of the state, northwestern California contains three species that bear well and provided a staple food for the aboriginal Tolowa: valley oak, *Quercus lobata;* canyon oak, *Q. chrysolepus;* and tanbark oak, *Lithocarpus densiflora.* The last-named species is most abundant in the area inhabited by the Tolowa. Groves of these trees occur in small, grass-covered flats alongside the Smith and Klamath rivers and their branches, in some small clearings along the east side of the redwood belt, and dispersed along the slopes of various canyons. The dispersed trees were little used by the Indians, since they grow on slopes too steep for easy movement or collection, but the groves on the flats were heavily exploited. Farther inland are large oak groves covering portions of the open, grassy bald areas on the tops of many hills and low mountains; these were exploited by certain groups of Coast Yurok and other groups from the interior. Few of the best oak groves from former times remain intact today, because bark was stripped from the tanbark oak for commercial purposes and roads and residences were built on these precious parcels of level land.

The oaks drop their acorns in late fall, and the nuts must be collected fairly fast, since they may be infested by weevils if left on the ground for long. Tanbark oak acorns are thick-shelled, however, and less susceptible to spoilage than those of other species (Wolf, 1945:51). Acorn-collecting was a group activity for the Indians, although not as formal or organized as ocean hunting of sea lions. Families congregated at the oak groves and harvested the acorns, and the transport and processing of the acorns into edible form was performed on an individual or family basis. An oak grove near the present Gasquet Flat, about 15 miles from the sea, was the farthest inland to be used regularly by the Tolowa. Women with baskets full of acorns moved constantly back and forth between the oak groves and their villages on the coast during the collecting period, processing and storing the acorns in their villages. Before leaving an oak grove after the annual acorn collection, they burned the grass over the entire flat. Tolowa informants claim that this reduced underbrush and kept the grass from growing too high, so that the fallen acorns could easily be located during the next year's harvest. A similar practice has been reported for the Kacha Pomo of Redwood Valley (Kniffen, 1939:378).

As the literature on California Indians makes clear, acorns require processing before they can be eaten. The Tolowa, like other California groups, pounded and leached the acorn meat until it was free of tannic acid, using ground stone pestles and large flat rocks as mortars, with basketry hoppers to contain the acorn meat as it was being pounded. This elaborate process was easily accomplished by the wives and children of one Tolowa family.

Wolf (1945:51, 63) estimates that 45.0 kg of whole *Lithocarpus densiflora* acorns will yield 31.1 kg of food material when dried: 2.93% protein, 12.08% fat, 20.14% fiber, and 54.43% carbohydrates, with the remaining 10.42% consisting of water and ash. Tanbark oak acorns contain fewer nutrients than other species of oak, largely because of the unusually high percentage of fiber in the thick shell, but they are still a significant contribution to a diet otherwise rich in fats and proteins and somewhat short in carbohydrates. California acorns are generally high in calories, approximately 5,000 kcal/kg (Baumhoff, 1963:163).

Wolf (1945:31–33, 51) estimates further that the production of acorns by tanbark oak trees was about equivalent to that of the Kellogg oak (*Q. kelloggii*), a tree whose productivity is slightly less than that of the blue or Douglas oak (*Q. douglasii*), which can provide 72.0 kg per tree per season. In 1972 I counted more than 200 mature oak trees in two surviving groves of tanbark oak, one at Pappas Flat on the Middle Fork of the Smith River and the other near Big Flat, on the South Fork of the Smith River, while at a smaller flat near Indian Bar on the South Fork I noted approximately 70 mature trees. These observations are minimum estimates, since all three areas had been at least partially logged in historic times. Still, if a conservative estimate of 56.3 kg of acorns per tree (slightly below the productivity of Douglas and Kellogg oak) is applied to these three remnant groves (minimum number, 470 trees), the result is about 26,460 kg of acorns per season, or about 18,290 kg of usable food materials when dried. Incomplete though they are, these estimates indicate the enormous magnitude of the acorn harvest under good conditions. Informants have also pointed out the locations of five additional flats that once contained much larger oak groves than those I observed in 1972, and several others along the lower Klamath River are known to have been important to the Coast Yurok.

Procurement System No. 4: Anadromous Fish. Both the Klamath and the Smith River are frequented by all the major anadromous species of fish (those which ascend rivers in order to breed) in this region, including salmon that run both in fall and in spring. Of overwhelming importance were king salmon (*Oncorhynchus tschawytscha*) and coho salmon (*O. kisutch*). These fish often ran in large numbers on the Smith River and were taken by the Tolowa with spears, net-traps, and various kinds of weirs (Kroeber and Barrett, 1960). Most of these devices were built and used by small groups of closely related persons, mainly individual families, but Drucker describes a communal fish weir at a spot called munsontun about 8 km upstream from the mouth of the Smith River:

Communal weir . . . built at summer low water on riffle at munsontun and/or militcuntun (latter site probably older). Owner gathered, prepared materials; called kin and friends to put in. Anyone who helped given fish. V-shaped row of alder stakes, supported by slanting braces on downstream side, supported panels of hazel wickerwork. Point of V was downstream. 2 center stakes driven first, to accompaniment of formula; if easily set, weir was successful. Basketry "trap" a rectangular wicker mat doubled, end and part of side sewn together to make wide-mouthed closed cyclinder, placed in apex of weir. Men went upstream, heated rocks in fire, with formulas, from canoes threw rocks in deep holes, shouted, splashed, to drive fish into weir. . . . Weir left to be swept away by higher water. (1937:232)

While this device is not as elaborate as either the Tolowa ocean-going canoes for sea lion hunting or the Kepel fish weir of the Yurok, it is certainly a "facility" as defined earlier. Present informants are uncertain in their recollections of this device, and the social organization involved in its construction and use remains incompletely known.

Salmon meat is rich in calories, averaging 2,200 kcal/kg (Rostlund, 1952:4). Like other freshwater fish, salmon are rich in a wide array of vitamins (A, D, B_1, B_2, and even some C in the roe), protein (about 15–20%

in edible portions), and fat (this component is highly variable according to season, feeding grounds, and other factors), but are generally lacking in carbohydrates. Rostlund concludes: "The table of calories shows that the high-calorie fishes are the very ones that characterize first-class fishing regions such as the Atlantic and Pacific anadromous areas" (1952:5–6), and the Smith and Klamath rivers lie in the heart of one such region.

Other anadromous fish were also taken. Steelhead (*Salmo gairdnerii*), candlefish (*Thaleichthys pacificus*), and Western sea lamprey (*Entosphenus tridentatus*) were caught regularly, though never in quantities approaching those of salmon. Hewes (in Kroeber and Barrett, 1960:25–26) describes an unusual Tolowa technique for catching lamprey, using a gaffing chute in shallow water over a white pebble floor. This was a night-fishing technique, and informants have shown me the shallow riffles where it was used at the confluence of the Middle and South Forks of the Smith River, where these white pebbles occur naturally. This technique, like most other fishing methods of the Tolowa, required only a few individuals and could be carried out by members of a single family. With the possible exception of the salmon weir at munsontun, Tolowa riverine fishing did not require large groups of families to reside together at special camps near the place where the fish were taken.

Procurement System No. 5: Waterfowl. Various species of ducks, geese, rails, and murres were caught by the northwestern California Indians, but cormorants (*Phalacrocorax* sp.) were by far the most important waterfowl in the total diet. Cormorants were captured at their nests on rocks and sea stacks not far offshore during a brief period in midsummer when the nestlings were unable to fly and could be taken easily (Gould, 1966a:84–85; Howard, 1929:378–83). No dietary data are available for cormorants, but there is no doubt that they were a staple food during the time they were collected. The Indians went out to the cormorant nesting areas in small river canoes, either individually or in family groups, and used clubs to take the immature birds. Aside from the element of timing, no special techniques or organization were required to make efficient use of this resource.

Procurement System No. 6: Surf Fish. Abundant runs of smelt (*Spirinchus starksi* and *Allosmerus attenuatus*) appear along the beaches of northwestern California in late summer, although the size of these runs varies considerably from year to year. The fish were easily taken in the surf by Indians using the traditional V-shaped dip net, an efficient technique that has been widely adopted and used by whites living in the area today. These nets may be used without any organized effort above the level of the individual fisherman, but the catch can be so massive that transporting it may be difficult. In 1965 and again in 1972, years when the smelt runs were large, I observed a single man net as much as 90 kg of fish in less than half an hour, although, of course, some time must be spent beforehand in locating the best runs along the beach. Many Indians continue to live along the beaches during August and early September in order to catch smelt, which are still much sought after. Today they use small trucks or 4-wheel-drive vehicles to transport the heavy tubs of fish to camp, but in former times this was done by women using baskets. Fish not eaten fresh are spread out on driftwood logs to dry in the sun while women and children living at the camp shoo away seagulls. Final drying is done on the sand, and the fish are covered at night to keep off the fog. This part of the operation takes several days, depending on the amount of sun, and involves constant attention but little labor. Thus, to exploit smelt efficiently, people must be camped in reasonably large numbers nearby, although no organized group effort is needed to collect or process the fish.

Sea perch, particularly the redtail surfperch (*Holconotus rhodoterus*), were caught off the beaches by individual aboriginal fishermen, and this practice continues today among both Indians and whites, especially in the summer. Sometimes the total catch of fish may be large—the largest I have seen weighed 34 kg and was taken in about 4 hours by one fisherman—but this was and still is of secondary importance compared to smelting.

Secondary Procurement Systems. The Tolowa frequently obtained various land mammals, edible berries and plants, and ocean fish, although not in amounts that could approach those of the items designated here as staples. Deer and elk were hunted in the interior, and Lewis (1973:49–56) has suggested that burning of this region by the Indians may have been an important means of enhancing the game resource, by improving the browse. However, deer and elk are solitary game and cannot be hunted *en masse*. Stalking and pit-snares were used by individual hunters to good effect, but total amounts of meat taken in this way cannot have been great compared to even the least productive of the staple food procurement systems.

Ocean fishing, like the hunting of land mammals, was often an individual task and may also have been a pastime during organized sea lion hunts, but the total catch was probably not large. Various sharks, hake, halibut, rockfish, lingcod, sculpin, and other kinds of fish were caught, some from boats when the sea was calm and some directly from the rocky parts of the shoreline.

Finally, women collected salal berries, salmon berries, huckleberries, the edible bulbs of camas lilies, and other edible plants during the summer months, to supplement and add flavor to the overall diet.

The Tolowa seem to have collected almost every kind of edible food that was available, with a few exceptions. Informants were emphatic that bear, raccoon, skunk, and porcupine were taboo because the forelimbs of these animals look like human hands and thus there was something vaguely cannibalistic about eating them. Drucker (1937:232) observed similar restrictions, although his list of tabooed foods is longer and also include dog, coyote, cougar, sea gulls, and all birds of prey, as well as land bird eggs, snakes, frogs, dove, and octopus. None of these species were potentially staple food resources. However, faunal remains recovered from the protohistoric Tolowa levels excavated at the Point St. George site included black bear, raccoon, coyote, and probably also sea gulls (Gould, 1966a:81–84). This suggests that these food restrictions were limited in some way and that at least some of the species tabooed in historic times were consumed by the aboriginal inhabitants of this region.

Seasonality and Tenure of Resources

The approximate seasonal occurrence of the major staple foods is summarized in table 11.2, but the exact periods of availability varied slightly from year to year. Marine shellfish were available all year, but in some years the poisonous period, especially for mussels, would have eliminated this resource during the period indicated. The dotted line for anadromous fish indicates that some salmon were available all year, at sea and at the mouth and lower reaches of the Smith River. The fall and spring salmon runs are shown in the figure as solid blocks, but the time of the steelhead run was uncertain, so it has not been included. Western sea lamprey run up the Smith River in July and August but are not shown either, since their numbers did not approach those of the salmon. Only cormorants are indicated under "waterfowl,' and only smelt are shown under "surf fish," since these were the main species taken in each case.

Table 11.2 also shows that staple foods of one kind or another were available to the Tolowa, the Tututni, and the Coast Yurok continuously throughout the year. Peak harvesting periods occurred from mid-June to mid-September (sea lions, cormorants, and smelt) and from early September to early November (acorns, salmon), with the latter peak representing the only period when interior resources predominated over coastal ones. Note, too, that more than one staple was available in harvestable quantities for over six months of the year. Such staple species were often found close together (e.g., oak flats invariably lay close to salmon-bearing streams), but in some years the scheduling of resource collection became a problem. In late August and early September, for instance, a particularly fine smelt run might continue into the beginning of the acorn harvest. These two resources occur far enough apart that both cannot be harvested simultaneously. Such scheduling problems were the exception rather than the rule, which for at least half the year was *simultaneous harvesting whenever possible.*

Only procurement system no. 3 (acorns) required any wholesale movement of people away from the coast, and then only for a few weeks during

Table 11.2. Staple food procurement systems of the Indians of the northwestern California coast

Economic calendar

Staple foods	J	F	M	A	M	J	J	A	S	O	N	D
1. Large sea mammals												
2. Marine shellfish[a]												
3. Acorns												
4. Anadromous fish (available at sea during rest of year)												
5. Waterfowl												
6. Surf fish												

[a]poisonous from July to September.

Note: Species taken within each procurement system:

1. Large sea mammals: mainly Steller sea lion, *Eumetopias jubata.* Also some whales (washed ashore) and sea otter, *Enhydra lutris;* California sea lion, *Zalophus californianus;* Northern fur seal, *Callorhinus ursinus;* and harbor seal, *Phoca vitulina.*

2. Marine shellfish: mainly California sea mussel, *Mytilus californianus.* Also common littleneck, *Protothaca staminea;* northern razor clam, *Siliqua patula;* rock scallop, *Hinnites multrugosa;* Washington clam, *Saxidomus* sp.; giant chiton, *Cryptochiton stelleri;* shortspine sea urchin, *Strongilo sintrodus,* etc.

3. Acorns: mainly tanbark oak, *Lithocarpus densiflora.* Also valley oak, *Quercus lobata,* and canyon oak, *Q. chrysolepus.*

4. Anadromous fish: mainly king salmon, *Oncorhynchus tschawytscha,* and coho salmon, *O kisutch.* Also steelhead, *Salmo gairdnerii;* Western sea lamprey, *Entosphenus tridentatus;* and candlefish, *Thaleichthys pacificus.*

5. Waterfowl: mainly cormorant, *Phalacrocorax* sp.

6. Surf fish: mainly smelt, *Spirinchus starksi,* and *Allosmerus attenuatus.* Also redtail surfperch, *Holconotus rhodoterus.*

late fall. Productive oak flats were a short distance from the coast, generally 8–25 km inland, so traveling distances were never great even between the most widely separated staple resources. In consequence, the northwestern California Indians followed a seasonally regular but narrowly circum- scribed pattern of movement between harvesting areas. In late summer, usually August, families moved from the large coastal villages onto the beaches to camp for several weeks while the smelt were running. Then they moved inland to various oak flats where they could collect acorns and, at the same time, fish during the fall salmon run. At the end of the acorn harvest, these families would make their way individually back to the coastal villages, where they remained for the remaining 9–10 months of the year.

These seasonal movements were not organized, large-scale movements of village populations. A wealthy headman generally took the initiative in such a move, but it was up to each family to move on its own, and no family moved to the beaches or the oak flats as part of a village; villages broke up in late summer and were reconstituted in the late fall upon return from the oak flats. Finally, movement away from the villages did not mean their total abandonment, since women constantly traveled back and forth between the collecting areas and the villages, carrying basketloads of fish and acorns to place in storage.

The seasonal pattern of village unity and dispersal is reflected in traditional concepts of land and resource tenure. Well-defined tracts of shoreline were claimed by particular villages and their boundaries were defended, especially in cases where whales became stranded on the beaches. With one exception, every village's shoreline tracts included both rocky headlands and sandy beach, thus ensuring that each one had access to the staple resources of each of these microenvironments. The single exception was the village of ?ectsŭuled, situated on a neck of land between Lake Earl and Lake Talawa, only a short distance from the ocean. These lakes may have furnished enough resources to offset this village's lack of a rocky foreshore, but the argument remains speculative. Individuals and individual families claimed ownership of particular oak groves (or even specific trees) as well as fishing and eeling places along the streams, and it was to these places that they moved in the late fall. There was no clear correlation between villages and interior collecting areas, and there were no bounded and defended village tracts in the interior. Individuals or families wishing to use interior resources not their own had to seek permission from the owners, and, although informants say this permission was often granted, they also stress that it was not granted automatically. Unfortunately our knowledge of the rules governing such permission remains vague, although we know that there were disputes (and subsequent indemnities) arising from ambiguities of ownership or failure to obtain permission.

Scarcity and Storage

As was true in most of California, the "lean" period of the year tended to be early spring, before the start of the salmon run (Baumhoff, 1963:161). However, "lean" in this case did not mean famine: informants agree that there was never any famine in this area, although we know that only a single staple, shellfish, was available in significant quantities for 4–5 months of the year, and amounts of any one staple (especially acorns, salmon, and smelt) might vary greatly from one year to the next. The diversity of resources and their general abundance ensured that natural failure of a staple such as the acorn crop would not undermine the economy to the extent of becoming a limiting factor. Shortages of a particular food resource may have led to temporary nutritional imbalances, but the caloric needs of the population were easily met at all times.

One important way to avoid food shortage is storage, and the Tolowa, Tututni, and Coast Yurok all had a well-developed technology for preparing and storing food. Shellfish, fish, and sea lion meat were all sun dried and/or smoked in large quantities as well as eaten fresh. Dried meat, fish, and acorns were kept in large storage baskets within the dwelling houses on the coast. In sunny weather, women periodically took acorns from their baskets and laid them on mats to dry, thus preventing or at least retarding damage from fungus and insects. Informants agree that the amounts of food thus stored were prodigious, filling many large baskets that stood atop the parapet lining the housepit in each dwelling house.

When shortages occurred, they affected only individual families rather than the society at large—though not commonplace, they were frequent enough for informants to recall (see e.g., Gould, 1966b:77–78)—and resulted more from improvidence by the families concerned than from any environmental scarcity. Each family harvested most of its own staple foods and prepared these for storage by itself. Only the hunting of large sea mammals (procurement system no. 1) and possibly the use of weirs for catching salmon (system no. 4) required families to unite their efforts, however temporarily, in food-getting activities. Similarly, food was not shared between families after a natural harvest except in the case of sea lions and stranded whales, creatures too large for any one family to handle effectively or to consume on its own. DuBois states that:

By subsistence economy is meant the exploitation of the plentiful natural resources available to any industrious individual. Although there were privately owned fishing sites, ordinarily these were used freely by any person within the village group. . . . Individuals who had been lazy or inefficient in gathering food . . . were forced to buy it [i.e., with prestige goods like dentalia shell beads, red-headed woodpecker scalps, and obsidian blades]. (1936:50)

although she later maintains that the Tolowa and Tututni

are not accustomed to translate the value of dried salmon or a basket into dentalia and then make exchanges whose dentalia equivalents are of equal value. In the realm of subsistence economy the Tolowa-Tututni were on a barter basis without translation into another medium. (Ibid.)

These statements are only apparently contradictory because there really was no "subsistence economy" among these Indians above the level of the individual family (i.e., a man, his wives, children, and close adherents). Except for the general division of shares of sea lion and whale meat there were no sharing or barter-based exchanges of food, although improvident families or individuals sometimes experienced shortages and were forced to "buy" food with their prestige goods.

THE CALIFORNIA COASTAL ADAPTATION

The subsistence system of the northwestern California coast Indians is an example of a "resource optimizing" strategy, seeking to derive the highest possible level of productivity without consideration of potential risk. Tolowa seasonal patterns of movement and residence, together with occasional efforts to organize at a supra-family level in the pursuit of particular resources (e.g., sea lions and salmon), were intended, consciously or unconsciously, to collect all harvestable resources at their time and place of maximum availability. To a very large extent this was a successful strategy. The Tolowa had little occasion to be concerned with scheduling, for they rarely had to choose among harvesting two or more resources that appeared simultaneously in widely separated localities. Yet their basic staples were varied and reliable and furnished a reasonably balanced diet. Few examples in the hunter/gatherer literature offer a picture of such affluence in subsistence with, at the same time, a minimum of risk. No shortages in any single resource or resource procurement system can be identified as limiting in either the short or long run of northwestern California Indian economic life.

WEALTH QUESTING AS AN AGGRANDIZIVE MECHANISM

Anthropologists (including myself) have tended to focus on the more conspicuous elements of northwestern California Indian social behavior— especially wealth-questing. The preceding discussion of Tolowa subsistence explores another side of their life and provides the basis for a reanalysis of these social activities. To what extent can wealth-questing and concomitant social behavior among the Tolowa be regarded as adaptive in the context of the total northwestern California coastal ecosystem?

Because of the balanced, abundant, and varied nature of their wild staple resources, the Tolowa did not experience famine or widespread shortages of food. Since each family was able to collect, prepare, and store its own food resources, largely by its own efforts, there was no compelling need for sharing networks between families. Before we can explain the existence of an aggrandizive system of resource procurement and use, however, we must first understand why a sharing system was not necessary. Not only was northwestern California an environment rich in natural resources, but these resources became available at times and places where they could be harvested economically by individuals and single families. Aside from sea lions and some salmon, no other staple food procurement system required the cooperation of more than one family in harvesting, preparation, or storage. Indeed, one could argue that individual families, because of their greater flexibility, were more responsive to fluctuations in resource availability. In all probability, large cooperative groups would have been unwieldy and without advantage. Economic success in Tolowa subsistence rested almost entirely on the efforts of individuals and families, and these efforts were as well or better rewarded than the efforts of larger, cooperative foraging and hunting groups. The partial adoption of this latter option for sea lion hunting and some types of salmon fishing shows that these Indians were ready to use cooperative techniques when they were clearly advantageous, but that otherwise such techniques were ignored.

On the other hand, personal and family aggrandizement of food resources by efficient collection, preparation, and storage met the needs of all but the most improvident or unlucky. Women were the primary producers in northwest California Indian society. Although men performed physically intense activities, such as sea lion and land-mammal hunting, and carried out most of the tasks related to canoe building, house construction, and salmon fishing (especially the construction of weirs), women collected the bulk of the acorn harvest and did most of the shellfish collecting. They also collected drift timber from the beaches for firewood. While men netted smelt in the surf, women carried the catch back to camp and took charge of drying it for storage. Similarly, women prepared acorns and all other foods for storage and consumption. Thus the amount of food a family could accumulate was directly dependent on the number of women in the household. A man with several hardworking wives and daughters could store up large reserves. Not only could he use these reserves as security against possible scarcities, but he could also commission "feasts" when he wished to recruit people to construct a large canoe or house. In a sense this amounted to redistribution of food, but this redistribution did not extend to those who needed food owing to shortages. Instead, all food was distributed with the clear expectation of *immediate* repayment, either in labor (as with canoe-building) or in prestige goods (as when an improvident family ran short of food). In those rare cases when a family was too poor to pay for the food, it was given grudgingly as a form of charity: "they were given food by others but they were looked down upon. 'Anybody could do what he liked with them'" (Du Bois, 1936:50).

In time, a man with several industrious wives and daughters could expect his household to accumulate larger reserves of food than families with fewer active women. Women were "working capital" in the fullest sense. As stressed elsewhere (Gould, 1966b), women were a source of bridewealth consisting of specific prestige goods—redheaded woodpecker scalps, dentalia, and obsidian blades, to mention the more commonly circulated items. Direct exchange of prestige goods for food occurred but was uncommon. More important was indirect exchange through the purchase of women as primary producers, by means of prestige goods. A man purchased a wife in the hope that she would work hard to maintain his family's domestic food supply, but he also bought rights to the bridewealth that would eventually be attracted by any daughters she might bear. Direct patrilineal inheritance, indemnities, trade, gambling, and other schemes were also important avenues to wealth in so-called prestige goods, although views differ about the relative importance of these approaches to wealth and the manner of their manipulation.

Du Bois (1936) distinguished between "prestige" and "subsistence" economies within Tolowa and Tututni society. The prestige economy was based on transactions involving the special goods mentioned above, whereas subsistence consisted of barter, and there were no exchanges between the two economies. Thus, Du Bois concluded, the prestige goods acquired and manipulated by the Tolowa were not all-purpose currency, to be subdivided and exchanged for goods of any kind. Drucker, however, while accepting Du Bois's basic distinction between prestige and subsistence goods, argued that prestige goods were true money (1937:241). He pointed out that kin-based exchanges of food could not be called a special economy, and that prestige goods could be used by the Tolowa to buy everything that was for sale and therefore were true money. While Du Bois emphasized the importance of manipulation and haggling by Tolowa men (1936:55–56), Drucker stressed direct, patrilineal inheritance as the principal means of becoming a wealthy man (1937:242). In my own analysis (1966b), I accepted Du Bois's emphasis on manipulation as an avenue to wealth but pointed out that bride-purchase is an important form of manipulation that tends to break down the sharp distinction Du Bois made between prestige and subsistence economies.

The eventual result of all these manipulations and direct inheritance was that wealth goods and food became concentrated in particular households—those of wealthy men, or *miixaˇsxə* as they were called by the Tolowa—and one such wealthy man usually appeared as paramount within each village. These men were not formal chiefs and lacked authority in most matters. But they acted as intermediaries in marriage negotiations and indemnity settlements and were in a position to initiate projects such as canoe- and house-building and the annual first sea lion hunt. Given the optimizing nature of traditional Tolowa subsistence procurement systems, the presence of a nonauthoritarian leader in each village who could take the initiative in the few subsistence activities requiring cooperative organization and who could marshal resources to construct the facilities necessary for these activities can be regarded as highly adaptive. The institution of a "wealthy man" in each village can be seen as more adaptive than a purely egalitarian system would have been in this society, since without some form of leadership, opportunities to harvest sea lions and salmon would have been severely limited.

Of course, environmental factors cannot "explain" all the particular manipulations and attendant symbolism of wealth-questing among coastal northwestern California Indians. I have tried to show, however, that the essentially aggrandizive nature of wealth-questing is consistently interrelated with the optimizing subsistence behavior of these people. Indeed, at least some aspects of wealth-questing, particularly the brideprice and the institution of the wealthy man, arise from and in turn support traditional northwestern California subsistence procurement systems. In this sense, wealth-questing, as an expanded form of a wider type of behavior I have termed "aggrandizive," is adaptive for hunter/gatherers living within the northwestern California coastal ecosystem.

CONCLUSIONS

The contrast between the risk-minimizing desert Aborigines of Australia and the resource-optimizing Indians of the northwestern California coast allows us to formulate the following proposition about food-sharing among hunter/gatherers, both past and present:

Aggrandizive behavior increases within a society in direct proportion to the opportunities for optimal harvesting with minimal risk by individual family or household groups. The extent of sharing above the level of the individual family is important in a society in direct proportion to the risk involved in obtaining basic resources within a given ecosystem.

This proposition can be tested against the existing literature on hunter/ gatherers. It can also be used to guide interpretations of prehistoric sharing of food and access to resources. If archaeologists and paleogeographers can reconstruct prehistoric ecosystems in enough detail to identify the potential limiting factors, and opportunities that confronted early humans, then these contrasting models can provide a basis for inferring the particular combination of sharing and aggrandizement that would have been most adaptive under the ecological conditions involved.

This essay also demonstrates the importance of behavioral information in understanding contemporary and prehistoric hunter/gatherer adaptations. Quantitative studies of nutritional intake are valuable, but only if considered in a behavioral context. A research strategy that assumes "you are what you eat, minus what you excrete," can easily distort the recognition of relationships between ecological variables and behavioral responses in human societies. I advocate here a balanced approach that empirically acquires both quantitative and behavioral data and uses them as a basis for positing general ecological relationships that can be tested by archaeologists and paleogeographers.

Acknowledgments

The Australian field research upon which this paper is based was carried out in 1966–1967 under a Social Science Research Council Fellowship, in 1969–1970 under a research grant from the Frederick G. Voss Fund for Anthropological Research of the American Museum of Natural History, and in 1973–1974 under National Science Foundation Research Grant no. GS-37105. Fieldwork in northwestern California was assisted in 1964–1965 by a National Science Foundation Graduate Fellowship and in 1972 by a University of Hawaii Research Travel Grant. I acknowledge this support with gratitude.

The arguments presented in this paper have benefited from discussions and criticism by many of my colleagues, especially George Schaller, Geza Teleki, Ronald M. Berndt, Robert Heizer, Lowell Bean, and Frederica de Laguna. The idea of "negative determinism" was proposed by Terry Grandstaff in the course of discussions about this paper and related matters. I thank Nicolas Peterson for his advice about recent revisions to the plant-species identifications for the Western Desert of Australia. Finally, and above all, I am deeply grateful to the many Western Desert Aborigines and the people of Indian descent in northwestern California who gave unstintingly of their time to aid this research. I hope that this paper gives a faithful and accurate account of their traditional adaptations and that it will provide a basis for informed appreciation of their cultures. However, I take full responsibility for the views expressed in the paper and any errors it may contain.

George Silberbauer

12.
Hunter/Gatherers of the Central Kalahari

The country of the G/wi Bushmen[1] is in the lower-lying, central area of the Kalahari and includes the northeastern Ghanzi ranches and part of the Central Kalahari Game Reserve. The former western portion of their land was settled in the late nineteenth century by white cattlemen. Before that time it had been intermittently penetrated by Bantu-speaking pastoralists from Ngamiland in the north. They moved down to the larger pans along the Ghanzi Ridge after seasons of good rain, and established temporary cattle posts where the ranches now are. More regularly they hunted elephant and rhinoceros, which were once fairly plentiful along the Ridge. The more remote part of the G/wi's land, out in the central desert, is waterless and more sparsely covered by vegetation, and its harshness and inhospitable nature provided an effective barrier to all but the briefest incursions by aliens.

Many people have assumed that the Bushmen of Botswana and neighboring countries are refugees, who were driven into the wastes of the Kalahari by the movement down Africa of Bantu-speaking peoples and the spread of white settlement northward from Table Bay. Iron-working Bantu were present in the vicinity of Pretoria 1,500 years ago (Mason, 1974), and the indications are that they, and Iron Age Bantu in other parts of the interior of South Africa, neither exterminated nor drove away the local Bushmen but coexisted with them. In the more recent past (i.e., after 1652) there is no record of Bushmen migrating away from settlement. On the contrary, they seem to have resisted displacement with great tenacity until war, disease, and hybridization overcame them. The gradation of dialects I found within the Central, or Tshu-khwe, language family and the regularity of the distribution of this and the other language families of the Kalahari Bushmen indicate that their speakers are no refugee population, dumped suddenly and chaotically into this region. The ordered state of linguistic relationships could only have developed over a very long period of stable occupation of present habitats. Archaeological evidence in the form of deposits of stone artifacts ranging in style from Lower Acheulean to Smithfield A, occurring in the northwestern, central, and east-central

Kalahari, shows that this part of Africa has been inhabited from very early times, and there is no reason to assume that it is so inhospitable as to be merely a last refuge.

It is therefore clear that the Bushmen have hunted and gathered in their present area for a very long time and could only have survived by successfully adapting to local conditions. This adaptation did not diminish the resources of the habitat but resulted in a reasonably stable set of interactions between the Bushmen and their environment.

The Habitat

The Kalahari is a basin some 1,200 m above sea level in the southern African plateau, the surrounding highlands of which rise a further 1,000 m. This basin is a vast plain of fine-grained red, white, and gray sands, formed into dunes in some localities, but flat or gently undulating elsewhere and broken in a few places by rocky protrusions. In Botswana the Kalahari lacks permanent surface water except for the Okavango-Botete system of swamps and rivers, and a few large pans in the northwest. Numerous shallow pans and interrupted, ancient drainages concentrate and hold small amounts of rainwater during the wet season. In the Central Kalahari Reserve this is the only surface water to be found and is present for only some 6–8 weeks of the year.

Climate. The climate of the Central Kalahari is arid. Winters are dry, with bitterly cold nights (the lowest minimum I recorded was −13° C) relieved by pleasantly warm days, except during the spells of gusty, chilly weather experienced several times each winter. The interval between the end of winter in late August or early September and the coming of the rains in late December is a time of great stress. Shade temperatures rise to 48° C by early October, while unshaded sand temperatures are 20–25° C higher. Relative humidity measured at 2 P.M. averages 18% in September, rising to 30% just before the onset of the rains. Fierce winds blow for most of the daylight hours, and blasts of stinging sand add to the discomfort of heat and dryness.

The mean annual rainfall in the Reserve is 400 mm, spread over a season of about 12 weeks. Most precipitation is from spectacular localized thunderstorms, and there is great variation in annual and local falls. Pike (1971) has calculated the annual seasonal variability in rainfall to be 60%.

Vegetation. The sandy soils of the Reserve are almost structureless and have an overall low nutrient content (Blair Rains and Yalala, 1972:67ff.), supporting a rather sparse vegetation. Most species are either ephemeral or markedly cold/dry deciduous. Woody plants are predominantly shrubs, and few trees reach heights of more than 8 m, most growing no higher than 4 m. For what seems an unpromising environment there is an unexpectedly wide range of species, especially among the ephemerals; they respond dramatically to the first good fall of rain, transforming the dreary black and brown waste of early summer with their prodigal, short-lived color and luxuriance.

Fauna. This vegetation feeds and shelters a great diversity of invertebrate and vertebrate herbivores, and a correspondingly broad range of predators prey on them. The animal populations fluctuate in phases that approximate, in period and magnitude, the seasonal changes in vegetation. The major part of the adult invertebrate population either dies or hibernates during winter, and the new generations hatch or the adults reappear in summer. In years of good rainfall the local irruptions of many species reach plague proportions. Many of the vertebrates also hibernate or become seasonally torpid, but migration into and out of the central desert accounts for most of the seasonal fluctuations in these populations. Of the 118 bird species that I noted in the Reserve, more than half are absent during winter, and huge herds of the six species of gregarious antelopes move down from the northeast in summer, leaving again before winter.

The People. The G/wi are hunter/gatherers and therefore must find their living in the unimproved resources of their environment. They have no means of countering the seasonal fluctuations in the flora and fauna which constitute their main sets of resources. Biologically they manifest no adaptation which is not common to other races (Tobias, 1964). Instead, they have had to develop a sociocultural system that enables them to meet the pressures exerted by their environment and to accommodate to the drastic seasonal changes in the state of their resource base.

Sociocultural adaptation raises certain problems which (in their extent, at least) are unique to mankind. Cultural behavior is learned, and hence variable. Prediction of an individual's response to another's actions is hazardous unless an agreed code or pattern of behavior restricts the range of variation, i.e., defines a response as appropriate to a specific situation or action, and establishes a hierarchy of choice among possible alternative responses. The assignment of meaning to behavior is more or less arbitrary, and the potential for misinterpretation and failure to comprehend action must be kept within tolerable limits. Humans are somewhat unspecialized animals, with few anatomical and physiological characteristics that enhance their chances of survival in isolation; they depend on a context of social order governing themselves and their fellows to implement their cultural means of survival. The necessary code of behavior can only be formulated, adjusted, and its operation maintained where there is a network of communication with a copious flow of information among those governed by the code. The members of the group must be in contact with one another under circumstances that permit this flow. They must, therefore, devise an appropriate residential strategy that will stabilize the range of interpersonal encounters and the interactions that result from them.

The minimum viable size of a group of hunter/gatherers has not been determined. Clearly there must be at least sufficient manpower for cooperative tasks and enough personnel to provide a collective memory for storing and recalling the knowledge on which cultural behavior depends. (Western society is rich in means of relieving the mind of the burden of remembering, and we perhaps overlook the problem of relying on memory for all the details of every technique of daily life.) Although we have not been able to quantify the minimal group size, it is nevertheless reasonable to assume a lower limit at which the efficiency of group action will decline and survival will be threatened.

Too large a group of hunter/gatherers, on the other hand, consumes resources too rapidly, requiring that more time and energy be spent to reach new supplies (the efficiency with which a given number searches and gathers declines as the radius of the search increases). Also, a larger group requires a more complex organization, the administration and main-tenance of which drain away yet more time and energy. (Increase in complexity of organizational structure is probably not simply proportional to size, but may progress in quanta, or steps.) The residential strategy of a community of hunter/gatherers must be such as to maintain the group size that will yield the greatest psychosocial and economic benefit at the lowest cost of time and energy spent in exploiting the requisite variety and amount of the habitat's resources.

In the case of the desert G/wi, the resources necessary to long-term survival are:

1. Food plants, in the variety, number, and density necessary to meet the population's nutritional needs in all seasons, within the wide range of rainfall and other climatic factors affecting vegetation.
2. Sufficient grazing and browsing to attract and sustain adequate numbers of antelopes and other herbivorous prey animals.
3. Trees for shade, shelter, and firewood, and as a source of raw material for artifacts.
4. Pans or other impervious drainage in which rainwater collects.
5. Considering the prevailing low density of floral and faunal popula-tions, sufficient space for adequate amounts of the above-mentioned resources.

It is obvious that these resources should occur in reasonably close proximity to each other if the community utilizing them is to be spared inordinate effort traveling between them and transporting the required food or other material back and forth (e.g., there is a limited distance one can afford to go to fetch firewood). In the Central Kalahari there is a limited number of localities where these resources occur in combination and in amounts adequate to the needs of communities above the minimum viable size. In the light of their hunter/gatherer lifestyle, this feature of their habitat strongly influences the G/wi choice of residential location.

In theory they have a choice of two residential strategies: large communities that migrate between several such major nexuses of resources, moving on as the supplies in each are exhausted, or small communities that could sustain themselves on what is to be found in a single resource-nexus. The G/wi have devised a compromise that accommodates the seasonal fluctuation in the amount and variety of resources. Each community, or band, occupies the country in which a major resource nexus occurs, and this is recognized by all others as being that band's territory. During the summer and autumn months of relative plenty (i.e., from about November to the first heavy frosts, which may occur at any time between April and July), the band members live together in a series of camps, migrating to a fresh one just before they have reduced the locally available supplies of food plants and other resources to scarcity. This phase normally lasts 7–9 months, and moves are made at intervals of 2–4 weeks.

When the aboveground plants are blighted by frost, the number of edible species is reduced by 75%, and the band must rely on those which have usable bulbs, tubers, or roots. These are so sparsely distributed that the band would have to move every few days if joint camps were to be continued. Instead, the constituent households separate, each going to its own campsite at which it remains, isolated from the others, until conditions again improve as midsummer approaches. In drought years when summer resources are too meager to support the whole membership in a single camp, the band forms a number of separate small camps, each consisting of a few families. In good summers, by contrast, a whole band can even migrate and temporarily join another band in its territory. Such mass visits do not occur more than once a year and only last a couple of weeks, which are spent in socializing, exchanging news and trade commodities, and in playing games. Differently motivated mass visits are sometimes made in times of localized drought. When one band suffers a shortage, it may seek succor in another's territory, but only when the host band has not been similarly afflicted and has enough resources to meet the needs of both populations. Although claims on this mutual insurance are seldom made, it is highly valued and is often mentioned as one of the reasons for maintaining good relationships among bands.

In short, the G/wi strategy is one of varying the size of the residential group (and, hence, the local population density) according to the seasonally prevailing density of food resources; at the cost of living in a part-time society, the band is able to sustain a membership far greater than would be possible in the lean seasons if it were a full-time society. The advantage of the bands having control over its own territory lies in its being able to coordinate households' choices of winter ranges and to arbitrate between conflicting claims and intentions of the member households. Isolated and joint campsites are selected on the basis of the current state of resources and change from year to year in response to the vagaries of rainfall. In this way the band accommodates the short-term variation in productivity of particular areas by avoiding the poorer, dry corners of the territory and taking advantage of those which experienced higher rainfall in the preceding wet season. In the long run, this practice serves to randomize areas of exploitation and avoids sustained pressure of use on particular ones.

SOCIAL ORGANIZATION

Each band is identified with its territory and has exclusive rights to the exploitation of its resources (table 12.1). Rights of occupation and exploitation are held equally by all households of the resident band. It is an open community in the sense that there are no exclusive qualifications for membership; theoretically anybody may join and is therefore also free to leave for another band. The size of the band is, of course, limited by the capacity of its territorial resources. (Maximum band size is also limited by its organizational nature to around 100 people; this factor would be constant for all G/wi bands, which share a common form of social organization.) In practice, band membership is fairly stable and the rate of change is normally small. There is evidence, however, that Bushmen all over Botswana (and, in the past, elsewhere in southern Africa) have experienced periodic and disastrous droughts and epidemics in which many died. The G/wi suffered heavy losses from smallpox and polio-myelitis in the early 1950s. It seems that the response to such calamities is a rapid redistribution of population, with the remnants of decimated bands forming new ones and abandoning many old territories. In all informants' accounts of these terrible times there was a clear picture of a coherent social fabric remaining intact and survivors coming together and integrating easily and smoothly in new communities, which must have mitigated the aftereffects of the epidemics.

The durability of social order in circumstances that might be expected to

Table 12.1. G/wi Bushman territories

Territory name	Area (km²)	Band population	Density (persons/km²)
≠xade	906	85	0.094
G!õsa	457	21	0.046
Easter Pan	777	50	0.064
Kxaotwe	1036	64	0.062
Tsxobe	725	70	0.097
Piper Pans	777	53	0.068

Note: Both modal and average densities approximate 0.07 persons/km², which is probably about the norm for the Central Kalahari.

bring severe dislocation is related to the problem inherent in the residential strategy of alternating between phases of joint- and single-household camps. Life in the united band must be sufficiently rewarding to bring the members together, yet not so attractive as to prevent their separating again in winter. The necessary independence of the isolated household, forced to self-reliance for 3–5 months (and longer in dry years) must be submerged in the intimacy and cooperation that is evident in the joint camp.

This facility for separation and reuniting is derived from several sources. One is the kinship system which, as is common among small-scale societies, is the principal means of organizing interpersonal relationships. The system furnishes definitions and models of status and behavior which help the individual choose his course of action and predict and interpret the behavior of others, and help the group to evaluate and comprehend the actions of the individual. A kinship system has two characteristics that are particularly suitable: First, kinship imposes lifelong relationships; they may be inactive through lack of interaction, but they can hardly be denied or eradicated once interaction occurs and (as we are enjoined on marrying) they must be accepted for better or for worse. Second, the way in which kin categories are defined by the system enables one to comprehend one's own position in relation to others, as well as the relative position of others among themselves.

It is not necessary to describe the details here; suffice it to say that the G/wi system accords a unique, exclusive character to intra-household relationships—those between spouses, parents and children, and among siblings. These cannot be easily shifted from one person to another. By contrast, there is a high incidence of equivalence among extra-household relationships and a great versatility of the corresponding roles. Potentially, the web of kinship spans the whole G/wi population; in practice it encompasses most, if not all, of the membership of any individual's band and the majority of his acquaintances. Bonds of friendships and of special affection may reduce the degree of real substitutability of some extra-household relationships, but the redundancy in the structure is such that one person, or a number of people, may join or leave a band and cause only minimal disruption of the social order. This aspect of the kinship system facilitates the formation of new combinations of households while also allowing already-formed groups to disperse.

The capacity of the household for economic independence in isolation is a function of the lack of specialization beyond a minimal age/sex division of labor; the combined manpower of the household possesses all the skills needed to meet the requirements of daily life, and the family does not need outside help for its survival.

Fission is made easier by the egalitarian character of the band and the absence of centralized, formal authority in its political organization. The band is a consensual polity, and leadership, which is diffused among the members, is an ephemeral role adopted by one or another in response to a particular situation when his or her opinion or advice is adopted by the rest of the band. On another occasion, facing a different problem, the band may be guided to consensus and decision by someone else's words. Experience, knowledge, and wisdom are the qualities of leadership; they are not evenly distributed among the membership, and in every band some people emerge as leaders more frequently than their fellows. But this does not gain them automatic power, nor does leadership in one field overflow into another. That a man's opinion on the best hunting strategy is often accepted and acted upon by his band does not mean that his views on other matters will necessarily carry weight, and the band does not see itself as relying on one man, or even a junta. If one leader drops out, another takes his place. Leadership is persuasive and authoritative, not authoritarian, and serves only to guide the band toward the consensus that is the real locus of decision. Therefore, a household's autonomy and self-reliance are not diminished by dependence on the authority and leadership of a headman, chief, or other central figure. Temporary fragmentation of the band is not subject to the constraint of dependence, nor are survivors of a catastrophe left helpless by the dismantling of a centralized, specialist authority structure.

The centripetal tendency that overcomes the autonomous, almost anarchistic, character of isolated households and brings band members together in one encampment derives from the clear advantages of increased manpower and information and from the very high value which the G/wi place on the company of their fellows. As indicated, the kinship system facilitates integration of the households into a single social entity.

When the band is in a common camp, much of the interaction between members involves the exchange of goods and services. There is also a network of exchange relationships that stretches across the Central Kalahari, reaching ranches, cattle posts, and trading posts. This network provides the pathways for importation of tobacco, iron, and other commodities that are otherwise unobtainable, and for export of prepared game hides and other G/wi produce. Exchange of these goods at the point of contact with alien cultures is conducted as a trading transaction in which participants bargain to maximize their return in the form of specific, desired articles and in terms of minimal outlay of proffered goods.

Within the network, between bands and among band members, exchange is conducted on different lines. The principle of reciprocity still operates—something must be given in return for what is received—but exchanges are not directed toward acquiring specific commodities in return for others of a matching market value. Both goods and services serve as media of exchange, and their value is determined more by the current needs of the recipient than by other market factors. The situation is paradoxical: the actual flow of goods and services far exceeds the pragmatic needs of households which annually demonstrate their economic self-reliance. Utilitarian need for one another's help and possessions does not account for the volume of exchanges and would, in fact, make nonsense of some of the transactions. There must be a supplementary motivation, and this appears to stem from the psychosocial aspects of exchange. In addition to its undeniable material value, a gift or favor also affirms friendship and solidarity between giver and receiver. In G/wi society the establishment and maintenance of harmonious relationships is the supreme value and the ultimate rationale of much that people do. This consideration explains the "superfluous" quality of transactions and also the G/wi notion that a return prestation (Mauss, 1954) not only discharges a previous obligation but also creates a new one—a view that perpetuates the flow of exchanges indefinitely.

A wide range of goods and services serve as a versatile currency of exchange. Breakdowns and blockages that could otherwise stalemate transactions under conditions of over- and undersupply of particular commodities are circumvented by the breadth of prestations possible and by the temporal latitude allowed to debtors—the proper time to make a return is when the opportunity arises, and whether this is a day later or the next summer is not what matters.

The importance accorded to a recipient's needs in evaluating prestations inhibits the accumulation of individual wealth; the more he has, the less he needs and the less will be the relative value of what he receives. This standard of values inclines the flow of goods and services toward the "have-nots" and its equalizing tendency, combined with the fluctuations of individual fortunes and the varying needs of the seasons, brings about constant changes in the relative needs and abilities among people, facilitating further exchanges and maintaining an egalitarian economy.

In its psychosocial aspects—the expression of interpersonal relationships—the exchange network seems to me to supplement the organizational framework which the kinship system furnishes. I referred earlier to the redundancy in the categories provided by the kinship system and to how the substitutability of those bracketed in a category enhanced the capacity of extra-household relationships to combine, facilitating the processes of fission and fusion (the combining of households in joint camps and their subsequent dispersal into isolation) on which depends the G/wi strategy of adjusting population density to changing resource levels. This flexibility entails a cost in terms of inadequate social definition. In the intimate life of the band, relationships develop a richness and diversity whose expression requires an elaboration of the social fabric within the broad pattern prescribed by the kinship system. While households are camped together, the band members need a way to define more precisely the current gradations in social and emotional distance which distinguish bonds of greater or lesser intensity. Such a way must be responsive to the dynamic nature of the web of relationships, accommodating and expressing fluctuations in emotional levels as affections strengthen or wane, as friendships change in alignment, and as band members come or go on visits. The exchange of goods and services provides a means of simultaneously expressing and ordering relationships with the requisite versatility and diversity of definition. Exchanges do not impair the flexibility imparted by the kinship system, but do meet the need to overcome its redundancy. Later I shall discuss the importance of exchanges of gifts of meat and, hence, of hunting in the maintenance of social order.

WORLD VIEW

Mankind's Place in the World

In G/wi belief, N!adima is the supreme being who created the fabric of the universe, its features and its creatures. It was he who ordained and set in operation all the natural systems of the seasons, weather, night and day, growth and reproduction of living things, etc. He is omnipresent and omniscient and, within the limits of the order he imposed, is all-powerful. He cannot, for instance, cause a man to give birth or make a stone speak, but he can send a lion to kill a man or withhold the rains when their season is due. As his creation, all the land and the living things in it belong to him. He is a remote deity who does not often intervene in the lives of his creatures, having, as it were, set them on their paths at the time of creation.

The G/wi see themselves as sharing the common lot of the deity's creatures and not at all as enjoying a position of primacy or special favor in his scheme. In relation to the land, they are his sufferance tenants. They may use the resources, for it is part of the order of creation that some living things destroy or kill others in order to live. Humans are just another species of predator or herbivore in this respect, and are permitted to meet their needs from what they find about them. The purpose of life is a mystery which cannot be known, but the means of life are clear: the universe is seen as a systematic, interacting whole in which all living things have to devise for themselves the optimal *modus vivendi* within the confines of natural, N!adima-given order. These confines are:

1. The creature's characteristic abilities and needs, ordained at the time of creation.
2. The obligation to coexist with other creatures, arising out of their common status as N!adima's property, to which due respect must be shown.

3. The complex of interspecies and intraspecies dependencies.
4. The operation of astronomical, climatic, biological, and other systems.
5. The pressure of appropriate sanctions "built in" by N!adima against wanton destruction or unseemly disturbance of his creatures and disrespect toward his creation and property and, by inference, himself.

It is not surprising that this reads like a charter for conservation; hunter/gatherers face short lives if penalty clause 5 is invoked.

Theirs is a poignantly lonely view of their place in the world: separated from other people by the distances and difficulties of travel in the Central Kalahari, subject to the disinterested order of an unapproachable deity, and responsible for their own survival without any promise that he will intervene to save them, understandably the G/wi place a very high value on the harmony and the company of one another.

Attitudes and Beliefs about Prey

Our Western view of the relationships among living things is vertical and ranked. Mankind stands at the top of a genealogical tree, for our theology has us at the pinnacle of creation with "dominion over the fish of the sea, the fowl of the air, and over every living thing that moveth upon the earth." The G/wi construct is horizontal, with complementary rather than ranked statuses. It is anthropocentric in that it views the world from a human perspective, but does not view it as a world *for* mankind. For heuristic purposes their construct could be depicted as a series of concentric rings with humans at the center. Working outward, successive rings would represent other mammals, then birds, chelonians, snakes and legless lizards, legged lizards, batrachians, invertebrates and, finally, the flora. Proximity to the center represents the relative extent to which each group resembles us. As is apparent from the placing of snakes and legless skinks before the legged lizards, classification is not purely morphological (lizards, with four limbs, are closer in their gross anatomy) but reflects the belief, by no means unique to the G/wi (see Matthew 10:16), that snakes are psychologically closer to mankind than are the subsequent groups.

Proximity to the center also relates to the extent of vernacular knowledge of each group. Some 75 species of animals occur in the Central Kalahari. Excepting the bats, dormice, mice, rats, and gerbils (which are generically named, as they are here in English), each is individually named. G/wi nomenclature for all life-forms tends toward monomorphemic, specific terms for those species which are prominent because they are frequently encountered, because of their contribution or threat to human survival, or because they have habits or appearances considered to be remarkable. The less prominent species mostly have polymorphemic, derived names or are included in generic groupings.

G/wi ethology is strongly anthropomorphic. Animal behavior is perceived as rational and purposive and as being directed by motives based largely on values which the G/wi themselves hold, with empathetic modification or transformation to fit the vernacular version of the circumstances of the animals concerned. Each species has its "customs," within which there is the same range of individual variation as exists among people. Both mammals and birds are credited with species-specific languages, and there is thought to be a measure of mutual intelligibility among these. Baboons are the most capable of animal polyglots; they eavesdrop on G/wi hunters and pass the latter's plans on to the intended prey. (This is not done out of altruism, but is an expression of the baboon's proclivity for trickery and teasing.)

Some animals are believed to possess special powers which they discovered at some time in the past through rational thought-processes or serendipitous accident. These discoveries became institutionalized as elements in the animals' "customs" and are passed on from generation to generation by parents in the normal training and socialization of the young. The complex hunting repertoire of the wild dog, *Lycaon pictus*, is mimicked in G/wi musical play. In these performances the players fit G/wi words to the astonishing variety of calls uttered by these dogs, discussing hunting tactics, commenting on the progress of the hunt, and explaining it all to the grown pups. As a European, I could not accept the anthropomorphism explicit in the G/wi view, but there certainly was a close correspondence between their mimicry and what I had seen and heard of the hunting dogs' behavior.

Duikers practice sorcery against their animal enemies and even against conspecific rivals, and some steenbok know magical means of protecting themselves from a hunter's arrows.

Prey animals are innately hostile to mankind. N!adima warned them that men would hunt them, saying, "Hate them when you see them and when you see their fires at night." Each is expected to use its strength and wits in the manner characteristic of its species and to do its best to avoid the hunter. He, in turn, expects to manage to overcome the challenge which the animal's behavior and other difficulties of the hunt present to his skill, cunning, and endurance, but is aware that there is always the chance of being outwitted or otherwise frustrated by an idiosyncratic quirk of his quarry. A gemsbok which uncharacteristically and inexplicably doubled back on its tracks when it seemed highly likely to walk into an ambush was praised as being /xudi ("ingenious"). However, another hunter described a hartebeest as/xan ("useless, stupid") for not conforming to its species-typical pattern of behavior. I have known hunters, watching herds of antelope before selecting their target, to classify individual animals and reject them because they had qualities of character or personality which would make them difficult targets. Some were contrary, too courageous, or too cowardly; others were said to be conceited, insolent, or cheats and might be good targets. I noted 18 terms in this typology which categorizes the quarry's expected behavior before and after it has been shot. In my observation the predictions about those judged to be favorable targets were nearly all accurate, and it was often apparent from their subsequent behavior that the rejected specimens would have been difficult or impossible to stalk. As any dairy farmer will confirm, every cow in a milking herd has her individual peculiarities; horses are notoriously variable in temperament. Discerning cattlemen and riders can recognize some traits, but we are not usually close observers of the behavior of even these domesticated animals and have a slender vocabulary by which to type their differences. I could not fathom much of the G/wi typology although the hunters obviously knew the signs diagnostic of each type and state, and their behavior connotations, and tried often enough to explain them to me.

There are some puzzling errors in vernacular ethology. Steenbok, for instance, are believed to have a regular breeding season, while in fact these small antelopes drop their fawns in all months of the year. Among lions, whose group behavior is explained in terms and concepts of the G/wi household, the male is said to do most of the hunting. Schaller's impressive study of the Serengeti lion (Schaller, 1972) unequivocally refutes this belief. Nevertheless, despite occasional error and a heavy anthropomorphic bias, G/wi ethology accounts for animal behavior accurately enough to be an effective aid in hunting, in anticipating the actions of dangerous species, and in interpreting the connotations of interactions between species. It has withstood the rigorous test of use by people who depend on its validity.

Knowledge of Prey Anatomy and Physiology

Mammalian anatomy and physiological processes are equated with those of human beings. In the course of cleaning dead animals I have been given the name of each larger organ of the prey animals together with an account of its function. Where appropriate (to zoology, rather than to etiquette—we had some very bawdy conversations when woman and girls were present or close enough to be teased), the position of the human homologue was indicated and its matching functions described. Organs are linked in conceptualized systems approximately isomorphic with those of Western zoology. The G/wi account of the cardiovascular-respiratory system differs in having blood flow from the heart through the veins, whose semilunar valves are seen as pumps assisting the action of the heart. The darker hue of venous blood explained by its nutrient load which is shed on the outward journey. "Empty," lighter-colored arterial blood returns for a fresh supply from the liver and lungs. The reproductive tract and its functions are accounted for in terms closer to our views. I was struck by the fact that human beings are known to be monogastric, in contrast to the four-chambered structure of the stomachs in the ruminants which are the animals most commonly dissected. Laughlin (1962) ascribed the extensive anatomical knowledge of Manchurian Tungus and Aleutian Islanders to their practice of human, as well as animal, postmortem dissection. But the G/wi do not dissect their dead and would seldom encounter them dismembered. Perhaps their knowledge is derived from palpation of living patients, which is an important source of information (and means of treatment) in their medical practice.

ECONOMICS

Subsistence: Gathering

Gathered plants constitute the main part of the subsistence base (table 12.2). In terms of mass, these provide 75–100% of the diet, depending on the time of year and the fortunes of hunters. Plant foods are the main (and sometimes only) source of fluids during the greater part of the year, when no rainwater is to be had. Many species are used intermittently [Tanaka (1976) lists 67 identified species; plus 12 unidentified ones], and 35 are gathered regularly. A dozen of the latter have the status of staples, i.e., they are of major importance in the diet. There is seasonal variation in the number available, from an autumn maximum of 28 (of which 10 are staples) down to an early summer minimum of 5 (2 staples). When food plants are relatively plentiful, the household's needs (i.e., for the plants eaten at home during meals) are met by each wife's gathering for her own family. At these times men gather only snacks for themselves while out hunting for the day, or for their meals while traveling. (Some men do sporadically bring home greater or smaller amounts of plant food, and most men gather any delicacies they encounter while hunting, but the brunt of the work is borne by the women.) In the seasons of scarcity, however, edible plants are so sparsely scattered that only the combined efforts of husband and wife are sufficient to meet the household's needs, and in these times men do as much gathering as their wives and older unmarried daughters. The mass of plant food gathered each day is fairly constant throughout the year, at 3.5–5 kg per person. Tanaka (1976:112), however, estimated average daily intake to be 800 g. The discrepancy may be due to Tanaka's having subtracted the amount of plant food eaten to meet fluid requirements. The day's collection is normally only enough for the evening and the following morning's meals, so gathering is a daily task. In any case, most plant foods spoil quickly and the G/wi have no means of preserving them. Melons are an exception, and when *tsamas* (*Citrullus lanatus*) are plentiful, gathering need only be done every second day and the intake is often considerably above 5 kg. Good *tsama* seasons, however, are not common [Leistner (1967:106) estimated that only one year in five brings abundance], and gathering is normally a chore taking up 4–8 hours of each woman's day.

Food plants are ranked by the G/wi in terms of their thirst- and hunger-allaying properties, the ease with which they can be utilized and, least important, their flavor. The first and third criteria are self-explanatory. The second is a function of the energy cost, which varies with the position of the edible portion (if above ground, whether within or beyond reach, and the degree of difficulty in detaching the portion; if below ground, the depth at which the portion lies), the size and weight of each portion, the density of distribution of edible material on the plant, the density of the species population and, last, the ease or difficulty with which the edible portion is prepared for eating. The distribution of the highest-ranking available species is the main determinant of the pattern of daily gathering and is the most commonly invoked factor in deciding the areas in which the band's successive camps are located. Availability of a high-ranking species, one that yields much food for little effort, allows women to avoid monotonous menus by adding tasty but less nutritious or less easily won items, and it is only in the lean seasons that households are regularly confronted by the same dish at each meal.

Gathering is nearly always physically demanding. There is no rhythm in the work—walk, stop, squat and dig or reach and pluck, and then walk on farther with the load growing heavier at each stop. The gathered material is not trimmed but is usually carried home with an added burden of leaves, scales, or whatever still adheres (like carrying home bunches of beets or carrots with the tops still on), to be stripped at the cooking fire in the camp. To the load of plant food must be added the required amount of firewood. At the end of the day a woman will come home with nearly the equal of her own weight piled on her shoulders and slung in her antelope-hide cloak, and less than half of this is food.

The distance covered to win this food varies with the season, the skill (or luck) with which the camp is located, and a woman's conscientiousness in adding variety to her family's meals. Seasonal variation in the area searched to find one day's ration of plant food for one person is of this order:

September	0.414 km²
December	0.026 km²
March	0.033 km²
May	0.009 km²
May (prolific *tsamas*)	0.0014 km²

Searches are not random but are narrowed by the gatherer's local

Table 12.2. Period of availability of G/wi plant foods

	Sept.	Oct.	Nov.	Dec.	Jan.	Feb.	Mar.	Apr.	May	Jun.	Jul.	Aug.
Fruits												
*Boscia albitrunca			+	+	+	+	+	+	+	+		
*Grewia flavescens (vars.)					+	+						
Momordica balsamina			+		+	+						
Strychnos sp.			+	+								
Trochomeria macrocarpa					+	+						
*Ximenia caffra					+	+	+					
Zizyphus mucronata									+	+		
(Melons)												
*Citrullus lanatus						+	+	+	+	+		
*C. naudinianus							+	+	+			
Cucumis hookerii								+	+	+	+	
C. metuliferus					+	+	+	+	+			
Seeds												
*Bauhinia esculenta					+	+	+	+	+	+	+	+
*B. macrantha						+	+	+	+	+	+	
Leaves												
Aloe rubrolutea	+	+	+	+	+	+	+	+	+	+	+	+
A. zebrina			+	+	+	+	+	+	+	+	+	
Caralluma lutea					+	+	+	+	+	+	+	+

Species	1	2	3	4	5	6	7	8	9	10
Duvalia polita	+	+	+	+	+	+	+	+		
Talinum arnotii		+			+	+	+	+		
Talinum sp.					+	+				
Terminalia sericea							+	+	+	+
Tribulus terristris							+	+	+	+
Roots and storage organs										
Bauhiniae sculenta	+	+	+	+	+	+	+	+		
Brachystelma barberiae		+	+	+	+	+	+	+		
Ceropegia spp.		+	+	+	+	+	+	+		
Coccinea rehmannii	+	+	+	+	+	+	+	+	+	
C. sessifolia	+	+	+	+	+	+	+	+	+	
Commiphora pyracanthoides	+		+	+	+	+	+	+	+	
Cyphia stenopetala		+	+	+	+					
Lapeirousin bainesii				+	+					
Ipomoea transvaalensis		+	+	+	+	+	+	+		
Raphionacme burkei	+	+	+	+	+	+	+	+	+	
Scilla sp.	+	+		+	+					
Terfezia sp.				+	+	+				
Vigna sp.			+			+				
Wallera nutans				+	+	+				

Note: * denotes a species of major importance in the G/wi diet.
+ denotes the period when the plant food is available.

knowledge of the country. The need for the husband's help in gathering in early summer is clear from the fact that an area of nearly half a mile square must be searched to find enough to meet just one person's daily requirement, and this must be done during the 3–4 hours after sunrise, or the 2 hours before sunset, because the midday heat is too trying for work and walking.

Subsistence: Hunting

Main Techniques. The most-used hunting technique is shooting game animals with bow and poisoned arrow. Snaring small terrestrial birds and small antelopes is resorted to when poison supplies are exhausted and when time and energy cannot be spared for the long, demanding hours needed for bow-and-arrow hunting. Springhares are hunted by means of long, barbed probes thrust into the warrens to hook and hold the prey fast until it can be dug out. Running-down, spearing, and clubbing are less commonly used techniques. Other predators, notably lions, are occasionally robbed of their kills, which is a dramatic but not always rewarding way of getting meat.

The G/wi bow is a light, single-curve stave made from the wood of the raisin-bush (*Grewia flava*). It is tapered from near the center to form a point at each end; these ends and the central hand-hold are bound with sinew from the splenius muscle of gemsbok. A short stick, forming a "thumb," is let into the foot of the bow and is bound fast. The bowstring of two-ply twisted sinew from the longissimus dorsii and costarum muscles of eland has an eye spliced at one end, and this is looped over the head of the stave to anchor that end. The free end goes between the "thumb" and bowstave and is wound around the lower part of the foot of the bow. The string is tightened by twisting the windings and pushing them against the "thumb", which pinches the string and keeps it from slackening. Correct tension is recognized by the musical pitch of the plucked string. The weight, or pull, of a tuned bow is about 9 kg at its draw of some 20 cm, which will carry an arrow to the 100-m mark. Accurate range, however, is limited to a quarter of that distance by the characteristics of the arrow.

The arrow consists of four sections: the head, sleeve, linkshaft, and mainshaft. Broadheads (barbed) are commonest, but piles (simple point) are also made for hunting birds and other small game. The usual material for broadheads is now no. 8 gauge steel fencing wire (4.1-mm diameter), but the ancient art of making arrowheads from the bone core (processus cornus) of gemsbok horn is still practiced by some. In making a wire arrowhead, a length of 12–13 cm is heated in a pit of wood coals, brought to maximum temperature by a blowpipe, until the wire becomes bright red or yellow. Using one block of quartzite as an anvil and another as hammer (both imported from the distant Ghanzi Ridge), the smith draws the wire to a point and then thins and spreads the barbs. The remaining length behind the barbs is slightly flattened, or squared to give a firmer hold when poison is applied and also to make the head sit more securely in the sleeve once it is fitted. Some men obtained pieces of steel, such as abandoned kingpins from my vehicles, and used these as hammers, and others acquired files for finishing their arrowheads, but most can give fine points and edges to their arrows using only the crude stone tools. Fencing-wire is more durable than bone and, being malleable, takes a sharper point and edges. It has become the perferred material and is a valued exchange commodity.

The sleeve of the arrow is a short tubular section of reed that fits over the shaft of the arrowhead and over the point of the linkshaft, connecting the two. To prevent its bursting on impact, the sleeve is served, or bound, with sinew.

A 5-cm spindle of hard wood (e.g., *Grewia*) or bone forms the linkshaft. Its rearward point fits snugly into the mainshaft but not so tightly as to prevent its being detached, since the purpose of this part is to allow the mainshaft to come away from the head once the arrow has lodged in its target. The precious mainshaft can then be recovered undamaged, and the wounded prey is also prevented from using the leverage of the mainshaft to remove the arrow and its load of poison.

The mainshaft is about 45 cm long and is made of reed or the culm of one of the suitably stout grasses. Both materials are somewhat scarce in the Central Kalahari, and a wand of raisin-bush serves as substitute if neither is available. The arrow is not fletched or flighted in any way. Being light, it has small momentum, and probably the increased accuracy which flights might give would not materially increase the weapon's efficiency.

The arrow is not intended to inflict a mortal wound; it is a means of injecting a load of poison which, in time, kills the prey. Poison is made from the intestines of the larval grubs of the beetle *Diamphidia simplex*. Men dig up the larvae from under the *Commiphora pyracanthoides* bush, leaving them stored in their cocoons until they are to be used. The cocoon is then broken open and the grub removed. It is gently squeezed and rolled to break up the innards without tearing the skin. The head is nipped off and the pulped insides are squeezed out, like blobs of toothpaste from a tube, onto the shaft of the arrowhead. To lessen the chance of accident, the poison is only applied behind the barbs, and the sharp parts of the arrowhead are left clean. The blobs of poison are smoothed over, forming a spindle-shaped thickening on the shaft, given a protective coating of juice from the leaf of *Aloe zebrina*, and then gently dried and hardened over warm coals and ashes. Eight larvae are used to arm an arrow and, provided the poison does not go stale, this dose normally proves lethal to all prey animals if the arrow is accurately placed in a fleshy part where it can penetrate to a depth of 8–10 cm, so that the poison can be dissolved and carried by the animal's bloodstream.

Breyer-Brandwijk (1937) analyzed *Diamphidia* poison and reported that it was of the toxalbuminous type with a high degree of toxicity, producing general paralysis, much local irritation around the wound, and hemolysis. Shaw, Woolley, and Rae (1963) reviewed the literature on Bushman arrow poisons and reported their tests of 18 poison samples. The *Diamphidia* sample was not tested but, as it was 42 years old, perhaps a test would not have had much validity (although a 143-year-old sample of another type of poison killed a mouse within 3 minutes!).

Each man arms his own arrows and, contrary to some reports, no secrecy or ritual accompanies this work. The source, method of preparation, and dangerous properties of poison are general knowledge and are known to all children old enough to understand.

It requires considerable skill to hunt with weapons of such limited range and accuracy. Most game animals shift their grazing grounds too often and range over too wide an area for G/wi hunters to predict their movements with the precision that would make it possible to organize beats in which animals might be driven toward bowmen concealed at prearranged locations [although this reportedly was done in other, better-favored parts of southern Africa (Livingstone, 1857; Stow, 1905)]. The game must be taken where it is found, and to find it at all needs luck, knowledge of the country and of the habits of the various prey species, and up-to-date information on their movements, gained from others' observations and from the hunter's own interpretation of the signs of the animals' movements.

There are two hunting strategies: the day sortie and the *biltong* hunt. Men making day sorties usually hunt in pairs. When the band occupies a joint camp, several pairs may go out in the morning, each having determined its area and direction of hunting in discussion during the previous evening. Men, women, and children habitually scan their surroundings, are sensitive to a wide spectrum of information, and are alert to the presence of game. All news is passed on to the hunters and is taken into account, together with other general and specific knowledge, when formulating plans. Each party's intentions are fully disclosed, to prevent one inadvertently interfering with another. Conflict of intention is usually resolved by according precedence to the acknowledged best hunters. Although the tactics of the actual hunt are decided on the spot by the pair concerned and are individualistic to that extent, the strategy of hunting by band members is a cooperative matter in which most adult members of the band participate. It is seldom difficult to reach consensus, as the number of hunting pairs in the field on the same day rarely exceeds four and is usually fewer, and the hunting range in which they operate covers anything up to 800 km² around the camp.

No two hunts are alike, and no informant was able to give me a concise, coherent account of the principles of hunting tactics. What follows is a synthesis of what I learned from discussion, from observation during hunts in which I participated, and from fireside conversation and questions about innumerable others in which I did not take part.

A hunter carries his arrows, ready-poisoned, in a bark quiver sewn into his steenbok-hide hunting satchel. Slung across his left shoulder, this also holds his bow, club, digging-stick, and a smaller quiver containing a repair kit consisting of spare portions of arrows, lengths of prepared sinew for repairing a bowstring or bindings, a small supply of poison-grubs, and plant gum for fixing the bindings. Loops and a small sheath attached to the satchel hold a spear, and a knife is carried in a sheath strapped to the hunter's waist. The spatulate blades of both these weapons are hammered out from appropriate lengths of 9–15-mm diameter soft iron rod, which, like fencing-wire, is an important trade commodity.

A pair leaves for its chosen hunting ground not long after sunrise, walking at a good pace, with the second man treading exactly in the footsteps of the first to minimize noise and to avoid thorns. If they speak at all it is in muted tones; most communication is by facial expression, gesture, and specific hand signals. Tracks encountered are commented upon: the direction taken by the animal is shown by a wave, a fast movement for a gallop and a slow, wavering sweep of the hand for a grazing animal. The distance which the animal is judged to have traveled since making the spoor is indicated by the extent of the follow-through of the wave. A flick of the fingers shows that the tracks are very fresh and their maker must be close by; an upturned palm means an old or fruitless sets of marks. There is a separate hand signal for each species of large mammal and for the small mammals and birds that are normally hunted. In general the fingers are held in positions imitating the shape of the head (or horns, where appropriate), and the hand is moved in imitation of the animal's distinctive gait.

Hunters have the habit of wariness; on approaching the area in which they expect to find their quarry they carefully and unobtrusively scout the land ahead, climbing into trees or edging over the tops of dunes to peer through covering vegetation, always careful not to betray their presence by sight, sound, or scent, keeping clear of the upwind side of a possible target. When the quarry is sighted, the pair makes a reconnaissance, noting the size and position of the herd (most bow-and-arrow hunting is in pursuit of large antelopes, all of which are gregarious), whether the herd is grazing or resting, quiet or nervous, the disposition of sentries, the "personalities" of likely prey, and many other factors. An animal positioned on the flank of the herd is preferred to one on the downwind extremity—the hindmost beast is nearly always conscious of his vulnerability and, hence, more difficult to approach within range of a telling shot. Herds generally move upwind, and the foremost animals are likewise watchful. Furthermore, the hunters' scent is likely to be carried down to the herd before the front-grazers can be approached, so they too are not favored targets. A lamed but not emaciated animal is a good prospect, since it will not run as far after being wounded as would a healthy specimen, but it may graze well inside the perimeter of the herd, seeking protection in its vulnerable state, and therefore be harder to approach successfully.

Whether a bull or a cow is easier to hunt depends on the species and the time of the year; kudu bulls are more alert when in mixed herds before the cows separate to drop their calves, but cows run farther when wounded. This is also true of gemsbok. By contrast, a hartebeest cow may run only a short distance after being shot and, if she has not detected the hunters and the source of her pain, may stop and stand for a while, offering the chance of a second shot. Wildebeest cows and bulls are equally tenacious of life, and the sex of the target makes no difference here.

After reconnoitering, the hunters plan their approach. The steadiness or fitfulness of the wind, its speed and direction must be considered, as well as the state of the herd and the amount of cover standing along the route of their interception of the herd. Assessment is rapid, almost automatic, and the attack is worked out in a series of gestures and a whispered word or two. G/wi hunters stalk at surprising speed through the sparest cover without disturbing their quarry. Bodies bent almost double, they advance in stages, taking advantage of the shaking of grass and the quivering of shrubs in the wind to mask their movement. The trick is to remain unnoticed; it is not necessarily a matter of invisibility, as animals seem to discern humans and other potential dangers more by scent and movement than by shape, size, or color. Crouching, the hunter slips from one scrap of cover to the next until he is so close to his quarry that he must sink to all fours and then get right down and wriggle forward on his elbows, bow in one hand and the other holding the arrow, nocked ready to the bowstring.

The commonest approach is a pincers movement that allows both men the chance of a shot. Ideally each puts an arrow into the target, doubling the dose of poison and insuring against the mishap of a miss or of an arrow's working loose and falling out before its poison is absorbed. They do not attempt to shoot simultaneously; this is unnecessary, and the complexities of signaling the moment are too great a burden to add to the difficulties of stalking to within range. When both are positioned, one slowly moves to give himself a clear line of arrow-flight, strains his arrow against the string, rises a little and lets fly. His partner shoots as soon after this as he can, and both hunters try to remain unnoticed by their prey. A further chance might present itself and, more importantly, the herd may not take flight if no danger is discerned, so that the wounded animal will remain close by and not career off on the start of what could become a long and grueling chase.

But flight and pursuit are the normal course. The hunters note the tracks of the wounded animal for future recognition. If the day is still young, they follow, not too closely for fear of startling the beast into running farther and faster; well back, out of sight and hearing, they let the tracks tell the tale of what is happening, how the poison is working and whether there are others who are becoming interested in their quarry. Toward the end, particularly, a predator or scavenger might be attracted to the prospect of an easy feed and make its move before the hunters make theirs. If the hunt takes place in late afternoon, the men usually camp on the spoor and take it up again at first light the next day. But if they are close to the band's camp, they will return home, to come back with helpers the next day. They abstain from food and, if their thirst is tolerable, from drink, since the G/wi believe that a hunter partaking of these strengthens his quarry, perhaps sufficiently for it to recover and escape. If the chase is long, lasting more than a whole day, they are forced to eat and drink, despite the expected effect on the prey, or they will become too weak to continue.

When it is clear from the tracks that an animal is very ill and weakened by the poison, the hunters close in and spear or club it to death. One remains to guard the kill and begins the process of skinning, cleaning, and dismembering the carcass while his partner returns to camp to fetch help in bringing in the meat (if this has not been done the previous night). Knives and spears are the butchers' main tools. The hide is peeled off the carcass by pulling, after a few blows from a club, spear butt, or even a large bone have loosened the tougher subcutaneous attachments. Joints and long bones are severed by a light hand-axe. The flesh around the arrowhead is cut away and discarded, as it is invariably foul and suppurating. The carcass is first flayed and then cut through the brisket and belly. The offal is carefully lifted out so as not to rupture any of the soft organs and sacs. Blood drains to the bottom of the cavity and is also saved, either to be drunk on the spot or poured into cleaned sacs for later baking at home. The intestine is cleaned out below the duodenum which, with the small intestine, is roasted and eaten, if there are a number of mouths to feed. (Utilization of the carcass is most efficient when the kill is near enough to camp to allow the hunters and their helpers to carry in not only the meat but the other portions as well.) The stomach of a large antelope is removed and placed on a bed of branches to keep it away from the sand; even in the driest season it holds 90–160 liters of liquor[2] which, although not very pleasant-tasting, is a welcome substitute for water.

In dismembering of the carcass, the fore- and hindquarters are first separated and the neck is then severed behind the atlas bone. The ribcage is split down the brisket and spine and is then quartered. The portions are now of portable size, and if the camp is not too far away (i.e., within about 20 km) they are taken home for further division. If the kill lies farther from camp, the meat is cut into strips 3–5 cm wide and hung out on branches to dry for the night, in summer, or for a day or two in winter. It is then tied into bundles for the homeward journey.

Biltong hunts are larger-scale affairs than the daily sorties. Between two and four are made between March and June. A party consisting of most of the active hunters in the band spends a week or two hunting in the remote parts of the band's territory. Operating out of one camp or a series of temporary camps, they make daily sorties in the manner described above. The meat taken is cut into strips and thoroughly dried before being tied into bundles. These expeditions are looked on as something of a holiday for the men, who enjoy a brief spell of one another's company away from their families. Nevertheless, they bring back a good deal of meat without putting any strain on the game resources within daily hunting-range of the band camp, and the expedition serves as a patrol of the territory. The information which the men bring back is of particular use in deciding the disposition of households during the coming period of separation and isolation.

Bow-and-arrow hunting is normally restricted to the season in which poison-grubs are gathered and for some 6 months after this. Supplies seldom last longer, and the poison itself goes stale and loses some of its toxicity. The early summer months of most years are, in any case, too hot and trying to permit the day-long exertion of this type of hunting. Instead, hunters resort to snaring game.

Other hunting techniques. Although most snaring is done by men, whose prey is steenbok and duiker, adolescent boys and girls also set snares for small mammals and birds, especially gallinaceous birds. All use the same type of spring-loaded noose made of twine spun from *Sansevieria* fibers. The noose is pegged out around the bait (for small mammals and birds) or a concealed pit (for small antelopes), anchored by a trigger-peg, while the free end is tied to a stout stick or small sapling that is bent over to provide the spring. When the bait is disturbed or the weight of a hoof treads into the concealed pit, the trigger-peg is released, the spring flies up, and the noose is tightened around the neck of the bird or small mammal, or around the pastern of the antelope, and the unfortunate animal is jerked into the air.

Snares are baited with a ball of *Acacia* gum set in a place frequented by the intended prey. Duiker and steenbok have regular pathways across their territories, and these make good sites for snares. Otherwise the hunter sets up an unobtrusive barrier of branches and twigs to guide the buck onto his trap. Trap-lines are checked four or five times a day. Apart from the fear of offending N!adima, the deity, by causing one of his creatures unnecessary suffering, leaving a trap unattended for longer may give the prey time to struggle free or provide a scavenger or predator with a free meal.

Springhares are caught by means of long, barbed probes. Several straight, peeled raisin-bush wands are scarfed together and the joints bound with *Terminalia sericea* bark, forming a supple stick 4–5 m long. A steenbok horn is bound to one end, forming a sharp barb. The probe is pushed into an occupied warren and jiggled about until the barb hooks an occupant, whose position is indicated by the length of stick pushed down the hole and the turns it has taken following the passage (deduced from the length and lie of the part of the stick which remains protruding from the hole). Then all that remains is to dig a shaft down from the surface above the calculated position. As this can involve quite a lot of digging, a springhare seems small return for all the work; still, this is a very popular method of hunting.

G/wi hunters occasionally club small mammals and birds to death, either striking them down with a thrown club as they pass within range, or stalking up to the prey and hitting it. Spears are seldom used as primary weapons but are usually employed to give the *coup de grâce* to quarry weakened by arrow poison. Relatively slow-moving animals, such as ant bears and porcupines, can be fairly easily overtaken when encountered in open country and are either speared or clubbed. Animals that are run down are killed by the same weapons. This last technique is not often used, but G/wi men, like other Bushmen, have remarkable tenacity and do manage to chase larger antelopes, such as eland, kudu, and hartebeest, until the animal can go no further.

Meat-robbing is a technique worth mentioning more for its dramatic impact than its economic value. Some two or three times a year, men encounter lions with fresh kills and drive them off by rushing up and furiously waving and shouting. The trick apparently lies in correctly judging the moment; if challenged too early in his meal, a lion will defend (and perhaps extend) his dinner, and if left until sated and lazy he is likely to get angry. Scavenging in this manner is a great game. Vultures dropping down tell the tale of a fresh kill, and if the distance is not too great, all able-bodied men grab their spears and clubs and go tearing off through the bush, whooping and yelling in high excitement. The wives' responses vary from ho-hum indifference to their men's silliness to obvious fears of imminent widowhood. On most occasions the men return empty-handed and rather sheepishly explain that the kill was too old or too small.

Bird's nests are robbed of eggs during the laying season. Ostrich eggs are particularly valued, not only for their food content (each holding the equivalent of about two dozen hen's eggs) but because they make handy water-containers when, some 3 months later, the wet season arrives. The usual clutch is between 10 and 15, of which only 2 or 3 are taken.

Large numbers of tortoises are caught during summer and autumn. They are simply picked up when encountered by men, women, and children, to be carried back to camp and roasted alive on the coals (this is the most effective method of killing these hardy creatures and is, in any case, a mercifully quick death in the great heat of the pit-oven).

Utilization of Game

Flesh. All meat of prey animals is cooked and eaten, excepting the flesh surrounding the arrow wound in those which have been shot. Meat is roasted on coals, stewed in plant juice, or chopped into mincemeat and fricasseed.

Skin. The hides of many of the antelopes which are killed are made into leather for clothing and a variety of other articles. Dried uncured hide of larger antelopes (preferably gemsbok) and of giraffe is used for the soles of sandals. When food is scarce, uncured hide is roasted, ground into powder and eaten. Giraffe hide is cut into narrow strips and used as an item of exchange, eventually finding a ready market at trading-stores for the manufacture of stockwhips. Furred pelts, notably those of jackals and foxes, are cured and made into headgear and fur blankets for exchange and eventual sale. Hides of larger antelopes are also made into riems, stout rawhide thongs that are eventually sold outside the Central Kalahari as trek gear.

Head. Larger antelopes are decapitated and their heads roasted entire in pit-ovens. The brains, tongue, all the muscles, and the cheek skin are eaten.

Rumen. The cud is removed from the rumen of larger antelopes, and squeezed into the cupped hand to expel the liquor, which is drunk.

Reticulum and pancreas. The reticula and pancreas of larger antelopes are cleaned, dried, and broken up to be cooked with stews.

Colon. Lengths of cleaned colon are used as substitutes for stronger sinew bindings when these are unobtainable.

Lungs and heart. The pluck is treated as meat.

Blood. It is drunk or baked.

Liver. This is one of the first organs to be removed from the carcass and is often roasted on the spot as a snack for the men busy with butchering.

Kidneys. Also baked on an open fire.

Bladder. The bladders of springhares are cleaned, dried, and used as water containers during the wet season. Those of small antelopes are used as containers of lightweight articles.

Udder. The udder of a lactating larger antelope is a delicacy and is baked on an open fire. If there is milk in the udder, it is squeezed out and drunk before flaying commences.

Amniotic fluid and fetus. The amniotic fluid of a gravid cow is drunk as a substitute for water. If sufficiently developed, the fetus is treated as a small antelope and is eaten as veal.

Testicles. Some regard animal testicles as great prizes and rejoice at the opportunity to eat them while others, even others in the same band, are disgusted at the prospect and throw them away. This contrast in attitudes is remarkable in people with so homogeneous a culture, but I have not been able to discover whether anything more than personal taste and fastidiousness is involved.

Skeleton. As mentioned above, the processus cornus of gemsbok is made into arrowheads if no iron is to be had. The hyoid bone of a large antelope killed during a boy's initiation school is sometimes given to him to remind him of the school's teachings. The sixth to thirteenth ribs of giraffe are cut up and the ventral ends trimmed to a length of about 15 cm, to be used as sweat-scrapers by women. The scapula of eland is sometimes used as a chopper during dissection (A. C. Campbell, personal communication) and is later discarded. Humerus, radius, metacarpus, femur, tibia, and metatarsus of antelope are split open and their marrow extracted for food, or for use in treating leather.

This extent of utilization is only possible when hunting is based at the home camp; on *biltong* hunts, many portions are thrown away because they can neither be used in the field nor taken home. Other parts of kills are also used for occasional, special purposes. The carapaces of the smaller geometric and leopard tortoises serve as ladles and drinking-bowls, and the long foot bones of springhares are strung as decorative tassels on girls' skirts. Tobacco pipes are fashioned from short sections of the femur of small antelopes, and long slivers of bone are used as leather-working awls when iron is not available.

How much do G/wi hunt?

While girls, boys, and women snare birds and catch snakes and tortoises, bow-and-arrow hunting and snaring antelope is exclusively the work of men. A man's life as an effective hunter begins when he has acquired the necessary skills, knowledge, and experience. This is usually not before he is 17, 18, or even older. He starts to learn the arts of the hunter as a small boy shooting beetles, small birds, and rodents with a toy bow and arrows made for him by his father. Later he goes after larger game with weapons he has made for himself, and bags birds and small mammals. Until puberty is reached, hunting is a game played with other children. An adolescent ranges farther from home, alone or with a partner, and hunts to feed himself—or tries to feed himself. After marriage, at the age of 14–16, he is the apprentice of his father-in-law, and is not regarded as a trustworthy and reliable partner until he has had a year proving and increasing his ability.

A man is at the peak of his hunting career in his late 20s. With good sight, hearing, and wind and with his strength undiminished, he has the confidence and experience to handle every situation he is likely to encounter. At 35 he is past his best and begins to restrict his hunting, and within about 5 years will be forced to rely on springhares and trapping and be able to succeed in only the easiest bow-and-arrow hunting.

In any band, the majority of men will be in that 20-year span of active hunting, and the remainder will be either too old or too young. The proportions vary; a newly formed band has almost all of its men in their prime, and an old established band could perhaps count only three-quarters of its men as fully active.

Hunting weapons are not made of durable materials and are subjected to hard wear. Their service life depends a great deal on the individual hunter's manner of using them and also on the quality of materials selected and the skill devoted to their manufacture, but all require considerable maintenance. With luck a bow stave will last a year or even longer before losing its spring, but the string frays quickly and could be replaced twice or even three times in that period. Minor repairs are needed after each hunt. Arrow-poison goes stale, or shakes loose when arrows are carried in a quiver, despite careful packing in shock-absorbing felt made from the nest of the penduline tit (*Anthoscopus caroli*) or from animal fur. Bindings work loose, and mainshafts warp even without use. After hitting an animal, an arrow usually requires partial or complete remaking. All this tinkering keeps men from hunting, but it is the manufacture of other artifacts which really takes up time. The work is inescapably time-consuming, but the amount of pottering which goes on makes it more so. Most jobs could be done in half the time they take. By this I do not mean that G/wi men are idle—they can, and do, work very hard indeed when it is necessary; my point is that hunting does not take up the greater part of their time, and they have no expectation that it should.

There is an overall seasonal rhythm which limits the time available for hunting. The difficult months of early summer provide least opportunity; poison is scarce or entirely used up, a good number of the 6 hours in which work can be done must be spent in gathering plant food and, in any case, most of the herds of larger antelope are absent from the Reserve, having migrated to the northeast. Conditions improve as the wet season approaches and are at their best between the end of the rains and the onset of cold weather. Hunting is restricted by wet weather; game is impossibly wary under an overcast sky, and rain ruins a bow. In autumn, more daylight hours are devoted to hunting than any other activity except "make and mend" (i.e., work connected with the processing of raw materials and making and maintaining tools, weapons, and other artifacts).

Within that broad annual pattern, hunting programs are idiosyncratic and highly variable. A few men may be described as inveterate hunters and go out whenever season, weather, and the state of their weapons permit. Some behave in this way for as long as 10 weeks and then switch over to "make and mend" occupations. This normally happens when a man has accumulated a stock of hides and then concentrates on working them, but there were instances when no discernible reason could be found to explain the change in habits. The men simply said they were tired of hunting. It is an arduous job and that is a good enough reason, but why did they decide to stop at that juncture? Others average only 5–10 days hunting per month in seasons when regular hunting is possible.

The level of band hunting activity is equally variable. Between two and six sorties (each involving a pair or a solitary hunter and lasting 4–10 hours) are made on most days when conditions permit. In contrast to the annual pattern, in which there is some correlation between hunting activity and prey numbers, this short-term fluctuation bears no apparent relationship to the amount of meat in camp, the number of animals killed, or the amount of game currently in the hunting range.

It is evident that hunting is neither a full-time, nor even a consistently followed, occupation among G/wi men but is subject to seasonal restrictions, competing demands on available time, and an absence of inclination to seize every opportunity presented.

It was impossible for me to count all the kills of any one band throughout the year, let alone monitor all the hunters in every band. I could not remain in the field continuously but had to return to my base periodically to replenish my supplies, and during the phase of band separation and household isolation, I could only observe one household at a time. Gaps in my observations were filled by hunters' reports, which appeared to be reasonably reliable. Table 12.3 lists various species bagged in a year by a band of 80 members, of which 16 were hunters, calculated as an average for the years 1958–1966. This is an atypically large band, and the kill total is therefore abnormally high. It is possible that the company of so many hunters in one band stimulated an unusual amount of hunting activity; the larger population may have favored success by providing an exceptionally wide intelligence-cover of game movements. The presence of so many helpers to bring meat back from distant kills may have encouraged more hunting of large antelopes then would be the case in smaller bands. However, comparison with other bands on a per capita basis indicates that the species range and number of kills are representative. I surmise that the factors mentioned above could indeed produce differences between very small bands and the larger ones, but that the differential is insignificant once 8 or 10 hunters are working the same territory. Nevertheless, it must be noted that Tanaka's (1976:111) observations indicate a much smaller number of kills, particularly of larger antelopes. The difference may only reflect the variation in hunting conditions from one year to another but should also serve as a warning that there is no certainty about the pressure which G/wi hunting exerts on game populations (figure 12.1).

I have some misgivings about the meat values I have assigned to the kills.

Table 12.3. Animals caught in one year by a band of 80 G/wi Bushmen

Species	Sept.	Oct.	Nov.	Dec.	Jan.	Feb.	Mar.	Apr.	May	Jun.	Jul.	Aug.	Total
Giraffe (Giraffa camelopardalis)	—	—	—	—	1 (400)	—	—	—	—	—	—	—	1 (400)
Eland (Taurotragus oryx)	—	—	—	1 (250)	2 (500)	1 (264)	—	1 (264)	3 (792)	1 (260)	—	—	9 (2,330)
Kudu (Strepsiceros strepsiceros)	—	—	—	—	—	1 (130)	—	1 (132)	1 (132)	—	—	—	3 (394)
Gemsbok (Oryx gazella)	—	—	—	3 (240)	2 (170)	4 (330)	2 (180)	1 (90)	—	3 (260)	3 (255)	2 (145)	20 (1,670)
Hartebeest (Alcelaphus buselaphus)	—	—	—	1 (60)	—	—	2 (130)	1 (66)	2 (130)	2 (130)	2 (125)	1 (60)	11 (701)
Wildebeest (Connochaetes taurinus)	—	—	—	1 (110)	1 (115)	—	3 (350)	2 (236)	—	2 (230)	2 (220)	1 (105)	12 (1,366)
Springbok (Antidorcas marsupialis)	—	—	—	1 (15)	4 (62)	2 (32)	6 (90)	6 (96)	4 (64)	6 (90)	2 (28)	1 (14)	32 (491)
Duiker (Sylvicapra grimmia)	12 (87)	10 (73)	12 (90)	4 (30)	5 (40)	4 (32)	3 (24)	7 (57)	2 (16)	3 (25)	1 (8)	2 (15)	65 (497)
Steenbok (Raphicerus campestris)	8 (38)	10 (48)	15 (73)	3 (15)	3 (15)	4 (20)	3 (15)	6 (30)	8 (40)	2 (10)	4 (19)	2 (9)	68 (332)

Springhare (*Pedetes capensis*)	3 (1.4)	—	8 (10.9)	32 (43.5)	30 (19)	24 (15)	28 (17.6)	30 (19)	26 (16.4)	22 (13)	15 (9)	4 (2.5)	222 (167.3)
Porcupine (*Hystrix africaeaustralis*)	—	—	—	—	—	—	1 (6)	—	1 (6)	—	—	—	2 (12)
Warthog (*Phacochoerus aethiopicus*)	—	—	—	—	—	—	—	1 (31)	—	—	—	—	1 (31)
Bat-eared fox (*Otocyon megalotis*)	2 (3.6)	1 (1.8)	4 (7.2)	—	—	—	—	4 (7)	—	3 (5.5)	1 (1.8)	3 (5.5)	18 (32.4)
Jackal (*Canis mesomelas*)	4 (12)	—	—	—	—	—	2 (6)	—	1 (3)	2 (6)	2 (6)	3 (9)	14 (42)
Rodents	(0.8)	(0.8)	(1.5)	(1.5)	(1)	(1.5)	(1.5)	(1.5)	(2)	(1)	(1)	(0.8)	(14.9)
Birds	(3.6)	(4.0)	(4.5)	(1.8)	(4)	(5)	(3)	(3.1)	(1.5)	(2.7)	(1)	(2.7)	(36.9)
Tortoises	—	—	(5.6)	(10.2)	(10.2)	(10.2)	(9)	(4.5)	(1.5)	(2.7)	(1)	—	(49.7)
Snakes	—	—	(1.3)	(0.9)	(1.8)	(0.9)	—	(1.8)	(2.2)	(1.8)	(0.5)	—	(11.2)
Invertebrates	—	—	(0.2)	(2.0)	(50)	(2)	(0.2)	—	—	—	—	—	(54.4)
Total quantity (kg)	146.4	127.6	194.2	779.9	1,388	842.6	832.3	1,038.9	1,205.1	1,035	674.3	368.5	8,632.8
Meat available per capita (kg)	1.83	1.60	2.43	9.75	17.35	10.53	10.40	12.99	15.06	12.94	8.43	4.61	107.9

Note: Figures in parentheses refer to kilograms of meat.

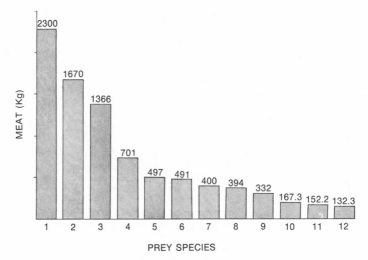

Figure 12.1. Prey species taken annually by a band of G/wi hunters, ranked by weight of available meat. *1*, Eland; *2*, gemsbok; *3*, wildebeest; *4*, hartebeest; *5*, duiker; *6*, springbok; *7*, giraffe; *8*, kudu; *9*, steenbok; *10*, springhare; *11*, birds, reptiles, invertebrates; *12*, other mammals.

Larger cuts presented no problems but it was beyond my means to do better than guess, for instance, the weight of the edible content of a roasted gemsbok head. My earlier figures were more conservative than are these values, which are largely derived from von La Chevallerie's lists of carcass weights of relevant mammal species (1970:73–87). He calculates the average lean meat content of carcasses to be 77–83% (1970:83), to which I have added 7–8% for edible portions of head, feet, knees, and entrails, blood, pluck, and marrow (Beattie, 1971:432). ("Meat" here includes all the portions of vertebrates and invertebrates customarily eaten by the G/wi, which gives the term a broader meaning than is usual in our own culinary practice.) On this basis, average annual consumption is 107.9 kg per capita, which approximates the 1938–1939 figure for white Australians (Beattie, 1971:436). Tanaka (1976) calculates meat consumption at a rate equivalent to 81.92 kg per captia annually.

The pattern of meat consumption is quite different, however, from that of Australians, and reflects both seasonal fluctuations and the day-to-day irregularities in the supply of meat. In general the G/wi eat large (but not gargantuan) quantities of meat at irregular intervals in the seasons when it is plentiful and smaller quantities at longer intervals when it is scarce.

Even in January, when meat was most plentiful, it contributed a maximum of 10% by weight of the food eaten in that month. In September, by contrast, it made up only 0.75% of the diet. If meat were the only source

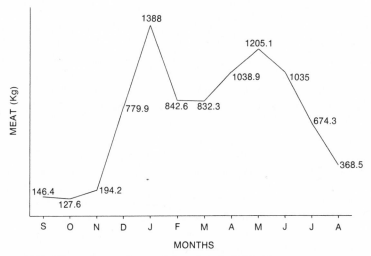

Figure 12.2. Meat taken each month by a band of G/wi hunters.

of protein, individual monthly intake would have to be 3.27 kg to meet the calculated adult requirement of protein (Thomas and Corden, 1970:54). Less than this amount is eaten in the 3 months of early summer (September–November) when available plant food is restricted almost entirely to roots and tubers of low nutritive value (figure 12.2). Depressed levels of protein intake could be advantageous in this very dry season, as the end-products of nitrogen metabolism are diuretic. A carbohydrate diet, on the other land limits ketosis and diuresis, which is a desirable circumstance when body fluid must be conserved.

The significance of rumen liquor from large antelopes is considerable in the waterless months (late March–late December). Rumen contents of the autumn and winter kills of these species were estimated to total 2,800 liters, of which approximately 1,500 liters were extracted for drinking. Almost all was consumed by hunters and their helpers (rumen liquor is not normally carried back to camp with the edible portions).

CENTRAL KALAHARI ECOLOGY AND G/WI PREDATION

The topography of the Central Kalahari Game Reserve is dominated by the Deception and Okwa valleys which, with the several tributaries of the Okwa, are the remnants of the drainage axes of this shallow basin into the Lake Xau and Makgadikgadi depression. It is possible that the main valleys lie along faults or other comparable geological discontinuities, for they quarter the Reserve into definite regions, each with its distinctive topographical, soil, floral, and faunal characteristics. West of the northward-trending Okwa, the valleys mark the boundaries between the northern dunelands, the central grassland plain, and the savannah thornveld south of the Okwa. Where the Okwa turns north, it is joined by the Merran, which rises far to the south in the Kweneng District. This section of the drainage forms a less distinct, longitudinal boundary, east of which the central plain gradually gives way to savannah and forest, and the thorn veld is replaced by a more heavily wooded area of low dunes in the southeastern corner of the Reserve.

Water no longer flows down any of these valleys, but the hard, flat floors of the Deception and the Okwa's tributaries, together with the many smaller and larger pans in the Reserve, hold water for up to 2 weeks after a good rainfall. Hollows have formed (and some have been excavated by Bushmen) in the calcrete floors of many pans and hold several thousand liters; these supplies last somewhat longer before evaporating, and water is available for about 6–8 weeks in most years. The Piper Pans complex (over 1000 km^2) on the northern edge of the central plain is by far the largest area of pans in the Reserve; others range from single pans of a couple of hectares up to complexes covering 30–40 km^2, with individual pans of up to 10 km^2 in size.

Within each of the two zones south of Deception Valley, these pans and valleys are the only ecologically distinctive features (except on a micro-environmental scale, where contrast is often drastic in nature and extent). Not only are they the only sources of water, but their unique tufaceous soils support a flora which includes some specialized species and provide more secure burrows for fossorial mammals than do the structureless sands found elsewhere in these two zones. Some of the pan-dwellers are surprisingly specialized in what is otherwise a rather undifferentiated environment (e.g., the Cape terrapin, *Pelomedusa subrufa,* which depends on standing water for its survival and reproduction.) For hunters, the meaning of the distinctiveness of the pans is that their vicinity is marked by changes in the distribution, density and, very often, the behavior of prey species.

Away from the pans and valleys, environmental differentiation is gradual and of modest extent on the grasslands and savannah. Almost the whole of the flora consists of ephemerals and cold-dry deciduous species. Dry-season plant communities are generally simple in structure. The somewhat stunted habit of most species of woody plants obviates any complexity of stratification, and the prevailing low density (average coverage varies from approximately 5 to 25%) and the frequency of competitive exclusion restrict localized variation or abundance of species. One of the factors limiting vegetational density appears to be water, which is present in adequate amounts only during the wet season and for the few subsequent months that it is held in the fine-grained sand. After rain the ground-layer is greatly enriched by the rapid emergence and growth of ephemerals, and coverage increases to between 50 and 100%. Upper strata are changed by refoliation of deciduous shrubs and trees and only marginally enriched by ephemeral or previously dormant climbers. The structure of communities is altered by the greater number and diversity of plants filling the empty space, mainly at ground level, but there is no radical change in stratification. There is, as it were, an elasticity in the environment which permits seasonal alternation between filling and emptying space without disrupting the essential structure of the communities.

The fauna responds to the seasonal rise and fall in crop level with its own ebb and flow. Invertebrates hatch, hibernating species emerge, and migrating mammals and birds return to the Central Kalahari from their wintering ranges between October and January, all combining to create an enormous expansion of biomass, which remains steady for a while and then contracts with increasing rapidity under the tightening grip of winter, which may arrive as early as mid-April or as late as July.

If we ignore the microenvironment and consider only the larger-scale aspects, the rather simple structure and minor localized differentiation of plant communities leads to a correspondingly large overlap in the niches of many of the mammal species. The larger antelopes are all gregarious grazers and browsers that feed off approximately the same range of vegetation. Springbok, particularly when in large herds, favor the vicinity of pans, and kudu have a marked preference for thick bush, but all species will be seen in a given locality at different times. Gemsbok can use their sharp hooves to dig out roots, bulbs, and tubers more effectively than can other antelopes. Wildebeest and springbok form the largest herds and graze more intensively than do other species, sometimes temporarily devastating an area. But none of these antelopes is highly specialized in its feeding habits. The potential for competition in this functional overlapping of niches is reduced by separation of the species (and, indeed, of herds of the same species) in space and time. If one locality is occupied or has been stripped, there are other equivalent areas of pasture nearby. These are migratory animals, and mobility is their means of avoiding the competition offered by other herds. Early rain, which is highly localized, does tend to encourage temporary clustering of antelopes, but once the wet season is established the equivalence of localities increases and the disposition of herds is more nearly random within their preferred types of country.

The smaller antelopes, duiker and steenbok, are tenaciously territorial. Both are browsers and grazers, feeding off a wide band of the vegetational spectrum. Their territories are small and steenbok are distributed almost uniformly throughout the Reserve. Duiker tend to prefer wooded country and are less commonly encountered on the grassland plain.

I have characterized the environment as structurally simple and, excepting the pans and drainages, showing only a small measure of localized differentiation in vegetation and the distribution of animals. I stated earlier that the G/wi are predisposed to occupy as their band territories the limited number of areas in which a nexus of requisite resources exists. This is one of the reasons why space must be considered among the requisite resources; a territory must be large enough to counterbalance localized uniformity, include the necessary diversity of community types, and provide a hunting range spacious enough to cover the probable distribution of the almost randomly placed herds of large antelopes. Territory size therefore is not only a matter of carrying capacity (a clear enough concept in relation to numbers of domesticated stock feeding off a known variety and quantity of pasture in a paddock, but a very hazy notion when applied to hunter/gatherers) but is directly related to the needed *variety* of resources.

The elasticity of the environment derives from structural simplicity, and redundancy imparts a certain level of stability. Fluctuations of sizes and variety of species populations are extreme, but the integrity and coherence of the ecosystem remain stable enough for the G/wi to follow a consistent strategy of occupation of one territory by each band and for the bands to follow the same pattern of intraterritorial migration and matching of residential density to the current state of resources. Perturbations beyond the G/wi range of tolerance do occur; disease and drought have taken their toll, but the ecosystem is stable enough for the G/wi to live in their customary style for decades without disruption.

It is clear that the G/wi have lived in their present country for a long time without substantially altering it. They have no means of manipulating its productivity to their advantage and, had they brought about a long-term decline in resources, they would have faced the prospect of moving out or dying out. Their presence does lead, however, to localized and temporary change. It is obvious that the occupation of a campsite by a band results in extermination of ephemerals and considerable denudation of trees and shrubs at and around the camp. Their activities also concentrate nutrients in the form of wood ash, feces, and vegetable detritus (hut thatch and uneaten portions of gathered plants). Small seeds that are not damaged by digestion (e.g., *Grewia* spp.) are deposited with fecal material around the camp. Campsites normally are not reused until memory and material indications of occupation have faded, so there is ample time for the vegetation to recover. The composition of plant communities at the site may well be altered, but occupation does not appear to lead to any other changes.

As hunters and gatherers the G/wi occupy both herbivore and carnivore trophic levels and are in competition with invertebrate and vertebrate herbivores and mammalian and avian carnivores. The Bushmen compete directly by consuming food that might otherwise be eaten by other plant- and meat-eaters. They also utilize grass and shrub foliage for thatching huts and covering shelters. Perhaps more importantly, they compete with those species which are frightened away by their presence and thus close off food and shelter that would otherwise be available to the animals which are chased away. Two factors lessen the intensity of competition offered by the G/wi: their periodic migration out of one locality into another (or, put another way, their low residential density over time), and their imperfect efficiency as gatherers. While the total number of plant species eaten and used in other ways approaches 100, and while they utilize fruits ranging in size from the smallest *Grewia* berries to the largest *Citrullus* melons, they are highly selective in their choice of individual specimens, rejecting damaged or unripe ones. Where the storage organ is the part eaten (e.g., roots, tubers, and bulbs), the whole plant is destroyed, although only a small portion is utilized. Furthermore, the increasing cost and decreasing benefit precludes total cropping of any edible species, and the G/wi abandon a locality long before their gathering threatens to exhaust the crop, or exterminate a species. (The importance of the religious prohibition of extermination is probably slight compared with the pragmatic balance of cost and benefit.)

Comparable direct and interference competition is offered to carnivores, and the interference or opportunity factor is here even more important, for not only are the predators themselves scared away but their prey is also disturbed. This last consideration is reciprocal; lions or other large predators in the vicinity make game just as wary as does human hunting. Furthermore, the G/wi must handle their highly mobile prey cautiously lest harassment cause the animals to leave the band's hunting range in search of more secure, peaceful pastures. A herd must be given time to recover from the shock of a hunt before it is next exploited. Sedentary and territorial species do not enjoy this protection, but their status as less highly prized prey confers another type of protection when more valued targets are to be had.

A set of taboos on the eating of meat of some species by specific age-grades also confers a measure of protection. The taboos are not complete protection, as there are always a substantial number of people who may eat any meat. The presence of those subject to the taboo reduces the utility of a carcass, however, and hence the motivation to hunt that species. The differential applicability of taboos encourages the hunting of a variety of species so that one category's inability to eat this kill will be compensated for by freedom to eat the next. This is not quite correct with respect to snakes, which may be eaten only by older men and women (who are free of all taboos). But snake-catching is not without hazard. The worthy prize is the large snake and these are either venomous or savage-tempered and capable of inflicting nasty lacerations with a good chance of blood-poisoning, which might end up being as bad for the hunter as a dose of venom could be. Consequently the younger hunter only catches a snake when a windfall opportunity occurs, or when affection or intention of wily ingratiation impels him.

In the Kalahari, hunting is a means of livelihood, and hunters have a businesslike attitude toward it. They select the prey that will give the greatest reward for the least cost; this means the species of large antelope which is most numerous in the current hunting range at the time. The numbers of all species fluctuate in response to environmental factors such as drought or good rains. Additional changes in species populations are not understood but are not in phase with the overall fluctuations. The "treks" of springbok that occurred in the past when these animals became particularly numerous are well documented and are part of southern African folklore. Other species (e.g., hartebeest) appear to fluctuate in comparable, though less dramatic, fashion. In their preference for the locally most easily encountered species, G/wi hunters tend to dampen population peaks. The effect is minimal, however, because the intensity of hunting activity is not always proportional to the local density of prey populations. The point is merely that differential pressures are imposed on prey populations—lightest on the scarcer species and heaviest on the most common.

Knowledge of the game's habits and the extensive intelligence service provided by the combined manpower of the band reduce the area of uncertainty to a comparatively small part of the hunting range. Search is therefore highly directed, and the probability of encounter is heavily biased toward a specific prey category. Within the selected category the choice of target is determined by such factors as size, sex, position in the herd, and "personality" (the least two factors probably being interdependent). The personality factor is possibly susceptible to variation in interpretation by different hunters (which would help to explain why I found it so difficult to understand). Whatever the case, the G/wi stock of ranked personality types must spread the preference of targets wider than would a choice based only on size, and thus makes hunting a less narrow selective pressure on the populations of large antelopes.

Such considerations are absent in the case of smaller prey. The vulnerability of steenbok and duiker is primarily a matter of proximity to the hunter or trapper's camp and is, in a sense, dependent on species and residential densities. Hunting pressure on springhares is more complex; this species prefers open country that is judged poor for campsites by the G/wi. Consequently those springhares which make their warrens near pans are the ones most likely to be hunted. (The small number hunted in winter and spring reflects the G/wi preference for more wooded, heavily grassed country during winter isolation.) Butynski (1973) reports much heavier hunting by Bushmen in other areas, but he does not indicate whether they are autonomous bands or Bushmen attached in some way to a fixed location, such as a cattle post. The central desert G/wi are potentially capable of more intensive springhare hunting, which would become relatively more important when other game became scarce, but the figures given here are representative of typical conditions for these people. Under normal conditions they do most of their springhare hunting some distance away from the campsites, in the habitat most favored by the species, and thus apply their heaviest hunting pressure to the most populous category.

The place of G/wi predation in the Central Kalahari ecology is clearly not the the simple predator–prey relationship modeled in the Lotka-Volterra equations (Odum, 1971). Population cycles of the nature predicted by the equations do not occur, and the role of the G/wi hunter differs in many respects from that of the typical predator of ecological theory. The Bushman's use of manufactured weapons increases his actual killing capacity far beyond that provided by the slight degree of human anatomical development in that direction. A bow and poisoned arrow compensate for lack of speed, strength, and effective fangs or claws; the spear and club stretch the hunter's reach far beyond the length of his arm. The ability to transmit knowledge symbolically in a sociocultural context and his high intelligence enable the Bushman to develop a large repertoire of general and species-specific search images and to elaborate these by inclusion of data (e.g., spoor recognition, interpretation of other animal's behavior as indicating the presence or proximity of prey, knowledge of prey habits as the basis for predicting its movements and other behavior) which help to circumvent the restrictions which time and space impose on other terrestrial predators. That these search images are employed in a social context virtually multiplies the hunter by the number of members in his band, all of whom add their information to what he gathers for himself, freeing him yet further from temporal and spatial considerations. His predatory efficiency is potentially very high and could produce a most unstable relationship between human and prey populations. However, this efficiency is applied in a way that reduces the intensity of the relationship while still benefiting the hunter. The G/wi do not have to hunt in order to eat; the predominance of plant foods in their diet weakens the subsistence tie that so closely interrelates the state of other predator populations with that of their prey. It is apparent from table 12.3 that the G/wi can switch prey with a good deal of versatility and that this greatly reduces the predation load carried by any one species. Their manner of utilizing kills is fairly efficient (more so than our own, for example) and thereby also reduces predation pressure. Hunters' concern not to scare antelope herds out of the band territory by excessive or careless hunting is indicative of the degrees of freedom they have to minimize this pressure. It is obvious that this concern is well founded; the ease with which the herds can find refuge in local and seasonal migration that puts them beyond the reach of G/wi hunters makes self-restraint imperative.

The combined effect of these factors and of the residential strategy followed by the G/wi is to reduce the intensity of hunter–prey interaction in terms of any one species to a level at which it is unlikely that the relationship produces any very significant effects on either population. This is perhaps not true in times of severe drought or epidemics—the interaction could then become relatively much more intense, and shortage of meat or predation pressure could become final and critical factors affecting the fate of the hunters and/or their prey populations. But under more nearly normal circumstances, it seems that G/wi hunting is a minor factor in the population dynamics of the animals they hunt.

THE PLACE OF HUNTING IN THE G/WI LIFE

The G/wi do not make heroes of their hunters, but hunting is nevertheless a prestigious activity. Small boys imbue it with some of the glamour once associated with driving steam locomotives and fighting fires in English or American society, and the successful hunter is respected and admired by adults as well. Virtuoso dancers, handy artisans, and those endowed with that rare sense called common are almost as highly esteemed.

The G/wi are hungry for meat, and any description of the "good life" always includes mention of a plentiful supply of it. It has a symbolic value far greater than its nutritional value or the pleasure it imparts to the palate. I have seen women involuntarily urinate with excitement at the sight of a kill being brought into camp, at a time when meat had not been scarce. And yet a tasty melon or a bowl of *morama* nuts is consumed with about the same enthusiasm and satisfaction as a generous portion of venison. The stimulus to excitement is the presence of meat, not the eating of it. It seems to me that this can be explained by its status as an exchange commodity. I described earlier how the needs of the recipient are included in the criteria of the transaction and how the return of a gift or favor not only discharges a previous obligation but also creates a new one. In the absence of a means of preserving meat, these factors combine to make meat acceptable in any transaction, to protect it from any threat of glut and stagnation of the exchange network, and to create a permanent need for it as an exchange commodity.

There are two modes in which the meat of large game is distributed: the individual gift and, less commonly, the men's feast. The division of a gemsbok shot by a hunter named //aũdze (assisted by his partner, Kamadwe) is a typical example of the first mode:

//aũdze took, and distributed 42 kg	
His own share, for his household	5 kg
His widowed mother	2
His wife's two younger married brothers	9
His elder married brother	5
His two married initiation mates	9
His married sister	3.5
N//ien/u, the oldest woman in the band	2
≠xwa:, a bachelor who is always given meat	1.5
Khwakhwe, who helped carry meat	5
Kamadwe took, and distributed, 27.5 kg	
His own share, for his household	5
His married daughter and her husband	3
!ao and his household	3.5
N/haukhwa and Kinin/u, who helped butcher and carry	7
!auka, to divide among his people	
who were visiting the band	9

In this division, married persons with dependent children were given larger portions (about 5 kg); couples without children had smaller shares (about 3 kg), and the smallest gifts went to single people. !auka, of the visiting band, was a close friend of both hunters and was therefore chosen as the representative of his people. !ao was an unusually old man to still have dependent children. Although he kept his household well supplied with springhares and other small mammals, he was no longer fit for regular bow-and-arrow hunting. Without a partner, he seldom killed anything worth dividing and could seldom give gifts of meat. He was a handy craftsman, however, and made artifacts for other people. This present of meat was in partial return for a winnowing mat given to Kamadwe for his wife. ≠xwa: was divorced and lived with the bachelors at the time. He was the nominal hunter of all that I shot (which greatly simplified my task of distributing meat) and had given a portion to //aũdze some time previously.

Many of the recipients (e.g., the single people) further divided their portions and passed on small amounts of raw meat to others so that, by the evening meal, many more households had at least something of the kill. (Cooked meat, like gathered food, normally is not shared outside the household except as tidbits for young children.)

The smaller game is not usually divided, but whole carcasses are given as gifts. Raw meat from these does pass, however, between close kin (e.g., siblings, parents and independent children) when hunters are incapacitated through age or illness or when their wives are menstruating.

The men's feast is given by the hunter, acting alone or in concert with his partner, who announces it and issues invitations. In the afternoon of the day after the kill a cooking fire is made outside the host's shelter and the invited men gather to cook pieces of meat. After they have eaten for a while, their wives and dependent children return from food-gathering and play and drift to the fringe of the gathering. Each guest is then given a portion of raw meat which he passes on to his wife or sends home with a child. In this way the host (and his associate) can deal with a number of obligations simultaneously and also derive prestige from having provided a pleasant social occasion. Feast-giving is also a means of repairing strained relations. When a quarrel is in its final stages, after hostile exchanges have ceased, the estranged men are invited. Etiquette demands that all guests behave in friendly fashion, a requirement which gives an opportunity for rapprochement with decorum, neither protagonist being forced to back down and lose face. (Although G/wi society is characterized by the rarity of aggression and lack of competitiveness, the vanity of most men is keen and tender.) The festive atmosphere is deliberately manipulated to help rebuild the bond threatened by the late quarrel.

Relations between people both create and consist of obligations and expectations which are partially fulfilled by the exchange of gifts and favors, this exchange also expressing feelings of goodwill and fellowship. The quality of the relationship is not expressed by the size or value of the gift, but by the frequency of exchange. In distributing meat, there is reciprocation of goods and services received by the hunters, which has the color of a business transaction (e.g., paying !ao for the winnowing mat), and there are also gifts to kin which have no commercial connotations. The value of gift-giving as a means of creating and maintaining social solidarity is amply documented in anthropological literature. As discussed earlier, gift exchange, with its interpersonal specificity, operates as a differentiator within the G/wi kinship system. By enabling people to discriminate among those grouped together in the broader kin categories and to express more precisely the quality of their relationship, exchange serves as a supplementary source of information to overcome redundancy and to more finely order the society.

In providing meat to be used as an item of exchange, large-game hunting plays an important part in creating and maintaining the social harmony that the G/wi value so highly. It seems to me that meat symbolizes this harmony, and this is the reason why the carcass of a large kill causes excitement so out of proportion to its gastronomic and nutritional importance. The fact that public exultation is confined to the large kills, such as giraffe or the bigger antelopes, supports the hypothesized symbolic link.

If the assertion is valid, and the hunter is motivated by a desire to feed his family and others and also to maintain in good condition the delicate fabric of society, it casts some doubt on the assumption that hunting is necessarily a demonstration of man's aggressiveness. The G/wi view of the world as a system of interdependent subsystems permits the taking of life where this is necessary to survival. Hunting is killing, and violence is obviously done to the prey. But the argument is not about the nature of the deed; it is about the state of mind of the hunter. The myth of the aggressive hunter is either a product of an affluent society in which hunting is a recreation, or else it stems from a rather muddled ping-pong projection of human values to nonhuman predators and then back again to the human hunter. Killing at a distance is by no means the same thing as hand-to-hand combat. If predation by humans entailed falling on the prey and strangling it, or even stabbing it, then the hunter might well be "fierce as ten furies, terrible as hell" but, in shooting an antelope with bow and arrow, he has no more need for lethal lust and endocrine hyperactivity than has the archer aiming for the gold.

EPILOGUE

The "ethnographic present" reported here is the period between 1958 and late 1966 when I was engaged in fieldwork on behalf of the Bechuanaland Protectorate Government. Radical change has since occurred in the Central Kalahari Game Reserve and in the pattern of life of many G/wi Bushmen of the area. Tanaka, who followed me into the field a year later, mentions goats and dogs being kept. Bantu-speaking cattlemen later moved in with their stock and settled at the borehole near ≠xade Pan in the middle of the Reserve. What had previously been a small, locally migratory population, whose isolation was broken by sporadic and brief visits of small groups of aliens and by my regular periods of fieldwork, is now faced with the continuing presence of a comparatively aggressive, well-organized number of settlers with a culture quite different from their own. The cattle which accompanied the settlers are highly selective grazers, the goats are less discriminating, and the combined pressure of grazing and browsing is severe. Damage done by trampling as stock passes between water and pasture is catastrophic. The cattlemen are mounted on horses or donkeys and armed with rifles (mostly single-shot muzzle-loaders or Martini-Henrys, but also modern magazine weapons); they are avid hunters of antelopes for the meat and hides. Medium and larger predators are also hunted for their pelts, or to protect stock. Hunting and the permanence of settlement have combined to reduce drastically the numbers and range of species of game animals available to the G/wi.

Disruption of the delicate web of social relations in the G/wi communities, removal of plant foods which provided the major part of their diet, and the local decimation of the game population have transformed the post-settlement life of the G/wi into something quite different from that which I observed and report here.

NOTES

1. *"Bushman" vs. "San."* I have retained the older term, "Bushman," in favor of "San," which Wilson and Thompson (1969), Lee (1976a), and many others have adopted. Lee (1967a:5) refers to Theophilus Hahn's study as the authority for "San" having the meaning of "aborigines" or "settlers proper" (Hahn, 1881:3). However, Hahn goes on to point out in his next paragraph that "the word Sa(b) has also acquired a low meaning, and is not considered to be very complimentary. The Khoikhoi often speak of *!Uri-Sān* (white Bushmen) and mean low white vagabonds and runaway sailors who visit their country as traders. One also often hears, '*Khoikhoi tamab, Sab* (sic) *ke,*' (he is no Khoikhoi, he is a sā), which means, '*he is no gentleman, he is of low extraction,* or *he is a rascal*'" (1881:3). Wilson and the others rejected "Bushman" because of the racist connotations they found in the word. Having lived in southern Africa among English- and Afrikaans-speaking European and Coloured South Africans, my experience has been that "Bushman" (and the Afrikaans "Boesman") has no more or less racist connotation than has "Englishman," "American," or "German." These last do not necessarily mean "Limey," "Yank," or "Kraut" any more than "Italian" and "Egyptian" are the equivalents of "Dago" and "Wog." Certainly, the label of any national, ethnic, or social group can be used in a pejorative sense. To coin or adopt a new usage because the older one has been misused by hostile, ignorant, or mischievous speakers is to embark with van der Decken on the *Flying Dutchman's* unending voyage. By the logic of Wilson et al., "San" can only remain current until somebody uses it as a swearword. Since it had already been used as such a century ago, it seems to me to be more profitable to stick to "Bushman" and by contributing to public knowledge and appreciation of the Bushmen's way of life, give the lie to those who would use them as exemplars of persons "of low extraction" and rascality. By coincidence, *G/wikhwe* translates literally as "bush-men" ("bush" in the Australian sense, which is the same as that of seventeenth-century Dutch *bosjes,* from which the Afrikaans "Boesman" and English "Bushman" are derived).

2. Calculated on the basis of a gastric capacity of 136.5–182 liters for medium-sized cattle (Sisson and Grossman, 1953:456). Smaller antelopes may be compared with sheep, which have a gastric capacity of ca. 15 liters (Sisson and Grossman, 1953:479).

Reizo Harako

13

The Cultural Ecology of Hunting Behavior among Mbuti Pygmies in the Ituri Forest, Zaïre

From October 1972 to September 1973 I participated in an ecological and anthropological investigation of Mbuti hunter/gatherers in the Ituri Forest, in northeast Zaïre. It hardly needs saying that further anthropological research on hunter/gatherers is urgently needed at this time, because all such populations are declining rapidly and undergoing considerable change in behavior and culture. It is especially important to provide clear descriptions of the ecological foundations of the hunter/gatherer mode of life before it disappears altogether.

The Mbuti Pygmies of the Ituri Forest have long been considered the nucleus of pygmy groups in equatorial Africa, and have been studied by Schebesta (1941), Gusinde (1956), Putnam (1954), and Turnbull (1965a), among others. These studies focused mainly on somatometrical measurement or descriptions of social behavior, culture, and religion, and for the most part overlooked ecological parameters.

Colin Turnbull's monograph, "The Mbuti Pygmies: An Ethnographic Survey" (1965a) divides the Mbuti people into net hunters and archers, and summarizes ethnographic data gathered by Schebesta and Putnam, which he then uses to compare the two groups. He stresses that the hunting/gathering economy exerts a great influence on Mbuti society and ideology, tending to regulate their way of life, but his data and analysis of actual hunting activities do not seem sufficient to prove the point.

This problem is commonly encountered in anthropological research on band societies. It has often been stated, for example, that the hunting/gathering economy is based on nomadism, division of labor according to sex, cooperation in subsistence activities, egalitarianism, food-sharing within the group, etc. Yet few studies provide enough data to document

Revised from "The Mbuti as Hunters: A Study of Ecological Anthropology of the Mbuti Pygmies," which appeared in *Kyoto University African Studies,* vol. 10 (edited by Y. Tani), 1976.

these phenomena in terms of environmental constraints. Systematic investigation of the various hunting and gathering activities that compose this type of subsistence economy remains quite rare. Anthropologists who express interest in the cultural ecology of hunter/gatherers are likely to discuss some relationships between a given society and its natural environment, but even they tend to give only a cursory description of ecological parameters.

This report is the first in a series of ecological/anthropological studies of the Mbuti. The project will eventually cover such diverse topics as economy, social behavior, and ideology. Here I shall concentrate on their hunting behavior, which, together with the gathering of plant foods, is perhaps most closely related to environmental factors. My study examined how different hunting techniques operate and how they contribute to the survival of an Mbuti band. Tadashi Tanno (1976) provides additional details on net hunting methods in a neighboring study area.

SCHEDULE AND METHODS

I gathered as much data as possible by direct observation, which entailed living with a particular band and accompanying the males on hunting expeditions in order to understand and master their methods. When this was not feasible, I obtained additional information by inquiry. The investigation ran for a full year, from October 1972 to September 1973, so that all seasons would be covered. The study periods and general aims of the investigation were:

1. December 1972–March 1973, observation of net hunters along the lower streams of the Lolwa River.
2. April–July 1973, observation of archers and spear hunters along the upper streams of the Lolwa River.
3. October–December 1972 and August–September 1973, an extensive survey of the Ituri region.

The languages spoken by the Mbuti of Ituri Forest include Kibila[1] (used by the Bila tribe and by Mbuti net hunters), Kilese (used by the Lese tribe and by Mbuti archers), and Kingwana (a common Swahili dialect). Most Mbuti can speak the latter, so I used Kingwana to conduct much of the investigation. However, I also gathered as much Kibila vocabulary as possible, trying to record technical terms and proper nouns in both languages. Special tools and techniques are sometimes labeled with Kibila terms in this report.[2] Abbreviations are used for each language where necessary: KBL for Kibila, KLS for Kilese, and KGN for Kingwana.

HABITATS AND BANDS

The Ituri Forest Environment

The locations of the Ituri Forest and the main study area within it are shown in figure 13.1. If we travel up the western escarpment of the Great Rift Valley from Lake Edward, we can follow a route along the ridges of a 1,500-m-high plateau northward to Butenbo, past Beni, and down to Komanda at an elevation of 500 m. This route runs between the watersheds of the Congo and Nile river systems. As we move westward, down the plateau, the vegetation becomes typical tropical rain forest at about 1,000 m elevation, and from there follows a gentle slope down to the Congo Basin.

The Ituri River is a northeastern tributary of the Aruwimi River, which in turn is a branch of the Congo River. The Ituri Forest covers the drainage basin of the Ituri River, extending over an area of approximately 100,000 km^2 and varying in altitude from 600 m to 1,000 m. The forest boundaries are roughly delineated by the following settlements: Ishiro, Watsa, Komanda, Beni, Bafwasende, and Nia-Nia. To the east of Komanda there is open land as far as Lake Albert, and to the east of Beni a forest stretches from the Semuliki River to the Ruwenzori Massif. The roads shown in figure 13.2 follow the gently rolling ridges in the forest, and the agricultural[3]

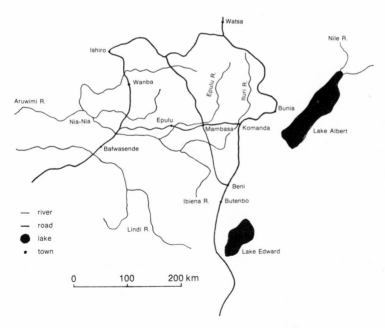

Figure 13.1. The location of the Ituri Forest in northeastern Zaïre.

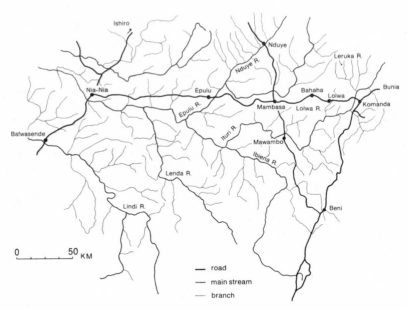

Figure 13.2. Rivers and streams in the Ituri Forest.

settlements of the Bantu and Sudanic tribes are concentrated along these roads.

Today villages are seldom isolated in the forest. Instead, they are situated along roads, with slash-and-burn cultivation extending 2–3 km in all directions, encircling the village(s). Secondary forest encroaches on neglected fields, and in some cases even invades currently cultivated areas. From an aerial perspective, the Ituri region is a vast primary forest dotted with fields and secondary forest growth. These altered sections are sometimes 4–5 km wide. The subsistence activities of agricultural tribes are limited to these belts or patches, while the subsistence activities of the Mbuti occur mainly in the surrounding primary forest.

The climax vegetation of the Ituri Forest is characterized by tall trees of the family Caesalpineaceae, reaching 40 m in height. Along the upper sections of the Ituri River, in the northeast, *Cynometra alexandri* is predominant, and in the southwestern reaches of the forest *Gilbertiodendron dewevrei* occurs in pure stands. Between the two sections, a distinct zone of *Brachystegia laurentii* can be observed. Other trees of medium height, shrubs, and undergrowth vary in height and density according to the prevalent climax species, providing floral diversity within the forest. Two other features are noteworthy. First, many species of Maranthaceae grow abundantly as undergrowth in the *Cynometra* forest but are seldom present in the *Gilbertiodendron* forest. Second, according to the Bila people, *Cynometra* grows in black soil, *Brachystegia* in reddish brown soil, and *Gilbertiodendron* in white sandy soil. My observations confirmed these distributions.

Swamp forest vegetation occurs rarely and is restricted to riverbanks and swamps within the Ituri area. These forests are densely overgrown with lianas and heavily populated by wild palms and ferns. Secondary forest patches are scattered about where traditional villages and Mbuti camps have been abandoned, and in these areas shrubs and bushes are dispersed among tall trees, and lianas and underbrush are abundant.

Maps of African vegetation distribution indicate that the Ituri Forest lies at the eastern end of the central rain-forest region. Yet the interior of this forest is relatively dry, and often the floor is only sparsely covered with underbrush. According to J. Itani (1974), the Caesalpineaceae forest should be distinguished from what is commonly called tropical rain forest. It differs in being relatively drier and having marked seasonality. It borders on dry deciduous woodland, which is covered with grasses and forms the transition zone between forest and savannah. The Ituri Forest is more of an evergreen high forest with no grasses growing on its floor. The Caesalpineaceae forest extends toward the central section of the Congo Basin, forming a vegetation mosaic with swamp forests. Itani points out that this Caesalpineaceae forest is always habitable for humans and other ground-living Hominoidea.

In the Ituri region the year can be divided broadly into two seasons: a dry season from December to March and a rainy season from April to November. Rainfall is particularly high from August to October, so this period constitutes the major rainy season. Even during the dry season some rain is likely to fall on most days, but the amounts are small and showers are brief.

From August to October the rivers are swollen from the heavy rains, and it becomes impossible to traverse many sections of the forest. Water levels fall rapidly in early December. The November shift from wet to dry season is abrupt and obvious, but the shift from dry to wet season in March is gradual.

One feature of the Ituri Forest requires special emphasis here. Turnbull (1965a) maintains that the Ituri Forest is homogeneous and that seasonal changes are slight, providing a uniform environment for all Mbuti bands within the region. According to my observations, there are definite seasons and the forest is quite diversified, with many vegetation and habitat zones. These are discussed later in more detail.

The Mbuti People

Schebesta (1933) called all the Ituri Pygmies the "Bambuti," and divided them into three linguistically different groups: Efé, Sua, and Akka.

Turnbull (1965a,b) simply classified them by their subsistence activities, either as archers (applied to Efé) or as net hunters (Sua), since he thought that Schebesta's classification showed only the interrelationships with Bantu or Sudanic tribes, the peoples with whom the Mbuti are linked socially. The archers are Lese-speaking Mbuti of the northeastern district, and the net hunters are Bila-speaking Mbuti of the central and southwestern district; I think that to classify them in this way is more accurate and useful.

The spatial relationship between an Mbuti band and a village of agriculturalists corresponds to that between a farm belt and a primary forest zone, as shown in figure 13.3. Within this region it is now illegal to buy and sell the meat of wild animals during certain periods of the year. In principle, while prohibiting the villagers from trading meat between the end of August and the beginning of December, this law allows the Mbuti to continue hunting activities during that time. However, enforcement is very perfunctory. The law was enacted to discourage hunting in the breeding season of the duiker, and the Mbuti are well aware of this. It is interesting that this period coincides with the rainy season, while duiker hunting is allowed in the dry season. This pattern accords with the nomadic cycle of the Mbuti, who dislike hunting in the rain.

In the major rainy season, most of the Mbuti bands return to their usual campsites near villages. These "base camps" are located on the outskirts of the secondary forest, and the surrounding primary forest constitutes the

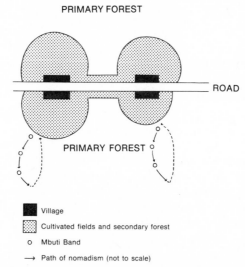

Figure 13.3. Schematic diagram of spatial relationships among villages and Mbuti bands.

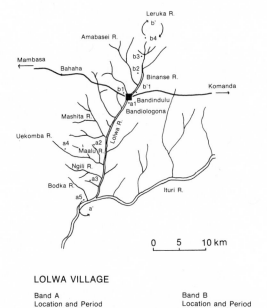

LOLWA VILLAGE

Band A Location and Period		Band B Location and Period	
a1:	1972 Aug-Nov	b1:	1972 Sep-Nov
a2:	Dec-Jan 1973	b'1:	Nov-Dec
a3:	1973 Jan-Feb (2 weeks)	b2:	Dec-Jan 1973
a4:	Feb-Mar	b3:	1973 Feb-Apr
a5:	Apr-Jun	b4:	May-July
a':	June (move for a short time)	b':	Aug (move for a short time)
a3:	again Jun-July	b2:	again Aug-
a1:	again Aug-		

Figure 13.4. Campsites and dates of residence for two Mbuti bands during the study.

hunting range of the band. While living at the base camp, the Mbuti depend largely on the food produced by the agriculturalists. The nomadism of Mbuti bands seems to have an annual cycle: during the major rainy season they stay near the village(s) at the border of their home range, while during the dry season and the minor rainy season they move into the interior of their hunting range (fig. 13.4).

Each band regularly associates with and depends on one village, and it is usually the tribal name of this village that the band adopts. Bambuti Babila, for example, signifies Bila-related Mbuti as well as Bila-speaking Mbuti. But Bila-speaking Mbuti can also be Lese-related, in which case they may still be called "Bambuti Babila" because "speaking" indicates an earlier historical association and is regarded as more important. Sometimes the name of the subtribe to which the village belongs is used by an Mbuti band, or even the more specific lineage name. Some bands are simply labeled by place names, but these are often also associated with villages.

Observation of Two Mbuti Bands

According to the present administrative system, Lolwa is the name of the village situated on the facing banks of the Lolwa River. It thus serves as the label for two lineages of the Bila tribe—Bandindulu and Bandilongona—which belong to the Bayaku,[4] one of the subtribes of the Bila. The two bands I studied intensively had a special relationship with this village, but the ties were between Mbuti families and Bila families rather than between the entire band and the entire village.

Band A: Net hunters. All members of this band are native speakers of the Kibila language. They are said to be originally Bambuti Bahaha,[5] although at present they are described as Bambuti Lolwa. They are also called Bapusoki, which means "people of Pusoki" and is equivalent to the lineage name of the villagers.

The lower segment of the Lolwa River is the hunting range for this band. Their campsites in 1972 and 1973 are depicted in figure 13.4, a_1–a_5. The area is at the eastern limit of the distribution of net-hunting bands.

During my study, this band fluctuated in size from 5 to 10 families, including 37 to 62 members. It had the largest membership at campsite a_4. The composition and genealogy appear in table 13.1 and figure 13.5. The three camps I joined for observation of hunting activities were a_1, a_2, and a_4. The a_1 campsite included 5 families, with a total membership of 37

Table 13.1. Families and individuals constituting Camp Uekomba (Campsite a_4) in February 1973

Families	Adult		Youth		Children		Total
	male	female	male	female	male	female	
1a	2	2	1	4	2	1	
a′		1	0	1	0	1	15
2b	1	2	2	0	0	0	
b′		1	0	0	0	2	8
3	1	1	0	1	1	0	4
4	1	1	0	0	1	3	6
5	1	1	1	3	2	0	8
6	1	1	0	0	0	1	3
7	1	1	1	1	0	0	4
8	1	1	0	2	1	1	6
9	1	1	0	0	0	0	2
10	2	2	1	0	1	0	6
Total	12	15	6	12	8	9	62

Note: Adults include all married individuals or widows; *youths* include unmarried boys and girls who are old enough to participate in group hunting activities; and *children* include all individuals below those ages. For family relationships, see figure 13.5.

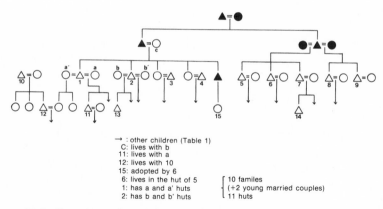

→ : other children (Table 1)
C: lives with b
11: lives with a
12: lives with 10
15: adopted by 6
6: lives in the hut of 5
1: has a and a' huts
2: has b and b' huts

⎡ 10 familes
⎬ (+2 young married couples)
⎣ 11 huts

Figure 13.5. Genealogy of band A.

individuals; a_2 campsite had 6 families, or 48 members; and a_4 campsite contained 10 families, or 62 members. Campsites a_3 and a_5, which I only visited for brief periods, included 10 families and almost the same number of individuals as a_4.

Band B: Archers. The members of this band speak both Kilese and Kibila, but elders use Kilese as their native language. They were originally Lese-related Mbuti, but developed ties with the Bila people about 20 years ago.

This band used a hunting range in the upper section of the Lolwa River, including its tributary, the Ieruka River. Their movements in 1972 and 1973 are charted in figure 13.4, b_1–b_4. The number of families fluctuated between 8 and 12, and the total membership between 33 and 45. I joined campsites b_3 and b_4 for detailed observations. Campsite b_3 included 8 families, having 33 members in all. The composition and genealogy of families at b_4 appear in table 13.2 and figure 13.6.

Observations at campsites b_1 and $b_{1'}$—which are the base camps of this band—were not as detailed as those at the base camp of band A. In November and December 1972 my study focused on band A, and I visited the base camp of band B only once during that time. Band B arrived at campsite b_1 around September 1972, then moved to campsite $b_{1'}$ in mid-November. Camp b_1, known as Bapûlai, was very large and was located near the roadside fields just west of Lolwa village. I counted 25 semi-spherical huts[6] and estimated that 100 or more members were present. The camp included three subgroups: band B; a band led by band A individual 15 (fig. 13.6); and a band led by an elder, Alomba. By the end of my survey in September 1973, band B was located at campsite b_2.

Camp Bapûlai also included many visitors, and many regular members of the camp were out visiting other camps. In mid-November band B, then

Table 13.2. Families and individuals composing Camp Kandilekandile (Campsite b_4) in June 1973

Families[a]	Adult		Youth		Children		Total
	male	female	male	female	male	female	
7a	1	1	2	1	1	0	
a′		1	1	0	0	0	8
6	1	1	3	0	0	0	5
8	1	1	0	1	0	0	3
9	1	1	0	1	0	0	3
10	1	1	0	0	0	1	3
11	1	1	0	0	0	0	2
16	1	1	0	0	0	1	3
4	1	0	0	1	0	0	2
26	1	1	0	0	2	3	7
27	1	2	0	0	1	0	4
Subtotal	10	11	6	4	4	5	40
Visitors							
13, 14, 15	3	1	0	0	0	1	5
Total	13	12	6	4	4	6	45

[a]See figure 13.6.

composed of 8 families (30 people), moved to campsite $b_{1'}$ on the northern outskirts of Lolwa village (Bandilongona plus Bandindulu, fig. 13.4). The move took about an hour, as one had to walk around fields and patches of secondary forest. Campsite $b_{1'}$ served as a transitional staging ground for moves between the traditional base camp (b_1) and the hunting camp (b_2) in the forest.

PREY SPECIES

The larger mammals, birds, and reptiles inhabiting the Ituri area are listed in table 13.3. Most are hunted by the Mbuti, notable exceptions being some of the Carnivora. In addition, many kinds of small animals, such as rodents, are hunted with bow and arrow, but these were not identified during the study.

It is noteworthy that the prey list includes 14 species of primates and 8 species of antelopes. Of the latter, 6 species are duikers (*Cephalophus* spp.).

The last column in table 13.3 shows how each species is usually hunted. Of the five main hunting techniques, spears are used for large animals, nets for terrestrial animals of various size, and arrows for small and medium prey of which some are arboreal. Duikers are the most important game

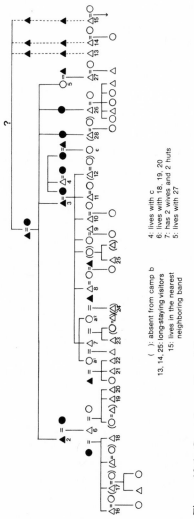

( ): absent from camp b
13, 14, 25: long-staying visitors
15: lives in the nearest
     neighboring band

4: lives with c
6: lives with 18, 19, 20
7: has 2 wives and 2 huts
5: lives with 27

Figure 13.6. Genealogy of band B.

Table 13.3. Game species available in the Ituri Forest

Scientific name	English name	Kibila name	Hunting method[a]
Order Primates			
Pan troglodytes	chimpanzee	siko *or* shiko	S, (B)
Colobus abyssinicus	Abyssinian colobus	bûlû	B
C. angolensis	Angolan colobus	mbela	B
C. badius	red colobus	aboi, amasako, akocha	B
Papio anubis	olive baboon	abula	N, S, (B)
Cercocebus albigena	gray-cheeked mangabey	akbutu	B
C. galeritus	crested mangabey	angala	B
Cercopithecus hamlyni	Hamlyn's monkey	mundupi	B, N
C. ascanius	red-tailed monkey	kide	B
C. mitis	blue monkey	aSaba	B
C. mona denti	Dent's monkey	mbengi	B
Galago demidovii	Demidov's galago	epinje	
G. inustus	needle-clawed galago	apanga	
Perodicticus potto	potto	abuku or abaku	(B)
Order Pholidota			
Manis tricuspis	tree pangolin	eboso	b′, S
M. gigantea	giant pangolin	tope	b′, S
Order Tubulidentata			
Orycteropus afer	aardvark	ngibo	b′, S
Order Hyracoidea			
Dendrohyrax arboreus	tree hyrax	sūka	(B)

Order Proboscidea			
Loxodonta africana cyclotis	African forest elephant	bongo *or* mbongo	S
Order Artiodactyla			
Hippopotamus amphibius	hippopotamus	?(kiboko: KGN)	(S)
Okapia johnstoni	okapi	mbote	S
Syncerus caffer nanus	dwarf forest buffalo	njali	S
Hylochoerus meinertzhageni	giant forest hog	ekuma	S (B)
Potamochoerus porcus	bush pig	ngoya	N (B)
Haemoschus aquaticus	chevrotain	ahele	S, (B, N)
Boocercus euryceros	bongo	soli	N, B
Neotragus batesi	Bate's pygmy antelope	ambilû	N, B
Cephalophus nigrifrons	black-fronted duiker	nge	N, B
C. dorsalis	bay duiker	kūfa	N, B
C. leucogaster	Gabon duiker	seke	N, B
C. callipygus	Peter's duiker	apole or aposo	N, B
C. sylvicultor	yellow-backed duiker	moimbo (adili: KGN)	N, B
C. monticola	blue duiker	buluku	N, B
Order Carnivora			
Crocuta crocuta	spotted hyena	?	
Panthera pardus	leopard	moli	(B)
Genetta spp.	genet	asimba	
	genet	?esele	
	genet	?apembe (kachimba)	
Crossarchus obscurus	dark mongoose	kpolokpolo	B, N
Atilax palidinosus	marsh mongoose	?ndele	B, N
?	mongoose	panbundundu	B, N

Table 13.3 (Continued)

Scientific name	English name	Kibila name	Hunting method[a]
Order Rodentia			
Atherurus sp.	brush-tailed porcupine	njiko	B, (N)
?*Hystrix* sp.	crested porcupine	njingi	B, (N)
	squirrels	pangu	B
		amapipi	B
		amakachacha	B
Larger birds and reptiles			
	guinea fowls	kanga	N, B
		endonbi *or* entobe	N, B
		amakikoale	N, B
	francolins	bolata	N, B
		ekonbi	N, B
		mgbemgbemgbe	N, B
	great blue turaco	kulukokō	B
	black and		
	white-casqued hornbill	gawa	(B)
	crocodile	ngwende	S
	python	mbia	S
	monitor	amaongaonga	b'
	lizards	amakiligbeki	b'
		maipongo	b'
	tortoise	amatie	G

Note: The data were compiled by J. Itani, T. Tanno, and R. Harako.

[a]Key to hunting method by Mbuti people:

S: Spearing   *b'*: Stick-beat

B: Bow and arrow   *G*: Gathering

N: Netting   ( ): Rare case

species for the Mbuti, and can be classified in relative terms as small (blue duiker), medium (black-fronted, bay, Gabon, and Peter's duikers), and large (yellow-backed duiker).

HUNTING TECHNOLOGY

The five main items of hunting equipment, plus the use of dogs, are described in this section. The plants used to make hunting tools are recorded in some cases without scientific names. Identification of these is under way and will be included in a future report about utilization of plant resources.

The Net (*kuya* in KBL)

The average height of a net is 1.2 m; the length is optional, with an average section being 50–100 m long. The nets are woven with twisted string obtained from the fibrous cambium of Euphorbiaceae vines (*Manniophyton fulvum*), called *kusa* in KBL.

The Spear (*ekonga* in KBL)

Spears are 130–160 cm long, the shaft being 100–120 cm. The iron blade is 30–50 cm long, and at most about 15 cm wide. The wooden shafts are made from four types of plants: *Pancovia harmsiana* (*engango* in KBL), *Cola sciaphila* (*janjalinja* in KBL), *Vepris louisii* (*mutuluka* in KBL), and a plant known locally as *mbutu* in KBL. The first three belong to the families Sapindaceae, Sterculiaceae, and Rutaceae, respectively.

The Bow (*mangé* in KBL)

Bows are 80–90 cm long, made of wood from *Vepris louisii* trees or *karu* (KBL) trees. Bowstrings are made of bark peeled from four kinds of liana palms. A plant known as *rekwe* (KBL) is used most commonly, although substitute materials can be obtained from other species: *Ancistrophyllum secundiflorum* (*koko* in KBL), *Eremospatha yanganbiensis* (*asuku* in KBL), and *Eremospatha haullevilleana* (*nbopi* in KBL).

The Arrow (*api* or *sûa* in KBL)

Arrows are about 50 cm long. Some are tipped with iron heads (*api*) while others are merely sharpened (*sûa*). (Unfinished shafts are also called *sûa*.) Wooden shafts are made from the pith of palms, *Raphia* spp. (Palmae). Wild palms (*bambu* in KBL) are used in the forest, cultivated palms (*mabondo* in KGN) at village sites. Substitute woods can be obtained from *Strychnos* sp. (*koha* in KBL) and *Grewia* sp. (*bembu* in KBL), which are members of the Loganiaceae and Tiliaceae, respectively.

Feathering is provided by tree leaves (*efofo* in KBL), which are cut into isosceles triangles around the leaf stems and stuck into the shaft. Wrist protectors (*asuba* in KBL) are fashioned from monkey skins, and quivers (*baba* or *bolobolo* in KBL) are made from duiker skins. Bark quivers are made from *Malantochloa congensis* (*toto* in KBL). Wrist protectors and quivers are used more for decorative than actual hunting purposes.

The Arrow Poison (*mutali* in KBL)

Several plants are used to produce poisons, but only one has been identified so far. Arrow poison is a liquid squeezed from the bark of a woody liana, *Partiquetina nigrescens* (*mutali* in KBL), with the roots, bark, and leaves of other plants mixed in. To prepare the liquid, these materials are finely shaved, pounded with a wooden stick until soft, and pushed through a mesh made from the stalk of *Malantochloa congensis*. The liquid is then spread onto the shaft, which has been covered with powdered wild pepper, and is dried gently at a fire.

The Dog (*imbwa* in KBL)

Dogs are the only domesticated animals used by the Mbuti.[7] They are seldom fed, and survive largely by scavenging around campsites. As trackers, dogs are indispensable to archers and are sometimes used by net hunters to flush the game as well. When young dogs are trained for hunting, the juice squeezed from *Strychnos* leaves (*pango* in KBL) is poured into their nasal passages. According to the Mbuti, the juice acts as a stimulant and makes the dogs fearless when confronted by game.

Dogs wear wooden bells (*lele* in KBL) around their necks during hunting expeditions. The material is from either of two trees, *ngomangoma* (KBL) or *ekimo* (KBL) (*Alstonia boonei*). Two or three hardwood sticks, made of *karu* (KBL) or *apalele* (KBL), are hung inside the bells to produce sound.

HUNTING METHODS

The Mbuti commonly hunt by one of three methods: net hunting, bow-and-arrow hunting, and spear hunting. Trapping is also practiced, but this method is used mainly by village specialists. When the Mbuti participate, they do so only to help villagers select localities and to act as standby assistants.

Net Hunting

Net hunting is a group activity involving men, women, and children. Even the very old can participate, as no particular skills are needed. Women always act as beaters, driving all kinds of game through an opening into a ring of nets by shouting and beating on bushes and trees. Men are stationed around the ring to catch suitable game that becomes entangled. A dog is occasionally taken along to assist in driving the game.

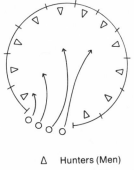

△   Hunters (Men)

○   Beaters (Women)

〔   one unit of net

Figure 13.7. Schematic diagram of net hunting tactics.

As shown in figure 13.7, about 10 nets are linked together to form a roughly shaped ring with a circumference approaching 1 km. One section of netting is omitted, and the beaters follow the driven game into the ring, thereby forcing the prey to attempt escape. A variety of prey can be captured by this method (see table 13.3), but it is most useful for catching duikers. The method is more consistently profitable than other hunting methods. Although there are seldom large differences between "good hunting" and "poor hunting" days, the method does require large numbers of individuals and some net maintenance.

Bow-and-Arrow Hunting

In contrast to the simplicity of net hunting, use of the bow and arrow involves considerable choice of technique. The bow-and-arrow hunter is faced with the following options: individual or collective activity, use of plain or poisoned arrows, and mode of pursuit. The latter may consist of an ambush, a stealthy approach, imitating animal calls as a lure, tracking, and driving. One or a combination of these basic methods can be applied on any given foray, depending on what prey species are sought or encountered.

Walking alone through the forest is the most basic pattern of Mbuti hunting. Lone archers sometimes carry all three types of arrows, using iron-tipped ones, poisoned ones, or plain sharpened shafts as the situation demands. The hunter may stalk or ambush game, or lure it within range with appropriate animal calls. When no game is encountered on a hunting expedition, the Mbuti collect other foods—such as plants, nuts, honey, termites, insect larvae—and check what resources will soon be available at various locations. Lone hunters also note animal movements and distributions in preparation for subsequent collective hunts. Mbuti men carry bow and arrows wherever they go, whatever the occasion.

Collective hunting (*motá* in KBL) usually involves about 10 archers. As

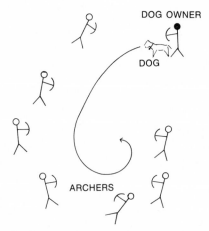

Figure 13.8. Schematic diagram of *Mota* bow-and-arrow hunting tactics.

shown in figure 13.8, the archers take up positions encircling a preselected area, and the game is flushed toward them by a dog, its owner, and sometimes several boys. Its wooden bell clattering, the dog rushes about within the circle and each archer shoots whatever comes his way. The tactics are somewhat similar to net hunting.

Archers shoot mainly at small to medium-sized duikers and other small game such as mongoose, porcupine, guinea fowl, and rodents. Iron-tipped rather than poisoned arrows are used, and so most animals are not instantly killed. The dog tracks wounded animals, followed by the nearest archer(s), until the prey can be cornered and killed.

Collective hunting varies in relation to the number of participants. The most complex type (*begbe* in KBL) involves large numbers of people; women and children attend as beaters, using the same tactics as in net hunting to flush game toward the ring of archers. This method is seldom used, and then only in the early dry season. At such times there may be cooperation between bands, and the affair becomes a festive event. Sometimes only five or six archers participate in collective hunting and, since the encircling formation is incomplete, the archers may have to vary their tactics. A small group of hunters must often resort to chasing the game, with a dog in the lead. Tracking may also be necessary, especially with prey species the dogs can harry by themselves, such as mongoose, porcupine, and guinea fowl.

Motá hunting is basically similar to net hunting, but the tactics are more flexible. Prey can be pursued beyond the immediate area ringed by the hunters, and is sometimes chased or tracked for considerable distances.

Poisoned arrows are used mainly by lone archers seeking arboreal game.

The tactic is simple but requires considerable skill: after locating suitable prey, the archer stealthily approaches and shoots into the tree. All the diurnal primates, especially those living in social groups, are hunted in this manner (see table 13.3). Red colobus monkeys are highly prized. Chimpanzees too are shot, but this may be a recent development because these apes are considered unsuitable for archery hunting by the Mbuti; chimpanzees are instead hunted with spears. Other small arboreal animals, such as birds and squirrels, are hunted with unpoisoned, untipped arrows.

Special tactics are applied to ambushing prey. A hunter selects a foothold (*ebaka* in KBL) in a suitable tree, usually on a branch 2–3 m above the ground, then stands on it waiting for duikers to pass by underneath.[8] These *ebaka* sites must be carefully selected, the main prerequisite being the presence of an animal trail with fruit-bearing trees near it and fruit scattered around and on the trail. It is also important that the site be near camp because tracking is necessary after the first hit. After the prey is wounded, the archer can call out to others at the campsite, and men and dogs come to assist in tracking the game. This method is practiced only in the early morning and late afternoon, when duikers forage.

The ambush method is sometimes combined with imitation of prey calls in an attempt to lure animals, especially blue duikers, to a waiting archer. This tactic (*kamiso* in KBL) is, I believe, rarely successful. One call is used for each type of prey. A group of archers will sometimes attempt this method, one producing the calls and others waiting near a trail to ambush the prey.

In summary, bow-and-arrow hunting is the most common method used by males, alone or in groups, and thus provides an opportunity to study the most basic patterns of Mbuti hunting behavior. The method is highly flexible, incorporating a variety of tactics, and can be performed by young and old band members. Poisoned arrows are used for arboreal prey, mainly primates, and iron-tipped arrows for terrestrial prey. These are always collected afterward, whereas poisoned arrows and sharpened shafts are not. Nearly all small and medium species can be hunted in this manner.

Spear Hunting

Spears are used for large game that cannot be killed efficiently with bow and arrow. Elephant, buffalo, okapi, giant forest hog, and bush pig are typically hunted with spears (table 13.3).[9] Other species marked with an *S* in the table are rarely taken by this method, and more by chance than by intention.

Spear hunters will either thrust or throw their weapons, depending on the situation at hand. Stalking and thrusting occur mainly with elephant, buffalo, and sometimes okapi, while throwing occurs with giant forest hog, bush pig, and okapi. Prey must be closely approached, usually within 5 m, even when spears are thrown. Tracking large game in dense vegetation is difficult and at times quite dangerous, so spear hunting involves considerable skill. Hunters usually begin by tracking potential prey, trying to move in an approximately correct direction even though they can seldom see the animal. When the prey is close enough to be heard, the hunter determines its location and direction of movement, then tries to outflank it with great stealth in order to set up an ambush. The hunter waits under cover, thrusting or throwing his spear as the animal passes.

Since speared prey seldom falls down on the spot, further tracking is usually necessary. When alone, a hunter will prepare a second spear to bring down the wounded prey, but spear hunting is more commonly done with a partner who can assist by giving signals. Tracking may continue for several kilometers until a kill is made, but rarely extends into a second day. Thus, the nature of the initial wound is critical: its location and depth determine success or failure. Some hunters consider the bladder and the hind leg tendons to be the most vital targets in spear hunting, but most try to wound the prey in the abdomen, which is large and soft and therefore provides the surest target. A kill is assured if the intestines drop from the abdominal cavity.

Because hunters must approach large game so closely, this method involves greater risk than any other. Serious injuries and fatal wounds occur only when this method is used. Spear hunters involved in the initial attack are experienced males, although boys may accompany them as apprentices.

Spear hunting is not a daily activity, especially when it is done by an organized group. Groups of spear hunters can be small or large, depending on the availability of people and the type of animal to be killed. Membership is highly variable, with one or more bands being involved. In the latter case, members consist of individuals who are on friendly terms, and this kind of multi-band cooperation definitely has a festive mood. Elephants are usually hunted in this manner.

Spear hunting by large groups involves specific formations, especially in the case of elephants but sometimes also buffalo. In such cases, group members usually divide into two or more subgroups, with one team in charge of the first spear attack and the other group(s), which often include boys, working as backup teams. Everyone advances, keeping a set distance from one another, until word of a successful spear attack spreads, whereupon all subgroups converge and begin tracking the wounded prey. If the team best situated for the first attack includes boys, they are prohibited from participating in the front line. According to the Mbuti, children are most useful as lookouts, climbing trees and directing the backup teams to the wounded animal.[10]

Spear hunting may also be practiced by small groups of 4–5 specialists who stalk stealthily through the forest in search of buffalo, okapi, giant forest hog, or bush pig. If they encounter an elephant they will of course give chase, but this opportunism is unlike an organized elephant hunt. Because the team includes only experienced specialists, such a small group is more mobile and more flexible in its maneuvers. In other respects, such as methods of ambush, attack, and tracking, they behave much like the large groups described above.

Spear hunting may also be attempted by a single individual, although this tends to occur only when a hunter is out gathering food or making preliminary observations on game availability. Those who specialize in this method always carry their spears when traveling in the forest.

To summarize, spear hunting focuses on large game and involves considerable risk. Skills are developed through apprenticeship to experienced specialists who are in charge of cooperative ventures and work on the front line of the attack. Tracking and stalking skills are especially important, and because silence is necessary, dogs are not used. Spear hunting is not a daily activity, although individuals are always ready for a good opportunity. Large groups may include several bands, and these hunts can readily turn into festive occasions.

HUNTING BEHAVIOR

In this section I provide some concrete examples of common hunting activities recorded in the two bands I studied most intensively.

Observations on Band A

The hunting range used by band A lies on the western bank of the lower Lolwa River and includes about 100–150 km^2 of forest (see fig. 13.4). The hunting season covers about 9 months, from December to August, and I was with the band from December 1972 to March 1973. Net hunting was practiced daily by all members except young children. In addition, individuals frequently went out to shoot monkeys.

Hunting with Nets. I observed 17 cases of net hunting between December 28 and March 2 (table 13.4), and the following descriptions are drawn from this sample. The number of nets corresponds to the number of families in a band. At Camp Maálu (fig. 13.4, site a_2) there were 8 net units, and at Camp Uekomba (site a_4) there were 10 net units. Each unit is handled by two persons, usually an adult man and woman, and table 13.4 shows that 20 is an average group size for net-hunting expeditions. At campsite a_2 there were 5 old men and women who seldom went hunting, 32 mature adults, and 15 children who were too young to go. At campsite a_4 the demographic breakdown was 11, 34, and 17, respectively. Thus, about 10 persons capable of participating in net hunting were held in reserve at each

Table 13.4. Net-hunting activities in band A

Case no.	Date	Departure (A.M.)	Arrival (P.M.)	Duration hr.	min.	Hunting Group male	female	total
1	28 Dec. 1972	8:35	4:50	8	15	10	12	22
2	29 Dec.	8:00	3:07	7	07	8	6	14
3	30 Dec.	7:00	5:10	10	10	10	11	21
4	3 Jan. 1973	8:20	4:55	8	35	8	11	19
5	5 Jan.	7:30	5:40	10	10	9	10	19
6	14 Feb.	7:00	6:00	11	00	10	12	22
7	18 Feb.	8:00	5:00	9	00	9	11	20
8	21 Feb.	7:00	(10:45 A.M.)ᶜ	(3	45)			
9	22 Feb.	8:30	3:10	6	40	8	7	15
10	23 Feb.	9:00	3:00	6	00	10	13	23
11	24 Feb.	8:00	5:15	9	15	10	12	22
12	25 Feb.	9:45	4:15	6	30	10	10	20
13	26 Feb.	(1:05 P.M.)	5:20	(4	15)	8	8	16
14	27 Feb.	7:20	3:40	8	20	10	11	21
15	28 Feb.	9:00	3:50	6	50	10	10	20
16	1 Mar.	10:05	4:56	6	51	11	12	23
17	2 Mar.	8:45	5:05	8	20	10	12	22
Average		8:14	4:35	8	12	9.4	10.5	19.9

ᵃNumber of times for netting.
ᵇBLD: blue duiker
  BFD: black-fronted duiker ⎫
  BYD: bay duiker   ⎬ MDD: middle-sized duiker
  GD: Gabon duiker   ⎭
ᶜ(   ): Excluded from calculation of average.

campsite. Parents whose children are old enough to participate tend to be the ones who remain in camp, but couples with no offspring may let youngsters from other families use their nets on some days while they rest.

The main requirement is that all available net units be manned for every hunting expedition. The Mbuti believe that a shortage of personnel will seriously reduce hunting success. In cases 2 and 9 (table 13.4), individuals who remained in camp were later blamed for the small yields on those days. Rotation of personnel is accepted, but a shortage is frowned upon.

Net hunting does not require much tactical skill or technical knowledge, so the minimum age limit for participation is low. I could not determine exact ages in most cases, but based on comparison with physical and social development in other human groups, I would guess that the minimum age is around 10 years. Both sexes participate, although their activities may differ to some extent, as mentioned earlier.

When the sun rises around 6:00 A.M. the band members are already up

Table 13.4 (Continued)

Netting[a]	Catches[b]	Fail to catch	Notes
8	BLD 1	4	
7	BLD 1	10	women were scolded after hunt
9	BLD 4	10	
8	BLD 3, BFD 2	6	
7	BLD 4		
9	BLD 2, GD 1		women departed 8:30 A.M.
8	BLD 5, BYD 1		python was killed heavy rain 10:30 A.M.
4	0		that night: speech and dance for good catch
6	BLD 2, BYD 1		
8	BLD 6	7	individual C also participated
7	BLD 3	2	
5	BFD 1	0	raining in the morning
7	BLD 5, GD 1	6	heavy rain 3:00 P.M.
5	0	0	no game because of evil dream
7	BLD 3, BFD 1		individual no. 1 participated
12	BLD 3, GD 1, BFD 1		gathering many kinds of food
7.3	BLD 2.6, MDD 0.63	5	

and sitting near their fires. One of them soon goes to light the first hunting fire (*kungya* in KBL) in the forest. The hunters then depart, followed by the women, and all participants are on their way by 7:00 to 9:00 A.M.[11] They do not necessarily depart together, or advance in a line, but rather disappear into the forest in twos and threes. Several factors, including dew, temperature, hunger, and especially rain, affect departure times. If it rains heavily in the morning, everyone usually remains in camp all day, although I saw one hunting party (case 13) depart in the afternoon.

The average duration of a hunting expedition is 8.4 hours from departure to return. During this time the nets are set up an average of 7.3 separate times. The frequency is usually related to the number of working hours per expedition but is also influenced by such factors as distance traveled, time spent on gathering plant foods or wandering about in the forest, number of rest stops, and unforeseen incidents (case 7). In table 13.4 the lowest frequencies appear in case 9, where there was a shortage of members, and in case 15, where no game were netted. After case 9 the elders recited evening prayers to ensure success the next day, whereas case 15 was attributed to a bad dream about an elephant.[12]

Duikers, and especially blue duikers, are the most common prey in net hunting. The 16 successful expeditions logged in table 13.4 yielded 42 small duikers (an average of 2.6 per day) and 10 medium-sized duikers (0.6 per day), for a total catch of 52 (3.2 per day). Given that blue duikers weigh about 4 kg and the medium-sized duikers weigh about 18 kg, and that hunting parties averaged 20 members while the bands averaged 57 members, the yields can be estimated as 1.06 kg per hunter per day or 0.37 kg per band member per day.

The numbers of working hours and the numbers of captures are not necessarily related, although it is unusual to complete a day of net hunting with no success at all (e.g., case 15). The numbers of participants, and hence the numbers of nets used, may correlate more closely with the frequency of kills but additional data are needed to verify this point.

The rate of failure is more difficult to determine, because accurate counts of elusive prey are not always available. Table 13.4 suggests, however, that more prey may escape than are caught per day. An average of 3.2 duikers were killed in 16 days of net hunting, while at least 45 duikers, or an average of 5 per day, managed to escape in 9 days. If these data are accurate, the success/failure ratio for this method is about 62%.

Hunting with Bow and Arrows. Members of band A also hunted monkeys with poisoned arrows. Table 13.5 shows the numbers and species of primates killed in this manner between February 15 and March 6, 1973. Each archer hunted alone, and each foray included some food-gathering and prey surveillance. Direction and duration are matters of individual choice. I only accompanied hunters 8, 9, and 13.

Since net hunting had priority during this season, lone archers went out only before or after net hunting expeditions or when taking a day off from net hunting. Only individual 6, an old male, never went net hunting on these 20 days, but he was out every day with bow and arrows. In table 13.5, male archers are classified as elders (*mangese* in KBL, which also means "great man"), mature hunters, young husbands, and youths. Band A included 5 elders (1, 2, 5, 6, 10 in fig. 13.6), of whom 3 had retired from daily hunting altogether. The youngest elder, individual 2, usually went net hunting but left the net to his son and acted instead as quasi-leader of the whole group.

The 4 mature hunters were all net owners, unlike the 4 young husbands and youths. These 8 males usually went net hunting, one or another doing bow-and-arrow hunting on his day off. Thus, with the exception of individual 6, who considered himself a specialist in archery, the 9 males who hunted primates with poisoned arrows did so on a part-time basis.

Archery hunting consists mainly of seeking, locating, and stalking prey. The hunter must be stealthy and needs to have good hearing and eyesight to pinpoint prey in dense vegetation. If a monkey is seen in a tree higher than 30 m, the hunter waits until it descends within range of the bow. According to the Mbuti, monkeys are likely to descend twice daily, early morning and late afternoon, in order to feed in low trees and shrubs. They are most

Table 13.5. Primates killed with poisoned arrows by band A males between February 15 and March 6, 1973

Individual archers[a]	Prey shot				
	Red colobus	Angolan colobus	Blue monkey	Crested mangabey	Totals
Elders					
2	—	—	1	—	1
6	6	—	—	—	6
Mature hunters					
3	2	—	—	—	2
4	1	1	—	1	3
8	3	1	—	—	4
9	—	1	—	—	1
Young husbands					
11	1	—	—	1	2
12	1	—	1	—	2
Youths					
13	1	—	—	—	1
14	—	1	—	—	1
Totals					
10	15	4	2	2	23
Percentages	65	17	9	9	100

[a]See figure 13.5.

difficult to locate on rainy or windy days, so prime hunting conditions are clear and still mornings and afternoons.

A detailed analysis of the poison used by archers will be reported elsewhere. I want to point out, however, that a notion held by many writers since Stanley's travels (1890) may be a myth. The poison is effective in slowing down and eventually immobilizing the prey, but it is not strong enough to cause swift death.[13] The main function of the poison is to ease the task of tracking and to ensure a kill that might otherwise be quite dangerous or impossible.

The 10 archers killed 23 primates, including one small infant, in 20 days (table 13.5). Thus, each archer made 0.12 kills per day, and the cumulative yield of their efforts was about 1 monkey per day for the band. Red colobus monkeys accounted for 65% of the prey taken by archers, probably because this species lives in large, cohesive troops that are easily located.[14] The average weight of a red colobus is about 10 kg, so the daily contribution of the archers was close to that figure. As a result, net hunters and archery hunters together contributed about 31 kg of game per day to the band's larder, which amounts to 0.54 kg per person per day in a 57-member band.[15]

Observations on Band B

The hunting range of band B lies on the upper Lolwa River, covering a forest area of about 200 km^2 (see fig. 13.4). The hunting season lasts about 10 months, from December to September. I joined the band at the end of March and stayed to the end of July, 1973. Archery hunting is the mainstay of this band, supplemented by periodic spear hunting. There were numerous opportunities to observe the former, but I was not permitted to join in spear hunting expeditions because they are considered dangerous. I therefore collected data on spear hunting at camp by interviewing the hunters and asking for demonstrations of technique after their return each day. Narrations of successful hunts were, in any case, told, sung, and acted out for several days after an expedition. In some cases I visited the kill site later to gather more information.

Hunting with Bow and Arrow. I observed 29 cases of bow-and-arrow hunting between April 17 and June 23 (table 13.6), and the following descriptions are drawn from this sample.

Campsites b_3 and b_4 contained 33 and 45 persons, respectively, while I was there to study hunting behavior. Archers were men and youths, or about 40% of the population (see table 13.2), although young boys regularly went out to shoot birds. An example is case 25, where a group of boys walked around the camp area to hunt birds feeding on high concentrations of insects. These activities provide practice and training, but probably do not contribute substantially to the band's larder.

Adult males hunt alone or in groups, using the *ebaka* and *motá* methods. However, since both methods utilize dogs and human trackers after the prey is wounded, it is not quite correct to label *ebaka* as individual hunting. When tracking small game, such as porcupine, mongoose, or guinea fowl, one or more hunters and a dog go out together. Iron-tipped arrows are used for this purpose. Primates, on the other hand, are hunted with sharpened shafts, or *sûa* (KBL). Unlike band A archers, who purposely hunted primates, band B archers did so opportunistically, concentrating instead on other prey species (table 13.6). A few monkeys were shot when they approached the campsite (cases 1, 3, 19), and one monkey was taken from an eagle (case 28).

Table 13.6 illustrates that the *ebaka* method of ambushing game is used mainly in the morning and evening hours, probably coinciding with the feeding schedules of prey species, while the collective *motá* method is used in the daytime. Given that archers may practice both methods on any given day, each hunter is likely to start or end the day with about an hour of *ebaka* hunting and then go on a tracking or *motá* hunting expedition during the day. The average duration for small-game tracking was 3.5 hours, while *motá* hunting usually required 4.3 hours. Incidental shooting of monkeys, squirrels, and birds occurred throughout the day except during *motá* hunting, when all participants must coordinate their actions. No archer spent more than 7 hours hunting per day.

The following description of a 4.5-hour *motá* hunt, observed on May 6, 1973 (case 18), shows how activities are distributed in time and space. Traveling in a semicircle away from and back to camp, the group killed 1 blue duiker, 1 guinea fowl, and 1 squirrel, and missed 4 blue duikers and 1 bay duiker because arrows thrice went wide of their marks and twice there was no chance to shoot. It is almost impossible to hit a duiker from more than 10 m away when it is flushed abruptly from the undergrowth.

10:15 A.M.	A group of 19 hunters enters the forest and starts a hunting fire to request success from the forest.
10:30	The hunters take up positions encircling a selected area of forest.
10:50	A blue duiker is flushed, but it flees and no one has a chance to shoot.
11:00	The group moves to another location.
11:10	The hunters again take up positions.
11:45	A blue duiker bolts, and there is again no chance to shoot. The formation begins to break up.
12:00 P.M.	Another blue duiker flees, and no one can shoot in time.
12:05	The hunters break formation and gather mushrooms.
12:10	A blue duiker bolts. One archer scores a direct hit from about 4 m away and another leaps on the wounded prey and seizes its legs.
12:20	The duiker is gutted.
12:35	The hunt is resumed.
12:45	A blue duiker flees and escapes after a miss.
12:47	The dog has tracked down a guinea fowl, which a hunter kills.
1:00	The hunters take up positions again.
1:40	One archer shoots at a rat, but it escapes.
1:55	A bay duiker bolts but there is no hit.
2:10	Rain begins and the hunt ends.
2:20	The group starts home. One archer kills a squirrel, and others collect mushrooms and nuts on the way to camp.
2:45	The group arrives in camp.

This episode illustrates the flexibility of the *motá* method, which, unlike net hunting, combines individual and group activities to maximum advantage.

Although it is not stressed above, the dog is an important aid to archers.

Table 13.6. Bow-and-arrow hunting activities in band B

Case no.	Date	Target	Technique	Time	Catch	Area of body hit	Tracking by dog	Notes
1	Apr. 17	monkey	sûa	6:00 P.M.	×			near camp (blue monkey)
2	18	duiker	motá	(10:46 A.M.– 4:05 P.M.)	×			hunting ritual before hunt
3	18	monkey	sûa	5:10 P.M.	×			near camp (blue monkey)
4	18	duiker	ebaka	5:35 P.M.	blue duiker	abdomen		
5	19	small game	tracking	(9:26 A.M.– 2:05 P.M.)	squirrel	penetration	(+)	on the way for nut-gathering
6	20	duiker	ebaka	7:00 P.M.	×			
7	20	duiker	motá	(11:15 A.M.– 4:15 P.M.)	×			hunting ritual after hunt
8	21	duiker	ebaka	6:45 A.M.	blue duiker	heart	(−)	died on the spot
9	21	duiker	ebaka	7:37 A.M.	(−)	back	(+)	hit on but ran away (blue duiker)
10	21	duiker	motá	(10:18 A.M.– 3:30 P.M.)	blue duiker	abdomen	(+)	
11	22	small game	tracking	(12:00– 2:49 P.M.)	porcupine	abdomen	(+)	tracked into hole of tree
12	25	potto	sûa	6:00 A.M.	×			near camp
13	May 3	duiker	motá	(1:30 P.M.– 4:50)	bay duiker	abdomen	(+)	
14	3	duiker	ebaka	5:27 P.M.	(−)			
15	4	duiker	motá	(11:40 A.M.– 2:05 P.M.)	×			blue duiker

Date	Target	Method	Time	Prey / result	Injury		Remarks
16	duiker	ebaka	7:00 A.M.	blue duiker	heart	(−)	died on the spot
17	duiker	ebaka	5:00 P.M.	(−)			blue duiker
18	duiker	motá	(10:15 A.M.– 2:45 P.M.)	blue duiker	neck	(−)	caught by hand
				guinea fowl	penetration	(+)	wounded by dog
				squirrel	abdomen		
June 10	monkey	sûa	5:20 P.M.	red colobus		(+)	near camp
10	duiker	ebaka	4:40 P.M.	Gabon duiker	hind limb	(−)	dog was absent
10	duiker	ebaka	5:15 P.M.	(−)			dog was wounded
11	squirrel	sûa	1:00 P.M.	squirrel	penetration	(+)	dog was wounded
13	small game	tracking	(1:00– 4:45 P.M.)	2 mongooses	abdomen	(+)	on the way for honey-collecting (porcupine)
16	small game	tracking	(8:05– 9:10 A.M.)	(−)			boys' group
18	birds	sûa	(11:00 A.M.– 12:43 P.M.)	×			boys' group
20	birds	sûa	(10:30 A.M.– 2:00 P.M.)	birds	penetration		
21	squirrel	sûa	5:05 P.M.	×			
22	monkey	sûa	2:05 P.M.	red colobus	killed by eagle		eagle was driven away
23	squirrel	sûa	10:00 A.M.	squirrel	penetration		

Key: ×: Fail to hit.
(−): Hit but not caught.

Only twice were duikers killed by the first arrow hits (cases 8 and 16), and only once did a hunter manage to grab a wounded prey (case 18). On nine occasions dogs with wooden bells tracked down prey successfully, and only twice (cases 9 and 24) were the hunters unable to kill these prey. In hunting porcupines, mongooses, guinea fowls, and other small terrestrial prey, the dog is invaluable to the archer.

Table 13.6 shows that wide variety of prey species, from small to large, are hunted by archers. Birds were the smallest and bay duikers were the largest prey which I observed being taken by archers. The yellow-backed duiker, which at 50 kg or more is the largest *Cephalophus* available to the Mbuti, tends to be the upper limit for arrows, although I was informed that on rare occasions a bush pig (about 70 kg) can be killed with an iron-tipped arrow.

If weight estimates of the prey in table 13.6 are tabulated, the total weight of game obtained by band B archers in 20 days is about 87 kg (table 13.7), which amounts to about 4.4 kg per day. Given an average band size of 39 for campsites b_3 and b_4, the yield is about 0.11 kg per person per day. This does not appear to compare favorably with the estimate obtained for net hunting in band A (0.37 kg/person per day), but archery hunting does not involve as high a percentage of band members, leaving women and girls free to gather other foods, and it is supplemented by spear hunting.

Hunting with Spears. I observed 11 cases of spear hunting between March 22 and June 18, 1973, and the following descriptions are based on this sample (table 13.8).

A spear-hunting party is usually composed of all male members of the band, other than children. In band B two elders (individuals 4 and 6, see fig. 13.6) also abstained, so the hunting parties included 16 adult males and youths plus whatever male visitors were on hand (see table 13.2).

Table 13.7. Estimated yield of hunting by band B archers in a 20-day period (see table 13.6)

Prey	No. killed	Estimated weight (kg) per prey	Total weight (kg)
Blue duiker	5	4	20
Other duikers	2	18	36
Red colobus	2	10	20
Porcupine	1	2	2
Mongoose	2	2	4
Squirrel	4	1	4
Guinea fowl	1	1	1
Totals	17		87

Table 13.8. Spear-hunting activities in band **B**

A. Successful Kills

Case no.	Date	Departure (A.M.)	Arrival (P.M.)	Duration (hr)	Group	1st spear	Catch	Technique	Area of body hit
A1	22 March	7:12	5:59	10.8	all members	no. 7	bush pig	throw	back
A2	18 April	?	?	?	3 hunters	no. 7	bush pig	throw	abdomen
A3	7 May	7:40	8:15	12.6	all members	—	dead buffalo	—	—
A4	28 May	7:30	6:05	10.6	all members	no. 16	buffalo	throw	abdomen
A5	18 June	8:37	6:20	9.7	3 hunters	no. 14	large ungulate	throw	abdomen

B. Unsuccessful Attempts

Case no.	Date	Departure (A.M.)	Arrival (P.M.)	Duration (hr)	Group	Animal	Approach	Technique
B1	11 June	8:40	5:54	9.2	main team	elephant	near	(−)
					no. 10	giant forest hog	far	throw
					no. 11	buffalo	far	throw
B2	12 June	8:40	3:55	7.2	main team	(−)	(−)	(−)
					no. 11	elephant	near	thrust
B3	13 June	7:20	5:30	10.2	main team	(−)	(−)	(−)
					no. 7	giant forest hog	far	throw
B4	15 June	8:33	6:20	9.8	3 hunters	giant forest hog	near	throw
B5	16 June	3:25 (P.M.)	6:00	2.5	no. 7	giant forest hog	near	throw
B6	17 June	9:30	7:00	9.5	no. 14	(−)	(−)	(−)

Sometimes another band cooperates in a large spear hunt (case B1), but this is not common. In such cases the party will divide into two subgroups, with a small team of several skilled adults and a main team including youths moving forward on parallel paths, and with the small team being in charge of the first spear attack. This tactic is also used by a single band.

Each boy is assigned to a specific adult so that he is not lost or left behind when subgroups separate. These units stay together throughout the expedition. The Mbuti describe this relationship with the terms "lunch owner" and "lunch carrier," for it is necessary to take along the remains of breakfast or last night's supper, wrapped in *ngongo* or *kasabulu* (KBL) leaves, on long expeditions.[16] These apprenticeships last from about age 10 to age 20.

Since all members of a band take note of the skills and successes of each hunter, I was able to obtain a reasonably accurate record of large-game kills made in the past by band B (table 13.9). One source of potential error is the term "innumerable," which the Mbuti use for any number above 10 kills. However, if we assume that all "innumerable" counts represent 10 kills apiece, it becomes apparent that this band hunts many elephants (>64), fewer giant forest hogs (>38) and bush pigs (>32), and relatively few buffalo (>15). These figures may in part reflect relative accuracy of memory, however, with the most highly prized game being best remembered.

The raw data in table 13.9 also suggest that spear-hunting efficiency increases with age, although some individuals (e.g., 9 and 27) have little success despite their status. Table 13.10 lends some support to this premise, but a larger sample of individuals is needed to firmly establish the point.

Spear hunting expeditions are long and arduous, starting at dawn or shortly afterward, usually between 7:00 and 9:00 A.M., and ending at dusk. Sometimes hunters return to camp several hours after sunset (e.g., case A3, table 13.8). On such nights the old man, individual 6, who no longer goes group spear hunting, calls toward the forest at regular intervals to guide the hunters back with his voice.

The average duration of spear-hunting expeditions is 11 hours. Upon their return to camp, spear hunters usually show great fatigue and sink exhausted around the fire—a situation that rarely happens after net or bow hunting expeditions. When spear hunters have been unsuccessful despite much work and effort, they tend to be unusually quiet in the evening, neither singing nor dancing. This high energy expenditure results in part from the need to travel long distances to good hunting areas, and in part from the necessity to move about constantly during the hunt. The distance traveled to the hunting site is often as much as 10 km as the crow flies, and probably several times as much in reality. These are the reasons, in addition to the danger, that old persons and children (and myself) were not allowed

Table 13.9. Lifetime spear-hunting records for male members of band B

Individual[a]	Estimated age	Classification	Elephant		Buffalo	Giant forest hog	Bush pig
			1st spear	2nd spear			
6	50	M,R	10+	10+	2	10+	10+
7	35–40	M	10+	10+	10+	10+	10+
27	35–40	M	0	1	0	1	0
9	35–40	M	0	1	0	1	0
8	30–35	M	3	10+	1	5	10+
26	30–35	M	1	0	0	1	0
14	30–35	M	2	2	0	3	1
13	30–35	U	0	0	0	0	0
16	25–30	M	0	2	1	2	0
10	25–30	M	1*	1	1	1	1
11	20–25	M	0	0	0	2	0
18	20	U	0	0	0	1	0
25	20	U	0	0	0	0	0
19	15–20	B	0	0	0	1#	0
21	10–15	B	0	0	0	0	0
23	10–15	B	0	0	0	0	0
22	10	B	0	0	0	0	0

[a]See figure 13.6.

Key: M: married
R: retired spear hunter
U: unmarried
B: boy
+: "innumerable" (Mbuti expression for more than 10)
*: wounded but ran away
#: baby animal

Table 13.10. Probability of spear hunting success relative to age in band B

Age grades (years)	No. of males	Cumulative no. of years[a]	No. of kills	Probability of success
40–50	1	45	42	.93
30–40	7	245	92	.38
20–30	5	125	13	.10
10–20	4	60	1	.02

[a]Based on the midpoint value for each 10-year interval.

to go spear hunting. This may be why band B went bow hunting routinely and spear hunting only periodically.

The Mbuti claim it is best to drive spears directly into large prey, especially elephant and buffalo, but the cases described to me involved spear throwing from distances of 8 m or less. In one instance, case B2, the spear bent and broke after piercing an elephant, and in cases B4 and B5 the hunters got close enough to throw several spears but missed the prey. Throwing clearly reduces the risk of injury for the hunter, but the probability of missing is increased by rough terrain and poor visibility, and obstacles such as trees and bushes. However, most of the failures in table 13.8B happened because the hunters could not get close enough to throw *or* thrust their spears at the prey.

Of the five successes listed in table 13.8A, case A3 involved the discovery and subsequent scavenging of a buffalo which the Mbuti estimated had been dead for a day or two. In the other cases, the prey were speared in the back or abdomen. The latter is considered more effective, in part because the spear shaft catches on vegetation and slows the prey, making tracking easier, especially if the point penetrates the abdominal cavity. The hunter carrying the second spear then tracks the wounded animal, following its sounds, blood, and spoor in the trampled vegetation. Spearing a wounded animal requires great bravery, according to the Mbuti, and so the owner of the second spear has high priority when the meat is distributed.

In band B, spear hunting is a periodic activity that supplements the yield from archery hunting. According to the data in table 13.8A, spear hunters contribute large game to the band's larder about once every 20 days. In all cases except A3, (the dead buffalo), band members held festivities for 3–7 days after the kill. Singing and dancing also occur on nights before a spear hunting expedition. However, the circumstances surrounding each expedition can differ considerably. In case A1 there was much singing and dancing the night before, and the next morning two bands jointly tracked an elephant while a small group of three hunters went off separately to chase and kill a bush pig. Case A2 involved the tracking and killing of another bush pig by three hunters after 3 days of work. Case A3 was

Table 13.11. Estimated yield of hunting by band B spear hunters in a 111-day period (see table 13.8)

Prey	No. killed	Estimated weight (kg) per prey	Total weight (kg)
Bush pig	2	70	140
Dwarf forest buffalo	2	300	600
Large ungulate	1	200	200
Totals	5		940

preceded by an evening of hunting songs, but the party discovered a dead buffalo the next day and did not perform any festivities that night. Case A4 involved the killing of a buffalo after 2 days of effort. And case A5 resulted in a kill only after 8 days of failure (see cases B1–B6).

Similar degrees of variability are apparent in the unsuccessful cases. For example, case B1 failed because one boy startled the game; he was severely scolded when the party returned to camp. In case B2 an elephant was speared but the spear broke, and that night everyone examined their spears and talked about the enormous strength of the elephant. Table 13.8B also suggests that spear hunting by lone individuals (case B5) or by single hunters working apart from the main team (case B1) tends to be unsuccessful. This seems to contrast with archery hunting, in which individuals are not as handicapped (see table 13.6).

During 111 days of observation, from March 22 to July 10, members of band B acquired 5 large game animals estimated to weigh a total of 940 kg (table 13.11). Thus, spear hunters contributed about 8.5 kg of game each day to the band's larder. Using an average band size of 39, this amounts to 0.22 kg per person per day, which is double the yield of archery hunting in that band.

Some of the meat brought in by spear hunters is eaten immediately and some is dried for storage. In case A4, a buffalo kill, a small quantity still remained after two weeks, but in most cases the meat is consumed within a week. There are festive days, after which the males resume archery hunting as a daily activity until another spear hunt is organized.

Comparison of Yields from Different Hunting Methods

Table 13.12 shows the estimated yields from various hunting methods used by band A and band B. (Note that all estimates represent gross amounts of animal products obtained by the bands and do not represent actual amounts of meat intake by individuals.)

The combination of net hunting and archery hunting in band A seems to

Table 13.12. Comparison of yields from different hunting methods used by bands A and B

Method	Band A yield (kg/person per day)	Band B yield (kg/person per day)
Archery	.17	.11
Nets	.37	—
Spears	—	.22
Totals	.54	.33

yield more than the combination of archery hunting and spear hunting used by band B. If the comparison is restricted to the main methods used by each band on a regular basis—i.e., nets in band A and archery in band B—the yields differ even more. Both comparisons indicate that net hunting is the more effective technique, and that net hunting bands produce more surplus for trade with agriculturalists.

TRANSPORTATION OF GAME

The Mbuti do not use special equipment for transporting game back to their campsites. When going net hunting, women sometimes carry baskets on their backs in anticipation of bringing meat home, but in most cases they simply make string from *Marantochloa congensis* (*toto* in KBL) at the kill site. Whole or segmented carcasses are trussed up and hauled home, sometimes wrapped in leaves of *Chaumatococcus danielli* (*ngongo* in KBL) for protection. In net hunting, a man and a woman are in charge of one net unit, and the woman is responsible for carrying back all game captured that day while the man carries the net. Most commonly the woman is the wife of the net owner.

In bow-and-arrow hunting, the archer who kills the game will most likely carry it back to camp. However, a successful *motá* hunt may require additional assistance, and a son may carry game shot by his father, or a younger brother the game shot by his older brother.

Nothing larger than a medium-sized duiker (16–20 kg) is likely to be killed by net hunters and archers, and small carcasses can be easily transported without gutting or segmenting them. With large game taken by spear hunters, the hunting party begins to butcher and clean the carcass immediately and transport as much as possible back to camp that day. Pieces up to 40 kg are portioned out to available workers, men or women. The 70-kg bush pigs listed in table 13.8A were carried by 3-man teams, but 17 individuals assisted in transporting a 300-kg buffalo. When an elephant is killed, and sometimes a buffalo, the entire band travels to the site to retrieve the carcass.

If part of the carcass remains behind, another team returns the next day, and this time the women do most of the carrying. After 3 spear hunters killed a 200-kg ungulate, for example, a team of 4 men and 4 women went out the next morning to get the animal: the men carried only small items while the women carried heavy loads. Carcass segments were apportioned as follows: (1) forequarters carried by the wife of individual 7; (2) hindquarters carried by the second wife of individual 7; (3) chest and its internal organs carried by the wife of individual 14, the first spear hunter; (4) loins, stomach, liver, and most of the abdominal wall carried by the wife of individual 8, the second spear hunter; (5) only part of the abdominal wall, the intestines, some internal organs, and a few scraps wrapped in *ngongo* leaves were carried by the men. And only one man assisted his wife at all during the trek home.

Transportation distances vary greatly, depending on where the kill was made. Small game can often be obtained near campsites by hunters working alone or in small groups, but spear hunters may travel 10 km or more in search of large game. More data are needed to determine what the threshold distance is for seeking and transporting game versus relocating campsites, but the spacing of campsites within the forest (see fig. 13.4) indicates that camps are moved when hunting and/or gathering activities become difficult within a 5 km radius.

DISTRIBUTION OF MEAT

Initial Distribution

Primary ownership of a carcass is determined by involvement in wounding and/or killing the prey, although the borrowing of hunting equipment alters this to some extent. In most instances those who own and use nets, spears, and arrows are also those who wound or kill the game, so it is clear that the net hunter, the first spear hunter, or the first arrow hunter owns the game. Net borrowing is common among the Mbuti, however, and the rule is that the borrower gets one leg and the net owner the rest. If four prey are captured in one day, the net borrower gets one carcass. Spear or arrow borrowing is rare, but when it happens the owner of the equipment gets only forelegs and the borrower retains the rest. The difference here is presumably related to degrees of prowess and risk involved, with individual variability greatest in archery and spear hunting.

Another convention is that the person who makes the morning hunting fire (*kungya* in KBL) before a net hunt gets all the heads of animals captured that day.

The archer whose arrow first hits the prey becomes the owner if no one else wounds or kills it. But the hunter who makes the second arrow attack receives the loins (*n'be* in KBL) and haunches. When a dog tracks and brings down the prey after it was wounded by the first and second arrows, the dog's owner keeps the loins, the owner of the second arrow receives a section of the hips, and the owner of the first arrow gets the rest. If a dog tracks down prey without human assistance and the first arrow kills it, the carcass belongs to the dog's owner and the archer gets the loins.

Similar conventions apply to spear hunting. The hunter who thrusts or throws the first spear to wound the prey has primary ownership, and the hunter using the second spear receives the loins. In the case of an elephant kill, the hunter using the second spear also gets the head and neck, although the primary owner of the carcass can retain the trunk if he wants it.

Redistribution

After transportation to the base camp, the primary owners of carcasses or carcass sections redistribute portions until all band members have received a share. There are no prescribed rules for redistribution, and the Mbuti frequently remark that this depends on a person's generosity. In fact, however, the primary owner does not physically participate in the further sectioning of carcasses. He sits instead at the public fire and feigns indifference. Such behavior is standard among hunters who have just returned from a successful expedition. The person most responsible for the kill speaks little or not at all, and the other hunters must describe the details of the expedition. When hunters return from a successful day without bringing the game to camp, women sometimes learn what happened only by the appearance of the weapons. Thus, even though primary ownership of the game is formally established, the impression is given that the catch actually belongs to all band members, and everyone expresses pleasure in the successful hunt. Alternatively, one could say that the personal rights established by the rules of initial distribution function mainly as a formal way of socially honoring the successful hunter.

Despite this absence of strict rules to govern redistribution, there are some generally accepted conventions. One is that men eat the heads of animals. These are cooked on the communal fire (*téle* in KBL, *baraza* in KGN) and then eaten at places reserved for men. The heads of large game are always eaten this way, in a festive atmosphere, while the heads of small game, from duikers on downward, are cooked and eaten at family fires. The man given animal heads because he built the hunting fire before a net hunting expedition shares these with other men at the communal fire. Another convention is that women and children eat the intestines. A third is that elders usually eat highly valued internal organs such as hearts and livers, and sometimes kidneys. In some cases the wives of carcass owners get to eat a liver or a heart, but it is generally acknowledged that the band elders have access to whatever parts they like.

There appear to be no set values regarding different cuts of meat or the order in which these are eaten. All muscle tissue is considered equally good. Cuts of meat are redistributed to all family members while still attached to bones.

Balanced Reciprocity

In addition to the reciprocity (Sahlins, 1965) established by meat redistribution within a band, other kinds of reciprocity occur when the Mbuti distribute meat to villagers. I observed this only once, at camp a_4 of band A. Villagers brought plantains, cassava, loincloths, pans, and leaf tobacco to the Mbuti camp and in return received cuts of duiker meat (excluding the heads, internal organs, abdominal walls, toes, and fur). Each carcass owner is the principal in the exchange, receiving village goods on behalf of all band members. He retains ownership only of the loincloth, but others frequently borrow even this item.

Among the net hunting bands west of Bahaha village, a village representative who conducts regular exchanges often lives at the Mbuti camp. This does not occur among archer bands, such as band B, and may reflect the greater efficiency of the net-hunting method. The net hunting yield shown in table 13.12 could conceivably include a surplus of 0.14 kg per person per day if the band B yield is taken as the base meat requirement for the Mbuti. Villagers' attitudes reflect this as well, for net hunters are viewed as good sources of meat while archers are considered highly unstable suppliers.

CONSUMPTION OF MEAT

Small-game hunting is a rather routine activity for the Mbuti, in both net hunting and spear hunting bands. Individuals and small parties go hunting whenever there is opportunity, sometimes taking days off from group hunting ventures. Small game are therefore distributed and consumed in a routine fashion.

When band A was at a hunting camp in the forest, they sang every night, and the singing usually escalated to dancing.[17] The festivals and feasts in band B were more intense, however, focusing on the large game brought in by spear hunters. In all the cases listed in table 13.8A, the festivities lasted several days and large quantities of meat were consumed. When an elephant is killed, the subsequent festivities may include several bands from surrounding ranges and numerous villagers. The cases I observed, where buffalo, pigs, and an ungulate were the prey, did not involve such larger gatherings.

Of all the hunting methods, spear hunting appears to have the most festive atmosphere, and such expeditions are greatly anticipated by band members. The night before, they perform songs, an elephant hunting dance, a fire dance, and other hunting rituals. After a kill the first spear hunter takes the leading part in singing and dancing, with others harmonizing to his melodies. Most of the songs are extemporaneous, the objective being to recite the roles played in the hunting episode: finding the prey and how it reacted, the stealthy approach and spear thrust, the animal's strength and fighting ability, the prowess needed to track and kill it, and so on. During this time the hunter is regarded as a hero, but only in singing and dancing scenes; at all other times he resumes his normal role.

DISCUSSION

The main purposes here are to summarize my observations from the 1972–1973 study period and to compare these to previous studies of the Mbuti. My work supplements and to some extent corrects the anthropological view of the Mbuti as hunters subsisting in a tropical forest environment. Comparisons with band societies living in other habitats serve to highlight the special adaptations of the Mbuti.

Habitats and Hunting Habits

The prey most consistently exploited by Mbuti hunters is the duiker. Both the net and bow hunting techniques are geared to efficient exploitation of *Cephalophus* species, which are widespread and numerous in the Ituri region. One might even characterize the Mbuti as duiker hunters who have developed some added capabilities for utilizing other prey species on a supplementary basis.

Duikers have not been extensively studied, but there is some general information about their behavior (Dorst and Dandelot, 1970). These animals are primarily nocturnal or crepuscular, the only diurnal one being the black-fronted duiker. They withdraw into the underbrush during the day, and their main escape tactic is to run into dense brush with their heads down, where they freeze until flushed again. Several species feed at dawn and dusk.

Net hunting and *motá* bow hunting tactics make use of these habits. Beaters in the former case and dogs with wooden bells in the latter serve to flush the game, which must then try to elude the rings of netters or archers. The *ebaka* tactic is used to ambush lone duikers that are browsing on leaves, shoots, buds, seeds, fruits, and bark at dawn and dusk. For this tactic to be successful, the hunter must know much about the feeding and ranging habits of duikers, and the Mbuti are skillful observers of these prey. Applied at different times of day, these tactics are complementary and virtually guarantee a steady meat supply for the band.

In contrast to the relatively dry, sparsely vegetated habitats exploited by other hunter/gatherer societies such as the Kalahari Bushmen and the

Hadza, the Ituri Forest is a lush, densely overgrown area. Mbuti hunting tactics must therefore be functional in a three-dimensional zone in which there is limited visibility and maneuverability. Also, many of the available prey are arboreal, and hunters cannot approach these species closely. Archery hunting by individuals or small parties is especially suited to these conditions, and the use of poison arrows provides a crucial advantage. Tracking can be exceedingly difficult in these adverse conditions, and the use of poison reduces the risk of losing wounded prey. What is adverse for the hunter can also be adverse for the prey, however, and the Mbuti often make use of dense cover and rugged terrain in stalking or ambushing game. These tactics are particularly highly developed by spear hunters, who take considerable risks in approaching formidable prey in order to thrust or throw their weapons accurately.

The forest animals hunted by the Mbuti differ in several ways from species inhabiting open grasslands and woodlands, and these differences are reflected in Mbuti hunting tactics. Most of the prey in the Ituri Forest are solitary and do not form large social groups. This is especially true for terrestrial species. Their home ranges tend to be small, and few species migrate seasonally. Accurate, current information on the distribution and abundance of prey is therefore vital, and the Mbuti take every opportunity to gather such information during their routine activities. Hunting tends to be a localized activity, the distances covered being relatively short as compared to hunting on open terrain (e.g., the 10–24-km hunts of the G/wi, described by Silberbauer, in this volume).

Mbuti hunters must operate within the limitations set by their forest environment, and are careful about selecting the most appropriate hunting method for a given set of conditions. There was, nonetheless, more failure than success in band A and band B during my study, and this is probably true for all bands in the area. Net hunting seems to be the most reliable, but its success is closely related to amount of participation (10–40 persons) and degree of organization. It is the combination of hunting methods used by a band that is significant, however, not any single method, and it is this combination that best characterizes the Mbuti adaptation to their forest environment. Mbuti hunting behavior typically consists of the following stages:

1. *Seeking out and locating prey.* The Mbuti are excellent trackers, but tracks merely show the direction taken and the time of passage, and hunters can rarely locate game by tracking alone. In most cases the hunters travel to a promising area and first locate the prey by hearing or seeing it.

2. *Pursuing prey.* Once a suitable prey is located, the hunters have several options depending on the species, the local conditions, and the weapons at hand. The number of available hunters is also decisive. The

object is to net, shoot, or spear the prey, but this can be accomplished by ambushing, luring, stalking, or simply flushing the prey so that it passes within a required distance of the hunter(s).

3. *Wounding or killing the prey.* The primary objective is, of course, to kill the game, but only net hunting is likely to accomplish this immediately. In most cases the prey is initially wounded by an arrow or spear, and must then be tracked. In addition to flushing prey, dogs serve a vital role in tracking wounded animals. The use of poison further increases the likelihood of success, and substitutes for tracking when the prey is arboreal. In these forest conditions it is usual for an animal wounded in the first attack to be found and killed by the second day.

4. *Transporting, distributing, and consuming the prey.* Small game is transported intact, while large game is dismembered at the kill site and initially divided among the hunters. Further dismantling occurs back at camp, until all members of the band have received a share. Some meat is consumed immediately, but large game supplies so much meat that some must be prepared for later consumption.

Comparison of these activities with the hunting behavior of Kalahari Bushmen (Tanaka, 1971) indicates that differences occur largely in the initial stages. For instance, the Bushmen, Tanaka observed commonly locate prey visually from a considerable distance. Approaching the game from a downwind angle, the hunter(s) carefully observe behavior and movement. Upon returning to camp, they convey this information to others, and the next day several hunters may go out to track the prey down. The tracking may take several days before hunters can maneuver into a suitable position for a bow shot. Thus, the hunting tactics Tanaka describes for the Central Kalahari and those I observed in the Ituri Forest differ in many respects, but each is admirably suited to the local conditions.

As mentioned previously, the Ituri biome is not entirely homogeneous, and some of these variations may affect Mbuti hunting behavior. In broad terms the Ituri Forest can be divided into a *Cynometra* zone, a *Brachystegia* zone, and a *Gilbertiodendron* zone, of which the first and the third are the most different in vegetation. It is therefore of some interest that net hunters occur mainly in the *Gilbertiodendron* forest and to some extent in the *Cynometra* forest, while archers occur only in the *Cynometra* forest. The data I obtained from my surveys are unfortunately insufficient to establish this relationship or to explore how it operates, but the distributions of plants used in hunting technology provide some insights. Consider the following examples.

A *Raphia* species (Palmae), known locally as *bambu* (KBL), occurs mainly in the *Cynometra* forest. In the Lolwa River basin, dense patches occur in marshy areas near small rivers, but the plant is absent south of the Ituri River. The Mbuti are aware of this distribution pattern, for the leafstalk of this wild palm is used in making arrow shafts, or *sûa*. The only good substitute for *bambu* is another *Raphia* species known locally as *mabondo* (KGN), a cultivated palm that grows near villages located in *Brachystegia* forest and *Gilbertiodendron* forest. Since neither species grows south of the Ituri River, the hunters there must use *Strychnos* or *Grewia* trees (*koha* and *bembu* in KBL, respectively) for making arrow shafts. The work required to collect and modify these materials is much greater, however, so the Mbuti prefer to use *bambu*. Archers in bands A and B were therefore inclined to hunt in areas north of the Ituri River, preferably where *bambu* stands were readily accessible.

An *Eremospatha* species (Palmae), known locally as *rekwe* (KBL), occurs only in *Cynometra* forest and is considered essential in making bowstrings by hunters operating in the Lolwa River basin. It apparently does not occur south of the Ituri River, where the bands studied by Tanno were unable to find *rekwe* upon request. According to Tanno (personal communication), the southern Mbuti use three kinds of liana palms (*koko, asuki,* or *nbopi* in KBL) as substitutes for *rekwe,* but from my observations these plants are difficult to work into bowstrings. The *nbopi* materials are particularly coarse and dry, and prone to cracking when bent or twisted. Archers thus prefer to hunt in areas north of the Ituri River, where *rekwe* is readily available, while bands living south of the river prefer to use the net hunting method (Tanno, 1976).

Manniophyton fluvum (Euphorbiaceae), called *kusa* (KBL), occurs all over the Ituri area, especially between the Mambasa River and Ibiena River basins, and is used to make net strings. My impression was that *kusa* is more abundant in the *Gilbertiodendron* forest than in the *Cynometra* forest, in which case there would be a correlation with the distribution of net hunters, but this conclusion may be premature.

Several species of plants are used for thatching on huts and for wrapping various items, but leaves of *Chaumatococcus danielli* (Maranthaceae) or *ngongo* (KBL), are probably the most suitable. These are abundant in the *Cynometra* zone and scarce elsewhere, especially in the undergrowth of *Gilbertiodendron* forest.

These observations suggest that the distribution of Mbuti bands, and of predominant hunting methods, are influenced by patterns of vegetation distribution within the Ituri Forest. Additional research on the distribution of flora used by the Mbuti, combined with detailed study of the distribution and availability of fauna hunted by different methods, may verify some of these relationships and refute others.

Tactical and Behavioral Aspects of Net Hunting versus Archery Hunting

Throughout the Ituri Forest, the male members of Mbuti bands hunt game with bows and arrows. While in some areas archery hunting predominates, in others net hunting is much more common and productive. In some net hunting bands, archery is only rarely practiced. These differences can be examined in functional and historical terms.

As one of several methods in the hunting repertoire of the Mbuti, archery is clearly the most flexible. It requires little preparation and organization, and individuals or small parties can launch expeditions on short notice. Tactics are highly variable, and can be changed immediately to fit new circumstances. And the prey hunted by archers includes a wide range of species and sizes, especially if poison is used. The overall success rate may not be high relative to net hunting, but archery is perhaps best suited to the floral and faunal conditions encountered in the Ituri Forest. A band of archers does not rely on any specific hunting tactic or on any particular type of prey and is therefore basically unspecialized. When other methods fail, the Mbuti can fall back on a technique that is bound to yield some meat, at least on a temporary if not permanent basis, for a band of 20–60 individuals (Harako, 1977).

The *begbe* tactic of archery hunting, in which men, women, and children from neighboring bands cooperate to encircle and flush prey from a preselected area, is the most complicated and infrequently used. It is actually an elaborate version of the *motá* tactic, in which 10 or more men plus a dog encircle and ambush prey flushed from the underbrush by one hunter and his dog. These archery tactics are quite similar to net hunting, and may have been derived from that method.

Among bands that practice net hunting, this tactic is now a primary hunting activity. It occurs daily, and sometimes several times per day. The method is simple, requiring little skill or knowledge, but a large number of persons must be available. Even if more than half of the animals flushed by the beaters manage to escape, the method provides a surplus of meat in the long run. There is some division of labor, in that nets are carried by males and kills are usually made by males, but these are not rigidly established.[18] The price paid for this efficiency seems to be a degree of specialization, where all band members concentrate on one type of subsistence activity.

These observations suggest that archery hunting predates net hunting in the Ituri region, and imply that the Mbuti were originally archers in prehistoric times. This premise is further supported by Bantu oral traditions, according to which the Bila practiced net hunting long ago and taught it to the Mbuti.[19] This would account for the fact that the Bantu-related Mbuti now practice net hunting while the Sudanic-related Mbuti remained archers. Iron arrowheads and spear blades, on the other hand, were probably introduced by Sudanic peoples, causing little change in Mbuti hunting tactics except perhaps to reduce the importance of poison.

The historical steps whereby net hunting entered the Ituri area and spread through Mbuti society remain hypothetical. It is possible that iron weapons were initially introduced by Sudanic peoples, who were then displaced toward the east and north by Bantu tribes who brought the net hunting technique with them and transmitted it to the indigenous Mbuti hunter/gatherer bands inhabiting the central and southwestern sections of the forest. If the Mbuti archers were already using the *mota* tactic at that time, net hunting, which is only a variation on the same theme, might have become quickly and firmly established. However, it is also possible that the *mota* tactic developed after the arrival of net hunting, with the behavioral but not always the technological component being borrowed by Mbuti archers, some of whom eventually specialized in the new technique. Given the relatively high productivity of net hunting, its adoption by the Bantu-related Mbuti would be understandable. There remains some doubt, however, about why the method did not spread throughout the entire Ituri region. When asked, archers simply say, "We are not accustomed to using nets."

If archery was the standard Mbuti hunting technique prior to the advent of net hunting, the transition was probably accompanied by changes in Mbuti social life, perhaps the most prominent being the introduction of female participation in routine hunting activities. These changes may in turn have intensified the economic symbiosis between bands and villages. The productivity and reliability of net hunting provided an economic base for regular exchange of goods with villagers, with meat moving in one direction and vegetables and other trade items moving in the other direction. Amplification of changes would presumably occur automatically once this system became established. For example, females whose primary role used to be gathering of plant foods could participate more and more in communal hunting expeditions as the trade network supplied more and more vegetables from villages. This scenario tentatively accounts for the unusual status of some Mbuti bands as "commercial hunter/gatherers" (Hayden, in this volume), but there are many nuances to be explored by further research.

Two points made by Turnbull (1965b) warrant attention here. The first is that the importance of the economic symbiosis between bands and villages has been overemphasized since it was initially described by Schebesta (1936). My work supports his conclusion by showing that relationships with villages are not the same for all bands, some having much stronger economic ties than others. Moreover, only a limited number of Mbuti bands are truly dependent on villagers for vital commodities. His second point is that the symbiosis is stronger among bow hunters than net hunters. My work demonstrates that exactly the opposite is true.

Tactical and Social Aspects of Spear Hunting as a Specialized Activity

Unlike bow hunting, which all Mbuti males do on a full-time or part-time basis, or net hunting, which is a communal activity involving nearly all age classes and both sexes, spear hunting is an intermittent activity performed by professionals. Boys must go through an apprenticeship period that lasts until they reach about 20 years of age. The best spear hunters in the band launch the first attack, as the risk of injury is considered high and skills must be finely honed. The fame of a hunter who can kill elephants spreads far and wide, and he is honored both within and beyond his own band. All the bands and villages in an area can identify the best spear hunters. In fact, only through skillful spear hunting can a male Mbuti achieve such distinction and be called by the honorary name of *tûma* (KBL). In contrast, an adept spear hunter who has not yet killed an elephant has a reputation only within his own band, where all members keep track of each person's hunting record. The reputation of a *tûma* spreads much farther, perhaps because other bands as well as villagers are routinely invited to elephant feasts.[20]

In band B, only individuals 6 and 7 were considered *tûma* hunters. Since individual 6 was retired, individual 7 acted as the leader of spear hunting parties. The core of such a party consisted of individual 7 and his brothers, and the sons of individual 6, with several boys accompanying them as apprentices. The composition of such a hunting party varies according to the number of available individuals in the band, although the standard party fielded by a given band may at times be augmented by visiting spear hunters. Band B, for example, was composed mainly of individual 6 and his children, individual 7 and his brothers' families, and some of the latter's paternal and maternal relatives (see fig. 13.6).[21] At campsite b_4 the core group of spear hunters was joined by individuals 13 and 14, who were probably relatives of the grandfather (individual 1) on the paternal side. Thus, band B could field a maximum of 9 experienced spear hunters during my study, of which 7 males were permanent members. These hunting parties were accompanied by a maximum of 7 apprentices whose ages ranged from 10 to 20 years. Larger bands can of course field more spear hunters, and the total number may double or even triple when bands cooperate in an elephant hunt.

The emphasis placed on spear hunting by band B is unusual for modern Mbuti. Spear hunting may always have been the specialty of certain bands in the Ituri region, but it appears to be declining in popularity these days despite the honor and fame associated with it. Although every band claims to have a spear hunter even today, which is probably the case if we do not take into account whether he is famous or unknown, practicing or retired, few bands include a true *tûma*. Since only spear hunting prowess can lead to such high status, not even the best archers and net hunters are widely known in an area. This situation is well illustrated by band A, in which individuals 1, 2, 5, and 6 were elders who had retired from hunting activities (see fig. 13.5). These *mangese* (KBL) were once spear hunters as well, and it is said that individual 1 was a renowned *tûma* throughout the district. This band routinely used the net hunting method in the old days, as they do now, but they maintain that elephant hunting with spears was more common in previous generations. As it was described to me, the reason for this decline was that about 10 years prior to my study individual 1 was badly wounded in the abdomen while elephant hunting and, having so narrowly escaped death, he took this opportunity to retire.[22] Upon the retirement of their *tûma*, the band all but quit spear hunting because no other hunter was in a position to take over the leadership of hunting parties. Individuals 1–9 had some experience in spear hunting when this happened, with individuals 1 and 5 having killed one elephant apiece, but all were net owners who preferred to use that method regularly. The only prey speared during my study was a python—killed by individual 2, who always carried a spear on net hunting expeditions. A small spear-hunting party (individuals 1, 3, and 5) went out on January 2, 1972, with no success.

The presence of a *tûma* is vital to an Mbuti band that intends to practice large-game hunting, and the above-mentioned case illustrates how rapidly the method can die out if such a man is not available. A *tûma* serves as leader of spear hunting expeditions and attracts others to the band. Band B, for example, included several dependents of the *tûma*: individual 4, his mother's brother, and individuals 21, 22, and 24, the children brought by his two wives. The presence of a famous *tûma* is likely to swell band membership, with the result that more males are available for forming hunting parties and for apprenticeships. Kinship, and especially paternal kinship, is therefore an important aspect of band composition, and the *tûma* is a central figure in this process, acting as the nucleus of the band by attracting maternal relatives, in-laws, and female relatives on the paternal side, as was the case with individual 7 in band B (see fig. 13.6).

Despite his fame and status, and the informal responsibility he bears for supporting the band, the authority of a *tûma* is not institutionalized and not conspicuous in routine camp life. Outside of hunting activities his status is emphasized only in an abstract sense, via singing and dancing. During routine activities his behavior is just like that of others in the same generation. Thus, when disputes arose in band B, in which individual 7 ranked as the *tûma*, these were arbitrated by individual 6, whose status as a respected elder, rather than as a retired *tûma*, gave him the right to present opinions.

This situation changes dramatically, however, when interactions between Mbuti bands and villages occur. The leadership of the *tûma* becomes more overt, in part because he acts as negotiator in economic and social contexts. This occurs to some extent also in interactions with other bands, for the status of the *tûma* in effect reflects on the reputation of his band.

The function and influence of the *tûma* is most apparent when other

Mbuti and villagers join in the festivities following an elephant kill. After the elephant has been butchered and largely consumed in the forest, all the participants travel to the local village for further celebrations. Together with his hunting companions, the *tûma* who killed the elephant enters the village in a stately procession. Then the festivities begin, with the *tûma* being the guest of honor (see Putnam, 1954). In reward for the successful hunt, and for sharing the meat, the hunters, their wives, and their children are allowed to take home whatever they need from the village. The villagers expect the Mbuti to take farm products, such as plantains, because they were allowed to partake of the elephant.

The economic system of exchanging forest products and farm products is typified at these celebrations, but the reciprocity has only minor economic significance in the long run because elephants are killed infrequently in any given area. Even if we account for some delayed reciprocity, whereby the villagers supply some farm products to the band during the rest of the year, the primary feature of these celebrations is social reciprocity. The *tûma*'s status is reinforced and other social ties are established, especially between villagers and the close relatives of the *tûma*. These ties reach into many aspects of Mbuti life other than subsistence.

According to my observations of bands A and B, and information obtained from other informants, Mbuti bands are composed of individuals whose biological relationships are readily traceable even though membership is neither formally determined nor limited to a single lineage. Kinship ties are apt to be closest in bands practicing spear hunting, for two reasons: the technique is based on formal apprenticeships, with skills being passed preferably from father to son, and the technique requires expert skill and manpower, drawn mainly from paternal relatives. Since these male relatives form the nucleus of the band, the composition of the entire band is directly affected by the membership of the core hunting group. This pattern differs markedly from the territorial aspect of band composition among the Epulu net hunters described by Turnbull (1965b), to which I shall return.

Seasonal Variability, Band Mobility, and Band Fluidity

The nomadic movements of bands A and B were charted in figure 13.4, on which campsites a_1 and b_1 are base camps. Both bands occupied their base camps during the major rainy season (August–October) and returned to their forest hunting camps at the beginning of the dry season (December). Base camp a_1 contained 37 individuals (5 families), base camp b_1 perhaps as many as 100 individuals (25 huts counted). The hunting camp sizes for band A ranged from 48 to 62 individuals (6–10 families), for band B from 30 to 41 individuals (8–10 families). Hunting camps are periodically moved to new sites within the home range, and the composition of the settlement changes regularly as families arrive and depart. Another cause of shifting composition is the irregular movement of individuals who may temporarily visit one campsite or another. To these patterns of fluidity can be added differences in grouping habits when bands associate with villages. At Lolwa Village, band A formed into small groups which then coalesced into a larger band of about 10 families when the hunting season began. On the northern periphery of Lolwa Village, band B formed a large encampment which then segmented into smaller units containing about 8 families during the hunting season. Base camps are also likely to contain some visitors from other areas, and some permanent members may be absent at any given time. A schematic diagram of these fission–fusion patterns appears in figure 13.9.

The Mbuti bands inhabiting the Ituri Forest are both fluid in composition and mobile within their home ranges, in part because their social structure and kinship system are relatively informal. According to Turnbull (1965a–c), the nuclear family is the basic social unit of Mbuti society. With few exceptions, as when an adoption occurs or when a man takes two or three wives, this social unit consists of a husband, a wife, and their children. These units are themselves quite cohesive, but each unit exhibits considerable freedom of movement within a home range and to some extent even across "territorial" boundaries. So it is more practical to consider band composition in terms of family units than individuals. The concept of territoriality is apparently applied by Turnbull because spatial integrity is more obvious to an observer than social cohesiveness. Our interpretations overlap to the extent that there are spatial limits on mobility and fluidity, but it should be noted that this is not a standard zoological application of the concept (Bates, 1970; Carpenter, 1964; Jewell, 1966).

Turnbull (1965a–c) also points out that net hunters form larger bands than archers because the tactical and behavioral requirements of these subsistence activities differ, one being a group activity and the other an

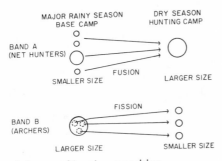

Figure 13.9. Seasonal change of band composition.

individual activity. The annual *begbe* hunt performed by archers is perceived as an exception to the rule. My work confirms this general picture, but there are a number of complications and some differences of opinion regarding certain details.

One point on which we differ is the timing and importance of the honey season. Turnbull (1965b) writes that the large bands of net hunters split into smaller units while the small bands of bow hunters congregate into larger units during the honey-collecting season. He does not fix the time of this season, but his description implies that these changes in band composition occur between April and July (see Turnbull, 1965b:168). He also maintains that hunting activities virtually cease during this period. During my study, honey-collecting was started in March by band A (campsite a_4 in the lower basin of the Lolwa River) and was at its height in May and June for band B (campsite b_4 in the upper basin of the Lolwa River). These dates coincide with Turnbull's, but they do not necessarily establish a general rule. As far as I could determine from supplementary information, the honey season occurs at different times in different sections of the Ituri Forest, in accordance with local blossoming cycles. *Cynometra* usually blooms in March, *Brachystegia* slightly later, and *Gilbertiodendron* in April, but there are variations resulting from altitude and other environmental factors. If local patterns are lumped into a single period, the best time for honey-collecting within the Ituri region is the minor rainy season, from April through July.

More importantly, the honey season did not particularly alter the hunting routines of the bands observed during my study, nor did the honey season entail more frequent and intense festivities in bands A and B. The band composition changes noted by Turnbull did occur, but not to the degree that I observed when hunting camps were being set up at the beginning of the dry season. Shifts in composition are greater when the Mbuti leave the villages than at any other time of year.

Some of these differences can probably be attributed to real changes in Mbuti subsistence and society since Turnbull's fieldwork in the 1950s. For instance, the buying and selling of meat is now legally prohibited during the major rainy season, and the law has had some effect on Mbuti behavior even though it is not strictly enforced. According to the local villagers I interviewed, the Mbuti spent less time at village campsites before the law was established. However, since the Mbuti are still allowed to hunt for their own needs during this period, I find it difficult to believe that trade has ceased entirely. Other differences can perhaps be attributed to opposing views of the Ituri Forest environment. Turnbull (1965a, 1968) regards this region as homogeneous in its vegetation, climate, and terrain, while I found enough heterogeneity in the habitat to make some tentative interpretations of the variations observed in Mbuti hunting habits. It may be appropriate to characterize the Ituri region as relatively homogeneous in comparison to arid habitats such as the Kalahari, but such generalization obscures subtle relationships between environmental and behavioral features.

Drawing on his study of the Epulu band and his incidental observations of other bands in the area, Turnbull (1965a–c) concluded that Mbuti band membership is not based on lineage. The Epulu band was very large, containing 65 married males, 66 married females, and 121 children, and comprising 27 lineages. The number of huts was consistent with the number of families, as well as lineages, within the band. More than 50% of the huts were occupied by male household heads from different patrilineages. Thus, a band containing 10 nuclear families is not likely to contain two family heads from the same lineage. Due to this complexity, and to the possibility that the concepts of lineage and totem were borrowed from villagers, Turnbull regarded the Mbuti band as a territorial unit. In my study, bands A and B were not comprised of single lineages but each was clearly consanguineous. Based on the large number of important positions held by adult male kin in these bands, my interpretation is that patrilineage is an important element in band composition. And in my view, the presence of so many lineages in the Epulu band suggests that it was actually composed of several different bands which perhaps congregated as a temporary social unit during Turnbull's study. It also seems relevant, in this regard, that the base camp used by the Epulu band was a permanent settlement, while the two bands I studied abandoned their base camps completely during the hunting season. Permanent occupation of a base camp may be the rule for large net-hunting bands, however; Tanno (personal communication) found that some members of the Mawambo band, which associates with a village about 50 km south of Mambasa (fig. 13.1), can always be found at the base camp. Moreover, two of the bands in Tanno's study area combined forces in the hunting season even though their base camps were separate. This observation supports my contention that net hunters tend to form the largest bands because this hunting technique depends on the availability of many participants. The differences observed in the bands studied by Tanno and myself can be explained in functional terms, and the principles governing their composition were similar; none was composed of the random assortment of families and individuals described by Turnbull (1965b).

More precise comparison of the bands studied by Turnbull, Tanno, and myself will be possible only when Tanno's data become available, but it is already apparent that the composition and structure of Mbuti society is not as simple and straightforward as some authors claim. Bands vary in size and composition, according to geography, season, and hunting methods. This flexibility and mobility are probably key adaptations to the Ituri Forest environment, and enable the Mbuti to maintain a high population density in a region where plant and animal resources are widely dispersed, by matching exploitative efficiency with resource availability.

The seasonal patterns of fission and fusion observed by Tanno and myself are illustrated in figure 13.10. From types A, B, and C it is possible to reconstruct earlier patterns that are no longer observable today. I would speculate that the shift from type E to type D was related to colonization of the Ituri area by agriculturalists, whereas the shift from type D to the three contemporary types was related to construction of roads by the Belgian colonial government. According to the local missionaries, the road between Bunia and Mambasa was opened in 1930 and was extended from Bunia to Kisangani by 1934. The agricultural groups that were previously scattered about in the forest soon moved their settlements to this road, and the Mbuti bands associating with these agriculturalists subsequently

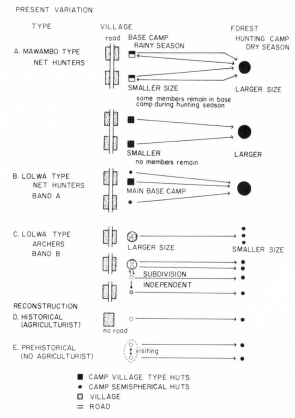

Figure 13.10. Seasonal patterns of fission and fusion in Mbuti bands; with a comparison of observed contemporary patterns and reconstructed historical patterns.

moved their base camps to the vicinity of the villages. The roads in this and other areas of Ituri Forest led to further changes in Mbuti society and subsistence, establishing new patterns of movement and trade. I suspect that the current pattern of nomadic migration from base camp to hunting camps reflects some of the original distributions of villages and band home ranges, but I also heard that some Mbuti bands shifted their home ranges and established new hunting camps when they followed the villagers to roadside settlements. These changes continue at present.

The missionaries in my study area said that the two Mbuti camps at Lolwa village, Bandindulu and Bandilongona, were moved there in 1929 from forest sites about 10 km to the north (marked as campsite b_3 in fig. 13.4). This section of the forest, known as Bekdebekde, serves as an informal boundary between the lands used by the Bila and Lese tribes. Band B, composed of Lese-related Mbuti, once utilized a home range extending northwestward from camp b_4, but now the area between that campsite and the Mambasa–Komanda road is also within their home range. In this case the move to Lolwa village resulted in changes in patterns of home range utilization. That was not the case with band A, composed of Bila-related Mbuti who were associating with Bahaha village before their recent move to Lolwa village. They relocated the base camp without altering the home range, which lies west of the Lolwa River. A footpath from camp a_4 to Bahaha village was still in use when I conducted my work there in 1972–1973. The area utilized by band A is bounded on the west by the home ranges of the Bandipoli and Batumbu bands, both composed of Lolwa-related, Lese-speaking Mbuti.

During prehistoric times, before agriculturalists settled in the Ituri Forest, small Mbuti bands probably moved continuously within their home ranges, not yet using more permanent base camps. Although each band probably had some stability and identity, its composition would change periodically as families and individuals moved about even more freely. Interband relationships were most likely based on such subunit nomadism coupled with seasonal contacts between neighboring bands. The shifting seasons may also have stimulated changes in behavior, such as alternating periods of hunting activity and social festivity.

Some of these prehistoric patterns survived historic change and are now observable in the fission–fusion sequences illustrated in figure 13.10. At present, interband communication and interaction is most intense during the major rainy season even though festivities occur most frequently during the early dry season. Regular interaction in the major rainy season has an economic basis, for it is then that bands move to the vicinity of villages and supplement low meat intake with agricultural produce. In prehistoric times interactions were probably most intense during the early dry season, when bands congregated to celebrate successful kills of large game.

All Mbuti bands exhibit a seasonal fission–fusion cycle, but the timing differs for net hunters and bow hunters (see figs. 13.9 and 13.10). Net hunters aggregate when they move to hunting camps in the dry season, then break up into small camps when they return to their village campsites in the rainy season. Bow hunters form small hunting camps in the dry season and congregate in larger camps near villages during the wet season. This difference is strictly functional, stemming from traditional hunting preferences and specializations in each band. Both cycles reflect current relationships between bands and agriculturalists but are probably rooted in prehistoric patterns of movement established when all Mbuti were archers.

In the Mbuti bands I studied, environmental and social factors combined to regulate seasonal nomadism and fission–fusion cycles. I would postulate that Mbuti movements within the forest are influenced primarily by social parameters linked to hunting traditions, with environmental constraints playing a lesser though important role. These adaptations appear similar to those observed by Radcliffe-Brown (1933) among the Andamanese bands ("local groups") living in forest and coastal areas. There are no radical changes in their habitat, yet the bands are seasonally mobile and hold festivities in the cooler months, from November to March, during which interband contact is frequent. Other band societies, such as the Kalahari Bushmen and the Netsilik Eskimos (Bicchieri, 1972; Lee and DeVore, 1968a, 1976), which live in harsher and seasonally more variable environments, are probably affected more directly by environmental factors that regulate individual, family, and band movements. According to Tanaka (1971, 1976), patterns of band fission–fusion and nomadism in the Central Kalahari are primarily influenced by the seasonal availability of plant resources and water. The northern Kalahari Bushmen studied by Lee (1969) are also restricted by water availability, their movements centering on permanent watering sites. Other examples are discussed by Hayden (in this volume), who compares patterns of band mobility and fluidity among the Mbuti with an array of hunter/gatherer societies.

Reconstructing the Origins of Mbuti Society and Subsistence

In the absence of archaeological evidence from the Ituri region, there is no alternative to ethnographic reconstruction of Mbuti prehistory, but I stress that the following sketch is highly speculative. More substantial data on behavioral and ecological parameters must be obtained in the near future if these speculations are to be refined before radical changes occur in Mbuti society and subsistence habits.

Prehistoric Mbuti bands containing 30–60 individuals, or about 5–15 families, probably subsisted largely on plant foods gathered by women and men and on small and medium-sized game hunted by men equipped with bows and arrows. No information on the introduction of spear hunting is available, and ethnographic data cannot be used to determine whether untipped wooden spears came into use before, at the same time as, or after archery became established. Thus, it is also impossible to determine the extent to which prehistoric bands exploited large-game species.

Each band probably utilized a large home range, including a core hunting area of perhaps 100–200 km^2 into which other bands rarely traveled. It is unlikely that these home ranges were mutually exclusive territories; fringe areas may have been used by neighboring bands in different years, or perhaps even simultaneously. Contact between bands was maintained in much the same manner as today, with some visiting by individuals and families, seasonal relocation of families, pair bonding or marrying members of other bands, seasonal patterns of fission and fusion, and occasional festive aggregation of two or more bands. Hunting was probably emphasized during the dry season, with exploitation of plant resources predominating in the major rainy season, at which time social interaction within and between bands was perhaps most frequent.

When the Sudanic agriculturalists colonized the Ituri region in historic times, the Mbuti developed affiliations with village settlements, probably to gain economic and social benefits. Thus began the cycle of establishing hunting camps in the drier months and returning to village campsites in the wettest months, much as the archer bands do today. When the Sudanic tribes were later displaced by Bantu peoples, the Mbuti developed similar ties with these agriculturalists, setting up trade networks to exchange forest products for agricultural products. Refinements in hunting techniques, especially via the introduction of new technology such as metal spear and arrow points, accompanied these affiliative relationships with agriculturalists. The net hunting technique in particular brought changes to those Mbuti bands that learned to specialize in this method of harvesting game. In contrast to the bow hunters, whose present life-style is perhaps most representative of prehistoric subsistence habits, the net hunters formed large bands of 100 or more individuals to ensure adequate manpower. The shift in size was not absolute, however, for these large bands break up into small subunits during wet months, when the net hunters return to their village campsites.

Still in the midst of change, Mbuti society and subsistence cannot be simply characterized because no single pattern represents all bands living in the Ituri Forest. Indeed, the forest itself is less homogeneous than it might appear to the casual observer of Mbuti gathering and hunting activities. The relationships between Mbuti subsistence habits and specific elements of the Ituri Forest habitat must be further explored if the unique aspects of human adaptation in this swiftly changing region are to be more fully understood.

Acknowledgments

I am grateful to all who assisted me in this field study: Ntika Mkumu, Director General of I.R.S.A.C., who kindly accepted me as a research associate at the Institute and helped with my surveys in Zaire; J. Bokdam of the National University of Zaïre, who identified my plant specimens; Prof. Takagi and Dr. Hamaguchi of Tohoku University, who had worked with I.R.S.A.C. in 1972 and advised me on my first trip to Ituri; J. Itani, director of the expedition, who kindly supported my research program; J. Ikeda, T. Tanno, and all my colleagues at the Laboratory of Physical Anthropology, Kyoto University, whose suggestions and comments were so useful. Thanks are also due to the many friendly people in the Ituri Forest who so kindly accepted my presence there. This research was financed by the Scientific Research Fund of the Ministry of Education, Japan.

NOTES

1. Turnbull and other use the spelling "Bira" while I use "Bila."

2. In Kibila, $\hat{u}$ signifies the intermediate tone of o and u, and dl the intermediate tone of d and l.

3. Judging from the distribution of various tribes of agriculturalists in this region, the area can be characterized as a mixture of Central Sudanic peoples and Equatorial Bantu peoples. In the heart of the Ituri, the Bila (Equatorial Bantu) inhabit the central and southern sections, the Lese (Central Sudanic) inhabit the northeastern section, and the Ndaka (Equatorial Bantu) inhabit the western section. Along the southwestern edge of the forest live the Bali (Equatorial Bantu), north of which are the Budu (Equatorial Bantu). Even farther north are the Mangbetu and Lendu (both Central Sudanic). In the open lands east of Komanda are the Bela, a tribe normally classified with the Bira. I refer to this group as Babela because that name is used by neighboring tribes. To the south of Ituri, the area is settled mainly by the Nande (Bantu) from Butenbo.

4. The Bila tribe can be segmented into four large subtribes: Bakwanza, Bayaku, Babonbi, and Bakaiku.

5. Bahaha is the name of the village lying at the center of the area occupied by the Bakwanza subtribe (see figs. 13.2, 13.4).

6. These semispherical huts are made of braided twigs interwoven with *ngongo* leaves. At base camp a_1, band A huts are small and square, with roofs and walls modeled after villagers' houses. These are referred to as village-type huts. In forest hunting camps, members of band A and band B constructed only semispherical huts.

7. However, sometimes fowl left in their care by villagers range freely about the campsite.

8. Each hunter has his own *ebaka* location, and the Mbuti refer to this technique as "stand on a foothold."

9. I frequently heard that people formerly hunted the hippopotamus with spears, although this is no longer done because the species is very scarce. Villagers would prepare a canoe, and a hunting group would be organized with Mbuti spear hunters as the main constituents.

10. I know of one instance where an elephant was killed by a single spear in August 1973.

11. The average starting time was 8:14 A.M. for male hunters carrying nets. Women start somewhat later.

12. Failure in this case was blamed on the young man who had the bad dream, but dreams are a common reason for not going hunting.

13. I conducted some experiments with laboratory rats in Japan, using poison specimens obtained from the Mbuti, and found that none died quickly.

14. Teleki (1973a,b) has noted a similar phenomenon in chimpanzee predation on baboons.

15. These estimates include all animal products, not just edible matter, so each individual probably consumes much less than 0.54 kg (1.2 lb) of meat.

16. I collected data on five such adult/boy units, as follows: (1) 7, 14, 23*; (2) 8, 21*, 22; (3) 16, 19*, 20; (4) 10, 11°, 18*; (5) 9°, 27°. The asterisk refers to individuals who carry lunches for adults, and the degree mark to individuals who carry their own lunches, always hung around their waists. The name applied to these apprentices, *atanabi na akotû lake* (KBL), means both "to carry the lunch of the man" and "to learn about the forest from the man."

17. Net hunters do have festivals, and these are sometimes akin to religious functions (*molimo* in KBL) performed on days when the men did not go hunting (see Turnbull, 1965a–c, for details). Games such as tug-of-war, plays, and other forms of recreation occurred in these days.

18. There is division of labor in other activities performed by net hunting bands. For example, women build houses, gather firewood and carry burdens, while men collect honey, etc.

19. Biebuyck (1973) reports that the Lega (Equatorial Bantu) still practice net hunting, and my conversation with a Lega informant living in Lolwa Village substantiated this.

20. When I asked for information about how a hunter acquires the status of a true *tûma*, I received the following reply: "Our grandfather, Alungu (individual 1), was a true *tûma*. His successor was his second son, Atoteatai (individual 3). His first son, Atupa (individual 2), was also an excellent hunter but his hunting success was limited. Atoteatai therefore taught his brother's son (individual 6) about the forest, and it was a great honor for him to be named after Atoteatai. When the younger Atoteatai (individual 6) became a *tûma*, the sons of the older Atoteatai (including individual 7 and others) grew up one after another, and the younger Atoteatai helped to train them in spear hunting. When the younger Atoteatai retired from spear hunting, the oldest son (individual 7) of the older Atoteatai was already a *tûma*. Now another son (individual 8) is soon to become a *tûma*. Meanwhile the sons of the younger Atoteatai (individual 6) have grown up enough to carry the lunches of the older Atoteatai's youngest sons (individuals 7 and 8)." Thus, spear hunting skills were passed from male to male in band B, preferably but not always to direct descendants.

21. The core membership of band B was based on paternal relationships, but also included a few relatives on the maternal side (individuals 4 and 29), a man who married into the band (individual 9), the sister of one man's (individual 7) father, and the family of her child. All of these people are described as "Bakba Tata kadli" (KBL), which means that they are descendants of the same grandfather, and refer to one another as brother, sister, parent, and child. The succession of male names in band B illustrates the paternal principle. The names Alungu (individual 1), Atupa (individual 2) and Atoteatai (individual 3) are passed down as follows: Alungu to individuals 7 and 20, Atupa to individual 17, and Atoteatai to individual 6. In addition, the name Abeli went to individuals 11 and 19, and Atowani to individuals 16 and 23. Thus, males are usually named after their grandfathers, uncles, or elder cousins; in no case is a son named after his father. This system is clearly apparent in the membership of band B, although membership in an Mbuti band is not strictly determined by paternal lineage.

22. The fame of this *tûma* spread far beyond band A, for he had not only killed "innumerable" (i.e., 10 or more) elephants but had speared 2 on a single day.

David Webster

14.
Late Pleistocene Extinction and Human Predation: A Critical Overview

Those concerned with the problem of human predation usually emphasize its effects on the evolution and structure of human biology, behavior, and culture. This paper investigates another dimension of the problem: the potential effects of human predation on ecosystems. I am specifically concerned with the controversial question of the role of human predation in Pleistocene extinctions of large vertebrate fauna—what Paul S. Martin (1967) has called "prehistoric overkill." This controversy is a venerable one, beginning over a century ago, by which time sufficient paleontological data had accumulated to indicate a significant reduction of Pleistocene megafauna in late glacial or early postglacial times. My analysis covers recent literature on the overkill problem (for a summary see P. S. Martin and Wright, 1967), with special emphasis on the work of Paul Martin, who is currently the most outspoken proponent of prehistoric overkill as *the* causal mechanism of late Pleistocene extinction (P. S. Martin, 1958, 1966, 1967, 1968, 1973; Mosimann and Martin, 1975).

The overkill issue is one of those scientific controversies fueled by the paucity or ambiguity of relevant data; the amount written on the subject (to which I am uncomfortably aware that I am contributing) is in inverse proportion to the hard evidence. Here I intend to evaluate the way in which this evidence is used as well as to discuss the evidence itself, along with pertinent material from ethnographic observation of modern hunter/gatherers (which has been notably absent in other considerations of the problem). My own biases will become clear in the discussion that follows, but two viewpoints should be stated now. First, I remain skeptical of the general proposition that human predation alone caused the massive extinctions proposed by Martin and others. Second, my perspective is that of an anthropologist and archaeologist rather than an ecologist.

THE OVERKILL HYPOTHESIS

Before we consider the overkill hypothesis in detail, the concepts of "overkill" and "extinction" should be examined. "Overkill" has two

556

possible implications that are not mutually exclusive: human predator populations were so large in proportion to their various prey species that constant predation caused extinction; human predators developed such effective hunting techniques that they were able to kill wastefully—i.e., to destroy many more animals than they required. In either case, predation levels exceeded the reproductive and survival potentials of the prey populations.

"Extinction," in the strict sense, refers to the disappearance of a genus or species with no direct phylogenetic replacement. But the word is loosely used to refer to at least three other phenomena: (1) continent-wide loss of a particular form (e.g., the disappearance of the horse and various camelids from the New World); (2) extensive modifications of geographical range (e.g., horse and reindeer populations are "extinct" in France, which was formerly within their range), and (3) the disappearance of a particular form even though it *may* have left behind a modern descendant (e.g., at least one of the "extinct" Pleistocene bison forms produced *Bison bison*). In the case of continental or hemisphere-wide extinction as referred to in (1) above, the processes involved probably are often very similar in form and magnitude to true extinction processes that eliminate *all* members of a genus or species, so we may reasonably accept this extension of meaning. For (2) and (3) above, the concept should not be applied.

The central and undeniable fact upon which the overkill hypothesis rests is the disappearance of a wide variety of fauna, most conspicuously large herbivores and associated carnivores, during late Pleistocene and early Holocene times (Martin, 1967). Although these episodes were worldwide phenomena, they varied considerably in timing and magnitude. Martin's conception of the major extinction processes is summarized in table 14.1. Note the short duration of various extinction episodes, especially the New World ones, which might be more properly called extinction "events" in evolutionary terms.

Although extinction is a common evolutionary phenomenon, Martin (1958, 1967) identifies what he thinks are unusual characteristics of the late Pleistocene–early Holocene extinction pattern:

1. Particularly heavy loss of large animal genera, especially large herbivores with adult weights of over 50 kg.
2. The narrow chronological span in which extinctions occurred.
3. The phenomenon of removal without replacement, resulting in "empty" ecological niches.
4. The lack of clear-cut evidence for associated drastic environmental changes that could explain disappearance of so many genera, especially since many forms had successfully survived previous multiple glaciations.

Confronted with these apparently unique circumstances, Martin seeks a

Table 14.1. The timing of major faunal extinctions according to Martin

	Years B.P.
Old World continental extinctions	
Africa	40,000–60,000
Northern Eurasia/Europe	11,000–13,000
Southwest and Southeast Asia	?
Australia	ca. 13,000
Insular Extinctions	
West Indies	"mid-postglacial"
New Zealand	ca. 400–900
Madagascar	800
New World continental extinctions	
North America	11,000–12,000
South America	10,000–11,000

Source: Data are from Martin (1967) and Mosimann and Martin (1975).

unique cause, and invokes man the hunter, maintaining that all of the extinction episodes coincided either with the first appearance of human populations (e.g., in Australia, the New World, and several island environments) or with a climax period of hunting efficiency (e.g., in Africa). Martin concludes:

The thought that prehistoric hunters ten to fifteen thousand years ago (and in Africa over forty thousand years ago) exterminated far more large animals than has modern man with modern weapons and advanced technology is certainly provocative and perhaps even deeply disturbing. With a certain inadmissible pride we may prefer to regard ourselves, not our remote predecessors, as holding uncontested claim to being the arch destroyers of native fauna. But this seems not to be the case. Have we dismissed too casually the possibility of prehistoric overkill? The late-Pleistocene extinction pattern leaves little room for any other explanation. (1967:115)

Martin's overkill hypothesis is indeed disturbing. At issue are some fundamental assumptions about human hunting/gathering systems. First, Martin invokes the traditional concept of "man the hunter," the arch-predator who prefers big game to other resources, a concept that has fallen into disrepute recently as a result of ethnographic studies in Africa and elsewhere (Bicchieri, 1972; Lee and DeVore, 1968a). More important is the question of whether human hunter/gatherers behave according to, or are constrained by, the same ecological principles as nonhuman species; specifically, can they be expected to achieve some sort of equilibrium between population and resources, thus avoiding environmental distur-bances that would be disadvantageous? I tend to view hunting/gathering subsistence systems in general as equilibrium systems, while admitting that under unusual circumstances some such systems may experience stresses (e.g., through population growth) that evoke adaptive cultural responses resulting in new equilibrium levels and economic strategies (e.g., the adoption of food production).

In regard to the overkill hypothesis, most anthropologists familiar with the literature on hunter/gatherers would certainly not subscribe to the myth of primitive man as always a natural conservationist who carefully husbands his resources (and especially his faunal resources); the literature contains too many instances to the contrary. Quimby (1960:122), for example, cites a group of Chippewa Indians on the Upper Great Lakes who snared the prodigious quantity of 2,400 moose in the winter of 1670–1671.

It seems undeniable that hunting, and especially the hunting of large animals, frequently results in some level of overkill in the sense that more prey individuals may be taken than are energetically necessary. Various factors that can lead to wastage include:

1. Spoilage of edible meat before it can be consumed or processed for storage.
2. Loss to scavengers.
3. Inability to transport all edible parts of a carcass to the consuming population, or vice versa.
4. Killing strategies that destroy more animals than can possibly be utilized (e.g., mass kills).
5. Game that eludes hunters, even though mortally wounded.
6. Selective utilization only of preferred edible portions of acquired prey.
7. The killing of some animals for by-products, such as hide, bone, or horn, rather than for food.

Even though all these factors promote some degree of overkill in a limited sense, it is expected that levels of predation will normally be low enough to counteract their effects, either because human predator densities are very low, or because several prey species are utilized (as well as plant resources), thus relieving massive pressure on any particular one. Factor 4 is most significant in reference to the overkill argument as propounded by Martin and his supporters.

Several distinct positions have emerged with regard to the causes of late Pleistocene—early Holocene extinctions:

1. Humans, through their hunting activities, were *directly* responsible for the destruction of late Pleistocene fauna—that is, without their presence the animal populations would not have become extinct when they did.
2. Human predation had no significant effect on the prey species; extinction was caused by some natural factor(s) such as environmental change or disease.

3. Ecological stress, probably related to environmental change, reduced animal populations to the point where human predation pushed them over the brink to extinction.
4. *Indirect* effects of human presence, such as the introduction of non-human predator or competitor species (e.g., dogs, rats), or modification of habitats (e.g., through burning or agricultural activities) caused extinction in the absence of natural ecological pressures.
5. Latent effects of selective human predation caused new patterns of intense, destructive competition *among the prey species themselves*, driving some into extinction [see Krantz (1970) for an elaboration of this ingenious argument].

A SURVEY OF AVAILABLE EVIDENCE

Archaeological Evidence

Various sorts of evidence can be used to support or refute the overkill hypothesis. Theoretically, archaeology could contribute two important kinds of evidence. The first is essentially chronological. Martin's argument is based on the assumption that extinction episodes occurred at the same time as initial human occupation of an area, or a climax period of human hunting efficiency. If one could demonstrate that such correlations did not exist, the overkill hypothesis would be very seriously weakened. Considerable evidence now at hand suggests that, in fact, these events are not correlated, and it is reviewed below.

A second kind of evidence, and one much more difficult to acquire, bears on the paleoanthropology of those prehistoric societies presumably involved in the extinction processes. Such evidence is pivotal because even if extinctions are correlated chronologically with human predation, it still must be shown that predatory behavior caused the extinctions. We need more information concerning subsistence resources and strategies, group size, regional population densities, and rates of prehistoric population increase in order to evaluate whether or not destructive levels of predation were achieved and maintained.

For example, an assumption fundamental to the overkill hypothesis is that those human populations responsible for the extinction of the Pleistocene fauna were "big-game hunters," in the literal sense that they were primarily dependent on megafauna [i.e., animals with adult body weight over 50 kg (Martin, 1967:77)] for most, or all, of their energetic requirements. This assumption is unsupported. In North America, late Pleistocene cultural material is unquestionably associated with only a few extinct forms, particularly mammoth and bison, although it is circumstantially associated with a number of others. Most sites are special-purpose kill or butchering sites. Our sample is thus biased toward specific functional types of sites which are relatively easy to find, and in which remains of megafauna are probably overrepresented, besides being more obvious and more durable than the remains of small fauna or plant resources.

Ethnographic Evidence

The implications of ethnographic studies of hunter/gatherers are, in my opinion, crucial to the investigation of the overkill hypothesis, but unfortunately have not been systematically applied to the issue. This seems largely a result of a deep distrust of the facile and simplistic use of ethnographic analogy by some authors. Since I refer below to ethnographic data, my own position regarding ethnographic analogy should be made clear. There is no question that traditional use of ethnographic analogy has often been uncritical, unconvincing, and unproductive. The reasons seem clear, and usually concern the lack of a strong theoretical framework to structure, select, and validate the analogies themselves. Given such a theoretical framework, it is possible to generate, and to defend, what I call "systemic analogies"—i.e., analogies that are productive because they are validated and constrained by theoretical principles which should be universally operable. Such "analogies" can properly be viewed as systemic isomorphisms.

Suppose, for example, that one wishes to demonstrate that prehistoric hunter/gatherers had low overall population densities, under $2/km^2$. One could argue this point by simple analogy; for instance, a large sample of ethnographically observed hunter/gatherers (Australian Aborigines, Bushmen, Eskimo, etc.) characteristically have low densities, and hence this must have been true in the past. Now these observations *themselves*, however numerous, are insufficient reasons for accepting the validity of the analogy, and hence the proposition about prehistoric densities. But if we take the next step and specify that observed hunter/gatherers possess low population densities because there are natural, ecological constraints upon their resource bases, then we are setting up a convincing systemic isomorphism which validates theoretically the conceptual linkage between the behavior of past and present systems. In this specific case it could be convincingly demonstrated that prehistoric hunter/gatherers had low population densities, *even if* we possessed no ethnographic analogues at all, by reasoning from ecological principles and environmental data alone. It is in the framework of proposed systemic isomorphisms that I shall later relate ethnographic information to the question of prehistoric overkill.

Ecological and Paleo-ecological Evidence

Much of the evidence bearing on the overkill controversy falls into this category and includes recovery of distributional and chronological information on extinct forms, delimitation of their ecological requirements, and reconstruction of prehistoric environments and processes of environmental change. As we shall see, the present state of this category of evidence, which is theoretically capable of resolving the overkill question, is inadequate, in that it stimulates a variety of interpretations (often divergent) without substantiating any of them. Before we evaluate this evidence, it is only fair to Martin to note that much of his early work on Pleistocene extinctions predates a good deal of the pertinent evidence discussed here. His tendency in recent work, however (e.g., Mosimann and Martin, 1975), has been to ignore or dismiss recently published pertinent data (e.g., studies on hunter/gatherer ecology or new Paleoindian discoveries in the New World) while holding strongly to his earlier views.

PATTERNS OF GLOBAL EXTINCTION

Martin has discussed worldwide extinction episodes in an attempt to demonstrate that this overall patterning is consistent with his hypothesis of human overkill. Before a detailed examination of the New World evidence, these global patterns must be briefly evaluated.

Old World Continental Extinctions

Africa, where Martin assumes the human species had its origins, has always been a weak point in the overkill hypothesis because of the absence of terminal Pleistocene or Holocene extinctions. Noting, however, that the number of genera has declined by about 30% from mid-Pleistocene times, Martin offers the following explanation: "Extinction in Africa seems to coincide with the maximum development of the most advanced early Stone Age hunting cultures, the evolved Acheulian, of abundant, continent-wide distribution" (1967:110). In other words, Martin (1966, 1967) identifies a significant wave of African extinctions dating to approximately 60,000–40,000 B.P., and relates them to a new threshold of hunting efficiency.

The validity of this interpretation is questionable. On the one hand, there is convincing evidence that, in technological terms, the evolved Acheulean traditions were more advanced than their predecessors in sub-Saharan Africa (J. Clark, 1970:108). Specifically, stone tools were more varied and specialized, and stone-working techniques more sophisticated. Specialized toolkits reflect increasingly distinctive and widespread regional adaptations, coincident with larger populations. On the other hand, there is no indication of any technological innovation that would have revolutionized hunting efficiency; in fact, potentially revolutionary innovations such as hafting seem to be related to numerous technological changes of the so-called African Middle Stone Age, after ca. 35,000 B.P.

One reasonable response to this criticism would be that hunting efficiency is as much a function of behavioral or organizational capabilities as technological ones. Unfortunately for Martin's chronology, however, archaeological evidence suggests that the capability of undertaking successful big-game hunts, and perhaps even mass hunts, seems to have emerged much earlier in human societies. It appears to have been present, for example, at Torralba and Ambrona, European Acheulean sites several hundred thousand years older than those of the evolved African Acheulean (F. C. Howell, 1966). So far as I know, available faunal inventories from African sites are too little known to document increased dependence on big-game hunting or intensive predation involving extinct forms for the period from 60,000 to 40,000 B.P.

Complicating the picture is evidence for continent-wide climatic changes near the beginning of the last glacial period (ca. 60,000 B.P.) which undoubtedly affected, in ways still poorly understood, both floral and faunal populations (J. Clark, 1970:105–7). That such climatic shifts could have had important ecological effects is demonstrated by the deterioration of a highly productive Saharan environment at the *end* of the Pleistocene, as documented by Axelrod (1967).

Even assuming that the African Acheulean did include the rise of sophisticated hunting cultures, a serious problem is the paucity of subsequent extinctions. Since there were very few (Martin, 1967:110), it could only be argued that hunting techniques declined in effectiveness (which seems highly unlikely), that subsistence patterns radically shifted away from dependence on big-game hunting (also highly unlikely if large herbivores were still abundant, and efficient means of taking them still available), or that the surviving species were somehow particularly resistant to the effects of human predation. In fact, the modern African fauna has proved surprisingly durable in historical times, even under intense pressure from expanding agriculturalists and pastoralists as well as European hunters.

Presumably southern Asia would have been the next global zone to suffer extinction, but this immense region is poorly known, both in archaeological and paleontological terms.

Subsequent extinction episodes occur, in Martin's scheme, very rapidly and roughly synchronously. The immense region of northern Eurasia has spotty archaeological and paleontological coverage. Only the European data are complete enough to discuss here, and Europe, like Africa, poses some knotty problems for the overkill hypothesis.

To begin with, there is the matter of progressive extinctions throughout the Pleistocene, which makes it difficult to isolate a clear extinction "event" (although Martin identifies one between about 13,000 and 11,000 B.P.). Guilday (1967:136) points out that, of the large mammal genera that were lost, fully 50% died out in the Günz glaciation and 25% in the Riss-Würm; and of the 32 genera which still existed in Europe during the late

Pleistocene, only three, or 9% (some would count four or five genera), became extinct. Yet it was precisely during this latter period that, according to excellent archaeological evidence, the advanced hunting cultures flourished, some of them highly specialized in terms of prey species, with remarkably dense populations. Butzer (1964:393) speculates that there may have been a 10-fold increase in population between middle and late Würm times in western Europe. Such dramatic demographic growth must have been related to increasingly efficient techniques of mass hunting, which are archaeologically well attested.

Kowalski has remarked on the peculiar pattern of European extinctions:

Reindeer, red deer, aurochs, wild horses—all extensively hunted—were able to survive, whereas some mammals, which were probably more difficult for primitive man to kill (mammoth, woolly rhinoceros, cave bear) or were of no interest to him (lion, hyena), became extinct. (1967:349–50)

He concludes that the cause of this extinction was "the disappearance of the specific habitat represented by the 'steppe-tundra' of the Pleistocene" (1967:350). Butzer maintains that tundra conditions "spasmodically deteriorated during a 4000 year interval, from the beginning of the Bölling to the close of the Pre-Boreal" (1964:410). He supports Kowalski in observing that the extinction of the steppe-tundra forms was probably a result of ecological change. Reed concurs (1970:284) and notes that the rapid disappearance of the steppe-tundra forms coincides with the warm Alleröd interval (ca. 13,500/12,500–10,800/10,150 B.P.). In the Soviet Union, large late-Pleistocene accumulations of mammal bone occur without cultural association, reinforcing the contention that local populations were experiencing high levels of mortality from natural causes (Vereschagin, 1967:373).

The reindeer and the horse, the two economically most important species for the advanced hunting cultures of western and central Europe, escaped extinction. Both species did experience marked changes in range, with the reindeer withdrawing to the north and the horse to the east—both consistent with the replacement of the European steppe-tundra by forest. At this point, advocates of the overkill hypothesis might well ask why species such as the mammoth could not have escaped extinction, as the reindeer did, simply by migrating north. The answer may be that the present high-latitude tundra of northern Europe differs significantly in important niche components (e.g., seasonality, length of day) from the Pleistocene low-latitude steppe-tundra. Perhaps the reindeer was the only animal capable of making the adjustment. But here we are speculating about the ethology of prehistoric fauna, a hazardous undertaking at best.

Important extinction episodes also affected Australia, one of the last continental land-masses to be colonized by human hunter/gatherers. As is discussed later, Martin accepts Birdsell's (1957) model of rapid expansion of frontier populations, and feels that rapid colonization of what was, in human terms, an open niche, led to destruction of some native fauna at about 12,000 B.P.

An assumption of this argument is that human colonization of Australia was a process of the terminal Pleistocene (Martin, 1967:105–7). More recent archaeological evidence indicates a far greater antiquity for aboriginal Australians than Martin would allow. Gould (1973:8) notes that the earliest well-dated skeletal remains date to 25,500 ± 1,000 B.P. and Tindale (1972:239) would put the initial penetration of the continent back to 40,000–30,000 B.P. Tindale's estimate is supported by radiocarbon dates from New South Wales, indicating human occupation at 31,000 B.C. (Gillespie et al., 1978:1044). There is, then, no correspondence between initial waves of colonization and extinction, if we accept Martin's chronology for the latter.

R. Jones (1968) has reviewed the evidence for the disappearance, in late-glacial times, of an impressive number of large Australian marsupials and concludes that the chronology of these extinctions is poorly documented. However, he notes that "when fauna is found in archaeological sites spanning the last 20,000 years it is modern" (1968:203). He is unable to demonstrate a single clear case of association between extinct fauna and early man in Australia. Nevertheless, Jones remains open-minded with regard to the causes of extinction, and does not rule out the possibility that human populations caused extensive environmental disturbances, particularly through the use of fire. Gould (1973:5) notes that although about 33% of the marsupial megafauna died off in the late Pleistocene, there is no convincing evidence that early Aborigine populations were heavily dependent on big game. Nor were there any obvious improvements in the rather rudimentary Australian technology which would have made hunting more efficient and destructive. Recent faunal studies (Gillespie et al., 1978) indicate that early Australian human populations and elements of the now-extinct Australian megafauna coexisted for some 7,000 years.

Insular Extinctions

Martin has extended the overkill hypothesis to three highly restricted extinction episodes which seem undeniably related to human presence in the island habitats of New Zealand, Madagascar, and the West Indies. Human colonization of these islands was quite late, and in each case distinctive elements of the native fauna disappeared. New Zealand was inhabited by many species of large, flightless birds (moas) that apparently proved ideal prey for early hunters, beginning at or slightly before 1,000 A.D. Their remains are conspicuous in midden deposits for about five centuries, at which point the last survivors were killed (Martin, 1967:104).

A similar late penetration of Madagascar exposed a vulnerable fauna, of which seven genera of lemurs, two species of tortoises, one species of pygmy hippopotamus, and two species of flightless birds disappeared (Martin, 1967:111). In the West Indies the casualties included a tortoise and several small mammals, birds, and lizards (Martin, 1967:109).

These examples of insular extinction are obviously advanced to add plausibility to the thesis of primitive man as destroyer, and in these instances Martin is almost certainly correct. But the fact that some populations were able to kill off lumbering, flightless birds in New Zealand or Madagascar scarcely validates the contention that other human hunters were capable of eliminating Pleistocene megafauna from the grasslands and forests of North America. In fact, some of the New Zealand extinctions coincide with the spread of agricultural economies. The environmental disturbances and high-density populations of agriculturalists clearly may produce stresses on fauna of a completely different degree than those produced by hunter/gatherer bands. Moreover, as Krantz cogently notes, "only agriculturalists can eliminate, with reasonable impunity, important elements of the natural ecosystems, since they have their own artificial ecosystems to fall back on" (1970:169).

For the Old World, then, the overkill argument remains unconvincing, and for insular environments it is applicable only in highly particular ways. Extinctions were widespread in time, space, and magnitude, and do not coincide well either with initial waves of human colonization or with climax periods of high population density and hunting efficiency. Moreover, some extinction events, such as those in Europe, seem clearly associated with rapid environmental changes that provide much more suitable explanations for megafaunal extinctions.

New World Continental Extinctions

Martin is on his most defensible ground in the New World, and especially in North America. Two recent elaborations of the overkill hypothesis (Martin, 1973; Mosimann and Martin, 1975) have considered only the New World evidence. In North America a good case can be made for spectacular megafaunal extinctions at the end of the Pleistocene (ca. 12,000–10,000 B.P.). The magnitude of late Pleistocene North American extinctions, in terms of megafaunal genera lost, varies somewhat according to the counts of individual authors and is a product of different taxonomic schemes, chronological interpretations, and definitions of extinction. Reed (1970:284) lists 24 genera, while Martin lists 31 genera of herbivores alone (1967:77). Axelrod (1967) counts 30 genera, but 6 of these survived in the Old World. No matter whose figures are accepted, however, it is apparent that a greater variety of fauna disappeared than in Europe or Australia. Note that these figures indicate a very high level of megafaunal diversity for

North America—comparable, for example, to that found in herbivore ecosystems in a modern East African savannah habitat. If all of these animals did indeed coexist chronologically, the level of generic diversity reflects the continent-wide environmental diversity typical of an area the size of North America, and therefore the range of habitats to which early human populations would have had to adapt to be responsible for widespread extinction.

Extinction characterizes the entire North American Pleistocene as well as the late Pliocene. "As now known, the fossil record indicates that 18% of the genera of large mammals recorded from North America did not survive the late Pliocene; approximately 23% made their last appearance in late Blancan time (early Kansan); 18% in Rancho La Brean time; and 30% in postglacial time" (Axelrod, 1967:2).

Martin (1967:77–78) points out what he feels are a number of distinctive features concerning the rash of extinctions (at ca. 12,000–11,000 B.P.) at the end of the North American Pleistocene, in addition to its surprising magnitude. First, differential extinction occurred: all the mammals known to be involved were large herbivores (except for two carnivores—both sabertooths—and one omnivore—a bear). Second, the extinctions involved loss *without replacement;* that is, vacant ecological niches were not filled by other or new species, as would normally be the case. Third, the time range postulated for extinctions is narrow (see table 14.1). Finally, most of the animals involved had already successfully survived the stress of multiple climatic changes associated with previous glaciations. The only event that can satisfactorily resolve these puzzling features is, according to Martin, the appearance of human hunting cultures in a wave of explosive colonization at the very end of the Wisconsin glacial period (Martin, 1973; Mosimann and Martin, 1975).

CRITICAL EVALUATION OF
THE HYPOTHESIS

Let us examine the validity of these "unusual" characteristics of the late Pleistocene New World extinction process, granting their surprising magnitude.

Chronology

Martin (1958) originally proposed 8,000 B.P. as a reasonable estimate (on the basis of existing carbon-14 dates) for the end of the spectacular wave of North American extinctions. He did allow that some species probably lingered on in favorable refuge areas long after this time, particularly in the southeast. Hester (1960), in a review of available carbon-14 dates, came to much the same conclusion. Since these early estimates, many more dates (and more reliable ones) have accumulated, and Martin (1967) has pushed back his terminal extinction date to ca. 11,000 B.P. He does this by discounting late dates, such as those associated with mastodon in the southeastern United States, on the basis that most of them were derived from bone samples susceptible to contamination that makes them appear younger, and that some mastodon dates are incompatible with associated palynological data (Martin, 1967:96–98). This chronological readjustment makes Pleistocene extinction appear to be an abrupt event that coincided with the florescence of the first *well-documented*, widespread hunter/gatherer cultures of North America, a picture which is more consistent with the overkill hypothesis than with an extended extinction process.

Another consideration in this chronological realignment was, I would guess, the uncomfortable proximity of the 8,000 B.P. date to the beginning of the Altithermal, a period of about 7500–4500 B.P. when worldwide temperatures were somewhat higher than today (Antevs, 1955; Baumhoff and Heizer, 1965; Bryan and Gruhn, 1964). Although Antevs' original concept of the Altithermal as a period of widespread increased warmth and dryness in North America was oversimplified, a variety of regional climatic changes associated with generally higher temperatures do seem likely and could be adduced as a cause of extinctions during the early-to-middle Holocene, long after the arrival of the first human population.

To support his chronology, Martin has assembled a list of 85 dates for now-extinct megafauna in North America for late Wisconsin times (1967:90–94). After elimination of those he considers questionable, the rest average out nicely to the hypothetical terminal stages of the extinction event at ca. 11,000 B.P. Guilday (1967) has emphasized, however, that factors of preservation, deposition, and research orientation have produced a chronological sample that is not representative of the actual extinction processes. Dated fossil finds usually come from archaeological sites or from late- or post-Wisconsin bog or cave deposits providing unusually good environments for preservation. "As a result we have a relatively rich fauna from a limited horizon, with two sharply artificial cutoff points associated with the appearance and disappearance of the Paleoindian hunting tradition" (Guilday, 1967:135). The validity of this criticism is borne out by Martin's own list of dates. Out of 85 dates, only 3 fall into the time range of 20,000–15,000 B.P. This is well before extinction is supposed to have taken place, and the remains of Pleistocene fauna should be abundant. And in fact, Mosimann and Martin's most recent argument (1975:312–13) substantiates Guilday's claim, for they insist that animals dying of natural (i.e., nonhuman) causes in the millennia before the extinction episode would contribute immeasurably more recoverable remains than those deposited during the short extinction episode.

Wilkinson (1973) has pointed out that although we have a rough idea of the *terminal* dates for widespread extinction, we know almost nothing about the chronological onset of massive, late Pleistocene extinction, which is essential for any understanding of it. His own evaluation of the available data suggests that extinctions began well before 20,000 B.P., indicating long-term patterns of extinction incompatible with the overkill scenario.

Another problem is the general paucity of dates. Martin (1967:89) admits that "the majority of extinct late-Pleistocene genera and species have not been critically dated by radiocarbon." It is obviously somewhat risky to generalize about the disappearance of 30 genera when we have data on only 12.

Extinction and Vacant Niches

Perhaps because I am not an ecologist, I find Martin's concept of extinction without replacement, in the sense of "empty" ecological niches, somewhat baffling. As an abstract concept, "ecological niche" refers to a set of biological, physical, and chemical parameters (e.g., temperature, topography, nutrients) affecting an organism in a given habitat (Boughey, 1968:81–87). The concept is thus essentially a structural/functional description of the manner in which an organism survives under a particular set of environmental conditions. Normally, when extinction occurs, it is assumed that some essential component(s) of the niche disappear, or that one organism or population succeeds in replacing another by direct or indirect competition for those essential components which are in short supply.

The "existence" of an ecological niche may be clearly demonstrated under two sets of conditions. First, if a population is present in or successfully colonizes a given habitat, it is axiomatic that the population occupies a niche. In this application the niche concept betrays its most serious weakness—its essentially tautological overtones. Second, if all of the niche parameters of a given population are known, an ecological niche suitable for colonization may reasonably be said to exist in another habitat, *provided* that all the requisite niche components can be shown to be present in that habitat.

In the case of extinct Pleistocene megafauna, we possess only the most rudimentary and general information about the niche requirements of the various genera, the nature of their habitats, and the details of environmental change that occurred at the end of the Pleistocene. To conclude, in the absence of such information, that niches for the extinct forms still exist seems to me to be logically unwarranted.

A counterargument might be advanced along the following lines. Horses were widespread in the New World some 12,000 years ago, and subsequently became extinct there. The species was successfully reintroduced in the sixteenth century by European colonists, and feral populations quickly proliferated. Therefore the niche for horses was obviously present, but vacant, between the end of the Pleistocene and the time of reintroduction by Europeans. Such reasoning is incomplete, however, since one still must show that the niche requirements of ancient and modern horses are essentially similar, and that appropriate habitat conditions existed *continuously* throughout the time horses were absent.

What seems to have impressed Martin is the impoverishment of the modern American megafauna (in terms of its diversity) in comparison with its Pleistocene antecedents, and the presence, especially in the arid West and Southwest, of ubiquitous plant communities that are avoided by the existing native (and domestic) fauna as energy sources (Martin, 1968). Neither, in my opinion, justifies the "empty niche" contention.

In any case, the chronological perspective of the past 10,000 years is too short to draw any conclusions about empty niches and the lack of megafaunal diversity. Given the normal evolutionary perspective of hundreds of thousands or even millions of years, the diversity of the native fauna might well increase; lowered species diversity might be expected after any major set of extinctions, no matter why they happened.

Selective Extinction

A cornerstone of the overkill hypothesis is the apparent extinction of herbivore megafauna while smaller mammalian and nonmammalian fauna were relatively unaffected in the New World. The crucial questions concerning selective extinction are whether it does exist and, if so, whether factors other than human predation could have caused it.

With regard to the first question, I cannot evaluate the present state of comparative paleontological studies of American fauna. There is suggestive evidence, however, that small fauna may also have suffered unusual stresses at the end of the Pleistocene. After a recent study of Pleistocene bird extinction, Grayson (1977) concluded that although ·extinctions increased throughout the Pleistocene, fully 45% of the missing avian genera disappeared between about 13,000 and 10,000 B.P. Of the progressive mammalian extinctions that occurred throughout the Pleistocene, about that same percentage falls at the very end of the epoch. This evidence indicates stresses other than human predation.

Wilkinson (1973) maintains that the taxa on which extinction studies usually focus (genera, species) may have different adaptive significance where small mammals are concerned, and cites evidence suggesting that small mammals (under 50-kg adult body weight) were affected at the same time as megafauna, but suffered only distributional changes and extinction of local populations. Axelrod (1967), among others, proposed that small mammals may possess adaptive buffers against rapid environmental changes, and that differential extinction could thus occur in the absence of human predation. At the very least it would seem prudent to suspend judgment about the existence and implications of selective extinction until more extensive and reliable paleontological data are obtained.

Human Colonization of the New World

Another critical problem for the overkill hypothesis involves the timing of human colonization of the New World. Although a northeastern Asian origin for the earliest New World colonists is almost universally accepted by American archaeologists, there are conflicting views about the chronology of colonization. These positions can be labeled the *late entry hypothesis* and the *early entry hypothesis.* The former is the more traditional, and its proponents hold that rapid population movements colonized the New World at the very end of the last (Wisconsin) glacial period. Acceptance of this idea is crucial to the overkill argument and is vigorously defended by its supporters (Martin, 1967; Mosimann and Martin, 1975) for several reasons.

Granting for the moment that Martin's extinction chronology is correct, the assumption of a late, massive, rapid colonization juxtaposes, chronologically, two unique "events"—the late Pleistocene extinctions and the appearance of humans, the new super-predators. It also supports the contentions that early human populations were technologically sophisticated in terms of hunting abilities, that they retained a supposed Arctic or Subarctic emphasis on big game as the prime subsistence resource as they colonized temperate and tropical zones, and, most importantly, that the New World fauna was suddenly exposed to an unfamiliar predator species, to whose behavior patterns many prey species could not adapt quickly enough to avoid extinction. Such populations are represented archaeologically by the first well-known cultural horizon in North America—the Llano and Llano-related "cultures," dating to about 12,000–10,000 B.P.

Alternatively, the early entry hypothesis postulates a much earlier *initial* colonization (while not ruling out later, additional ones). Until fairly recently, this has been the minority position. Its initial appeal lay in its ability to connect several loose ends of evidence which the late entry hypothesis leaves dangling. First, the highly distinctive fluted point technology which characterizes the (supposedly) intrusive Llano horizon has no obvious close prototypes in northeastern Asia, its supposed area of origin. Second, not all material on the Llano *chronological horizon* can be forced into the Llano technological tradition (especially in the eastern United States); at this early stage there was already considerable cultural diversity that is difficult to explain given the assumption of a late, explosive radiation of human populations into North America. Cultural (and probably physical) diversity was well developed over the entire New World by about 9,000 B.P. (MacNeish, 1976), and the emergence of regional cultures with highly specialized adaptations is most explicable given a long, rather than short, time perspective. Third, numerous problematical sites in North and South America have produced artifact assemblages characterized by rough core or flake tools, which lack projectile points; such sites, with their crude technologies and (sometimes) associated early dates, provided the stimulus for identification of a "pre-projectile point horizon" predating the Llano horizon (Krieger, 1964).

Most of the evidence for the early entry hypothesis is circumstantial. The sites, taken one at a time, present problems: artifact samples are small, stratigraphy is absent or confused, associations between dated material and obvious cultural remains are uncertain. Nevertheless, the combined weight of the circumstantial evidence, when all sites are taken into consideration, is compelling and has convinced many, including myself, of the validity of the early entry hypothesis (for general reviews, see Bryan, 1969; MacNeish, 1976; Wilkinson, 1973).

Additional evidence for the existence of an early, pre-projectile point horizon has come from highland Peru. MacNeish has produced a long stratigraphic sequence from two sites in the Ayacucho Valley which indicates a surprisingly long history of occupation (MacNeish, 1971; MacNeish, Nelker-Turner, and Cook, 1970). Although, like many archaeologists, I am skeptical of the validity of the earliest cultural components identified by MacNeish, which date before 16,000 B.P., I feel that stratigraphic, technological, and radiocarbon evidence from his sites clearly indicates human presence as early as 15,000–10,000 B.P. (the Ayacucho Complex material). Supporting data are also available from Guitarrero Cave, also in the Peruvian highlands, where early cultural levels date between 11,000 and 10,000 B.C. (Lynch and Kennedy, 1970). More recently, associations of human cultural material and a butchered mastodon from the site of Taima-Taima, Venezuela, have been dated to *at least* 13,000 B.P. (11,000 B.C.), leading the excavators to conclude that "the Martin model of the earliest peopling of the New World is thereby refuted by field evidence" (Bryan et al., 1978:1277).

If early human populations were already exploiting South American environments by ca. 13,000–11,000 B.C., how much earlier was the initial colonization of North America? Two sets of factors bear on this question, the first being cultural/demographic and the second involving opportunity. One view—and this is Martin's own—stresses an enormous capacity for explosive demographic increases and rapid cultural adaptation of New World colonists. Granting this assumption for the sake of argument, initial penetration of North American could have occurred only a short time earlier—say about 20,000 B.P. or even later. But considerably more time is necessary if one doubts these assumptions, which brings us to the question of opportunity.

Assuming a northeastern Asian area of origin and a terrestrial migration route into the New World across the Bering Straits, two considerations affect the colonization of continental North America. The first concerns the timing of the emergence of the Bering Straits land connection during the Wisconsin glacial period. Pleistocene geologists do not agree on this issue, but for our purposes it is sufficient to note that two periods of emergence seem highly probable: an early one at ca. 50,000–40,000 B.P., and a late one at ca. 28,000–10,000 B.P. (Müller-Beck, 1966). Access to unglaciated portions of Alaska would potentially have been available at some time during either period.

Now we are faced with an important but as yet unresolved problem— whether or not there was an ice-free Canadian corridor allowing further migrations south during times of glacial maxima (i.e., when the land bridge was exposed). If, as Bryan has argued (1969), there was a late Pleistocene ice barrier during the Wisconsin glacial maximum which blocked human access to the south, then an initial entry of human populations into Alaska during the *earlier* period of emergence would seem most plausible. This interpretation is apparently favored by MacNeish, although there is wide disagreement concerning the ice-barrier question. It can only be said that initial colonization of North America *could* have been as early as 50,000–40,000 B.P., but was almost certainly well under way by about 20,000 B.P.

The point I want to stress here is that either interpretation is virtually lethal to the overkill argument as presented by Martin because, even if we use his own extinction chronology, human predator populations were present long before the proposed extinction "event" at ca. 12,000–11,000 B.P. This undercuts his contention that the North American fauna was suddenly confronted with a new super-predator against whom it had no innate defenses (which has always seemed to me to grossly underrate the intelligence and behavioral flexibility of the resident fauna), and that the early human populations were the immediate heirs of an Arctic or Subarctic tradition in which big game was the preferred subsistence resource, there having been insufficient time to adopt a more broad-spectrum subsistence strategy.

Martin, expectably, has firmly rejected such an early occupation, recognizing that it tends to demolish his argument (Martin, 1973; Mosimann and Martin, 1975). He could of course argue, even in the face of early colonization, that extinctions might not have been possible for some time, given the poorly developed technological skills of the earliest human colonists of North America. But his own scenario for African extinctions, in which evolved Acheulean populations are the supposed culprits, effectively seals off this approach to a solution. However crude the technologies of the first New World immigrants, it is unlikely that they were less effective than the African ones of 60,000–40,000 B.P. Consequently his defense is the extreme one of simply dismissing the early-entry data entirely.

Martin's approach (1973:973) is not to refute the existing evidence (especially MacNeish's) by detailed examination but to assert, in effect, that objective interpretation of the archaeological data is rendered difficult or impossible because of the biases of the excavators, who find what they want to find. This rationale could be applied to virtually any of the sciences, and someone familiar with the palynological and paleontological literature could, if uncharitably inclined, apply it equally easily to Martin's own work. He further asserts that all sites should be regarded as suspect until excavations are replicated (i.e., sites are reexcavated), which he should know is often impossible because of their small size. Moreover, this polemic against archaeology is double-edged, since it could be used to criticize most of the sites which he himself cites to bolster his overkill hypothesis.

SIMULATIONS OF PLEISTOCENE OVERKILL

In an attempt to make the overkill argument more rigorous, Martin (1973) proposed a preliminary simulation model of the process, which has recently been elaborated by Mosimann and Martin (1975). I shall restrict my comments to the latter.

As Mosimann and Martin quite correctly observe (1975:313), simulations do not constitute proof of a hypothetical process. Rather, their purpose is to indicate whether a certain result is plausible, given a set of specific components (demographic factors, predation/consumption rates, patterns of dispersal of populations, etc.) that can be assigned certain values or ranges of values. The plausibility of the outcome is, of course, contingent on, first, selection of the proper components for the model and, second, assignment of values which either are known to be or are reasonably likely to be correct.

In part, a simulation model is a methodological device to suggest alternative *testable* hypotheses. As used by Mosimann and Martin, however, it seems to be an end in itself, since they present elaborate arguments that the hypothetical extinction/overkill event is "invisible" and will always remain so in terms of hard evidence. For example, acceptance of the overkill scenario implies logically that human predator populations were very large, thus placing undue stress on prey, and/or that efficient means of killing were available. It follows logically that the appropriate segment of the archaeological record should provide evidence for dense human populations and/or extremely high predation rates for the extinct fauna (e.g., mass kills). In fact it does not. Undaunted by this negative evidence, Martin and Mosimann assert that neither kind of evidence is recoverable.

Rather than offering a simulation of my own, I would like to examine the values Mosimann and Martin attach to the components of their simulation, many of which I feel are unreasonable. It is at this point that ethnographic data can be fruitfully integrated into the argument.

Chronological Variables

The two basic chronological components of Martin's hypothesis are the timing of the extinction event, assumed to fall between 12,000 and 11,000 B.P., and the initial penetration of the New World by the first human migrants around 12,000 B.P. The first component is based on insufficient data, and may have been of much longer duration; the second ignores additional evidence for a much greater antiquity for human populations in the New World.

Geographical Variables

The most important geographical variable in the Mosimann-Martin model is that of the moving "front." This concept [borrowed from ecological models of the expansion of animal populations into open environments (see Mosimann and Martin, 1975:306)] involves the sweep of a continuous wave of a rapidly expanding population, with highest densities and rates of increase concentrated along the advancing front itself, where there is sustained possibility for population spin-offs. While the front has a geographic dimension, it is also density-dependent; that is, if densities do not reach certain critical values, no front is formed (Mosimann and Martin, 1975:311). The advance of the front proceeds as local game populations are exhausted. In the Mosimann-Martin simulation not only are animal populations on the front eradicated, but because of the *continuous* nature of the front there are no refuge areas left behind the sweep or any leakage through it. Thus the total environment available for animal exploitation is continually reduced in size as the front advances.

One obvious weakness in this concept is its blatant artificiality and its oversimplification of the patterns of population expansion into a vast expanse of vacant habitats. Even if rates of human population growth and density increase were sufficient to form such a front, humans would obviously not distribute their movements continuously over the varied landscapes of a continent. These movements would instead be unevenly channeled by optimal environmental characteristics such as resource and shelter availability, and ease of movement. Many areas marginal to human survival would be neglected or avoided. Such selective patterns of movement would not generate the enormous predation pressure along a hypothetical front, and extinction of fauna would no longer be plausible. Any realistic simulation would involve a discontinuous expansion pattern, which could be modeled statistically even if it proved impossible to assess reasonable migration routes through terminal Pleistocene environments.

Subsistence Variables

A fundamental part of the overkill argument, as applied to the New World and especially to the simulation of North American data, is the assumption that early human colonists placed extraordinarily severe pressure on the indigenous herbivorous megafauna. This pressure has been linked to several factors. One is that the earliest migrants emerged from an Arctic or Subarctic cultural tradition that relied largely, perhaps even exclusively, on large vertebrate fauna as energy sources. A corollary is that a classic "big-game hunting strategy" obtained until larger fauna disappeared. Another is that a very high rate of predation resulted from extremely dense predator populations being concentrated along a rapidly expanding, continuous, and impermeable front. A third is the claim that hunting groups expanding into a frontier previously devoid of human populations encountered prey populations with no adequate behavioral defenses, rendering them exceedingly vulnerable to extinction under new conditions of efficient predation.

The notion that hunter/gatherers emphasize hunting over all other subsistence activities has recently been called into question (Bicchieri, 1972; Lee and DeVore, 1968a). Primarily as a result of modern ethnographic studies, many have adopted the counterposition that, for hunter/gatherer economics in general, energy derived from large fauna is subordinate to other energy sources, particularly plant foods.

After reviewing some of the pertinent literature, I think that some of these new conclusions are questionable. One serious problem is sampling. Lee, for example, actually measured !Kung Bushman intake for a period of one month (during a year which was unusually dry) and it is from this possibly nonrepresentative sample that he determined that only about 30% of caloric intake was derived from hunting (Lee, 1968). Silberbauer (1972; in this volume) conducted more extensive sampling but noted the difficulty of monitoring the details of day-to-day food intake. Assuming that sampling in studies such as these is representative, the results must be interpreted with care. For example Silberbauer (1972) found that the Central Kalahari G/wi, who apparently have more large prey at their disposal than the !Kung, also rely heavily on plant foods although they lack a plant resource as productive as the mongongo nut. According to Silberbauer, the dry-season plant intake (6–8 lb. per capita per day) functions in large part to supply required liquids in an environment singularly lacking in water sources. Thus the G/wi and !Kung diets do resemble one another in that both are heavily dependent (at least during some seasons of the year) on plant food, but this dependence seems very differently motivated. The G/wi presumably have no choice in the consumption of calories in the form of plant food, since this is unavoidably associated with water intake. If we accept Lee's data, the !Kung dependence on the mongongo nut derives, by contrast, from its productivity. This particular example also serves to illustrate the considerable variation in the responses of hunter/gatherer populations to variations in environmental stresses or opportunities even within a relatively small region.

Despite problems of sampling and interpretation with recently acquired ethnographic data, many anthropologists have adopted radically different perspectives on hunter/gatherer subsistence from those held a generation ago, particularly with regard to the importance of hunting. A consensus has developed that Lee (1968) is correct in his assessment, based upon cross-cultural surveys, that caloric intake from hunting is almost universally much less important than that derived from gathering of plant food. The reasoning behind this consensus seems to be based upon several considerations:

1. Exclusive reliance on big-game hunting is a wasteful strategy if it is a male-specific activity (as usually seems the case) and if alternative resources exist. A large segment of potential female producers is not utilized while a heavy burden is placed on males, which lowers efficiency and creates a life-style characterized by negative reciprocity.
2. Generalized subsistence strategies in which many species of flora and fauna are utilized are more efficient in energy production per unit of exploitable landscape. They should also be more efficient in terms of energy expenditure, given a suitable division of labor, since, on the productive landscape as a whole, eclectic resources should be more widely and abundantly distributed.
3. Generalized strategies should be more reliable than specialized strategies since they are more capable of counteracting short- or long-term variations in the resource base. Successful systems (human or otherwise) adapt to ranges of variation in essential variables, not to average or maximal conditions.
4. Dependence on big-game hunting often necessitates a high degree of mobility for human groups, and would in turn impose severe constraints on group size, fertility, and social interaction.
5. Exploitative strategies that partially focus on primary producers in the food chain (i.e., plant species) avoid the energy losses involved in processing of primary production by herbivores, and thus tap more abundant energy supplies.

Granted that some societies are forced to rely heavily on big game because of environmental constraints, these theoretical considerations have suggested to many that when alternative energy sources are available there should be rapid selection for generalized subsistence behavior. Such seems to be the case for the Hadza, who depend on gathered resources even though game is abundant and meat is valued. Acceptance of this picture of hunter/gatherer subsistence obviously undermines the necessary "big-game" assumption underlying the overkill hypothesis.

Since we have so few studies of hunter/gatherer subsistence, and since these are often from regions which in terms of available megafauna are marginal compared to the Pleistocene environments featured in the overkill hypothesis, other interpretations are possible. I am personally uncomfortable with several aspects of the above arguments. In the initial enthusiasm over rapidly accumulating ethnographic data on hunter/gatherers, many anthropologists (myself included) adopted the perspective championed by Sahlins (1972:1–39) and emphasized hunter/gatherer subsistence as extremely efficient. More sober considerations of human subsistence costs, in terms of time and energy, make it clear that in fact hunter/gatherers like the Bushmen are much *less* efficient than many primitive agriculturalists (Ruddle et al., 1978:65).

Perhaps the most serious difficulty is poor information on the time/energy costs of predation in environments rich in big game, since it is quite possible that highly efficient, and therefore attractive, hunting opportunities did exist in such areas in the past—a point of view which Martin holds and which, in all fairness to him, may be plausibly defended. Lacking predation data from the ethnographic record, we may fall back on predation models developed in ecology. Of the several models available (e.g., Krebs, 1973), one which I find extremely interesting and potentially fruitful is optimal foraging theory.

Optimal foraging theory is concerned with determining optimal strategies of energy acquisition (Smith, 1979). One basic assumption is that if an organism or population is energy-limited (i.e., would experience increased reproductive fitness if the energy budget were increased), there will be adaptive pressures to seek strategies which increase net energy supply, if increased fitness results; this is a concept implicit in many considerations of human energy acquisition (e.g., Boserup, 1965). Smith (1979) has offered and tested a variation of this concept in which he argues that even where energy is not limiting, strategies will be adopted which increase net acquisition *rates* (now factoring in time as an essential variable) if time is an important constraint. Here the assumption is that increased net acquisition creates free time which may then be devoted to other behaviors which facilitate fitness.

An implication of optimal foraging theory is that foragers rank alternative resources in highly selective ways (note that while the model is generally used to investigate predation, it is just as applicable, among humans, to gathering of plant food or even agricultural economies). Choices are made on the basis of time/energy efficiency among the alternatives available, focusing on the most desirable (i.e., highly ranked) alternatives. Thus there may in fact be a high degree of specialization and dependence on one or a few subsistence options, and these might well be big game in a game-rich environment. That such specialization has occurred among some human hunter/gatherers is suggested by faunal assemblages from many European sites of the late Upper Paleolithic.

A high degree of specialization does not necessarily involve high risk, it should be noted in passing, since uncontrollable perturbations in availability of optimal items can be counteracted by "dropping down" to lower-ranked food items that are abundant but simply more costly to obtain. As long as population densities are low and high selectivity is possible, hunter/gatherer subsistence systems are in fact buffered very well against resource instability.

An implication of optimal foraging theory for the evolution of preagricultural subsistence systems is that as human densities rise, optimal resources become less abundant and more costly to obtain. This results in a new set of choices; while formerly optimal items will still be taken when encountered, formerly suboptimal items will now be increasingly taken as well. Consequently the subsistence system broadens out (i.e., becomes more diversified or less specialized) as human densities increase. This may be precisely what is reflected in the economic trends seen in a number of late Paleolithic and "Epipaleolithic" archaeological sequences in the Near East (see Redman, 1978:51–87, for a review). From the perspective of optimal foraging theory the Bushmen, with their low dependence on costly hunting and high dependence on diversified plant resources may, in fact, represent hunter/gatherers who have, in the marginal Kalahari environment, already broadened out their subsistence options considerably.

Interestingly enough, optimal foraging theory also may explain some evolutionary "reversals" that have long puzzled anthropologists. An example is the adoption of a high degree of dependence on bison hunting on the American Great Plains by groups that previously had mixed hunter/gatherer-horticultural economies. The simplest explanation is that the sudden availability of the horse (and later of guns) involved the rapid reranking of bison from a suboptimal resource to a highly desirable one.

At first glance it would seem that the implications of optimal foraging theory are highly consistent with the overkill hypothesis. Humans may indeed, in some environments, specialize on big game. There are, however, several major objections to the overkill scenario as proposed by Mosimann and Martin (1975), even if this assumption is made. First, human hunters in the New World would certainly have specialized on only one or a few species of Pleistocene megafauna available in a given region. To indiscriminately hunt all of them is inconsistent with the idea of ranking. Second, we have seen that an essential element of the overkill scenario is the advancing "front" which jumps forward as megafauna are eradicated. In the Mosimann and Martin model, the front moves when *all* megafauna are taken. Optimal foraging strategies would predict that the movement of the front would be motivated by the eradication of the optimally ranked species alone, thus leaving behind intact populations of less desirable megafauna. Even if the whole front notion is abandoned and human densities are allowed to increase in a given region, it is not necessarily the case that extinction would result, since prey-switching would occur not when optimal prey items were completely eliminated, but when they became scarce enough that the cost of procuring them became too great. Finally, the basic assumptions of optimal foraging theory involve time/ energy efficiency. As I demonstrate below, the Mosimann-Martin model involves extreme inefficiency.

Obviously we have a long way to go before we can reconstruct the range of choices which particular hunter/gatherers made in their subsistence strategies and the motivations behind them, and our current views should be regarded as no more than hypothetical. This inadequacy in our data notwithstanding, I feel Mosimann and Martin's predation scenario is extremely unconvincing.

Let us now further examine Mosimann and Martin's (1975) suggested patterns of predation and associated consumption, wherein they claim that the human populations responsible for faunal extinctions depended almost entirely on meat from large prey.[2] Various levels of prey biomass and prey replacement rates are postulated, based on analogies with modern herbivore demographic figures derived from animal populations in the United States and Africa. Mosimann and Martin's biomass figures, 4.39–8.78 metric tons/km[2], fall nicely into the range of modern African savannah populations (Bourliere and Hadley, 1970:table 2; Butzer, 1964:145) and are accepted here as reasonable.

Two predation levels are simulated—namely, levels of 7 and 13 *animal units* per person per year, one animal unit being 450 kg (1,000 lb).

Simple mathematical computation indicates that the suggested predation rates are unreasonably high. Tables 14.2–14.4 provide some energetic calculations based upon these predation rates, articulated with a range of human energetic requirements. In determining energy yields I have used calculations for deer (1,500 kcal/kg), and for cattle (2,000 kcal/kg). These figures are derived from Wu Leung (1971). Three figures are provided for average daily energy requirements for human hunter/gatherers. The range of 1,700 kcal (about minimum for known human populations) to 2,700 kcal [which Kemp (1971) measured for Eskimo populations experiencing high activity levels and cold stress] presumably encompasses the requirements of

Table 14.2. Total caloric yields per person per year of high predation rate (13 animal units) and low predation rate (7 animal units), assuming 50% edible meat per animal unit

	High predation rate	*Low predation rate*
1,500 kcal/kg (deer)	4,387,500 kcal (225 kg × 1,500 × 13)	2,362,500 kcal (225 kg × 1,500 × 7)
2,000 kcal/kg (cattle)	5,850,000 kcal (225 kg × 2,000 × 13)	3,150,000 kcal (225 kg × 2,000 × 7)

all human populations. The 2,000 kcal/day figure is slightly less than Lee's estimate for the Bushmen (1968:39). Table 14.4 indicates that even if nothing but meat is consumed, these predation levels will result in a 58–89% waste (i.e., energy loss) of *edible meat*. If we make the more conservative assumption that, by analogy with known hunter/gatherer populations, the diet consisted of 50% or less meat, but keep predation on the same level, the wastage is absolutely incredible.

Only naive conceptions of the time and labor (not to mention risk) involved in hunting megafauna (including elephants) could lead to the proposal of such high predation levels. At the risk of being facetious, this is practically equivalent to going out and killing a fresh animal for dinner rather than eating leftovers from the one killed for breakfast. Any resource exploitation system that operated in this fashion would have a very high ratio of energy expenditure to energy return and would thus be highly inefficient. In other words, people would work much harder and longer than necessary for the dubious advantage of always eating the choicest cuts. Moreover, such a pattern would require high mobility, which seems to be one of the major stresses on hunter/gatherer populations and one which they attempt to counteract through various biological, social, and cultural adjustments.

Let me propose a slightly (but not much) more realistic situation. Still assuming 50% wastage of edible meat (probably too high), a 2,700 kcal daily requirement per person (certainly too high), and no energy intake apart from megafaunal sources (extremely unlikely), an individual could

Table 14.3. Annual energy requirements for an individual at various levels of energy expenditure

Average daily energy expenditure (kcal/day)	*Yearly requirement (kcal/day × 365)*
1,700	620,500
2,000	730,000
2,700	985,500

Table 14.4. Percentage of energy wasted (using data from tables 14.2 and 14.3), assuming that 50% of each animal unit is edible

	Daily energy requirement		
	1,700 kcal	*2,000 kcal*	*2,700 kcal*
High predation, 1,500 kcal/kg	86%	83%	78%
High predation, 2,000 kcal/kg	89%	88%	83%
Low predation, 1,500 kcal/kg	74%	69%	58%
Low predation, 2,000 kcal/kg	80%	77%	69%

actually be supported for one year by 4–5.8 animal units (cattle and deer values, respectively). These figures fall far below the simulation estimates. If there was only a 50% dependence on megafaunal energy sources, the level of necessary yearly predation would drop to 2–2.9 animal units; at 35% dependence, the respective requirements would be 1.4–2 animal units per person per year.

My basic point is that hunting is work, and why work if there is already food in the larder? The general pattern among ethnographically observed hunter/gatherer bands is to take advantage of an abundance of resources (meat or otherwise) by indulging in leisurely social interaction (facilitated by high levels of sharing) until the food runs out. Sometimes meat is processed for preservation (a skill which Martin and Mosimann attribute to the early American hunters); alternatively it may simply be consumed at camp over an extended period. Thus, the Mbuti may keep an animal for up to 7 days in a hot, humid climate (Harako, in this volume), and the !Kung Bushmen for 4 days in a hot, dry climate (Lee, 1972a:349). The overall strategy of the !Kung Bushmen seems to be to minimize labor (and hence consumption) in order to maximize a valued life-style involving high levels of social interaction (Lee, 1968, 1972a).

By far the most unlikely claim made by Mosimann and Martin (1975:309) is that the meat rations required by early migrant populations averaged 4.5 kg (10 lb)/day per person. This incredibly high figure is based on meat rations for several historically known American frontier populations, and Mosimann and Martin seem to suggest *consumption* on this level. While there may have been rations in this amount in historic times (with meat easily acquired with firearms and transported by horses), most of it was certainly wasted or diverted to nonhuman uses (e.g., feeding dogs). The energy yield from 4.5 kg of meat would be about 6,750–9,000 kcal. An extremely active adult male Eskimo under severe cold stress could perhaps need 3,500 kcal/day, and I suppose a famished "mountain man" might occasionally have gorged himself on an entire deer haunch. But no conceivable activity level by any normal human population as a whole could ever have expended, and thus required, energy equivalent to 4.5 kg of meat per day on average.

We might, at this point, examine some consumption/predation rates for known hunter/gatherer societies. For a G/wi Bushmen group of about 85 members, the yearly consumption was 4,528 kg, for a daily average intake of about 0.15 kg per person (Silberbauer, 1972). Twenty of Mosimann and Martin's animal units would be required to provision the Bushmen at this rate of intake (assuming that 50% of each animal unit is inedible), for an average of about 0.24 animal units per person per year. Actually, most of this yield was taken from 221 small bovids (Silberbauer, 1972:286). During the month that Lee (1972a:348) measured meat intake, the !Kung averaged almost exactly the same consumption rate as the G/wi. For the Mbuti, Tanno (1976:126) reports that cooperative net-hunting, involving both males and females, yields an average daily ration of 0.8 kg of meat while people are actually in a hunting camp. Harako (in this volume, table 13.12) reports yields of 0.32–0.46 kg/person per day from various hunting techniques used by the two Mbuti bands he observed for extended periods. Tanaka (1976:111) estimates daily intake totals of 0.22 kg/person per day for the G/wi.

To counter the objection that Bushmen or Pygmies are hardly representative of the kinds of northern temperate zone hunters Martin and Mosimann are talking about, let us turn to some Subarctic groups with heavy dependence on meat and especially megafauna. Using Helm's figures (1972:62) for caribou predation among the Dogrib, the yearly take of caribou per hunter (36.7) would potentially yield about 1,670 kg of edible meat. Figuring one hunter per four consumers, the average yearly ration would be about 405 kg per person, with no wastage. This is the yield equivalent of about 1.8 animal units and, if fully consumed, would provide virtually full energy support for a single person. Figuring 50% wastage, as in our earlier calculations, a Dogrib individual could be fully supported by only 3.6 animal units annually—far below the levels proposed by Mosimann and Martin. Actually, although the Dogrib are heavily dependent on caribou (not only for themselves but for their dogs), they, like most Arctic and Subarctic peoples, exploit a wide variety of faunal resources including small game and fish. Thus very low megafaunal predation levels are characteristic of the Dogrib, despite their dependence on caribou, and the relative ease with which they may be taken and transported with rifle and sled. E. Rogers' estimates for the Mistassini Cree indicate similar low predation levels (1972).

Another factor seemingly not considered by Mosimann and Martin is that game, even when abundant, may not be a reliable resource. Burch (1972) analyzed the problems of caribou hunting for some Arctic groups and discovered that complete reliance on them was difficult for two reasons. First, caribou are much too mobile for any human population to keep up with on foot. Second, it is difficult to predict consistently the whereabout, movements, or sizes of caribou herds. Consequently, these

Arctic populations emphasize the situational exploitation of a wide variety of available resources apart from megafauna.

This observation leads us to another point made by Mosimann and Martin—namely, that northern peoples are predominantly hunters of megafauna because little else is available, and that a preference for large game would therefore be carried over into lower-latitude environments as long as game held out. It seems to me that the traditional subsistence systems of high-latitude hunter/gatherers stress the exploitation, either regularly or situationally, of just about every usable resource, including plant foods (either from seasonally available vegetation or the stomach contents of animals). If one makes the dubious argument that there would be a strong "traditional" carry-over of subsistence strategies in low-latitude environments, emphasis could just as well be placed on the broad-spectrum omnivorous dimension rather than the "big-game" meat-eating. In a richer environmental setting, eclectic dietary habits would be energetically and nutritionally more efficient, and would also provide greater opportunities for the intensive social interaction that seems to be highly valued in hunter/gatherer populations.

Turning to the Great Plains of the continental United States, which constituted the greatest megafaunal reservoir of both historic and prehistoric times, Hester (1967:179) cites estimates of a bison herd of 30–40 million for the early 1870s, and human predation (not counting animals killed for commercial markets) amounted to approximately 321,000 animals per year, or about 0.8–1.07% of the total herd. This predation rate is far below the biomass replacement rates for bison and for prehistoric megafauna estimated by Mosimann and Martin (5–30%), and should have had no serious effects on bison populations.

According to Kroeber (1947:142), the contact-period human population of the Plains–Prairie region was about 103,500. Assuming the average bison to be the equivalent of 1 animal unit (450 kg), overall average rates of predation would be just over 3 animal units per person per year, which is certainly low considering the fact that bison were a major staple for these populations. To this would have to be added smaller amounts of meat derived from other large game (e.g., elk, bear, deer) and small game (e.g., rabbits, birds, antelopes).

Although the Plains Indians provide us with perhaps the most archetypal models for "big-game" hunting societies, it is clear that they were by no means fully dependent on megafaunal predation, or even on hunting. I know of no measurements of energy intake for any Plains society, but plant foods seem to have been an important component in the diet, especially when processed for use over the long winters when mobility was limited and bison hunting difficult (Hoeble, 1960; Spencer and Jennings, 1965; Wedel, 1961). Not only were wild plants used, but maize was acquired from sedentary farming populations during visits or through raiding or extortion. Bison provided an unstable year-round resource; in some seasons hunting these prey was difficult, unproductive, or dangerous, and consequently great efforts were made to preserve as much meat as possible to counteract shortages, thus reducing predation by reducing wastage. This pattern is visible archaeologically (Wheat, 1972). Moreover bison, like caribou, do not seem to have been highly predictable in their movements or local abundance, a circumstance which Newcomb (1950) links to Plains Indian warfare.

It would seem, then, that the much celebrated "big-game hunters" of the Plains, even with horses and firearms, did not rely completely on megafaunal resources, especially bison, for their energetic needs, and that their levels of predation were far below those necessary to drive any Plains species into extinction. Mosimann and Martin's contention that their more poorly equipped ancestors found it possible or necessary to exterminate a Pleistocene megafauna of comparable size and greater diversity seems completely unfounded. I have never been able to understand why, if one accepts Martin's overkill arguments, bison and several other surviving large herbivores were not brought to extinction prior to the arrival of Europeans in the New World. We certainly have good archaeological evidence that they have been a major food source since the end of the Pleistocene.

In a tangential approach to the overkill hypothesis, Krantz (1970) has suggested that human predation may have caused some extinctions indirectly by increasing competition among megafaunal populations. Briefly, his argument is that if humans specialized in hunting one or a few prey species, patterns of cropping may have actually *increased* prey populations by eliminating unfit individuals which otherwise competed with healthy and reproductively capable individuals. Rapid population expansion of a favored prey species, such as bison, could thus have caused competitive imbalances that drove other species into extinction. I bring up this ingenious argument not because there is good evidence to support it, but rather because it illustrates how complex the extinction processes might have been.

Another proposition made by Mosimann and Martin is that the North American fauna was exceedingly vulnerable because these species had no experience with, and consequently no "natural" defenses against, human predators. Aside from being unprovable, this argument assumes that prey adaptations are relatively inflexible and that learning is an unimportant component. It further assumes that human predatory behavior was so different from that of nonhuman predators that the prey's existing avoidance tactics were inappropriate. These claims are, to say the least, debatable. If a longer chronology for the colonization of the New World is accepted (as suggested above), this argument is vitiated, for the species that became extinct at the end of the Pleistocene would already have been exposed to human predation for thousands of years.

On what, then, does the assumption rest that late Pleistocene populations in the New World were primarily big-game hunters? Not on ethnographic or energetic considerations, and certainly not on the sparse and ambiguous archaeological evidence. Apart from the traditional and questionable myth that humans are predators *par excellence*, I suggest that for Mosimann and Martin the reasoning is essentially circular. Massive extinction occurred and (in their view) the only unique factor was a human predator population, which must therefore have been responsible. Succinctly put: since the animals disappeared, the humans must have been megafauna hunters; and since they were big-game hunters, they must have had the capability to eliminate the megafaunal populations.

Demographic Variables

Even with high rates of predation, extinction would not occur unless certain demographic conditions were met. These include: very high, sustained rates of human population growth, producing the large absolute numbers of human predators to decimate the Pleistocene fauna; and very dense *concentrations* of human population along the advancing "front."

Mosimann and Martin (1975) have based their calculations of rates of population increase (as well as other elements of their simulation) on Birdsell's model for the colonization of Australia (1957). Birdsell was concerned with population dynamics in a frontier situation where excess population could bud off into new, unoccupied habitats. On the basis of historical data involving the colonization of several small island environments, notably Tristan da Cunha and Pitcairn, he concluded that annual rates of increase on the order of 3.5% could have been reached and maintained, enabling populations to double every 20 years.[3] A number of scholars, in addition to Mosimann and Martin, have uncritically accepted Birdsell's figures and applied them to various problems [see, e.g., Ammerman and Cavalli-Sforza's simulation of the Neolithic colonization of Europe (1973)].

It seems unwise to generalize from Birdsell's examples to human colonizing populations in general, and particularly to hunter/gatherer demography (Roberts, 1968). First, these cases of colonization involved primarily agricultural groups, or groups trading for agricultural commodities, which occupied small, relatively homogeneous island environments. Such environments do not present diverse problems of adaptation, particularly for food-producers, and may be relatively free of certain kinds of biological stresses, such as endemic diseases with animal vectors. Second, the population structures, particularly in the earliest phases of colonization, were weighted heavily toward individuals of reproductive age, thus facilitating rapid initial growth rates. As more normal population structures were established in subsequent generations, growth rates declined. Emigration and immigration were conspicuous factors influencing fertility. Finally, the populations involved were very small, to the extent that the fertility of single individuals had exaggerated effects on overall rates of increase, even though these fertility levels were nonrepresentative.

In assessing the usefulness of Birdsell's estimates, we might look at measured maximum growth rates for some recent populations. The Hutterites show a crude annual rate of increase of about 4.15% per year, probably the highest known for any population (Eaton and Mayer, 1953). This rate of increase is in part a product of their very high fertility rate (although it is not the highest ever observed), but more importantly reflects exceedingly low crude death rates of 4.4% per year. As Eaton and Mayer observe:

They show how a human population might grow if people believe in procreation without interference with biological reproductive potential, but live under technological conditions that give such a growing population good economic and medical support. Hutterites can therefore be viewed as a modern population in their death rates but primitive in their birth rates. (1953:244)

Hutterite rates of population growth, which have been measured for several generations, have also been enhanced by the same factor noted for Birdsell's populations—an unusual population structure initially weighted heavily toward reproductively viable adults.

Recent studies of rapidly expanding agricultural populations in southern Peru indicate short-term rates of increase of about 2.5–3.0% per year (Baker and Dutt, 1972; Dutt, 1976). These rates are probably more directly pertinent for prehistoric demographic studies, since the populations involved exhibit high fertility but also high mortality as a result of premodern medical conditions and the capacity for continued emigration for excess population increments.

L. Cole (1954), in a general examination of demographic problems, concluded that maximum rates of intrinsic population increase among humans would vary between 2% and 4% annually, with the latter figure very seldom achieved. Baker and Sanders (1972:162) note that studies of colonizing agricultural peoples show growth profiles much lower than Birdsell's, with doubling occurring at approximately 100-year rather than 20-year intervals.

Only one thing is certain about *average* annual rates of population growth during the Paleolithic: they were minuscule, often close to zero (Acsadi and Nemeskeri, 1970; Coale, 1974; Hassan, 1973; Weiss, 1976).

Most authors assume that these low rates of increase resulted from high, virtually unrestrained fertility counterbalanced by high mortality. Mortality itself was conditioned by various sorts of uncontrolled losses (e.g., disease, starvation, accidents) as well as by socially induced mortality (e.g., infanticide).

Although we have very little detailed information on the demography of hunter/gatherer populations, some recent studies suggest that fairly low rates of growth may be caused by limitations on fertility which are, at least in part, cultural. Lee (1972:335) reports occasional infanticide among the Bushmen but cites extended periods of nursing as a major cause of wide birth-spacing (4–5 years between births). Such spacing obviously limits the number of pregnancies a woman will experience during her reproductive span. Even though additional children may be desired, and the environment is seen as productive enough to support them, more children would limit mobility while at the same time necessitating additional food procurement, which is itself dependent on mobility. Given such options, there is a trade-off between the affective attraction of more children and a life-style characterized by relatively low expenditure of labor and abundant leisure time. N. Howell (1976a) has presented a somewhat different interpretation of Bushman demographic patterns, and cites a recent growth rate of 0.5% annually, which implies a doubling of population about every 140 years. While this is a slow rate of growth compared to those of many modern peasant societies, sustained rates even of this magnitude would undoubtedly have major effects on Bushman adaptation over a period of, say, 1,000 years.

Hayden (1972, and in this volume), in a general review of population control among hunter/gatherers, maintains that the situation described by Lee is widespread and that it indirectly functions to keep population levels in some reasonable equilibrium with resources. He suggests that a division of labor weighted toward female producers is a prime factor in inhibiting rapid rates of growth for many primitive societies. With a shortage of large prehistoric skeletal populations and of systematic demographic observations of modern hunters/gatherers, we unfortunately cannot determine the extent to which either high mortality or conscious constraints on fertility have affected long-term growth rates. We are equally ignorant concerning causes of mortality among hunter/gatherers (Dunn, 1968). It seems reasonable that mobile, low-density populations would experience comparatively low uncontrolled losses as a result of contagious diseases. On the other hand, high mobility itself seems to impose stresses on women, resulting not only in avoidance of pregnancy but also in elimination of a significant proportion of children at or before birth. For groups that live in extreme environments and depend heavily on game, such as the Eskimo, adult male mortality may be very high because of accidents (Kemp, 1971).

Starvation, to judge from ethnographic accounts, is rather rare among hunter/gatherers in general, but we have poor data concerning mortality in temperate or Subarctic populations who experience both seasonal food shortages and climatic stresses.

Mosimann and Martin are of course concerned less with average than with extreme conditions of population growth. Their contention is that open frontiers (i.e., vacant niches) stimulate rapid population increase, although they do not say why. The fundamental assumption seems to be that fertility and, especially, mortality are constrained *only* by limitations of space for absorbing surplus population, and by the total biomass of food resources on the landscape. Such an assumption is at best a great oversimplification.

If one wishes to estimate maximum rates of population growth for the Pleistocene, and to assume that fertility was unconstrained, I suggest that an annual mortality of at least 25/1,000 is likely. Acsadi and Nemeskeri (1970) report that annual death rates of 20–25/1,000 were typical of developed areas of Europe and North America until quite recently. It is difficult to believe that mortality rates would have been more favorable for temperate or Subarctic Paleolithic populations, although undoubtedly the causes of mortality were quite different. Even at peak fertility—say an annual rate of 4.5%—maximum overall annual increases given these mortality levels would be about 2% per year, and average rates much lower. Mosimann and Martin appear to have postulated unreasonably high rates of sustained increase, and estimates of 1% or less per annum would be more realistic.

The other major demographic factor cited by Mosimann and Martin is population density, their position being that critical densities are necessary to form a "front" and to guarantee predation levels consistent with extinction. In one of their basic simulations (1975:311), Mosimann and Martin postulate a critical density level of 2.02 persons/mi^2 or 0.78/km^2. These are *overall* densities in the sense that they are uniformly maintained over thousands of square kilometers. This density estimate and others of theirs seem unreasonably high. For example, Kroeber's reconstructions (1947:142) of overall Plains–Prairie human densities range from 0.093 to 0.12 persons/mi^2 (0.036–0.046/km^2). These estimates are strikingly small for populations that had available, by Mosimann and Martin's own admission, a prey biomass comparable to the Pleistocene one and that were certainly better-equipped technologically. Even if we cautiously calculate that Kroeber underestimated these populations by a factor of 2, it is still apparent that the figures used in the simulations are considerably too high.

Finally, another feature of the density problem brings us back to Birdsell's original model, in which rapid population growth and fissioning into an open environment are prime components. As Birdsell himself noted: "To assume that a native population would not begin to colonize adjacent favorable and unspoiled hunting territories prior to attaining a maximum carrying capacity is untenable" (1957:54). Accordingly, in the construction of his model he simulated fissioning at 40–80% of carrying capacity, and similar assumptions have been used by other authors working with demographic problems (e.g., Binford, 1968b). In contrast, Mosimann and Martin propose that the "front" does not advance until local megafaunal resources are completely exhausted—i.e., not until 100% of local carrying capacity is attained (in terms of the traditional subsistence system) and not until maximum faunal depletion occurs. Obviously extinction would be facilitated by such conditions, but again the assumption is unrealistic.

My impression of the North American simulation model is that the values attached to its various components are virtually geared to produce an extinction outcome and that, in general, little attention was devoted to critically evaluating their accuracy or consistency with known data. Although I cannot offer an alternative set of simulations here, it is apparent that slight modifications in basic values will yield the result of no extinction. Mosimann and Martin have neither proved that extinction took place according to the overkill scenario nor demonstrated its *plausibility* via the simulation exercise.

ALTERNATIVES TO OVERKILL

The most common alternative explanation to the overkill hypothesis, and the one most frequently applied to large-scale extinction of megafauna within the span of human evolution, is that of environmental change—specifically, terminal Pleistocene climatic changes with all of their potential stresses on floral and faunal communities. Martin and Wright's (1967) overview of the extinction controversy can be basically characterized as overkill vs. climatic change. I will accordingly restrict my comments to this alternative to overkill, with special reference to the New World.

There seems little doubt that, in broad terms, the climate of the earth in general, and of high-latitude regions in particular, experienced considerable change during the terminal Pleistocene–Holocene transition. Martin, himself an expert in paleo-ecological reconstruction, originally postulated "a lack of evidence of major climatic change during the extinction period" (1958:413). He later adopted the somewhat more conservative position that "while it [extinction] occurred at a time of climatic change, the pattern appears to be independent of a climatic cause" (1967:114). Evidence for this independence is seen in the (supposed) selectivity of extinction, and the fact that many of the extinct forms had already survived multiple glaciations.

Northern Europe, where the best and most extensive work on paleo-ecological reconstruction has been done, seems to be one region in which the correlation of rapid, drastic environmental change with extinction is so convincing that a causal relationship is almost certain. Unfortunately, environmental change in most other regions of the Old World (as well as South America) has been less thoroughly documented by paleo-climatologists.

For North America a great deal of evidence exists, derived from geological, botanical, faunal, and especially palynological studies, which strongly suggests substantial climatic change associated with the end of the Pleistocene.[4] A detailed consideration of these data is beyond the scope of this article, but I shall examine some of the reasons why this information is insufficient to sort out obvious climatic causes for extinction.

One fundamental difficulty involves the interpretive leap from clear physical markers indicating prehistoric environmental change to pin-pointing exactly what kind of change is involved. For example, a pollen core might clearly show an increase in pine pollen in a sequence previously dominated by grass; this could indicate either an expansion of pine forest (and hence an increase in moisture), or a decline in local grass vegetation caused by drought, which might result in increased relative frequencies of windborne pine-pollen values. Similarly, arroyo cutting might be explained by increased aridity, which destroys vegetation cover and promotes rapid run-off, but arroyos may also form on the lower reaches of rivers under humid conditions when stream beds are lowered and water volume is increased.

Another problem is the spottiness of paleoclimatic research. For example, in the continental United States we have reasonably good paleo-environmental data from the Southwest, the Western Plains, and the Great Lakes Region; these areas seem to have experienced rather dramatic changes with the onset of modern conditions. For the Southeast, however, there is a comparative lack of good data concerning terminal Pleistocene climatic change, and much of the available information suggests that changes were less severe and rapid than elsewhere. Even within regions where a great deal of research has been done, local sequences are often contradictory. For example Antevs (1962) discusses two very different pollen diagrams taken from deposits less than a kilometer apart. Fortu-nately these problems reflect the present state of the art and should be eventually resolvable. Unfortunately paleo-environmentalists have often made unconvincing generalizations based on insufficient evidence, just as do supporters of the overkill hypothesis. The "equability" hypothesis, discussed below, is an example.

As I have noted, Martin argues against climatic causes for extinctions by pointing out that the animals in question had survived multiple glaciations and that large herbivores were more drastically affected than other genera. Other authors, most notably Axelrod (1967), have circumvented these issues by denying that the Pleistocene-Holocene transition was necessarily similar to earlier glacial transitions and by focusing on a critical factor known as "equability." Regions of high equability are characterized by absences of extreme heat and cold, and lack abrupt transitions between seasons. Axelrod's main argument is that there are severe stresses on reproduction, particularly among large mammals, if conditions of high climatic equability quickly shift toward greater seasonality (i.e., marked and abrupt fluctuation in temperature).

Since Darwin's time, botanists and biologists have been disturbed by the problem that many ancient floral and faunal assemblages include species which would today be segregated into tropical and temperate environments (Axelrod, 1967:12–21). One explanation offered by Axelrod (1967:5–8) is that these ancient assemblages existed during periods of high equability: "Under conditions of high equability, temperatures are neither so high as to discourage temperate forms, or so low as to prevent the success of tropical ones." He concludes that "a change in the factor that explains the associations of animals and plants of tropical and temperate requirements in Quaternary and Tertiary communities may be responsible for the widespread selective extinctions of the Quaternary." He cites sub-Saharan Africa, which has maintained impressive levels of herbivore biomass and diversity (Bourliere and Hadley, 1970) as a high-equability region and offers meteorological data to support his contention. For regions of the United States, Leopold's plant studies (1967:235) and Taylor's mollusk studies (1965:611) offer tentative support for a rapid increase in late Quaternary seasonality as postulated by Axelrod.

The equability hypothesis is immediately appealing because it appears to resolve such sticky problems as the apparent selective extinction of large herbivores. Slaughter (1967:163) has noted that under equable conditions many mammals have mating seasons which are unrestricted or are limited by factors other than temperature. Bourliere and Hadley (1970:147), in a review of the ecology of tropical savannahs, support Slaughter's contention with data from African savannah habitats.

Mammals with such "equable" reproductive habits, and especially large mammals with long gestation periods, would be subject to severe reproductive stress if rapid increases in seasonality occurred. Similarly, mammals with inflexible mating seasons would be adversely affected in regions such as North America if equability were quickly lowered. Those bearing young in the fall would suffer from the onset of earlier, more severe winters, while spring births would be endangered by increasingly late and frequent spring blizzards. Large mammals in open habitats would suffer from exposure. Periods of drought would reduce browse and pasture, causing overgrazing and throwing larger herbivores into unusually intense competition. Axelrod discusses several well-documented cases in which unusual episodes of cold or drought have decimated deer and antelope populations, and maintains that if such conditions became commonplace then extinctions might well occur.

According to the equability hypothesis, small mammals would not be as severely affected as large ones because their breeding habits are more flexible, gestation periods are shorter, and more young are produced. Other buffers against increased seasonality include the construction of shelters (dens, nests), storage of food, and the fact that breeding populations can be maintained in very restricted habitats. Slaughter concludes that "it is hardly a coincidence that essentially modern ranges of extinct animals were established during the most intense period of megafaunal extinction. The advent of essentially modern continental climate qualifies as a fundamental cause of these extinctions" (1967:162).

Although the equability argument is intriguing on a theoretical level, as originally presented by Axelrod it is also full of unresolved problems, including some rather facile assumptions concerning the tolerances and distributions of living and extinct species, and a failure to consider the undoubted seasonality of glacial periods with which earlier Pleistocene extinctions are associated [see Reed (1969:345–46), for a detailed critique of Axelrod's hypothesis]. Wilkinson (1973) maintains that high continentality was characteristic of the final (Wisconsin) glacial episode in North America, and that extinction probably began much earlier than has been thought. We simply do not know in detail how and when (or perhaps even *if*) ancient climates shifted toward greater seasonality.

Even if we did possess adequate reconstructions of prehistoric environmental changes, we would still have to be able to specify exactly *what* selective environmental factors were operating on the populations involved, in order to generate explanations of extinction. Such specification requires reasonably detailed information about the physiological requirements and behavior of extinct faunal populations. Why, for example, did the moose survive in the eastern woodlands of the United States while the mastodon did not? Needless to say, our present knowledge concerning the tolerances and behaviors of prehistoric animal populations is quite limited, and may remain so for a long time to come. Reconstructions of the interplay between environmental and ethological factors which do exist are currently much too general [e.g., Dreimanis's model of mastodon extinction (1968)] to be applied in causal models of the overkill hypothesis.

CONCLUSIONS

My own conclusion is that the overkill controversy is premature, in the sense that our present level of knowledge is inadequate to allow formulation of productive questions about the causes of extinction processes, much less to provide convincing answers. Its only value, and perhaps a considerable one despite its faults, lies in the attention it has focused on the intriguing problem of terminal Pleistocene extinctions. The overkill hypothesis, especially as elaborated by Martin (1967) and Mosimann and Martin (1975), is seriously flawed, both in terms of its basic assumptions and in the nature and use of the supportive data. It is, fortunately, a hypothesis susceptible to refutation, and I expect that it will be soon rejected, at least in its present form. I am less sanguine about the possibilities of quickly confirming alternative hypotheses, especially those involving climatic change, but I hope that such confirmation will be possible as techniques of paleo-environmental reconstruction become more refined and widely applied.

My preference, after a critical review of the evidence, is the conservative position that *if* human predation was involved in the terminal Pleistocene extinctions of megafauna, it was in the nature of an indirect cause. Human predation may well have driven certain animal populations—already under severe natural stress—over the brink of extinction, but its basic effect was merely to accelerate a process already under way. The overkill explanation is attractive because it is both simple and dramatic, but the principles of parsimony and elegance are perhaps less common in the real world than we might wish.

NOTES

1. Because these data represent intake during only 1 month (albeit during a lean year), they should be used cautiously.

2. Seemingly in contradiction they maintain at one point that "it is not necessary that the hunters actually eat all, or even any, of their prey" (1975:304–5). The only sense I can make of this cryptic remark is that many prey individuals may be "wasted" in energetic terms due to some combination of the factors outlined above.

3. Birdsell has since suggested even higher rates (Birdsell, 1968).

4. For an extensive collection of such data, see Wright and Frey (1965).

References

Acsadi, Gy., and J. Nemeskeri
1970   History of Human Life Span and Mortality. Budapest: Akademei Kaido.

Alcalde del Río, H., H. Breuil, and L. Sierra
1911   Les Cavernes de la Région Cantabrique (Espagne). Monaco: Prince Albert 1er.

Aldrich-Blake, F. P. G., T. K. Bunn, R. I. M. Dunbar, and P. M. Headley
1971   Observations on Baboons, *Papio anubis*, in an Arid Region in Ethiopia. Folia Primatologica 15:1–35.

Alexander, R.
1974   The Evolution of Social Behavior. Annual Review of Ecology and Systematics 5:325–383.

Allen, H.
1974   The Bagundji of the Darling Basin: Cereal Gatherers in an Uncertain Environment. World Archaeology 5:309–322.

Almagro, M., R. Fryxell, H. Irwin, and M. Serna
1970   Avance a la Investigación Arqueológica, Geocronológica y Ecólogica de la Cueva de Cariguela (Piñar, Granada). Trabajos de Préhistoria 27:45–60.

Altmann, J.
1974   Observational Study of Behavior: Sampling Methods. Behaviour 49: 227–67.

Altmann, S. A., and J. Altmann
1970   Baboon Ecology: African Field Research. Chicago: University of Chicago Press.

Altuna, J.
1971   Los Mamíferos del Yacimiento Prehistórico de Morín (Santander). *In* J. González Echegaray et al., eds., 1971. Pp. 367–398.

1972   Fauna de Mamíferos de los Yacimientos Prehistóricos de Guipuzcoa, con Catálogo de los Mamíferos Cuaternarios del Cantábrico y Pirenéo Occidental. Munibe 24:1–464.

1973   Fauna de Mamíferos de la Cueva de Morín. *In* J. González Echegaray et al., eds., 1973. Pp. 279–290.

1976   Los Mamíferos del Yacimiento Prehistórico de Tito Bustillo (Asturias). *In* Excavaciones en la Ceuva de "Tito Bustillo" (Asturias): Trabajos 1975. Pp. 149–194. Oviedo: Instituto de Estudios Asturianos.

Altuna, J., and L. Straus
1975   The Solutrean of Altamira: The Artifactual and Faunal Evidence. Zephyrus 26–27:175–182.

595

Amerasinghe, F. B., B. W. B. Van Cuylenberg, and C. M. Hladik
1971   Comparative Histology of the Alimentary Tract of Ceylon Primates in Correlation with Diet. Ceylon Journal of Science 9:75–87.

Ames, K. M.
1976   Stable and Resilient Systems along the Skeena: The Gitksan/Carrier Boundary. Paper presented at the 9th Annual Conference of the University of Calgary Archaeological Association, November, 1976.

Ammerman, A., and L. Cavalli-Sforza
1973   A Population Model for the Diffusion of Early Farming into Europe. *In* The Explanation of Culture Change. C. Renfrew, ed. Pp. 343–358. London: Duckworth.

Andrews, P.
1971   *Ramapithecus wickeri* Mandible from Fort Ternan, Kenya. Nature 231: 192–194.

Andrews, P., and E. N. Evans
1979   The Environment of *Ramapithecus* in Africa. Paleobiology 5:22–30.

Andrews, P., and I. Tekkaya
1976   *Ramapithecus* in Kenya and Turkey. *In* Les Plus Anciens Hominidés. Nice: Colloque VI, IX Congrés, Union Internationale des Sciences Préhistoriques et Protohistoriques. P. V. Tobias and Y. Coppens, eds. Paris: Centre National de la Recherche Scientifique.

Andrews, P., and H. Tobien
1977   New Miocene Locality in Turkey with Evidence on the Origin of *Ramapithecus* and *Sivapithecus*. Nature 268:699–701.

Andrews, P., and J. H. van Couvering
1975   Paleoenvironments in the East African Miocene. *In* Approaches to Primate Paleobiology. F. Szalay, ed. Basel: S. Karger.

Andrews, P., and A. Walker
1976   The Primate and Other Fauna from Fort Ternan, Kenya. *In* G.Ll. Isaac and E.R. McCown, eds., 1976. Pp. 279–304.

Antevs, E.
1955   Geologic-Climatic Method of Dating. Tucson: University of Arizona Physical Science Bulletin No. 2.
1962   Late Quaternary Climates in Arizona. American Antiquity 28:193–198.

Ardrey, R.
1961   African Genesis: A Personal Investigation into the Animal Origins and Nature of Man. New York: Atheneum.
1976   The Hunting Hypothesis. New York: Atheneum.

Axelrod, D.
1967   Quaternary Extinction of Large Mammals. University of California Publications in Geological Science, 74.

Azpeitia, P.
1958   Estudio de los Restos Paleontológicos de la Trinchera I. *In* P. Janssens and J. González Echegaray, eds., 1958. Pp. 101–117.

Badrian, A., and N. Badrian
1977 Pygmy Chimpanzees. Oryx 12:463–468.

Bailey, K. V.
1963 Nutrition in New Guinea. Food and Nutrition Notes and Reviews 20:89.

Baker, P., and J. Dutt
1972 Demographic Variables as Measures of Biological Adaptation: A Case Study of High Altitude Human Populations. *In* The Structure of Human Populations. G. A. Harrison and A. J. Boyce, eds. Pp. 352–378. Oxford: Oxford University Press.

Baker, P., and W. T. Sanders
1972 Demographic Studies in Anthropology. Annual Reviews of Anthropology 1:51–178.

Baldus, H.
1943 Sinopse da Cultura Guayaki. Sociologia (São Paulo) 5:147–153.

Baldwin, J. D., and J. Baldwin
1972 The Ecology and Behavior of Squirrel Monkeys (*Saimiri oerstedi*) in a Natural Forest in Western Panama. Folia Primatologica 18:161–184.

Baldwin, L. A., and G. Teleki
1973 Field Research on Chimpanzees and Gorillas: An Historical, Geographical, and Bibliographical Listing. Primates 14:315–320.

Balikci, A.
1968 The Netsilik Eskimos: Adaptive Processes. *In* R. B. Lee and I. DeVore, eds., 1968a. Pp. 78–82.

Balout, L.
1955 Préhistoire de l'Afrique du Nord. Paris: Arts et Métiers Graphiques.

Bang, P., and P. Dahlström
1975 Huellas y Señales de los Animales de Europa. Barcelona: Ediciones Omega.

Barandiarán, I.
1975 El Abrigo de Eudoviges (Alacon, Teruel), Noticia Preliminar. Miscelanea Arqueológica Dedicada al Profesor Antonio Beltran. Pp. 29–47.

Barbour, G. B.
1949 Ape or Man? An Incomplete Chapter of Human Ancestry from South Africa. Yearbook of Physical Anthropology 5:117–133.

Barrett, S. A.
1964 The Beautiful Tree: Chishkale (motion picture). Berkeley: University of California Extension Media Center.

Bartholomew, G. A., and J. B. Birdsell
1953 Ecology and the Protohominids. American Anthropologist 55:481–498.

Bar-Yosef, O.
1975 Archaeological Occurrences of the Middle Pleistocene of Israel. *In* K. W. Butzer and G.Ll. Isaac, eds., 1975. Pp. 571–604.

Basedow, H.
1925   The Australian Aboriginal. Adelaide: F. W. Preece.

Bates, B. C.
1970   Territorial Behavior in Primates: A Review of Recent Field Studies. Primates 11:271–284.

Bauchop, T., and R. W. Martucci
1968   Ruminant-like Digestion of the Langur Monkey. Science 161:698–699.

Bauer, H. R.
1975   Behavioral Changes about the Time of Reunion in Parties of Chimpanzees in the Gombe Stream National Park. *In* S. Kondo, M. Kawai, and A. Ehara, eds., 1975.
1977   Chimpanzee Bipedal Locomotion in the Gombe National Park, Tanzania. Primates 18:913–921.

Baumhoff, M. A.
1963   Ecological Determinants of Aboriginal California Populations. University of California Publications in American Archaeology and Ethnology 49:155–236.

Baumhoff, M., and P. Heizer
1965   Postglacial Climate and Archaeology in the Desert West. *In* Quaternary of the United States. H. E. Wright and D. Frey, eds. Pp. 697–708. Princeton: Princeton University Press.

Beard, G.
1898   Sexual Neurasthenia, 5th ed. New York: E. B. Treat and Co.

Beard, M. E. J., and H. J. Huser
1970   Studies on Folate and Vitamin B12 Metabolism in Primates. II. Vitamin B12 Binding Proteins. Folia Primatologica 12:305–312.

Bearder, S. K., and G. A. Doyle
1974   Ecology of Bushbabies, *Galago senegalensis* and *Galago crassicaudatus*, with Some Notes on Their Behaviour in the Field. *In* R. D. Martin, G. A. Doyle, and A. C. Walker, eds., 1974. Pp. 109–136.

Beattie, W. A.
1971   Beef Cattle Breeding and Management, 3d ed. Melbourne: Pastoral Review Australia Pty.

Beck, B. B.
1975   Primate Tool Behavior. *In* R. Tuttle, ed., 1975b. Pp. 414–447.

Behrensmeyer, A. K.
1975   The Taphonomy and Paleoecology of Plio-Pleistocene Vertebrate Assemblages East of Lake Rudolf, Kenya. Bulletin of the Museum of Comparative Zoology (Harvard University) 146, No. 10.
1976a   Fossil Assemblages in Relation to Sedimentary Environments in the Lake Rudolf Succession. *In* Y. Coppens et al., eds., 1976. Pp. 383–401.
1976b   The Recent Bones of Amboseli Park, Kenya in Relation to East African Paleoecology. Paper prepared for the Wenner-Gren Foundation Burg Wartenstein Symposium No. 69, 1976.

1978   The Habitat of Plio-Pleistocene Hominids in East Africa: Taphonomic and Micro-Stratigraphic Evidence. *In* C. J. Jolly, ed., 1978. Pp. 165–189.

Beltrán Martínez, A., and I. Barandiarán Maestú
1968   Avance al Estudio de las Cuevas Paleolíticas de la Hoz y los Cásares (Guadalajara). Excavaciones Arqueológicas en España.

Berndt, R.
1959   The Concept of the Tribe in the Western Desert of Australia. Oceania 30:82–107.

Berndt, R. M., and C. H. Berndt
1964   The World of the First Australians. Sydney: Ure Smith.

Bernstein, I. S.
1968   The Lutong of Kuala Selangor. Behaviour 32:1–16.

Bertrand, M.
1969   Behavioral Repertoire of the Stumptail Macaque, *Macaca speciosa.* Bibliotheca Primatologica 11. Basel: S. Karger.

Biberson, P.
1961   Le Paléolithique Inférieur du Maroc Atlantique. Rabat: Pub. Services des Antiquités du Maroc, Fasc. 17.

Bicchieri, M. G.
1969   A Cultural Ecological Comparative Study of Three African Foraging Societies. *In* Contributions to Anthropology: Band Societies. D. Damas, ed. Pp. 172–179. Ottawa: National Museums of Canada Bulletin 228, Anthropological Ser. 84.
1972   (Ed.) Hunters and Gatherers Today. New York: Holt, Rinehart and Winston.

Biebuyck, D.
1973   Lega Culture. Los Angeles: University of California Press.

Bigot, L., and P. Jouventin
1974   Quelques Expériences de Comestibilité de Lépidoptères Gabonais Faites avec le Mandrill, le Cercocèbe à Joues Grises et le Garde-Boeufs. La Terre et la Vie 28:521–543.

Bilbey, L. W.
1968   A Pilot Scheme to Investigate the Diets of Some of the Mammals at the London Zoo. I. Primate Diets. *In* M. A. Crawford, ed., 1968. Pp. 63–75.

Binford, L. R.
1968a   Methodological Considerations of the Archaeological Use of Ethnographic Data. *In* R. B. Lee and I. DeVore, eds., 1968a. Pp. 268–273.
1968b   Post-Pleistocene Adaptations. *In* New Perspectives in Archaeology. L. R. Binford and S. Binford, eds. Chicago: Aldine.
1972   Contemporary Model Building: Paradigms and the Current State of Paleolithic Research. *In* Models in Archaeology. D. L. Clarke, ed. Pp. 109–166. London: Methuen.
1978   Olorgesailie Deserves More Than a Review. Journal of Anthropological Research 33:493–502.

Binford, L. R., and W. Chasko, Jr.
1976 Nunamiut Demographic History: A Provocative Case. *In* Demographic Anthropology. E. Zubrow, ed. Pp. 63–143. Albuquerque: University of New Mexico Press.

Bird, J.
1963 The Alacaluf. *In* Handbook of South American Indians, Vol. 1. Smithsonian Institution, Bureau of American Ethnology, Bulletin 143. Pp. 555–579.

Birdsell, J. B.
1953 Some Environmental and Cultural Factors Influencing the Structuring of Australian Aboriginal Populations. American Naturalist 87:169–207.
1957 Some Population Problems Involving Pleistocene Man. *In* Population Studies: Animal Ecology and Demography. Cold Spring Harbor Symposium on Quantitative Biology 22:47–69.
1968a Comment. *In* R. B. Lee and I. DeVore, eds., 1968a. P. 94.
1968b Some Predictions for the Pleistocene Based on Equilibrium Systems among Recent Hunter-Gatherers. *In* R. B. Lee and I. DeVore, eds., 1968a. Pp. 229–240.
1975 A Preliminary Report on New Research on Man–Land Relations in Aboriginal Australia. *In* Population Studies in Archaeology and Biological Anthropology: A Symposium. A. Swedlund, ed. Pp. 34–37. American Antiquity, Memoir 30.

Bishop, A.
1964 Use of the Hand in Lower Primates. *In* Evolutionary and Genetic Biology of Primates. J. Buettner-Janusch, ed. Pp. 133–225. New York: Academic Press.

Bishop, W. W.
1967 The Later Tertiary in East Africa: Volcanics, Sediments, and Faunal Inventory. *In* Background to Evolution in Africa. W. W. Bishop and J. D. Clark, eds. Chicago: University of Chicago Press. Pp. 31–56.

Bishop, W. W., M. Pickford, and A. Hill
1975 New Evidence Regarding the Quaternary Geology, Archaeology, and Hominids of Chesowanja, Kenya. Nature 258:204–208.

Bitterman, M. E.
1975 The Comparative Analysis of Learning. Science 188:699–709.

Blair Rains, A., and A. M. Yalala
1972 The Central and Southern State Lands, Botswana. Land Resource Study No. 11. Surrey: Surbiton.

Blankenship, L. and C. R. Field
1972 Factors Affecting the Distribution of Wild Ungulates on a Ranch in Kenya. Preliminary Report. Zoologica Africana 7(1):281–302.

Blankenship, L., and S. Qvortrup
1974 Resource Management on a Kenya Ranch. Journal of the South African Wildlife Management Association 4:185–190.

Blaxter, K.
1975 Protein from Non-Domesticated Herbivores. *In* Food Protein Sources. N. Pirie, ed. Pp. 147–156. Cambridge: Cambridge University Press.

Blundell, V.
1975 Aboriginal Adaptation in Northwest Australia. Ph.D. dissertation, University of Wisconsin.

Boas, F.
1964 The Central Eskimo. Lincoln: University of Nebraska Press.

Boaz, N., and J. Hampel
1978 Strontium Contents of Tooth Enamel and Diet in Early Hominids. Journal of Paleontology 52:928–933.

Bodenheimer, F. S.
1951 Insects as Human Food. The Hague: W. Junk.

Boesch, C.
1978 Nouvelles Observations sur les Chimpanzés de la Forêt de Tai (Côte-D'Ivoire). La Terre et la Vie 32:195–201.

Bogert, L. J., G. M. Briggs, and D. H. Calloway
1973 Nutrition and Physical Fitness, 9th ed. Philadelphia: W. B. Saunders.

Bonnefille, R.
1972 Associations Polliniques Actuelles et Quaternaires en Ethiopie (Vallées de l'Awash et de l'Omo). Paris: Centre National de la Recherche Scientifique, doc. no. A07229.
1976a Implications of Pollen Assemblages from the Koobi Fora Formation, East Rudolf, Kenya. Nature 264:403–407.
1976b Palynological Evidence for an Important Change in the Vegetation of the Omo Basin Between 2.5 and 2 Million Years. *In* Y. Coppens et al., eds., 1976. Pp. 421–431.

Bonucci, E., and G. Graziani
1976 Comparative Thermogravimetric, X-Ray Diffraction and Electron Microscope Investigations of Burnt Bones from Recent, Ancient and Prehistoric Age. Atti dell'Accademia Nazionale dei Lincei 59:517–532.

Booth, A. H.
1956 The Cercopithecidae of the Gold and Ivory Coast: Geographic and Systematic Observations. Annals and Magazine of Natural History 9:476–480.
1957 Observations on the Natural History of the Olive Colobus Monkey, *Procolobus verus* (Van Beneden). Proceedings of the Zoological Society of London 129:421–430.

Bordes, F.
1968 The Old Stone Age. New York: McGraw-Hill.

Boserup, E.
1965 The Conditions of Agricultural Growth. Chicago: Aldine.

Boughey, A.
1968 Ecology of Populations. New York: Macmillan Co.

Bourliere, F., and M. Hadley
   1970   The Ecology of Tropical Savannas. Annual Review of Ecology and Systematics 1.

Bourliere, F., C. Hunkeler, and M. Bertrand
   1970   Ecology and Behavior of Lowe's Guenon (*Cercopithecus campbelli lowei*) in the Ivory Coast. *In* J. R. Napier and P. H. Napier, eds., 1970. Pp. 297–350.

Bowdler, S.
   1976   Hook, Line and Dilly Bag: An Interpretation of an Australian Coastal Shell Midden. Mankind 10:248–258.

Braidwood, R., and G. Willey
   1962   Conclusions and Afterthoughts. *In* Courses Toward Urban Life. R. Braidwood and G. Willey, eds. Viking Fund Publications in Anthropology, 32. Pp. 330–59. Chicago: Aldine.

Brain, C. K.
   1958   The Transvaal Ape-Man-Bearing Deposits. Pretoria: Transvaal Museum Memoir 11.
   1967   Hottentot Food Remains and their Meaning in the Interpretation of Fossil Bone Assemblages. Pretoria: Scientific Papers of the Namib Desert Research Station 32:1–11.
   1969a   The Contribution of Namib Desert Hottentots to an Understanding of Australopithecine Bone Accumulations. Pretoria: Scientific Papers of the Namib Desert Research Station 39:13–22.
   1969b   Faunal Remains from the Bushman Rock Shelter, Eastern Transvaal. South African Archaeological Bulletin 24:52–55.
   1969c   Faunal Remains from the Wilton Large Rock Shelter. *In* Re-excavation and Description of the Wilton Type-Site, Albany District, Eastern Cape, by J. Deacon. M. A. thesis, University of Cape Town.
   1970   New Finds at Swartkrans Australopithecine Site. Nature 225:1112–1118.
   1974   Some Suggested Procedures in the Analysis of Bone Accumulations from Southern African Quaternary Sites. Annals of the Transvaal Museum 29:1–5.
   1976a   Some Principles in the Interpretation of Bone Accumulations Associated with Man. *In* G.Ll. Isaac and E. R. McCown, eds., 1976. Pp. 97–116.
   1976b   A Re-interpretation of the Swartkrans Site and Its Remains. South African Journal of Science 72:141–146.
   1978   Some Aspects of the South African Australopithecine Sites and Their Bone Accumulations. *In* C. Jolly, ed., 1978. Pp. 131–164.

Brain, C. K., C. van Riet Lowe, and R. A. Dart
   1955   Kafuan Stone Artefacts in the Post-Australopithecine Breccia at Makapansgat. Nature 175:16–18.

Breuil, H., and R. Lantier
   1959   Les Hommes de la Pierre Ancienne. Paris: Payot.

Breuil, H. and H. Obermaier
   1935   The Cave of Altamira at Santillana del Mar, Spain. Junta de las Cuevas

de Altamira. Madrid: Hispanic Society of America and Academia de la Historia.

Breuil, H., and G. Willey
1955   The Cave of Altamira at Santillana del Mar, Spain. Junta de las Cuevas de Altamira. Madrid: Hispanic Society of America and Academia de la Historia.

Brewer, S.
1978   The Chimps of Mt. Asserik. New York: Alfred A. Knopf.

Breyer-Brandwijk, M. G.
1937   A Note on the Bushman Arrow Poison, *Diamphidia simplex* Peringuey. *In* Bushmen of the Southern Kalahari. J. D. Rheinallt Jones and C. M. Doke, eds. Johannesburg: Witwatersrand University Press.

Britton, D., and E. Richards
1969   Optical Emission Spectroscopy and the Study of Metallurgy in the European Bronze Age. *In* D. R. Brothwell and E. Higgs, eds., 1969. Pp. 603–613.

Brolly, R.
n.d.   Eastern Athapaskan Settlement Patterns as a Functional Ecological Response of Predator-Prey Relationships. Manuscript on file with the Department of Archaeology, Simon Fraser University, Burnaby, British Columbia.

Broom, R.
1925   Some Notes on the Taungs Skull. Nature 115:569–571.

Brosset, A.
1966   La Biologie des Chiroptères. Paris: Masson.

Brothwell, D. R., and E. Higgs, eds.
1969   Science in Archaeology, rev. ed. New York: Praeger.

Brothwell, D. R., T. Molleson, P. Gray, and R. Harcourt
1969   The Application of X-Rays to the Study of Archaeological Materials. *In* D. R. Brothwell and E. Higgs, eds., 1969. Pp. 513–525.

Brouwer, A.
1966   General Palaeontology. Chicago: University of Chicago Press.

Brown, A.
1973   Bone Strontium Content as a Dietary Indicator in Skeletal Populations. Ph.D. dissertation, University of Michigan.

Brown, F. H., and K. R. Lajoie
1971   Radiometric Age Determinations on Pliocene/Pleistocene Formations in the Lower Omo Basin, Ethiopia. Science 229:483–485.

Brown, L. H.
1971   The Relations of the Crowned Eagle *Stephanaoetus coronatus* and Some of its Prey Animals. Ibis 113:240–243.

Bryan, A. L.
1969   Early Man in America and the Late Pleistocene Chronology of Western Canada and Alaska. Current Anthropology 10:339–367.

Bryan, A. L., and R. Gruhn
1964   Problems Relating to the Neothermal Climatic Sequence. American Antiquity 29:307–316.

Bryan, A. L., R. Casamiquela, J. Cruxent, R. Gruhn, and C. Ochsenius
1978   An El Jobo Mastodon Kill at Taima-Taima, Venezuela. Science 200: 1275–1277.

Burch, E. S., Jr.
1972   The Caribou/Wild Reindeer as a Human Resource. American Antiquity 37:339–368.

Burrows, W.
1968   Textbook of Microbiology, 19th ed. Philadelphia: W. B. Saunders.

Burton, F. D., and M. J. Bick
1972   A Drift in Time can Define a Deme: The Implications of Tradition Drift in Primate Societies for Hominid Evolution. Journal of Human Evolution 1:53–59.

Busse, C. D.
1977   Chimpanzee Predation as a Possible Factor in the Evolution of Red Colobus Monkey Social Organization. Evolution 31:907–911.
1978   Do Chimpanzees Hunt Cooperatively? American Naturalist 112:771–774.

Butynski, T. M.
1973   Life History and Economic Value of the Springhare (*Pedetes capensis* Forster) in Botswana. Botswana Notes and Records 5:209.

Butzer, K. W.
1964   Environment and Archaeology: An Introduction to Pleistocene Geography. Chicago: Aldine.
1971a   Environment and Archaeology: An Introduction to Pleistocene Geography. 2nd ed. Chicago: Aldine.
1971b   Comunicación Preliminar Sobre la Geología de Cueva Morín (Santander). *In* J. González Echegaray et al., eds., 1971. Pp. 343–356.
1974   Paleoecology of South African Australopithecines: Taung Revisited. Current Anthropology 15:367–382.
1975   Geological and Ecological Perspectives on the Middle Pleistocene. *In* K. W. Butzer and G.Ll. Isaac, eds., 1975. Pp. 847–873.
1976   Lithostratigraphy of the Swartkrans Formation. South African Journal of Science 72:136–141.
1978   Geo-Ecological Interpretation of Early Hominid Paleo-Ecology: Background, Realizations, Prospects. *In* C. Jolly, ed., 1978. Pp. 191–218.

Butzer, K. W., and G.Ll. Isaac, eds.
1975   After the Australopithecines: Stratigraphy, Ecology, and Culture Change in the Middle Pleistocene. The Hague: Mouton.

Buxton, A. P.
1952 Observations on the Diurnal Behavior of the Redtail Monkey (*Cerco-pithecus ascanius schmidti*) in a Small Forest in Uganda. Journal of Animal Ecology 21:25–58.

Bygott, J. D.
1972 Cannibalism among Wild Chimpanzees. Nature 238:410–411.

Campbell, B. G.
1966 Human Evolution. Chicago: Aldine.
1974 Human Evolution, 2d ed. Chicago: Aldine.

Campbell, I., D. Crozier, and R. Caton
1976 Abnormal Fatty Acid Composition and Impaired Oxygen Supply in Cystic Fibrosis Patients. Pediatrics 57:480–486.

Campbell, J. A.
1974 Approaches in Revising Dietary Standards. Journal of the American Dietetic Association 64:175–178.

Canal i Roquet, J., and N. Soler i Masferrer
1976 El Paleolític a les Comarques Gironines. Girona: Caixa de'Estalvis Provincial.

Caraco, T., and L. Wolf
1975 Ecological Determinants of Group Sizes of Foraging Lions. American Naturalist 109:343–352.

Carbonell, E.
1976 Materials Paleolítics de les Comarques Gironines. Barcelona: Biblioteca de Catalunya.

Carnegie, D.
1898 Spinnifex and Sand: A Narrative of Five Years' Pioneering and Explora-tion in Western Australia. London: Pearson.

Carpenter, C. R.
1934 A Field Study of the Behavior and Social Relations of Howling Monkeys. Comparative Psychology Monographs 10:1–168.
1935 Behavior of the Red Spider Monkey (*Ateles geoffroyi*) in Panama. Journal of Mammalogy 16:171–180.
1940 A Field Study in Siam of the Behavior and Social Relations of the Gibbon, *Hylobates lar*. Comparative Psychology Monographs 16:1–212.
1964 Territoriality: A Review of Concepts and Problems. *In* Naturalistic Behavior of Nonhuman Primates. C. R. Carpenter, ed. Pp. 224–250. Uni-versity Park: Pennsylvania State University Press.

Cartmill, M.
1974 Rethinking Primate Origins. Science 184:436–443.

Casimir, M. J.
1975 Feeding Ecology and Nutrition of an Eastern Gorilla Group in the Mt. Kahuzi Region (République du Zaïre). Folia Primatologica 24:81–137.

Cates, R. G., and G. H. Orians
1975   Successional Status and the Palatability of Plants to Generalized Herbivores. Ecology 56:410–418.

Caughley, G.
1966   Mortality Patterns in Mammals. Ecology 47:906–918.
1970   Eruption of Ungulate Populations, with Emphasis on Himalayan Tahr in New Zealand. Ecology 51:53–72.

Chalmers, N. R.
1968   Group Composition, Ecology and Daily Activity of Free Living Mangabeys in Uganda. Folia Primatologica 8:247–262.

Chang, K. C.
1967   Rethinking Archaeology. New York: Random House.

Chaplin, R. E.
1971   The Study of Animal Bones from Archaeological Sites. London: Seminar Press.

Chapman, V.
1964   Coastal Vegetation. New York: Macmillan.

Chard, C.
1969   Man in Prehistory. New York: McGraw-Hill.

Charles-Dominique, P.
1966   Analyse des Contenus Stomacaux d'*Arctocebus calabarensis, Perodicticus potto, Galago alleni, Galago elegantulus, Galago demidovii*. Biologica Gabonica 2:347–353.
1971   Eco-Éthologie des Prosimiens du Gabon. Biologica Gabonica 7:121–228.
1972   Ecologie et Vie Sociale de *Galago demidovii* (Fischer 1808; Prosimii). *In* Behaviour and Ecology of Nocturnal Prosimians. Advances in Ethology, 9. P. Charles-Dominique and R. D. Martin, eds. Pp. 7–41. Berlin: Verlag Paul Parey.
1974   Ecology and Feeding Behaviour of Five Sympatric Lorisids in Gabon. *In* R. D. Martin, G. A. Doyle, and A. C. Walker, eds. Pp. 131–150.
1975   Nocturnality and Diurnality: An Ecological Interpretation of These Two Modes of Life by an Analysis of the Higher Vertebrate Fauna in Tropical Forest Ecosystems. *In* Phylogeny of the Primates: An Interdisciplinary Approach. W. P. Luckett and F. S. Szalay, eds. Pp. 69–88. New York: Plenum Publishing Co.
1977   Ecology and Behaviour of Nocturnal Primates. New York: Columbia University Press.
1978   Solitary and Gregarious Prosimians: Evolution of Social Structure in Primates. *In* Recent Advances in Primatology. Vol. 3: Evolution. D. J. Chivers and K. A. Joysey, eds. Pp. 139–150. London: Academic Press.

Charles-Dominique, P., and C. M. Hladik
1971   Le *Lepilemur* du Sud de Madagascar: Ecologie, Alimentation et Vie Sociale. La Terre et la Vie 25:3–66.

Charles-Dominique, P., and R. D. Martin
1970   Evolution of Lorises and Lemurs. Nature 227:257–260.

Charles-Dominique, P., and J.-J. Petter
in press Ecology and Social Life of *Phaner furcifer*. *In* Ecology, Physiology, and Behavior of Five Nocturnal Lemurs of the West Coast of Madagascar. P. Charles-Dominique, ed. Basel: S. Karger.

Chavaillon, J.
1975 La Site Paléolithique Ancien l'Omo 84 (Éthiopie). Documents pour Servir á l'Histoire des Civilisations Éthiopiennes. Paris: Centre National de la Recherche Scientifique, Fasc. 6:9–18.
1976a Evidence for the Technical Practices of Early Pleistocene Hominids: Shungura Formation, Lower Valley of the Omo, Ethiopia. *In* Y. Coppens et al., eds., 1976. Pp. 565–573.
1976b (Ed.) L'Éthiopie avant l'Histoire. Cahier No. 1. Bellevue, France: Centre National de la Recherche Scientifique.

Chewings, C.
1936 Back in the Stone Age. Sydney: Angus and Robertson.

Chivers, D. J.
1973 An Introduction to the Socio-Ecology of Malayan Forest Primates. *In* R. P. Michael and J. H. Crook, eds., 1973. Pp. 101–146.
1974 The Siamang in Malaya. Contributions to Primatology 4. Basel: S. Karger.
1977 The Feeding Behaviour of Siamang. *In* T. H. Clutton-Brock, ed., 1977. Pp. 355–383.

Chivers, D. J., and J. Herbert, eds.
1978 Recent Advances in Primatology. Vol. 1: Behaviour. London: Academic Press.

Chivers, D. J., and C. M. Hladik
in prep. Morphology of the Gastro-Intestinal Tract in Primates: Comparisons with Other Mammals in Relation to Diet.

Chivers, D. J., J. J. Raemaekers, and F. P. G. Aldrich-Blake
1975 Long-Term Observations of Siamang Behavior. Folia Primatologica 23:1–49.

Chorazyna, H., and G. U. Kurup
1975 Observations on the Ecology and Behavior of *Anathana ellioti* in the Wild. *In* S. Kondo, M. Kawai, and A. Ehara, eds., 1975. Pp. 342–344.

Clark, G.
1971 The Asturian of Cantabria: A Re-Evaluation. Ph.D. dissertation, University of Chicago.

Clark, J. D.
1959 The Prehistory of Southern Africa. Baltimore: Penguin.
1960 Human Ecology during Pleistocene and Later Times in Africa South of the Sahara. Current Anthropology 1:307–321.
1970 The Prehistory of Africa. New York: Praeger.
1972a Paleolithic Butchery Practices. *In* P. J. Ucko, R. Tringham, and G. W. Dimbleby, eds., 1972, Pp. 149–156.
1972b Mobility and Settlement Patterns in Sub-Saharan Africa: A Com-

parison of Late Prehistoric Hunter-Gatherers and Early Agricultural Occupation Units. *In* P. J. Ucko, R. Tringham, and G. W. Dimbleby, eds., 1972. Pp. 127–148.

Clark, J. D., and C. V. Haynes, Jr.
1969   An Elephant Butchery Site at Mwanganda's Village, Karonga, Malawi, and Its Relevance for Palaeolithic Archaeology. World Archaeology 1: 390–411.

Clark, J. D., and H. Kurashina
1976   New Plio-Pleistocene Archaeological Occurrences from the Plain of Gadeb, Upper Webi Shebele Basin, Ethiopia. *In* Les Plus Anciennes Industries en Afrique. J. D. Clark and G.Ll. Isaac, eds. Nice: Preprint of the IX Congrès, Union Internationale des Sciences Préhistoriques et Protohistoriques.

Clark, J. G. D.
1953   The Economic Approach to Prehistory. Proceedings, British Academy 39:215–238.

Clark, W. E. Le Gros
1967   Man-Apes or Ape Men? New York: Holt, Rinehart and Winston.

Clastres, D.
1972   The Guayaki. *In* M. G. Bicchieri, ed., 1972. Pp. 138–174.

Clutton-Brock, T. H.
1973   Feeding Levels and Feeding Sites of Red Colobus (*Colobus badius tephrosceles*) in the Gombe National Park. Folia Primatologica 19:368–379.
1975a   Feeding Behavior of Red Colobus and Black and White Colobus in East Africa. Folia Primatologica 23:165–208.
1975b   Ranging Behavior of Red Colobus Monkeys. Animal Behaviour 23: 706–722.
1977   (Ed.) Primate Ecology. New York: Academic Press.

Coale, A.
1974   The History of the Human Population. Scientific American 231(3):40–52.

Coe, M. J., and F. M. Isaac
1965   Pollination of the Baobab (*Adansonia digitata* L.) by the Lesser Bush Baby (*Galago crassicaudatus* E. Geoffroy). East African Wildlife Journal 3:123–124.

Coelho, A.
1975   Energy Budgets of Guatemalan Howler and Spider Monkeys: A Socio-Bioenergetic Analysis. Ph.D. dissertation, University of Texas, Austin.

Coimbra-Filho, A. F., and R. A. Mittermeier
1973a   Distribution and Ecology of the Genus *Leontopithecus* Lesson, 1840 in Brazil. Primates 14:47–66.
1973b   New Data on the Taxonomy of the Brazilian Marmosets of the Genus *Callithrix* Erxleben, 1777. Folia Primatologica 20:241–264.

Cole, L.
1954   The Population Consequences of Life History Phenomena. Quarterly Review of Biology 29:103–137.

Cole, S.
1963 The Prehistory of East Africa. New York: Macmillan.

Coles, J.
1973 Archeology by Experiment. New York: Charles Scribner's Sons.

Conklin, H.
1954 An Ethnoecological Approach to Shifting Agriculture. Transactions, New York Academy of Sciences, n.s. 17:133–142.

Cooke, H. B. S.
1962 Notes on the Faunal Material from the Cave of Hearths and Kalkbank. *In* Prehistory of the Transvaal. R. Mason, ed. Pp. 447–453. Johannesburg: Witwatersrand University Press.
1963 Pleistocene Mammal Faunas of Africa, with Particular Reference to Southern Africa. *In* African Ecology and Human Evolution. F. C. Howell and F. Bourliere, eds. Pp. 65–116. Chicago: Aldine.

Cooper, H.
in press Learning Abilities of Prosimians. *In* Cognition and Learning. A. M. Schrier and R. E. Passingham, eds. London: Academic Press.

Cooper, J. M.
1917 Analytical and Critical Bibliography of the Tribes of Tierra del Fuego and Adjacent Territory. Washington, D.C.: Smithsonian Institution, Bureau of American Ethnology, Bulletin 63.

Coppens, Y., F. C. Howell, G. Ll. Isaac, and R. E. F. Leakey, eds.
1976 Earliest Man and Environments in the Lake Rudolf Basin: Stratigraphy, Paleoecology, and Evolution. Chicago: University of Chicago Press.

Coryndon, S. C.
1976 Fossil Hippopotamidae from the Plio-Pleistocene Successions of the Rudolf Basin. *In* Y. Coppens et al., eds., 1976. Pp. 238–250.

Coursey, D. G.
1973 Hominid Evolution and Hypogeous Plant Foods. Man 8:634–635.

Crader, D. C.
in prep. A Comparative Study of Later Stone Age Bone Refuse and Its Implications for Prehistoric Economy in South Central Africa. Ph.D. dissertation, University of California, Berkeley.

Crawford, M. A., ed.
1968 Comparative Nutrition of Wild Animals. London: Symposia of the Zoological Society of London, No. 21.

Crook, J. H.
1966 Cooperation in Primates. Eugenics Quarterly 58:63–70
1970 The Socio-Ecology of Primates. *In* Social Behaviour in Birds and Mammals. J. H. Crook, ed. Pp. 103–159. New York: Academic Press.

Crook, J. H., and P. Aldrich-Blake
1968 Ecological and Behavioral Contrasts between Sympatric Ground Dwelling Primates in Ethiopia. Folia Primatologica 8:192–227.

Crook, J. H., and S. Gartlan
  1966   Evolution of Primate Societies. Nature 210:1200–1203.

Curtin, S. H.
  1976   Niche Differentiation and Social Organization in Sympatric Malaysian Colobines. Ph.D. dissertation, University of California, Berkeley.
  1977   Niche Separation in Sympatric Malaysian Leaf-Monkeys (*Presbytis obscura* and *P. melalophus*). Yearbook of Physical Anthropology 20:421–439.

Curtin, S. H., and D. J. Chivers
  1978   Leaf-Eating Primates of Peninsular Malaysia. *In* G. G. Montgomery, ed., 1978. Pp. 441–464.

Dahlberg, F.
  1976   More on Mechanisms of Population Growth. Current Anthropology 17:164–166.

Damas, D.
  1972   The Copper Eskimos. *In* M. G. Bicchieri, ed., 1972. Pp. 3–50.

Dantín Cereceda, J.
  1948   Resumen Fisiográfico de la Península Ibérica. Madrid: Consejo Superior de Investigacions Científicas.

Dare, R.
  1974   The Ecology and Evolution of Food Sharing. California Anthropologist 2:13–25.

Dart, R. A.
  1925   *Australopithecus africanus*: The Man-Ape of South Africa. Nature 115:195–199.
  1926   Taungs and Its Significance. Natural History 26:315–327.
  1940   The Status of *Australopithecus*. American Journal of Physical Anthropology 26:167–186.
  1949   The Predatory Implemental Technique of *Australopithecus*. American Journal of Physical Anthropology 7:1–38.
  1953   The Predatory Transition from Ape to Man. International Anthropological and Linguistic Review 1:201–217.
  1957   The Osteodontokeratic Culture of *Australopithecus prometheus*. Pretoria: Transvaal Museum Memoir 10.
  1959   Adventures with the Missing Link. New York: Viking Press.
  1963   The Carnivorous Propensity of Baboons. Symposia of the Zoological Society of London 10:49–56.

Dart, R. A., and J. W. Kitching
  1958   Bone Tools at the Kalkbank Middle Stone Age Site and the Makapansgat Australopithecine Locality, Central Transvaal. Part 2: The Osteondontokeratic Contribution. South African Archaeological Bulletin 8:94–116.

Darwin, C.
  1871   The Descent of Man. (Published with the Origin of Species.) Reprinted, New York: Random House, Modern Library.

Davenport, R. K., Jr.
1967   The Orang-utan in Sabah. Fola Primatologica 5:247–263.

Davidson, D. S.
1935   Archaeological Problems of Northern Australia. Journal, Royal Anthropological Institute of Great Britain and Ireland 65:145–184.

Day, M., R. E. F. Leakey, and B. Wood
1975   New Hominid from East Rudolf Kenya, I.   American Journal of Physical Anthropology 42:461–476.

Day, M., R. E. F. Leakey, A. Walker, and B. Wood
1976   New Hominids from East Turkana, Kenya. American Journal of Physical Anthropology 45:369–436.

Deacon, H. J.
1972   A Review of the Post-Pleistocene in South Africa. South African Archaeological Society, Goodwin ser. 1:26–45.
1976   Where Hunters Gathered: A Study of Stone Age People in the Eastern Cape. South African Archaeological Society, Monograph Ser. 1:1–232.

Deacon, J.
1974   Patterning in the Radiocarbon Dates for the Wilton/Smithfield Complex in Southern Africa. South African Archaeological Bulletin 28:3–18.

Deag, J. M.
1974   A Study of the Social Behaviour and Ecology of the Wild Barbary Macaque, *Macaca sylvannus* L.   Ph.D. dissertation, University of Bristol.

Deag, J. M., and J. H. Crook
1971   Social Behavior and "Agonistic Buffering" in Wild Barbary Macaque, *Macaca sylvanus* L.   Folia Primatologica 15:183–200.

Deevey, E., Jr.
1968   Discussion. *In* R. B. Lee and I. DeVore, eds., 1968a. Pp. 94–95.

de la Vega del Sella, C.
1923   El Asturiense. Neuva Industria Preneolítica. Comisíon de Investigacions Paleontológicas y Prehistóricas, Memoira 32.

Delibes Castro, M.
1975   Alimentación del Milano Negro (*Milvus migrans*) en Doñana (Huelva, España). *In* Ornitología y Conservación de la Naturaleza Hoy (special issue of Ardeola), Vol. 1. I. Bernis, I. M. Fernández Cruz, S. Maluquer, and R. Saez Royuela, eds. Pp. 183–207.

de Lumley, H.
1966   Les Fouilles de Terra Amata à Nice. Premiers Résultats. Bulletin du Musée d'Anthropologie Préhistorique de Monaco 13:29–51.
1969a   Étude de l'Outillage Moustérienne de la Grotte de Carigüela (Piñar, Grenade). L'Anthropologie 74:165–206, 325–364.
1969b   A Paleolithic Camp at Nice. Scientific American 2205:42–50.

de Lumley, H., and E. Ripoll
1962   Le Remplissage et l'Industrie Moustérienne de l'Abri Romaní (Province de Barcelone). L'Anthropologie 66:1–35.

de Pelham, A., and F. D. Burton
1976   More on Predatory Behavior in Nonhuman Primates. Current Anthropology 17:512–513.
1977   Reply to: Still More on Predatory Behavior in Nonhuman Primates (by G. Teleki). Current Anthropology 18:108–109.

de Terán, M., et al.
1968   Geografía Regional de España. Barcelona: Ariel.

DeVore, I.
1963   Mother–Infant Relations in Free-Ranging Baboons. *In* Maternal Behavior in Mammals. H. Rheingold, ed. Pp. 305–335. New York: Wiley.
1965 (Ed.)   Primate Behavior. New York: Holt, Rinehart and Winston.

DeVore, I., and K. R. L. Hall
1965   Baboon Ecology. *In* I. DeVore, ed., 1965. Pp. 20–52.

DeVore, I., and S. L. Washburn
1963   Baboon Ecology and Human Evolution. *In* African Ecology and Human Evolution. F. C. Howell and F. Bourliere, eds. Pp. 335–367. Chicago: Aldine.

DeVos, A., and A. Omar
1971   Territories and Movements of Sykes Monkeys (*Cercopithecus mitis kolbi* Neuman) in Kenya. Folia Primatologica 16:196–205.

Dimuzio, J.
n.d.   A Biochemical Approach to Determination of Predation Frequency of Free-Ranging Baboons (*Papio anubis*). School of Veterinary Medicine, University of Pennsylvania. Manuscript.

Dittus, W. P. J.
1974   The Ecology and Behavior of the Toque Monkey, *Macaca sinica.* Ph.D. dissertation, University of Maryland.
1977   The Socioecological Basis for the Conservation of the Toque Monkey (*Macaca sinica*) of Sri Lanka (Ceylon). *In* Primate Conservation. H. S. H. Prince Rainier III and G. Bourne, eds. Pp. 237–265. London: Academic Press.

Dobkin de Rios, M.
1976   Female Odors and the Origin of the Sexual Division of Labor in *Homo sapiens.* Human Ecology 4:261–262.

Dorst, J., and P. Dandelot
1970   A Field Guide to the Larger Mammals of Africa. London: Collins.

Dowling, J. H.
1968   Individual Ownership and the Sharing of Game in Hunting Societies. American Anthropologist 70:502–507.

Doyle, G. A.
1979   Development of Behaviour in Prosimians with Special Reference to the Lesser Bushbaby. *In* The Study of Prosimian Behaviour. G. A. Doyle and R. D. Martin, eds. London: Academic Press.

Draper, H. H.
1977   The Aboriginal Eskimo Diet in Modern Perspective. American Anthropologist 79:309–316.

Draper, P.
1976 Social and Economic Constraints on Child Life Among the !Kung. *In* R. B. Lee and I. DeVore, eds., 1976. Pp. 199–217.

Dreimanis, A.
1968 Extinction of Mastodon in the Eastern United States. Ohio Journal of Science 68:257–272.

Drucker, P.
1937 The Tolowa and Their Southwest Oregon Kin. University of California Publications in American Archaeology and Ethnology 36:221–300.
1951 The Northern and Central Nootkan Tribes. Washington, D.C.: Smithsonian Institution, Bureau of American Ethnology, Bulletin 144.

D'Souza, F.
1974 A Preliminary Field Report of the Lesser Tree Shrew (*Tupaia minor*). *In* R. D. Martin, G. A. Doyle, and A. C. Walker, eds., 1974. Pp. 167–182.

Du Bois, C.
1936 The Wealth Concept as an Integrative Factor in Tolowa-Tutuni Culture. *In* Essays in Anthropology Presented to A. L. Kroeber. R. Lowie, ed. Pp. 49–65. Berkeley: University of California Press.

du Boulay, G. H., and M. A. Crawford
1968 Nutritional Bone Diseases in Captive Primates. *In* M.A. Crawford, ed., 1968. Pp. 223–236.

Dunbar, R. I. M.
1974 Observations on the Ecology and Social Organization of the Green Monkey, *Cercopithecus sabaeus*, in Senegal. Primates 15:341–350.
1977 Feeding Ecology of Gelada Baboons: A Preliminary Report. *In* T. H. Clutton-Brock, ed., 1977. Pp. 251–273.

Dunbar, R. I. M., and E. P. Dunbar
1974 Ecology and Population Dynamics of *Colobus quereza* in Ethiopia. Folia Primatologica 21:188–208.

Dunn, F.
1968 Epidemiological factors: Health and Disease in Hunter-Gatherers. *In* R. B. Lee and I. DeVore, eds., 1968a. Pp. 221–228.

Durnin, J. V. G. A., O. G. Edholm, D. S. Miller, and J. C. Waterlow
1973 How Much Food Does Man Require? Nature 242:418.

Dutt, J.
1976 Population Movement and Gene Flow. *In* Man in the Andes. P. Baker and M. Little, eds. Stroudsburg, Pa.: Dowden, Hutchinson, and Ross.

Eaton, J., and A. Mayer
1953 High Fertility among the Hutterites. Human Biology 25:206–263.

Eaton, R. L.
1974 The Cheetah: The Biology, Ecology, and Behavior of an Endangered Species. New York: Van Nostrand Reinhold.

Eibl-Eibesfeldt, I.
1974 The Myth of the Aggression-Free Hunter and Gatherer Society. *In*

Primate Aggression, Territorality, and Xenophobia. R. Holloway, ed. New York: Academic Press.

Eisenberg, J. F., N. A. Muckenhirn, and R. Rudran
  1972   The Relations Between Ecology and Social Structure in Primates. Science 176:863–874.

Elkin, A. P.
  1964   The Australian Aborigines. New York: Doubleday.

Ellefson, J. O.
  1974   A Natural History of White-Handed Gibbons in the Malayan Peninsula. *In* Gibbon and Siamang, Vol. 3. D. M. Rumbaugh, ed. Pp. 1–136. Basel: S. Karger.

Elliot, O., and M. Elliot
  1967   Field Notes on the Slow Loris in Malaysia. Journal of Mammalogy 48:497–498.

Emlen, S. T., and N. J. Demong
  1975   Adaptive Significance of Synchronized Breeding in a Colonial Bird: A New Hypothesis. Science 188:1029–1031.

Estrada, A., and R. Estrada
  1976   Establishment of a Free-Ranging Colony of Stumptail Macaques (*Macaca arctoides*): Relations to the Ecology I.   Primates 17:337–355.
  1977   Patterns of Predation in a Free-Ranging Colony of Stumtail Macaques (*Macaca arctoides*): Relations to the Ecology II.   Primates 18:633–646.

Estrada, A., J. M. Sandoval, and D. Manzolillo
  1978   Further Data on Predation by Free-Ranging Stumptail Macaques (*Macaca arctoides*). Primates 19:401–407.

Evans, I. H. N.
  1937   The Negritos of Malaya. London: Frank Cass.

Eyre, E. J.
  1845   Journals of Expeditions of Discovery into Central Australia and Overland from Adelaide to King George's Sound, in the Years 1840–1. London: T. and W. Boone.

Fagan, B. M.
  1974   Men of the Earth. Boston: Little, Brown.

Fagan, B. M., and F. L. Van Noten
  1971   The Hunter-Gatherers of Gwisho. Tervuren, Belgium: Musée Royal de l'Afrique Centrale. Annales, Ser. IN-8, Sciences Humaines, No. 74.

FAO/WHO (Food and Agricultural Organization/World Health Organization)
  1975   Handbook on Human Nutritional Requirements, 1974. Nutritional Reviews 33:147–157.

Fernandez, C., and F. Lynch
  1972   Tasaday. Philippine Sociological Review 20:275–330.

Finlayson, H. H.
1935 The Red Centre: Man and Beast in the Heart of Australia. Sydney: Angus and Robertson.

Fitzhugh, W.
1972 Environmental Archaeology and Cultural Systems in Hamilton Inlet, Labrador. Washington, D.C.: Smithsonian Contributions to Anthropology, No. 16.

Fitzpatrick, E. A., and H. A. Nix
1973 The Climatic Factor in Australian Grassland Ecology. *In* Australian Grasslands. R. M. Moore, ed. Pp. 3–26. Canberra: Australian National University Press.

Flannery, K. V.
1968 Archaeological Systems Theory and Early Mesoamerica. *In* Anthropological Archaeology in the Americas. B. J. Meggars, ed. Pp. 67–87. Washington, D.C.: Anthropological Society of Washington.

Flood, J. M.
1973 The Moth Hunters. Ph.D. dissertation, Research School of Pacific Studies, Australian National University.

Fogden, M. P. L.
1974 A Preliminary Field Study of the Western Tarsier, *Tarsius bancanus* Horsefield. *In* R. D. Martin, G. A. Doyle, and A. C. Walker, eds. Pp. 151–165.

Foley, R.
1977 Space and Energy: A Method for Analysing Habitat Value and Utilization in Relation to Archaeological Sites. *In* Spatial Archaeology. D. L. Clarke, ed. Pp. 163–187. New York: Academic Press.

Food and Nutrition Board of the National Research Council
1974 Recommended Dietary Allowances, 8th ed. Washington, D.C.: National Academy of Sciences.

Fooden, J.
1964 Stomach Contents and Gastro-Intestinal Proportions in Wild-Shot Guianian Monkeys. American Journal of Physical Anthropology 22:227–232.
1971 Report on the Primates Collected in Western Thailand, January–April, 1967. Fieldiana. ser. Zoology 59:62.

Forde, C. D.
1934 Habitat, Economy, and Society: A Geographical Introduction to Ethnology. London: Methuen.
1954 Foraging, Hunting and Fishing. *In* A History of Technology, Vol. 1. C. Singer, ed. Pp. 154–186. Oxford: Clarendon Press.

Forrest, Sir John
1875 Explorations in Australia. London: Low, Marston & Searle.

Fortea Pérez, J., and F. Jordá Cerdá
1976 La Cueva de Les Mallaetes y los Problemas del Paleolítico Superior del Mediterráneo Español. Zephyrus 26–27:129–166.

Fossey, D.
1974   Observations on the Home Range of One Group of Mountain Gorillas (*Gorilla gorilla beringei*). Animal Behaviour 22:568–581.

Fossey, D., and A. H. Harcourt
1977   Feeding Ecology of Free-Ranging Mountain Gorilla (*Gorilla gorilla beringei*). *In* T. H. Clutton-Brock, ed., 1977. Pp. 415–447.

Fowler, D., and C. Fowler
1971   Anthropology of the Numa: John Wesley Powell's Manuscripts on the Numic Peoples of Western North America, 1868–1880. Smithsonian Contributions to Anthropology, No. 14. Washington, D.C.: Smithsonian Institution.

Fox, M. W., ed.
1975   The Wild Canids: Their Systematics, Behavioral Ecology and Evolution. New York: Van Nostrand Reinhold.

Fox, R.
1967   In the Beginning: Aspects of Hominid Behavioral Evolution. Man 2:415–433.

Freeman, L.
1973   The Significance of Mammalian Faunas from Paleolithic Occupations in Cantabrian Spain. American Antiquity 38:3–44.
1975a   By Their Works You Shall Know Them: Cultural Developments in the Paleolithic. *In* Hominisation und Verhalten. G. Kurth and I. Eibl-Eibesfeldt, eds. Pp. 234–261. Stuttgart: Gustav Fischer.
1975b   Acheulian Sites and Stratigraphy in Iberia and the Maghreb. *In* K. W. Butzer and G. Ll. Isaac, eds., 1975. Pp. 661–743.
1977   Contribucíon al Estudio de Niveles Paleolíticos en la Cueva del Conde (Oviedo). Boletin del Instituto de Estudios Asturianos 90–91:431–488.

Freeman, L., and K. Butzer
1966   The Acheulean Station of Torralba (Spain). A Progress Report. Quaternaria 8:9–21.

Freeman, L., and J. González Echegaray
1968   La Industria Musteriense de la Cueva de la Flecha (Puente-Viesgo, Santander). Zephyrus 18:43–61.
1970   Aurignacian Structural Features and Burials at Cueva Morín (Santander, Spain). Nature 226:722–726.
in prep.   Life and Death at Cueva Morín.

Freese, C.
1976   Censusing *Alouatta palliata*, *Ateles geoffroyi*, and *Cebus capucinus* in the Costa Rican Dry Forest. *In* Neotropical Primates: Field Studies and Conservation. R. W. Thorington and P. G. Heltne, eds. Pp. 4–9. Washington, D.C.: National Academy of Sciences.

Frisch, J.
1968   Individual Behavior and Intertroop Variability in Japanese Macaques. *In* Primates: Studies in Adaptation and Variability. P. Jay, ed. Pp. 243–252. New York: Holt, Rinehart and Winston.

Frisch, R. E.
1973 The Critical Weight at Menarche and the Initiation of the Adolescent Growth Spurt, and the Control of Puberty. *In* The Control and Onset of Puberty. M. Crumback et al., eds. New York: Wiley-Interscience.
1975 Demographic Implications of the Biological Determinants of Female Fecundity. Social Biology 22:17–22.

Frisch, R. E., and J. W. McArthur
1974 Menstrual Cycles: Fatness as a Determinant of Minimum Weight for Height Necessary for their Maintenance or Onset. Science 185:949–951.

Furuya, Y.
1965 Social Organization of the Crab-Eating Monkey. Primates 6:285–337.

Galat, G., and A. Galat-Luong
1976 La Colonisation de la Mangrove par *Cercopithecus aethiops sabaeus* au Senegal. La Terre et la Vie 30:3–30.

Galdikas-Brindamour, B., and R. Brindamour
1975 Orangutans, Indonesia's "People of the Forest." National Geographic 148:444–473.

Galdikas, B., and G. Teleki
1981 Variations in the Subsistence Activities of Female and Male Pongids: New Perspectives on the Origins of Hominid Labor Division. Current Anthropology 22(3): in press.

Galef, B. G., R. A. Mittermeier, and R. C. Bailey
1976 Predation by the Tayra (*Eira barbara*). Journal of Mammalogy 57:760–761.

Garcia, J., W. G. Hankins, and K. W. Rusiniak
1974 Behavioral Regulation of the Milieu Interne in Man and Rat. Science 185:824–831.

García Sánchez, M.
1960 Restos Humanos del Paleolítico Medio y Superior y del Neo-Eneolítico de Piñar (Granada). Trabajos del Instituto "Bernardino de Sahagun," 15:17–72.

Gardner, P. M.
1972 The Paliyans. *In* M. G. Bicchieri, ed., 1972. Pp. 404–447.

Garrod, D., L. Buxton, E. Smith, and D. Babe
1928 Excavation of a Mousterian Rock Shelter at Devil's Tower, Gibraltar. Journal of the Royal Anthropological Institute 58:33–113.

Gartlan, J. S.
1970 Preliminary Notes on the Ecology and Behavior of the Drill, *Mandrillus leucophaeus* Ritgen 1824. *In* J. R. Napier and P. H. Napier, eds., 1970. Pp. 445–480.

Gartlan, J. S., and C. K. Brain
1968 Ecology and Social Variability in *Cercopithecus aethiops* and *C. mitis. In* Primates: Studies in Adaptation and Variability. P. Jay, ed. Pp. 253–292. New York: Holt, Rinehart, and Winston.

Gartlan, J. S., D. B. McKey, and P. G. Waterman
  1978   Soils, Forest Structures and Feeding Behaviour of Primates in a Cameroon Coastal Rain-Forest. *In* D. J. Chivers and J. Herbert, eds., 1978. Pp. 259–267.

Gartlan, J. S., and T. T. Struhsaker
  1972   Polyspecific Associations and Niche Separation of Rain-Forest Anthropoids in Cameroon, West Africa. Journal of Zoology (London) 168:221–266.

Gaulin, S. J. C., and M. Konner
  1977   On the Natural Diet of Primates, Including Humans. *In* Nutrition and the Brain, Vol. 1. R. J. Wurtman and J. J. Wurtman, eds. Pp. 1–86. New York: Raven Press.

Gaulin, S. J. C., and J. A. Kurland
  1976   Primate Predation and Bioenergetics. Science 191:314–315.

Gautier, J.P., and A. Gautier-Hoin
  1969   Associations Polyspécifiques chez les Cercopithèques du Gabon. La Terre et la Vie 23:164–201.

Gautier-Hion, A.
  1966   L'Écologie et l'Éthologie du Talapoin (*Miopithecus talapoin talapoin*). Revue Biologique du Gabon 2:311–329.
  1971   L'Ecologie de Talapoin du Gabon. La Terre et la Vie 25:427–490.
  1973   Social and Ecological Features of the Talapoin Monkey: Comparisons with Sympatric Cercopithecines. *In* R. P. Michael and J. H. Crook, eds., 1973. Pp. 147–170.
  1977   Données sur le Régime Alimentaire de *Cercocebus albigena* dans le Nord-Est du Gabon. La Terre et la Vie 31:579–585.
  1978   Food Niche and Co-Existence in Sympatric Primates in Gabon. *In* D. J. Chivers and J. Herbert, eds., 1978. Pp. 269–286.

Gautier-Hion, A., and J. P. Gautier
  1974   Les Associations Polyspécifiques de Cercopithèques du Plateau de M'passa (Gabon). Folia Primatologica 22:134–177.

Geist, V.
  1975   Mountain Sheep and Man in the Northern Wilds. Ithaca, N.Y.: Cornell University Press.

Gentilli, J.
  1972   Australian Climate Patterns. Melbourne: Thomas Nelson.

Gibbs, W. J.
  1969   Meteorology and Climatology. *In* Lands of Australia. R. O. Slayter and R. A. Perry, eds. Pp. 33–54. Canberra: Australian National University Press.

Gier, H. T.
  1975   Ecology and Behavior of the Coyote (*Canis latrans*). *In* The Wild Canids: Their Systematics, Behavioral Ecology and Evolution. M. W. Fox, ed. New York: Van Nostrand Reinhold.

Gifford, D. P.
1977 Observations of Modern Human Settlements as an Aid to Archaeological Interpretation. Ph.D. dissertation, University of California, Berkeley.

Gifford, D., G. Ll. Isaac and C. M. Nelson
in press Hunters and Herders: Late Stone Age Faunal Remains at Prolonged Drift, Elmenteita, Kenya. Azania.

Gillespie, R., D. R. Horton, P. Ladd, P. G. Macumber, T. H. Rich, R. Thorne, and R. V. S. Wright
1978 Lanafield Swamp and the Extinction of Australian Megafauna. Science 200:1044–1047.

Glander, K.
1975 Habitat Description and Resource Utilization: A Preliminary Report on Mantled Howling Monkey Ecology. *In* R. H. Tuttle, ed., 1975b. Pp. 37–58.
1977 Poison in a Monkey's Garden of Eden. Natural History 86:35–41.
1978 Howling Monkey Feeding Behavior and Plant Secondary Compounds: A View of Strategies. *In* G. G. Montgomery, ed., 1978. Pp. 561–574.

Glaser, D.
1972 Die Reaktionen bei einigen Primaten auf Zwei Künstliche Süssstoffe und H_2O Dest. Folia Primatologica 18:433–443.

Glaser, D., and G. Hellekant
1977 Verhaltens—und Elektrophysiologische Experimente über den Geschmackssinn bei *Saguinus tamarin* (Callitrichidae). Folia Primatologica 28:42–51.

Glob, P. V.
1969 The Bog People. Ithaca, N.Y.: Cornell University Press.

Goggin, J., and W. Sturtevant
1964 The Calusa: A Stratified Nonagricultural Society. *In* Explorations in Cultural Anthropology. W. H. Goodenough, ed. Pp. 179–219. New York: McGraw-Hill.

Göksu, H., J. Fremlin, H. Irwin, and R. Fryxell
1974 Age Determination of Burned Flint by a Thermoluminescent Method. Science 183:651–654.

González Echegaray, J.
1972 Consideraciones Climáticas y Ecológicas Sobre el Magdaleniense III en el Norte de España. Zephyrus 23–24:167–187.
1977 La Estratigrafia del Yacimiento Tardiglaciar de la Cueva del Rascaño (Santander). *In* La Fin des Temps Glaciaires en Europe. Colloque Internationale du Centre National de la Recherche Scientifique. Pp. 448–452.

González Echegaray, J., and L. G. Freeman
1978 Vida y Muerte en Cueva Morín. Santander: Institución Cultural de Cantabria.

González Echegaray, J., L. G. Freeman, K. W. Butzer, A. Leroi-Gourhan, J. Altuna, B. Madariaga, and J. Apellaniz, eds.

1971   Cueva Morín: Excavaciones 1966–1968. Santander: Patronato de las Cuevas Prehistóricas.

González Echegaray, J., L. G. Freeman, B. Madariaga, K. W. Butzer and J. Altuna, eds.
1973   Cueva Morín: Excavaciones 1969. Santander: Patronato de las Cuevas Prehistóricas.

Goodall, A. G.
1977   Feeding and Ranging Behaviour of a Mountain Gorilla Group (*Gorilla gorilla beringei*) in the Tshibinda-Kahuzi Region (Zaïre). *In* T. H. Clutton-Brock, ed., 1977. Pp. 449–479.

Goodall, J. (*see also* van Lawick-Goodall, J.)
1963a   My Life among Wild Chimpanzees. National Geographic 124:272–308.
1963b   Feeding Behavior of Wild Chimpanzees: A Preliminary Report. Symposia of the Zoological Society of London 10:39–47.
1964   Tool-Using and Aimed Throwing in a Community of Free-Living Chimpanzees. Nature 201:1264–1266.
1965   Chimpanzees of the Gombe Stream Reserve. *In* I. DeVore, ed., 1965. Pp. 425–473.
1976   Continuities between Chimpanzee and Human Behavior. *In* G. Ll. Isaac and E. R. McCown, eds., 1976. Pp. 81–95.
1977   Infant Killing and Cannibalism in Free-Living Chimpanzees. Folia Primatologica 28:259–282.

Goodall, J., and D. A. Hamburg
1975   Chimpanzee Behavior as a Model for the Behavior of Early Man: New Evidence of Possible Origins of Human Behavior. American Handbook of Psychiatry 6:14–43.

Gould, R. A.
1966a   Archaeology of the Point St. George Site, and Tolowa Prehistory. University of California Publications in Anthropology 4.
1966b   The Wealth Quest Among the Tolowa Indians of Northwestern California. Proceedings of the American Philosophical Society 110:68–89.
1966c   Notes on Hunting, Butchering, and Sharing of Game among the Ngatatjara and Their Neighbors in the Western Australian Desert. Kroeber Anthropological Society Papers 36:41–63.
1968a   Chipping Stones in the Outback. Natural History 77:42–49.
1968b   Living Archaeology: The Ngatatjara of Western Australia. Southwestern Journal of Anthropology 24:101–122.
1968c   Seagoing Canoes among the Indians of Northwestern California. Ethnohistory 15:11–42.
1969a   Subsistence Behaviour among the Western Desert Aborigines of Australia. Oceania 39:253–274.
1969b   Yiwara: Foragers of the Australian Desert. New York: Scribner's.
1970a   Spears and Spear-Throwers of the Western Desert Aborigines of Australia. American Museum Novitates 2403:1–42.
1970b   Journey to Pulykara. Natural History 79:56–67.

1973 Australian Archaeology in Ecological And Geographical Perspective. Warner Modular Publication No. 7.

Gould, R. A., D. A. Koster, and A. H. L. Sontz
1971 Lithic Assemblage of the Western Desert Aborigines of Australia. American Antiquity 36:149–169.

Graczyk, E.
1971 Fungal Spores as Contextual Archeological Evidence. Bachelor's Honors Paper, Department of Anthropology, University of Chicago.

Graham, A.
1962 The Role of Fungal Spores in Palynology. Journal of Paleontology 36:60–68.

Grayson, D.
1977 Pleistocene Avifaunas and the Overkill Hypothesis. Science 195:691–693.

Green, S.
1975 Dialects in Japanese Monkeys: Vocal Learning and Cultural Transmission of Locale-Specific Vocal Behavior. Zeitschrift für Tierpsychologie 38:304–314.

Greengo, R. E.
1952 Shellfish Foods of the California Indians. Kroeber Anthropological Society Papers 7:63–114.

Greig-Smith, P.
1971 Application of Numerical Methods to Tropical Forests. *In* Statistical Ecology. G. P. Patil, E. C. Pielou, and W. E. Waters, eds. State College: Pennsylvania State University Press.

Grey, G.
1841 Journals of Two Expeditions of Discovery in Northwest and Western Australia during the Years 1837, 38 and 39. 2 vols. London: T. and W. Boone.

Groves, C. P.
1973 Notes on the Ecology and Behavior of the Angola Colobus (*Colobus angolensis* P. L. Sclater 1860) in N. E. Tanzania. Folia Primatologica 20:12–26.

Grubb, P.
1973 Distribution, Divergence and Speciation of the Drill and Mandrill. Folia Primatologica 20:161–177.

Guilday, J. E.
1967 Differential Extinction during Late-Pleistocene and Recent Times. *In* P. S. Martin and H. E. Wright, eds., 1967. Pp. 121–140.
1970 Animal Remains from Archaeological Excavations at Fort Ligonier. Annals of Carnegie Museum 42:177–186.

Gunderson-Coolen, V.
1977 Some Observations on the Ecology of *Colobus badius temmincki*, Abuko Nature Reserve, The Gambia, West Africa. Primates 18:305–314.

Gunther, E.
1926 An Analysis of the First Salmon Ceremony. American Anthropologist 28:605–617.

Gusinde, M.
1956 Die Twiden: Pygmäen und Pygmoide im Tropischen Afrika. Vienna: Wilhelm Braumüller.

Guyton, A. C.
1966 Textbook of Medical Physiology. Philadelphia: W. B. Saunders.

Haddow, A. J.
1952 Field and Laboratory Studies on an African Monkey, *Cercopithecus ascanius schmidti* Matschie. Proceedings of the Zoological Society of London 122:297–394.

Hahn, T.
1881 Tsuni-//Goam: The Supreme Being of the Khoi-Khoi. London: Trubner and Co.

Hall, K. R. L.
1962 Numerical Data, Maintenance Activities and Locomotion of the Wild Chacma Baboon, *Papio ursinus*. Proceedings of the Zoological Society of London 139:181–220.
1963a Observational Learning in Monkeys and Apes. British Journal of Psychology 54:201–226.
1963b Variations in the Ecology of the Chacma Baboon, *Papio ursinus*. Symposia of the Zoological Society of London 10:1–28.
1965 Behavior and Ecology of the Wild Patas Monkey, *Erythrocebus patas*, in Uganda. Journal of Zoology 148:15–87.
1968 Social Learning in Monkeys. *In* Primates: Studies in Adaptation and Variability. P. Jay, ed. Pp. 383–397. New York: Holt, Rinehart and Winston.

Hall, K. R. L., and J. S. Gartlan
1965 Ecology and Behavior of the Vervet Monkey, *Cercopithecus aethiops*, Lolui Island, Lake Victoria. Proceedings of the Zoological Society of London 145:37–56.

Halstead, L. B.
1969 The Pattern of Vertebrate Evolution. Edinburgh: Oliver and Boyd.

Harako, R.
1976 Mbuti as Hunters: A Study of the Economic Anthropology of the Mbuti Pygmies. Kyoto University African Studies 10:37–99.
1977 Ecology and Society of the Mbuti. *In* Handbook of Anthropology, Vol. 12: Ecological Anthropology. H. Watanabe, ed. Tokyo: Yazankaku.

Hardesty, D. L.
1975 The Niche Concept: Suggestions for its Use in Human Ecology. Human Ecology 3:71–85.

Harding, R. S. O.
1973a Predation by a Troop of Olive Baboons (*Papio anubis*). American Journal of Physical Anthropology 38:587–592.

1973b Range Utilization by a Troop of Olive Baboons (*Papio anubis*). Ph.D. dissertation, University of California, Berkeley.

1974 The Predatory Baboon. Expedition 16:30–39.

1975 Meat-Eating and Hunting in Baboons. *In* R. H. Tuttle, ed., 1975b. Pp. 245–258.

1976 Ranging Patterns of a Troop of Baboons (*Papio anubis*) in Kenya. Folia Primatologica 25:143–185.

1977 Patterns of Movement in Open Country Baboons. American Journal of Physical Anthropology 47:349–353.

Harding, R. S. O., and S. C. Strum
1976 The Predatory Baboons of Kekopey. Natural History 85:46–53.

Harris, J. W. K.
1978 The Karari Industry and Its Place in East African Prehistory. Ph.D. dissertation, University of California, Berkeley.

Harris, J. W. K., and G. Ll. Isaac
1976 The Karari Industry: Early Pleistocene Archaeological Evidence from the Terrain East of Lake Turkana, Kenya. Nature 262:102–107.

Harris, M.
1971 Culture, Men and Nature. New York: Crowell.

1975 Culture, People, and Nature. New York: Crowell.

Harrison, T.
1962 Leaf Monkeys at Fraser's Hill. Malaysian Nature Journal 16:120–125.

Hassan, F.
1973 On Mechanics of Population Growth during the Neolithic. Current Anthropology 14:5.

Hartmann, R.
1886 Anthropoid Apes. New York: D. Appleton.

Hausfater, G.
1975 Dominance and Reproduction in Baboons. Contributions to Primatology 7. Basel: S. Karger.

1976 Predatory Behavior of Yellow Baboons. Behaviour 56:440–468.

Hawkes, C.
1954 Archaeological Theory and Method: Some Suggestions from the Old World. American Anthropologist 56:155–168.

Hay, R. L.
1973 Lithofacies and Environments of Bed I, Olduvai Gorge, Tanzania. Quaternary Research 3:541–560.

1976 Geology of the Olduvai Gorge. Berkeley: University of California Press.

Hayden, B.
1972 Population Control Among Hunter/Gatherers. World Archaeology 4:205–221.

1975 The Carrying Capacity Dilemma. *In* Population Studies in Archaeology and Biological Anthropology: A Symposium. A. Swedlund, ed. Pp. 11–21. American Antiquity, Memoir 30.

1976 Comment on K. Hutterer's An Evolutionary Approach to the Southeast Asian Cultural Sequence. Current Anthropology 17:232–233.

1977 Sticks and Stones and Ground Edge Axes: The Upper Paleolithic in Southeast Asia? *In* Sunda and Sahul: Prehistoric Studies in Southeast Asia, Melanesia and Australia. J. Allen, J. Golson, and R. Jones, eds. Pp. 73–109. New York: Academic Press.

1978 Bigger is Better? Factors Determining Ontario Iroquois Site Sizes. Canadian Journal of Archaeology 2:107–116.

Hedgepeth, J. W.
1962 Introduction to Seashore Life of the San Francisco Bay Region and the Coast of Northern California. Berkeley: University of California Press.

Hegsted, D. M.
1972 Problems in the Use and Interpretation of the Recommended Dietary Allowances. Ecology of Food and Nutrition 1:255-265.

Heinz, H. J.
1972 Territoriality among the Bushmen in General and the !Ko in Particular. Anthropos 67:405–416.

Helbaek, H.
1969 Palaeo-Ethnobotany. *In* D. R. Brothwell and E. Higgs, eds., 1969. Pp. 206–214.

Helm, J.
1972 The Dogrib Indians. *In* M. G. Bicchieri, ed., 1972. Pp. 51–89.

Helms, R.
1896 Anthropology of the Elder Exploring Expedition. Transactions of the Royal Society of South Australia 16:327–332.

Hendey, Q. B., and R. Singer
1965 The Faunal Assemblages from the Gamtoos Valley Shelters. South African Archaeological Bulletin 20:206–213.

Herbert, V.
1968 Nutritional Requirements for Vitamin B 12 and Folic Acid. American Journal of Clinical Nutrition 21:743–752.

Hernandez-Camacho, J., and R. W. Cooper
1976 The Nonhuman Primates of Colombia. *In* Neotropical Primates: Field Studies and Conservation. R. W. Thorington and P. G. Heltne, eds. Pp. 35–69. Washington, D.C.: National Academy of Sciences.

Herrero, S.
1972 Bears: Their Biology and Management. IUCN Publication, N.S. No. 23. Morges: International Union for the Conservation of Nature.

Hester, J.
1960 Pleistocene Extinction and Radiocarbon Dating. American Antiquity 26:58–77.

1967 The Agency of Man in Animal Extinctions. *In* P. S. Martin and H. E. Wright, eds., 1967. Pp. 189–192.

Hewes, G.
1942 Economic and Geographical Relations of Aboriginal Fishing in Northern California. California Fish and Game 28:103–110.
1961 Food Transport and the Origin of Hominid Bipedalism. American Anthropologist 63:687–710.

Hiatt, B.
1967 The Food Quest and the Economy of the Tasmanian Aborigines. Oceania 38:190–219.
1970 Woman the Gatherer. *In* Woman's Role in Aboriginal Society. F. Gale, ed. Pp. 2–8. Australian Aboriginal Studies No. 36. Canberra: Australian Institute of Aboriginal Studies.

Hiatt, L. R.
1962 Local Organization among the Australian Aborigines. Oceania 32: 267–286.

Hickerson, H.
1962 The Southwestern Chippewa: An Ethnohistorical Study. American Anthropological Association Memoir No. 92. American Anthropologist 64(3), pt. 2.

Higgs, E. S., ed.
1975 Paleoeconomy. Cambridge: Cambridge University Press.

Higgs, E. S., and C. Vita-Finzi
1972 Prehistoric Economies: A Territorial Approach. *In* Papers in Economic Prehistory. E. S. Higgs, ed. Pp. 27–36. Cambridge: Cambridge University Press.

Hilditch, T. P., and P. N. Williams
1964 The Chemical Composition of Natural Fats, 4th ed. London: Chapman and Hall.

Hill, A.
1975 Taphonomy of Contemporary and Late Cenozoic East African Vertebrates. Ph.D. dissertation, University of London.

Hill, J.
1966 A Prehistoric Community in Eastern Arizona. Southwestern Journal of Anthropology 22:9–30.

Hinde, R. A.
1966 Animal Behaviour: A Synthesis of Ethology and Comparative Psychology. New York: McGraw-Hill.

Hipsley, E. H. and N. E. Kirk
1965 Studies of Dietary Intake and the Expenditure of Energy by the New Guineans. Noumea: South Pacific Commission Technical Paper 147.

Hladik, A.
1978a Phenology of Leaf Production in Rain Forest of Gabon: Distribution and Composition of Food for Folivores. *In* G. G. Montgomery, ed., 1978. Pp. 51–71.

1978b   Distribution of Plants Available as Food to Different Primate Species: A Mathematical Approach. *In* D. J. Chivers and J. Herbert, eds., 1978. Pp. 391–398.

Hladik, A., and C. M. Hladik
1969   Rapports Trophiques Entre Végétation et Primates dans la Forêt de Barro Colorado (Panama). La Terre et la Vie 1:25–117.
1977   Signification Écologique des Teneurs en Alcaloïdes des Végétaux de la Forêt Dense: Résultats des Tests Préliminaires Éffectués au Gabon. La Terre et la Vie 31:515–555.

Hladik, C. M.
1966   Observations sur la Muqueuse du Tractus Digestif de Quelques Primates et Corrélations avec le Régime Alimentaire. Thèse de 3ème Cycle, Université de Paris.
1967   Surface Relative du Tractus Digestif de Quelques Primates, Morphologie des Villosités Intestinales et Corrélations avec le Regime Alimentaire. Mammalia 31:120–147.
1968   Recherche des Caractéristiques Histochimiques et Cytologiques de la Muqueuse Intestinale des Primates et des Corrélations avec le Régime Alimentaire. Mémoires du Museum National d'Histoire Naturelle, n.s., ser. A 52:1–69.
1973   Alimentation et Activité d'un Groupe de Chimpanzés Réintroduits en Forêt Gabonaise. La Terre et la Vie 27:343–413.
1974   La Vie d'un Groupe de Chimpanzés dans la Forêt du Gabon. Science et Nature 121:5–14.
1975   Ecology, Diet and Social Patterning in Old and New World Primates. *In* R. H. Tuttle, ed., 1975b. Pp. 3–35.
1977a   A Comparative Study of the Feeding Strategies of Two Sympatric Species of Leaf Monkeys: *Presbytis senex* and *Presbytis entellus. In* T. H. Clutton-Brock, ed., 1977. Pp. 324–353.
1977b   Chimpanzees of Gabon and Chimpanzees of Gombe: Some Comparative Date on the Diet. *In* T. H. Clutton-Brock, ed., 1977. Pp. 481–501.
1978   Adaptive Strategies of Primates in Relation to Leaf Eating. *In* G. G. Montgomery, ed., 1978. Pp. 373–395.
1979   Diet and Ecology of Prosimians. *In* The Study of Prosimian Behaviour. G. A. Doyle and R. D. Martin, eds. Pp. 307–357. London: Academic Press.

Hladik, C. M., and P. Charles-Dominique
1974   The Behavior and Ecology of the Sportive Lemur (*Lepilemur mustelinus*) in Relation to its Dietary Peculiarities. *In* R. D. Martin, G. A. Doyle, and A. C. Walker, eds., 1974. Pp. 23–39.

Hladik, C. M., P. Charles-Dominique, and J.-J. Petter
in press   Feeding Strategies of Five Nocturnal Lemurs in the Dry Forest of the West Coast of Madagascar. *In* Nocturnal Malagasy Lemurs: Ecology, Physiology, and Behavior. P. Charles-Dominique et al., eds. New York: Academic Press.

Hladik, C. M., and D. J. Chivers
1978a Corrélations Entre le Régime Alimentaire et les Proportions du Tractus Digestif des Mammifères et Définitions des Tendances Ecophysiologiques des Primates. Comptes-Rendus de l'Académie des Sciences.

Hladik, C. M., and D. J. Chivers
1978b Concluding Discussion: Ecological Factors and Specific Behavioural Patterns Determining Primate Diet. *In* D. J. Chivers and J. Herbert, eds., 1978. Pp. 433–444.

Hladik, C. M., and L. Gueguen
1974 Géophagie et Nutrition Minérale Chez les Primates Sauvages. Comptes-Rendus de l'Académie des Sciences, ser. D 279:1393–1396.

Hladik, C. M., and A. Hladik
1967 Observations sur le Rôle des Primates dans la Dissémination des Végétaux de la Forêt Gabonaise. Biologica Gabonica 3:43–58.
1972 Disponibilités Alimentaires et Domaines Vitaux des Primates à Ceylan. La Terre et la Vie 26:149–215.

Hladik, C. M., and J.-J. Petter
1970 Le Loris Tardigrade: Observations de Terrains Effectuées à Ceylan. Science et Nature 101:10–17.

Hladik, C. M., and G. Viroben
1974 L'Alimentation Protéique de Chimpanzé dans son Environnement Forestier Naturel. Comptes-Rendus de l'Académie des Sciences, ser. D 279:1475–1478.

Hladik, C. M., P. Charles-Dominique, P. Valdebouze, J. Delort-Laval, and J. Flanzy
1971 La Caecotrophie Chez un Primate Phyllophage du Genre *Lepilemur* et les Corrélations avec les Particularités de son Appareil Digestif. Paris: Comptes-Rendus de l'Académie des Sciences 272:3191–3194.

Hladik, C. M., A. Hladik, J. Bousset, P. Valdebouze, G. Viroben, and J. Delort-Laval
1971 Le Régime Alimentaire des Primates de L'Île de Barro-Colorado (Panama): Résultats des Analyses Quantitatives. Folia Primatologica 16:85–122.

Hoebel, E. A.
1960 The Cheyennes. New York: Holt, Rinehart and Winston.

Hollings, C. S.
1973 Resilience and Stability of Ecological Systems. Annual Review of Ecology and Systematics 4:1–23.

Holloway, R. L.
1966 Cranial Capacity, Neural Reorganization, and Hominid Evolution: A Search for More Suitable Parameters. American Anthropologist 68:103–121.
1969 Culture: A Human Domain. Current Anthropology 10:395–412.

Hooton, E. A.
  1931 Up from the Ape. New York: Macmillan.

Horn, H. S.
  1968 The Adaptive Significance of Colonial Nesting in the Brewer's Blackbird (*Euphagus cyanocephalus*). Ecology 49:682–694.

Horr, D. A.
  1972 The Borneo Orang-Utan. Paper presented at the Annual Meeting of the American Association of Physical Anthropologists, Lawrence, Kansas.

Howard, H.
  1929 The Avifauna of Emeryville Shellmound. University of California Publications in Zoology 32:378–383.

Howell, F. C.
  1966 Observations on the Earlier Phases of the European Lower Paleolithic. American Anthropologist 68:88–201.
  1967 Recent Advances in Human Evolutionary Studies. Quarterly Review of Biology 42:471–513.
  1968 Early Man. New York: Time-Life Books.
  1969 Remains of Hominidae from Pliocene/Pleistocene Formations in the Lower Omo Basin, Ethiopia. Nature 223:1234–1239.
  1972 Pliocene-Pleistocene Hominidae in Eastern Africa: Absolute and Relative Ages. *In* Calibration of Hominoid Evolution. W. W. Bishop and J. A. Miller, eds. Pp. 331–368. Edinburgh: Scottish University Press.
  1976 An Overview of the Pliocene and Earlier Pleistocene of the Lower Omo Basin, Southern Ethiopia. *In* G. Ll. Isaac and E. R. McCown, eds. 1976. Pp. 227–268.
  1979 Hominidae. *In* Mammalian Evolution in Africa. H. B. S. Cooke and V. Maglio, eds. Cambridge, Mass.: Harvard University Press.

Howell, F. C., and J. D. Clark
  1963 Acheulian Hunter-Gatherers of Sub-Saharan Africa. *In* African Ecology and Human Evolution. F. C. Howell and F. Bourliere, eds. Pp. 458–533. Chicago: Aldine.

Howell, F. C., and Y. Coppens
  1976 An Overview of Hominidae from the Omo Succession, Ethiopia. *In* Y. Coppens et al., eds., 1976. Pp. 522–532.

Howell, N.
  1976a The Population of the Dobe Area !Kung. *In* R. B. Lee and I. DeVore, eds., 1976. Pp. 137–151.
  1976b Toward a Uniformitarian Theory of Human Paleodemography. Journal of Human Evolution 5:25–40.

Howells, W. W.
  1967 Mankind in the Making. New York: Doubleday.

Hrdy, S. B.
  1974 Male-Male Competition and Infanticide Among the Langurs (*Presbytis entellus*) of Abu, Rajasthan. Folia Primatologica 22:19–58.

Hughes, A. R., and P. V. Tobias
1977 A Fossil Skull Probably of the Genus *Homo* from Sterkfontein, Transvaal. Nature 265:310–312.

Humphrey, N. K.
1976 The Social Function of Intellect. *In* Growing Points in Ethology. P. P. G. Bateson and R. A. Hinde, eds., Pp. 303–317. Cambridge: Cambridge University Press.

Hutchinson, G. E.
1957 Concluding Remarks. Cold Spring Harbor Symposium on Quantitative Biology 22:415–427.

Hutterer, K.
1976 An Evolutionary Approach to the Southwest Asian Cultural Sequence. Current Anthropology 17:221–242.

Irwin, G.
1974 The Emergence of a Central Place in Coastal Papuan Prehistory: A Theoretical Approach. Mankind 9:268–272.

Isaac, G. Ll.
1966 New Evidence from Olorgesailie Relating to the Character of Acheulean Occupation Sites. Actas del V Congreso Panafricano de Prehistoria y de Estudio del Cuaternario, Vol. 2, Pp. 135–146.
1967a Towards the Interpretation of Occupation Debris: Some Experiments and Observations. Kroeber Anthropological Society Papers 37:31–57
1967b The Stratigraphy of the Peninj Group: Early Middle Pleistocene Formations West of Lake Natron, Tanzania. *In* Background to Evolution in Africa. W. W. Bishop and J. D. Clark, eds. Pp. 229–258. Chicago: University of Chicago Press.
1968 Traces of Pleistocene Hunters: An East African Example. *In* R. B. Lee and I. DeVore, eds., 1968a. Pp. 253–261.
1969 Studies of Early Culture in East Africa. World Archaeology 1:1–28.
1971 The Diet of Early Man: Aspects of Archaeological Evidence from Lower and Middle Pleistocene Sites in Africa. World Archaeology 2:270–299.
1972 Comparative Studies of Pleistocene Site Locations in East Africa. *In* P. J. Ucko, R. Tringham, and G. W. Dimbleby, eds., 1972. Pp. 165–176.
1975 Stratigraphy and Cultural Patterns in East Africa during the Middle Ranges of Pleistocene Time. *In* K. W. Butzer and G. Ll. Isaac, eds., 1975. Pp. 495–542.
1976a The Activities of Early African Hominids: A Review of Archaeological Evidence from the Time Span Two and a Half to One Million Years Ago. *In* G. Ll. Isaac and E. R. McCown, eds., 1976. Pp. 462–514.
1976b Early Stone Tools: An Adaptive Threshold? *In* Problems in Economic and Social Archaeology. G. de G. Sieveking, I. H. Longworth and K. E. Wilson, eds. Pp. 39–47. London: Duckworth.
1976c Plio-Pleistocene Artifact Assemblages from East Rudolf, Kenya. *In* Y. Coppens et al., eds., 1976. Pp. 552–564.
1976d Stages of Cultural Elaboration in the Pleistocene: Possible Archaeo-

logical Indicators of the Development of Language Capabilities. *In* Origins and Evolution of Language and Speech. Annals of the New York Academy of Sciences 280:275–288.

1978 The Food-Sharing Behavior of Protohuman Hominids. Scientific American 238(4):90–108.

Isaac, G. Ll., and J. W. K. Harris

1978 Archaeology. *In* Koobi Fora Research Project. Vol. 1: The Fossil Hominds and an Introduction to their Context, 1968–1974. M. D. Leakey and R. E. F. Leakey, eds. Pp. 64–85. Oxford: Clarendon Press.

Isaac, G. Ll., and E. R. McCown, eds.

1976 Human Origins: Louis Leakey and the East African Evidence. Menlo Park, Calif.: W. A. Benjamin.

Itani, J.

1974 A Sketch of Ituri Forest. Seibutsu Kagaku (Biological Science), No. 26.

Itani, J., and A. Nishimura

1973 The Study of Infrahuman Culture in Japan. *In* Precultural Primate Behavior. Symposia of the Fourth International Congress of Primatology, Vol. 1. E. W. Menzel, ed. Pp. 26–50. Basel: S. Karger.

Iwamoto, T.

1974 A Bioeconomic Study in a Provisioned Troop of Japanese Monkeys (*Macaca fuscata fuscata*) at Koshima Islet, Miyazaki. Primates 15:241–262.

1975 Food Resources and the Feeding Activity. Studies of the Gelada Society (III). *In* S. Kondo, M. Kawai, and A. Ehara, eds., 1975. Pp. 475–480.

1978 Food Availability as a Limiting Factor on Population Density of the Japanese Monkey and Gelada Baboon. *In* D. J. Chivers and J. Herbert, eds., 1978. Pp. 287–303.

Izawa, K.

1972 Japanese Monkeys Living in the Okoppe Basin of the Shimokita Peninsula: The Second Report of the Winter Follow-up Survey after the Aerial Spraying of Herbicide. Primates 13:201–212.

1975 Foods and Feeding Behavior of Monkeys in the Upper Amazon Basin. Primates 18:295–316.

Izawa, K., and J. Itani

1966 Chimpanzees in Kasakati Basin, Tanganyika: (I) Ecological Study in the Rainy Season, 1963–1964. Kyoto University Studies 1:73–156.

Izawa, K., and T. Nishida

1963 Monkeys Living in the Northern Limits of Their Distribution. Primates 4:67–88.

Jaeger, J.-J.

1975 The Mammalian Faunas and Hominid Fossils of the Middle Pleistocene of the Maghreb. *In* K. W. Butzer and G. Ll. Isaac, eds., 1975. Pp. 399–418.

James, W. W.

1960 The Jaws and Teeth of Primates. London: Pitman Medical Publishing Co.

Janssens, P., and J. Gonzáles Echegaray
1958 Memoria de las Excavaciones de la Cueva del Juyo (1955–1956). Santander: Patronato de las Cuevas Prehistóricas.

Janzen, D. H.
1971 Seed Predation by Animals. Annual Review of Ecology and Systematics 2:465–492.
1975 Ecology of Plants in the Tropics. London: Edward Arnold.

Jay, J.
1970 Modern Food Microbiology. New York: Van Nostrand Reinhold.

Jay, P. C.
1962 Aspects of Maternal Behavior Among Langurs. Annals of the New York Academy of Sciences 102:468–476.
1963 Mother-Infant Relations in Langurs. In Maternal Behavior in Mammals. H. Rheingold, ed. Pp. 282–304. New York: Wiley.
1968 (Ed.) Primates: Studies in Adaptation and Variability. New York: Holt, Rinehart and Winston.

Jerome, N. W.
1976 An Ecological Approach to Nutritional Anthropology. Paper presented at the Advanced Seminar on Anthropological Aspects of Human Nutrition. School of American Research, Santa Fe, New Mexico.

Jervis, R. E., et al.
1963 Computer Analysis of Complex Gamma Ray Spectra. Paper presented at the 11th Annual Meeting of the Society for Applied Spectroscopy.

Jewell, P. A.
1966 The Concept of Home Range in Mammals. In Play, Exploration, and Territory in Mammals. P. A. Jewell and C. Loizos, eds. New York: Academic Press.

Jewell, P. A., and J. F. Oates
1969 Ecological Observations on the Lorisoid Primates of African Lowland Forest. Zoological Africana 4:231–248.

Jewitt, J. R.
1974 The Adventures and Sufferings of John R. Jewitt, Captive Among the Nootka, 1803–1805. Journals edited by Derik Smith. Toronto: McClelland and Stewart.

Johanson, D. C., and Y. Coppens
1976 A Preliminary Anatomical Diagnosis of the First Plio/Pleistocene Hominid Discoveries in the Central Afar, Ethiopia. American Journal of Physical Anthropology 45:217–233.

Johanson, D. C., and M. Taieb
1976 Plio-Pleistocene Hominid Discoveries in Hadar, Ethiopia. Nature 260:293–297.

Johanson, D. C., M. Taieb, and Y. Coppens
1978 Plio/Pleistocene Hominid Discoveries in Hadar, Ethiopia. In C. Jolly, ed., 1978.

Johanson, D. C., and T. D. White
  1979   A Systematic Assessment of Early African Hominids. Science 202: 321–330.

Johanson, D. C., T. D. White, and Y. Coppens
  1978   A New Species of the Genus *Australopithecus* (Primates: Hominidae) from the Pliocene of Eastern Africa. Kirtlandia 28:1–14.

Johnson, G. D., and R. G. H. Raynolds
  1976   Late Cenozic Environments of the Koobi Fora Formation. *In* Y. Coppens et al., eds., 1976. Pp. 115–122.

Jolly, A.
  1966   Lemur Behavior: A Madagascar Field Study. Chicago: University of Chicago Press.
  1972   The Evolution of Primate Behavior. New York: Macmillan.

Jolly, C. J.
  1970   The Seed-Eaters: A New Model of Hominid Differentiation Based on a Baboon Analogy. Man 5:5–26.
  1972   Changing Views of Hominid Origins. Yearbook of Physical Anthropology 16:1–17.
  1978   (Ed.) Early Hominids of Africa. New York: St. Martin's Press.

Jones, C.
  1970   Stomach Contents and Gastro-Intestinal Relationships of Monkeys Collected in Rio Muni, West Africa. Mammalia 34:107–117.
  1972   Natural Diets of Wild Primates. *In* Pathology of Simian Primates. R. N. T.-W. Fiennes, ed. Pp. 58–77. Basel: S. Karger.

Jones, C. and J. Sabater Pi
  1968   Comparative Ecology of *Cercocebus albigena* (Gray) and *Cercocebus torquatus* (Kerr) in Rio Muni, West Africa. Folia Primatologica 9:99–113.
  1971   Comparative Ecology of *Gorilla gorilla* (Savage and Wyman) and *Pan troglodytes* (Blumenbach) in Rio Muni, West Africa. Bibliotheca Primatologica 13:1–96.

Jones, R.
  1968   The Geographical Background to the Arrival of Man in Australia and Tasmania. Archaeology and Physical Anthropology in Oceania 3:186–215.

Jonkel, C. J., and I. McT. Cowan
  1971   The Black Bear in the Spruce Fir Forest. Wildlife Monographs 27:1–57.

Jordá Cerdá, F.
  1947   El Musteriense de la "Còva de la Pechina" (Bellus). Comunicaciones del S.I.P. al l[er] Congreso Arqueológico del Levante. Pp. 7–14.

Jouventin, P.
  1975   Observations Sur la Socio-Écologie du Mandrill. La Terre et la Vie 29:493–532.

Kano, T.
  1971a   The Chimpanzee of Filabanga, Western Tanzania. Primates 12:229–246.

1971b   Distribution of the Primates in the Eastern Shore of Lake Tanganyika. Primates 12:281-304.

Kavanagh, M.
1972   Food-Sharing Behaviour Within a Group of Douc Monkeys (*Pygathrix nemaeus nemaeus*). Nature 239:406-407.

Kawabe, M.
1966   One Observed Case of Hunting Behavior Among Wild Chimpanzees Living in the Savanna Woodland of Western Tanzania. Primates 7:393-396.

Kawabe, M., and T. Mano
1972   A Study of the Wild Proboscis Monkey, *Nasalis larvatus* (Wurmb), in Sabah. Primates 13:213-229.

Kawai, M.
1965   Newly Acquired Pre-Cultural Behavior of the Natural Troop of Japanese Monkeys on Koshima Islet. Primates 6:1-30.

Kawai, M., and H. Mizuhara
1959   An Ecological Study of the Wild Mountain Gorilla (*Gorilla gorilla beringei*). Primates 2:1-43.

Kawamura, S.
1959   The Process of Sub-Culture Propagation Among Japanese Macaques. Primates 2:43-60.

Kay R. F.
1973   Mastication, Molar Tooth Structure and Diet in Primates. Ph.D. dissertation, Yale University.
1978   Molar Structure and Diet in Extant Cercopithecidae. *In* Development, Function, and Evolution of Teeth. P. M. Butler and K. A. Joysey, eds. New York: Academic Press. Pp. 309-339.

Kay, R. F., and W. Hylander
1978   The Dental Structure of Mammalian Folivores with Special Reference to Primates and Phalangeroids (Marsupialia). *In* G. G. Montgomery, ed., 1978. Pp. 173-191.

Keeley, L. H.
1977   The Functions of Paleolithic Flint and Tools. Scientific American 237(5):108-126.

Kemp, W.
1971   The Flow of Energy in a Hunting Society. Scientific American 225(3):104-115.

Kern, J. A.
1964   Observations on the Habits of the Proboscis Monkey, *Nasalis larvatus* (Wurmb), Made in the Brunei Bay Area, Borneo. Zoologia 49:183-192.

King, G. E.
1975   Socioterritorial Units Among Carnivores and Early Hominids. Journal of Antrhopological Research 31:69-87.

Kinzey, W. G.
  1977   Diet and Feeding Behavior of *Callicebus torquatus. In* T. H. Clutton-Brock, ed., 1977. Pp. 127–152.
  1978   Feeding Behavior and Molar Features in Two Species of Titi Monkey. *In* D. J. Chivers and J. Herbert, eds., 1978. Pp. 373–385.

Kinzey, W. G., A. L. Rosenberger, and M. Ramirez
  1975   Vertical Clinging and Leaping in a Neotropical Anthropoid. Nature 225:327–328.

Kleiman, D. G., and J. F. Eisenberg
  1973   Comparisons of Canid and Felid Social Systems from an Evolutionary Perspective. Animal Behaviour 21:637–659.

Klein, L. L.
  1972   The Ecology and Social Organization of the Spider Monkey, *Ateles belzebuth.* Ph.D. dissertation, University of California, Berkeley.

Klein, L. L., and D. J. Klein
  1975   Social and Ecological Contrasts Between Four Taxa of Neotropical Primates. *In* R. H. Tuttle, ed., 1975b. Pp. 59–85.

Klein, R. G.
  1972   The Late Quaternary Mammalian Fauna of Nelson Bay Cave (Cape Province, South Africa): Its Implications for Megafaunal Extinctions and Environmental and Cultural Change. Quaternary Research 2:135–142.
  1974a   Environment and Subsistence of Prehistoric Man in the Southern Cape Province, South Africa. World Archaeology 5:249–284.
  1974b   A Provisional Statement on Terminal Pleistocene Mammalian Extinctions in the Cape Biotic Zone (Southern Cape Province, South Africa). South African Archaeological Society, Goodwin ser. 2:39–45.
  1975a   Ecology of Stone Age Man at the Southern Tip of Africa. Archaeology 28:238–247.
  1975b   Paleoanthropological Implications of the Non-Archeological Bone Assemblage from Swartklip 1, South-Western Cape Province, South Africa. Quaternary Research 5:275–288.
  1975c   Middle Stone Age Man-Animal Relationships in Southern Africa: Evidence from Klasies River Mouth and Die Kelders. Science 190:265–267.
  1976a   The Mammalian Fauna of the Klasies River Mouth Sites, Southern Cape Province, South Africa. South African Archaeological Bulletin 31:75–98.
  1976b   The Fossil History of *Raphicerus* H. Smith, 1827 (Bovidae, Mammalia) in the Cape Biotic Zone. Annals of the South African Museum 71:169–191.
  1976c   A Preliminary Report on the "Middle Stone Age" Open-Air Site of Duinefontein 2 (Melkberstrand, South-Western Cape Province). South African Archaeological Bulletin 31:12–20.
  1977a   The Ecology of Early Man in Southern Africa. Science 197:115–126.
  1977b   The Mammalian Fauna from the Middle and Later Stone Age (Later Pleistocene) Levels of Border Cave, Natal Province, South Africa. South African Archaeological Bulletin 32:14–27.

1980 The Interpretation of Mammalian Faunas from Stone Age Archaeological Sites, with Special Reference to Sites in the Southern Cape Province, South Africa. *In* Fossils in the Making. A. K. Behrensmeyer and A. Hill, eds. Chicago: University of Chicago Press.

n.d. Mammalian Fauna. *In* Cueva del Juyo: Excavaciones 1978/1979. I. Barandiarán et al., eds.

Kleindienst, M.
1961 Variability Within the Late Acheulian Assemblage in Eastern Africa. South African Archaeological Bulletin 16:35–52.

Klíma, B.
1963 Dolní Věstonice. Praha: Československé Akademie Věd.

Kniffen, F. B.
1939 Pomo Geography. University of California Publications in American Archaeology and Ethnology 36:353–399.

Koenigswald, G. H. R. von
1972 Ein Unterkiefer Eines Fossilen Hominoiden aus dem Unterpliozän Griechenlands. Proceedings of the Koninklijke Nederlandse Akademie van Wetenschappen, ser. B 75:385–394.

Koganezawa, M.
1975 Food Habits of Japanese Monkey (*Macaca fuscata*) in the Boso Mountains. *In* S. Kondo, M. Kawai, and A. Ehara, eds., 1975. Pp. 380–383.

Kondo, S., M. Kawai, and A. Ehara, eds.
1975 Contemporary Primatology. Basel: S. Karger.

Kormondy, E.
1969 Concepts of Ecology. Englewood Cliffs, N.J.: Prentice Hall.

Kortlandt, A.
1967 Experimentation with Chimpanzees in the Wild. *In* Neue Ergebnisse der Primatologie. D. Starck, R. Schneider, and H. J. Kuhn, eds. Stuttgart: Gustav Fischer.
1972 New Perspectives on Ape and Human Evolution. Amsterdam: Stichting voor Psychobiologie.

Kortlandt, A., and M. Kooij
1963 Protohominid Behavior in Primates. Symposia of the Zoological Society of London 10:61–88.

Kowalski, K.
1967 The Pleistocene Extinctions of Mammals in Europe. *In* P. S. Martin and H. E. Wright, eds., 1967. Pp. 349–364.

Krantz, G.
1970 Human Activities and Megafaunal Extinctions. American Scientist 58:164–170.

Krebs, J. R.
1973 Behavioral Aspects of Predation. *In* Perspectives in Ethology. P. G. Bateson and P. H. Klopfer, eds. New York: Plenum Press. Pp. 73–111.

Kretzoi, M.
  1975   New Ramapithecines and *Pliopithecus* from the Lower Pliocene of Rudabanya in North-Eastern Hungary. Nature 257:578–581.

Krieger, A.
  1964   Early Man in the New World. *In* Prehistoric Man in the New World. J. D. Jennings and E. Norbeck, eds. Houston: Rice University Press.

Kroeber, A. L.
  1947   Cultural and Natural Areas of Native North America. Berkeley: University of California Press.
  1953   Handbook of the Indians of California. Reprint of 1925 ed. Berkeley: California Book Co.

Kroeber, A. L., and S. A. Barrett
  1960   Fishing among the Indians of Northwestern California. University of California Anthropological Records 21(1).

Kruuk, H.
  1972   The Spotted Hyena: A Study of Predation and Social Behavior. Chicago: University of Chicago Press.

Kummer, H.
  1968   Social Organization of Hamadryas Baboons. Chicago: University of Chicago Press.

Kurland, J. A.
  1973   A Natural History of Kra Macaques (*Macaca fascicularis* Raffles, 1821) at the Kutai Reserve, Kalimantan, Timur, Indonesia. Primates 14:245–262.

Lack, D.
  1954   The Natural Regulation of Animal Numbers. Cambridge: Cambridge University Press.

Lancaster, J. B.
  1968   On the Evolution of Tool-Using Behavior. American Anthropologist 70:56-66.
  1975   Primate Behavior and the Emergence of Human Culture. New York: Holt, Rinehart and Winston.
  1978   Carrying and Sharing in Human Evolution. Human Nature 1:83–89.

Landes, R.
  1938   The Ojibwa Woman. New York: Columbia University Press.

Laughlin, W. S.
  1962   Acquisition of Anatomical Knowledge by Ancient Man. *In* Social Life of Early Man. S. L. Washburn, ed. Pp. 150–175. Chicago: Aldine.
  1968   Hunting: An Integrating Bio-Behavior System and its Evolutionary Importance. *In* R. B. Lee and I. DeVore, eds., 1968a. Pp. 304–320.

Lautensach, H.
  1967   Geografía de España y Portugal. Barcelona: Vicens-Vives.

Lavelle, C. L. B.
  1975   A Study of Molar Tooth Form. Bulletin de la Groupe Européene de la Recherche Scientifique pour Stomatologie et Odontologie, 18:155–163.

Laws, R. M.
1966 Age Criteria for the African Elephant, *Loxodonta africana*. East African Wild Life Journal 4:1–37.

Leakey, L. S. B.
1935 The Stone Age Races of Kenya. Oxford: Clarendon Press.
1951 Olduvai Gorge: A Report of the Evolution of the Handaxe Culture in Beds I–IV. Cambridge: Cambridge University Press.
1961 Exploring 1,750,000 Years into Man's Past. National Geographic 120:564–589.
1962 A New Lower Pliocene Fossil Primate from Kenya. Annals and Magazine of Natural History 13:689–696.
1967a Development of Aggression as a Factor in Early Human and Prehuman Evolution. *In* Aggression and Defense. C. Clemente and D. Lindsley, eds. Los Angeles: University of California Press.
1967b An Early Miocene Member of the Hominidae. Nature 213:155–163.
1968 Upper Miocene Primates from Kenya. Nature 218:527–528.
1969 Animals of East Africa. Washington, D.C.: National Geographic Society.

Leakey, L. S. B., P. V. Tobias, and J. R. Napier
1964 A New Species of Genus *Homo* from Olduvai Gorge. Nature 202:7–9.

Leakey, M. D.
1971 Olduvai Gorge, Vol. 3. Cambridge: Cambridge University Press.
1976 A Summary and Discussion of the Archaeological Evidence from Bed I and Bed II, Olduvai Gorge, Tanzania. *In* G. Ll. Isaac and E. R. McCown, eds., 1976. Pp. 431–459.

Leakey, R. E. F.
1971 Further Evidence of Lower Pleistocene Hominids from East Rudolf, North Kenya. Nature 231:241–245.
1972 Further Evidence of Lower Pleistocene Hominids from East Rudolf, North Kenya. Nature 237:264–269.
1973 Evidence for an Advanced Plio-Pleistocene Hominid from East Rudolf, Kenya. Nature 242:223–224.
1976 New Hominid Fossils from the Koobi Fora Formation in Northern Kenya. Nature 261:574–576.

Leakey, R. E. F., and R. Lewin
1977 Origins. New York: E. P. Dutton.

Leakey, R. E. F., and A. Walker
1976 *Australopithecus, Homo erectus* and the Single Species Hypothesis. Nature 261:572–574.

Lebra, T. S.
1975 An Alternative Approach to Reciprocity. American Anthropologist 77:550–565.

Lee, R. B.
1968 What Hunters Do for a Living, or How to Make Out on Scarce Resources. *In* R. B. Lee and I. DeVore, eds., 1968a. Pp. 30–48.
1969 !Kung Bushman Subsistence: An Input-Output Analysis. *In* Environment and Cultural Behavior. A. P. Vayda, ed. New York: Natural History Press.

1972a   The !Kung Bushmen of Botswana. *In* M. G. Bicchieri, ed., 1972. Pp. 326–368.

1972b   Population Growth and the Beginnings of Sedentary Life among the !Kung Bushmen. *In* Population Growth: Anthropological Implications. B. Spooner, ed. Pp. 329–342. Cambridge, Mass: MIT Press.

1972c   Work Effort, Group Structure and Land Use in Contemporary Hunter-Gatherers. *In* P. J. Ucko, R. Tringham, and G. W. Dimbleby, eds., 1972. Pp. 177–185.

1972d   !Kung Spatial Organization: An Ecological and Historical Perspective. Human Ecology 1:125–147.

1973   Mongongo: The Ethnography of a Major Wild Food Resource. Ecology of Food and Nutrition 2:307–321.

1976a   Introduction. *In* R. B. Lee and I. DeVore, eds., 1976. Pp. 3–24.

1976b   !Kung Spatial Organization. *In* R. B. Lee and I. DeVore, eds., 1976. Pp. 73–97.

Lee, R. B., and I. DeVore
1968a   (Eds.) Man the Hunter. Chicago: Aldine.

1968b   Problems in the Study of Hunters and Gatherers. *In* R. B. Lee and I. DeVore, eds., 1968a. Pp. 3–12.

1976   (Eds.) Kalahari Hunter-Gatherers. Cambridge, Mass: Harvard University Press.

Leigh, E. G., and N. Smythe
1978   Leaf Production, Leaf Consumption, and the Regulation of Folivory on Barro Colorado Island. *In* G. G. Montgomery, ed., 1978. Pp. 33–50.

Leistner, O. A.
1967   The Plant Ecology of the Southern Kalahari. Pretoria: Botanical Survey Memoir No. 38.

Leopold, A. C., and R. Ardrey
1974   Toxic Substances in Plants and the Food Habits of Early Man. Science 176:512–514.

Leopold, E.
1967   Late-Cenozoic Patterns of Plant Extinction. *In* P. S. Martin and H. E. Wright, eds., 1967. Pp. 203–246.

Leroi-Gourhan, A.
1964   Le Geste et la Parole: Technique et Langage. Paris: Editions Albin Michel.

1975   The Flowers Found with Shanidar IV, a Neanderthal Burial in Iraq. Science 190:562–564.

Lewis, H. T.
1973   Patterns of Indian Burning in California: Ecology and Ethnohistory. Ballena Press Anthropological Papers, 1. Ramona, Calif.: Ballena Press.

Lieberman, P., and E. S. Crelin
1971   On the Speech of Neanderthal Man. Linguistic Inquiry 2:203–222.

Linares, O.
1976   "Garden Hunting" in the American Tropics. Human Ecology 4:331–349.

Lindburg, D. G.
1971 The Rhesus Monkey in North India: An Ecological and Behavioral Study. *In* Primate Behavior: Developments in Field and Laboratory Research, Vol. 2. L. A. Rosenblum, ed. Pp. 2–106. New York: Academic Press.

Livingstone, D.
1857 Missionary Travels and Researches in South Africa. London: James Murray.

Long, J.
1971 Arid Region Aborigines: The Pintubi. *In* Aboriginal Man and Environment in Australia. D. J. Mulvaney and J. Golson, eds. Pp. 262–270. Canberra: Australian National University Press.

Lorenz, K.
1966 On Aggression. New York: Harcourt, Brace.

Lorenz, R.
1971 Goeldi's Monkey, *Callimico goeldii,* Preying on Snakes. Folia Primatologica 15:133–142.

Lough, A. K., and G. A. Garton
1968 Digestion and Metabolism of Feed Lipids in Ruminants and Non-Ruminants. *In* M. A. Crawford, ed., 1968. Pp. 163–173.

Lynch, T., and A. Kennedy
1970 Early Human Cultural and Skeletal Remains from Guitarerro Cave, Northern Peru. Science 169:1307–1309.

McArthur, M.
1960 Food Consumption and Dietary Levels of Groups of Aborigines Living on Naturally Occurring Foods. *In* Records of the American-Australian Scientific Expedition to Arnhem Land, Vol. 2: Anthropology and Nutrition. C. P. Mountford, ed. Pp. 90–135. Melbourne: Melbourne University Press.

MacArthur, R. H.
1972 Geographical Ecology. New York: Harper and Row.

MacArthur, R. H., and J. H. Connell
1966 Biology of Populations. New York: John Wiley.

MacArthur, R. H., and E. O. Wilson
1967 The Theory of Island Biogeography. Princeton: Princeton University Press.

McCarthy, F., and M. McArthur
1960 The Food Quest and the Time Factor in Aboriginal Economic Life. American-Australian Scientific Expedition to Arnhem Land Records 2.

McGrew, W. C.
1974 Tool Use by Wild Chimpanzees in Feeding upon Driver Ants. Journal of Human Evolution 3:501–508.
1975 Patterns of Plant Food Sharing by Wild Chimpanzees. *In* S. Kondo, M. Kawai, and A. Ehara, eds., 1975. Pp. 304–309.
1977 Socialization and Object Manipulation of Wild Chimpanzees. *In* Primate

Bio-Social Development: Biological, Social, and Ecological Determinants. S. Chevalier-Skolnikoff and F. E. Poirier, eds. New York: Garland.
1979   Evolutionary Implications of Sex Differences in Chimpanzee Predation and Tool Use. *In* The Great Apes. D. A. Hamburg and E. R. McCown, eds. Pp. 441-464. Menlo Park, Calif.: Benjamin/Cummings.

McGrew, W. C., and C. E. G. Tutin
1978   Evidence for a Social Custom in Wild Chimpanzees? Man 13:234-251.

McGrew, W. C., C. E. G. Tutin, P. J. Baldwin, M. J. Sharman, and A. Whiten
in press   Primates Preying Upon Vertebrates: New Records from West Africa (*Pan troglodytes, Papio papio, Cercopithecus sabaeus*). Carnivore.

McHenry, H. M.
1976   Early Hominid Body Weight and Encephalization. American Journal of Physical Anthropology 45:77-84.

McKey, D.
1978   Soils, Vegetation and Seed-Eating by Black Colobus Monkeys. *In* G. G. Montgomery, ed., 1978. Pp. 423-437.

Mackey, W.
1976   The Adult Male-Child Bond: An Example of Convergent Evolution. Journal of Anthropological Research 32:58-73.

MacKinnon, J. R.
1971   The Orang-utan in Sabah Today. Oryx 11:141-191.
1973   Orang-utans in Sumatra. Oryx 12:234-242.
1974   The Behaviour and Ecology of Wild Orang-utans (*Pongo pygmaeus*). Animal Behaviour 22:3-74.

MacKinnon, J. R., and K. S. MacKinnon
1978   Comparative Feeding Ecology of Six Sympatric Primates in West Malaysia. *In* D. J. Chivers and J. Herbert, eds., 1978. Pp. 305-321.

MacNeish, R. S.
1967   A Summary of the Subsistence. *In* The Prehistory of the Tehuacan Valley, Vol. 1: Environment and Subsistence. D. S. Byers, ed. Austin: University of Texas Press.
1971   Early Man in the Andes. Scientific American 224(4):36-46.
1976   Early Man in the New World. American Scientist 64:316-327.

MacNeish, R. S., A. Nelker-Terner, and A. Cook
1970   Second Annual Report of the Ayacucho Archaeological-Botanical Project. Andover, Mass.: Peabody Foundation for Archaeology.

Madariaga de la Campa, B.
1971   La Fauna Marina de la Cueva de Morín. *In* J. González Echegaray et al., eds., 1971. Pp. 399-415.
1975   Estudio de la Fauna Marina de la Cuevade "Tito Bustillo" (Oviedo). *In* Excavaciones en la Cueva de "Tito Bustillo" (Campañas de 1972 y 1974). J. Moure, ed. Pp. 89-107.
1976   Estudio de la Fauna Marina de la Cueva de "Tito Bustillo" (Oviedo). Campaña de 1975. *In* Excavaciones en la Cueva de "Tito Bustillo" (Asturias). J. Moure, ed. Pp. 209-227.

Maglio, V. J.
1972 Vertebrate Faunas and Chronology of Hominid-Bearing Sediments East of Lake Rudolf, Kenya. Nature 239:379–385.

Magnen, J. Le
1966 Les Bases Sensorielles de l'Analyse de Qualités Organoleptiques. *In* Méthodes Subjectives et Objectives d'Appréciation des Caractères Organoleptiques des Denrées Alimentaires. Journées Scientifiques du Centre National de Coordination des Études sur l'Alimentation. Paris: Centre National de Recherches Scientifiques 14:1–54.

Maguire, B.
1968 The Lithic Industry in the Makapansgat Limeworks Breccias and Overlying Surface Soil. Palaeontologia Africana 11:99–125.

Mann, A. E.
1970 "Telanthropus" and the Single Species Hypothesis: A Further Comment. American Anthropologist 72:607–609.
1971 *Homo erectus. In* Background for Man. P. Dolhinow and V. Sarich, eds. Pp. 166–177. Boston: Little, Brown.
1972 Hominid and Cultural Origins. Man 7:379–386.
1975 Paleodemographic Aspects of the South African Australopithecines. Philadelphia: University of Pennsylvania Publications in Anthropology, No. 1.

Marais, E.
1939 My Friends the Baboons. London: Methuen.

Marks, S. A.
1976 Large Mammals and a Brave People. Seattle: University of Washington Press.

Marshall, L.
1961 Sharing, Talking and Giving: Relief of Social Tension Among !Kung Bushmen. Africa 1:231–249.
1976 The !Kung of Nyae Nyae. Cambridge, Mass.: Harvard University Press.

Martin, P. S.
1958 Pleistocene Ecology and Biogeography of North America. American Association for the Advancement of Science, Publication 51:375–420.
1966 Africa and Pleistocene Overkill. Nature 212:339–342.
1967 Prehistoric Overkill. *In* P. S. Martin and H. E. Wright, eds., 1967. Pp. 75–120.
1968 The Meaning of Empty Niches. Paper presented at the Pleistocene Man–Environment Relationship Symposium, Columbus, Ohio, September, 1968.
1973 The Discovery of America. Science 179:969–974.

Martin, P. S., and H. E. Wright, eds.
1967 Pleistocene Extinctions. New Haven: Yale University Press.

Martin, R. D.
1972 A Preliminary Field-Study of the Lesser Mouse Lemur (*Microcebus murinus* J. F. Miller 1777). *In* Behaviour and Ecology of Nocturnal

Prosimians. Advances in Ethology 9. P. Charles-Dominique and R. D. Martin, eds. Pp. 43–89. Berlin: Verlag Paul Parey.
1973   A Review of the Behaviour and Ecology of the Lesser Mouse Lemur. *In* R. P. Michael and J. H. Crook, eds., 1973. Pp. 2–68.

Martin, R. D., G. A. Doyle, and A. C. Walker, eds.
1974   Prosimian Biology. London: Duckworth.

Mason, R. J.
1962   Australopithecines and Artefacts at Sterkfontein. Pt. II: The Sterkfontein Stone Artefacts and Their Maker. South African Archaeological Bulletin 17:109–125.
1965   Makapansgat Limeworks Fractured Stone Objects and Natural Fracture in Africa. South African Archaeological Bulletin 20(1):3–16.
1974   Background to the Transvaal Iron Age: New Discoveries at Olifantspoort and Broederstroom. Journal of the South African Institute of Mining and Metallurgy 74.

Matheron, G.
1970   La Théorie des Variables Régionalisées et ses Applications. Les Cahiers du Centre de Morphologie Mathématique de Fontainebleau, 5. Paris: École Nationale des Mines de Paris.

Maugh, T. H.
1973   Vitamin B12: After 25 Years, the First Synthesis. Science 179:266–267.

Mauss, M.
1954   The Gift: Forms and Functions of Exchange in Archaic Societies. I. Cunnison, transl. Glencoe, Ill.: Free Press.

Mech, L.
1970   The Wolf. Garden City, N.Y.: Natural History Press.

Medway, Lord
1970   Breeding of the Silvered Leaf Monkey, *Presbytis cristata,* in Malaya. Journal of Mammalogy 51:630–632.

Mentis, M. T.
1972   A Review of Some Life History Features of the Large Herbivores of Africa. Lammergeyer 16:1–89.

Merrick, H. V.
1976   Recent Archaeological Research in the Plio-Pleistocene Deposits of the Lower Omo Valley, Southwestern Ethiopia. *In* G. Ll. Isaac and E. R. McCown, eds., 1976. Pp. 461–481.

Merrick, H V., and J. S. Merrick
1976   Archaeological Occurrences of Earlier Pleistocene Age from the Shungura Formation. *In* Y. Coppens et al., 1976. Pp. 574–584.

Merrick, H. V., J. de Heinzelin, P. Haesarts, and F. C. Howell
1973   Archaeological Occurrences of Early Pleistocene Age from the Shungura Formation, Lower Omo Valley, Ethiopia. Nature 242:572–575.

Meyer-Rochow, V. B.
1973 Edible Insects in Three Different Ethnic Groups of Papua and New Guinea. American Journal of Clinical Nutrition 26:673–677.

Michael, R. P., and J. H. Crook, eds.
1973 Comparative Ecology and Behaviour of Primates. London: Academic Press.

Milton, K., and M. L. May
1976 Body Weight, Diet and Home Range Area in Primates. Nature 259:459–462.

Moir, R. J.
1967 Ruminant Digestion and Evolution. *In* Handbook of Physiology, Sect. 6: Alimentary Canal. C. F. Code, ed. Pp. 2673–2694. Washington, D.C.: American Physiological Society.

Montgomery, G. G., ed.
1978 The Ecology of Arboreal Folivores. Washington, D.C.: Smithsonian Institution.

Moore, O. K.
1965 Divination: A New Perspective. American Anthropologist 67:69–74.

Moreno-Black, G., and W. R. Maples
1977 Differential Habitat Utilization of Four Cercopithecidae in a Kenyan Forest. Folia Primatologica 27:85–107.

Morgan, E.
1972 The Descent of Woman. New York: Stein and Day.

Morris, D.
1967 The Naked Ape. New York: McGraw-Hill.

Morris, K., and J. Goodall
1977 Competition for Meat between Chimpanzees and Baboons of the Gombe National Park. Folia Primatologica 28:109–121.

Morris, R., and D. Morris
1966 Men and Apes. New York: McGraw-Hill.

Mosimann, J., and P. S. Martin
1975 Simulating Overkill by Paleoindians. American Scientist 63:304–313.

Moss, R.
1972 Social Organization of Willow Ptarmigan on their Breeding Grounds in Interior Alaska. Condor 74:144–151.

Moure Romanillo, J., and M. Cano Herrera
n.d. Upper Magdalenian Habitation Structure from the Cave of Tito Bustillo (Asturias, Spain). Manuscript.

Moure Romanillo, J. A. and G. Delibes de Castro
1972 El Yacimiento Musteriense de la Cueva de la Ermita (Hortigüela, Burgos). Noticiario Arqueológico Hispánico, Prehistoria, 1:10–44.

Mowat, F.
1951   People of the Deer. New York: Pyramid Books.
1963   Never Cry Wolf. New York: Dell Publishing Co.

Moynihan, M.
1976   The New World Primates. Princeton: Princeton University Press.

Mukherjee, R. P., and S. S. Saha
1974   The Golden Langurs (*Presbytis geei* Khajuria, 1956) of Assam. Primates 15:327–340.

Müller-Beck, H.
1966   Paleohunters in America: Origins and Diffusion. Science 152:37–56.

Mulvaney, D. J.
1969   The Prehistory of Australia. London: Thames and Hudson.

Muñoz, A. and M. Pericot
1975   Excavaciones de la Cueva de "Els Ermitons" (Sadernas, Gerona). Pyrenae 11:7–42.

Myers, F.
1976   To Have and to Hold: A Study of Persistence and Change in Pintupi Social Life. Ph.D. dissertation, Bryn Mawr College.

Nagel, U.
1973   A Comparison of Anubis Baboons, Hamadryas Baboons and Their Hybrids at a Species Border in Ethiopia. Folia Primatologica 19:104–165.

Napier, J. R., and P. H. Napier
1967   A Handbook of Living Primates. New York: Academic Press.
1970   (Eds.) Old World Monkeys: Evolution, Systematics, and Behavior. New York: Academic Press.

Nelson, C. M.
1971   Fourth Bulletin of the Commission on Nomenclature of the Pan African Congress on Prehistory, Berkeley, California: University of California. Mimeographed.

Nelson, E.
1899   The Eskimo about the Bering Strait. Smithsonian Institution, Bureau of American Ethnology. Annual Report 18 (for 1896–97).

Neville, M. K.
1968   Ecology and Activity of Himalayan Foothill Rhesus Monkeys (*Macaca mulatta*). Ecology 49:110–123.

Newcomb, W.
1950   A Re-Examination of the Causes and Consequences of Plains Warfare. American Anthropologist 52:317–330.

Newkirk, J., III
1973   A Possible Case of Predation in the Gibbon. Primates 14:301–304.

Nickerson, N. H., N. H. Rowe, and E. A. Richter
1973   Native Plants in the Diets of North Alaskan Eskimos. *In* Man and His Foods. C. E. Smith, Jr., ed. University, Ala.: University of Alabama Press.

Nie, N. H., C. H. Hull, J. G. Jenkins, K. Steinbrenner, and D. H. Bent
1975 A Statistical Package for the Social Sciences. New York: McGraw-Hill.

Nishida, T.
1969 The Monkeys of Kasoge (in Japanese). Monkey 13:5–15.
1972a The Ant-Gathering Behavior by the Use of Tools among Wild Chimpanzees of the Mahali Mountains. Journal of Human Evolution 2:357–370.
1972b A Note on the Ecology of the Red Colobus Monkeys (*Colobus badius tephrosceles*) Living in the Mahali Mountains. Primates 13:57–64.
1972c Preliminary Information of the Pygmy Chimpanzees (*Pan paniscus*) of the Congo Basin. Primates 13:415–425.
1974 Ecology of Wild Chimpanzees (in Japanese). *In* Human Ecology. A. Ohtsuka, T. Tanaka, and T. Nishida, eds. Tokyo: Kyoritsu-Shuppan.
1976 The Bark-Eating Habits in Primates, with Special Reference to Their Status in the Diet of Wild Chimpanzees. Folia Primatologica 25:277–287.
in press Local Differences in Water-Oriented Attitude among Wild Chimpanzees. Primates.

Nishida, T., S. Uehara, and R. Nyundo
1978 Predatory Behavior among Wild Chimpanzees of the Mahale Mountains. Primates 20:1–20.

Oakley, K.
1961 On Man's Use of Fire, with Comments on Tool-Making and Hunting. *In* Social Life of Early Man. S. L. Washburn, ed. Chicago: Aldine. Pp. 176–193.

Oates, J. F.
1969 The Lower Primates of Eastern Nigeria. African Wildlife 23:321–332.
1977 The Guereza and Its Food. *In* T. H. Clutton-Brock, ed., 1977. Pp. 276–321.

Oatley, T. B.
1970 Predatory Behavior by the Samango Monkey *Cercopithecus mitis*. Lammergeyer 11.

Oberg, K.
1973 The Social Economy of the Tlingit Indians. Seattle: University of Washington Press.

Odum, E. P.
1971 Fundamentals of Ecology, 3d ed. Philadelphia: W. B. Saunders.

Oldeman, R. A. A.
1974 Écotopes des Arbres et Gradients Écologiques Verticaux en Forêt Guyanaise. La Terre et la Vie 28:487–520.
1977 Architecture and Energy Exchange of Dicotyledonous Trees in the Forest. *In* Tropical Trees as Living Systems. P. B. Tomlinson and M. H. Zimmerman, eds. Cambridge: Cambridge University Press.

Oliviera, J. F. S., J. Passos de Carvalho, R. F. X. Bruno de Sousa, and M. Madalena Simão
1976 The Nutritional Value of Four Species of Insects Consumed in Angola. Ecology of Food and Nutrition 5:91–97.

Olson, E. C.
1966   Community Evolution and the Origin of Mammals. Ecology 47:291–302.

Oomen, H. A. P. C.
1961   The Papuan Child as a Survivor. Journal of Tropical Pediatrics 6:103.

Oppenheimer, J. R.
1969   Behavior and Ecology of the White Faced Monkey, *Cebus capucinus*, on Barro Colorado Island, C. Z.   Dissertation Abstracts International 830: 442–443.

Osborn, A.
1977   Strandloopers, Mermaids and Other Fairy Tales: Ecological Determinants of Marine Resource Utilization—the Peruvian Case. *In* For Theory Building in Archaeology. L. R. Binford, ed. Pp. 157–205. New York: Academic Press.

Osborn, R.
1963   Observations of the Behaviour of the Mountain Gorilla. Symposia of the Zoological Society of London 10:29–38.

Osgood, C.
1936   Contribution to the Ethnography of the Kutchin. New Haven: Yale University Publications in Anthropology, No. 14.
1937   The Ethnography of the Tanaina. New Haven: Yale University Publications in Anthropology, No. 16.

Osman Hill, W. C.
1972   Evolutionary Biology of the Primates. New York: Academic Press.

Pariente, G. F.
1976   Étude Éco-Physiologique de la Vision chez les Prosimiens Malgaches. Ph.D. dissertation, Université des Sciences et Techniques de Languedoc. Centre National de la Recherche Scientifique doc. no. A.O. 12352.

Parkington, J. E.
1977   Follow the San. Ph.D. dissertation, University of Cambridge.

Parkington, J., and C. Poggenpoel
1971   Excavations at De Hangen, 1968. South African Archaeological Bulletin 26:3–36.

Parra, R.
1978   Comparison of Foregut and Hindgut Fermentation in Herbivores. *In* G. G. Montgomery, ed., 1978. Pp. 205–229.

Passmore, R., B. M. Nicol, M. Narayana Roa, G. H. Beaton, and E. M. Demayer
1974   Handbook on Human Nutritional Requirements. World Health Monograph Series, No. 61. Geneva: World Health Organization.

Paul, P. C., and H. H. Palmer, eds.
1972   Food Theory and Applications. New York: Wiley.

Pauling, L.
1970   Vitamin C and the Common Cold. San Francisco: W. H. Freeman.

Pearson, A. M.
  1975 The Northern Interior Grizzly Bear *Ursus arctos* L.   Canada Wild Life
  Service Report Series No. 34:86.

Pericot García, L.
  1942 La Cueva del Parpalló. Madrid: C.S.I.C., Instituto Diego Velázquez.

Perkins, D., and P. Daly
  1968 A Hunter's Village in Neolithic Turkey. Scientific American 219(5):
  96–106.

Perles, C.
  1976 Le Feu. *In* La Préhistoire Française, Vol. I. H. de Lumley, ed. Pp.
  679–683. Paris: Editions du C.N.R.S.

Perper, T., and C. Schrire
  1977 The Nimrod Connection: Myth and Science in the Hunting Model. *In* The
  Chemical Senses and Nutrition. M. R. Kare and O. Maller, eds. Pp. 447–459.
  New York: Academic Press.

Perret, M.
  1974 Variation of Endocrine Glands in the Lesser Mouse Lemur *Microcebus
  murinus*. *In* R. D. Martin, G. A. Doyle, and A. C. Walker, eds., 1974. Pp.
  375–387.

Peters, R., and L. Mech
  1975 Behavioral and Intellectual Adaptations of Selected Mammalian Predators to the Problem of Hunting Large Animals. *In* R. H. Tuttle, ed.,
  1975b. Pp. 279–300.

Peterson, N.
  1972 Totemism Yesterday: Sentiment and Local Organization among the
  Australian Aborigines. Man 7:12–32.
  1975 Hunter-Gatherer Territoriality: The Perspective from Australia. American
  Anthropologist 77:53–68.

Peterson, R., G. Mountfort, and P. Hollom
  1962 Guide des Oiseaux d'Europe. Neuchatel: Delachaux et Niestlé.

Petter, J.-J.
  1962a Remarques sur l'Écologie et l'Ethnologie des Lémuriens Malgaches.
  Paris: Mémoires du Museum Nationale d'Histoire Naturelle 27:1–146.
  1962b Remarques sur l'Écologie et l'Ethnologie Comparées des Lémuriens
  Malgaches. La Terre et la Vie 109:394–416.
  1965 The Lemurs of Madagascar. *In* I. DeVore, ed., 1965. Pp. 292–319.
  1978 Ecological and Physiological Adaptations of Five Sympatric Nocturnal
  Lemurs to Seasonal Variations in Food Production. *In* D. J. Chivers and
  J. Herbert, eds., 1978. Pp. 211–223.

Petter, J.-J., and C. M. Hladik
  1970 Observations sur le Domaine Vital et la Densité de Population de *Loris
  tardigradus* dans les Forêts de Ceylan. Mammalia 34:394–409.

Petter, J.-J., and A. Peyrieras

1970a   Observations Éco-Éthologiques sur les Lémuriens Malgaches du Genre *Hapalemur*. La Terre et la Vie 17:356–382.

1970b   Nouvelle Contribution a l'Étude d'un Lémurien Malgache, le Aye-Aye (*Daubentonia madagascariensis* E. Geoffroy). Mammalia 34:167–193.

1975   Preliminary Notes on the Behavior and Ecology of *Hapalemur griseus*. *In* Lemur Biology. I. Tattersall and R. W. Sussman, eds. Pp. 281–286. New York: Plenum Press.

Petter, J.-J., A. Schilling, and G. Pariente

1971   Observations Eco-Éthologiques sur Deux Lémuriens Malgaches Nocturnes Peu Connus: *Phaner furcifer* et *Microcebus coquereli*. La Terre et la Vie 25:287–327.

1975   Observations on Behavior and Ecology of *Phaner furcifer*. *In* Lemur Biology. I. Tattersall and R. W. Sussman, eds. Pp. 209–218. New York: Plenum Press.

Peyrony, D.

1930   Le Moustier: Ses Gisements, Ses Industries, Ses Couches Géologiques. Revue Anthropologique 1–3, 48–76.

1934   La Ferrassie: Mousterien, Perigordien, et Aurignacien. Préhistoire 3:1–92.

Pfaffmann, C.

1960   The Pleasures of Sensation. Psychological Review 67:253–268.

Pfeiffer, J.

1969   The Emergence of Man, 1st ed. New York: Harper and Row.

1977   The Emergence of Society. New York: McGraw-Hill.

1978   The Emergence of Man, 3d ed. New York: Harper and Row.

Pianka, E.

1974   Evolutionary Ecology. New York: Harper and Row.

Pike, J. G.

1971   Rainfall over Botswana. *In* Proceedings of the Conference on Sustained Production from Semi-Arid Areas. Botswana Notes and Records, Special Ed. No. 1. Pp. 69–76.

Pilbeam, D. R.

1970   The Evolution of Man. New York: Funk and Wagnalls.

1972   The Ascent of Man: An Introduction to Human Evolution. New York: Macmillan.

1975   Middle Pleistocene Hominids. *In* K. W. Butzer and G. Ll. Isaac, eds., 1975. Pp. 809–856.

Pilbeam, D. R., and E. L. Simons

1965   Some Problems of Hominid Classification. American Scientist 53: 237–259.

Pilbeam, D., J. Barry, G. E. Meyer, S. M. Ibrahim Shah, M. H. L. Pickford, W. W. Bishop, H. Thomas, and L. L. Jacobs

1977   Geology and Paleontology of Neogene Strata of Pakistan. Nature 270:684–689.

Pilbeam, D., G. E. Meyer, C. Badgley, M. D. Rose, M. H. L. Pickford, A. K.
Behrensmeyer, and S. M. Ibrahim Shah
1977   New Hominoid Primates from the Siwaliks of Pakistan and Their Bearing
on Hominoid Evolution. Nature 270:689–695.

Piperno, M., and G. M. Bulgarelli Piperno
1974–1975   First Approach to the Ecological and Cultural Significance of the
Early Palaeolithic Occupation Site of Garba IV at Melka Kunturé (Ethiopia).
Quaternaria 18:347–382.

Plooij, F. X.
1978   Tool-Use During Chimpanzees' Bushpig Hunt. Carnivore 1:103–106.

Poiner, G.
1971   The Process of the Year. B. A. Honours Thesis, Department of
Anthropology, University of Sydney.

Poirier, F. E.
1969   Behavioral Flexibility and Intertroop Variation Among Nilgiri Langurs
(*Presbytis johnii*) of South India. Folia Primatologica 11:119–133.
1970   The Nilgiri Langur (*Presbytis johnii*) of South India. *In* Primate
Behavior: Developments in Field and Laboratory Research, Vol. 1. L. A.
Rosenblum, ed. Pp. 251–383. New York: Academic Press.
1972   The St. Kitt's Green Monkey (*Cercopithecus aethiops sabaeus*): Ecology,
Population Dynamics, and Selected Behavioral Traits. Folia Primatologica
17:20–55.

Poirier, F. E., and E. O. Smith
1974   The Crab-Eating Macaques (*Macaca fascicularis*) of Angaur Island,
Pelau, Micronesia. Folia Primatologica 22:258–306.

Pollock, J. I.
1975   Field Observations on *Indri indri*: A Preliminary Report. *In* Lemur
Biology. I. Tattersall and R. W. Sussman, eds. Pp. 287–311. New York:
Plenum Press.

Portman, O. W.
1970a   Nutritional Requirements (NRC) of Non-Human Primates. *In* Feeding
and Nutrition of Nonhuman Primates. R. S. Harris, ed. Pp. 87–115. New
York: Academic Press.
1970b   Nutritional Requirements of Squirrel and Woolly Monkeys. *In* Feeding
and Nutrition of Nonhuman Primates. R. S. Harris, ed. Pp. 159–174. New
York: Academic Press.

Powers, S.
1877   Tribes of California. *Reprinted in* Contributions to North American
Ethnology 3. Washington, D.C.: United States Geographical and Geological
Survey of the Rocky Mountain Region.

Puget, A.
1971   Observations sur le Macaque Rhesus, *Macaca mulatta,* en Afghanistan.
Mammalia 35:199–203.

Putnam, A. E.
1954   Madami: My Eight Years of Adventure with the Congo Pigmies. Englewood Cliffs, N.J.: Prentice-Hall.

Quimby, G.
1960   Indian Life in the Upper Great Lakes: 11,000 B.C. to 1800 A.D. Chicago: University of Chicago Press.

Radcliffe-Brown, A. R.
1922   The Andaman Islanders. Cambridge: Cambridge University Press.
1933   The Andaman Islanders, 2d ed. Cambridge: Cambridge University Press.

Ransom, T. W.
1971   Ecology and Social Behavior of Baboons (*Papio anubis*) at the Gombe National Park. Ph.D. dissertation, University of California, Berkeley.

Rappaport, R.
1968   Pigs for the Ancestors. New Haven: Yale University Press.

Read-Martin, C. E., and D. W. Read
1975   Australopithecine Scavenging and Human Evolution: An Approach from Faunal Analysis. Current Anthropology 16:359–368.

Redman, C.
1978   The Rise of Civilization. San Francisco: W. H. Freeman.

Reed, C.
1969   They Never Found the Ark. Ecology 50:343–345.
1970   Extinction of Mammalian Megafauna in the Old World Late Quaternary. BioScience, 20(5):284–288.

Reynolds, V.
1965   Budongo: An African Forest and Its Chimpanzees. New York: Natural History Press.
1966   Open Groups in Hominid Evolution. Man 1:441–452.
1975   How Wild are the Gombe Chimpanzees? Man 10:123–125.

Reynolds, V., and F. Reynolds
1965   Chimpanzees of the Budongo Forest. *In* I. DeVore, ed., 1965. Pp. 368–424.

Richard, A.
1970   A Comparative Study of the Activity Patterns and Behavior of *Alouatta villosa* and *Ateles geoffroyi*. Folia Primatologica 12:241–263.
1974   Intraspecific Variation in the Social Organization and Ecology of *Propithecus verreauxi*. Folia Primatologica 22:178–207.

Ripley, S.
1967   Intertroop Encounters Among Ceylon Gray Langurs (*Presbytis entellus*). *In* Social Communication in Primates. S. A. Altmann, ed. Pp. 237–253. Chicago: University of Chicago Press.
1970   Leaves and Leaf-Monkeys: The Social Organization of Foraging in Gray Langurs, *Presbytis entellus thersites*. *In* J. R. Napier and P. H. Napier, eds., 1970. Pp. 481–509.

Ripoll Perelló, E.
1961 Excavaciones en la Cueva de Ambriosio (Velez Blanco, Almeria), Campañas 1958 y 1960. Ampurias 22-23.

Ripoll Perelló, E., and H. de Lumley
1964 El Paleolítico Medio en Cataluña. Ampurias 26-27:1-70.

Riss, D. C., and C. D. Busse
1977 Fifty-Day Observation of a Free-Living Adult Male Chimpanzee. Folia Primatologica 28:283-297.

Ritenbaugh, C.
1978 Human Foodways: A Window on Evolution. *In* The Anthropology of Health. E. E. Bauwens, ed. St. Louis: C. V. Mosby.

Roberts, D.
1968 Genetic Fitness in a Colonizing Human Population. Human Biology 40:494-507.

Robinson, J. T.
1954 The Genera and Species of the Australopithecinae. American Journal of Physical Anthropology 12:181-200.
1956 The Dentition of the Australopithecinae. Pretoria: Transvaal Museum Memoir No. 9.
1962 Australopithecines and Artefacts at Sterkfontein. Part I: Sterkfontein Stratigraphy and the Significance of the Extension Site. South African Archaeological Bulletin 17:87-107.
1963 Adaptive Radiation in the Australopithecines and the Origin of Man. *In* African Ecology and Human Evolution. F. C. Howell and F. Bourliere, eds. Pp. 385-416. Chicago: Aldine.
1967 Variation and Taxonomy of the Early Hominids. *In* Evolutionary Biology, Vol. 1. T. Dobzhansky, M. K. Hecht, and W. C. Steere, eds. Pp. 69-100. New York: Appleton-Century-Crofts.
1968 The Origin and Adaptive Radiation of the Australopithecines. *In* Evolution und Hominisation. G. Kurth, ed. Stuttgart: Gustav Fischer Verlag.
1972 Early Hominid Posture and Locomotion. Chicago: University of Chicago Press.

Robson, J. R. K., and D. E. Yen
1976 Some Nutritional Aspects of the Philippine Tasaday Diet. Ecology of Food and Nutrition 5:83-89.

Roche, H., and J.-J. Tiercelin
1977 Découverte d'une Industrie Lithique Ancienne in Situ dans la Formation d'Hadar, Afar Central, Éthiopie. Comptes-Rendus de l'Academie des Sciences, Ser. D, 284:1871-1874.

Rodman, P. S.
1973a Synecology of Bornean Primates. Ph.D. dissertation, Harvard University.
1973b Population Composition and Adaptive Organisation Among Orang-utans of the Kutai Reserve. *In* R. P. Michael and J. H. Crook, eds., 1973. Pp. 171-209.

Rogers, C. M.
  1973   Implications of a Primate Early Rearing Experiment for the Concept of Culture. *In* Precultural Primate Behavior. E. W. Menzel, ed. Pp. 185–191. Basel: S. Karger.

Rogers, E. S.
  1972   The Mistassini Cree. *In* M. G. Bicchieri, ed., 1972. Pp. 90–137.

Rogers, E. S., and M. Black
  1976   Subsistence Strategy in the Fish and Hare Period, Northern Ontario: The Weagamow Ojibwa, 1880–1920. Journal of Anthropological Research 32:1–43.

Rollet, B.
  1974   L'Architecture des Forêts Denses Humides Sempervirentes de Plaine. Nogent: Centre de Technique Forestier Tropical.

Roonwal, M. L., and S. M. Mohnot
  1977   Primates of South Asia. Cambridge, Mass.: Harvard University Press.

Rose, M. D.
  1976   Bipedal Behavior of Olive Baboons (*Papio anubis*) and its Relevance to an Understanding of the Evolution of Human Bipedalism. American Journal of Physical Anthropology 44:247–262.
  1977   Positional Behavior of Olive Baboons (*Papio anubis*) and its Relationship to Maintenance and Social Activities. Primates 18:59–116.
  1978   The Roots of Primate Predatory Behavior. Journal of Human Evolution 7:179–189.

Rosenblum, L. A., and R. W. Cooper, eds.
  1968   The Squirrel Monkey. New York: Academic Press.

Ross, E. B.
  1978   Food Taboos, Diet, and Hunting Strategy: The Adaptation to Animals in Amazon Cultural Ecology. Current Anthropology 19:1–16.

Rostlund, E.
  1952   Freshwater Fish and Fishing in Native North America. University of California Publications in Geography 9.

Roth, W.
  1897   Ethnological Studies among the North-West-Central Queensland Aborigines. Brisbane: Edmund Gregory, Government Printer.
  1901   Food: Its Search, Capture, and Preparation. North Queensland Ethnography, Bulletin No. 3. Brisbane: Government Printer.

Rousseau, J.-J.
  1755   Discours sur l'Origine et les Fondaments de l'Inégalité parmi les Hommes. *In* The Social Contract and Discourses. G. D. H. Cole, transl. London: Dent, 1973.

Rowell, T. E.
  1966   Forest Living Baboons in Uganda. Journal of Zoology (London) 149:344–364.
  1972   Toward a Natural History of the Talapoin Monkey in Cameroon. Annales de la Faculté des Sciences du Cameroun 10:121–134.

Ruddle, K., D. Johnson, P. Townsend, and J. Rees
1978   Palm Sago. Honolulu: University Press of Hawaii.

Rudran, R.
1970   Aspects of the Ecology of Two Subspecies of Purple-Faced Langurs (*Presbytis senex*). M.Sc. thesis, University of Ceylon, Colombo.

Rumbaugh, D. M.
1975   The Learning and Symbolizing Capacities of Apes and Monkeys. *In* R. H. Tuttle, ed., 1975b. Pp. 352–365.

Sabater Pi, J.
1972   Contribution to the Ecology of *Mandrillus sphinx* Linnaeus 1758 of Rio Muni. Folia Primatologica 17:304–319.
1973   Contributions to the Ecology of *Colobus polykomos satanas* of Rio Muni, Republic of Equatorial Guinea. Folia Primatologica 19:193–207.
1974   An Elementary Industry of the Chimpanzees in the Okorobiko Mountains, Rio Muni (Republic of Equatorial Guinea). Primates 15:351–364.

Sabater Pi, J.
1977   Contribution to the Study of Alimentation of Lowland Gorillas in the Natural State, in Rio Muni, Republic of Equatorial Guinea (West Africa). Primates 18:183–204.
1978   Observaciones y Comentarios a un Inventario de los Alimentos Consumidos en la Naturaleza por los Chimpances (*Pan troglodytes troglodytes*) de Rio Muni, Africa Occidental Ecuatorial. Zoo 23:15–17.

Sade, D. S., and R. W. Hildrech
1965   Notes on the Green Monkey (*Cercopithecus aethiops sabaeus*) on St. Kitt's, West Indies. Caribbean Journal of Science 5:67–81.

Santonja Gómez, M., N. López and A. Perez González
1978   Acheulean Occupation Sites in the Jarama Valley. Current Anthropology 19:394–395.

Sahlins, M. D.
1960   The Origin of Society. Scientific American 203(3):76–87.
1965   On the Sociology of Primitive Exchange. *In* The Relevance of Models for Social Anthropology. M. Banton, ed. Pp. 139–236. London: Tavistock.
1972   Stone Age Economics. Chicago: Aldine-Atherton.

Sampson, C. G.
1974   The Stone Age Archaeology of Southern Africa. New York: Academic Press.

Sarich, V. M.
1971   A Molecular Approach to the Question of Human Origins. *In* Background for Man. P. Dolhinow and V. M. Sarich, eds. Boston: Little, Brown.

Sauer, C.
1969   Seeds, Spades, Hearths, and Herds. Cambridge, Mass.: MIT Press.

Sauer, E. G. F., and E. M. Sauer
1963   The Southwest African Bush-Baby of the *Galago senegalensis* Group. Journal of the South West African Science Society 16:5–36, 104–107.

Schaeffer, V. B.

1958   Seals, Sea-Lions, and Walruses. Palo Alto: Stanford University Press.

Schaller, G. B.

1963   The Mountain Gorilla: Ecology and Behavior. Chicago: University of Chicago Press.

1972   The Serengeti Lion: A Study of Predator–Prey Relations. Chicago: University of Chicago Press.

1973   Golden Shadows, Flying Hooves. New York: Alfred A. Knopf.

Schaller, G. B., and G. P. Lowther

1969   The Relevance of Carnivore Behavior to the Study of Early Hominids. Southwestern Journal of Anthropology 25:307–340.

Schebesta, P.

1933   Among Congo Pygmies. London: Hutchinson.

1936   My Pygmy and Negro Hosts. London: Hutchinson.

1941   Die Bambuti-Pygmäen vom Ituri: Ethnographie der Ituri-Bambuti, die Wirtschaft der Ituri-Bambuti. Mémoires de l'Institut Royal Colonial Belge, Section des Sciences Morales et Politiques, Vol. 2.

Schoener, T.

1971   Theory of Feeding Strategies. Annual Review of Ecology and Systematics 2:369–404.

Schroeder, H. A.

1973   Trace Elements and Nutrition. London: Faber and Faber.

Schultz, L.

1891   Aborigines of the Upper and Middle Finke River. Transactions, Royal Society of South Australia 14:210–246.

Schweitzer, F. R.

1974   Archaeological Evidence for Sheep at the Cape. South African Archaeological Bulletin 29:75–82.

1976   The Ecology of Post-Pleistocene Peoples on the Gansbaai Coast, South-Western Cape. M.A. thesis, University of Stellenbosch.

Schweitzer, F. R., and K. Scott

1973   Early Occurrence of Domestic Sheep in Sub-Saharan Africa. Nature 241:547–548.

Scrimshaw, N. S., and V. R. Young

1976   The Requirements of Human Nutrition. Scientific American 235(3): 50–64.

Semenov, S. A.

1964   Prehistoric Technology. New York: Barnes and Noble.

1968   Razvitie Tekhniki v Kamennom Veke. Moscow: Institut Arkheologii, Akademiya Nauk, SSSR.

Sen, S.

1962   Land and People of the Andamans. Calcutta: Post-Graduate Book Mart.

Service, E. R.
1966 The Hunters. Englewood Cliffs, N.J.: Prentice-Hall.

Shaw, E. M., P. L. Woolley, and R. A. Rae
1963 Bushman Arrow Poisons. Cimbebasia (Windhoek) 7.

Shepard, P.
1973 The Tender Carnivore and the Sacred Game. New York: Charles Scribner's Sons.

Shipman, P.
1975 Implication of Drought for Vertebrate Fossil Assemblages. Nature 257:667–668.

Shipman, P., and J. E. Phillips
1976 On Scavenging by Hominids and Other Carnivores. Current Anthropology 17:170–171.

Shipman, P., and J. Phillips-Conroy
1977 Hominid Tool-Making Versus Carnivore Scavenging. American Journal of Physical Anthropology 46:77–86.

Short, D. J.
1968 Experience with Cubed Diets for Laboratory Primates. In M. A. Crawford, ed., 1968. Pp. 13–20.

Silberbauer, G.
1972 The G/wi Bushmen. In M. G. Bicchieri, ed., 1972. Pp. 271–326.

Simonds, P.
1965 The Bonnet Macaques in South India. In I. DeVore, ed., 1965. Pp. 175–196.
1974 The Social Primates. New York: Harper and Row.

Simons, E. L.
1961 The Phyletic Position of *Ramapithecus*. Postilla 57:1–9.
1964 On the Mandible of *Ramapithecus*. Proceedings of the National Academy of Science 51:528–535.
1972 Primate Evolution. New York: Macmillan.
1976 *Ramapithecus*. Scientific American 236(5):28–35.

Sinha, D. F.
1972 The Birhors. In M. G. Bicchieri, ed., 1972. Pp. 371–403.

Sisson, S., and J. D. Grossman
1953 The Anatomy of the Domestic Animals, 4th ed. Philadelphia: W. B. Saunders.

Slaughter, B. H.
1967 Animal Ranges as a Clue to Late-Pleistocene Extinctions. In P. S. Martin and H. E. Wright, eds., 1967. Pp. 155–168.

Smith, E.
1979 Human Adaptation and Energetic Efficiency. Human Ecology 7:53–54.

Smith, J. R.
1929 Tree Crops, A Permanent Agriculture. New York: Harcourt and Brace.

Snodderly, M.
1978 Color Discriminations During Food Foraging by a New World Monkey. *In* D. J. Chivers and J. Herbert, eds., 1978. Pp. 369–372.

Soler, N.
1976a El Cau de les Goges. *In* El Paleolític a les Comarques Gironines. J. Canal and N. Soler, eds. Pp. 61–62.
1976b La Bora Gran d'en Carreres. *In* El Paleolític a les Comarques Gironines. J. Canal and N. Soler, eds. Pp. 156–158.
1976c L'Abreda. *In* El Paleolític a les Comarques Gironines. J. Canal and N. Soler, eds. Pp. 148–152.

Soler García, J. M.
1956 El Yacimiento Musteriense de "la Cueva del Cochino" (Villena, Alicante). Valencia: Servicio de Investigación Prehistórica del C.S.I.C.

Spencer, R.
1959 The North Alaskan Eskimo: A Study in Ecology and Society. Washington, D.C.: Smithsonian Institution, Bureau of American Ethnology, Bulletin 171.

Spencer, R., and J. Jennings, eds.
1965 The Native Americans. New York: Harper and Row.

Spencer, W. B., and F. J. Gillen
1899 The Native Tribes of Central Australia. London: Macmillan.
1927 The Arunta. London: Macmillan.

Speth, J. D., and D. D. Davis
1976 Seasonal Variability in Early Hominid Predation. Science 192:441–445.

Spuhler, J. N., ed.
1965 The Evolution of Man's Capacity for Culture. Detroit: Wayne State University Press.

Stanley, H. M.
1890 In Darkest Africa or the Quest, Rescue and Retreat of Emin, Governor of Equatoria. London: Sampson Low.

Stanner, W. E.
1965 Aboriginal Territorial Organization: Estate, Range, Domain and Regime. Oceania 36:1–26.

Stearns, C., and D. L. Thurber
1967 Th 230/U 234 Dates of Late Pleistocene Marine Fossils from the Mediterranean and Moroccan Littorals. *In* Progress in Oceanography, Vol. 4. M. Sears, ed. Pp. 293–306.

Stefansson, V.
1962 My Life with the Eskimo (originally published 1913). New York: Collier.

Steward, J.
1938 Basin-Plateau Aboriginal Sociopolitcal Groups. Washington, D.C.: Smithsonian Institute, Bureau of American Ethnology, Bulletin 120.

Stoltz, L. P., and G. S. Saayman
1970 Ecology and Behaviour of Baboons in the Northern Transvaal. Annals of the Transvaal Museum 26:99–143.

Stone, I.
1965 Studies of a Mammalian Enzyme System for Producing Evolutionary Evidence on Man. American Journal of Physical Anthropology 23:83.

Stow, G. W.
1905 The Native Races of South Africa. London: Swan Sonnenschein.

Straus, L.
1974 Notas Preliminares Sobre el Solutrense de Asturias. Boletín del Instituto de Estudios Asturianos 82:483–504.
1975 Solutrense o Magdaleniense Inferior Cantábrico? Significado de las "Diferencias." Boletín del Instituto de Estudios Asturianos 86:781–790.
1976 Análisis Arqueológico de la Fauna Paleolítica del Norte de la Península Ibérica. Munibe 28:277–285.
1977 Of Deerslayers and Mountain Men: Paleolithic Faunal Exploitation in Cantabrian Spain. In For Theory Building in Archaeology. L. Binford, ed. Pp. 41–76. New York: Academic Press.

Strehlow, T. G. H.
1965 Culture, Social Structure and Environment in Aboriginal Central Australia. In Aboriginal Man in Australia. R. Berndt and C. Berndt, eds. Pp. 121–145. Sydney: Angus and Robertson.

Struever, S.
1968 Flotation Techniques for the Recovery of Small-Scale Archaeological Remains. American Antiquity 33:353–362.

Struhsaker, T. T.
1967 Ecology of Vervet Monkeys (Cercopithecus aethiops) in the Masai-Amboseli Game Reserve, Kenya. Ecology 48:891–904.
1975 The Red Colobus Monkey. Chicago: University of Chicago Press.
1978 Food Habits of Five Monkey Species in the Kibale Forest, Uganda. In D. J. Chivers and J. Herbert, eds., 1978. Pp. 225–248.

Struhsaker, T. T., and P. Hunkeler
1971 Evidence of Tool-Using by Chimpanzees on the Ivory Coast. Folia Primatologica 15:212–219.

Strum, S. C.
1975a Life with the Pumphouse Gang: New Insights into Baboon Behavior. National Geographic 147:672–691.
1975b Primate Predation: Interim Report on the Development of a Tradition in a Troop of Olive Baboons. Science 187:755–757.
1976a Predatory Behavior of Olive Baboons (Papio anubis) at Gilgil, Kenya. Ph.D. dissertation, University of California, Berkeley.

1976b   Primate Predation and Bioenergetics. Science 191:314–317.

1978   Dominance Hierarchy and Social Organization: Strong or Weak Inference. Paper presented at Wenner-Gren Conference, "Baboon Field Research: Myths and Models."

n.d.   Agonistic Dominance in Male Baboons: an Alternate View. Manuscript submitted to International Journal of Primatology.

Sugiyama, Y.

1968   The Ecology of the Lion-Tailed Macaque (*Macaca silenus* Linnaeus): a Pilot Study. Journal of the Bombay Natural History Society 65:283–292.

1971   Characteristics of the Social Life of Bonnet Macaques (*Macaca radiata*). Primates 12:247–266.

1973   The Social Structure of Wild Chimpanzees: A Review of Field Studies. *In* R. P. Michael and J. H. Crook, eds., 1973. Pp. 375–410.

Summers, R. W., and M. K. Neville

1978   On the Sympatry of Early Hominids. American Anthropologist 80:657–660.

Sussman, R. W.

1974   Ecological Distinctions in Sympatric Species of *Lemur*. *In* R. D. Martin, G. A. Doyle, and A. C. Walker, eds., 1974. Pp. 75–108.

1975   A Preliminary Study of the Behavior and Ecology of *Lemur fulvus rufus* Audebert 1800. *In* Lemur Biology. I. Tattersall and R. W. Sussman, eds. Pp. 237–258. New York: Plenum Press.

1977   Feeding Behaviour of *Lemur catta* and *Lemur fulvus*. *In* T. H. Clutton-Brock, ed., 1977. Pp. 1–36.

1978   Nectar-Feeding by *Lemur mongoz mongoz* and Its Evolutionary Implications. *In* Recent Advances in Primatology. Vol. 3: Evolution. D. J. Chivers and K. A. Joysey, eds. London: Academic Press.

Sussman, R. W., and I. Tattersall

1976   Cycles of Activity, Group Composition and Diet of *Lemur mongoz mongoz* in Madagascar. Folia Primatologica 26:270–283.

Sutcliffe, A. J.

1972   Spotted Hyena: Crusher, Gnawer, Digester, and Collector of Bones. *In* Perspectives on Human Evolution, Vol. 2. S. L. Washburn and P. Dolhinow, eds. Pp. 141–150. New York: Holt, Rinehart and Winston.

Suttles, W.

1968   Coping with Abundance: Subsistence on the Northwest Coast. *In* R. B. Lee and I. DeVore, eds., 1968a. Pp. 56–68.

Suzuki, A.

1965   An Ecological Study of Wild Japanese Monkeys in Snowy Areas: Focused on Their Food Habits. Primates 6:31–72.

1966   On the Insect-Eating Habits among Wild Chimpanzees Living in the Savanna Woodland of Western Tanzania. Primates 7:481–487.

1968   A Mystery in Budongo Forest: Meat Eating and Cannibalism among the Chimpanzees (in Japanese). Monkey 103:5–13.

1969   An Ecological Study of Chimpanzees in Savanna Woodland. Primates 10:103–148.

1971 Carnivority and Cannibalism Observed Among Forest-Living Chimpanzees. Journal of the Anthropological Society of Nippon 79:30–48.
1975 The Origin of Hominid Hunting: A Primatological Perspective. *In* R. H. Tuttle, ed., 1975b. Pp. 259–278.
1976 Chimpanzee Hunting Behavior. Scientific American (Japanese Edition) 6:18–29.

Swartz, M. J., and D. K. Jordan
1976 Anthropology: Perspective on Humanity. New York: Wiley.

Szalay, F. S.
1975 Hunting-Scavenging Protohominids: A Model for Hominid Origins. Man 10:420–429.

Taieb, M., D. C. Johanson, Y. Coppens, and J. L. Aronson
1976 Geological and Paleontological Background of Hadar Hominid Site, Afar, Ethiopia. Nature 260:289–293.

Taieb, M., D. C. Johanson, Y. Coppens, and J.-J. Tiercelin
1978 Chronostratigraphie des Gisements à Hominidés Pliocènes d'Hadar et Corrélations avec les Sites Préhistoriques du Kada Gona. Comptes Rendus de l'Academie des Sciences, ser. D, 287:459–461.

Tanaka, J.
1971 The Bushmen (in Japanese). Tokyo: Shisakusha.
1976 Subsistence Ecology of Central Kalahari San. *In* R. B. Lee and I. DeVore, eds., 1976. Pp. 98–119.

Tankard, A. J., and F. R. Schweitzer
1974 The Geology of Die Kelders Cave and Environs: A Palaeoenvironmental Study. South African Journal of Science 70:365–369.
1976 Textural Analysis of Cave Sediments: Die Kelders, Cape Province, South Africa. *In* Geoarchaeology. D. A. Davidson and M. L. Shackley, eds. Pp. 298–316. London: Duckworth.

Tanner, N., and A. Zihlman
1976 Women in Evolution. Part I: Innovation and Selection in Human Origins. Signs 1:585–608.

Tanno, T.
1976 The Mbuti Net-Hunters in the Ituri Forest, Eastern Zaïre. Kyoto University African Studies 10:101–136.

Tattersall, I., and R. W. Sussman
1975 Observations on the Ecology and Behavior of the Mongoose Lemur *Lemur mongoz mongoz* Linnaeus at Ampijoroa, Madagascar. Anthropological Papers of the American Museum of Natural History 52:195–216.

Taub, D. M.
1977 Geographic Distribution and Habitat Diversity of the Barbary Macaque *Macaca sylvanus* L. Folia Primatologica 27:108–133.

Taylor, D.
1965 The Study in Pleistocene Nonmarine Mollusks in North America. *In* Quaternary of the United States. H. E. Wright and D. Frey, eds. Princeton: Princeton University Press.

Teitelbaum, P., and A. N. Epstein
   1963   The Role of Taste and Smell in the Regulation of Food and Water Intake. *In* Proceedings of the First International Symposium on Olfaction and Taste. Y. Zotterman, ed. Pp. 347–360. Oxford: Pergamon Press.

Teleki, G.
   1973a   The Predatory Behavior of Wild Chimpanzees. Lewisburg: Bucknell University Press.
   1973b   The Omnivorous Chimpanzee. Scientific American 228(1):32–42.
   1973c   Notes on Chimpanzee Interactions with Small Carnivores in Gombe National Park, Tanzania. Primates 14:407–411.
   1973d   Group Response to the Accidental Death of a Chimpanzee in Gombe National Park, Tanzania. Folia Primatologica 20:81–94.
   1974   Chimpanzee Subsistence Technology: Materials and Skills. Journal of Human Evolution 3:575–594.
   1975   Primate Subsistence Patterns: Collector-Predators and Gatherer-Hunters. Journal of Human Evolution 4:125–184.
   1977a   Spatial and Temporal Dimensions of Routine Activities Performed by Chimpanzees in Gombe National Park, Tanzania: An Ethological Study of Adaptive Strategy. Ph.D. dissertation, Pennsylvania State University.
   1977b   Still More on Predatory Behavior in Nonhuman Primates. Current Anthropology 18:107–108.
   1978   Response to: Carrying and Sharing in Human Evolution (by J. B. Lancaster). Human Nature 1:8.
   in press.   The Organized Utilization of Natural Resources by Primate Societies. *In* Modes of Production: Method and Theory. J. Silverberg, ed. New York: Queens College Press.

Teleki, G., E. E. Hunt, and J. H. Pfifferling
   1976   Demographic Observations (1963–1973) on the Chimpanzees of Gombe National Park, Tanzania. Journal of Human Evolution 5:559–598.

Tenaza, R. R., and W. J. Hamilton III
   1971   Preliminary Observations of the Mentawai Islands Gibbon, *Hylobates klossii*. Folia Primatologica 15:201–211.

Thomas, S., and M. Corden
   1970   Tables of Composition of Australian Foods. Canberra: Commonwealth Department of Health.

Thompson, P. R.
   1975   A Cross-Species Analysis of Carnivore, Primate, and Hominid Behavior. Journal of Human Evolution 4:113–124.

Thomson, D. F.
   1939   The Seasonal Factor in Human Culture. Proceedings of the Prehistoric Society 5:209–222.
   1949   Economic Structure and the Ceremonial Exchange Cycle in Arnhem Land. Melbourne: Macmillan.
   1962   The Bindibu Expedition. Geographical Journal 128:1–14, 143–157, 262–278.

Thorington, R. W.
  1967   Feeding and Activity of *Cebus* and *Saimiri* in a Colombian Forest. *In*
    Neue Ergebnisse der Primatologie. D. Starck, R. Schneider, and H. J. Kuhn,
    eds. Pp. 180–184. Stuttgart: Gustav Fischer Verlag.
  1968   Observations of Squirrel Monkeys in a Colombian Forest. *In* The
    Squirrel Monkey. L. A. Rosenblum and R. W. Cooper, eds. Pp. 69–85. New
    York: Academic Press.
  1970   Feeding Behavior of Nonhuman Primates in the Wild. *In* Feeding and
    Nutrition of Nonhuman Primates. R. S. Harris, ed. New York: Academic
    Press.

Tiger, L.
  1969   Men in Groups. New York: Random House.

Tiger, L., and R. Fox
  1971   The Imperial Animal. New York: Holt, Rinehart and Winston.

Tindale, N.
  1972   The Pitjandjara. *In* M. G. Bicchieri, ed., 1972. Pp. 217–268.

Tobias, P. V.
  1964   Bushman Hunter-Gatherers: A Study in Human Ecology. *In* Ecological
    Studies in Southern Africa. D. H. S. Davis, ed. Pp. 67–86. The Hague: W.
    Junk.
  1967   The Cranium and Maxillary Dentition of *Australopithecus* (*Zinjan-
    thropus*) *boisei*. Olduvai Gorge, Vol. 2. Cambridge: Cambridge University
    Press.
  1968   Cultural Hominization Among the Earliest African Pleistocene Hominids.
    Proceedings of the Prehistoric Society 33:367–376.
  1973a   Implications of the New Age Estimates of the Early South African
    Hominids. Nature 246:79–83.
  1973b   New Developments in Hominid Paleontology in South and East Africa.
    Annual Reviews of Anthropology 2:311–334.
  1976   African Hominids: Dating and Phylogeny. *In* G. Ll. Isaac and E. R.
    McCown, eds., 1976. Pp. 377–422.

Tobias, P. V., and A. R. Hughes
  1969   The New Witwatersrand University Excavations at Sterkfontein. South
    African Archaeological Bulletin 24:158–169.

Tomita, K.
  1966   The Sources of Food for the Hadzapi Tribe: The Life of a Hunting Tribe
    in East Africa. Kyoto University African Studies 1:157–171.

Toots, H., and M. R. Voorhies
  1965   Strontium in Fossil Bones and the Reconstruction of Food Chains.
    Science 149:854–855.

Tringham, R., G. Cooper, G. Odell, B. Voytek, and A. Whitman
  1974   Experimentation in the Formation of Edge Damage: A New Approach to
    Lithic Analysis. Journal of Field Archaeology 1(1/2):171–196.

Truswell, A. S., and J. D. L. Hansen
    1976   Medical Research among the !Kung. *In* R. B. Lee and I. DeVore, eds., 1976. Pp. 166–194.

Tucker, V. A.
    1970   Energetic Cost of Locomotion in Animals. Comparative Biochemistry and Physiology 34:841–846.

Turnbull, C. M.
    1965a   The Mbuti Pygmies: An Ethnographic Survey. Anthropological Papers of the American Museum of Natural History 50:139–282.
    1965b   Wayward Servant. New York: Natural History Press.
    1965c   The Mbuti Pygmies of the Congo. *In* Peoples of Africa. J. L. Gibbs, ed. New York: Holt, Rinehart and Winston.
    1968   The Importance of Flux in Two Hunting Societies. *In* R. B. Lee and I. DeVore, eds., 1968. Pp. 132–137.
    1973   The Mountain People. London: Jonathan Cape.

Tuttle, R. H., ed.
    1975a   Paleoanthropology, Morphology and Paleoecology. The Hague: Mouton.
    1975b   Socioecology and Psychology of Primates. The Hague: Mouton.

Ucko, P. J., R. Tringham, and G. W. Dimbleby, eds.
    1972   Man, Settlement, and Urbanism. London: Duckworth.

van Couvering, J. A. H., and J. A. van Couvering
    1976   Early Miocene Mammal Fossils from East Africa: Aspects of Geology, Faunistics and Paleoecology. *In* G. Ll. Isaac and E. R. McCown, eds., 1976. Pp. 155–207.

van Lawick-Goodall, J.
    1968   The Behavior of Free-Living Chimpanzees in the Gombe Stream Reserve. Animal Behaviour Monographs 1:161–311.
    1970   Tool-Using in Primates and Other Vertebrates. *In* Advances in the Study of Behaviour. Vol. 3. D. S. Lehrman, R. A. Hinde, and E. Shaw, eds. Pp. 195–249. London: Academic Press.
    1971   In the Shadow of Man. Boston: Hougton Mifflin.
    1973   Cultural Elements in a Chimpanzee Community. *In* Precultural Primate Behavior. E. W. Menzel, ed. Symposia of the 4th International Congress of Primatology, Vol. 1. Pp. 144–184. Basel: S. Karger.
    1975   The Behaviour of the Chimpanzee. *In* Hominisation und Verhalten. G. Kurth and I. Eibl-Eibesfeldt, eds., Pp. 74–136. Stuttgart: Gustav Fischer.

Vanstone, J.
    1974   Athapaskan Adaptations. Chicago: Aldine.

Vaufrey, R.
    1950   La Faune de Sidi Zin. *In* Le Gisement de Sidi Zin. E. G. Gobert, ed. Karthago 1:1–63.

Vellard, J.
    1939   Une Civilisation du Miel. Paris: Gallimard.

Vereschagin, N.
1967 Primitive Hunters and Pleistocene Extinction in the Soviet Union. *In* P. S. Martin and H. E. Wright, eds., 1967. Pp. 365–398.

Villa, A.
1976 Mollet I. *In* El Paleolític a les Comarques Gironines. J. Canal i Roquet and N. Soler i Masferrer, eds., 1976. Pp. 139–142.

Viñes Masip, G., F. Jordá Cerdá, and J. Royo Gómez
1947 Cova Negra de Bellús. Valencia: Servicio de Investigación Prehistórica del C.S.I.C.

Vita-Finzi, C., and E. S. Higgs
1970 Prehistoric Economy in the Mount Carmel Area of Palestine: Site Catchment Analysis. Proceedings of the Prehistoric Society 36: 1–37.

Von La Chevallerie, M.
1970 Meat Production from Wild Ungulates. Proceedings of the South African Society of Animal Production 9:73–87.

Vrba, E. S.
1974 Chronological and Ecological Implications of the Fossil Bovidae at the Sterkfontein Australopithecine Site. Nature 250:19–23.
1975 Some Evidence of Chronology and Paleoecology of Sterkfontein, Swartkrans and Kromdraai from the Fossil Bovidae. Nature 254:301–304.

Waechter, J.
1964 The Excavation of Gorham's Cave, Gibraltar, 1951–54. Bulletin of the Institute of Archaeology 4:189–221.

Walker, A.
1969 The Locomotion of the Lorises, with Special Reference to the Potto. East African Wildlife Journal 8:1–5.

Walker, A., and P. Andrews
1973 Reconstruction of the Dental Arcades of *Ramapithecus wickeri*. Nature 224:313–314.

Walker, A., H. N. Hoeck, and L. Perez
1978 Microwear of Mammalian Teeth as an Indicator of Diet. Science 201:908–910.

Walker, A., and R. E. F. Leakey
1978 The Hominids of East Turkana. Scientific American 239(2):54–66.

Walker, E. P.
1968 Mammals of the World, 2 vols. Baltimore: Johns Hopkins Press.

Wallace, J. A.
1973 Tooth Chipping in the Australopithecines. Nature 244:117–118.

Walther, F. R.
1969 Flight Behaviour and Avoidance of Predators in Thomson's Gazelle. Behaviour 34:184–221.

Warner, W. L.
1958   A Black Civilization. New York: Harper.

Waser, P. M.
1974   Intergroup Interaction in a Forest Monkey: The Mangabey *Cercocebus albigena*. Ph.D. dissertation, Rockefeller University.
1975   Monthly Variation in Feeding and Activity Patterns of the Mangabey, *Cercocebus albigena* (Lydekker). East African Wildlife Journal 13:249–263.

Washburn, S. L.
1951   The Analysis of Primate Evolution with Particular Reference to the Origin of Man. Cold Spring Harbor Symposia on Quantitative Biology 15:67–77.
1957   Australopithecines: The Hunters or the Hunted? American Anthropologist 59:612–614.
1968   The Study of Human Evolution. Eugene, Ore.: University of Oregon, Condon Lectures.

Washburn, S. L., and V. Avis
1958   Evolution of Human Behavior. *In* Behavior and Evolution. A. Roe and G. G. Simpson, eds. Pp. 421–436. New Haven: Yale University Press.

Washburn, S. L., and I. DeVore
1961   Social Behavior of Baboons and Early Man. *In* Social Life of Early Man. S. L. Washburn, ed. Pp. 91–105. Chicago: Aldine.

Washburn, S. L., and D. Hamburg
1965   The Study of Primate Behavior. *In* I. DeVore, ed., 1965. Pp. 1–13.

Washburn, S. L., and C. S. Lancaster
1968   The Evolution of Hunting. *In* R. B. Lee and I. DeVore, eds., 1968. Pp. 293–303.

Watanabe, H.
1968   Subsistence and Ecology of Northern Food Gatherers with Special Reference to the Ainu. *In* R. B. Lee and I. DeVore, eds., 1968. Pp. 69–77.
1972   The Ainu. *In* M. G. Bicchieri, ed., 1972. Pp. 448–484.

Waterman, T. T., and A. L. Kroeber
1938   The Kepel Fish Dam. University of California Publications in American Archaeology and Ethnography 35:49–80.

Wedel, W.
1961   Prehistoric Man on the Great Plains. Norman: University of Oklahoma Press.

Wehmeyer, A. S., R. B. Lee and M. Whiting
1969   The Nutrient Composition and Dietary Importance of Some Vegetable Foods Eaten by the !Kung Bushmen. South African Medical Journal (Supplement—South African Journal of Nutrition) 95:1529–1530.

Weiss, K.
1976   Demographic Theory and Anthropological Influence. Annual Review of Anthropology 5:351–381.

Weiss, M. L., and A. E. Mann
  1978 Human Biology and Behavior: An Anthropological Perspective, 2d ed. Boston: Little, Brown.

Wharton, C. H.
  1950 Notes on the Philippine Tree Shrew *Urogale everetti* (Thomas, 1892). Journal of Mammalogy 31:352–354.

Wheat, J. B.
  1972 The Olsen-Chubbuck Site: A Paleo-Indian Bison Kill. American Antiquity 37(1), pt. 2:1–180.

White, L. A., and B. Dillingham
  1973 The Concept of Culture. Minneapolis: Burgess Publishing Co.

Whiting, M. G.
  1958 A Cross-Cultural Nutrition Survey. Ph.D. dissertation, Harvard School of Public Health.

Whittaker, R. H., and P. P. Feeny
  1971 Allelochemics: Chemical Interaction Between Species. Science 171: 757–770.

WHO Expert Committee on Trace Elements in Human Nutrition
  1973 World Health Organization Technical Report Series, No. 532.

Wilkerson, B. J., and D. M. Rumbaugh
  1978 Learning and Intelligence in Prosimians. *In* The Study of Prosimian Behaviour. G. A. Doyle and R. D. Martin, eds. Pp. 207–246. London: Academic Press.

Wilkinson, P.
  1973 Ecosystem Models and Demographic Hypotheses: Predation and Prehistory in North America. *In* The Explanation of Culture Change. C. Renfrew, ed. London: Duckworth.

Williams, B. J.
  1969 The Birhor of Hazaribagh. *In* Contributions of Anthropology: Band Societies. D. Damas, ed. National Museums of Canada, Bulletin 228.

Wilmsen, E.
  1973 Interaction, Spacing Behavior, and the Organization of Hunting Bands. Journal of Anthropological Research 29:1–31.

Wilson, E. O.
  1975 Sociobiology: The New Synthesis. Cambridge: Harvard University Press.
  1978 On Human Nature. Cambridge: Harvard University Press.

Wilson, M., and L. Thompson
  1969 The Oxford History of South Africa, 2 vols. Oxford: Oxford University Press.

Wintrobe, M. M.
  1970 Harrison's Principles of Internal Medicine. New York: McGraw-Hill.

Wolberg, D. L.
1970   The Hypothesised Osteodontokeratic Culture of the Australopithecines: A Look at the Evidence and the Opinions. Current Anthropology 11:23–37.

Wolf, C. B.
1945   California Wild Tree Crops. Anaheim: Rancho Santa Ana Botanic Garden of the Native Plants of California.

Wolpoff, M. H.
1970   The Evidence for Multiple Hominid Taxa at Swartkrans. American Anthropologist 72:576–607.
1971   Competitive Exclusion among Lower Pleistocene Hominids: The Single Species Hypothesis. Man 6:601–614.
1973a   Posterior Tooth Size, Body Size and Diet in South African Gracile Australopithecines. American Journal of Physical Anthropology 39:375–394.
1973b   The Single Species Hypothesis and Early Hominid Evolution. *In* Variation in Anthropology. D. W. Lathrap and J. Douglas, eds. Pp. 5–15. Urbana: Illinois Archaeological Survey.
1976   Primate Models for Australopithecine Sexual Dimorphism. American Journal of Physical Anthropology 45:497–510.

Woodburn, J.
1968a   An Introduction to Hadza Ecology. *In* R. B. Lee and I. DeVore, eds., 1968a. Pp. 49–55.
1968b   Stability and Flexibility in Hadza Residential Groupings. *In* R. B. Lee and I. DeVore, eds., 1968a. Pp. 103–110.
1972   Ecology, Nomadic Movement, and the Composition of the Local Group among Hunters and Gatherers. *In* P. Ucko, R. Tringham, and G. W. Dimbleby, eds., 1972. Pp. 193–206.

Wood Jones, F.
1926   Arboreal Man. London: Edward Arnold and Co.

Wrangham, R.
1974   Artificial Feeding of Chimpanzees and Baboons in Their Natural Habitat. Animal Behaviour 22:83–93.
1975   The Behavioural Ecology of Chimpanzees in Gombe National Park, Tanzania. Ph.D. dissertation, University of Cambridge.
1977   Feeding Behaviour of Chimpanzees in Gombe National Park, Tanzania. *In* T. H. Clutton-Brock, ed., 1977. Pp. 504–538.

Wright, H. E., and D. Frey, eds.
1965   The Quaternary of the United States. Princeton: Princeton University Press.

Wu Leung, W.
1971   Food Composition Tables for Use in Latin America. Bethesda, Md.: Interdepartmental Committee on Nutrition for National Defense and the Institute on Nutrition for Central America and Panama.

Wynne-Edwards, V. C.
1962   Animal Dispersion in Relation to Social Behavior. Edinburgh: Oliver and Boyd.

Yellen, J. E.
1976 Settlement Patterns of the !Kung: An Archaeological Perspective. *In* R. B. Lee and I. DeVore, eds., 1976. Pp. 47–72.
1977 Archaeological Approaches to the Present. New York: Academic Press.

Yellen, J. E., and R. B. Lee
1976 The Dobe-Du/da Environment. *In* R. B. Lee and I. DeVore, eds., 1976. Pp. 27–46.

Yen, D. E.
1976 The Ethnobotany of the Tasaday: III. Notes on the Subsistence System. *In* Further Studies on the Tasaday. D. E. Yen and J. Nance, eds. Pp. 159–183. Makati, Rizal, Philippines: Panamin Foundation Research Series, No. 2.

Yengoyan, A.
1968 Demographic and Ecological Influences on Aboriginal Australian Marriage Sections. *In* R. B. Lee and I. DeVore, eds., 1968a. Pp. 185–199.

Yoshiba, K.
1968 Local and Intertroop Variability in Ecology and Social Behavior of Common Indian Langurs. *In* Primates: Studies in Adaptation and Variability. P. Jay, ed. Pp. 217–242. New York: Holt, Rinehart and Winston.

Zeuner, F.
1953 The Chronology of the Mousterian at Gorham's Cave, Gibraltar. Proceedings of the Prehistoric Society 19:180–188.

Zihlman, A. L., and N. Tanner
in press Gathering and the Hominid Adaptation. *In* Female Hierarchies. L. Tiger, ed. Chicago: Aldine.

Zihlman, A. L., J. E. Cronin, D. L. Cramer, and V. M. Sarich
1978 Pygmy Chimpanzee as a Possible Prototype for the Common Ancestor of Humans, Chimpanzees and Gorillas. Nature 275:744–746.

Zingeser, M. R.
1973 Dentition of *Brachyteles arachnoides* with Reference to Alouattine and Ateline Affinities. Folia Primatologica 20:351–390.

Zipf, G. K.
1949 Human Behavior and the Principle of Least Effort. Reading, Mass.: Addison-Wesley.

Index

669